**STREET & SMITH'S
GUIDE TO PRO BASKETBALL
1994–95**

STREET & SMITH'S GUIDE TO PRO BASKETBALL 1994 – 95

By the editors of
Street & Smith's

Consulting Editor: Reuben Lattimore

BALLANTINE BOOKS • NEW YORK

Copyright © 1994 by Condé Nast Publications, Inc.

All rights reserved under International and Pan-American Copyright Conventions. Published in the United States of America by Ballantine Books, a division of Random House, Inc., New York, and simultaneously in Canada by Random House of Canada Limited, Toronto.

Library of Congress Catalog Card Number: 94–94424

ISBN 345–38619–1

Manufactured in the United States of America

Cover photo of Shaquille O'Neal © Jerry Wachter/Focus on Sports

Player photos appear courtesy of NBA Photos and individual player's team.

All team trademarks used with permission of the teams.

First Edition: November 1994

10 9 8 7 6 5 4 3 2 1

TABLE OF CONTENTS

ACKNOWLEDGMENTS

We'd like to thank the Directors of Public Relations and Media Relations of all the teams in the National Basketball Association. NBA Photos was particularly helpful in providing us with player photos—and extensions to our deadlines. The staff at Creative Graphics worked long and hard on this project. Myles McDonnell answered our call yet again. To all of you, we are grateful.

Finally, many people at Ballantine Books contributed boundless energy and knowledge to this book. We'd like to thank Cathy Repetti, Caron Harris, George Davidson, Nora Reichard, and Scott Gray, who made it happen.

EDITOR'S NOTE

1994–95 statistical projections are based on the individual player's 1993–94 performance, as measured on a per-minute basis, combined with the degree of change in an individual category over a player's career. We take into account the rate of increase in a player's playing time in creating our projection. 1993 stats were thrown out in projecting 1994 stats for projected 1994 starters who were injured for most of 1993 (such as Tim Hardaway). But players with a history of injuries, or who have seen a steady decline in playing time for other reasons, are projected to continue that decline in playing time and stats. There are no projections for rookies and second-year players, because they lack the statistical differences over two or more years that form the basis of our projections.

Our 1994 projections are just that—projections. They indicate continuations of past trends. Although projected numbers could be used as a forecast of a player's 1994–95 performance, they are best used as a general indication of whether or not a player is likely to improve on his 1993–94 performance. This is particularly true for players entering their third and fourth years in the NBA. The longer a player's career, the less likely our projections are skewed by a one-time spike in a player's performance.

This guide should give you a comprehensive preview of the 1994–95 season from training camp to the NBA finals. Due to a tight schedule, we've probably missed some late free agent signings, trades, and other developments. If you can't find a player under his new team, look in the player index and you'll find the page he's on under his old team.

1993–94 NBA RECAP

EASTERN CONFERENCE

ATLANTIC DIVISION

	W	L	PCT	GB	HOME		ROAD		DIV	
Y-New York	57	25	.695	—	32	9	25	16	18	10
X-Orlando	50	32	.610	7	31	10	19	22	20	8
X-New Jersey	45	37	.549	12	29	12	16	25	17	11
X-Miami	42	40	.512	15	22	19	20	21	16	12
Boston	32	50	.390	25	18	23	14	27	12	16
Philadelphia	25	57	.305	32	15	26	10	31	7	21
Washington	24	58	.293	33	17	24	7	34	8	20

CENTRAL DIVISION

	W	L	PCT	GB	HOME		ROAD		DIV	
Y-Atlanta	57	25	.695	—	36	5	21	20	21	7
X-Chicago	55	27	.671	2	31	10	24	17	21	7
X-Indiana	47	35	.573	10	29	12	18	23	15	13
X-Cleveland	47	35	.573	10	31	10	16	25	16	12
Charlotte	41	41	.500	16	28	13	13	28	12	16
Detroit	20	62	.244	37	10	31	10	31	4	24
Milwaukee	20	62	.244	37	11	30	9	32	9	19

WESTERN CONFERENCE

MIDWEST DIVISION

	W	L	PCT	GB	HOME		ROAD		DIV	
Y-Houston	58	24	.707	—	35	6	23	18	15	11
X-San Antonio	55	27	.671	3	32	9	23	18	16	10
X-Utah	53	29	.646	5	33	8	20	21	21	5
X-Denver	42	40	.512	16	28	13	14	27	14	12
Minnesota	20	62	.244	38	13	28	7	34	5	21
Dallas	13	69	.159	45	6	35	7	34	7	19

PACIFIC DIVISION

	W	L	PCT	GB	HOME		ROAD		DIV	
Y-Seattle	63	19	.768	—	37	4	26	15	25	5
X-Phoenix	56	26	.683	7	36	5	20	21	19	11
X-Golden St.	50	32	.610	13	29	12	21	20	19	11
X-Portland	47	35	.573	16	30	11	17	24	17	13
LA Lakers	33	49	.402	30	21	20	12	29	7	23
Sacramento	28	54	.341	35	20	21	8	33	9	21
LA Clippers	27	55	.329	36	17	24	10	31	9	21

Y–Division winner, X–Playoff team

Playoff Results

EASTERN CONFERENCE FIRST ROUND

Atlanta 3, Miami 2

Th	Apr. 28	Miami 93	Atlanta 88
Sat	Apr. 30	Atlanta 104	Miami 86
Tu	May 3	Miami 90	Atlanta 86
Th	May 5	Atlanta 103	Miami 89
Sun	May 8	Atlanta 102	Miami 91

New York 3, New Jersey 1

Fri	Apr. 29	New York 91	New Jersey 80
Sun	May 1	New York 90	New Jersey 81
Wed	May 4	New Jersey 93	New York 92
Fri	May 6	New York 102	New Jersey 92

Chicago 3, Cleveland 0

Fri	Apr. 29	Chicago 104	Cleveland 96
Sun	May 1	Chicago 105	Cleveland 96
Tu	May 3	Chicago 95	Cleveland 92 (OT)

Indiana 3, Orlando 0

Th	Apr. 28	Indiana 89	Orlando 88
Sat	Apr. 30	Indiana 103	Orlando 101
Mon	May 2	Indiana 99	Orlando 86

EASTERN CONFERENCE SEMIFINALS

New York 4, Chicago 3

Sun	May 8	New York 90	Chicago 86
Wed	May 11	New York 96	Chicago 91
Fri	May 13	Chicago 104	New York 102
Sun	May 15	Chicago 95	New York 83
Wed	May 18	New York 87	Chicago 86
Fri	May 20	Chicago 93	New York 79
Sun	May 22	New York 87	Chicago 77

Indiana 4, Atlanta 2

Tu	May 10	Indiana 96	Atlanta 85
Th	May 12	Atlanta 92	Indiana 69
Sat	May 14	Indiana 101	Atlanta 81
Sun	May 15	Indiana 102	Atlanta 86
Tu	May 17	Atlanta 88	Indiana 76
Th	May 19	Indiana 98	Atlanta 79

EASTERN CONFERENCE FINALS

New York 4, Indiana 3

Tu	May 24	New York 100	Indiana 89
Th	May 26	New York 89	Indiana 78
Sat	May 28	Indiana 88	New York 68
Mon	May 30	Indiana 83	New York 77
Wed	June 1	Indiana 93	New York 86
Fri	June 3	New York 98	Indiana 91
Sun	June 5	New York 94	Indiana 90

WESTERN CONFERENCE FIRST ROUND

Denver 3, Seattle 2

Th	Apr. 28	Seattle 106	Denver 82
Sat	Apr. 30	Seattle 97	Denver 87
Mon	May 2	Denver 110	Seattle 93
Th	May 5	Denver 94	Seattle 85 (OT)
Sat	May 7	Denver 98	Seattle 94 (OT)

Houston 3, Portland 1

Fri	Apr. 29	Houston 114	Portland 104
Sun	May 1	Houston 115	Portland 104
Tu	May 3	Portland 118	Houston 115
Fri	May 6	Houston 92	Portland 89

Phoenix 3, Golden State 0

Fri	Apr. 29	Phoenix 111	Golden St. 104
Sun	May 1	Phoenix 117	Golden St. 111
Wed	May 4	Phoenix 140	Golden St. 133

Utah 3, San Antonio 1

Th	Apr. 28	San Antonio 106	Utah 89
Sat	Apr. 30	Utah 96	San Antonio 84
Tu	May 3	Utah 105	San Antonio 72
Th	May 5	Utah 95	San Antonio 90

WESTERN CONFERENCE SEMIFINALS

Houston 4, Phoenix 3

Sun	May 8	Phoenix 91	Houston 87
Wed	May 11	Phoenix 124	Houston 117 (OT)
Fri	May 13	Houston 118	Phoenix 102
Sun	May 15	Houston 107	Phoenix 96
Tu	May 17	Houston 109	Phoenix 86
Th	May 19	Phoenix 103	Houston 89
Sat	May 21	Houston 104	Phoenix 94

Utah 4, Denver 3

Tu	May 10	Utah 100	Denver 91
Th	May 12	Utah 104	Denver 94
Sat	May 14	Utah 111	Denver 109 (OT)
Sun	May 15	Denver 83	Utah 82
Tu	May 17	Denver 109	Utah 101 (OT)
Th	May 19	Denver 94	Utah 91
Sat	May 21	Utah 91	Denver 81

WESTERN CONFERENCE FINALS

Houston 4, Utah 1

Mon	May 23	Houston 100	Utah 88
Wed	May 25	Houston 104	Utah 99
Fri	May 27	Utah 95	Houston 86
Sun	May 29	Houston 80	Utah 78
Tu	May 31	Houston 94	Utah 83

NBA FINALS

Houston 4, New York 3

Wed	June 8	Houston 85	New York 78
Fri	June 10	New York 91	Houston 83
Sun	June 12	Houston 93	New York 89
Wed	June 15	New York 91	Houston 82
Fri	June 17	New York 91	Houston 84
Sun	June 19	Houston 86	New York 84
Wed	June 22	Houston 90	New York 84

Atlantic Division

New York: New York went undefeated in March on the way to a 15-game winning streak and finished up first in the Atlantic Division at 57–25. The Knicks lost the season series to New Jersey, 4–1, but defeated the Nets 3–1 in the first round of the playoffs. They beat Chicago and Indiana in tough 7 game series before losing in game 7 of the NBA finals.

Orlando: Anfernee Hardaway was January Rookie of the Month as the Magic went 10–5 for their best month ever. The Magic finished strong, going 9–4 in April to end up second in the Atlantic Division at 50–32. The Magic ran into a hot Indiana club in the first round of the playoffs, losing 3 straight to close out their first playoff appearance.

New Jersey: The Nets put it together after the All-Star break, going 20–13 to finish third in the Atlantic Division (45–37) and winning their third straight playoff berth. But they lost in the first round to the Knicks, 3–1.

Miami: The Heat got strong all-around play from Steve Smith and Rony Seikaly to finish fourth in the Atlantic Division at 42–40 and return to the playoffs as the eighth seed. They gave Central Division champ Atlanta a scare, winning the first game in Atlanta before ultimately succumbing in 5 games in the first round of the playoffs.

Boston: The Celtics stumbled in the second half, going winless in February on the way to 13 losses in a row. Once invincible at home, the Celtics had their first losing season at Boston Garden since the '69–70 season. They wound up 32–50, fifth in the Atlantic Division.

Philadelphia: Philadelphia was 20–27 at the All-Star break, but went 5–30 to close out a 25–57 season. They dropped 15 in a row between February 9 and March 13, beat Washington, and then lost another 10 in a row. Losing Shawn Bradley for the season on February 18 with a dislocated left kneecap was a big reason for Philly's second-half swoon.

Washington: The Bullets lost 10 in a row in December, and things never got better after that. Kevin Duckworth didn't turn into the force at center the Bullets had hoped for, and Pervis Ellison's knee problems continued. The Bullets wound up in last place in the Atlantic Division with a 24–58 record.

Central Division

Atlanta: The Hawks won 14 in a row between November 16 and December 14, and stopped Houston's record setting 15–0 start along the way. They ended up with the best record in the Eastern Conference, 57–25 (winning a tie breaker with New York). But they struggled in the first round against Miami and were punched out against Indiana in the conference semifinals.

Chicago: Michael Jordan's retirement looked like it would scuttle Chicago's season, but the Bulls remained one of the league's elite teams. They put together 2 10-game winning streaks, one in December, and one from late March to mid-April. They remained in contention for the conference lead up to the season's final weekend, ending up 55–27. Chicago swept Cleveland in the first round of the playoffs, but lost to the Knicks on the way to a 7 game loss in the conference semifinals.

Indiana: The Pacers finished strong, winning the season's final 8 games, and were 47–35 for the season. They surprised Orlando 3–0 in the first round. Indiana then upset Atlanta, the regular season conference champs, in 6 games, and had a 3–2 lead in the Eastern Conference finals against New York before losing in game 7.

Cleveland: The Cavs started to perk after the All-Star break, winning 11 in a row between February 18 and March 11. But in March, the Cavs lost Brad Daugherty for the season with a herniated disk in his back, and Larry Nance went down with torn cartilage in his knee. The Cavs finished the season at 47–35, only to be swept 3–0 by Chicago in the first round of the playoffs.

Charlotte: Injuries to Larry Johnson (back) and Alonzo Mourning (torn calf muscle) derailed what started out as an impressive season. Charlotte was just 1–10 in February when Mourning and Johnson were both out. But the Hornets bounced back after Mourning, and then Johnson, returned. They were 10–4 in April and ended up at 41–41, missing the playoffs by a single game.

Detroit: Shaken by the retirement of Bill Laimbeer, Detroit lost 14 games in a row between December 20 and January 18. The Pistons limped to the gate, losing their final 12 games and ending the year 20–62. Injury-plagued Isiah Thomas retired after the season.

Milwaukee: The Bucks started slow, losing their first 10 games in a row, and finished slow, going 3–24 in March and April and ending up at 20–62. They were one of the worst shooting teams in the league and were woefully undermanned up front, especially when Frank Brickowski was traded.

Midwest Division

Houston: The Rockets opened the season by winning 15 games in a row, tying the NBA record for consecutive wins to open a season. They cruised through the rest of the season and into the playoffs with a 58–24 record, until they lost the first 2 games of the Western Conference semifinals to Phoenix. But they shook the Choke City label by winning 4 of the next 5 over Phoenix, beating Utah in 5 games in the Western Conference finals, and ultimately defeating New York in the NBA finals.

San Antonio: The Spurs put together a 13-game winning streak between January 22 and February 21. But San Antonio may have peaked too soon; they were just 4–7 in April, ended the season at 55–27 (second in the Midwest Division), and fell 3–1 to Utah in the first round of the playoffs.

Utah: The Jazz started the season 20–8 in November and December. After a lackluster January, the Jazz won 10 in a row between February 19 and March 8. They finished with a 9–2 April record to end up 53–29, third in the Midwest Division. They beat San Antonio and Denver in the playoffs before losing in the Western Conference finals to Houston, 4–1.

Denver: The Nuggets managed to go 20–15 after the All-Star break and finished 42–40, fourth in the Midwest Division. The Nuggets surprised Seattle in the first round of the playoffs, rebounding from a 0–2 deficit to win 3 straight and beat the Sonics 3–2. They nearly turned the same trick against Utah in the semifinals, falling behind 0–3 to the Jazz before they won 3 straight and took Utah to a seventh game.

Minnesota: The Timberwolves were 6–7 in January to stand at 14–27. But they slumped after that, going 6–30 after the All-Star break and ending up 20–62, fifth in the Midwest Division.

Dallas: Quinn Buckner brought Bobby Knight's approach to the NBA—and it didn't work. Dallas had the 3 longest losing streaks of the season: 20 games in a row from November 13 to December 22, 16 games in a row from December 28 to January 27, and 17 games in a row from February 26 to April 5. Those three losing skids accounted for 53 losses. Dallas finished with a 13–69 mark, and ended up last in the Midwest Division.

Pacific Division

Seattle: The Sonics started off strong, winning their first 10 games. They finished with the NBA's best record, 63–19, and were first in the Pacific Division. But they drew Denver as their first-round opponent, and after going 2–0, lost 3 in a row to the Nuggets in the biggest upset of the playoffs.

Phoenix: Injuries to Charles Barkley (knee) and Kevin Johnson (ankle) slowed Phoenix in January, when they were just 7–8. They finished strong, going 10–3 in April and ending up 56–26, second in the Pacific Division . The Suns swept Golden State 3–0 in the first round, and looked like they would do the same to Houston, winning the first 2 games of the Western Conference semifinals on the road. But the Rockets bounced back with 2 wins in Phoenix, eventually beating Phoenix in 7 games.

Golden State: The Warriors were 36–19 after January 1 to finish 50–32, third in the Pacific Division. In the playoffs, Phoenix swept the Warriors 3–0 in the first round.

Portland: A sprained ankle slowed down Clyde Drexler, who didn't resemble the "Clyde the Glide" of old. The Blazers went 20–15 after the All–Star break to finish 47–35, fourth in the Pacific Division. Portland lost in the first round of the playoffs to eventual champ Houston, 4–1.

LA Lakers: The Lakers started off badly, going 9–19 in November and December. With a playoff spot still a possibility, the Lakers replaced coach Randy Pfund with Magic Johnson on March 23. The

Lakers won 5 of their first 6 under Johnson, but their push for a playoff spot quickly faded as they lost their final 10 games and finished 33–49, fifth in the Pacific Division, and the second-worst record in club history.

Sacramento: Kings point guard Bobby Hurley, the team's top draft choice, was nearly killed in an auto accident after a game on December 12. The Kings had a losing record every month except February, when they were 7–6. They finished 28–54, sixth in the Pacific Division. It was the first time the team had finished out of last place in the division since the '88–89 season.

LA Clippers: Danny Manning told management he wouldn't return, and Ron Harper claimed playing with the Clippers was like serving jail time. Manning was traded to Atlanta for Dominique Wilkins, and Harper was suspended for a game. By season's end, the Clippers had thrown in the towel, going 2–10 in April and finishing last in the Pacific Division with a 27–55 record.

1994–95 NBA PROJECTIONS

Atlantic	Central	Midwest	Pacific
Y-New York	Y-Cleveland	Y-Houston	Y-Seattle
X-Orlando	X-Indiana	X-San Antonio	X-Golden State
X-Miami	X-Atlanta	X-Denver	X-Phoenix
New Jersey	X-Charlotte	X-Utah	X-Portland
Philadelphia	X-Chicago	Dallas	LA Lakers
Washington	Milwaukee	Minnesota	Sacramento
Boston	Detroit		LA Clippers

Y–Division winner, X–Playoff team

Playoff Forecast

	Eastern Conference	Western Conference
First round	New York over New Jersey	Seattle over Portland
	Cleveland over Miami	Golden State over Utah
	Indiana over Charlotte	Phoenix over Denver
	Orlando over Atlanta	Houston over San Antonio
Semifinals	New York over Orlando	Seattle over Houston
	Indiana over Cleveland	Golden State over Phoenix
Conf. finals	New York over Indiana	Seattle over Golden State
NBA finals	New York over Seattle	

Defense has become the name of the game in the NBA. Last season, 10 teams held opponents to 100 points or less per game; the season before, only 3 did. Shooting percentages dropped from 47.3 percent in '92–93 to 46.6 percent last season, and average points per game declined from 105.3 to 101.5.

Tough, stifling defense is a trend in the NBA because, quite simply, it's an effective way to win. The Laker and Celtic championship teams of the '80s always played great defense, although their offensive abilities overshadowed their defensive prowess. But Detroit showed that a team with modest offensive talent could win a title by playing aggressive defense. And Pat Riley's Knicks have picked up that theme.

You need a variety of scoring threats to win consistently in the NBA. When you rely on just a couple of guys for your points, you'll have problems. Dallas is a case in point. They were 1 of only 2 NBA teams to have 2 scorers in the top 18: Jamal Mashburn and Jim Jackson, who both averaged 19.2 points per game to finish tied at eighteenth. Yet, they finished just 13–69. Who was the other team with 2 scorers in the top 18? The L.A. Clippers, who finished 27–55 with Dominique Wilkins (fourth) and Ron Harper (fifteenth).

The NBA's elite all have most or all of these characteristics: chemistry, 3 offensive weapons, tough defensive rebounding, good defense, and 3 quality players off the bench. Having all 5 makes you a championship contender, 4 out of 5 gives you a shot at the title, and 3 out of 5 makes you a playoff team. New York had 4 out of 5 last season; they lacked only that third offensive option. We think they'll come up with the perimeter bomber they've been looking for and win the NBA championship.

Here's how we think the rest of the league will shape up:

Atlantic Division

The Knicks should have enough to hold off a challenge from Orlando. The Magic will be stronger with the addition of Horace Grant, but they're still a year away from being able to play with the New York core of Ewing, Oakley, and Starks. Miami should slip past New Jersey to take over third place. The Heat's young players are just getting better, and with a new long-term contract, they know

Kevin Loughery's not going anywhere. Meanwhile, the Nets will feel the loss of Chuck Daly and have to adjust to new coach Butch Beard and rookie center Yinka Dare. Clarence Weatherspoon and Shawn Bradley should help Philadelphia finish ahead of Washington and Boston. With players like Don MacLean, Rex Chapman, Tom Gugliotta, and Juwan Howard, the Bullets have a lot of young talent, and could contend for a playoff spot—if everything breaks right for them. Boston added Dominique Wilkins and Pervis Ellison, but adding aging free agents to a losing team is not a path to long-term success.

Central Division

Brad Daugherty should lead the Cavs to the top of the division. But they'll have to hold off Indiana, who gained confidence during their impressive playoff run. The Pacers will have powerful weapons with Reggie Miller, Derrick McKey, and Mark Jackson. The Hawks will stumble without Dominique Wilkins and Danny Manning, but the guard tandem of Stacey Augmon and Mookie Blaylock should continue to improve. Charlotte should return to the playoffs, with Robert Parish backing up Alonzo Mourning. They could finish higher if Larry Johnson can shake off the effects of his back problem. After losing Michael Jordan and Horace Grant in consecutive years, Chicago stands to slide all the way to fifth place. The Bucks will be better with the addition of Glenn "Big Dog" Robinson, but they still have too many holes to contend for a playoff spot. Detroit, in the middle of a major rebuilding job, should bring up the rear, despite improved play from Lindsay Hunter and Allen Houston.

Midwest Division

With the league's most dominating player in Hakeem Olajuwon, defending NBA champ Houston should repeat as division champs. San Antonio has David Robinson and Dennis Rodman (and Sean Elliott has returned to the team), but they don't get championship-caliber play from their guards; and they'll have to adjust to a new coach, Bob Hill. Another year of experience for Dikembe Mutombo should help improving Denver pass Utah for third place. The Jazz are a slow team, out of place in the fast-paced Western Conference, and their stars, Karl Malone and John Stockton, aren't getting any younger. Dallas should pass Minnesota and finish fifth. The Mavs, under Dick Motta, have Jim Jackson, Jamal Mashburn, and '94 draft pick Jason Kidd, but are probably a year away from contending for a playoff spot. The Timberwolves have Christian Laettner and Isaiah Rider, but they lack chemistry and have to adjust to their fourth coach in 5 years, Bill Blair.

Pacific Division

Seattle has the most talented, versatile players in the NBA. With stars like Shawn Kemp and Gary Payton, they should repeat as Pacific Division champs. Golden State should give them a run for their money, though. They'll welcome back Tim Hardaway, who missed the entire '93–94 season. Phoenix will have another good season, and figures to finish third in a competitive division, provided that Charles Barkley's back doesn't sideline him for a significant number of games. Portland should finish fourth, largely by default. With aging stars like Clyde Drexler, Buck Williams, and Terry Porter, the Blazers have more talent than the Lakers. Nick Van Exel and Anthony Peeler are going to be stars in the NBA, but the Lakers need to upgrade themselves in the frontcourt. Sacramento should repeat their sixth place finish; despite stars like Mitch Richmond, Lionel Simmons, and Spud Webb, the Kings lack the depth to contend for a playoff spot. The Clippers are cleaning house, and they've brought in Bill Fitch to establish order. They may take a year to adjust to the new way of doing things.

Atlanta *HAWKS*

Atlanta Hawks

1994–95 Scouting Report

Frontcourt

Overall, the Hawks are one of the NBA's better rebounding teams. Power forward Kevin Willis is a first-rate rebounder, and last season was his best offensively. Kenny Norman takes over at small forward for the departed Dominique Wilkins and Danny Manning. But he's not the scorer they were, so Atlanta figures to fall off in that department. Center Jon Koncak is the weak link of the frontcourt. He's extremely limited offensively; although he can block shots and rebound a little, he's not a championship-caliber center. The bench is average. Adam Keefe is the reserve power forward; he showed little in his rookie season to justify picking him over Harold Miner in the '93 draft. Duane Ferrell comes off the bench to play small forward. He's able to contribute on defense, and he turned into a perimeter threat last season. Andrew Lang is Koncak's backup. 1993 first-round pick Doug Edwards was plagued by injuries on the way to a disappointing rookie year.

Backcourt

Stacey Augmon plays tough defense, and he's becoming a first rate offensive threat. He's great driving to the basket, and his jump shot is getting better and better. Mookie Blaylock is one of the NBA's better point guards, and should be even better in his second year in Atlanta. Craig Ehlo backs up Blaylock at point guard, although he's been around, and should start to see his minutes decline. Snoopy Graham will come off the bench to add instant offense, especially from the perimeter. And they'll have to find a spot for first-round draft pick Gaylon Nickerson.

Defense

Lenny Wilkens brought that old-time defensive religion to Atlanta last season. Formerly one of the league's weaker defensive teams, the Hawks played tenacious defense last year. They held opponents under 100 points 58 times last year, and limited opponents to a 96.2 points per game average, fourth lowest in the NBA and breaking the old team record by over 4 points. The Hawks were second in the NBA in forcing turnovers (17.9 per game). Atlanta's defensive FG percentage was eighth in the NBA (it was twenty-sixth the previous season). They stole the ball 11.2 times a game (second in the NBA), while suffering steals just 7.8 times per game.

1994–95 Prospects

Atlanta may have been last season's biggest surprise. Lenny Wilkens got them to play defense, got a career year from Kevin Willis, and tied a franchise record for wins by a coach with 57. And the Hawks feasted on the NBA's weaker teams, going 27–1 against Boston, Detroit, Milwaukee, Philadelphia, Washington, Dallas, Minnesota, and Sacramento. On the other hand, Atlanta was 30-24 against the rest of the league. Maybe that was a harbinger of their problems in the playoffs. After putting up the Eastern Conference's best record last season, Atlanta was a disappointment in the play-offs, struggling against Miami and not putting up much of a fight against Indiana.

Atlanta appears ill-situated to repeat last season's success. Without Dominique Wilkins or Danny Manning, the Hawks lack the offensive firepower to compete with the best teams in the NBA. Atlanta still has Dominique Wilkins' $3.5 million salary slot to fill. They're antici-pating using it to facilitate a trade before the trading deadline in February. They're looking for a backup point guard and a shooter off the bench. They'll count on scoring from Kevin Willis, Stacey Augmon, Kenny Norman, and Mookie Blaylock. But Willis had a career year last season, and he may not be able to do it all two years in a row. Depth is also a problem; Duane Ferrell and Craig Ehlo are quality reserves, but after them, the bench drops off sharply.

Atlanta should have a winning record again, but they won't go 57–25 this season. The Hawks don't figure to beat out Cleveland for the Central Division crown. We think they will make the playoffs, but continue their streak of having never made it past the conference semifinals since they moved to Atlanta from St. Louis in 1968.

Team Directory

Owner: R. E. (Ted) Turner
President: Stan Kasten
VP/General manager: Pete Babcock

Chairman of the board: J. M. Gearon
Exec. vice president: Lee Douglas
Dir., media rel.: Arthur Triche, Jr.

1993–94 Review

EASTERN CONFERENCE						WESTERN CONFERENCE					
ATLANTIC DIV.			CENTRAL DIV.			MIDWEST DIV.			PACIFIC DIV.		
	W	L		W	L		W	L		W	L
NY	2	2	ATL	-	-	HOU	1	1	SEA	1	1
ORL	3	1	CHI	2	3	SAN	1	0	PHO	1	1
NJ	1	3	CLE	3	1	UTAH	1	1	GS	0	2
MIA	3	1	IND	3	2	DEN	1	1	POR	1	1
BOS	4	0	CHA	4	1	MIN	2	0	LAL	1	1
PHI	4	0	DET	4	0	DAL	2	0	SAC	2	1
WAS	4	0	MIL	5	0				LAC	1	1
	21	7		21	7		8	3		7	8

1993–94 finish: 57–25 (36–5 home, 21–20 away), first in Central Div.

1994–95 Schedule

11/4	Indiana	7:30 pm	12/30	@ Cleveland	7:30 pm	3/3	Detroit	7:30 pm
11/5	Detroit	7:30 pm	1/3	Portland	7:30 pm	3/5	@ Orlando	7:30 pm
11/7	@ Utah	9:00 pm	1/4	@ New York	7:30 pm	3/8	Denver	7:30 pm
11/9	@ Phoenix	9:00 pm	1/6	Wash.	7:30 pm	3/10	New York	7:30 pm
11/10	@ LA Clip.	10:30 pm	1/7	New Jersey	7:30 pm	3/12	@ Boston	2:30 pm
11/12	@ Sacra.	10:30 pm	1/10	@ Wash.	7:30 pm	3/13	Houston	8:00 pm
11/15	Boston	7:30 pm	1/13	Orlando	7:30 pm	3/15	@ Chicago	8:30 pm
11/18	Milw.	7:30 pm	1/16	Miami	3:30 pm	3/18	Phoenix	7:30 pm
11/19	@ New York	8:30 pm	1/18	Phila.	7:30 pm	3/20	LA Clip.	7:30 pm
11/22	Phila.	7:30 pm	1/20	@ Indiana	7:30 pm	3/22	Miami	7:30 pm
11/23	@ Minn.	8:00 pm	1/21	Boston	7:30 pm	3/24	@ Cleveland	7:30 pm
11/25	LA Lakers	7:30 pm	1/25	@ Charlotte	7:30 pm	3/25	Chicago	7:30 pm
11/29	Charlotte	7:30 pm	1/26	Cleveland	7:30 pm	3/28	@ Portland	10:00 pm
12/2	@ Chicago	8:30 pm	1/28	Charlotte	7:30 pm	3/30	@ Gold. St.	8:00 pm
12/3	Orlando	7:30 pm	1/30	@ Miami	7:30 pm	3/31	@ LA Lakers	10:30 pm
12/6	@ New Jersey	7:30 pm	2/1	Gold. St.	7:30 pm	4/2	@ Seattle	4:00 pm
12/7	@ Boston	7:30 pm	2/3	Seattle	8:00 pm	4/5	Cleveland	7:30 pm
12/9	New York	7:30 pm	2/4	@ Detroit	7:30 pm	4/7	Indiana	8:00 pm
12/10	@ Orlando	7:30 pm	2/6	@ Phila.	7:30 pm	4/9	@ Milw.	1:00 pm
12/13	Minn.	7:30 pm	2/8	New Jersey	7:30 pm	4/11	@ Phila.	7:30 pm
12/14	@ Indiana	7:30 pm	2/14	@ Denver	8:00 pm	4/12	Wash.	7:30 pm
12/16	Chicago	7:30 pm	2/17	@ Dallas	8:30 pm	4/14	@ Cleveland	7:30 pm
12/17	@ Miami	7:30 pm	2/18	@ San Ant.	8:30 pm	4/16	@ Charlotte	3:00 pm
12/20	Milw.	7:30 pm	2/21	Chicago	7:30 pm	4/19	@ New Jersey	7:30 pm
12/22	Utah	7:30 pm	2/23	Dallas	7:30 pm	4/21	Detroit	7:30 pm
12/23	@ Detroit	8:00 pm	2/24	@ Wash.	7:30 pm	4/23	@ Indiana	3:30 pm
12/27	@ Houston	8:30 pm	2/27	Sacra.	7:30 pm			
12/29	San Ant.	7:30 pm	3/2	@ Milw.	8:30 pm			

1993–94 Team Stats

NAME	G	MIN	FG	FGA	FG%	3FG	3FGA	3FG%	FT	FTA	FT%	ORB	TRB	AST	PF	STL	BLK	TO	PTS	AVG
Wilkins	49	1687	430	996	43.2	61	198	30.8	275	322	85.4	119	305	114	87	63	22	120	1196	24.4
Willis	80	2867	627	1257	49.9	9	24	37.5	268	376	71.3	335	963	150	250	79	38	188	1531	19.1
Manning	26	925	177	372	47.6	1	3	33.3	54	83	65.1	49	169	85	93	46	25	86	409	15.7
Augmon	82	2605	439	861	51.0	1	7	14.3	333	436	76.4	178	394	187	144	149	45	147	1212	14.8
Blaylock	81	2915	444	1079	41.1	114	341	33.4	116	159	73.0	117	424	789	161	212	44	196	1118	13.8
Ehlo	82	2147	316	708	44.6	77	221	34.8	112	154	72.7	71	279	273	85	136	26	130	821	10.0
Ferrell	72	1155	184	379	48.5	1	9	11.1	144	184	78.3	62	129	65	192	44	16	64	513	7.1
Lang	82	1608	215	458	46.9	1	4	25.0	73	106	68.9	126	313	51	179	38	87	81	504	6.1
Keefe	63	763	96	213	45.1	0	0	—	81	111	73.0	77	201	34	80	20	9	60	273	4.3
Koncak	82	1823	159	369	43.1	0	3	0.0	24	36	66.7	83	365	102	236	63	125	44	342	4.2
Whatley	82	1004	120	236	50.8	0	6	0.0	52	66	78.8	22	99	181	93	59	2	78	292	3.6
Graham	21	128	21	57	36.8	3	13	23.1	13	17	76.5	4	12	13	11	4	5	5	58	2.8
Edwards	16	107	17	49	34.7	0	1	0.0	9	16	56.3	7	18	8	9	9	5	6	43	2.7
Grace	3	8	2	3	66.7	0	0	—	0	2	0.0	0	1	1	3	0	0	0	4	1.3
Bagley	3	13	0	2	0.0	0	0	—	2	2	100.0	0	—	3	2	2	0	0	2	0.7
Hawks	82	19755	3247	7039	46.1	268	830	32.3	1556	2070	75.2	1250	3673	2056	1625	915	449	1252	8318	101.4
Opp.	82	19755	3163	6954	45.5	275	872	31.5	1285	1732	74.2	1157	3515	1897	1722	641	338	1465	7886	96.2

History

TITLES

1956–57 Western Div. champs
1957–58 NBA champs
1959–60 Western Div. champs
1960–61 Western Div. champs

1979–80 Central,Div. champs
1986–87 Central Div. champs
1993–94 Central Div. champs

ALL-TIME TEAM RECORDS

Career

Games played	Dominique Wilkins	882	1982–94
Total points	Dominique Wilkins	23,292	1982–94
Field goals made	Dominique Wilkins	8,752	1982–94
Field goals attempted	Dominique Wilkins	18,743	1982–94
Free throws made	Bob Pettit	6,182	1954–65
Free throws attempted	Bob Pettit	8,119	1954–65
Total rebounds	Bob Pettit	12,851	1954–65
Assists	Glenn (Doc) Rivers	3,866	1983–91
Steals	Dominique Wilkins	1,245	1982–94

Season

Total points	Bob Pettit	2,429	1961–62
Field goals made	Dominique Wilkins	909	1987–88
Free throws made	Bob Pettit	695	1961–62
Total rebounds	Bob Pettit	1,540	1960–61
Assists	Glenn (Doc) Rivers	823	1986–87
Steals	Mookie Blaylock	212	1993–94

Game

Total points	Dominique Wilkins	57	vs. Chicago, 12/10/86
	Dominique Wilkins	57	vs. New Jersey, 4/10/86
	Lou Hudson	57	vs. Chicago, 11/10/69
Field goals made	Lou Hudson	25	vs. Chicago, 11/10/69
Free throws made	Dominique Wilkins	23	vs. Chicago, 12/8/92
Total rebounds	Kevin Willis	33	vs. Washington, 2/19/92
Assists	Mookie Blaylock	23	vs. Utah, 3/6/93
Steals	Glenn (Doc) Rivers	8	vs. Miami, 11/24/89

LEADING COACHES

	REGULAR SEASON				PLAYOFFS		
NAME	YEARS	W	L	PCT	W	L	PCT
Richie Guerin	1964–72	327	291	.529	26	34	.433
Mike Fratello	1983–90	324	250	.564	18	22	.450
Hubie Brown	1976–81	199	208	.489	6	10	.375
Cotton Fitzsimmons	1972–76	140	180	.438	2	4	.333
Bob Weiss	1990–93	124	122	.504	2	6	.250

Atlanta Hawks 1994–95 Roster

Head Coach: Lenny Wilkens

No.	Name	Pos.	Ht.	Wt.	Yrs.	Born	College
31	Adam Keefe	F	6-9	241	2	2/22/70	Stanford
28	Andrew Lang	C	6-11	250	6	6/28/66	Arkansas
41	Blair Rasmussen	C	7-0	250	8	11/13/62	Oregon
3	Craig Ehlo	G	6-7	205	11	8/11/61	Washington State
34	Doug Edwards	F	6-7	235	1	1/21/71	Florida State
33	Duane Ferrell	F	6-7	215	6	2/28/65	Georgia Tech
1	Ennis Whatley	G	6-3	180	8	8/11/62	Alabama
	Gaylon Nickerson	G	6-3	190	R	2/5/69	NW Oklahoma State
32	Jon Koncak	C	7-0	250	9	5/17/63	Southern Methodist
	Ken Norman	F	6-9	238	7	9/5/64	Illinois
42	Kevin Willis	F-C	7-0	240	10	9/6/62	Michigan State
10	Mookie Blaylock	G	6-1	185	6	3/20/67	Oklahoma
25	Paul Graham	F	6-6	200	3	11/28/67	Ohio
2	Stacey Augmon	G-F	6-8	205	3	8/1/68	Nevada-Las Vegas

Arena Information

The Omni (16,368)
Tickets: 404-249-6400, 800-249-6400
Ticket prices: $150, $55, $44, $33, $30, $25, $20, $15, $10

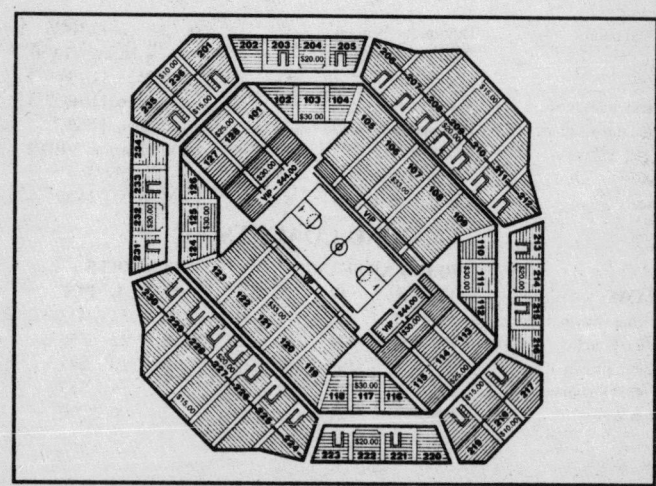

Mookie Blaylock

Full name: Daron Oshay Blaylock
HT: 6-1   **WT:** 185
Born: 3/20/67, Garland, TX
High school: Garland (TX)
College: Oklahoma

Blaylock is one of the best defensive point guards in the NBA. He's also a good passer. Last season, Blaylock set career highs in minutes, field goals made, field goals attempted, offensive rebounds (117), defensive rebounds (307), total rebounds, assists, steals (212, a Hawks record), blocks and points. Blaylock now ranks eleventh on the Hawks' all-time steals list. Blaylock started 81 games for Atlanta, and led the team in minutes, 3-point field goals made, 3-point field goals attempted, assists, and steals. His 789 assists were second highest in club history, his 114 3-point field goals made were third highest in team history, and his 341 3-point field goals attempted were a team record.

REGULAR SEASON	G	MIN	FG	FGx	3FG	3PTx	FT	FTx	REB	AST	STL	BLK	PTS	AVG
'89-90 NEW JERSEY	50	1267	212	37.1	18	22.5	63	77.8	140	210	82	14	505	10.1
'90-91 NEW JERSEY	72	2585	432	41.6	14	15.4	139	79.0	249	441	169	40	1017	14.1
'91-92 NEW JERSEY	72	2548	429	43.2	12	22.2	126	71.2	269	492	170	40	996	13.8
'92-93 ATLANTA	80	2820	414	42.9	118	37.5	123	72.8	280	671	203	23	1069	13.4
'93-94 ATLANTA	81	2915	444	41.1	114	33.4	116	73.0	424	789	212	44	1118	13.8
5 YR TOTALS	355	12135	1931	41.6	276	31.3	567	74.4	1362	2603	836	161	4705	13.3
'93-94 RANK NBA Gs	27	7	30	106	13	57	68	101	6	2	2	9	33	39
'94-95 PROJECTIONS	82	3115	465	40.6	158	36.1	112	72.3	524	945	233	53	1200	14.6

PLAYOFFS	G	MIN	FG	FGx	3FG	3PTx	FT	FTx	REB	AST	STL	BLK	PTS	AVG
'91-92 NEW JERSEY	4	148	17	30.9	1	16.7	3	75.0	16	31	15	2	38	9.5
'92-93 ATLANTA	3	99	9	36.0	4	33.3	5	83.3	13	13	3	4	27	9.0
'93-94 ATLANTA	11	415	48	34.0	22	34.4	25	83.3	55	98	24	5	143	13.0
TOTALS	18	662	74	33.5	27	32.9	33	82.5	84	142	42	11	208	11.6

Craig Ehlo

No. 3/G

Full name: Joel Craig Ehlo
HT: 6-7 **WT:** 205
Born: 8/11/61, Lubbock, TX
High school: Monterey (Lubbock)
College: Washington State

Last season was Ehlo's first as a Hawk; he had spent the previous 7 seasons with Cleveland under Coach Lenny Wilkins before landing with Atlanta as a free agent. Not known as particularly quick, Ehlo plays solid defense and has a good shot from 3-point range. He hit 77 3-point FGs last season, seventh highest in Hawks history. The 3-point shot deserted him late last season, though; he was only 10 for 58 (.147) from 3-point land in his last 24 games. Last season, Ehlo was 1 of only 5 Hawks to play in all 82 games. He had 136 steals, a career high. His 1.7 steals per game ranked third on the team and twenty-third in the league. He led the team in scoring twice and in rebounds once. He scored 20 points or more in 4 games.

REGULAR SEASON		G	MIN	FG	FG%	3FG	3PT%	FT	FT%	REB	AST	STL	BLK	PTS	AVG
'85-86	HOUSTON	36	199	36	42.9	3	33.3	23	79.3	46	29	11	4	98	2.7
'86-87	CLEVELAND	44	890	99	41.4	5	17.2	70	70.7	161	92	40	30	273	6.2
'87-88	CLEVELAND	79	1709	226	46.6	22	34.4	89	67.4	274	206	82	30	563	7.1
'88-89	CLEVELAND	82	1867	249	47.5	39	39.0	71	60.7	295	266	110	19	608	7.4
'89-90	CLEVELAND	81	2834	436	46.4	104	41.9	126	68.1	439	371	126	23	1102	13.6
'90-91	CLEVELAND	82	2766	344	44.5	49	32.9	95	67.9	388	376	121	34	832	10.1
'91-92	CLEVELAND	63	2016	310	45.3	69	41.3	87	70.7	307	238	78	22	776	12.3
'92-93	CLEVELAND	82	2559	385	49.0	93	38.1	86	71.7	403	254	104	22	949	11.6
'93-94	ATLANTA	82	2147	316	44.5	77	34.8	112	72.7	279	273	136	26	821	10.0
11 YR TOTALS		683	17299	2446	46.0	461	37.4	779	68.9	2626	2137	822	213	6132	9.0
'93-94	RANK NBA Gs	1	54	56	67	22	48	71	102	28	52	15	22	58	6.6
'94-95	PROJECTIONS	82	1962	288	43.3	73	33.0	118	73.8	232	264	147	26	767	9.4

PLAYOFFS		G	MIN	FG	FG%	3FG	3PT%	FT	FT%	REB	AST	STL	BLK	PTS	AVG
'84-85	HOUSTON	3	6	1	100.0	0	---	2	100.0	0	0	4	0	4	1.3
'85-86	HOUSTON	10	38	8	50.0	0	0.0	4	80.0	3	6	4	1	20	2.0
'87-88	CLEVELAND	5	128	17	42.5	0	0.0	10	62.5	18	17	5	0	44	8.8
'88-89	CLEVELAND	4	97	17	43.6	5	38.5	9	81.8	6	13	3	1	48	12.0
'89-90	CLEVELAND	5	196	26	41.9	5	23.3	12	63.2	32	32	6	0	69	13.8
'91-92	CLEVELAND	17	552	63	41.4	21	41.2	16	76.2	77	77	21	5	163	9.6
'92-93	CLEVELAND	9	289	38	41.8	10	38.5	12	80.0	31	25	12	4	98	10.9
'93-94	ATLANTA	11	317	50	42.4	8	34.8	17	70.8	30	40	11	0	125	11.4
TOTALS		64	1623	220	42.4	49	35.8	82	72.6	197	210	66	11	571	8.9

Jon Koncak

Full name: Jon Francis Koncak
HT: 7-0 **WT:** 250
Born: 5/17/63, Cedar Rapids, IA
High school: Center (Kansas City, MO)
College: Southern Methodist
Koncak is a big body in the middle who rebounds, plays defense and blocks shots. He posted 125 blocks, a new career-high. And he led the team in rebounding twice—pretty impressive when you play next to Kevin Willis. But he's weak offensively; his mid-range jumper is improving, but he's a weak ballhandler, a poor passer, and still not much of a scorer. 12 points was his top game last season (twice). He's durable; last season, Koncak was 1 of 5 Hawks who played in all 82 games, and he started in 78 of them. Koncak is eighth in Hawks history in games played, third in blocks, eighth in offensive rebounds (978), and sixth in defensive rebounds (2,422).

REGULAR SEASON		G	MIN	FG	FGx	3FG	3PTx	FT	FTx	REB	AST	STL	BLK	PTS	AVG
'85-86	ATLANTA	82	1695	263	50.7	0	0.0	156	60.7	467	55	37	69	682	8.3
'86-87	ATLANTA	82	1684	169	48.0	0	0.0	125	65.4	493	31	52	76	463	5.6
'87-88	ATLANTA	49	1073	98	48.3	0	0.0	83	61.0	333	19	36	56	279	5.7
'88-89	ATLANTA	74	1531	141	52.4	0	0.0	63	55.3	453	56	54	98	345	4.7
'89-90	ATLANTA	54	977	78	61.4	0	0.0	42	53.2	226	23	38	34	198	3.7
'90-91	ATLANTA	77	1931	140	43.6	1	12.5	32	59.3	375	124	74	76	313	4.1
'91-92	ATLANTA	77	1489	111	39.1	0	0.0	19	65.5	261	132	50	67	241	3.1
'92-93	ATLANTA	78	1975	124	46.4	3	37.5	24	48.0	427	140	75	100	275	3.5
'93-94	ATLANTA	82	1823	159	43.1	0	0.0	24	66.7	365	102	63	125	342	4.2
	9 YR TOTALS	655	14178	1283	47.3	4	10.3	568	60.0	3400	682	479	701	3138	4.8
'93-94	RANK NBA Cs	1	17	28	43	14	14	43	31	21	12	9	10	29	37
'94-95	PROJECTIONS	82	1871	177	41.5	0	0.0	19	73.1	370	93	62	151	373	4.5

PLAYOFFS		G	MIN	FG	FGx	3FG	3PTx	FT	FTx	REB	AST	STL	BLK	PTS	AVG
'85-86	ATLANTA	9	193	14	48.3	0	---	26	56.5	34	5	6	10	54	6.0
'86-87	ATLANTA	8	86	7	53.8	0	---	6	75.0	25	3	3	4	20	2.5
'88-89	ATLANTA	5	192	18	62.1	0	---	28	84.8	48	4	2	8	64	12.8
'90-91	ATLANTA	5	133	4	28.6	0	---	2	100.0	23	7	2	4	10	2.0
'92-93	ATLANTA	3	89	1	10.0	0	---	1	50.0	24	4	3	5	3	1.0
'93-94	ATLANTA	11	195	27	40.9	0	---	4	40.0	30	13	6	12	58	5.3
	TOTALS	41	888	71	44.1	0	---	67	66.3	184	36	22	43	209	5.1

Kevin Willis

No. 42/F-C

Full name: Kevin Alvin Willis
HT: 7-0 **WT:** 240
Born: 9/6/62, Los Angeles, CA
High school: Pershing (Detroit, MI)
College: Michigan State

Willis is the team's star now. Never much of a passer or ball handler, Willis may be the best rebounder in the NBA this side of Dennis Rodman. His 55 double-doubles was fourth highest in the NBA, behind Shaquille O'Neal, Hakeem Olajuwon, and Karl Malone. He's also the best scorer on the team, now that Dominique Wilkins and Danny Manning are gone. He runs the floor well for a player his size, and has a good jump shot. Last season was Willis' best. He led Atlanta in field goals made, field goals attempted, all rebounding categories, points, and points per game. And he set career highs in field goals made, field goals attempted, 3-pointers made, free throws attempted, steals, points and scoring average. Willis led Atlanta in scoring 24 times and in rebounding 71 times.

REGULAR SEASON		G	MIN	FG	FGx	3FG	3PTx	FT	FTx	REB	AST	STL	BLK	PTS	AVG
'84-85	ATLANTA	82	1785	322	46.7	2	22.2	119	65.7	522	36	31	49	765	9.3
'85-86	ATLANTA	62	2300	419	51.7	0	0.0	172	65.4	704	45	66	44	1010	12.3
'86-87	ATLANTA	81	2626	538	53.6	1	25.0	227	70.9	849	62	65	61	1304	16.1
'87-88	ATLANTA	75	2091	356	51.8	0	0.0	159	64.9	547	28	68	42	871	11.6
'88-89	ATLANTA	did not play -- injured													
'89-90	ATLANTA	81	2273	418	51.9	2	28.6	168	68.3	645	57	63	47	1006	12.4
'90-91	ATLANTA	80	2373	444	50.4	4	40.0	159	66.8	704	99	60	40	1051	13.1
'91-92	ATLANTA	81	2962	591	48.3	6	16.2	292	80.4	1258	173	72	54	1480	18.3
'92-93	ATLANTA	80	2878	616	50.6	7	24.1	196	65.3	1028	165	68	41	1435	17.9
'93-94	ATLANTA	80	2867	627	49.9	9	37.5	268	71.3	963	150	79	38	1531	19.1
10 YR TOTALS		722	22155	4331	50.5	31	24.2	1760	69.5	7220	815	572	416	10453	14.5
'93-94 RANK NBA Fs		23	8	5	37	41	11	14	69	3	41	27	56	7	10
'94-95 PROJECTIONS		80	2931	665	49.7	11	45.8	302	72.1	955	155	85	34	1643	20.5

PLAYOFFS		G	MIN	FG	FGx	3FG	3PTx	FT	FTx	REB	AST	STL	BLK	PTS	AVG
'85-86	ATLANTA	9	280	55	58.1	0	---	15	65.2	65	5	7	8	125	13.9
'86-87	ATLANTA	9	358	60	52.2	0	---	21	67.7	83	6	9	7	141	15.7
'87-88	ATLANTA	12	462	80	58.0	0	0.0	34	68.0	108	11	10	10	194	16.2
'90-91	ATLANTA	5	159	27	40.3	2	66.7	21	70.0	45	5	3	1	77	15.4
'92-93	ATLANTA	3	103	21	48.7	0	0.0	8	57.1	26	3	2	0	50	16.7
'93-94	ATLANTA	11	362	59	45.7	0	0.0	16	76.2	119	11	8	5	134	12.2
TOTALS		49	1722	302	51.0	2	20.0	115	68.0	446	41	39	31	721	14.7

Ken Norman

No. 3/F

Full name: Kenneth Darnel Norman
HT: 6-9   **WT:** 238
Born: 9/5/64, Chicago, IL
High school: Richard T. Crane
   (Chicago)
College: Illinois

Norman played for Milwaukee last season. He started 75 games for the Bucks. He started off fast, averaging 22.8 points and 8.2 rebounds in Milwaukee's first 5 games on 58.5 percent shooting. He also finished strong, averaging 17.5 points and 7.5 rebounds per game in the last 13 games of the season. He put up 189 3-point attempts, tops on the Bucks; his 63 3-pointers were second on the team. Both totals doubled the totals he entered the season with (31 for 145 heading into '93–94). His best game was March 31 vs. Portland, when he scored 37 points, most by a Buck last season. He also turned in the Bucks' best rebounding performance, snagging 18 boards at Charlotte February 18.

REGULAR SEASON		G	MIN	FG	FG%	3FG	3PT%	FT	FT%	REB	AST	STL	BLK	PTS	AVG
'87-88	LA CLIPPERS	66	1435	241	48.2	0	0.0	87	51.2	263	78	44	34	569	8.6
'88-89	LA CLIPPERS	80	3020	638	50.2	4	19.0	170	63.0	667	277	106	66	1450	18.1
'89-90	LA CLIPPERS	70	2334	484	51.0	7	43.8	153	63.2	470	160	78	59	1128	16.1
'90-91	LA CLIPPERS	70	2309	520	50.1	6	18.8	173	62.9	497	159	63	63	1219	17.4
'91-92	LA CLIPPERS	77	2009	402	49.0	4	14.3	121	53.5	448	125	53	66	929	12.1
'92-93	LA CLIPPERS	76	2477	498	51.1	10	26.3	131	59.5	571	165	59	58	1137	15.0
'93-94	MILWAUKEE	82	2539	412	44.8	63	33.3	92	50.3	500	222	58	46	979	11.9
7 YR TOTALS		521	16123	3195	49.4	94	28.1	927	58.4	3416	1186	461	392	7411	14.2
'93-94	RANK NBA Fs	1	27	28	50.9	8	22	75	132	31	18	52	46	32	39
'94-95	PROJECTIONS	82	2653	376	41.9	107	38.1	69	45.7	487	261	56	36	928	11.3

PLAYOFFS		G	MIN	FG	FG%	3FG	3PT%	FT	FT%	REB	AST	STL	BLK	PTS	AVG
'91-92	LA CLIPPERS	5	184	27	50.9	0	0.0	9	52.9	49	15	4	3	63	12.6
'92-93	LA CLIPPERS	5	164	25	37.3	3	37.5	11	50.0	41	12	4	0	64	12.8
TOTALS		10	348	52	43.3	3	30.0	20	51.3	90	27	8	3	127	12.7

Duane Ferrell   No. 33/F

HT: 6-7 **WT:** 215
Born: 2/28/65, Baltimore, MD
High school: Calvert Hall (Towson, MD)
College: Georgia Tech

Ferrell is a solid defender and one of Atlanta's best perimeter shooters. He played in 72 games, scored 20 points or more 6 times, and led the team in scoring 4 times.

REGULAR SEASON		G	MIN	FG	FG%	3FG	3PT%	FT	FT%	REB	AST	STL	BLK	PTS	AVG
'88-89	ATLANTA	41	231	35	42.2	0	---	30	68.2	41	10	7	6	100	2.4
'89-90	ATLANTA	14	29	5	35.7	0	0.0	2	33.3	7	2	1	0	12	0.9
'90-91	ATLANTA	78	1165	174	48.9	2	66.7	125	80.1	179	55	33	27	475	6.1
'91-92	ATLANTA	66	1598	331	52.4	11	33.3	166	76.1	210	92	49	17	839	12.7
'92-93	ATLANTA	82	1736	327	47.0	9	25.0	176	77.9	191	132	59	17	839	10.2
'93-94	ATLANTA	72	1155	184	48.5	1	11.1	144	78.3	129	65	44	16	513	7.1
	6 YR TOTALS	353	5914	1056	48.9	23	28.0	643	77.1	757	356	193	83	2778	7.9
'93-94	RANK NBA Fs	72	89	81	48	69	74	50	21	116	78	72	100	74	90
'94-95	PROJECTIONS	73	1024	148	43.2	0	0.0	141	81.5	100	52	42	16	437	6.0

PLAYOFFS		G	MIN	FG	FG%	3FG	3PT%	FT	FT%	REB	AST	STL	BLK	PTS	AVG
'90-91	ATLANTA	5	73	8	44.4	0	---	8	66.7	17	3	0	0	24	4.8
'92-93	ATLANTA	3	54	14	60.9	1	33.3	4	80.0	5	1	0	0	33	11.0
'93-94	ATLANTA	11	187	25	39.7	1	25.0	27	75.0	31	17	5	3	78	7.1
	TOTALS	19	314	47	45.2	2	28.6	39	73.6	53	21	5	3	135	7.1

Stacey Augmon No. 2/G-F

Full name: Stacey Orlando Augmon
HT: 6-8 **WT:** 205
Born: 8/1/68, Pasadena, CA
High school: John Muir (Pasadena)
College: UNLV

Augmon is a defensive stud (1.8 steals per game) who's improving as a shooter. He was the only Hawk to start all 82 games last year.

REGULAR SEASON		G	MIN	FG	FG%	3FG	3PT%	FT	FT%	REB	AST	STL	BLK	PTS	AVG
'91-92	ATLANTA	82	2505	440	48.9	1	16.7	213	66.6	420	201	124	27	1094	13.3
'92-93	ATLANTA	73	2112	397	50.1	0	0.0	227	73.9	287	170	91	18	1021	14.0
'93-94	ATLANTA	82	2605	439	51.0	1	14.3	333	76.4	394	187	149	45	1212	14.8
	3 YR TOTALS	237	7222	1276	50.0	2	11.8	773	72.7	1101	558	364	90	3327	14.0
'93-94	RANK NBA Gs	1	28	31	5	124	125	7	81	6	75	12	8	24	29
'94-95	PROJECTIONS	82	3075	481	51.9	2	20.0	463	80.0	476	201	203	72	1427	17.4

PLAYOFFS		G	MIN	FG	FG%	3FG	3PT%	FT	FT%	REB	AST	STL	BLK	PTS	AVG
'92-93	ATLANTA	3	93	14	45.2	0	---	8	66.7	8	5	4	0	36	12.0
'93-94	ATLANTA	11	324	46	51.7	0	---	27	71.1	29	28	7	2	119	10.8
	TOTALS	14	417	60	50.0	0	---	35	70.0	37	33	11	2	155	11.1

Adam Keefe   No. 31/F

Full name: Adam Thomas Keefe
HT: 6-9 **WT:** 241
Born: 2/22/70, Irvine, CA
High school: Woodbridge (Irvine)
College: Stanford

Keefe led Atlanta in rebounding 4 times. His performance slumped in his second season, and consequently his minutes decreased.

REGULAR SEASON		G	MIN	FG	FG%	3FG	3PT%	FT	FT%	REB	AST	STL	BLK	PTS	AVG
'92-93	ATLANTA	82	1549	188	50.0	0	0.0	166	70.0	432	80	57	16	542	6.6
'93-94	ATLANTA	63	763	96	45.1	0	0.0	81	73.0	201	34	20	9	273	4.3
2 YR TOTALS		145	2312	284	48.2	0	0.0	247	71.0	633	114	77	25	815	5.6
'93-94	RANK NBA Fs	99	112	110	90	78	78	86	55	97	108	110	120	105	112
'94-95	PROJECTIONS	44	-23	-3	42.9	0	0.0	-2	66.7	-6	-1	0	0	-8	-0.2

PLAYOFFS		G	MIN	FG	FG%	3FG	3PT%	FT	FT%	REB	AST	STL	BLK	PTS	AVG
'92-93	ATLANTA	3	53	7	53.8	0	---	4	66.7	13	6	1	0	18	6.0
'93-94	ATLANTA	7	62	6	60.0	0	---	4	44.4	13	2	1	1	16	2.3
TOTALS		10	115	13	56.5	0	---	8	53.3	26	8	2	1	34	3.4

Andrew Lang   No. 28/C

Full name: Andrew Charles Lang, Jr.
HT: 6-11 **WT:** 250
Born: 6/28/66, Pine Bluff, AR
High school: Dollarway (Pine Bluff)
College: Arkansas

Lang is a role player who comes off the bench to block shots and rebound. He runs pretty well for a player his size.

REGULAR SEASON		G	MIN	FG	FG%	3FG	3PT%	FT	FT%	REB	AST	STL	BLK	PTS	AVG
'89-90	PHOENIX	74	1011	97	55.7	0	---	64	65.3	271	21	22	133	258	3.5
'90-91	PHOENIX	63	1152	109	57.7	0	0.0	93	71.5	303	27	17	127	311	4.9
'91-92	PHOENIX	81	1965	248	52.2	0	0.0	126	76.8	546	43	48	201	622	7.7
'92-93	PHILADELPHIA	73	1861	149	42.5	1	20.0	87	76.3	436	79	46	141	386	5.3
'93-94	ATLANTA	82	1608	215	46.9	1	25.0	73	68.9	313	51	38	87	504	6.1
6 YR TOTALS		435	8123	878	49.8	2	18.2	482	71.7	2016	230	188	737	2240	5.1
'93-94	RANK NBA Cs	1	21	20	36	8	6	26	26	24	24	21	17	22	27
'94-95	PROJECTIONS	82	1575	240	46.0	2	40.0	61	65.6	258	50	38	52	543	6.6

PLAYOFFS		G	MIN	FG	FG%	3FG	3PT%	FT	FT%	REB	AST	STL	BLK	PTS	AVG
'88-89	PHOENIX	4	8	0	0.0	0	---	0	---	6	1	0	0	0	0.0
'89-90	PHOENIX	12	93	6	66.7	0	---	4	57.1	20	2	3	10	16	1.3
'90-91	PHOENIX	4	55	6	54.5	0	---	14	82.4	18	1	1	3	26	6.5
'91-92	PHOENIX	8	192	15	37.5	0	---	15	78.9	32	2	3	15	45	5.6
'93-94	ATLANTA	11	234	29	46.0	0	0.0	17	77.3	47	5	6	20	75	6.8
TOTALS		39	582	56	44.8	0	0.0	50	76.9	123	11	13	48	162	4.2

Ennis Whatley   No. 1/G

HT: 6-3 **WT:** 180
Born: 8/11/62, Birmingham, AL
High school: Phillips (Birmingham)
College: Alabama

Whatley is a valuable reserve who played in all 82 games without starting. This first-round pick in '83 has bounced around Israel, the CBA, and 7 different NBA teams.

REGULAR SEASON		G	MIN	FG	FGx	3FG	3PTx	FT	FTx	REB	AST	STL	BLK	PTS	AVG
'84-85	CHICAGO	70	1385	140	44.7	1	11.1	68	79.1	101	381	66	10	349	5.0
'85-86	CLE-WAS-SA	14	107	15	42.9	0	---	5	50.0	14	23	5	1	35	2.5
'86-87	WASHINGTON	73	1816	246	47.8	0	0.0	126	76.4	194	392	92	10	618	8.5
'87-88	ATLANTA	5	24	4	44.4	0	---	3	75.0	4	2	2	0	11	2.2
'88-89	LA CLIPPERS	8	90	12	36.4	0	---	10	90.9	16	22	7	1	34	4.3
'91-92	PORTLAND	23	209	21	41.2	0	---	27	87.1	21	34	14	3	69	3.0
'93-94	ATLANTA	82	1004	120	50.8	0	0.0	52	78.8	99	181	59	2	292	3.6
	8 YR TOTALS	355	6794	819	46.9	1	4.3	437	76.3	646	1697	364	44	2076	5.8
'93-94	RANK NBA Gs	1	103	113	6	131	131	108	65	104	77	78	115	113	124
'94-95	PROJECTIONS	82	1348	152	55.9	0	0.0	29	76.3	111	246	71	-3	333	4.1

PLAYOFFS		G	MIN	FG	FGx	3FG	3PTx	FT	FTx	REB	AST	STL	BLK	PTS	AVG
'86-87	WASHINGTON	2	32	3	25.0	0	---	0	---	3	6	2	0	6	3.0
'91-92	PORTLAND	15	96	6	30.0	0	0.0	4	100.0	10	13	7	0	16	1.1
'93-94	ATLANTA	11	113	9	32.1	0	---	6	75.0	14	12	7	0	24	2.2
	TOTALS	28	241	18	30.0	0	0.0	10	83.3	27	31	16	0	46	1.6

Lenny Wilkens   Coach

Full name: Leonard Randolph Wilkens
HT: 6-1 **WT:** 180
Born: 10/28/37, Brooklyn, NY
High school: Boys (Brooklyn)
College: Providence

Coach of the Year in '93–94, Wilkins needs just 12 more wins to pass Red Auerbach as the NBA's all-time winningest coach.

	REGULAR SEASON				PLAYOFFS			
YEAR	TEAM	W	L	PCT	FINISH	W	L	PCT	
'78-79	SEATTLE	52	30	.634	1st/Pacific Div.	12	5	.706	won NBA Finals over Washington, 4-1
'79-80	SEATTLE	56	26	.683	2nd/Pacific Div.	7	8	.467	lost Western Conf. finals to LA Lakers, 4-1
'80-81	SEATTLE	34	48	.415	6th/Pacific Div.				
'81-82	SEATTLE	52	30	.634	2nd/Pacific Div.	3	5	.375	lost Western Conf. semifinals to San Antonio, 4-1
'82-83	SEATTLE	48	34	.585	3rd/Pacific Div.	0	2	.000	lost Western Conf. first round to Portland, 2-0
'83-84	SEATTLE	42	40	.512	3rd/Pacific Div.	2	3	.400	lost Western Conf. first round to Dallas, 3-2
'84-85	SEATTLE	31	51	.378	4th/Pacific Div.				
'86-87	CLEVELAND	31	51	.378	6th/Central Div.				
'87-88	CLEVELAND	42	40	.512	T4th/Central Div.	2	3	.400	lost Eastern Conf. first round to Chicago, 3-2
'88-89	CLEVELAND	57	25	.695	2nd/Central Div.	2	3	.400	lost Eastern Conf. first round to Chicago, 3-2
'89-90	CLEVELAND	42	40	.512	T4th/Central Div.	2	3	.400	lost Eastern Conf. first round to Philadelphia, 3-2
'90-91	CLEVELAND	33	49	.402	6th/Central Div.				
'91-92	CLEVELAND	57	25	.695	2nd/Central Div.	9	8	.529	lost Eastern Conf. finals to Chicago, 4-2
'92-93	CLEVELAND	54	28	.659	2nd/Central Div.	3	6	.333	lost Eastern Conf. semifinals to Chicago, 4-0
'93-94	ATLANTA	57	25	.695	1st/Central Div.	6	5	.455	lost Eastern Conf. semifinals to Indiana, 4-2
	21 YR TOTALS	926	774	.545		60	61	.496	

Boston
CELTICS

1994–95 Scouting Report

Frontcourt

Boston is deep at small forward. Free agent acquisition Dominique Wilkins will give Boston a legitimate offensive threat in the frontcourt. Wilkins has the athletic ability to create his own shots. In addition, Boston has Xavier McDaniel to come off the bench; they also play free agent acquisition Blue Edwards and Kevin Gamble at small forward. The Celtics lack a first rate power forward. Before Dino Radja entered the NBA, he was touted as a player who could play anywhere. Actually, he has many problems. He's not physical enough to play center, he's too slow to play small forward, and his low-post game is too limited for him to be a force at power forward. McDaniel can play at power forward, although he's too small to play that position consistently.

Center is another question mark. The Celtics concluded that Robert Parish had come to the end of the road, so they obtained free agent Pervis Ellison to play center. Parish may have been old, but Ellison has a history of injury problems, and many think power forward is his true position. Acie Earl is limited; he's a weak ballhandler, and he's not mobile. Top draft pick Eric Montross will get a chance to see a lot of playing time. Derek Strong, who came over in the Blue Edwards deal, was the best frontcourt reserve on the Bucks. He had 15.7 points and 9.9 rebounds per 40 minutes played last season.

Backcourt

Backcourt is the Celtics' bright spot, with Kevin Brown and Blue Edwards at shooting guard and Sherman Douglas and Dee Brown at point guard. With Dominique Wilkins' acquisition, Kevin Gamble will see most of his playing time at shooting guard, a position he's more suited for than small forward. He's a consistent outside shooter. Boston's ability to score from the perimeter has been improved with the off-season acquisition of Blue Edwards. Edwards has a better inside game than Gamble. Rick Fox is a steady performer who will see some time as a backup, but he has yet to repeat the level of play that he showed as a rookie. The Celtics have good depth at point guard with Sherman Douglas and Dee Brown. Douglas beat out Brown for the starting job last season. Brown is a tremendous athlete who plays tough defense and can drive to the basket. Douglas is a better passer than Brown, and doesn't commit many turnovers, although he's not as good a defender. Neither Brown nor Douglas have the outside shot you'd like to see at the point guard position.

Defense

The Celtics are now one of the NBA's weaker defensive squads. Boston allowed 105.1 points per game last season, seventh worst in the NBA. Opponents shot 47.7 percent against the Celtics, sixth highest in the league. The Celtics were also a below average team in forcing turnovers (seventeenth in the NBA) and steals (twenty-first). Their defensive prospects for this season are dicey; Wilkins is not known for his defense, and neither is Blue Edwards. Ellison can play defense, when he's healthy, but it's questionable whether the Ellison that Boston will get will be any more of a defensive force than Parish was last season.

1994–95 Prospects

Boston's problem is that they have too many players who are too small to play forward and too slow to play guard. Boston's defensive woes are a result of a dearth of quality athletes who can play a pressing defense, or physical athletes who can body up opponents. They don't have a proven low-post player who can force the defense to sag in and take the defensive pressure off the perimeter shooters. The Celtics lack the complete offensive game to outscore opponents, and they have trouble stopping opponents on the defensive end. That's why last season the Celtics played best against mid-level NBA teams that didn't body up on defense. They'll be better this season, thanks to the acquisition of Wilkins, Edwards and Ellison, but they're still not a threat to make the playoffs.

Team Directory

Chairman of the board: Paul E. Gaston   Vice chairman: Paul R. Dupee, Jr.
Vice chairman of the board: Dave Gavitt   President: Red Auerbach
Dir., basketball operations: M.L. Carr   Media rel.: R. Jeffrey Twiss

1993–94 Review

EASTERN CONFERENCE						WESTERN CONFERENCE					
ATLANTIC DIV.			CENTRAL DIV.			MIDWEST DIV.			PACIFIC DIV.		
	W	L		W	L		W	L		W	L
NY	0	4	ATL	0	4	HOU	1	1	SEA	0	2
ORL	2	2	CHI	2	2	SAN	0	2	PHO	1	1
NJ	1	4	CLE	1	3	UTAH	0	2	GS	1	1
MIA	2	3	IND	0	4	DEN	1	1	POR	1	1
BOS	-	-	CHA	0	4	MIN	1	1	LAL	1	1
PHI	4	1	DET	3	1	DAL	2	0	SAC	1	1
WAS	3	2	MIL	3	1				LAC	1	1
	12	16		9	19		5	7		6	8

1993–94 finish: 32–50 (18–23 home, 14–27 away), fifth in Atlantic Div.

1994–95 Schedule

11/4	New York	7:30 pm	1/4	Miami	7:30 pm	3/4	@ Indiana	7:30 pm
11/5	@ Indiana	7:30 pm	1/6	Portland	7:30 pm	3/7	@ New York	7:30 pm
11/11	Houston	7:30 pm	1/7	@ Charlotte	7:30 pm	3/8	New York	7:30 pm
11/12	@ Minn.	8:00 pm	1/9	Wash.	7:30 pm	3/10	New Jersey	7:30 pm
11/15	@ Atlanta	7:30 pm	1/11	Indiana	7:30 pm	3/12	Atlanta	2:30 pm
11/16	Seattle	7:30 pm	1/13	Utah	8:00 pm	3/14	@ Seattle	10:00 pm
11/18	@ Miami	7:30 pm	1/15	Sacra.	7:00 pm	3/16	@ Portland	10:00 pm
11/19	@ Wash.	7:30 pm	1/17	San Ant.	7:30 pm	3/17	@ LA Lakers	10:30 pm
11/22	Milw.	7:30 pm	1/18	@ Miami	7:30 pm	3/19	@ Milw.	2:30 pm
11/23	Charlotte	7:30 pm	1/20	LA Lakers	7:30 pm	3/22	Chicago	7:30 pm
11/25	Orlando	7:30 pm	1/21	@ Atlanta	7:30 pm	3/24	@ Phila.	7:30 pm
11/26	@ Phila.	7:30 pm	1/24	@ Orlando	7:30 pm	3/25	@ Detroit	7:30 pm
11/30	Detroit	7:30 pm	1/25	LA Clip.	7:30 pm	3/28	@ Miami	7:30 pm
12/2	Phoenix	7:30 pm	1/27	Gold. St.	7:30 pm	3/30	@ Chicago	8:30 pm
12/3	@ Chicago	8:30 pm	2/1	Charlotte	7:30 pm	3/31	Miami	7:30 pm
12/6	@ New York	7:30 pm	2/4	@ New Jersey	8:00 pm	4/2	Dallas	4:00 pm
12/7	Atlanta	7:30 pm	2/5	Minn.	7:00 pm	4/4	@ Cleveland	7:30 pm
12/9	Cleveland	7:30 pm	2/8	Cleveland	7:30 pm	4/7	Phila.	7:30 pm
12/10	@ New Jersey	7:30 pm	2/14	@ Sacra.	10:30 pm	4/9	@ Wash.	1:00 pm
12/12	Denver	7:30 pm	2/15	@ Gold. St.	10:30 pm	4/10	@ Charlotte	7:30 pm
12/14	@ San Ant.	8:30 pm	2/17	@ LA Clip.	10:30 pm	4/13	Orlando	7:30 pm
12/15	@ Dallas	8:30 pm	2/18	@ Utah	9:00 pm	4/15	Detroit	7:30 pm
12/17	@ Houston	8:30 pm	2/21	@ Phoenix	9:00 pm	4/17	New Jersey	7:30 pm
12/19	@ Denver	9:00 pm	2/23	Orlando	7:30 pm	4/19	@ Milw.	8:30 pm
12/23	Phila.	7:30 pm	2/24	@ Orlando	7:30 pm	4/21	New York	7:30 pm
12/26	@ Cleveland	1:00 pm	2/27	Indiana	7:30 pm	4/23	@ New Jersey	6:00 pm
12/28	Chicago	7:30 pm	3/1	Wash.	7:30 pm			
12/30	@ Detroit	8:00 pm	3/3	Milw.	7:30 pm			

1993–94 Team Stats

NAME	G	MIN	FG	FGA	FG%	3FG	3FGA	3FG%	FT	FTA	FT%	ORB	TRB	AST	PF	STL	BLK	TO	PTS	AVG
Brown	77	2867	490	1021	48.0	30	96	31.3	182	219	83.1	63	300	347	207	156	47	126	1192	15.5
Radja	80	2303	491	942	52.1	0	1	0.0	226	301	75.1	191	577	114	276	70	67	149	1208	15.1
Douglas	78	2789	425	919	46.2	13	56	23.2	177	276	64.1	70	193	683	171	89	11	233	1040	13.3
Parish	74	1987	356	725	49.1	0	0	—	154	208	74.0	141	542	82	190	42	96	108	866	11.7
Gamble	75	1880	368	804	45.8	25	103	24.3	103	126	81.7	41	159	149	134	57	22	77	864	11.5
McDaniel	82	1971	387	839	46.1	10	41	24.4	144	213	67.6	142	400	126	193	48	39	116	928	11.3
Fox	82	2096	340	728	46.7	33	100	33.0	174	230	75.7	105	355	217	244	81	52	158	887	10.8
Harris	5	88	9	31	29.0	3	9	33.3	23	25	92.0	3	10	8	8	4	0	6	44	8.8
Earl	74	1149	151	372	40.6	0	1	0.0	108	160	67.5	85	247	12	178	24	53	72	410	5.5
Pinckney	76	1524	151	289	52.2	0	0	—	92	125	73.6	160	478	62	131	58	44	62	394	5.2
Abdelnaby	13	159	24	55	43.6	0	0	—	16	25	64.1	12	46	3	20	2	3	17	64	4.9
Oliver	44	540	89	214	41.6	13	32	40.6	25	33	75.8	8	46	33	39	16	1	21	216	4.9
Lichti	4	48	6	14	42.9	0	0	—	7	14	50.0	8	8	6	4	5	1	3	19	4.8
Corchiani	51	467	40	94	42.6	11	38	28.9	26	38	68.4	8	44	86	47	22	2	38	117	2.3
Wenstrom	11	37	6	10	60.0	0	0	—	6	10	60.0	6	12	0	7	0	2	4	18	1.6
Celtics	82	19905	3333	7057	47.2	138	477	28.9	1463	2003	73.0	1037	3417	1928	1849	674	440	1242	8267	100.8
Opp.	82	19905	3357	7034	47.7	231	665	34.7	1673	2218	75.4	1131	3639	2089	1738	690	414	1273	8618	105.1

HISTORY
TITLES

1956–57 NBA champs	1973–74 NBA champs
1957–58 Eastern Div. champs	1974–75 Atlantic Div. champs
1958–59 NBA champs	1975–76 NBA champs
1959–60 NBA champs	1979–80 Atlantic Div. champs
1960–61 NBA champs	1980–81 NBA champs
1961–62 NBA champs	1981–82 Atlantic Div. champs
1962–63 NBA champs	1983–84 NBA champs
1963–64 NBA champs	1984–85 Eastern Conf. champs
1964–65 NBA champs	1985–86 NBA champs
1965–66 NBA champs	1986–87 Eastern Conf. champs
1967–68 NBA champs	1987–88 Atlantic Div. champs
1968–69 NBA champs	1990–91 Atlantic Div. champs
1971–72 Atlantic Div. champs	1991–92 Atlantic Div. champs
1972–73 Atlantic Div. champs	

ALL-TIME TEAM RECORDS

Career

Games played	John Havlicek	1,270	1962–78
Total Points	John Havlicek	26,395	1962–78
Scoring average	Larry Bird	24.3	1979–92
Field goals made	John Havlicek	10,513	1962–78
Field goals attempted	John Havlicek	5,369	1962–78
Total rebounds	Bill Russell	21,620	1956–69
Assists	Bob Cousy	6,945	1950–63
Steals	Larry Bird	1,556	1979–92

Season

Total points	John Havlicek	2,338	1970–71
Scoring average	Larry Bird	29.9	1987–88
Total rebounds	Bill Russell	1,930	1959–60
Assists	Bob Cousy	715	1959–60
Steals	Larry Bird	166	1985–86

Game

Total points	Larry Bird	60	vs. Atlanta, 3/12/85
Total rebounds	Bill Russell	51	vs. Syracuse, 2/5/60
Assists	Bob Cousy	28	vs. Minneapolis, 2/27/59
Steals	Larry Bird	9	vs Utah, 2/18/85

LEADING COACHES

NAME	YEARS	REGULAR SEASON			PLAYOFFS		
		W	L	PCT	W	L	PCT
Red Auerbach	1950–66	795	397	.667	90	58	.608
Tom Heinsohn	1969–78	427	263	.619	47	33	.588
K. C. Jones	1983–88	308	102	.751	65	37	.637
Bill Fitch	1979–83	242	86	.738	26	19	.578
Chris Ford	1990–94	187	141	.57	12	13	.480

Boston Celtics 1994–95 Roster

Head Coach: Chris Ford

No.	Name	Pos.	Ht.	Wt.	Yrs.	Born	College
7	Dee Brown	G	6-1	161	4	11/29/68	Jacksonville
20	Sherman Douglas	G	6-1	180	5	9/15/66	Syracuse
55	Acie Earl	F	6-10	240	1	6/23/70	Iowa
	Blue Edwards	G-F	6-4	228	5	10/31/65	East Carolina
43	Pervis Ellison	F-C	6-10	225	5	4/3/67	Louisville
44	Rick Fox	F	6-7	231	3	7/24/69	North Carolina
34	Kevin Gamble	G-F	6-5	210	7	11/13/65	Iowa
31	Xavier McDaniel	F	6-7	205	9	6/4/63	Wichita State
0	Eric Montross	C	7-0	275	R	9/23/71	North Carolina
27	Jimmy Oliver	G	6-5	208	2	7/12/69	Purdue
40	Dino Radja	F	6-11	225	1	4/24/67	Croatia
45	Derek Strong	F	6-8	220	3	2/9/68	Xavier
50	Matt Wenstrom	C	7-1	250	1	11/4/70	North Carolina
	David Wesley	G	6-0	190	1	11/14/70	Baylor
12	Dominique Wilkins	F	6-8	215	12	1/12/60	Georgia

Arena Information

Boston Garden (14,890)
Tickets: 617-523-3030

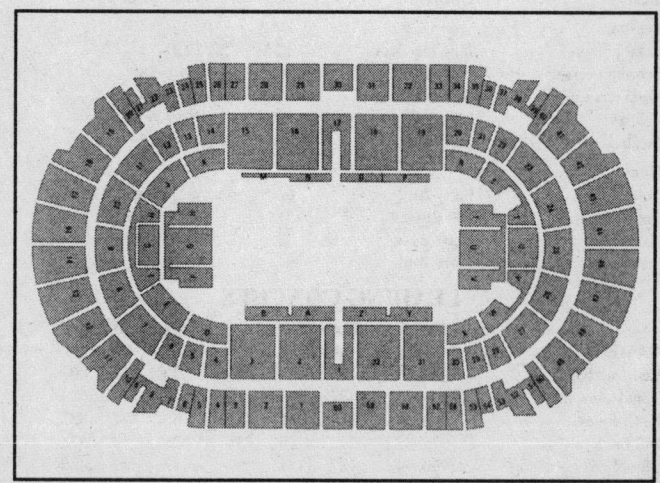

Blue Edwards

G-F

Full name: Theodore Edwards
HT: 6-4 **WT:** 228
Born: 10/31/65, Washington, DC
High school: Greene Central
(Snow Hill, NC)
College: East Carolina

Edwards is athletic enough to play off guard or small forward. He's a high-percentage shooter who can post up, or score from outside. He has problems turning over the ball. And like many players who can play off guard or small forward, he has trouble on defense. Edwards is durable; last season he appeared in all 82 games for the second straight year. He started 64 of them, after opening the season as the Bucks' sixth man. He averaged 13.8 points and 3.9 rebounds per game in that role, including scoring his season-high of 28 points vs. Atlanta on November 24. He scored 18 points in the third quarter against New York on March 17, which was a team season high for points scored in one quarter.

REGULAR SEASON		G	MIN	FG	FG%	3FG	3PT%	FT	FT%	REB	AST	STL	BLK	PTS	AVG
'89-90	UTAH	82	1889	286	50.7	9	30.0	146	71.9	251	145	76	36	727	8.9
'90-91	UTAH	62	1611	244	52.6	6	25.0	82	70.1	201	108	57	29	576	9.3
'91-92	UTAH	81	2283	433	52.2	39	37.9	113	77.4	298	137	81	46	1018	12.6
'92-93	MILWAUKEE	82	2729	554	51.2	37	34.9	237	79.0	382	214	129	45	1382	16.9
'93-94	MILWAUKEE	82	2322	382	47.8	38	35.8	151	79.3	329	171	83	27	953	11.6
5 YR TOTALS		389	10834	1899	50.8	129	35.0	729	76.3	1461	775	426	183	4656	12.0
'93-94	RANK NBA Gs	1	44	43	30	51	39	49	62	17	81	52	20	49	53
'94-95	PROJECTIONS	82	2311	356	45.8	45	37.5	143	81.7	336	172	75	19	900	11.0

PLAYOFFS		G	MIN	FG	FG%	3FG	3PT%	FT	FT%	REB	AST	STL	BLK	PTS	AVG
'89-90	UTAH	5	94	14	53.8	1	33.3	7	87.5	18	8	7	2	36	7.2
'90-91	UTAH	9	241	37	48.1	1	50.0	16	80.0	28	16	8	1	91	10.1
'91-92	UTAH	16	354	52	46.8	2	20.0	23	71.9	51	17	23	3	129	8.1
TOTALS		30	689	103	48.1	4	26.7	46	76.7	97	41	38	6	256	8.5

Dee Brown

No. 7/G

Full name: DeCovan Kadell Brown
HT: 6-1   **WT:** 161
Born: 11/29/68, Jacksonville, FL
High school: The Bolles School (Jacksonville)
College: Jacksonville

Brown has quickness, speed, and great leaping ability. Those talents help make him an above-average defender, and a threat on the fast break. But if you take away his drive to the basket, you can limit him as an offensive threat, because his jump shot needs improvement. Brown led the Celtics in scoring last season, and also in steals and free throw shooting percentage. His 30 3-pointers were second on the team, just 3 behind Rick Fox's 33. Brown was named to the 1991 NBA All-Rookie team. He gained instant notoriety by winning the Gatorade Slam Dunk Championship at the 1991 All-Star weekend in Charlotte.

REGULAR SEASON		G	MIN	FG	FG%	3FG	3PT%	FT	FT%	REB	AST	STL	BLK	PTS	AVG
'90-91	BOSTON	82	1945	284	46.4	7	20.6	137	87.3	182	344	83	14	712	8.7
'91-92	BOSTON	31	883	149	42.6	5	22.7	60	76.9	79	164	33	7	363	11.7
'92-93	BOSTON	80	2254	328	46.8	26	31.7	192	79.3	246	461	138	32	874	10.9
'93-94	BOSTON	77	2867	490	48.0	30	31.3	182	83.1	300	347	156	47	1192	15.5
4 YR TOTALS		270	7949	1251	46.6	68	29.1	571	82.0	807	1316	410	100	3141	11.6
'93-94	RANK NBA Gs	53	11	18	26	61	75	36	32	23	35	10	6	26	24
'94-95	PROJECTIONS	82	3504	640	49.5	42	33.6	189	84.8	375	267	197	69	1511	18.4

PLAYOFFS		G	MIN	FG	FG%	3FG	3PT%	FT	FT%	REB	AST	STL	BLK	PTS	AVG
'90-91	BOSTON	11	284	53	49.1	0	0.0	28	82.4	45	41	11	6	134	12.2
'91-92	BOSTON	6	120	22	50.0	0	0.0	4	66.7	12	31	1	4	48	8.0
'92-93	BOSTON	4	133	15	36.6	1	14.3	14	100.0	6	15	2	4	45	11.3
TOTALS		21	537	90	46.6	1	6.7	46	85.2	63	87	14	14	227	10.8

Sherman Douglas
No. 20/G

HT: 6-1 **WT:** 180
Born: 9/15/66, Washington, DC
High school: Spingarn
(Washington, DC)
College: Syracuse

Douglas is an excellent point guard who can score driving to the basket. He'd be an even better scorer if he had a better outside shot or was more consistent as a free throw shooter. Douglas passes well, and doesn't commit many turnovers. But he doesn't steal the ball very often, and needs improvement on defense. Douglas led Boston in assists last season, and also in turnovers; he was the Celtics' third-leading scorer. Douglas left Syracuse as the NCAA's all-time leader in assists with 960, and as Syracuse's career leader in scoring (2,060 points) and steals (235). He was a second-round pick by Miami in the 1988 draft, but was named to the NBA All-Rookie first team in 1989. Douglas came to the Celtics in exchange for Brian Shaw on January 10, 1992.

REGULAR SEASON	G	MIN	FG	FGx	3FG	3PTx	FT	FTx	REB	AST	STL	BLK	PTS	AVG
'89-90 MIAMI	81	2470	463	49.4	5	16.1	224	68.7	206	619	145	10	1155	14.3
'90-91 MIAMI	73	2562	532	50.4	4	12.9	284	68.6	209	624	121	5	1352	18.5
'91-92 MIA-BOS	42	752	117	46.2	1	10.0	73	68.2	63	172	25	9	308	7.3
'92-93 BOSTON	79	1932	264	49.8	6	20.7	84	56.0	162	508	49	10	618	7.8
'93-94 BOSTON	78	2789	425	46.2	13	23.2	177	64.1	193	683	89	11	1040	13.3
5 YR TOTALS	353	10505	1801	48.7	29	18.5	842	66.1	833	2606	429	45	4473	12.7
'93-94 RANK NBA Gs	48	16	35	46	84	101	40	124	54	6	45	68	40	43
'94-95 PROJECTIONS	82	3297	491	44.8	21	27.3	196	64.9	204	798	100	9	1199	14.6

PLAYOFFS	G	MIN	FG	FGx	3FG	3PTx	FT	FTx	REB	AST	STL	BLK	PTS	AVG
'91-92 BOSTON	6	65	9	36.0	0	0.0	1	50.0	4	10	0	0	19	3.2
'92-93 BOSTON	4	166	17	37.8	0	0.0	10	66.7	26	38	4	0	44	11.0
TOTALS	10	231	26	37.1	0	0.0	11	64.7	30	48	4	0	63	6.3

Pervis Ellison
No. 43/F-C

HT: 6-10   **WT:** 225
Born: 4/3/67, Savannah, GA
High school: Savannah (GA)
College: Louisville

When healthy, Ellison is an above-average NBA center. He's a good shooter around the basket, and a good shotblocker and rebounder. However, Ellison has suffered from chronic knee problems throughout his career as a pro. Ellison opened last season on the injured list rehabilitating from off season knee surgery to both knees, missing Washington's first 15 games. His best month was March; he averaged 9.9 points and 7.5 rebounds per game, and had his high game of the season March 1 when he scored 25 points against Philadelphia. But on March 24 he went on the injured list for the remainder of the season because of soreness in his knees. Despite appearing in only 47 games, and starting just 25, Ellison led the Bullets in rebounding 6 times and in steals 4 times.

REGULAR SEASON		G	MIN	FG	FG%	3FG	3PT%	FT	FT%	REB	AST	STL	BLK	PTS	AVG
'89-90	SACRAMENTO	34	866	111	44.2	0	0.0	49	62.8	196	65	16	57	271	8.0
'90-91	WASHINGTON	76	1942	326	51.3	0	0.0	139	65.0	585	102	49	157	791	10.4
'91-92	WASHINGTON	66	2511	547	53.9	1	33.3	227	72.8	740	190	62	177	1322	20.0
'92-93	WASHINGTON	49	1701	341	52.1	0	0.0	170	70.2	433	117	45	108	852	17.4
'93-94	WASHINGTON	47	1178	137	46.9	0	0.0	70	72.2	242	70	25	50	344	7.3
	5 YR TOTALS	272	8198	1462	51.3	1	5.6	655	69.5	2196	544	197	549	3580	13.2
'93-94	RANK NBA F s	118	88	98	67	78	78	91	62	83	76	100	36	99	77
'94-95	PROJECTIONS	43	836	69	44.5	0	0.0	37	74.0	144	46	16	24	175	4.1

Dominique Wilkins

No. 21/F

Full name: Jacques Dominique Wilkins

HT: 6-8   **WT:** 215

Born: 1/12/60, Paris, France

High school: Washington (NC)

College: Georgia

Wilkins is one of the best pure scorers in the NBA. He can drive to the basket or score from outside. He also gets his share of rebounds. The biggest knock on him is that he doesn't work hard on defense. But he's certainly not afraid of the ball in crunch time, a trait Atlanta missed in the '94 playoffs. Last season on April 18 he became the ninth man to score 24,000 points in the NBA. Wilkins was named to the All-Star team for the ninth time, and scored 11 points and dished 4 assists in 17 minutes as a reserve. He led the Hawks and the Clippers in scoring. In 25 games (all starts) with the Clippers, Wilkins averaged 29.1 points, 7.0 rebounds, 2.2 assists, 1.16 steals, and 37.9 minutes.

REGULAR SEASON		G	MIN	FG	FG%	3FG	3PT%	FT	FT%	REB	AST	STL	BLK	PTS	AVG
'84-85	ATLANTA	81	3023	853	45.1	25	30.9	486	80.6	557	200	135	54	2217	27.4
'85-86	ATLANTA	78	3049	888	46.8	13	18.6	577	81.8	618	206	138	49	2366	30.3
'86-87	ATLANTA	79	2969	828	46.3	31	29.2	607	81.8	494	261	117	51	2294	29.0
'87-88	ATLANTA	78	2948	909	46.4	38	29.5	541	82.6	502	224	103	47	2397	30.7
'88-89	ATLANTA	80	2997	814	46.4	29	27.6	442	84.4	553	211	117	52	2099	26.2
'89-90	ATLANTA	80	2888	810	48.4	59	32.2	459	80.7	521	200	126	47	2138	26.7
'90-91	ATLANTA	81	3078	770	47.0	85	34.1	476	82.9	732	265	123	65	2101	25.9
'91-92	ATLANTA	42	1601	424	46.4	37	28.9	294	83.5	295	158	52	24	1179	28.1
'92-93	ATLANTA	71	2647	741	46.8	120	38.0	519	82.8	482	227	70	27	2121	29.9
'93-94	ATL-LAC	74	2635	698	44.0	85	28.8	442	84.7	481	169	92	30	1923	26.0
	12 YR TOTALS	907	33493	9020	46.7	524	31.1	5455	81.3	6295	2376	1274	596	24019	26.5
'93-94	RANK NBA Fs	61	21	2	103	4	39	2	5	35	34	19	75	2	1
'94-95	PROJECTIONS	78	2709	707	42.4	84	25.9	434	85.8	482	142	39	27	1932	24.8

PLAYOFFS		G	MIN	FG	FG%	3FG	3PT%	FT	FT%	REB	AST	STL	BLK	PTS	AVG
'82-83	ATLANTA	3	109	17	40.5	1	100.0	12	85.7	15	1	2	1	47	15.7
'83-84	ATLANTA	5	197	35	41.7	0	0.0	26	83.9	41	11	12	1	96	19.2
'85-86	ATLANTA	9	360	94	43.3	1	20.0	68	86.1	54	25	9	2	257	28.6
'86-87	ATLANTA	9	360	86	41.0	3	30.0	66	89.2	70	25	16	8	241	26.8
'87-88	ATLANTA	12	473	137	45.7	4	22.2	96	76.8	77	34	16	6	374	31.2
'88-89	ATLANTA	5	212	52	44.8	5	29.4	27	71.1	27	17	4	8	136	27.2
'90-91	ATLANTA	5	195	35	37.2	2	13.3	32	91.4	32	13	9	5	104	20.8
'92-93	ATLANTA	3	113	32	42.7	3	25.0	23	76.7	16	9	3	1	90	30.0
	TOTALS	51	2019	488	42.9	19	24.1	350	82.2	332	135	71	32	1345	26.4

Dino Radja   No. 40/F

Full name: Dino Radja
HT: 6-11 **WT:** 225
Born: 4/24/67, Split, Yugoslavia
High school: Technical School Center (Split, Yugoslavia)
College: None
Radja has an effective offensive game, but his defense needs improvement.

REGULAR SEASON		G	MIN	FG	FG%	3FG	3PT%	FT	FT%	REB	AST	STL	BLK	PTS	AVG
'93-94	BOSTON	80	2303	491	52.1	0	0.0	226	75.1	577	114	70	67	1208	15.1
	1 YR TOTALS	80	2303	491	52.1	0	0.0	226	75.1	577	114	70	67	1208	15.1
'93-94	RANK NBA Fs	23	36	18	21	78	78	24	42	23	52	34	21	20	23

Acie Earl   No. 55/F

Full name: Acie Boyd Earl
HT: 6-10 **WT:** 240
Born: 6/23/70, Peoria, IL
High school: Moline (IL)
College: Iowa
Earl lacks speed, quickness, and jumping ability. But he's got a decent shot from outside to medium range, and he has good hands.

REGULAR SEASON		G	MIN	FG	FG%	3FG	3PT%	FT	FT%	REB	AST	STL	BLK	PTS	AVG
'93-94	BOSTON	74	1149	151	40.6	0	0.0	108	67.5	247	12	24	53	410	5.5
	1 YR TOTALS	74	1149	151	40.6	0	0.0	108	67.5	247	12	24	53	410	5.5
'93-94	RANK NBA Fs	61	90	89	125	78	78	66	94	82	129	103	31	88	96

Kevin Gamble   No. 34/G-F

Full name: Kevin Douglas Gamble
HT: 6-5   **WT:** 210
Born: 11/13/65, Springfield, IL
High school: Lanphier (Springfield)
College: Iowa

A reliable outside shooter, Gamble lacks the size to be a strong rebounder. His size also contributes to problems he has on defense.

REGULAR SEASON		G	MIN	FG	FG%	3FG	3PT%	FT	FT%	REB	AST	STL	BLK	PTS	AVG
'89-90	BOSTON	71	990	137	45.5	3	16.7	85	79.4	112	119	28	8	362	5.1
'90-91	BOSTON	82	2706	548	58.7	0	0.0	185	81.5	267	256	100	34	1281	15.6
'91-92	BOSTON	82	2496	480	52.9	9	29.0	139	88.5	286	219	75	37	1108	13.5
'92-93	BOSTON	82	2541	459	50.7	52	37.4	123	82.6	246	226	86	37	1093	13.3
'93-94	BOSTON	75	1880	368	45.8	25	24.3	103	81.7	159	143	57	22	864	11.5
7 YR TOTALS		445	11007	2067	51.8	91	29.4	670	81.6	1115	1004	362	141	4895	11.0
'93-94	RANK NBA Gs	65	66	46	52	68	99	78	48	69	85	83	30	53	55
'94-95	PROJECTIONS	72	1625	324	42.6	25	23.1	87	81.3	122	117	47	17	760	10.6

PLAYOFFS		G	MIN	FG	FG%	3FG	3PT%	FT	FT%	REB	AST	STL	BLK	PTS	AVG
'88-89	BOSTON	1	29	4	36.4	0	0.0	0	0.0	1	2	1	0	8	8.0
'89-90	BOSTON	3	8	3	60.0	0	—	0	—	1	2	0	0	6	2.0
'90-91	BOSTON	11	238	29	48.3	0	—	8	66.7	13	19	4	2	66	6.0
'91-92	BOSTON	10	335	62	47.3	0	0.0	12	80.0	42	23	12	6	136	13.6
'92-93	BOSTON	4	142	23	54.8	5	41.7	4	100.0	9	10	6	1	55	13.8
TOTALS		29	752	121	48.6	5	33.3	24	72.7	66	56	23	9	271	9.3

Xavier McDaniel   No. 31/F

Full name: Xavier Maurice McDaniel
HT: 6-7   **WT:** 205
Born: 6/4/63, Columbia, SC
High school: A.C. Flora (Columbia)
College: Wichita State

McDaniel has the tools. He's a physical player who can shoot and grab rebounds. He's not a good passer, though.

REGULAR SEASON		G	MIN	FG	FG%	3FG	3PT%	FT	FT%	REB	AST	STL	BLK	PTS	AVG
'89-90	SEATTLE	69	2432	611	49.6	5	29.4	244	73.3	447	171	73	36	1471	21.3
'90-91	SEA-PHE	81	2634	590	49.7	0	0.0	193	72.3	557	187	76	46	1373	17.0
'91-92	NEW YORK	82	2344	488	47.8	12	30.8	137	71.4	460	149	57	24	1125	13.7
'92-93	BOSTON	82	2215	457	49.5	6	27.3	191	79.3	489	163	72	51	1111	13.5
'93-94	BOSTON	82	1971	387	46.1	10	24.4	144	67.6	400	126	48	39	928	11.3
9 YR TOTALS		720	22421	5279	49.1	63	26.6	2027	71.8	4664	1593	722	377	12648	17.6
'93-94	RANK NBA Fs	1	49	32	76	39	54	50	93	51	47	66	54	38	47
'94-95	PROJECTIONS	82	1779	332	44.5	12	25.5	124	63.3	355	109	38	37	800	9.8

PLAYOFFS		G	MIN	FG	FG%	3FG	3PT%	FT	FT%	REB	AST	STL	BLK	PTS	AVG
'86-87	SEATTLE	14	528	124	48.8	2	20.0	34	60.7	117	42	21	9	284	20.3
'87-88	SEATTLE	5	180	45	55.6	4	50.0	12	50.0	48	25	3	1	106	21.2
'88-89	SEATTLE	8	281	58	40.3	3	33.3	31	75.6	67	22	2	5	150	18.8
'90-91	PHOENIX	4	101	17	41.5	0	0.0	4	66.7	15	5	0	2	38	9.5
'91-92	NEW YORK	12	458	94	47.7	2	25.0	36	73.5	86	23	9	2	226	18.8
'92-93	BOSTON	4	126	22	41.5	0	0.0	6	66.7	18	9	1	3	50	12.5
TOTALS		47	1674	360	46.8	11	28.9	123	66.5	351	126	36	22	854	18.2

Eric Montross   No. 0/C

HT: 7-0   **WT:** 275
Born: 9-23-71
College: North Carolina
Montross had a disappointing senior season, averaging just 13.6 points and 8.1 rebounds. A 58.5 percent shooter in college, Montross will probably play power forward as a pro.

REGULAR SEASON	G	MIN	FG	FGx	3FG	3PT%	FT	FT%	REB	AST	STL	BLK	PTS	AVG
ROOKIE -- NO NBA EXPERIENCE														

Chris Ford   Head Coach

Full name: Christopher Joseph Ford
HT: 6-5   **WT:** 190
Born: 1/11/49, Atlantic City, NJ
High school: Holy Spirit (Absecon, NJ)
College: Villanova
Celtics management gave Ford a contract extension. But he'll be expected to return Boston to the playoffs soon.

YEAR	REGULAR SEASON TEAM	W	L	PCT	PLAYOFFS FINISH	W	L	PCT	
'90-91	BOSTON	56	26	.683	1st/Atlantic Div.	5	6	.455	lost Eastern Conf. semifinals to Detroit, 4-2
'91-92	BOSTON	51	31	.622	T1st/Atlantic Div.	6	4	.600	lost Eastern Conf. semifinals to Cleveland, 4-3
'92-93	BOSTON	48	34	.585	2nd/Atlantic Div.	1	3	.250	lost Eastern Conf. first round to Charlotte, 3-1
'93-94	BOSTON	32	50	.390	5th/Atlantic Div.				
	4 YR TOTALS	187	141	.570		12	13	.480	

Charlotte
HORNETS

1994–95 Scouting Report

Frontcourt

Alonzo Mourning and Larry Johnson are two of the best frontcourt players in the NBA. Mourning missed 21 games, but still led the team in scoring, rebounding, and blocks. He has a good jump shot, and a jump hook that he can shoot with either hand. He's also a tough defender who gives Patrick Ewing fits. When he's healthy, Larry Johnson is one of the best forwards in the game. Unfortunately, early signs indicate that Johnson's back injury has hindered his mobility. Once known for brute strength, explosive moves, and rim-ringing dunks, he played hesitantly in the World Championships with Dream Team II. Kenny Gattison comes off the bench to play power forward. Gattison will be a better player now that he won't have to play center, thanks to the acquisition of ex-Celtic Robert Parish. He'll spell Mourning at center, and should be able to give Charlotte 12 quality minutes a game.

Backcourt

Hersey Hawkins is the starting shooting guard. He's an average scorer, but a good rebounder and defender. Rookie Darrin Hancock will also contend for playing time at shooting guard, and may see a lot of time at small forward if Johnson's back acts up again. Dell Curry is one of the NBA's better sixth men, able to score coming off the bench. And David Wingate is a reserve who can play defense against the other team's best guard and shut him down. Muggsy Bogues plays point guard. He was Charlotte's MVP for the second straight year, as he posted a career high in scoring and led the Eastern Conference in assists. Tony Bennett backs up Bogues.

Defense

Opponents put up a lot of points against Charlotte last season. Teams averaged 106.7 points against the Hornets, fourth highest in the

NBA. And they held opponents under 100 points only 27 times. That's largely due to the Hornets' wide-open tempo; opposing teams shot 47.1 percent from the floor against Charlotte, sixteenth in the league. Charlotte ranked eighteenth in the league in forcing turnovers, and twenty-fifth in stealing the ball. One problem spot is on the defensive boards; opponents grabbed 1,217 offensive rebounds against Charlotte, fourth highest in the league last season.

1994–95 Prospects

The Hornets looked like a title contender before last season, but injuries to Larry Johnson and Alonzo Mourning derailed their drive to the playoffs. With both players in the lineup, the Hornets were 31-19, but when both players were out, Charlotte was just 5-16. That just shows how irreplaceable Mourning and Johnson are. Newcomers Hersey Hawkins and Eddie Johnson averaged 36.8 points per game in the 21 games that Johnson and Mourning missed, nearly 11 points better than their season average.

The Hornets are too young to be an injury-prone team, so they should bounce back this year. And make no mistake, Charlotte has a lot of young talent and is an improving team. Two years ago, they were twenty-fourth in rebounds. Last season, with injuries that sidelined All-Stars Mourning and Johnson for much of the season, Charlotte ranked fifteenth in the NBA. Their biggest hole is at point guard, where there's no quality backup to Muggsy Bogues. The Hornets could also use a rebounding forward. And Charlotte needs insurance in case Johnson's back keeps him from returning to form.

Unless both Mourning and Johnson go out again for prolonged periods, the Hornets will make the playoffs this season. They were one of the hottest teams in the league at the end of last season, finishing 12-2 (including 3-1 on the road) and just missing the playoffs by one game. How far can they go? With Chicago and Atlanta slipping, they will challenge for the Central Division championship, and should be a high seed in the playoffs. But Coach Allen Bristow was an assistant under Doug Moe for six years; his team plays the same kind of unstructured passing game that has problems in the playoffs, when defensive intensity gets stepped up a notch. So don't be surprised if the Hornets lose in the Eastern Conference semifinals.

Team Directory

Owner: George Shinn
VP, business operations: Sam Russo
Dir., player pers.: Dave Twardzik

President: Spencer Stolpen
VP, finance: Wayne J. Deblander
Media relations: Harold Kaufman

1993–94 Review

EASTERN CONFERENCE						WESTERN CONFERENCE					
ATLANTIC DIV.			CENTRAL DIV.			MIDWEST DIV.			PACIFIC DIV.		
	W	L		W	L		W	L		W	L
NY	3	1	ATL	1	4	HOU	1	1	SEA	0	2
ORL	2	2	CHI	1	4	SAN	0	2	PHO	2	0
NJ	2	2	CLE	1	4	UTAH	1	1	GS	0	2
MIA	1	3	IND	2	2	DEN	1	1	POR	0	2
BOS	4	0	CHA	–	–	MIN	2	0	LAL	2	0
PHI	3	1	DET	4	0	DAL	1	1	SAC	1	1
WAS	2	2	MIL	3	2				LAC	1	1
	17	11		12	16		6	6		6	8

1993–94 finish: 41–41 (28–13 home, 13–28 away), fifth in Central Div.

1994–95 Schedule

11/4	@ Chicago	8:00 pm	1/4	Portland	7:30 pm	3/2	@ Portland	10:00 pm
11/5	Cleveland	7:30 pm	1/6	@ New Jersey	7:30 pm	3/3	@ Gold. St.	10:30 pm
11/9	Orlando	7:30 pm	1/7	Boston	7:30 pm	3/5	@ Sacra.	9:00 pm
11/11	@ Milwaukee	8:00 pm	1/10	@ Cleveland	7:30 pm	3/9	Seattle	7:30 pm
11/12	Detroit	7:30 pm	1/11	Minnesota	7:30 pm	3/11	Miami	7:30 pm
11/15	@ Cleveland	7:30 pm	1/14	Chicago	7:30 pm	3/13	Wash.	7:30 pm
11/17	LA Clip.	7:30 pm	1/17	@ Orlando	7:30 pm	3/14	@ Milwaukee	8:30 pm
11/19	Indiana	7:30 pm	1/18	San Ant.	7:30 pm	3/16	Phoenix	8:00 pm
11/22	Gold. St.	8:00 pm	1/20	New Jersey	7:30 pm	3/19	Utah	12:00 pm
11/23	@ Boston	7:30 pm	1/22	@ Minnesota	3:30 pm	3/21	@ New York	7:30 pm
11/26	@ New York	1:00 pm	1/23	LA Lakers	7:30 pm	3/23	@ Orlando	8:00 pm
11/29	@ Atlanta	7:30 pm	1/25	Atlanta	7:30 pm	3/25	Cleveland	7:30 pm
11/30	Miami	7:30 pm	1/27	New York	8:00 pm	3/29	@ Phila.	7:30 pm
12/3	@ Denver	9:00 pm	1/28	@ Atlanta	7:30 pm	3/30	Dallas	7:30 pm
12/5	@ LA Clip.	10:30 pm	1/31	@ Wash.	8:00 pm	4/2	@ Miami	6:00 pm
12/6	@ Utah	9:00 pm	2/1	@ Boston	7:30 pm	4/5	Phila.	7:30 pm
12/8	@ Houston	8:30 pm	2/3	Milwaukee	7:30 pm	4/7	@ Wash.	7:30 pm
12/10	@ Dallas	8:30 pm	2/5	Wash.	2:00 pm	4/9	@ Indiana	1:00 pm
12/13	Milwaukee	7:30 pm	2/7	Indiana	8:00 pm	4/10	Boston	7:30 pm
12/14	@ Detroit	7:30 pm	2/8	@ Detroit	7:30 pm	4/11	New Jersey	7:30 pm
12/16	@ Indiana	7:30 pm	2/14	@ New Jersey	7:30 pm	4/14	@ Detroit	8:00 pm
12/17	Denver	7:30 pm	2/16	Houston	8:00 pm	4/16	Atlanta	3:00 pm
12/20	Indiana	7:30 pm	2/18	Detroit	7:30 pm	4/17	@ Phila.	7:30 pm
12/22	Phila.	7:30 pm	2/20	Chicago	7:30 pm	4/20	New York	8:00 pm
12/23	@ Miami	7:30 pm	2/22	Sacra.	7:30 pm	4/22	@ Chicago	3:30 pm
12/27	@ San Ant.	8:30 pm	2/24	@ LA Lakers	10:30 pm	4/23	Cleveland	3:30 pm
12/29	Orlando	8:00 pm	2/26	@ Phoenix	3:30 pm			
12/30	@ Milwaukee	8:30 pm	2/27	@ Seattle	10:00 pm			

1993–94 Team Stats

NAME	G	MIN	FG	FGA	FG%	3FG	3FGA	3FG%	FT	FTA	FT%	ORB	TRB	AST	PF	STL	BLK	TO	PTS	AVG
Mourning	60	2018	427	845	50.5	0	2	0.0	433	568	76.2	177	610	86	207	27	188	199	1287	21.5
L. Johnson	51	1757	346	672	51.5	5	21	23.8	137	197	69.5	143	448	184	131	29	14	116	834	16.4
Curry	82	2173	533	1171	45.5	152	378	40.2	117	134	87.3	71	262	221	161	98	27	120	1335	16.3
Hawkins	82	2648	395	859	46.0	78	235	33.2	312	362	86.2	89	377	216	167	135	22	158	1180	14.4
Newman	18	429	91	174	52.3	4	16	25.0	48	59	81.4	21	58	29	44	18	5	28	234	13.0
E. Johnson	73	1460	339	738	45.9	59	150	39.3	99	127	78.0	80	224	125	143	36	8	84	836	11.5
Bogues	77	2746	354	751	47.1	2	12	16.7	125	155	80.6	78	313	780	147	133	7	171	835	10.8
Conlon	16	378	66	109	60.6	0	1	0.0	31	38	81.6	34	89	28	36	5	2	23	163	10.2
Brickowski	28	653	117	233	50.2	1	2	50.0	47	63	74.6	32	125	57	77	28	11	56	282	10.1
Gattison	77	1644	233	445	52.4	0	0	—	126	195	64.6	105	358	95	229	59	46	79	592	7.7
Wingate	50	1005	136	283	48.1	4	12	33.3	34	51	66.7	30	134	104	85	42	6	53	310	6.2
Burrell	51	767	98	234	41.9	2	6	33.3	46	70	65.7	46	132	62	88	37	16	45	244	4.8
Ellis	50	680	88	182	48.4	0	0	—	45	68	66.2	70	188	24	83	17	25	21	221	4.4
Gminski	21	255	31	79	39.2	0	0	—	11	14	78.6	19	59	11	20	13	13	11	73	3.5
Bennett	74	983	105	263	39.9	27	75	36.0	11	15	73.3	16	90	163	84	39	1	40	248	3.4
Kempton	9	103	9	26	34.6	0	0	—	7	10	70.0	6	14	6	25	4	0	4	25	2.8
Robinson	14	95	13	33	39.4	1	5	20.0	3	9	33.3	2	8	18	15	3	0	18	30	2.1
Henson	3	17	1	2	50.0	1	1	100.0	0	0	—	0	4	5	3	0	0	1	3	1.0
Williams	1	19	0	2	0.0	0	0	—	0	0	—	0	4	0	3	0	0	1	0	0.0
Hornets	82	19830	3382	7100	47.6	336	916	36.7	1632	2135	76.4	1019	3494	2214	1747	724	394	1266	8732	106.5
Opp.	82	19830	3463	7359	47.1	317	916	34.6	1507	2036	74.0	1217	3684	2116	1761	629	430	1260	8750	106.7

HISTORY
ALL-TIME TEAM RECORDS

Career

Games played	Muggsy Bogues	481	1988–94
Total points	Dell Curry	6,214	1988–94
Scoring average	Alonzo Mourning	21.2	1992–94
Field goals made	Dell Curry	2,589	1988–94
Field goals attempted	Dell Curry	5,537	1988–94
Free throws made	Kelly Tripucka	902	1988–91
Free throws attempted	Johnny Newman	1,083	1990–94
Total rebounds	Larry Johnson	2,211	1991–94
Assists	Muggsy Bogues	4,390	1988–94
Steals	Muggsy Bogues	878	1988–94
Personal fouls	Kenny Gattison	1,100	1989–94

Season

Total points	Larry Johnson	1,810	1992–93
Scoring average	Kelly Tripucka	22.6	1988–89
Field goals made	Larry Johnson	728	1992–93
Field goals attempted	Kendall Gill	1,427	1991–92
Free throws made	Alonzo Mourning	495	1992–93
Free throws attempted	Alonzo Mourning	634	1992–93
Total rebounds	Larry Johnson	899	1991–92
Assists	Muggsy Bogues	867	1989–90
Steals	Muggsy Bogues	170	1991–92
Personal fouls	J.R. Reid	292	1989–90

Game

Total points	Johnny Newman	41	vs. Indiana, 1/25/92
	Hersey Hawkins	41	vs. Golden State, 2/9/94
Field goals made	Rex Chapman	17	vs. New York, 11/27/89
Free throws made	Larry Johnson	18	vs. Golden State, 12/2/92
	Johnny Newman	18	vs. Dallas, 1/19/91
Total rebounds	Larry Johnson	23	vs. Minnesota, 3/10/92
Assists	Muggsy Bogues	19	vs. Boston, 4/23/89
	Muggsy Bogues	19	vs. LA Lakers, 11/24/93
	Muggsy Bogues	19	vs. Milwaukee, 2/18/94

LEADING COACHES

NAME	REGULAR SEASON				PLAYOFFS		
	YEARS	W	L	PCT	W	L	PCT
Allan Bristow	1991–94	116	130	.472	4	5	.444
Gene Littles	1990–91	37	87	.298	0	0	—
Dick Harter	1988–90	28	94	.230	0	0	—

Charlotte Hornets 1994–95 Roster

Head Coach: Allan Bristow

No.	Name	Pos.	Ht.	Wt.	Yrs.	Born	College
23	Michael Adams	G	5-10	175	9	1/19/63	Boston College
25	Tony Bennett	G	6-0	179	2	6/1/69	Wis.-Green Bay
1	Tyrone Bogues	G	5-3	144	7	1/9/65	Wake Forest
24	Scott Burrell	F	6-7	218	1	1/12/71	Connecticut
30	Dell Curry	G	6-5	210	8	6/25/64	Virginia Tech
44	Kenny Gattison	F	6-8	255	8	5/23/64	Old Dominion
32	Darrin Hancock	G	6-7	205	R	11/3/71	Kansas/France
3	Hersey Hawkins	G	6-3	190	6	9/29/66	Bradley
2	Larry Johnson	F	6-7	257	3	3/14/69	Nevada-Las Vegas
33	Alonzo Mourning	C	6-10	244	2	2/8/70	Georgetown
00	Robert Parish	C	7-1	230	18	8/30/53	Centenary
11	David Wingate	G	6-5	190	8	12/15/63	Georgetown

Arena Information

Charlotte Coliseum (23,698)
Tickets: 704-522-6500 (Ticketmaster)
Ticket prices: $44, $40, $31, $28, $26, $19, $15, $11, $8

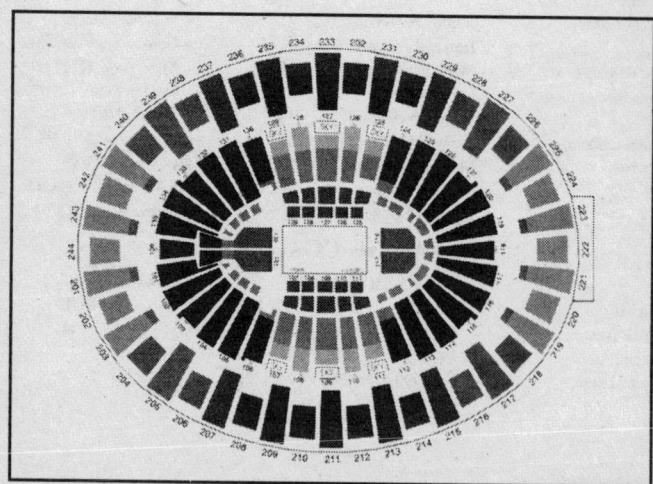

Muggsy Bogues

No. 1/G

Full name: Tyrone Bogues
HT: 5-3   **WT:** 144
Born: 1/9/65, Baltimore, MD
High school: Dunbar (Baltimore)
College: Wake Forest

Bogues may be the quickest player in basketball. He can score driving to the basket, he's an outstanding passer, he shoots well from the line, and doesn't turn over the ball much. His size leads to problems defensively; he gets a lot of steals, but can be exploited in crunch time because opponents can get a good look at the basket. Bogues was named Hornets Player of the Year for the second time after his best season as a pro. His 10.1 assists per game ranked second in the NBA, and his 10.8 points per game average was a career high. He tied his franchise-record (and career-high) of 19 assists in a single game twice (vs. the Lakers on November 24, and vs. Milwaukee on February 18).

REGULAR SEASON		G	MIN	FG	FG%	3FG	3PT%	FT	FT%	REB	AST	STL	BLK	PTS	AVG
'87-88	WASHINGTON	79	1628	166	39.0	3	18.8	58	78.4	136	404	127	3	393	5.0
'88-89	CHARLOTTE	79	1755	178	42.6	1	7.7	66	75.0	165	620	111	7	423	5.4
'89-90	CHARLOTTE	81	2743	326	49.1	5	19.2	106	79.1	207	867	166	3	763	9.4
'90-91	CHARLOTTE	81	2299	241	46.0	0	0.0	86	79.6	216	669	137	3	568	7.0
'91-92	CHARLOTTE	82	2790	317	47.2	2	7.4	94	78.3	235	743	170	6	730	8.9
'92-93	CHARLOTTE	81	2833	331	45.3	6	23.1	140	83.3	298	711	161	5	808	10.0
'93-94	CHARLOTTE	77	2746	354	47.1	2	16.7	125	80.6	313	780	133	2	835	10.8
	7 YR TOTALS	560	16794	1913	45.7	19	14.4	675	79.7	1570	4794	1005	29	4520	8.1
'93-94	RANK NBA Gs	53	20		36	117	121	64	55	20	4	18	115	57	60
'94-95	PROJECTIONS	75	2756	377	47.6	1	16.7	130	80.2	342	805	119	1	885	11.8

PLAYOFFS		G	MIN	FG	FG%	3FG	3PT%	FT	FT%	REB	AST	STL	BLK	PTS	AVG
'87-88	WASHINGTON	1	2	0	...	0	...	0	...	0	2	0	0	0	0.0
'92-93	CHARLOTTE	9	346	39	47.6	0	0.0	10	71.4	36	70	24	0	88	9.8
	TOTALS	10	348	39	47.6	0	0.0	10	71.4	36	72	24	0	88	8.8

Hersey Hawkins

No. 32/G

Full name: Hersey R. Hawkins, Jr.
HT: 6-3   **WT:** 190
Born: 9/29/66, Chicago, IL
High school: Westinghouse
   Vocational (Chicago)
College: Bradley

Hawkins is one of the best shots from 3-point range in the NBA, and deadly from the free throw line. His 86.2 FT percentage was eleventh best in the league. In fact, Hawkins set a team record for consecutive free throws made by hitting 37 straight. He also tied Johnny Newman's single game team scoring record when he scored 41 points vs. Golden State on February 9. Hawkins plays hard, is a good defender, and is usually among the league leaders in steals. Hawkins led the Hornets in steals and minutes played last season, was second in scoring, tied for third in rebounds, and fourth in assists. He played and started in all 82 games, which extended his streak of consecutive starts to 133 (eighth longest in the league).

REGULAR SEASON		G	MIN	FG	FGx	3FG	3PTx	FT	FTx	REB	AST	STL	BLK	PTS	AVG
'88-89	PHILADELPHIA	79	2577	442	45.5	71	42.8	241	83.1	225	239	120	37	1196	15.1
'89-90	PHILADELPHIA	82	2856	522	46.0	84	42.0	387	88.8	304	261	130	28	1515	18.5
'90-91	PHILADELPHIA	80	3110	590	47.2	108	40.0	479	87.1	310	299	178	39	1767	22.1
'91-92	PHILADELPHIA	81	3013	521	46.2	91	39.7	403	87.4	271	248	157	43	1536	19.0
'92-93	PHILADELPHIA	81	2977	551	47.0	122	39.7	419	86.0	346	317	137	30	1643	20.3
'93-94	CHARLOTTE	82	2648	395	46.0	78	33.2	312	86.2	377	216	135	22	1180	14.4
	6 YR TOTALS	485	17181	3021	46.4	554	39.4	2241	86.7	1833	1580	857	199	8837	18.2
'93-94	RANK NBA Gs	1	25	40	49	21	63	9	14	10	64	16	30	28	34
'94-95	PROJECTIONS	82	2469	326	45.5	64	29.5	262	85.9	398	181	128	16	978	11.9

PLAYOFFS		G	MIN	FG	FGx	3FG	3PTx	FT	FTx	REB	AST	STL	BLK	PTS	AVG
'88-89	PHILADELPHIA	3	72	3	12.5	0	0.0	2	100.0	5	4	3	1	8	2.7
'89-90	PHILADELPHIA	10	415	81	43.7	14	38.9	59	93.7	31	36	12	7	235	23.5
'90-91	PHILADELPHIA	8	329	47	46.5	14	53.8	59	93.7	46	27	20	10	167	20.9
	TOTALS	21	816	131	45.5	28	41.8	120	93.8	82	67	35	18	410	19.5

Larry Johnson

No. 2/F

Full name: Larry Demetric Johnson
HT: 6-7   **WT:** 257
Born: 3/14/69, Tyler, TX
High school: Skyline (Dallas)
College: Nevada-Las Vegas

When healthy, Johnson is a complete offensive force. He's got a terrific inside game, and is also a good passer, an excellent rebounder, and an aggressive defensive player. But if Johnson fully recovers from his back injury, it may not be this season. In the World Championships with Dream Team II, he didn't play with confidence on offense. And the injury seems to have affected his attitude, as well. Once known as one of the most affable players in the game, Johnson was surly and cocky while a member of Dream Team II. Charlotte officials have talked to Johnson about improving his relationship with the media and toning down the trash talk on the court.

REGULAR SEASON		G	MIN	FG	FG%	3FG	3PT%	FT	FT%	REB	AST	STL	BLK	PTS	AVG
'91-92	CHARLOTTE	82	3047	616	49.0	5	22.7	339	82.9	899	292	81	51	1576	19.2
'92-93	CHARLOTTE	82	3323	728	52.6	18	25.4	336	76.7	864	353	53	27	1810	22.1
'93-94	CHARLOTTE	51	1757	346	51.5	5	23.8	137	69.5	448	184	29	14	834	16.4
3 YR TOTALS		215	8127	1690	51.0	28	24.6	812	77.8	2211	829	163	92	4220	19.6
'93-94 RANK NBA Fs		110	58	43	23	51	56	53	77	40	29	96	105	46	21
'94-95 PROJECTIONS		28	1215	224	51.5	2	20.0	74	62.7	295	129	17	7	524	18.7

PLAYOFFS		G	MIN	FG	FG%	3FG	3PT%	FT	FT%	REB	AST	STL	BLK	PTS	AVG
'92-93	CHARLOTTE	9	348	68	55.7	1	25.0	41	78.8	62	30	5	2	178	19.8
TOTALS		9	348	68	55.7	1	25.0	41	78.8	62	30	5	2	178	19.8

Alonzo Mourning   No. 33/C

HT: 6-10   **WT:** 244
Born: 2/8/70, Chesapeake, VA
High school: Indian River
  (Chesapeake)
College: Georgetown
Mourning can do it all at center: score, shoot from the perimeter (his jumper eliminated Boston in the '93 playoffs), rebound, and block shots. He can even shoot from the free throw line, a rarity among Georgetown alumni. His biggest flaw is that he turns over the ball too much (453 turnovers in two seasons). Last season, Mourning led the Hornets in scoring, rebounding and blocks. His 3.13 blocks ranked fourth in the NBA. Mourning was named to the NBA All-Star team as a reserve, but the torn calf muscle that kept him out of 15 regular games prevented him from playing. He missed tying the Charlotte all-time single game scoring record when he tallied a career-high 39 points against Detroit on April 23. He scored 36 points in consecutive games at Denver on December 3 and at Utah on December 4.

REGULAR SEASON	G	MIN	FG	FG%	3FG	3PT%	FT	FT%	REB	AST	STL	BLK	PTS	AVG
'92-93 CHARLOTTE	78	2644	572	51.1	0	0.0	495	78.1	805	76	27	271	1639	21.0
'93-94 CHARLOTTE	60	2018	427	50.5	0	0.0	433	76.2	610	86	27	188	1287	21.5
2 YR TOTALS	138	4662	999	50.9	0	0.0	928	77.2	1415	162	54	459	2926	21.2
'93-94 RANK NBA Cs	28	11	7	2.0	14	14	4	14	10	15	29	6	5	5
'94-95 PROJECTIONS	42	1392	288	49.9	0	0.0	335	74.4	418	79	23	117	911	21.7

PLAYOFFS	G	MIN	FG	FG%	3FG	3PT%	FT	FT%	REB	AST	STL	BLK	PTS	AVG
'92-93 CHARLOTTE	9	367	71	48.0	0	0.0	72	77.4	89	13	6	31	214	23.8
TOTALS	9	367	71	48.0	0	0.0	72	77.4	89	13	6	31	214	23.8

Robert Parish

No. 00/C

Full name: Robert Lee Parish
HT: 7-1 **WT:** 230
Born: 8/30/53, Shreveport, LA
High school: Woodlawn (Shreveport)
College: Centenary

Parish, along with Larry Bird, Kevin McHale, and Dennis Johnson, was part of the core of the Celtics team that went to the NBA finals 5 times in the '80s and won 3 times. Although he's 41, Parish is still an effective scorer, rebounder and shot blocker. He can't run very much anymore—but neither could Kareem when he was Parish's age. He has trouble against the better young centers of the NBA. A backup role will perfectly fit his limited stamina. He became the twelfth man to score 22,000 points in the NBA last season. He went to the same high school as former Pittsburgh Steeler QB Terry Bradshaw.

REGULAR SEASON		G	MIN	FG	FGx	3FG	3PTx	FT	FTx	REB	AST	STL	BLK	PTS	AVG
'84-85	BOSTON	79	2850	551	54.2	0	---	292	74.3	840	125	56	101	1394	17.6
'85-86	BOSTON	81	2567	530	54.9	0	---	245	73.1	770	145	65	116	1305	16.1
'86-87	BOSTON	80	2995	588	55.6	0	0.0	227	73.5	851	173	64	144	1403	17.5
'87-88	BOSTON	74	2312	442	58.9	0	0.0	177	73.4	628	115	55	84	1061	14.3
'88-89	BOSTON	80	2840	596	57.0	0	---	294	71.9	996	175	79	116	1486	18.6
'89-90	BOSTON	79	2396	505	58.0	0	---	233	74.7	796	103	38	69	1243	15.7
'90-91	BOSTON	81	2441	485	59.8	0	0.0	237	76.7	856	66	66	103	1207	14.9
'91-92	BOSTON	79	2285	468	53.5	0	---	179	77.2	705	70	68	97	1115	14.1
'92-93	BOSTON	79	2146	416	53.5	0	---	162	68.9	740	61	57	107	994	12.6
'93-94	BOSTON	74	1987	356	49.1	0	---	154	74.0	542	82	42	96	866	11.7
	16 YR TOTALS	1254	39507	8547	54.5	0	0.0	3678	72.7	12750	1916	1031	2035	20772	16.6
'93-94	RANK NBA Cs	19	12	10	26	14	14	12	17	11	17	17	14	10	11
'94-95	PROJECTIONS	71	1847	311	46.0	0	0.0	139	74.7	443	87	34	93	761	10.7

PLAYOFFS		G	MIN	FG	FGx	3FG	3PTx	FT	FTx	REB	AST	STL	BLK	PTS	AVG
'84-85	BOSTON	21	803	136	49.3	0	---	87	78.4	219	31	21	34	359	17.1
'85-86	BOSTON	18	591	106	47.1	0	---	58	65.2	158	25	9	30	270	15.0
'86-87	BOSTON	21	734	149	56.7	0	0.0	79	76.7	198	28	18	35	377	18.0
'87-88	BOSTON	17	626	100	53.2	0	---	50	82.0	168	21	11	19	250	14.7
'88-89	BOSTON	3	112	20	45.5	0	---	7	77.8	26	6	4	2	47	15.7
'89-90	BOSTON	5	170	31	57.4	0	---	17	94.4	50	13	5	7	79	15.8
'90-91	BOSTON	10	296	58	59.8	0	---	42	68.9	92	6	8	7	158	15.8
'91-92	BOSTON	10	335	50	49.5	0	---	20	71.4	97	14	7	15	120	12.0
'92-93	BOSTON	4	146	31	54.4	0	---	6	85.7	38	5	1	6	68	17.0
	TOTALS	178	6088	1125	50.7	0	0.0	554	72.4	1752	233	145	303	2804	15.8

Michael Adams G

HT: 5-10 **WT:** 175
Born: 1/19/63, Hartford, CT
High school: Hartford Public (CT)
College: Boston College

Adams is a threat to put it up from anywhere. He's also a good free throw shooter. However, he's never been a high percentage shooter, and he's a defensive liability.

REGULAR SEASON		G	MIN	FG	FG%	3FG	3PT%	FT	FT%	REB	AST	STL	BLK	PTS	AVG
'87-88	DENVER	82	2778	416	44.9	139	36.7	166	83.4	223	503	168	16	1137	13.9
'88-89	DENVER	77	2787	468	43.3	166	35.6	322	81.9	283	490	166	11	1424	18.5
'89-90	DENVER	79	2690	398	40.2	158	36.6	267	85.0	225	495	121	5	1221	15.5
'90-91	DENVER	66	2346	560	39.4	167	29.6	465	87.9	256	693	147	6	1752	26.5
'91-92	WASHINGTON	78	2795	485	39.3	125	32.4	313	86.9	310	594	145	9	1408	18.1
'92-93	WASHINGTON	70	2499	365	43.9	68	32.1	237	85.6	240	526	100	4	1035	14.8
'93-94	WASHINGTON	70	2337	285	40.8	55	28.8	224	83.0	183	480	96	6	849	12.1
9 YR TOTALS		603	19674	3153	41.4	906	33.1	2107	85.0	1849	4047	1037	62	9319	15.5
'93-94 RANK NBA Gs		80	41	61	108	34	84	22	36	62	16	42	89	55	50
'94-95 PROJECTIONS		69	2216	217	40.4	33	26.6	190	81.2	148	437	84	6	657	9.5

PLAYOFFS		G	MIN	FG	FG%	3FG	3PT%	FT	FT%	REB	AST	STL	BLK	PTS	AVG
'87-88	DENVER	2	75	15	41.7	10	45.5	7	87.5	17	9	3	0	47	23.5
'88-89	DENVER	3	105	13	38.2	6	30.0	7	87.5	6	18	4	0	39	13.0
TOTALS		19	668	83	36.9	35	33.3	51	85.0	66	101	32	2	252	13.3

Dell Curry No. 30/G

Full name: Wardell Stephen Curry
HT: 6-5 **WT:** 210
Born: 6/25/64, Harrisonburg, VA
High school: Fort Defiance (VA)
College: Virginia Tech

Curry is a great outside shooter who comes off the bench to provide offense. He's also extremely reliable from the free throw line.

REGULAR SEASON		G	MIN	FG	FG%	3FG	3PT%	FT	FT%	REB	AST	STL	BLK	PTS	AVG
'86-87	UTAH	67	636	139	42.6	17	28.3	30	76.9	78	58	27	4	325	4.9
'87-88	CLEVELAND	79	1499	340	45.8	28	34.6	79	78.2	166	149	94	22	787	10.0
'88-89	CHARLOTTE	48	813	256	49.1	19	34.5	40	87.0	104	50	42	4	571	11.9
'89-90	CHARLOTTE	67	1860	461	46.6	52	35.4	96	92.3	168	159	98	26	1070	16.0
'90-91	CHARLOTTE	76	1515	337	47.1	32	37.2	96	84.2	199	166	75	25	802	10.6
'91-92	CHARLOTTE	77	2020	504	48.6	74	40.4	127	83.6	259	177	93	20	1209	15.7
'92-93	CHARLOTTE	80	2094	498	45.2	99	40.1	136	86.6	286	180	87	23	1227	15.3
'93-94	CHARLOTTE	82	2173	533	45.5	152	40.2	117	87.3	262	221	98	27	1335	16.3
8 YR TOTALS		576	12610	3068	46.4	469	38.2	721	85.2	1522	1160	614	151	7326	12.7
'93-94 RANK NBA Gs		1	52	8	56	3	17	67	10	32	61	40	20	13	20
'94-95 PROJECTIONS		82	2286	567	45.0	201	40.9	113	88.3	267	246	103	29	1448	17.7

PLAYOFFS		G	MIN	FG	FG%	3FG	3PT%	FT	FT%	REB	AST	STL	BLK	PTS	AVG
'86-87	UTAH	2	4	1	0.0	0	0.0	0	0.0	0	0	0	0	0	0.0
'87-88	CLEVELAND	2	17	1	25.0	0	0.0	0	---	1	2	0	1	2	1.0
'92-93	CHARLOTTE	9	222	42	43.3	6	28.6	9	81.8	32	18	13	0	99	11.0
TOTALS		13	243	43	41.3	6	26.1	9	75.0	33	20	13	1	101	7.8

Kenny Gattison   No. 44/F

Full name: Kenneth Clay Gattison
HT: 6-8   **WT:** 255
Born: 5/23/64, Wilmington, NC
High school: New Hanover (Wilmington)
College: Old Dominion

Gattison is a physical player who can set screens and rebound. He can score down low, although he's not much from outside.

REGULAR SEASON		G	MIN	FG	FG%	3FG	3PT%	FT	FT%	REB	AST	STL	BLK	PTS	AVG
'86-87	CHARLOTTE	77	1104	148	47.6	0	---	108	63.2	270	36	24	33	404	5.2
'87-88	CHARLOTTE	did not play -- injured													
'88-89	CHARLOTTE	2	9	0	0.0	0	0.0	1	50.0	1	0	0	0	1	0.5
'89-90	CHARLOTTE	63	941	148	55.0	1	100.0	75	68.2	197	39	35	31	372	5.9
'90-91	CHARLOTTE	72	1552	243	53.2	0	0.0	164	66.1	379	44	48	67	650	9.0
'91-92	CHARLOTTE	82	2223	423	52.9	0	0.0	196	68.8	580	131	59	69	1042	12.7
'92-93	CHARLOTTE	75	1475	203	52.9	0	0.0	102	60.4	353	68	48	55	508	6.8
'93-94	CHARLOTTE	77	1644	233	52.4	0	---	126	64.6	358	95	59	46	592	7.7
	8 YR TOTALS	448	8948	1398	52.4	1	9.1	772	65.4	2138	413	273	301	3569	8.0
'93-94	RANK NBA Fs	43	62	65	19	78	78	60	107	57	61	50	46	68	73
'94-95	PROJECTIONS	78	1665	224	51.9	0	0.0	124	64.6	342	107	64	39	572	7.3

PLAYOFFS		G	MIN	FG	FG%	3FG	3PT%	FT	FT%	REB	AST	STL	BLK	PTS	AVG
'92-93	CHARLOTTE	9	187	22	47.8	0	---	9	42.9	39	11	5	1	53	5.9
	TOTALS	9	187	22	47.8	0	---	9	42.9	39	11	5	1	53	5.9

Darrin Hancock   No. 32/G

HT: 6-7   **WT:** 205
Born: 11/3/71
College: Maurienne (France)/Kansas

National Junior College Player of the Year in France's Pro B League for Maurienne last season, Hancock played for Kansas during the 1992–93 season, starting for the Jayhawks' Final Four team.

REGULAR SEASON	G	MIN	FG	FG%	3FG	3PT%	FT	FT%	REB	AST	STL	BLK	PTS	AVG
ROOKIE -- NO NBA EXPERIENCE														

David Wingate   No. 55/G

Full name: David Grover Stacey Wingate, Jr.
HT: 6-5   **WT:** 190
Born: 12/15/63, Baltimore, MD
High school: Dunbar (Baltimore)
College: Georgetown

Wingate is a solid ballhandler, passer, and defender. Last season's .667 FT percent was a career low.

REGULAR SEASON		G	MIN	FG	FGx	3FG	3PTx	FT	FTx	REB	AST	STL	BLK	PTS	AVG
'88-89	PHILADELPHIA	33	372	54	47.0	2	33.3	27	79.4	37	73	9	2	137	4.2
'89-90	SAN ANTONIO	78	1856	220	44.8	0	0.0	87	77.7	195	208	89	18	527	6.8
'90-91	SAN ANTONIO	25	563	53	38.4	1	11.1	29	70.7	75	46	19	5	136	5.4
'91-92	WASHINGTON	81	2127	266	46.5	1	5.6	105	71.9	269	247	123	21	638	7.9
'92-93	CHARLOTTE	72	1471	180	53.6	1	16.7	79	73.8	174	183	66	9	440	6.1
'93-94	CHARLOTTE	50	1005	136	48.1	4	33.3	34	66.7	134	104	42	6	310	6.2
8 YR TOTALS		477	10425	1386	45.0	32	20.5	609	73.9	1141	1135	488	102	3413	7.2
'93-94	RANK NBA Gs	119	102	106	25	110	58	118	122	84	101	96	89	112	99
'94-95	PROJECTIONS	41	732	105	47.7	4	40.0	19	63.3	102	72	29	4	233	5.7

PLAYOFFS		G	MIN	FG	FGx	3FG	3PTx	FT	FTx	REB	AST	STL	BLK	PTS	AVG
'89-90	SAN ANTONIO	10	293	40	51.9	2	66.7	9	75.0	37	38	18	3	91	9.1
'90-91	SAN ANTONIO	3	38	6	50.0	0	---	2	66.7	3	1	1	0	14	4.7
'92-93	CHARLOTTE	9	117	18	36.4	0	---	3	37.5	12	15	4	1	19	2.1
TOTALS		27	538	69	46.6	4	80.0	23	62.2	64	63	28	5	165	6.1

Allan Bristow   Head Coach

Full name: Allan Mercer Bristow, Jr.
HT: 6-7   **WT:** 210
Born: 8/23/51, Richmond, VA
High school: Henrico (Richmond)
College: Virginia Tech

Bristow is now tied with Miami's Kevin Loughery for the sixth-longest head coaching term with one team (246 games).

	REGULAR SEASON				PLAYOFFS			
YEAR	TEAM	V	L	PCT	FINISH	V	L	PCT
'91-92	CHARLOTTE	31	51	378	T6th/Central Div.			
'92-93	CHARLOTTE	44	38	537	3rd/Central Div.	4	5	444	lost Eastern Conf. semifinals to New York, 4-1
'93-94	CHARLOTTE	41	41	500	5th/Central Div.			
3 YR TOTALS		116	130	472		4	5	444

Chicago *BULLS*

CHICAGO BULLS

1994–95 Scouting Report

Frontcourt

The Bulls have problems in the frontcourt. They're thin at forward, their lack of a quality center was exposed in the playoffs against the Knicks, and they now need a power forward to replace free-agent departure Horace Grant. Corie Blount, Chicago's top '93 draft pick, figures to take over the power forward duties. In college, Blount was a good defender and shotblocker, but just an average rebounder, and not much of a scorer. Luc Longley is at center. He doesn't score much but is a decent rebounder and shotblocker. Toni Kukoc will start at small forward. Kukoc is an outstanding passer with long arms. Swingman Pete Myers played well for Chicago last season, but has bounced around the NBA (6 different stops) and CBA throughout his pro career.

Backcourt

Scottie Pippen is the Bulls' starting shooting guard. He's a great scorer; blessed with size, speed, and leaping ability, Pippen is one of the league's best in the open court. He's also one of the best defenders in the league, and the most athletically gifted player on the team. His attitude, though, is a wild card, and some think he won't play his best unless he's the highest paid player on the Bulls. Steve Kerr, one of the NBA's best 3-point shooters, is a reserve. B.J. Armstrong, also one of the NBA's best 3-point shooters, plays point guard. He's a tough defender who's not reluctant to body up opponents. He was only second in assists on the Bulls, though; you want your point guard to lead the team in assists.

Defense

With Michael Jordan, the Bulls were one of the best defensive teams in the NBA. Without Jordan and his defensive ability, the Bulls had to slow down the pace and bang the glass to hold opponents' scoring down. Teams averaged 94.9 points against the Bulls, third lowest in the NBA. And they held opponents under 100 points 60 times. But opponents shot 46.3 from the floor against Chicago, just twelfth in the league. Why did they score so little? Because opposing teams averaged just 79.8 FGA against the Bulls, fourth lowest in the league. They'll see more shots this season with Horace Grant gone; Chicago led the league last year in defending their defensive glass, limiting opponents to 12 offensive rebounds per game. The Bulls were an average team in terms of disrupting their opponents' offenses; they ranked twelfth in the NBA in stealing the ball and forcing turnovers. And they're not intimidating underneath; their average of 4.3 blocks per game was twenty-fourth in the NBA.

1994–95 Prospects

Despite losing Michael Jordan, Chicago won 50 games for the fifth straight season. They made the playoffs for the tenth straight year, and their 24–17 road record (second best in the Eastern Conference and third best in the NBA) marked the fourth straight season that they've been .500 or better on the road. They were 13–4 in games decided by 3 points or less. The credit has to go to Coach Phil Jackson, who got his team to play with tremendous character.

One-by-one, the stars of the championship teams—Michael Jordan, Horace Grant, John Paxson, maybe Bill Cartwright, and even Scottie Pippen, by season's end—are all going. And the reserves are ill-equipped for starting responsibilities. Who's going to replace Horace Grant's rebounding production? There's no one left up front who's athletically gifted as a rebounder, let alone as a defensive intimidator. That means Chicago's defensive production stands to fall off dramatically this season. And who's going to score? The Bulls have Scottie Pippen (for now), B.J. Armstrong and Toni Kukoc. But only Pippen is a proven threat going to the basket, and it's hard to win consistently in the NBA shooting from outside. Chicago also has problems shooting free throws (70.6 percent in 1993–94).

Unfortunately, the Bulls look like they're in the middle of a Detroit-style meltdown. They might edge out a team like Miami for the last playoff spot with 45 wins or so, but their days of high playoff seeds are over. And they could be really bad in a couple of years.

Team Directory

Chairman: Jerry Reinsdorf   VP, financial & legal: Irwin Mandel
VP, mktg. & broad.: Steve Schanwald   VP, basketball op.: Jerry Krause
Dir., ticket sales: Keith Brown   Dir., media services: Tim Hallam

1993–94 Review

EASTERN CONFERENCE						WESTERN CONFERENCE					
ATLANTIC DIV.			CENTRAL DIV.			MIDWEST DIV.			PACIFIC DIV.		
	W	L		W	L		W	L		W	L
NY	1	3	ATL	3	2	HOU	1	1	SEA	1	1
ORL	2	2	CHI	-	-	SAN	1	1	PHO	1	1
NJ	3	1	CLE	1	3	UTAH	2	0	GS	2	0
MIA	2	2	IND	4	1	DEN	1	1	POR	0	2
BOS	2	2	CHA	4	1	MIN	2	0	LAL	1	1
PHI	3	1	DET	5	0	DAL	2	0	SAC	1	1
WAS	4	0	MIL	4	0				LAC	2	0
	17	11		21	7		9	3		8	6

1993–94 finish: 55–27 (31–10 home, 24–17 away), second in Central Div.

1994–95 Schedule

11/4	Charlotte	8:00 pm	1/4	Denver	8:30 pm	3/1	Miami	8:30 pm
11/5	Wash.	8:30 pm	1/6	Seattle	8:00 pm	3/2	@ New York	7:30 pm
11/7	Phila.	8:30 pm	1/7	@ Cleveland	7:30 pm	3/4	@ Phila.	7:30 pm
11/9	@ New Jersey	7:30 pm	1/10	Orlando	8:30 pm	3/6	Portland	8:30 pm
11/11	@ Minnesota	8:00 pm	1/11	@ Phila.	7:30 pm	3/10	Cleveland	8:30 pm
11/12	Dallas	8:30 pm	1/13	Sacra.	8:30 pm	3/11	LA Lakers	8:30 pm
11/16	@ San Ant.	8:30 pm	1/14	@ Charlotte	7:30 pm	3/14	@ Wash.	7:30 pm
11/17	@ Houston	8:00 pm	1/16	@ Wash.	1:00 pm	3/15	Atlanta	8:30 pm
11/19	@ Dallas	8:30 pm	1/18	Milwaukee	8:30 pm	3/17	Milwaukee	8:30 pm
11/22	@ LA Clip.	10:30 pm	1/20	Minnesota	8:30 pm	3/19	@ Indiana	12:00 pm
11/23	@ Denver	9:00 pm	1/22	Houston	1:00 pm	3/22	@ Boston	7:30 pm
11/25	@ Utah	9:00 pm	1/24	San Ant.	8:00 pm	3/24	Orlando	8:30 pm
11/30	Phoenix	8:00 pm	1/26	@ Orlando	8:00 pm	3/25	@ Atlanta	7:30 pm
12/2	Atlanta	8:30 pm	1/29	Gold. St.	2:30 pm	3/28	@ New York	8:00 pm
12/3	Boston	8:30 pm	1/31	@ LA Lakers	10:30 pm	3/30	Boston	8:30 pm
12/5	New Jersey	8:30 pm	2/2	@ Sacra.	10:30 pm	4/1	Phila.	8:30 pm
12/9	@ Detroit	8:00 pm	2/3	@ Phoenix	9:30 pm	4/5	@ New Jersey	7:30 pm
12/10	@ Milwaukee	8:30 pm	2/5	@ Gold. St.	8:00 pm	4/7	Cleveland	8:30 pm
12/13	Detroit	8:30 pm	2/8	@ Portland	10:00 pm	4/9	@ Cleveland	1:00 pm
12/16	@ Atlanta	7:30 pm	2/9	@ Seattle	10:00 pm	4/11	Indiana	8:30 pm
12/17	Utah	8:30 pm	2/15	Wash.	8:30 pm	4/12	@ Detroit	7:30 pm
12/19	Cleveland	8:30 pm	2/17	Detroit	8:30 pm	4/16	New York	5:30 pm
12/21	@ Indiana	7:30 pm	2/18	@ Milwaukee	8:30 pm	4/17	@ Miami	7:30 pm
12/23	Indiana	8:00 pm	2/20	@ Charlotte	7:30 pm	4/20	Detroit	8:30 pm
12/25	New York	6:30 pm	2/21	@ Atlanta	7:30 pm	4/22	Charlotte	3:30 pm
12/27	LA Clip.	8:30 pm	2/24	@ Miami	8:00 pm	4/23	@ Milwaukee	2:30 pm
12/28	@ Boston	7:30 pm	2/26	@ Orlando	1:00 pm			
12/30	Miami	8:30 pm	2/27	New Jersey	8:30 pm			

1993–94 Team Stats

NAME	G	MIN	FG	FGA	FG%	3FG	3FGA	3FG%	FT	FTA	FT%	ORB	TRB	AST	PF	STL	BLK	TO	PTS	AVG
Pippen	72	2759	627	1278	49.1	63	197	32.0	270	409	66.0	173	629	403	227	211	58	232	1587	22.0
Grant	70	2570	460	878	52.4	0	6	0.0	137	230	59.6	306	769	236	164	74	84	109	1057	15.1
Armstrong	82	2770	479	1007	47.6	60	135	44.4	194	227	85.5	28	170	323	147	80	9	131	1212	14.8
Kukoc	75	1808	313	726	43.1	32	118	27.1	156	210	74.3	98	297	252	122	81	33	167	814	10.9
Kerr	82	2036	287	577	49.7	52	124	41.9	83	97	85.6	26	131	210	97	75	3	57	709	8.6
Myers	82	2030	253	556	45.5	8	29	27.6	136	194	70.1	54	181	245	195	78	20	136	650	7.9
Williams	38	638	114	236	48.3	1	5	20.0	60	98	61.2	69	181	39	112	16	21	44	289	7.6
Longley	27	513	85	176	48.3	0	0	—	34	45	75.6	42	138	63	85	10	21	40	204	7.6
Wennington	76	1371	235	482	48.8	0	2	0.0	72	88	81.8	117	353	70	214	43	29	75	542	7.1
Cartwright	42	780	98	191	51.3	0	0	—	39	57	68.4	43	152	57	83	18	8	50	235	5.6
King	31	537	68	171	39.8	0	2	0.0	36	53	67.9	50	132	39	64	18	12	43	172	5.5
English	36	419	56	129	43.4	8	17	47.1	10	21	47.6	9	45	38	61	8	10	36	130	3.6
Blount	67	690	76	174	43.7	0	1	—	46	75	61.3	76	194	56	93	19	33	52	198	3.0
Johnson	17	119	17	54	31.5	0	0	0.0	13	21	61.9	9	16	4	7	4	0	9	47	2.8
Perdue	43	397	47	112	42.0	0	1	0.0	23	32	71.9	40	126	34	61	8	11	42	117	2.7
Paxson	27	343	30	68	44.1	9	22	40.9	1	2	50.0	3	20	33	18	7	2	6	70	2.6
Bulls	82	19780	3245	6815	47.6	233	659	35.4	1310	1859	70.5	1143	3534	2102	1750	740	354	1306	8033	98.0
Opp.	82	19780	3029	6542	46.3	252	780	32.3	1470	1987	74.0	985	3225	1840	1725	730	374	1335	7780	94.9

HISTORY

TITLES

1974–75 Midwest Div. champs	1991–92 NBA Eastern Conf. champs
1990–91 Midwest Div. champs	1991–92 NBA champs
1990–91 NBA Eastern Conf. champs	1992–93 Midwest Div. champs
1990–91 NBA champs	1992–93 NBA Eastern Conf. champs
1991–92 Midwest Div. champs	1992–93 NBA champs

ALL-TIME TEAM RECORDS

Career

Games played	Jerry Sloan	696	1966–76
Total points	Michael Jordan	21,541	1984–93
Field goals made	Michael Jordan	8,079	1984–93
Field goals attempted	Michael Jordan	15,647	1984–93
Free throws made	Michael Jordan	5,096	1984–93
Free throws attempted	Michael Jordan	6,025	1984–93
Total rebounds	Tom Boerwinkle	5,745	1968–78
Assists	Michael Jordan	3,935	1984–93
Steals	Michael Jordan	1,815	1984–93

Season

Total points	Michael Jordan	3,041	1986–87
Scoring average	Bob Love	43	1970–71
Field goals made	Michael Jordan	1,069	1987–88
Field goals attempted	Michael Jordan	1,998	1987–88
Free throws made	Michael Jordan	833	1986–87
Free throws attempted	Michael Jordan	972	1986–87
Total rebounds	Tom Boerwinkle	1,133	1970–71
Assists	Guy Rodgers	908	1966–67
Steals	Michael Jordan	259	1987–88

Game

Total points	Michael Jordan	69	vs. Cleveland (OT), 3/28/90
Field goals made	Michael Jordan	27	vs. Orlando, 1/16/93
Free throws made	Michael Jordan	26	vs. New Jersey, 2/26/87
Total rebounds	Tom Boerwinkle	37	vs. Phoenix, 1/8/90
Assists	Guy Rodgers	24	vs. New York, 12/21/66
Steals	Michael Jordan	10	vs. New Jersey, 1/29/88

LEADING COACHES

NAME	YEARS	REGULAR SEASON			PLAYOFFS		
		W	L	PCT	W	L	PCT
Dick Motta	1968–76	356	300	.543	18	29	.383
Phil Jackson	1989–94	295	115	.720	61	23	.726
Doug Collins	1968–89	137	109	.557	13	17	.433
Jerry Sloan	1979–82	94	122	.435	2	4	.333
Ed Badger	1976–78	84	80	.512	1	2	.333

Chicago Bulls 1994–95 Roster

Head Coach: Phil Jackson

No.	Name	Pos.	Ht.	Wt.	Yrs.	Born	College
10	B.J. Armstrong	G	6-2	185	6	9/9/67	Iowa
44	Corie Blount	F	6-10	242	2	1/4/69	Cincinnati
	Kris Bruton	G	NA	NA	R	NA	Benedict
24	Bill Cartwright	C	7-1	245	16	7/30/57	San Francisco
3	Jo Jo English	G	6-4	180	2	2/4/70	South Carolina
25	Steve Kerr	G	6-3	180	7	9/27/65	Arizona
7	Toni Kukoc	F-G	6-11	230	1	9/18/68	Croatia
13	Luc Longley	C	7-2	265	3	1/19/69	New Mexico
20	Pete Myers	G-F	6-6	180	7	9/15/63	Arkansas-Little Rock
32	Will Perdue	C	7-0	260	7	8/29/65	Vanderbilt
33	Scottie Pippen	F	6-7	225	8	9/25/65	Central Arkansas
	Dickie Simpkins	F	6-9	248	R	4/16/72	Providence
34	Bill Wennington	C	7-0	245	8	4/26/63	St. John's

Arena Information

United Center (21,500)
Tickets: 312-559-1212
Ticket prices: $325, $120, $65, $50, $40, $30, $20, $15

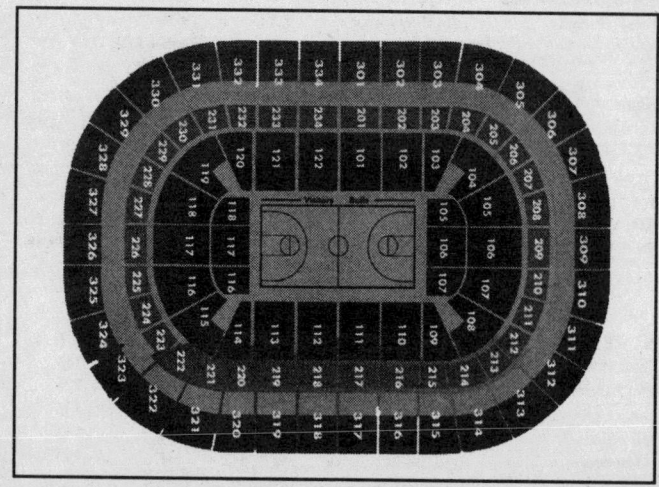

B.J. Armstrong

No. 10/G

Full name: Benjamin Roy Armstrong, Jr.

HT: 6-2 **WT:** 185

Born: 9/9/67, Detroit, MI

High school: Brother Rice (Birmingham, MI)

College: Iowa

Armstrong is quick, and a tenacious defender. He's one of the best jump-shooters in the NBA, especially from 3-point range. Armstrong's 44.4 3-point FG percentage was second in the NBA. He's also good from the free throw line; he hit 85.5 percent from the stripe last season, fourteenth best in the league. Last season, Armstrong was third on the team in scoring, second in assists, and third in steals. Armstrong was elected as a starter on the 1994 NBA All-Star Team. Despite his slight build, Armstrong is amazingly durable. He's played in 363 consecutive games, the longest streak of any Bull, and he has started 122 straight games, including all 82 games for Chicago last season.

REGULAR SEASON		G	MIN	FG	FG%	3FG	3PT%	FT	FT%	REB	AST	STL	BLK	PTS	AVG
'89-90	CHICAGO	81	1291	190	48.5	3	50.0	69	88.5	102	199	46	6	452	5.6
'90-91	CHICAGO	82	1731	304	48.1	15	50.0	97	87.4	149	301	70	4	720	8.8
'91-92	CHICAGO	82	1875	335	48.1	35	40.2	104	80.6	145	266	46	5	809	9.9
'92-93	CHICAGO	82	2492	408	43.9	63	45.3	130	86.1	149	330	66	6	1009	12.3
'93-94	CHICAGO	82	2770	479	47.6	60	44.4	194	85.5	170	323	80	9	1212	14.8
	5 YR TOTALS	409	10159	1716	48.4	176	44.3	594	85.3	715	1419	308	30	4202	10.3
'93-94	RANK NBA Gs	1	18	20	33	32	6	31	20	65	43	57	78	24	29
'94-95	PROJECTIONS	82	3130	550	46.8	73	44.2	246	85.7	177	320	90	11	1419	17.3

PLAYOFFS		G	MIN	FG	FG%	3FG	3PT%	FT	FT%	REB	AST	STL	BLK	PTS	AVG
'89-90	CHICAGO	16	217	21	33.9	0	0.0	22	91.7	20	23	10	0	64	4.0
'90-91	CHICAGO	17	273	35	50.0	3	60.0	20	80.0	27	43	19	1	93	5.5
'91-92	CHICAGO	22	434	63	45.3	5	29.4	30	78.9	24	47	14	0	161	7.3
'92-93	CHICAGO	19	643	88	52.4	21	51.2	20	90.9	28	62	19	2	217	11.4
'93-94	CHICAGO	10	360	55	51.9	7	58.3	36	81.8	24	25	8	0	153	15.3
	TOTALS	84	1927	262	48.1	36	45.6	128	83.7	123	206	70	3	688	8.2

Steve Kerr

No. 25/G

Full name: Stephen Douglas Kerr
HT: 6-3 **WT:** 180
Born: 9/27/65, Beirut, Lebanon
High school: Pacific Palisades (CA)
College: Arizona

Kerr played in all 82 games for Chicago. Although he never started, Kerr was the Bulls' fifth-leading scorer. Kerr is an accurate shooter who picks his shots well. He's virtually a career 45 percent shooter from 3-point range. Last season, Kerr's 41.9 3-point FG percentage ranked fourth in the NBA. (He was also third in the 3-point shootout competition held during the 1994 All-Star weekend.) He's also good from the free throw line, and he's a pretty good ballhandler and playmaker. Kerr has below-average speed and quickness for a guard, but he's not the defensive liability some think him to be.

REGULAR SEASON	G	MIN	FG	FG%	3FG	3PT%	FT	FT%	REB	AST	STL	BLK	PTS	AVG
'88-89 PHOENIX	26	157	20	43.5	8	47.1	6	66.7	17	24	7	0	54	2.1
'89-90 CLEVELAND	78	1664	192	44.4	73	50.7	63	86.3	98	248	45	7	520	6.7
'90-91 CLEVELAND	57	905	99	44.4	28	45.2	45	84.9	37	131	29	4	271	4.8
'91-92 CLEVELAND	48	847	121	51.1	32	43.2	45	83.3	78	110	27	10	319	6.6
'92-93 CLE-ORL	52	481	53	43.4	6	23.1	22	91.7	45	70	10	1	134	2.6
'93-94 CHICAGO	82	2036	287	49.7	52	41.9	83	85.6	131	210	75	3	709	8.6
6 YR TOTALS	343	6090	772	47.2	199	44.5	264	85.2	406	793	193	25	2007	5.9
'93-94 RANK NBA Gs	1	59	60	12	38	8	90	18	86	69	60	110	64	78
'94-95 PROJECTIONS	82	2691	413	51.9	70	45.5	100	84.0	150	223	114	-1	996	12.1

PLAYOFFS	G	MIN	FG	FG%	3FG	3PT%	FT	FT%	REB	AST	STL	BLK	PTS	AVG
'89-90 CLEVELAND	5	73	4	28.6	0	0.0	0	---	6	10	4	0	8	1.6
'91-92 CLEVELAND	12	149	18	43.9	3	27.3	5	100.0	6	10	5	0	44	3.7
'93-94 CHICAGO	10	186	13	36.1	6	37.5	3	100.0	14	10	7	0	35	3.5
TOTALS	27	408	35	38.5	9	30.0	8	100.0	26	30	16	0	87	3.2

Toni Kukoc

No. 7/F-G

HT: 6-11　　**WT:** 230
Born: 9/18/68, Split, Croatia
College: None

Kukoc can score, pass, and rebound. He was fourth on the Bulls in scoring, third in assists, and second in steals. He's also a good ballhandler, and can block shots. And he can shoot under pressure. He should improve on his rookie campaign. He's known as having one of the best outside shots in basketball, but was just 43.1 percent from the field last season. He was 27.1 percent from 3-point range last season, after averaging 40 percent from the closer 3-point arc in the Italian League. Kukoc was a member of 3 European Championship teams, and was European Player of the Year 3 times. He reportedly signed a contract over the offseason that makes him the highest paid Bull in history.

REGULAR SEASON	G	MIN	FG	FGx	3FG	3PTx	FT	FTx	REB	AST	STL	BLK	PTS	AVG
'93-94 CHICAGO	75	1808	313	43.1	32	27.1	156	74.3	297	252	81	33	814	10.9
1 YR TOTALS	75	1808	313	43.1	32	27.1	156	74.3	297	252	81	33	814	10.9
'93-94 RANK NBA Fs	55	55	51	112	25	45	47	45	70	15	24	65	48	50

PLAYOFFS	G	MIN	FG	FGx	3FG	3PTx	FT	FTx	REB	AST	STL	BLK	PTS	AVG
'93-94 CHICAGO	10	194	30	44.8	8	42.1	25	73.5	40	36	5	3	93	9.3
TOTALS	10	194	30	44.8	8	42.1	25	73.5	40	36	5	3	93	9.3

Luc Longley

No. 13/C

Full name: Lucien James Longley
HT: 7-2   **WT:** 265
Born: 1/19/69, Melbourne, Australia
High school: Scotch College
   (Perth, Australia)
College: New Mexico

Longley is a good rebounder and an outstanding shot blocker. He's also an excellent passer, and has a good shooting touch. But Longley is not an aggressive defender, and he's been inconsistent throughout his career. The 6.9 points and 5.7 rebounds that he averaged last season, modest production for a 7-2, 265 pound center, were both career highs. Longley's also foul-prone, averaging over 6.1 fouls per 40 minutes played over his short career. That's a big reason why he's averaged just 18 minutes per game over his career. Longley played for Australia in the '82 and '88 Summer Olympics basketball competition.

REGULAR SEASON		G	MIN	FG	FG%	3FG	3PT%	FT	FT%	REB	AST	STL	BLK	PTS	AVG
'91-92	MINNESOTA	66	991	114	45.8	0	---	53	66.3	257	53	35	64	281	4.3
'92-93	MINNESOTA	55	1045	133	45.5	0	---	53	71.6	240	51	47	77	319	5.8
'93-94	MIN-CHI	76	1502	219	47.1	0	0.0	90	72.0	433	109	45	79	528	6.9
	3 YR TOTALS	197	3538	466	46.3	0	0.0	196	70.3	930	213	127	220	1128	5.7
'93-94	RANK NBA Cs	16	22	19	35	14	14	20	19	19	11	14	19	20	25
'94-95	PROJECTIONS	82	1906	312	48.2	0	0.0	127	73.8	619	170	40	74	751	9.2

PLAYOFFS		G	MIN	FG	FG%	3FG	3PT%	FT	FT%	REB	AST	STL	BLK	PTS	AVG
'93-94	CHICAGO	10	170	25	50.0	0	---	13	72.2	45	18	6	8	63	6.3
	TOTALS	10	170	25	50.0	0	---	13	72.2	45	18	6	8	63	6.3

Scottie Pippen

No. 33/F

Full name: Scottie Pippen
HT: 6-7   **WT:** 225
Born: 9/25/65, Hamburg, AR
High school: Hamburg (AR)
College: Central Arkansas

One of the best players in the NBA, Pippen can score driving to the basket or from outside. He's also a great passer. He plays great defense, and gets a lot of steals. Pippen's ability has become overshadowed by his mercurial temperament. Oddly enough, Pippen's biggest controversy arose when he sulked and refused to play after Phil Jackson called a crunch time play for Toni Kukoc, not Pippen, vs. New York in the '94 Playoffs. It wasn't so long ago that Pippen was known as a disappearing act in the playoffs. Pippen has been the subject of trade talks involving Seattle, Miami, and Washington. In fact, he was apparently headed to Seattle for Shawn Kemp on draft day until Seattle management got cold feet after the proposed trade was lambasted on local sports talk radio.

REGULAR SEASON		G	MIN	FG	FGx	3FG	3PTx	FT	FTx	REB	AST	STL	BLK	PTS	AVG
'87-88	CHICAGO	79	1650	261	46.3	4	17.4	99	57.6	298	169	91	52	625	7.9
'88-89	CHICAGO	73	2413	413	47.6	21	27.3	201	66.8	445	256	139	61	1048	14.4
'89-90	CHICAGO	82	3148	562	48.9	28	25.0	199	67.5	547	444	211	101	1351	16.5
'90-91	CHICAGO	82	3014	600	52.0	21	30.9	240	70.6	595	511	193	93	1461	17.8
'91-92	CHICAGO	82	3164	687	50.6	16	20.0	330	76.0	630	572	155	93	1720	21.0
'92-93	CHICAGO	81	3123	628	47.3	22	23.7	232	66.3	621	507	173	73	1510	18.6
'93-94	CHICAGO	72	2759	627	49.1	63	32.0	270	66.0	629	403	211	58	1587	22.0
	7 YR TOTALS	551	19271	3778	49.1	175	26.9	1571	68.3	3765	2862	1173	531	9302	16.9
'93-94	RANK NBA Fs	72	14	5	41	8	31	13	101	19	1	1	27	5	3
'94-95	PROJECTIONS	67	2572	618	49.0	87	36.1	272	64.2	630	350	223	46	1595	23.8

PLAYOFFS		G	MIN	FG	FGx	3FG	3PTx	FT	FTx	REB	AST	STL	BLK	PTS	AVG
'87-88	CHICAGO	10	294	46	46.5	3	50.0	5	71.4	52	24	8	8	100	10.0
'88-89	CHICAGO	17	619	84	46.2	22	39.3	32	64.0	129	67	23	16	222	13.1
'89-90	CHICAGO	15	612	104	49.5	10	32.3	71	71.0	108	83	31	19	289	19.3
'90-91	CHICAGO	17	704	142	50.4	4	23.5	80	79.2	151	99	42	19	368	21.6
'91-92	CHICAGO	22	899	152	46.8	6	25.0	118	76.1	193	147	41	25	428	19.5
'92-93	CHICAGO	19	789	152	46.5	3	17.6	74	63.8	132	107	41	13	381	20.1
'93-94	CHICAGO	10	384	85	43.4	12	26.7	46	88.5	83	46	24	7	228	22.8
	TOTALS	110	4301	765	47.2	60	30.6	426	73.3	848	573	210	107	2016	18.3

Bill Cartwright No. 24/C

Full name: James William Cartwright
HT: 7-1 **WT:** 245
Born: 7/30/57, Lodi, CA
High school: Elk Grove (CA)
College: San Francisco

One of the worst rebounding big men in the NBA, Cartwright's always been knocked for having poor hands. He can still play defense.

REGULAR SEASON		G	MIN	FG	FGx	3FG	3PTx	FT	FTx	REB	AST	STL	BLK	PTS	AVG
'89-90	CHICAGO	71	2160	292	48.8	0	---	227	81.1	465	145	38	34	811	11.4
'90-91	CHICAGO	79	2273	318	49.0	0	---	124	69.7	486	126	32	15	760	9.6
'91-92	CHICAGO	64	1471	208	46.7	0	---	96	60.4	324	87	22	14	512	8.0
'92-93	CHICAGO	63	1253	141	41.1	0	---	72	73.5	233	83	20	10	354	5.6
'93-94	CHICAGO	42	780	98	51.3	0	---	39	68.4	152	57	8	8	235	5.6
15 YR TOTALS		934	27061	4629	52.6	0	0.0	3386	77.2	6019	1380	454	665	12644	13.5
'93-94 RANK NBA Cs		41	32	35	17	14	14	36	28	37	22	41	49	35	30
'94-95 PROJECTIONS		29	365	45	54.9	0	0.0	15	65.2	70	29	3	4	105	3.6

PLAYOFFS		G	MIN	FG	FGx	3FG	3PTx	FT	FTx	REB	AST	STL	BLK	PTS	AVG
'89-90	CHICAGO	16	462	50	41.3	0	---	29	67.4	75	16	5	4	129	8.1
'90-91	CHICAGO	17	511	70	51.9	0	---	22	68.8	80	32	9	7	162	9.5
'91-92	CHICAGO	22	612	55	47.4	0	---	13	41.9	98	38	11	4	123	5.6
'92-93	CHICAGO	19	444	46	46.5	0	---	28	77.8	85	29	11	3	120	6.3
		115	3307	403	49.0	0	0.0	253	72.1	624	151	51	55	1059	9.2

Jo Jo English No. 3/G

Full name: Stephen English
HT: 6-4 **WT:** 180
Born: 2/4/70, Frankfurt, West Germany
High school: Lower Richland (Columbia, SC)
College: South Carolina

English uses quickness to drive to the hoop or pull up for the jumper.

REGULAR SEASON		G	MIN	FG	FGx	3FG	3PTx	FT	FTx	REB	AST	STL	BLK	PTS	AVG
'92-93	CHICAGO	6	31	3	30.0	0	0.0	0	0.0	6	1	3	2	6	1.0
'93-94	CHICAGO	36	419	56	43.4	8	47.1	10	47.6	45	38	8	10	130	3.6
2 YR TOTALS		42	450	59	42.4	8	40.0	10	43.5	51	39	11	12	136	3.2
'93-94 RANK NBA Gs		130	125	125	82	95	4	135	136	122	127	134	73	129	122
'94-95 PROJECTIONS		66	807	135	57.0	-12	92.3	28	96.6	17	120	-47	-14	286	4.3

PLAYOFFS		G	MIN	FG	FGx	3FG	3PTx	FT	FTx	REB	AST	STL	BLK	PTS	AVG
'93-94	CHICAGO	7	58	5	41.7	1	25.0	3	50.0	3	2	1	1	14	2.0
TOTALS		7	58	5	41.7	1	25.0	3	50.0	3	2	1	1	14	2.0

Pete Myers   No. 20/G-F

Full name: Peter E. Myers
HT: 6-6   **WT:** 180
Born: 9/15/63, Mobile, AL
High school: Williamson (Mobile)
College: Arkansas-Little Rock

Myers had his best season in Chicago last year. He's a mediocre free throw shooter, but he compensates by working hard on defense.

REGULAR SEASON		G	MIN	FG	FG%	3FG	3PT%	FT	FT%	REB	AST	STL	BLK	PTS	AVG
'86-87	CHICAGO	29	155	19	36.5	0	0.0	28	65.1	17	21	14	2	66	2.3
'87-88	SAN ANTONIO	22	328	43	45.3	0	0.0	26	66.7	37	48	17	6	112	5.1
'88-89	PHILA-NY	33	270	31	42.5	0	0.0	33	68.8	33	48	20	2	95	2.9
'89-90	NY-NJ	52	751	89	39.6	0	0.0	66	66.0	96	135	35	11	244	4.7
'90-91	SAN ANTONIO	8	103	10	43.5	0	0.0	9	81.8	18	14	3	3	29	3.6
'93-94	CHICAGO	82	2030	253	45.5	8	27.6	136	70.1	181	245	78	20	650	7.9
6 YR TOTALS		226	3637	445	43.5	8	16.3	298	68.5	382	511	167	44	1196	5.3
'93-94	RANK NBA Gs	1	60	70	57	95	90	61	112	63	58	59	35	71	83
'94-95	PROJECTIONS	82	2925	389	47.0	21	42.9	158	67.8	172	302	105	12	957	11.7

PLAYOFFS		G	MIN	FG	FG%	3FG	3PT%	FT	FT%	REB	AST	STL	BLK	PTS	AVG
'86-87	CHICAGO	1	1	0	0.0	0	---	0	---	0	0	0	0	0	0.0
'88-89	NEW YORK	4	14	0	---	0	---	4	66.7	3	1	0	1	4	1.0
'93-94	CHICAGO	10	235	29	51.8	0	0.0	12	57.1	19	28	8	4	70	7.0
TOTALS		15	250	29	50.9	0	0.0	16	59.3	22	29	8	5	74	4.9

Dickie Simpkins   F

Full name: LuBara Dixon Simpkins
HT: 6-9   **WT:** 248
Born: 4/6/72, Washington, DC
High school: Friendly (Ft. Washington, MD)
College: Providence

Simpkins was a hit in postseason tournaments, averaging 20 points and 12.5 rebounds in Portsmouth.

REGULAR SEASON	G	MIN	FG	FG%	3FG	3PT%	FT	FT%	REB	AST	STL	BLK	PTS	AVG

ROOKIE — NO NBA EXPERIENCE

Bill Wennington   No. 34/C

Full name: William Percey Wennington
HT: 7-0 **WT:** 245
Born: 4/26/63, Montreal, Canada
High school: L.I. Lutheran (Brookville, NY)
College: St. John's
Wennington provides decent rebounding off the bench. He was 81.8 percent as a free throw shooter, third on the team.

REGULAR SEASON		G	MIN	FG	FG%	3FG	3PTx	FT	FTx	REB	AST	STL	BLK	PTS	AVG
'87-88	DALLAS	30	125	25	51.0	1	50.0	12	63.2	39	4	5	9	63	2.1
'88-89	DALLAS	65	1074	119	43.3	1	11.1	61	74.4	296	46	16	35	300	4.6
'89-90	DALLAS	60	814	105	44.9	0	0.0	60	80.0	198	41	20	21	270	4.5
'90-91	SACRAMENTO	77	1455	181	43.6	1	20.0	74	78.7	340	69	46	59	437	5.7
'93-94	CHICAGO	76	1371	235	48.8	0	0.0	72	81.8	353	70	43	29	542	7.1
7 YR TOTALS		422	5961	793	45.6	3	10.7	369	76.9	1477	275	154	165	1958	
'93-94	RANK NBA Cs	16	25	18	30	14	14	27	4	22	20	16	32	18	24
'94-95	PROJECTIONS	82	1522	295	50.8	0	0.0	69	84.1	397	82	50	18	659	8.0

PLAYOFFS		G	MIN	FG	FG%	3FG	3PTx	FT	FTx	REB	AST	STL	BLK	PTS	AVG
'86-87	DALLAS	4	47	6	50.0	0	---	3	60.0	10	4	0	3	15	3.8
'87-88	DALLAS	6	14	0	0.0	0	---	0	---	4	1	1	0	0	0.0
'89-90	DALLAS	3	25	1	20.0	0	---	0	---	3	1	0	1	2	0.7
'93-94	CHICAGO	7	47	3	50.0	0	---	2	66.7	7	4	0	1	8	1.1
TOTALS		26	151	12	36.4	1	100.0	7	70.0	29	10	1	5	32	1.2

Phil Jackson Head Coach

Full name: Philip D. Jackson
HT: 6-8 **WT:** 230
Born: 9/17/45, Deer Lodge, MT
High school: Williston (ND)
College: North Dakota
Jackson has now coached more Bulls games than anyone except Dick Motta. He was the first person to win NBA and CBA titles.

	REGULAR SEASON				PLAYOFFS			
YEAR	TEAM	W	L	PCT	FINISH	W	L	PCT	
'89-90	CHICAGO	55	27	671	2nd/Central Div.	10	6	625	lost Eastern Conf. finals to Detroit, 4-3
'90-91	CHICAGO	61	21	744	1st/Central Div.	15	2	882	won NBA Finals over LA Lakers, 4-1
'91-92	CHICAGO	67	15	817	1st/Central Div.	15	7	682	won NBA Finals over Portland, 4-2
'92-93	CHICAGO	57	25	695	1st/Central Div.	15	4	789	won NBA Finals over Phoenix, 4-2
'93-94	CHICAGO	55	27	671	2nd/Central Div.	6	4	600	lost Eastern Conf. semifinals to New York, 4-3
5 YR TOTALS		295	115	720		61	23	726	

Cleveland
CAVALIERS

1994–95 Scouting Report

Frontcourt

When everyone's healthy, Cleveland has one of the deepest front-courts in the league. Brad Daugherty is one of the top centers in the NBA. He's coming off a herniated disk, though, and it's not easy to recover from back problems. Tyrone Hill, the starting power forward, missed 25 games last season. He's one of the best defenders in the NBA. Chris Mills, '93 top draft pick, will probably move into the starting small forward role. Mills has a good outside shot, but may be too small to be effective at forward. Hot Rod Williams played well while filling in for the injured Daugherty, and he's available to fill in at power forward or center. Reserves include Danny Ferry and Michael Cage. Ferry can hit from the perimeter, although he's a defensive liability, while Cage gives Cleveland rebounding and defense off the bench.

Backcourt

Shooting guard Gerald Wilkins is an inconsistent scorer, but a tough defender who can take on the opponent's best shooting guard. John Battle, who missed 27 games last season due to a dislocated elbow, is available to add offense off the bench. Mark Price is one of the best point guards in the NBA. He was ninth in the league in assists, and he's deadly from outside. Terrell Brandon is his backup; despite starting at guard only 10 times last year, he led the team in assists in 14 games.

Defense

Cleveland's been accused of playing soft for some time. It's true that the Cavs were the seventh least penalized team in the league last year, and it's true that the Cavs ranked just fourteenth in blocked shots. The Cavs were just an average team when it came to disrupt-ing the other teams' offenses; they ranked sixteenth in the NBA in stealing the ball and fifteenth in the league in forcing turnovers. But Cleveland still managed to play well defensively, holding opponents to an average of just 97.1 points per game, seventh lowest in the NBA. Opposing teams shot 46.4 percent from the floor against Cleveland, thirteenth in the league. Cleveland was outstanding when it came to defending their defensive glass; they limited opponents to 12.9 offensive rebounds per game, fourth lowest in the league last season. That's one reason why opponents managed just 82.2 FGA per game, ninth lowest in the NBA. Blocks and rebounds should improve this year with Brad Daugherty's return. That means Cleveland should be an even tougher defensive team this season.

1994–95 Prospects

Last season, Cleveland started off slow, opening the year 7–14 and going 20–21 in their first 41 games. They missed Larry Nance for 23 games during this period after arthroscopic surgery to his right knee. They then put together an 8–3 run to stand at 28–24 before a herniated disk sidelined Brad Daugherty for the last 29 games of the season. Nance and Battle went out soon after. Hot Rod Williams did a yeoman's job filling in at center, notching 16.8 points, 8.4 rebounds and 1.86 blocks per game, and the Cavs went 18–11 in those games.

Cleveland should improve this year. They lost 223 player games due to injury last season, and that's not likely to happen again this season. Their frontline of Daugherty, Williams, Hill and Nance (when everyone is healthy), can score, rebound, block shots and play defense. And the Cavs have quality backcourt players in guards Mark Price, Gerald Wilkins, and John Battle. Cleveland consistently has the lowest turnover rates in the NBA (last year's 13.9 per game led the league). They were second in the NBA from the free throw line last year. They were also third in 3-point shooting. Their 4.0 point differential was eighth best in the NBA. (NBA champ Houston was sixth best, at 4.3.)

A healthy Cleveland squad should contend for the Central Division title and a spot in the NBA Finals. They could easily be a 50-win team this season; last year, they won 47 games despite going 1–10 in games decided by 3 points or less.

Team Directory

Chairman of the board: Gordon Gund Sr. vice chairman: George Gund III
Secy./Legal counsel: R. T. Watson   CEO: John W. Graham
Exec. VP/GM: Wayne Embry   Dir., public relations: Bob Price

1993–94 Review

EASTERN CONFERENCE							WESTERN CONFERENCE						
ATLANTIC DIV.			CENTRAL DIV.				MIDWEST DIV.				PACIFIC DIV.		
	W	L		W	L			W	L			W	L
NY	0	4	ATL	1	3		HOU	0	2		SEA	1	1
ORL	2	2	CHI	3	1		SAN	0	2		PHO	0	2
NJ	2	2	CLE	-	-		UTAH	1	1		GS	2	0
MIA	1	3	IND	2	3		DEN	1	1		POR	2	0
BOS	3	1	CHA	4	1		MIN	2	0		LAL	1	1
PHI	4	0	DET	3	2		DAL	2	0		SAC	2	0
WAS	3	1	MIL	3	2						LAC	2	0
	15	13		16	12			6	6			10	4

1993–94 finish: 47–35 (31–10 home, 16–25 away), third in Central Div.

1994–95 Schedule

11/5	@ Charlotte	7:30 pm	1/4	Seattle	7:30 pm	3/4	New York	7:30 pm
11/8	Houston	8:00 pm	1/6	New York	7:30 pm	3/7	Detroit	7:30 pm
11/10	Milwaukee	7:30 pm	1/7	Chicago	7:30 pm	3/9	San Ant.	8:00 pm
11/12	Indiana	7:30 pm	1/10	Charlotte	7:30 pm	3/10	@ Chicago	8:30 pm
11/15	Charlotte	7:30 pm	1/12	@ Phoenix	9:00 pm	3/12	@ Phila.	1:00 pm
11/17	@ Portland	10:00 pm	1/14	@ Gold. St.	10:30 pm	3/16	Utah	7:30 pm
11/18	@ LA Lakers	10:30 pm	1/17	@ Seattle	10:00 pm	3/17	@ Minnesota	8:00 pm
11/20	@ Sacra.	9:00 pm	1/18	@ LA Clip.	10:30 pm	3/19	@ Wash.	1:00 pm
11/22	Minnesota	7:30 pm	1/20	@ Utah	9:00 pm	3/20	Dallas	7:30 pm
11/23	@ Miami	7:30 pm	1/21	@ Denver	9:00 pm	3/22	Sacra.	7:30 pm
11/25	@ Wash.	7:30 pm	1/23	LA Clip.	7:30 pm	3/24	Atlanta	7:30 pm
11/26	Gold. St.	7:30 pm	1/26	@ Atlanta	7:30 pm	3/25	@ Charlotte	7:30 pm
11/30	LA Lakers	7:30 pm	1/27	Portland	7:30 pm	3/29	@ Indiana	7:30 pm
12/1	@ Milwaukee	8:30 pm	1/30	Phoenix	7:30 pm	3/31	Wash.	7:30 pm
12/3	Phila.	7:30 pm	2/1	@ Indiana	7:30 pm	4/2	Denver	4:00 pm
12/6	Orlando	7:30 pm	2/2	@ Detroit	7:30 pm	4/4	Boston	7:30 pm
12/7	@ Orlando	7:30 pm	2/4	Indiana	7:30 pm	4/5	@ Atlanta	7:30 pm
12/9	@ Boston	7:30 pm	2/7	Phila.	7:30 pm	4/7	@ Chicago	8:30 pm
12/10	Detroit	7:30 pm	2/8	@ Boston	7:30 pm	4/9	Chicago	1:00 pm
12/13	Indiana	7:30 pm	2/15	Orlando	7:30 pm	4/11	@ Orlando	7:30 pm
12/14	@ New Jersey	7:30 pm	2/16	@ Milwaukee	8:30 pm	4/13	@ Miami	7:30 pm
12/16	@ Phila.	7:30 pm	2/18	@ New Jersey	7:30 pm	4/14	Atlanta	7:30 pm
12/19	@ Chicago	8:30 pm	2/20	Miami	6:00 pm	4/18	@ Detroit	7:30 pm
12/22	@ New York	7:30 pm	2/21	@ New York	7:30 pm	4/19	Miami	7:30 pm
12/23	New Jersey	7:30 pm	2/25	New Jersey	7:30 pm	4/21	Milwaukee	7:30 pm
12/26	Boston	1:00 pm	2/27	@ Houston	8:30 pm	4/23	@ Charlotte	3:30 pm
12/28	Wash.	7:30 pm	2/28	@ San Ant.	8:30 pm			
12/30	Atlanta	7:30 pm	3/2	@ Dallas	8:30 pm			

1993–94 Team Stats

NAME	G	MIN	FG	FGA	FG%	3FG	3FGA	3FG%	FT	FTA	FT%	ORB	TRB	AST	PF	STL	BLK	TO	PTS	AVG
Price	76	2386	480	1005	47.8	118	297	39.7	238	268	88.8	39	228	589	93	103	11	189	1316	17.3
Daugherty	50	1838	296	606	48.8	0	0	—	256	326	78.5	128	508	149	145	41	36	110	848	17.0
Wilkins	82	2768	446	975	45.7	84	212	39.6	194	250	77.6	106	303	255	186	105	38	131	1170	14.3
Williams	76	2660	394	825	47.8	0	0	—	252	346	72.8	207	575	193	219	78	130	139	1040	13.7
Nance	33	909	153	314	48.7	0	0	—	64	85	75.3	77	227	49	96	27	55	38	370	11.2
Hill	57	1447	216	398	54.3	2	2	0.0	171	256	66.8	184	499	46	193	53	35	78	603	10.6
Mills	79	2022	284	677	41.9	38	122	31.1	137	176	77.8	134	401	128	232	54	50	89	743	9.4
Phills	72	1531	242	514	47.1	1	12	8.3	113	157	72.0	71	212	133	135	67	12	63	598	8.3
Brandon	73	1548	230	548	42.0	7	32	21.9	139	162	85.8	38	159	277	108	84	16	111	606	8.3
Battle	51	814	130	273	47.6	5	19	26.3	73	97	75.3	7	39	83	66	22	1	41	338	6.6
Higgins	36	547	71	163	43.6	22	50	44.0	31	42	73.8	25	82	36	53	25	14	21	195	5.4
Ferry	70	965	149	334	44.6	14	51	27.5	38	43	88.4	47	141	74	113	28	22	41	350	5.0
Kempton	4	33	6	12	50.0	0	0	—	2	6	33.3	4	10	3	8	2	1	7	14	3.5
Alexander	7	43	7	12	58.3	0	0	—	3	7	42.9	6	12	1	7	3	0	7	17	2.4
Madkins	22	149	11	31	35.5	5	15	33.3	8	10	80.0	1	11	19	16	9	0	13	35	1.6
Guidinger	32	131	16	32	50.0	0	0	—	15	21	71.4	15	33	3	23	4	5	16	47	1.5
Toney	12	64	2	12	16.7	0	1	0.0	6	6	100.0	1	3	11	8	0	0	5	6	0.5
Cavaliers	82	19855	3133	6731	46.5	294	813	36.2	1736	2254	77.0	1090	3443	2049	1701	705	426	1136	8296	101.2
Opp.	82	19855	3131	6741	46.4	258	729	35.4	1446	1967	73.5	1059	3394	2006	1797	628	461	1293	7966	97.1

HISTORY

TITLES

1975–76 Central Div. champs

ALL-TIME TEAM RECORDS

Career

Games played	Bobby "Bingo" Smith	720	1970–80
Total points	Austin Carr	10,265	1971–80
Scoring average	World B. Free	23	1982–86
Field goals made	Austin Carr	4,272	1971–80
Field goals attempted	Austin Carr	9,480	1971–80
Free throws made	Brad Daugherty	2,741	1986–94
Free throws attempted	Brad Daugherty	3,670	1986–94
Total rebounds	Brad Daugherty	5,227	1986–94
Assists	Mark Price	3,871	1986–94
Steals	"Foots" Walker	722	1974–80
Personal fouls	Bobby "Bingo" Smith	1,752	1970–80

Season

Total points	Mike Mitchell	2,012	1980–81
Scoring average	Mike Mitchell	24.5	1980–81
Field goals made	Mike Mitchell	853	1980–81
Field goals attempted	Mike Mitchell	1,791	1980–81
Free throws made	Brad Daugherty	435	1990–91
Free throws attempted	Brad Daugherty	579	1990–91
Total rebounds	Jim Brewer	891	1975–76
Assists	John Bagley	735	1985–86
Steals	Ron Harper	209	1986–87
Personal fouls	James Edwards	347	1981–82

Game

Total points	Walt Wesley	50	vs. Cincinnati, 2/19/71
Field goals made	Mike Mitchell	20	vs. Houston, 2/8/80
	Walt Wesley	20	vs. Cincinnati, 2/19/71
Free throws made	Mark Price	18	vs. Charlotte, 4/9/89
	Mark Price	18	vs. Atlanta, 11/17/89
Total rebounds	Rick Roberson	25	vs. Houston, 3/4/72
Assists	Geoff Huston	27	vs. Golden State, 1/27/82
Steals	Ron Harper	10	vs. Philadelphia, 3/10/87

LEADING COACHES

NAME	YEARS	REGULAR SEASON			PLAYOFFS		
		W	L	PCT	W	L	PCT
Lenny Wilkens	1986–93	316	258	.551	18	23	.439
Bill Fitch	1970–79	304	434	.412	7	11	.389
George Karl	1984–86	61	88	.409	1	3	.250
Tom Nissalke	1982–84	51	113	.311	0	0	—
Stan Albeck	1979–80	37	45	.451	0	0	—

Cleveland Cavaliers 1994–95 Roster

Head Coach: Mike Fratello

No.	Name	Pos.	Ht.	Wt.	Yrs.	Born	College
10	John Battle	G	6-2	190	9	11/9/69	Rutgers
11	Terrell Brandon	G	5-11	180	3	5/20/70	Oregon
44	Michael Cage	C-F	6-9	240	10	1/28/62	San Diego State
	Gary Collier	G	6-4	195	R	10/8/71	Tulsa
43	Brad Daugherty	C	7-0	263	8	10/19/65	North Carolina
35	Danny Ferry	F	6-10	236	4	10/17/66	Duke
23	Rod Higgins	F	6-7	215	12	1/31/60	Fresno State
32	Tyrone Hill	F	6-9	245	4	3/17/68	Xavier
8	Tim Kempton	F-C	6-10	255	5	1/25/64	Notre Dame
12	Gerald Madkins	G	6-4	200	1	4/18/69	UCLA
24	Chris Mills	F	6-6	216	1	1/25/70	Arizona
14	Bobby Phills	G	6-5	217	3	12/20/69	Southern
25	Mark Price	G	6-0	178	8	2/15/64	Georgia Tech
21	Gerald Wilkins	G	6-6	210	9	9/11/63	Tenn-Chattanooga
18	John Williams	F-C	6-11	245	8	8/9/62	Tulane

Arena Information

The Arena at Gateway (20,750)
Tickets: 216-420-CAVS
Ticket prices: $48, $35, $30, $26, $22, $16, $10

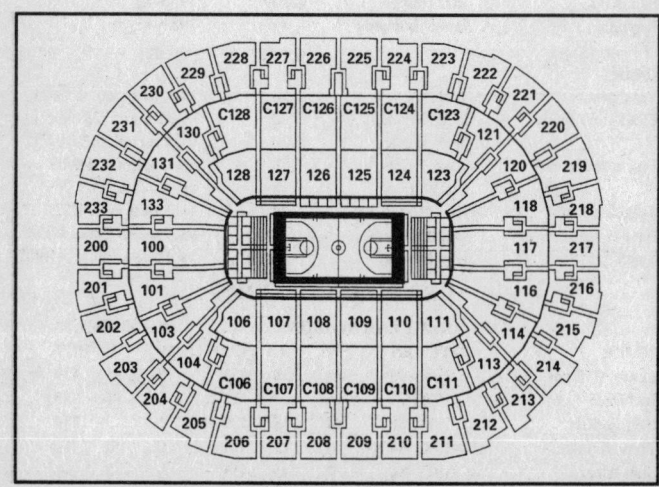

Brad Daugherty

No. 43/C

Full name: Bradley Lee Daugherty
HT: 7-0   **WT:** 263
Born: 10/19/65, Black Mountain, NC
High school: Charles D. Owen
   (Swannanoa, NC)
College: North Carolina

Daugherty is still a quality NBA center. He shoots for a high percentage and may be unequalled as a passer at his position. He simply suffers in comparison to more physical centers, such as Ewing, Olajuwon, and Shaquille O'Neal, who are more physical inside. Dougherty is just an average shot blocker, not as quick as Olajuwon or Robinson, and not as explosive as Patrick Ewing. Still, he can run the floor and fill the lanes on the fast break. He has good hands, can find open teammates with passes, and has an effective hook shot. He's also improved his low-post game over his career. His size (7-0, 265) makes him difficult to defend.

REGULAR SEASON		G	MIN	FG	FGx	3FG	3PTx	FT	FTx	REB	AST	STL	BLK	PTS	AVG
'86-87	CLEVELAND	80	2695	487	53.8	0	---	279	69.6	647	304	49	63	1253	15.7
'87-88	CLEVELAND	79	2957	551	51.0	0	0.0	378	71.6	665	333	48	56	1480	18.7
'88-89	CLEVELAND	78	2821	544	53.8	1	33.3	386	73.7	718	285	63	40	1475	18.9
'89-90	CLEVELAND	41	1438	244	47.9	0	0.0	202	70.4	373	130	29	22	690	16.8
'90-91	CLEVELAND	76	2946	605	52.4	0	0.0	435	75.1	830	253	74	46	1645	21.6
'91-92	CLEVELAND	73	2643	576	57.0	0	0.0	414	77.7	760	262	65	78	1566	21.5
'92-93	CLEVELAND	71	2691	520	57.1	1	50.0	391	79.5	726	312	53	56	1432	20.2
'93-94	CLEVELAND	50	1838	296	48.8	0	---	256	78.5	508	149	41	36	848	17.0
8 YR TOTALS		548	20029	3823	53.2	2	14.3	2741	74.7	5227	2028	422	397	10389	19.0
'93-94 RANK NBA Cs		33	16	12	27	14	14	7	8	12	8	19	26	11	6
'94-95 PROJECTIONS		40	1457	209	45.6	0	0.0	196	79.0	404	101	33	27	614	15.4

PLAYOFFS		G	MIN	FG	FGx	3FG	3PTx	FT	FTx	REB	AST	STL	BLK	PTS	AVG
'87-88	CLEVELAND	5	204	29	46.0	0	---	21	67.7	46	16	2	7	79	15.8
'88-89	CLEVELAND	5	167	17	36.2	0	0.0	21	60.0	46	12	6	5	55	11.0
'89-90	CLEVELAND	5	186	41	58.6	0	---	32	69.6	48	20	2	4	114	22.8
'91-92	CLEVELAND	17	687	124	52.8	0	0.0	118	81.4	174	58	11	17	366	21.5
'92-93	CLEVELAND	9	356	64	55.7	0	---	40	80.0	105	31	6	7	168	18.7
TOTALS		41	1600	275	51.9	0	0.0	232	75.6	419	137	27	40	782	19.1

Tyrone Hill

No. 32/F

HT: 6-9   **WT:** 245
Born: 3/17/68, Cincinnati, OH
High school: Withrow (Cincinnati)
College: Xavier

A physical player, Hill is a tough rebounder. Hill missed 18 games with a sprained left thumb, and three games with a hyperextended right knee. When he did play, only Dennis Rodman averaged more rebounds per 48 minutes among NBA forwards. Hill had ten or more rebounds 27 times; Cleveland was 18–9 in those games. He also plays hard on defense, although he commits his share of fouls. Hill's not much of a scorer; he lacks an outside shot and he has problems from the free throw line. But he can get points off of putbacks of offensive rebounds, and he led Cleveland in FG percentage at 54.3. Hill had 19 double-doubles and scored in double figures 29 times.

REGULAR SEASON		G	MIN	FG	FG%	3FG	3PT%	FT	FT%	REB	AST	STL	BLK	PTS	AVG
'90-91	GOLDEN STATE	74	1192	147	49.2	0	---	96	63.2	383	19	33	30	390	5.3
'91-92	GOLDEN STATE	82	1886	254	52.2	0	0.0	163	69.4	593	47	73	43	671	8.2
'92-93	GOLDEN STATE	74	2070	251	50.8	0	0.0	138	62.4	754	68	41	40	640	8.6
'93-94	CLEVELAND	57	1447	216	54.3	0	0.0	171	66.8	499	46	53	35	603	10.6
4 YR TOTALS		287	6595	868	51.7	0	0.0	568	65.7	2229	180	200	148	2304	8.0
'93-94 RANK NBA Fs		102	72	67	9	78	78	41	98	33	101	60	63	67	53
'94-95 PROJECTIONS		45	1195	197	56.3	0	0.0	175	68.4	414	41	51	31	569	12.6

PLAYOFFS		G	MIN	FG	FG%	3FG	3PT%	FT	FT%	REB	AST	STL	BLK	PTS	AVG
'90-91	GOLDEN STATE	9	80	9	64.3	0	0.0	4	66.7	23	2	3	4	22	2.4
'91-92	GOLDEN STATE	4	47	3	42.9	0	---	0	0.0	8	1	2	0	6	1.5
'93-94	CLEVELAND	3	123	11	40.7	0	---	20	54.1	31	4	1	1	42	14.0
TOTALS		16	250	23	47.9	0	0.0	24	53.3	62	7	6	5	70	4.4

Mark Price

No. 25/G

Full name: William Mark Price
HT: 6-0   **WT:** 178
Born: 2/15/64, Bartlesville, OK
High school: Enid (OK)
College: Georgia Tech

Price is still one of the best point guards in the NBA. He was named to the All-Star team for the third straight year, and for the fourth time. He's unsurpassed as a shooter at 3-point range and from the free throw line. In fact, Price is the leading active free throw shooter in the NBA, with a 90.6 career free throw percentage. And he's quick enough to drive to the hoop for baskets. Last season, Price led Cleveland in scoring, total points, 3-point FG shooting, and FT shooting. He broke 20 points in 31 games, and was his teams leading scorer 22 times. Price also led the Cavs in assists and was second in steals. Price is one of the smaller guards in the league, so he often has trouble defending taller guards.

REGULAR SEASON		G	MIN	FG	FGx	3FG	3PTx	FT	FTx	REB	AST	STL	BLK	PTS	AVG
'86-87	CLEVELAND	67	1217	173	40.8	23	32.9	95	83.3	117	202	43	4	464	6.9
'87-88	CLEVELAND	80	2626	493	50.6	72	48.6	221	87.7	180	480	99	12	1279	16.0
'88-89	CLEVELAND	75	2728	529	52.6	93	44.1	263	90.1	226	631	115	7	1414	18.9
'89-90	CLEVELAND	73	2706	489	45.9	152	40.6	300	88.8	251	666	114	5	1430	19.6
'90-91	CLEVELAND	16	571	97	49.7	19	34.0	59	95.2	45	166	42	2	271	16.9
'91-92	CLEVELAND	72	2138	438	48.8	101	38.7	270	94.7	173	535	94	12	1247	17.3
'92-93	CLEVELAND	75	2380	477	48.4	122	41.6	289	94.8	201	602	89	11	1365	18.2
'93-94	CLEVELAND	76	2386	480	47.8	118	39.7	238	88.8	228	589	103	11	1316	17.3
8 YR TOTALS		534	16752	3176	48.5	699	40.9	1735	90.6	1421	3871	699	64	8786	16.5
'93-94	RANK NBA Gs	61	40	19	29	12	21	19	7	42	9	36	68	15	13
'94-95	PROJECTIONS	82	2550	522	47.5	129	39.8	231	86.2	259	615	107	12	1404	17.1

PLAYOFFS		G	MIN	FG	FGx	3FG	3PTx	FT	FTx	REB	AST	STL	BLK	PTS	AVG
'87-88	CLEVELAND	5	205	38	56.7	5	41.7	24	96.0	18	38	3	0	105	21.0
'88-89	CLEVELAND	4	158	22	38.6	6	37.5	14	93.3	13	22	3	0	64	16.0
'89-90	CLEVELAND	5	192	32	52.5	6	35.3	30	100.0	14	44	9	1	100	20.0
'91-92	CLEVELAND	17	603	118	49.6	25	36.2	66	90.4	42	128	24	4	327	19.2
'92-93	CLEVELAND	9	288	43	44.3	8	30.8	23	95.8	19	55	15	0	117	13.0
'93-94	CLEVELAND	3	102	15	34.9	2	22.2	13	92.9	6	14	4	0	45	15.0
TOTALS		43	1548	268	47.6	52	34.9	170	93.9	112	301	58	5	758	17.6

Gerald Wilkins   No. 21/G

Full name: Gerald Bernard Wilkins
HT: 6-6   **WT:** 210
Born: 9/11/63, Atlanta, GA
High school: Mays (Atlanta)
College: Tenn.-Chattanooga

Wilkins is a gifted athlete who can run, drive the lane, dunk, and play ferocious defense. But he's an erratic shooter, and his ball handling and passing are just average. Wilkins led Cleveland in minutes played and steals. He was also third in scoring average and assists and second in total points. He was the only Cavalier to play in all 82 games. Wilkins' 38 points at Orlando on January 12 were the most points scored by a Cav last season, and Wilkins' most in a Cleveland uniform. Wilkins had his best season shooting 3-pointers: he had a career-high 84 3-pointers, and his career-best 39.6 percent from 3-point range ranked thirteenth in the NBA in 3-point FG percentage.

REGULAR SEASON		G	MIN	FG	FG%	3FG	3PT%	FT	FT%	REB	AST	STL	BLK	PTS	AVG
'85-86	NEW YORK	81	2025	437	46.8	7	28.0	132	55.7	208	161	68	9	1013	12.5
'86-87	NEW YORK	80	2758	633	48.6	26	35.1	235	70.1	294	354	88	18	1527	19.1
'87-88	NEW YORK	81	2703	591	44.6	39	30.2	191	78.6	270	326	90	22	1412	17.4
'88-89	NEW YORK	81	2414	462	45.1	51	29.7	186	75.6	244	274	115	22	1161	14.3
'89-90	NEW YORK	82	2609	472	45.7	39	31.2	208	80.3	371	330	95	21	1191	14.5
'90-91	NEW YORK	68	2164	380	47.3	9	20.9	169	82.0	207	275	82	23	938	13.8
'91-92	NEW YORK	82	2344	431	44.7	38	35.2	116	73.0	206	219	76	17	1016	12.4
'92-93	CLEVELAND	80	2079	361	45.3	16	27.6	152	84.0	214	183	78	18	890	11.1
'93-94	CLEVELAND	82	2768	446	45.7	84	39.6	194	77.6	303	255	105	38	1170	14.3
9 YR TOTALS		717	21864	4213	46.0	309	32.7	1583	74.8	2317	2377	797	188	10318	14.4
'93-94	RANK NBA Gs	1	19	29	53	19	22	31	73	22	56	35	11	29	35
'94-95	PROJECTIONS	82	3054	466	45.9	137	45.2	216	76.1	345	269	119	50	1285	15.7

PLAYOFFS		G	MIN	FG	FG%	3FG	3PT%	FT	FT%	REB	AST	STL	BLK	PTS	AVG
'87-88	NEW YORK	4	149	33	47.8	2	50.0	12	85.7	8	19	4	0	80	20.0
'88-89	NEW YORK	9	290	63	48.1	1	10.0	18	78.3	33	42	12	3	145	16.1
'89-90	NEW YORK	10	319	63	46.0	2	25.0	18	81.8	36	52	14	1	146	14.6
'90-91	NEW YORK	3	78	14	36.8	2	28.6	2	100.0	8	5	5	1	32	10.7
'91-92	NEW YORK	12	344	45	41.3	1	7.7	16	69.6	30	34	5	1	107	8.9
'92-93	CLEVELAND	9	236	38	43.7	4	33.3	13	76.5	16	24	9	2	93	10.3
'93-94	CLEVELAND	3	126	20	44.4	7	43.8	14	87.5	13	10	3	0	61	20.3
TOTALS		50	1542	276	44.8	19	27.1	93	79.5	144	186	52	8	664	13.3

Hot Rod Williams

No.18/F-C

Full name: John Williams
HT: 6–11 **WT:** 245
Born: 8/9/62, Sorrento, LA
High school: St. Amant (LA)
College: Tulane

Tremendously versatile, Williams played center and both forward spots for Cleveland last season after Brad Daugherty and Larry Nance went down with injuries. As Cleveland's starting center, Williams averaged 16.8 points, 8.4 rebounds, 3.3 assists and 1.86 blocks per game on 51.1 percent shooting in 38.6 minutes per game. Williams led Cleveland in scoring 14 times, scored in double figures 62 times, and broke 20 points 20 times. He was the Cavs' leading rebounder 20 times. Williams ranked thirteenth in the NBA with 1.71 blocks per game, and his 7.6 rebounds per game ranked thirtieth. He's Cleveland's all-time leader in offensive rebounds with 1,447.

REGULAR SEASON		G	MIN	FG	FG%	3FG	3PT%	FT	FT%	REB	AST	STL	BLK	PTS	AVG
'86-87	CLEVELAND	80	2714	435	48.5	0	0.0	298	74.5	629	154	58	167	1168	14.6
'87-88	CLEVELAND	77	2106	316	47.7	0	0.0	211	75.6	506	103	61	145	843	10.9
'88-89	CLEVELAND	82	2125	356	50.9	1	25.0	235	74.8	477	108	77	134	948	11.6
'89-90	CLEVELAND	82	2776	528	49.3	0	---	325	73.9	663	168	86	167	1381	16.8
'90-91	CLEVELAND	43	1293	199	46.3	0	0.0	107	65.2	290	100	36	69	505	11.7
'91-92	CLEVELAND	80	2432	341	50.3	0	0.0	270	75.2	607	196	60	182	952	11.9
'92-93	CLEVELAND	67	2055	263	47.0	0	---	212	71.6	415	152	48	105	738	11.0
'93-94	CLEVELAND	76	2660	394	47.8	0	---	252	72.8	575	193	78	130	1040	13.7
8 YR TOTALS		587	18161	2832	48.6	1	9.1	1910	73.5	4162	1174	504	1099	7575	12.9
'93-94	RANK NBA Fs	48	18	31	59	78	78	16	58	24	25	28	5	28	29
'94-95	PROJECTIONS	80	2946	445	47.6	0	0.0	266	73.5	629	211	93	130	1156	14.5
PLAYOFFS		G	MIN	FG	FG%	3FG	3PT%	FT	FT%	REB	AST	STL	BLK	PTS	AVG
'86-87	CLEVELAND	5	133	20	50.0	0	---	6	46.2	29	4	3	7	46	9.2
'87-88	CLEVELAND	5	161	21	46.7	0	---	13	72.2	34	10	2	7	55	11.0
'88-89	CLEVELAND	5	174	39	55.7	0	---	17	77.3	46	11	2	5	95	19.0
'91-92	CLEVELAND	17	567	84	54.5	0	---	87	79.8	130	42	24	17	255	15.0
'92-93	CLEVELAND	9	237	30	40.0	0	---	21	75.0	41	17	5	14	81	9.0
TOTALS		41	1272	194	50.5	0	---	144	75.8	280	84	36	50	532	13.0

Terrell Brandon   No. 11/G

Full name: Thomas Terrell Brandon
HT: 5-11 **WT:** 180
Born: 5/20/70, Portland, OR
High school: Grant (Portland)
College: Oregon

Brandon is an excellent playmaker and a strong backup at point guard. His shooting range is limited, but he's dangerous inside.

REGULAR SEASON	G	MIN	FG	FG%	3FG	3PT%	FT	FT%	REB	AST	STL	BLK	PTS	AVG
'91-92 CLEVELAND	82	1605	252	41.9	1	4.3	100	80.6	162	316	81	22	605	7.4
'92-93 CLEVELAND	82	1622	297	47.8	13	31.0	118	82.5	179	302	79	27	725	8.8
'93-94 CLEVELAND	73	1548	230	42.0	7	21.9	139	85.8	159	277	84	16	606	8.3
3 YR TOTALS	237	4775	779	44.0	21	21.6	357	83.2	500	895	244	65	1936	8.2
'93-94 RANK NBA Gs	71	75	78	92	99	108	59	16	69	49	50	46	77	82
'94-95 PROJECTIONS	66	1686	220	39.0	7	21.2	179	88.6	167	288	98	11	626	9.5

PLAYOFFS	G	MIN	FG	FG%	3FG	3PT%	FT	FT%	REB	AST	STL	BLK	PTS	AVG
'91-92 CLEVELAND	12	157	22	40.0	0	0.0	3	75.0	22	30	3	1	47	3.9
'92-93 CLEVELAND	8	132	20	43.5	2	40.0	9	100.0	17	17	7	3	51	6.4
'93-94 CLEVELAND	3	56	12	63.2	0	---	2	66.7	4	5	1	0	26	8.7
TOTALS	23	345	54	45.0	2	25.0	14	87.5	43	52	11	4	124	5.4

Michael Cage   No. 44/C-F

Full name: Michael Jerome Cage
HT: 6-9 **WT:** 240
Born: 2/28/62, West Memphis, AR
High school: West Memphis (AR)
College: San Diego State

Cage is a physical rebounder and a tough defender with a decent low-post game. His passing and ballhandling skills are limited.

REGULAR SEASON	G	MIN	FG	FG%	3FG	3PT%	FT	FT%	REB	AST	STL	BLK	PTS	AVG
'89-90 SEATTLE	82	2595	325	50.4	0	---	148	69.8	821	70	79	45	798	9.7
'90-91 SEATTLE	82	2141	226	50.8	0	---	70	62.5	558	89	85	58	522	6.4
'91-92 SEATTLE	82	2461	307	56.6	0	0.0	106	62.0	728	92	99	55	720	8.8
'92-93 SEATTLE	82	2156	219	52.6	0	0.0	61	46.9	659	69	76	46	499	6.1
'93-94 SEATTLE	82	1708	171	54.5	0	0.0	36	48.6	444	45	77	38	378	4.6
10 YR TOTALS	795	22355	2799	54.3	0	0.0	1499	61.6	6644	864	801	485	7097	8.9
'93-94 RANK NBA Cs	1	20	25	10	14	14	37	52	18	27	6	25	27	35
'94-95 PROJECTIONS	82	1410	133	55.2	0	0.0	21	45.7	339	31	70	32	287	3.5

PLAYOFFS	G	MIN	FG	FG%	3FG	3PT%	FT	FT%	REB	AST	STL	BLK	PTS	AVG
'90-91 SEATTLE	5	80	6	42.9	0	---	13	76.5	21	2	3	2	25	5.0
'91-92 SEATTLE	9	197	19	55.9	0	---	1	100.0	51	4	6	8	39	4.3
'92-93 SEATTLE	19	378	42	52.5	0	---	7	38.9	111	10	13	7	91	4.8
'93-94 SEATTLE	5	93	6	37.5	0	---	2	33.3	27	4	4	5	14	2.8
TOTALS	46	923	97	52.7	0	0.0	32	50.0	256	25	33	25	226	4.9

Danny Ferry No. 35/F

Full name: Daniel John Willard Ferry
HT: 6-10 **WT:** 236
Born: 10/17/66, Hyattsville, MD
High school: DeMatha Catholic (Hyattsville)
College: Duke

A smart player who passes well, with a good 3-point shot, Ferry's a bit too slow to play defense against quick small forwards.

REGULAR SEASON		G	MIN	FG	FGx	3FG	3PTx	FT	FTx	REB	AST	STL	BLK	PTS	AVG
'90-91	CLEVELAND	81	1661	275	42.8	23	29.9	124	81.6	286	142	43	25	697	8.6
'91-92	CLEVELAND	68	937	134	40.9	17	35.4	61	83.6	213	75	22	15	346	5.1
'92-93	CLEVELAND	76	1461	220	47.9	34	41.5	99	87.6	279	137	29	49	573	7.5
'93-94	CLEVELAND	70	965	149	44.6	14	27.5	38	89.4	141	74	28	22	350	5.0
4 YR TOTALS		295	5024	778	44.1	88	34.1	322	84.5	919	428	122	111	1966	6.7
'93-94	RANK NBA Fs	77	99	92	97	35	44	115	2	114	71	97	91	98	102
'94-95	PROJECTIONS	67	727	113	44.1	8	21.1	15	88.2	83	50	24	15	249	3.7

PLAYOFFS		G	MIN	FG	FGx	3FG	3PTx	FT	FTx	REB	AST	STL	BLK	PTS	AVG
'91-92	CLEVELAND	9	55	7	46.7	1	33.3	4	100.0	16	1	1	1	19	2.1
'92-93	CLEVELAND	8	118	13	38.2	4	44.4	9	90.0	25	14	4	3	39	4.9
'93-94	CLEVELAND	1	4	0	—	0	—	0	—	0	1	0	0	0	0.0
TOTALS		18	177	20	40.8	5	41.7	13	92.9	41	16	5	4	58	3.2

Chris Mills No. 24/F

Full name: Christopher Lemonte Mills
HT: 6-6 **WT:** 216
Born: 1/25/70, Los Angeles, CA
High school: Fairfax (Los Angeles)
College: Arizona

Despite his size, Mills is a pretty good rebounder. He was fourth on the team in rebounds, and third in offensive rebounds.

REGULAR SEASON		G	MIN	FG	FGx	3FG	3PTx	FT	FTx	REB	AST	STL	BLK	PTS	AVG
'93-94	CLEVELAND	79	2022	284	41.9	38	31.1	137	77.8	401	128	54	50	743	9.4
1 YR TOTALS		79	2022	284	41.9	38	31.1	137	77.8	401	128	54	50	743	9.4
'93-94	RANK NBA Fs	30	48	58	118	20	33	53	23	50	46	58	36	56	61

PLAYOFFS		G	MIN	FG	FGx	3FG	3PTx	FT	FTx	REB	AST	STL	BLK	PTS	AVG
'93-94	CLEVELAND	3	112	19	50.0	4	80.0	9	81.8	23	8	7	1	51	17.0
TOTALS		3	112	19	50.0	4	80.0	9	81.8	23	8	7	1	51	17.0

Bobby Phills   No. 14/G

Full name: Bobby Ray Phills II
HT: 6-5   **WT:** 217
Born: 12/20/69, Baton Rouge, LA
High school: Southern U. Lab (Baton Rouge)
College: Southern

Last season was Phills' best in Cleveland. He started 53 games, and scored a career-high 26 points vs. Golden State February 25.

REGULAR SEASON		G	MIN	FG	FG%	3FG	3PT%	FT	FT%	REB	AST	STL	BLK	PTS	AVG
'91-92	CLEVELAND	10	65	12	42.9	0	0.0	7	63.6	8	4	3	1	31	3.1
'92-93	CLEVELAND	31	139	38	46.3	2	40.0	15	60.0	17	10	10	2	93	3.0
'93-94	CLEVELAND	72	1531	242	47.1	1	8.3	113	72.0	212	133	67	12	598	8.3
	3 YR TOTALS	113	1735	292	46.8	3	15.8	135	63.9	237	147	80	15	722	6.4
'93-94	RANK NBA Gs	75	77	73	38	124	128	70	104	48	91	67	62	79	80
'94-95	PROJECTIONS	82	2409	216	48.5	2	-6.9	91	79.8	362	243	70	6	525	6.4

PLAYOFFS		G	MIN	FG	FG%	3FG	3PT%	FT	FT%	REB	AST	STL	BLK	PTS	AVG
'91-92	CLEVELAND	5	12	4	44.4	0	0.0	3	75.0	6	5	1	0	11	2.2
'92-93	CLEVELAND	2	9	1	33.3	0	---	2	100.0	0	0	0	0	4	2.0
'93-94	CLEVELAND	3	68	9	37.5	1	100.0	1	50.0	14	7	2	0	20	6.7
	TOTALS	10	89	14	38.9	1	50.0	6	75.0	20	12	3	0	35	3.5

Mike Fratello Head Coach

Full name: Michael Robert Fratello
HT: 5-7   **WT:** 150
Born: 2/24/47, Hackensack, NJ
High school: Hackensack (NJ)
College: Montclair State

Fratello's 47–35 record was the best ever by a Cleveland head coach in his first year. He's now had 6 straight winning seasons.

	REGULAR SEASON				PLAYOFFS			
YEAR	TEAM	W	L	PCT	FINISH	W	L	PCT
'80-81	ATLANTA	0	3	.000	4th/Central Div.			
'83-84	ATLANTA	40	42	.488	3rd/Central Div.	2	3	.400	lost Eastern Conf. first round to Milwaukee, 3-2
'84-85	ATLANTA	34	48	.415	5th/Central Div.			
'85-86	ATLANTA	50	32	.610	2nd/Central Div.	4	5	.444	lost Eastern Conf. semifinals to Boston, 4-1
'86-87	ATLANTA	57	25	.695	1st/Central Div.	4	5	.444	lost Eastern Conf. semifinals to Detroit, 4-1
'87-88	ATLANTA	50	32	.610	T2nd/Central Div.	6	6	.500	lost Eastern Conf. semifinals to Boston, 4-3
'88-89	ATLANTA	52	30	.634	3rd/Central Div.	2	3	.400	lost Eastern Conf. first round to Milwaukee, 3-2
'89-90	ATLANTA	41	41	.500	6th/Central Div.			
'93-94	CLEVELAND	47	35	.573	T3rd/Central Div.	0	3	.000	lost Eastern Conf. first round to Chicago, 3-0
	7 YR TOTALS	371	288	.563		18	25	.419	

Dallas
MAVERICKS

1994–95 Scouting Report

Frontcourt

Last season, the Mavericks lacked a first-rate center and power forward in their frontcourt. They hoped they'd solved the power forward problem with second round draft pick Deon Thomas out of Illinois, but it looks like he'll play in Europe this season. 1993 first-rounder Jamal Mashburn returns at small forward. Mashburn had 5 of the top 8 Maverick scoring performances last season on his way to a 19.2 points per game average—tops among NBA rookies. Sean Rooks started 28 games at center last season (he played in 19 other games and missed 35 games due to injuries). His role is to rebound and block shots. The starting power forward, Popeye Jones, is a rebounder whose 7.5 rebounds per game was third highest among all NBA rookies. Doug Smith comes off the bench to play forward; he brings rebounding and ballhandling to the Mavs. Lorenzo Williams is a CBA alumnus who's trying to hang on by working hard as a rebounder and shotblocker. As we go to press, Roy Tarpley's attempt to gain readmission to the NBA is still up in the air. Dallas would be helped by Tarpley's addition; he's a 7-footer who is quick, strong, a tremendous leaper, and a dominating rebounder.

Backcourt

The Mavs took Jason Kidd, the best draft prospect at point guard since Kenny Anderson in 1991, with their top pick in the draft. Jim Jackson effectively played point for Dallas' last season (he had seven of Dallas' top ten assist games), so Kidd's drafting will free Jackson to play a more effective off-guard. Dallas also drafted shooting guard Tony Dumas in the first round; Dumas is a scorer who can rebound, so the Mavericks are situated to play a three guard rotation this season with Kidd, Jackson (who can play point or shooting guard), and Dumas. Lucious Harris is a reserve guard who can play defense and pass.

Defense

Dallas has a group of young, athletic players who have the ability to force opponents to give up the ball. Dallas was third in the league in forcing turnovers, and sixth in steals. As a result, teams didn't get a whole lot of shots against the Mavericks—Dallas allowed the third fewest shots from the field last season, behind New York and Seattle. That's why teams averaged 103.8 points against the Mavericks, seventeenth lowest in the NBA. Why wasn't that total lower? Because Dallas doesn't have a big defensive presence down low; the Mavs were dead last in the NBA in blocked shots. So when they didn't turn over the ball, opponents shot for a high percentage against Dallas—49.4 percent, second highest in the league. But there's potential for defensive improvement, if Dallas can get a defensive intimidator underneath.

1994-95 Prospects

Really bad teams play poorly at home. That's because when a team is really bad, two things happen: (a) the home town fans stay away, and playing before empty seats depresses the home team, and (b) the fans who do show up turn on the home team at the first sign of adversity, depressing the home team more than any hostile road crowd. Last season, Dallas was 6–35 at home, and 7–34 on the road, the first time a team played better on the road since the '76–77 New York Nets (another really bad team) went 10–31 at home and 12–29 on the road). Fortunately, Dallas matched up well against Minnesota, against whom they were 5–1.

The good news is that Dallas is no longer a really bad team. They've got a good crop of rookies in Jason Kidd and Tony Dumas to complement second year F Jamal Mashburn and third year G Jim Jackson. The bad news is that they're a young team with a glaring hole at center and a rookie at point guard. There's virtually no depth on this team, and they desperately need rebounding help; the Mavs were last in the NBA in defensive rebounds last season, and of the bottom five teams in that category, only Seattle (fifth lowest) had a winning record; the other four teams, including Dallas, were 90–238, a .274 percentage. Dallas is headed in the right direction, but the Mavs are still a couple of years away from being any kind of force in the NBA. They'll be a lottery team again this year.

Team Directory

Owner/President: Donald Carter   COO/GM: Norm Sonju
Vice president/Counsel: Doug Adkins   Dir., player personnel: Keith Grant
Dir., finance: Jim Livingston   Dir., media services: Kevin Sullivan

1993–94 Review

WESTERN CONFERENCE   EASTERN CONFERENCE
MIDWEST DIV. PACIFIC DIV.   ATLANTIC DIV. CENTRAL DIV.

	W	L		W	L		W	L		W	L
HOU	1	4	SEA	0	4	NY	0	2	ATL	0	2
SAN	0	5	PHO	0	4	ORL	0	2	CHI	0	2
UTAH	0	5	GS	0	4	NJ	0	2	CLE	0	2
DEN	1	4	POR	1	3	MIA	0	2	IND	0	2
MIN	5	1	LAL	0	4	BOS	0	2	CHA	1	1
DAL	–	–	SAC	2	2	PHI	0	2	DET	1	1
			LAC	0	4	WAS	1	1	MIL	0	2
	7	19		3	25		1	13		2	12

1993–94 finish: 13–69 (6–35 home, 7–34 away), sixth in Midwest Div.

1994–95 Schedule

11/5	New Jersey	8:30 pm	1/9	@ Utah	9:00 pm	3/8	@ Utah	9:00 pm
11/8	Denver	8:30 pm	1/11	LA Clip.	8:30 pm	3/11	@ Houston	8:30 pm
11/11	@ Phila.	7:30 pm	1/12	@ Denver	9:00 pm	3/13	@ Gold. St.	10:30 pm
11/12	@ Chicago	8:30 pm	1/14	Miami	8:30 pm	3/14	@ Sacra.	10:30 pm
11/15	@ Miami	7:30 pm	1/15	@ San Ant.	7:00 pm	3/17	Phila.	8:30 pm
11/17	Sacra.	8:30 pm	1/18	Orlando	8:30 pm	3/18	@ San Ant.	8:30 pm
11/19	Chicago	8:30 pm	1/20	New York	8:30 pm	3/20	@ Cleveland	7:30 pm
11/23	@ LA Lakers	10:30 pm	1/21	Seattle	8:30 pm	3/22	@ Minn.	8:00 pm
11/25	Portland	8:30 pm	1/23	@ Utah	9:00 pm	3/23	@ Detroit	7:30 pm
11/26	@ Denver	9:00 pm	1/24	@ Sacra.	10:30 pm	3/25	Utah	8:30 pm
11/29	Minn.	8:30 pm	1/27	Minn.	8:30 pm	3/28	Milw.	8:30 pm
12/1	Denver	8:30 pm	1/28	Sacra.	8:30 pm	3/30	@ Charlotte	7:30 pm
12/3	Utah	8:30 pm	1/31	@ Milw.	8:30 pm	3/31	@ New York	7:30 pm
12/6	@ San Ant.	8:30 pm	2/1	@ Minn.	8:00 pm	4/2	@ Boston	4:00 pm
12/8	Wash.	8:30 pm	2/3	San Ant.	8:30 pm	4/5	LA Lakers	8:30 pm
12/10	Charlotte	8:30 pm	2/4	Utah	8:30 pm	4/7	Minn.	8:30 pm
12/13	LA Lakers	8:00 pm	2/7	Phoenix	8:30 pm	4/8	Seattle	8:30 pm
12/15	Boston	8:30 pm	2/8	@ Orlando	7:30 pm	4/10	Gold. St.	8:30 pm
12/17	@ LA Clip.	10:30 pm	2/14	Portland	8:30 pm	4/11	@ Houston	8:30 pm
12/20	@ Gold. St.	10:30 pm	2/17	Atlanta	8:30 pm	4/13	@ Seattle	10:00 pm
12/22	@ Seattle	10:00 pm	2/21	@ Wash.	7:30 pm	4/15	@ Portland	10:00 pm
12/23	@ Portland	10:00 pm	2/23	@ Atlanta	7:30 pm	4/16	@ LA Lakers	10:00 pm
12/26	@ Phoenix	9:00 pm	2/24	@ New Jersey	7:30 pm	4/18	LA Clip.	8:30 pm
12/27	Phoenix	8:30 pm	2/26	@ Indiana	2:30 pm	4/20	San Ant.	8:30 pm
12/30	Gold. St.	8:30 pm	2/28	Houston	8:30 pm	4/21	@ Phoenix	10:00 pm
01/3	Houston	8:30 pm	3/2	Cleveland	8:30 pm	4/23	@ LA Clip.	6:00 pm
01/5	@ Houston	8:30 pm	3/4	Detroit	8:30 pm			
01/6	Indiana	8:30 pm	3/7	Denver	8:30 pm			

1993–94 Team Stats

NAME	G	MIN	FG	FGA	FG%	3FG	3FGA	3FG%	FT	FTA	FT%	ORB	TRB	AST	PF	STL	BLK	TO	PTS	AVG
Jackson	82	3066	637	1432	44.5	17	60	28.3	285	347	82.1	169	388	374	161	87	25	334	1576	19.2
Mashburn	79	2896	561	1382	40.6	85	299	28.4	306	438	69.9	107	353	266	205	89	14	245	1513	19.2
Harper	28	893	130	342	38.0	37	105	35.2	28	50	56.0	10	55	98	46	45	4	54	325	11.6
Rooks	47	1255	193	393	49.1	0	1	0.0	150	210	71.4	84	259	49	109	21	44	80	536	11.4
Campbell	41	835	164	384	42.7	6	25	24.0	64	83	77.1	48	126	51	75	30	14	55	398	9.7
Smith	79	1684	295	678	43.5	2	9	22.2	106	127	83.5	114	349	119	287	82	38	93	698	8.8
Legler	79	1322	231	528	43.8	52	139	37.4	142	169	84.0	36	128	120	133	52	13	60	656	8.3
Lever	81	1947	227	557	40.8	26	74	35.1	75	98	76.5	83	283	213	155	159	15	88	555	6.9
White	18	320	45	112	40.2	6	20	30.0	19	33	57.6	30	83	11	46	10	10	18	115	6.4
Jones	81	1773	195	407	47.9	1	1	0.0	78	107	72.9	299	605	99	246	61	31	94	468	5.8
Harris	77	1165	162	385	42.1	7	33	21.2	87	119	73.1	45	157	106	117	49	10	78	418	5.4
Morningstar	22	363	38	81	46.9	0	0	—	18	30	60.0	31	80	15	69	14	2	19	94	4.3
Davis	15	286	24	59	40.7	0	0	—	8	12	66.7	30	74	6	27	9	1	5	56	3.7
Williams	34	678	48	103	46.6	0	0	—	12	28	42.9	92	209	23	87	15	41	21	108	3.2
Brown	1	10	4	4	100.0	0	0	—	1	1	100.0	0	1	0	2	0	0	0	3	3.0
Hodge	50	428	46	101	45.5	0	1	0.0	44	52	84.6	46	95	32	66	15	13	30	136	2.7
Dreiling	54	685	52	104	50.0	0	1	100.0	27	38	71.1	47	170	31	159	16	24	43	132	2.4
Wiley	12	124	6	21	28.6	2	6	33.3	0	0	—	0	6	16	17	13	0	11	14	1.2
Mavs	82	19730	3055	7070	43.2	241	773	31.2	1450	1942	74.7	1271	3421	1629	2007	767	299	1393	7801	95.1
Opp.	82	19730	3212	6508	49.4	249	688	36.2	1841	2498	73.7	1101	3604	1970	1649	782	507	1428	8514	103.8

HISTORY
TITLES

1986–87 Midwest Div. champs

ALL-TIME TEAM RECORDS

Career

Games played	Brad Davis	883	1980–92
Total points	Rolando Blackman	16,643	1981–92
Scoring average	Mark Aguirre	24.6	1981–89
Field goals made	Rolando Blackman	6,487	1981–92
Field goals attempted	Rolando Blackman	13,061	1981–92
Free throws made	Rolando Blackman	3,501	1981–92
Free throws attempted	Rolando Blackman	4,166	1981–92
Total rebounds	James Donaldson	4,589	1985–92
Assists	Derek Harper	4,790	1983–94
Steals	Derek Harper	1,459	1983–94
Personal fouls	Brad Davis	2,040	1980–92

Season

Total points	Mark Aguirre	2,330	1983–84
Scoring average	Mark Aguirre	29.5	1983–84
Field goals made	Mark Aguirre	925	1983–84
Field goals attempted	Mark Aguirre	1,765	1983–84
Free throws made	Mark Aguirre	465	1983–84
Free throws attempted	Mark Aguirre	621	1983–84
Total rebounds	James Donaldson	973	1986–87
Assists	Derek Harper	634	1987–88
Steals	Derek Harper	172	1988–89
Personal fouls	Roy Tarpley	313	1987–88

Game

Total points	Mark Aguirre	49	vs. Philadelphia, 1/28/85
Field goals made	Mark Aguirre	21	vs. Denver, 3/24/84
Free throws made	Rolando Blackman	22	vs. New Jersey, 2/17/86
Total rebounds	James Donaldson	27	vs. Portland, 12/29/89
Assists	Derek Harper	18	vs. Boston, 12/29/88
Steals	Fat Lever	9	vs. Washington, 2/10/94

LEADING COACHES

		REGULAR SEASON			PLAYOFFS		
NAME	YEARS	W	L	PCT	W	L	PCT
Dick Motta	1980–87	267	307	.465	11	17	.393
John MacLeod	1987–90	96	79	.549	10	7	.588
Richie Adubato	1989–93	94	170	.356	0	3	.000
Gar Heard	1992–93	9	44	.170	0	0	—
Quinn Buckner	1993–94	13	69	.159	0	0	—

Dallas Mavericks 1994-95 Roster

Head Coach: Dick Motta

No.	Name	Pos.	Ht.	Wt.	Yrs.	Born	College
43	Terry Davis	F-C	6-10	250	5	6/17/67	Virginia Union
7	Tony Dumas	G	6-6	190	R	8/25/72	Missouri-Kansas City
30	Lucious Harris	G	6-5	190	1	12/18/70	Long Beach State
35	Donald Hodge	F	7-0	239	3	2/25/69	Temple
24	Jim Jackson	G	6-6	220	2	10/14/70	Ohio State
54	Popeye Jones	F	6-8	250	1	6/17/70	Murray State
5	Jason Kidd	G	6-4	205	R	3/23/73	California
32	Jamal Mashburn	F	6-8	240	1	11/29/72	Kentucky
45	Sean Rooks	C	6-10	260	2	9/9/69	Arizona
34	Doug Smith	F	6-10	238	3	9/17/69	Missouri
20	Morlon Wiley	G	6-4	192	6	9/24/66	Long Beach State
44	Lorenzo Williams	F	6-9	200	2	7/15/69	Stetson

Arena Information

Reunion Arena (17,502)
Tickets: 214-939-2800
Ticket prices: $46, $36, $28, $24, $19, $15, $13, $5

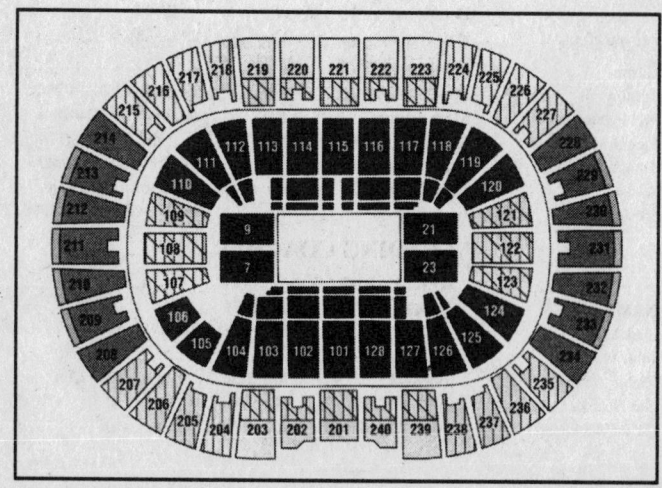

Jim Jackson

No. 24/G

Full name: James Arthur Jackson
HT: 6-6   **WT:** 220
Born: 10/14/70, Toledo, OH
High school: Macomber-Whitney (Toledo)
College: Ohio State

Although he turns over the ball too much to play point guard successfully, Jackson's probably the best all-around young guard in the NBA. A confident player, Jackson is strong and fluid. He can go around an opponent or right through him. He has good court sense, can score from anywhere, is an excellent rebounder, and can find the open man for the assist. He tied Jamal Mashburn for the team scoring lead, and led the team in total points scored and assists. He's started 110 straight games since signing with Dallas, the tenth longest active stretch of consecutive starts in the NBA (and 39 off Brad Davis' record of 149 from 2/8/81 through 11/25/83). His 3,066 minutes played last season set a team record.

REGULAR SEASON	G	MIN	FG	FG%	3FG	3PT%	FT	FT%	REB	AST	STL	BLK	PTS	AVG
'92-93 DALLAS	28	938	184	39.5	21	28.8	68	73.9	122	131	40	11	457	16.3
'93-94 DALLAS	82	3066	637	44.5	17	28.3	285	82.1	388	374	87	25	1576	19.2
2 YR TOTALS	110	4004	821	43.3	38	28.6	353	80.4	510	505	127	36	2033	18.5
'93-94 RANK NBA Gs	1	4	1	68	77	87	13	45	9	30	47	23	3	7
'94-95 PROJECTIONS	82	3936	852	49.5	-42	27.6	456	90.3	484	411	56	18	2118	25.8

Popeye Jones

No. 54/F

Full name: Ronald Jerome Jones
HT: 6-8   **WT:** 250
Born: 6/17/70, Martin, TN
High school: Dresden (TN)
College: Murray State

Jones can play both forward positions. He's a big, strong guy who gets good rebounding position. Jones tied Dallas' rookie rebounding record (set by Sam Perkins in '84–85) with 605 last season. His 7.5 rebounds per game was third highest among all NBA rookies, behind Chris Webber's 9.1 and Vin Baker's 7.6. Jones was the Mavs' leading rebounder last season; he had almost as many offensive rebounds (299) as defensive rebounds (306). Although Jones wasn't a big scorer in his rookie season, he has a good low-post game and passes well. He averaged 21.1 points and 13.3 rebounds with Milano Teorematour in the Italian League in the '92–93 season.

REGULAR SEASON	G	MIN	FG	FG%	3FG	3PT%	FT	FT%	REB	AST	STL	BLK	PTS	AVG
'93-94 DALLAS	81	1773	195	47.9	0	0.0	78	72.9	605	99	61	31	468	5.8
1 YR TOTALS	81	1773	195	47.9	0	0.0	78	72.9	605	99	61	31	468	5.8
'93-94 RANK NBA Fs	15	56	77	57	78		78	87	56	21	58	47	71	77	92

Jason Kidd

No. 5/G

HT: 6-4   **WT:** 205
Born: 3/23/73, San Francisco
College: California

How the Mavs handle Kidd will tell how successful they'll be in building this team over the long-term. What do Mookie Blaylock, Muggsy Bogues, Mark Jackson, and Rod Strickland all have in common? They're all star point guards today who were abandoned by the teams that drafted them after they struggled early in their careers. That shows a team can be tempted to give up too early on a point guard. Kidd was the top point guard in the NCAA when he declared for the NBA Draft after his sophomore season at Cal. An exceptional playmaker with uncommon maturity on the court, Kidd led the nation in assists per game (9.1) last season, and was fourth in steals per game (3.1). As a freshman, he led Cal to an upset of two-time defending champ Duke on the way to the Sweet 16 in the 1993 NCAA Tournament. He'll need to develop an outside shot in the NBA.

REGULAR SEASON	G	MIN	FG	FGx	3FG	3PTx	FT	FTx	REB	AST	STL	BLK	PTS	AVG
ROOKIE -- NO NBA EXPERIENCE														

Jamal Mashburn

No. 32/F

Full name: Jamal Mashburn
HT: 6-8 **WT:** 240
Born: 12/29/72, New York, NY
High school: Cardinal Hayes
  (Bronx, NY)
College: Kentucky

Mashburn is powerful, quick, and can score from outside. He also passes well and plays good defense. His 19.2 points per game average led all NBA rookies last year, and was exceeded during the past decade only by the rookie campaigns of Michael Jordan (28.2 in 1984–85), David Robinson (24.3 in '89–90), Shaquille O'Neal (23.4 in '92–93), Mitch Richmond (22.0 in '88–89), Ralph Sampson (21.0 in '83–84), Alonzo Mourning (21.0 in '92–93), Hakeem Olajuwon (20.6 in '84–85), and Patrick Ewing (20.0 in '85–86). Of these 8 players, only Jordan and Richmond played a position other than center. Mashburn is the Mavs' go-to guy; he was the Mavericks' scoring leader a team-best 37 times.

REGULAR SEASON	G	MIN	FG	FGx	3FG	3PTx	FT	FTx	REB	AST	STL	BLK	PTS	AVG
'93-94 DALLAS	79	2896	561	40.6	85	28.4	306	69.9	353	266	89	14	1513	19.2
1 YR TOTALS	79	2896	561	40.6	85	28.4	306	69.9	353	266	89	14	1513	19.2
'93-94 RANK NBA Fs	30	7	11	124	4	41	9	75	59	12	20	105	8	9

Sean Rooks

No. 45/C

Full name: Sean Lester Rooks
HT: 6-10 **WT:** 260
Born: 9/9/69, New York, NY
High school: Fontana (CA)
College: Arizona

Though he's not a prolific scorer, Rooks shoots for a decent percentage from the field. Although far from a dominating center, Rooks can score inside and is strong on both the offensive and defensive glass. He has also improved his free throw shooting. Injuries cost him nearly half of last season, so he could develop even more this year. The Mavericks need a shot-blocking presence in the middle, and Rooks averages 1.05 blocks per game. That figure will improve as he gains experience, but the Mavs will be happy if Rooks can remain injury free.

REGULAR SEASON		G	MIN	FG	FG%	3FG	3PT%	FT	FT%	REB	AST	STL	BLK	PTS	AVG
'92-93	DALLAS	72	2087	368	49.3	0	0.0	234	60.2	536	95	38	81	970	13.5
'93-94	DALLAS	47	1255	193	49.1	0	0.0	150	71.4	259	49	21	44	536	11.4
2 YR TOTALS		119	3342	561	49.2	0	0.0	384	64.1	795	144	59	125	1506	12.7
'93-94	RANK NBA Cs	35	27	23	25	14	14	14	22	30	25	30	24	19	13
'94-95	PROJECTIONS	22	423	56	49.1	0	0.0	52	82.5	66	14	6	13	164	7.5

Terry Davis   No. 43/F-C

HT: 6-10 **WT:** 250
Born: 6/17/67, Danville, VA
High school: George Washington (Danville)
College: Virginia Union
Davis shattered his left shooting elbow in a
car accident after the '92–93 season. He
came back in January, but after 15 games
the team returned him to the injured list.

REGULAR SEASON		G	MIN	FG	FG%	3FG	3PT%	FT	FT%	REB	AST	STL	BLK	PTS	AVG
'89-90	MIAMI	63	884	122	46.6	0	0.0	54	62.1	229	25	25	28	298	4.7
'90-91	MIAMI	55	996	115	48.7	1	50.0	69	55.6	266	39	18	28	300	5.5
'91-92	DALLAS	68	2149	256	48.2	0	0.0	181	63.5	672	57	26	29	693	10.2
'92-93	DALLAS	75	2462	393	45.5	2	25.0	167	59.4	701	68	36	28	955	12.7
'93-94	DALLAS	15	286	24	40.7	0	---	8	66.7	74	6	9	1	56	3.7
5 YR TOTALS		276	6777	910	46.6	3	18.8	479	60.7	1942	195	114	114	2302	8.3
'93-94	RANK NBA Fs	not ranked -- didn't appear in 25 games in '93-94													
'94-95	PROJECTIONS	-13	-587	-34	37.0	0	0.0	-1	100.0	-144	-10	-23	2	-69	5.3

Tony Dumas   No. 7/G

HT: 6-6   **WT:** 190
Born: 8/25/72
College: Missouri-Kansas City
Dumas was the nation's seventh-leading
scorer last season, averaging 26 points per
game. He averaged 21.8 points per game in
four years at Missouri-Kansas City; his 2,459
points and 576 rebounds are school records.

REGULAR SEASON	G	MIN	FG	FG%	3FG	3PT%	FT	FT%	REB	AST	STL	BLK	PTS	AVG

ROOKIE -- NO NBA EXPERIENCE

Lucious Harris No. 30/G

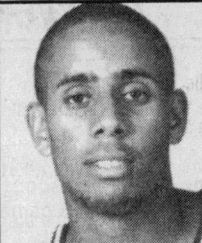

Full name: Lucious H. Harris, Jr.
HT: 6-5 **WT:** 190
Born: 12/18/70, Los Angeles, CA
High school: Cleveland (Los Angeles)
College: Long Beach State

Harris is a big-time scorer who struggled to find his range as a rookie. He's not quick enough to create his own shot off the dribble.

REGULAR SEASON		G	MIN	FG	FGx	3FG	3PTx	FT	FTx	REB	AST	STL	BLK	PTS	AVG
'93-94	DALLAS	77	1165	162	42.1	7	21.2	87	73.1	157	106	49	10	418	5.4
1 YR TOTALS		77	1165	162	42.1	7	21.2	87	73.1	157	106	49	10	418	5.4
'93-94 RANK NBA Gs		53	93	94	91	93	109	86	100	73	100	92	73	98	105

Doug Smith No. 34/F

Full name: Douglas Smith
HT: 6-10 **WT:** 238
Born: 9/17/69, Detroit, MI
High school: MacKenzie (Detroit)
College: Missouri

Smith plays aggressive defense: he had 82 steals last season. But he committed over 550 fouls over the last two years.

REGULAR SEASON		G	MIN	FG	FGx	3FG	3PTx	FT	FTx	REB	AST	STL	BLK	PTS	AVG
'91-92	DALLAS	76	1707	291	41.5	0	0.0	89	73.6	391	129	62	34	671	8.8
'92-93	DALLAS	61	1524	289	43.4	0	0.0	56	75.7	328	104	48	52	634	10.4
'93-94	DALLAS	79	1684	295	43.5	2	22.2	106	83.5	349	119	82	38	698	8.8
3 YR TOTALS		216	4915	875	42.8	2	8.3	251	78.0	1068	352	192	124	2003	9.3
'93-94 RANK NBA Fs		30	61	55	110	62	60	68	7	61	51	23	56	58	65
'94-95 PROJECTIONS		82	1921	324	44.0	5	41.7	155	89.6	380	136	116	34	808	9.9

Lorenzo Williams No. 44/F

HT: 6-9 **WT:** 200
Born: 7/15/69, Ocala, FL
High school: Forest (Ocala)
College: Stetson

Williams is a hard worker who was undrafted. He averaged 6.1 rebounds per game last season, second on the team. He was also second on the team in blocked shots.

REGULAR SEASON		G	MIN	FG	FGx	3FG	3PTx	FT	FTx	REB	AST	STL	BLK	PTS	AVG
'92-93	CHA-ORL-BOS	27	179	17	47.2	0	---	2	28.6	55	5	5	17	36	1.3
'93-94	ORL-CHA-DAL	38	716	49	44.5	0	0.0	12	42.9	217	25	18	46	110	2.9
	2 YR TOTALS	65	895	66	45.2	0	0.0	14	40.0	272	30	23	63	146	2.2
'93-94	RANK NBA Fs	124	115	127	98	78	78	135	136	93	119	116	46	128	125
'94-95	PROJECTIONS	49	1253	56	42.1	0	0.0	28	57.1	375	53	28	42	140	2.9

PLAYOFFS		G	MIN	FG	FGx	3FG	3PTx	FT	FTx	REB	AST	STL	BLK	PTS	AVG
'92-93	BOSTON	1	3	1	100.0	0	---	0	---	1	0	0	0	2	2.0
	TOTALS	1	3	1	100.0	0	---	0	---	1	0	0	0	2	2.0

Dick Motta   Head Coach

Full name: John Richard Motta
HT: 5-10 **WT:** 170
Born: 9/3/31, Medvale, UT
High school: Jordan (UT)
College: Utah State

A young team like Dallas needs a patient teacher as its coach. Motta displayed those qualities with the expansion Mavs.

	REGULAR SEASON				PLAYOFFS			
YEAR	TEAM	W	L	PCT	FINISH	W	L	PCT	
'77-78	WASHINGTON	44	38	.537	2nd/Central Div.	14	7	.667	won NBA Finals over Seattle, 4-3
'78-79	WASHINGTON	54	28	.659	1st/Atlantic Div.	9	10	.474	lost NBA Finals to Seattle, 4-1
'79-80	WASHINGTON	39	43	.476	3rd/Atlantic Div.	0	2	.000	lost Eastern Conf. first round to Philadelphia, 2-0
'80-81	DALLAS	15	67	.183	6th/Midwest Div.				
'81-82	DALLAS	28	54	.341	5th/Midwest Div.				
'82-83	DALLAS	38	44	.463	4th/Midwest Div.				
'83-84	DALLAS	43	39	.524	2nd/Midwest Div.	4	6	.400	lost Western Conf. semifinals to LA Lakers, 4-1
'84-85	DALLAS	44	38	.537	3rd/Midwest Div.	1	3	.250	lost Western Conf. first round to Portland, 3-1
'85-86	DALLAS	44	38	.537	3rd/Midwest Div.	5	5	.500	lost Western Conf. semifinals to LA Lakers, 4-2
'86-87	DALLAS	55	27	.671	1st/Midwest Div.	1	3	.250	lost Western Conf. first round to Seattle, 3-1
'89-90	SACRAMENTO	16	38	.296	7th/Pacific Div.				
'90-91	SACRAMENTO	25	57	.305	7th/Pacific Div.				
'91-92	SACRAMENTO	7	18	.280					
	22 YR TOTALS	856	863	.498		56	70	.444	

Denver
NUGGETS

1994–95 Scouting Report

Frontcourt

Dikembe Mutombo anchors the Denver frontline. Mutombo is a shotblocking ace who challenges anyone who drives the lane and changes as many shots as he blocks. He doesn't score much, but the Nuggets have other players to do that. Swingman Reggie Williams will start most of the time at small forward. Williams is a great defender, and a good scorer and passer. LaPhonso Ellis starts at power forward. He's a shotblocker who complements Mutombo, and he is the team's second leading scorer. '93 first rounder Rodney Rogers plays backup small forward; he's a powerful player who was Denver's leading scorer off the bench last season. Brian Williams comes off the bench to score and rebound at power forward. He was Denver's second leading shotblocker, despite starting in only one game.

Backcourt

Last year, the Nuggets backcourt lacked depth. Denver's biggest deficiency was the lack of a first rate point guard; Mahmoud Abdul-Rauf was really an off guard playing the point. Denver hopes they filled that gap by drafting 6-8 point guard Jalen Rose out of Michigan. Rose can do it all: pass, score, score from outside, and play defense. Rose could free up Abdul-Rauf (Denver's leading scorer) to play offguard. Or the 6-8 Rose, instead of the 6-1 Abdul-Rauf, could play shooting guard. Either move sends last year's starter, Bryant Stith, to the bench. He was fourth on the team in scoring last season. Robert Pack may become the odd man out in the Denver backcourt.

Defense

Denver is one of the best defensive teams in the NBA, and Dikembe Mutombo is a big, big reason. The Nuggets led the league in blocking shots, thanks to Mutombo, who led the league with 4.1 blocked shots per game. And thanks to the shots that Mutombo changed, Denver was second in defensive field goal percentage, holding teams to 43.8 percent from the field. Teams averaged 98.8 points against the Nuggets, tenth lowest in the NBA. And they held opponents under 100 points 48 times. They ranked seventh in the league in forcing turnovers, but just twentieth in the NBA in stealing the ball.

1994–95 Prospects

Last season, Denver was one of the biggest surprises in the playoffs (along with Indiana), but in retrospect, they shouldn't have been that much of a shock. When you're in the playoffs, where defensive intensity gets stepped up a notch, you'll perform better if you're one of the league's best defensive teams. (The five best defensive teams, measured by defensive FG percentage, were cumulatively 44–36 in the playoffs; the five best offensive teams, by FG percentage, were 15–19 in the playoffs, and only Phoenix and Indiana made it as far as the conference semi finals.) Their bugaboo was inconsistency. Interestingly, although the perception was that the Nuggets played up (or down) to the level of their opposition, the only elite teams they played well against during the regular season were Seattle and division rival Houston. Against teams that failed to make the playoffs, Denver was 23–11. Beating the weak sisters of the NBA consistently is a prerequisite to joining the NBA elite.

Denver is a young team that should continue to improve this season. Drafting Rose improves the team at two positions, point guard and shooting guard Rose should help correct a big problem for Denver last season, shooting from outside. They were just 28 percent shooting from 3-point range; no playoff team last year shot worse. The front court is solid, although Denver lacks a backup center to spell Dikembe Mutombo.

Denver is virtually a playoff lock this season; they'll be a better team than last season. But because they played so well against the league's weaker teams, they'll only move up in the standings by beating the league's better teams more often. If they can play with more consistency (as they should as they mature), they could finish as high as the fifth seed in the West, with an excellent chance to advance to the conference semifinals.

Team Directory

President: Timothy J. Leiweke   Executive VP: Shawn Hunter
VP, bus. operations: Gary Hunter   VP, CFO: Mark Waggoner
Sr. exec. VP/GM: Bernie Bickerstaff   Dir., Media relations: Jay L. Clark

1993–94 Review

WESTERN CONFERENCE						EASTERN CONFERENCE					
MIDWEST DIV.			PACIFIC DIV.			ATLANTIC DIV.			CENTRAL DIV.		
	W	L		W	L		W	L		W	L
HOU	3	2	SEA	2	2	NY	1	1	ATL	1	1
SAN	2	4	PHO	1	3	ORL	1	1	CHI	1	1
UTAH	1	4	GS	1	3	NJ	1	1	CLE	1	1
DEN	-	-	POR	1	3	MIA	1	1	IND	1	1
MIN	4	1	LAL	3	1	BOS	1	1	CHA	1	1
DAL	4	1	SAC	2	2	PHI	0	2	DET	2	0
			LAC	3	1	WAS	1	1	MIL	2	0
	14	12		13	15		6	8		9	5

1993–94 finish: 42–40 (28–13 home, 14–27 away), fourth in Midwest Div.

1994–95 Schedule

11/4	Minnesota	9:00 pm	1/4	@ Chicago	8:30 pm	3/4	@ LA Clip.	10:30 pm
11/5	Gold. St.	9:00 pm	1/7	Phoenix	9:00 pm	3/7	@ Dallas	8:30 pm
11/8	@ Dallas	8:30 pm	1/8	Milwaukee	9:00 pm	3/8	@ Atlanta	7:30 pm
11/11	@ LA Lakers	10:30 pm	1/11	@ Utah	9:00 pm	3/10	@ Detroit	8:00 pm
11/12	Utah	9:00 pm	1/12	Dallas	9:00 pm	3/12	@ Milwaukee	2:30 pm
11/15	San Ant.	8:00 pm	1/14	Houston	9:00 pm	3/14	@ New York	8:00 pm
11/17	Detroit	9:00 pm	1/16	@ Gold. St.	5:00 pm	3/16	Sacra.	9:00 pm
11/19	Houston	9:00 pm	1/17	@ Phoenix	9:00 pm	3/18	Portland	9:00 pm
11/23	Chicago	9:00 pm	1/20	Orlando	8:00 pm	3/20	@ Sacra.	10:30 pm
11/25	@ Sacra.	10:30 pm	1/21	Cleveland	9:00 pm	3/22	@ Utah	9:00 pm
11/26	Dallas	9:00 pm	1/24	@ Seattle	10:00 pm	3/23	New York	9:00 pm
11/29	@ Houston	8:30 pm	1/27	New Jersey	9:00 pm	3/26	@ Portland	8:00 pm
12/1	@ Dallas	8:30 pm	1/28	@ San Ant.	8:30 pm	3/27	LA Clip.	9:00 pm
12/3	Charlotte	9:00 pm	1/31	@ Houston	8:30 pm	3/31	@ Indiana	7:30 pm
12/6	@ Minnesota	8:00 pm	2/1	@ Utah	9:00 pm	4/2	@ Cleveland	4:00 pm
12/10	Wash.	9:00 pm	2/3	@ LA Lakers	10:30 pm	4/4	LA Lakers	9:00 pm
12/12	@ Boston	7:30 pm	2/7	LA Lakers	9:00 pm	4/6	Seattle	8:00 pm
12/14	@ Orlando	7:30 pm	2/9	Gold. St.	8:00 pm	4/9	Houston	3:30 pm
12/15	@ Miami	8:00 pm	2/14	Atlanta	8:00 pm	4/10	@ Minnesota	8:00 pm
12/17	@ Charlotte	7:30 pm	2/16	@ New Jersey	7:30 pm	4/13	@ LA Clip.	10:30 pm
12/19	Boston	9:00 pm	2/18	@ Phila.	7:30 pm	4/14	Phoenix	9:00 pm
12/21	San Ant.	9:00 pm	2/19	@ Wash.	6:00 pm	4/16	San Ant.	3:00 pm
12/23	@ Phoenix	9:00 pm	2/21	LA Clip.	9:00 pm	4/18	@ San Ant.	8:00 pm
12/25	Seattle	4:00 pm	2/23	Phila.	8:00 pm	4/19	Minnesota	9:00 pm
12/27	Indiana	9:00 pm	2/24	@ Seattle	10:00 pm	4/22	@ Gold. St.	3:30 pm
12/29	@ Portland	10:00 pm	2/26	Utah	3:30 pm	4/23	Sacra.	9:00 pm
12/30	Portland	9:00 pm	2/28	Minnesota	9:00 pm			
1/3	@ Minnesota	8:00 pm	3/3	Miami	9:00 pm			

1993–94 Team Stats

NAME	G	MIN	FG	FGA	FG%	3FG	3FGA	3FG%	FT	FTA	FT%	ORB	TRB	AST	PF	STL	BLK	TO	PTS	AVG
Abdul-Rauf	80	2617	588	1279	46.0	42	133	31.6	219	229	95.6	27	168	362	150	82	10	151	1437	18.0
Ellis	79	2699	483	963	50.2	7	23	30.4	242	359	67.4	220	682	167	304	63	80	172	1215	15.4
R. Williams	82	2654	418	1014	41.2	64	230	27.8	165	225	73.3	98	392	300	288	117	66	163	1065	13.0
Stith	82	2853	365	811	45.0	2	9	22.2	291	351	82.9	119	349	199	165	116	16	131	1023	12.5
Mutombo	82	2853	365	642	56.9	0	1	0.0	256	439	58.3	286	971	127	262	59	336	206	986	12.0
Pack	66	1382	223	503	44.3	6	29	20.7	179	236	75.8	25	123	356	147	81	9	204	631	9.6
Rogers	79	1406	239	545	43.9	35	92	38.0	127	189	67.2	90	226	101	195	63	48	131	640	8.1
B. Williams	80	1507	251	464	54.1	0	3	0.0	137	211	64.9	138	446	50	221	49	87	104	639	8.0
Macon	7	126	14	45	31.1	0	3	0.0	8	10	80.0	3	7	11	17	6	1	14	36	5.1
Hammonds	74	877	115	230	50.0	0	0	—	71	104	68.3	62	199	34	91	20	12	41	301	4.1
Liberty	3	11	4	7	57.1	0	1	0.0	1	2	50.0	0	5	2	5	0	0	2	9	3.0
Brooks	34	190	36	99	36.4	4	23	17.4	9	10	90.0	5	21	3	19	0	2	12	85	2.5
Jordan	6	79	6	23	26.1	3	10	30.0	0	—	—	5	6	19	6	0	1	6	15	2.5
Randall	28	155	17	50	34.0	2	14	14.3	22	28	78.6	9	22	11	18	8	3	10	58	2.1
Mee	38	285	28	88	31.8	5	24	20.8	12	27	44.4	17	35	16	34	15	13	18	73	1.9
Farmer	4	29	2	6	33.3	0	2	0.0	0	—	—	0	2	4	3	0	0	5	4	1.0
Marble	5	32	2	12	16.7	0	0	—	0	3	0.0	0	8	1	1	0	2	3	4	0.8
Nuggets	82	19755	3156	6781	46.5	170	597	28.5	1739	2423	71.8	1105	3662	1763	1926	679	686	1422	8221	100.3
Opp.	82	19755	3065	7000	43.8	208	717	29.0	1761	2349	75.0	1118	3449	1745	1957	725	502	1245	8099	98.8

HISTORY

TITLES

1969–70 ABA Western Div. regular season champs
1974–75 ABA Western Div. regular season champs
1975–76 ABA regular season champs
1976–77 Midwest Div. champs
1977–78 Midwest Div. champs
1984–85 Midwest Div. champs
1987–88 Midwest Div. champs

ALL-TIME TEAM RECORDS

Career

Games played	Alex English	837	1979–90
Total points	Alex English	21,645	1979–90
Field goals made	Alex English	8,953	1979–90
Field goals attempted	Alex English	17,604	1979–90
Free throws made	Dan Issel	4,214	1975–85
Free throws attempted	Dan Issel	5,277	1975–85
Total rebounds	Dan Issel	6,630	1975–85
Assists	Alex English	3,679	1979–90
Steals	Fat Lever	1,167	1984–90

Season

Total points	Spencer Haywood	2,519	1969–70
Field goals made	Spencer Haywood	986	1969–70
Free throws made	Larry Cannon	605	1970–71
Total rebounds	Spencer Haywood	1,637	1969–70
Assists	Michael Adams	693	1990–91
Steals	Fat Lever	223	1987–88

Game

Total points	David Thompson	73	vs. Detroit, 4/9/78
Field goals made	David Thompson	28	vs. Detroit, 4/9/78
Free throws made	Larry Cannon	21	vs. Virginia, 12/26/70
Total rebounds	Spencer Haywood	31	vs. Kentucky, 11/13/69
Assists	Fat Lever	23	vs. Golden State, 4/21/89
	Larry Brown	23	vs. Pittsburgh, 2/20/72
Steals	Fat Lever	10	vs. Indiana, 3/9/85

LEADING COACHES

	REGULAR SEASON				PLAYOFFS		
NAME	YEARS	W	L	PCT	W	L	PCT
Doug Moe	1981–90	432	357	.548	24	37	.393
Larry Brown	1974–79	251	134	.649	21	24	.467
Alex Hannum	1971–74	118	134	.468	4	8	.333
Bob Bass	1967–69	89	67	.571	5	7	.471
Dan Issel	1992–94	78	86	.476	6	6	.500

Denver Nuggets 1994–95 Roster

Head Coach: Dan Issel

No.	Name	Pos.	Ht.	Wt.	Yrs.	Born	College
3	M. Abdul-Rauf	G	6-1	162	4	3/9/69	Louisiana State
20	LaPhonso Ellis	F	6-8	240	2	5/5/70	Notre Dame
21	Tom Hammonds	F	6-9	225	5	3/27/67	Georgia Tech
4	Darnell Mee	G	6-5	175	1	2/11/71	Western Kentucky
55	Dikembe Mutombo	C	7-2	250	2	6/25/66	Georgetown
14	Robert Pack	G	6-2	190	3	2/3/69	Southern California
42	Mark Randall	F	6-9	235	3	9/30/67	Kansas
7	Alvin Robertson	G	6-4	208	10	7/22/62	Arkansas
54	Rodney Rogers	F	6-7	255	1	6/20/71	Wake Forest
5	Jalen Rose	G	6-8	210	R	1/20/73	Michigan
23	Bryant Stith	G	6-5	208	2	12/10/70	Virginia
8	Brian Williams	F	6-11	260	3	4/6/69	Arizona
34	Reggie Williams	F	6-7	195	7	3/5/64	Georgetown

Arena Information

McNichols Sports Arena (17,171)
Tickets: 303-893-3865, 303-290-TIXS (Ticketmaster)
Ticket prices: $115, Courtside (sold out); $85, End Courtside (sold out); $35, Prime Loge (sold out); $30, Center Loge (sold out); $25, Center Loge, End Risers (sold out); $20, End Loge, Center Balcony; $16.50, Corner Balcony; $12.50, Lower End Balcony; $8.50, Upper End Balcony

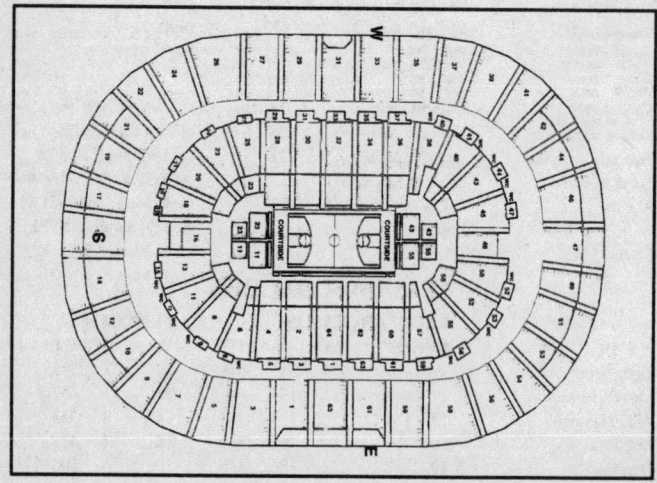

Mahmoud Abdul-Rauf

No. 3/G

Full name: Mahmoud Abdul-Rauf
HT: 6-1   **WT:** 162
Born: 3/9/69, Gulfport, MS
High school: Gulfport (MS)
College: Louisiana State

Denver's draft of Jalen Rose puts Abdul-Rauf's role up in the air. As a point guard, Abdul-Rauf is a great scorer. He's been Denver's leading scorer for two straight seasons, and was the best free throw shooter in the NBA last year. (He just missed breaking Calvin Murphy's NBA single season record for FT percentage.) He can score driving to the basket, or from outside. But although he handles the ball well, the knock on Abdul-Rauf is that he's not a true point guard. He plays defense like a gunner; that is, not much and not well. But he's too small to last long at shooting guard in the NBA; his defensive problems would be exacerbated against bigger shooting guards.

REGULAR SEASON		G	MIN	FG	FGx	3FG	3PTx	FT	FTx	REB	AST	STL	BLK	PTS	AVG
'90-91	DENVER	67	1505	417	41.3	24	24.0	84	85.7	121	206	55	4	942	14.1
'91-92	DENVER	81	1538	356	42.1	31	33.0	94	87.0	114	192	44	4	837	10.3
'92-93	DENVER	81	2710	633	45.0	70	35.5	217	93.5	225	344	84	8	1553	19.2
'93-94	DENVER	80	2617	588	46.0	42	31.6	219	95.6	168	362	82	10	1437	18.0
4 YR TOTALS		309	8370	1994	43.9	167	31.9	614	92.1	628	1104	265	26	4769	15.4
'93-94 RANK NBA Gs		33	27	4	50	46	73	23	1	66	32	54	73	7	12
'94-95 PROJECTIONS		81	2889	615	47.5	36	31.0	267	98.9	157	418	90	13	1533	18.9
PLAYOFFS		G	MIN	FG	FGx	3FG	3PTx	FT	FTx	REB	AST	STL	BLK	PTS	AVG
'93-94	DENVER	12	339	57	37.0	12	32.4	29	93.5	18	30	5	1	155	12.9
TOTALS		12	339	57	37.0	12	32.4	29	93.5	18	30	5	1	155	12.9

LaPhonso Ellis   No. 20/F

Full name: LaPhonso D. Ellis
HT: 6-8   **WT:** 240
Born: 5/5/70, East St. Louis, IL
High school: Lincoln (East St. Louis)
College: Notre Dame

Ellis is a good shotblocker and rebounder. Offensively, he has an outstanding low post game. Ellis followed a rookie season (in which he made NBA All-Rookie first team) with a terrific sophomore season, and looks like he'll be an outstanding pro for years to come. Ellis was the Nuggets' second leading scorer and rebounder, and third-leading shotblocker. He led the team in scoring 21 times, had 20 points or more 15 times, and scored in double figures in 70 of 79 games. He also had 31 double-doubles. Ellis had at least one blocked shot in 51 games. He's started in every game he's played as a pro.

REGULAR SEASON		G	MIN	FG	FG%	3FG	3PT%	FT	FT%	REB	AST	STL	BLK	PTS	AVG
'92-93	DENVER	82	2749	483	50.4	2	15.4	237	74.8	744	151	72	111	1205	14.7
'93-94	DENVER	79	2699	483	50.2	7	30.4	242	67.4	682	167	63	80	1215	15.4
	2 YR TOTALS	161	5448	966	50.3	9	25.0	479	70.9	1426	318	135	191	2420	15.0
'93-94	RANK NBA Fs	30	17	19	31	46	35	21	95	16	35	44	17	18	22
'94-95	PROJECTIONS	76	2649	482	49.8	15	45.5	240	60.2	622	182	54	50	1219	16.0

PLAYOFFS		G	MIN	FG	FG%	3FG	3PT%	FT	FT%	REB	AST	STL	BLK	PTS	AVG
'93-94	DENVER	12	436	68	47.9	3	50.0	38	70.4	97	26	9	11	177	14.8
	TOTALS	12	436	68	47.9	3	50.0	38	70.4	97	26	9	11	177	14.8

Dikembe Mutombo

No. 55/C

Full name: Dikembe Mutombo Mpolondo Mukamba Jean Jacque Wamutombo
HT: 7-2   **WT:** 250
Born: 6/25/66, Kinshasa, Zaire
High school: Institute Boboto (Kinshasa, Zaire)
College: Georgetown

Mutombo is one of the NBA's best defensive players. He led the NBA in blocked shots, was sixth in rebounding with 11.8 boards per game, and fourth in defensive rebounds with 685. In fact, he grabbed 27 percent of Denver's rebounds and 49 percent of Denver's blocked shots. Mutombo's defensive stats overshadow his offensive contribution. He collects his points from putbacks of offensive rebounds and a reliable hook shot. His 56.9 FG percentage was second in the league, and the fourth highest mark in Nuggets' NBA history. And he had 41 double-doubles last season. His offense should improve as he gains NBA experience.

REGULAR SEASON		G	MIN	FG	FGx	3FG	3PTx	FT	FTx	REB	AST	STL	BLK	PTS	AVG
'91-92	DENVER	71	2716	428	49.3	0	---	321	64.2	870	156	43	210	1177	16.6
'92-93	DENVER	82	3029	398	51.0	0	---	335	68.1	1070	147	43	287	1131	13.8
'93-94	DENVER	82	2853	365	56.9	0	0.0	256	58.3	971	127	59	336	986	12.0
3 YR TOTALS		235	8598	1191	52.0	0	0.0	912	63.7	2911	430	145	833	3294	14.0
'93-94	RANK NBA C±	1	5	5	6	14	14	7	45	2	10	10	1	9	10
'94-95	PROJECTIONS	82	3134	357	61.7	0	0.0	231	51.9	1062	123	79	437	945	11.5

PLAYOFFS		G	MIN	FG	FGx	3FG	3PTx	FT	FTx	REB	AST	STL	BLK	PTS	AVG
'93-94	DENVER	12	511	50	46.3	0	---	59	60.2	144	21	8	69	159	13.3
TOTALS		12	511	50	46.3	0	---	59	60.2	144	21	8	69	159	13.3

Bryant Stith

No. 23/G

Full name: Bryant Lamonica Stith
HT: 6-5   **WT:** 208
Born: 12/10/70, Emporia, VA
High school: Brunswick
   (Lawrenceville, VA)
College: Virginia

As a shooting guard, Stith is an above average defensive player. He has problems with his outside shot (he was just 22.2 percent from 3-point range) and is not an exceptional ballhandler. Stith was one of only two Nuggets to play and start in all 82 games (the other was Dikembe Mutombo). However, if Jalen Rose takes over the starting point guard role, Stith will undoubtedly end up on the bench as a reserve. He was fourth on the team in scoring, and second on the team in FT percentage. He led the Nuggets in scoring seven times, and scored 20 or more points in ten games. He posted a career high when he scored 33 points at San Antonio December 11.

REGULAR SEASON		G	MIN	FG	FGx	3FG	3PTx	FT	FTx	REB	AST	STL	BLK	PTS	AVG
'92-93	DENVER	39	865	124	44.6	0	0.0	99	83.2	124	49	24	5	347	8.9
'93-94	DENVER	82	2853	365	45.0	2	22.2	291	82.9	349	199	116	16	1023	12.5
	2 YR TOTALS	121	3718	489	44.9	2	15.4	390	83.0	473	248	140	21	1370	11.3
'93-94	RANK NBA Gs	1	13	47	62	117	103	11	38	14	71	30	46	41	49
'94-95	PROJECTIONS	82	3938	442	45.4	3	42.9	353	82.7	399	326	211	21	1240	15.1

PLAYOFFS		G	MIN	FG	FGx	3FG	3PTx	FT	FTx	REB	AST	STL	BLK	PTS	AVG
'93-94	DENVER	12	413	43	42.2	0	0.0	50	83.3	56	26	11	2	136	11.3
	TOTALS	12	413	43	42.2	0	0.0	50	83.3	56	26	11	2	136	11.3

Reggie Williams

No. 34/F

HT: 6-7   **WT:** 195
Born: 3/5/64, Baltimore, MD
High school: Dunbar (Baltimore)
College: Georgetown

Although Williams plays small forward, he seems better suited to shooting guard. Bigger forwards can outmuscle him for rebounds, and he relies on his jumper for his points. On the other hand, Williams is quick, steals the ball a lot, and is an exceptional passer for a small forward. Williams led the Nuggets in steals and was third on the team in scoring and assists. Williams is working harder than ever on defense, and that seems to have affected his concentration offensively. He's not the scorer he was three seasons ago, when he averaged 18.2 points per game. His FG and 3-point FG percentages have slipped, his average has dropped by over five points per game, and last season's FT percentage was his lowest since his rookie year.

REGULAR SEASON		G	MIN	FG	FG%	3FG	3PT%	FT	FT%	REB	AST	STL	BLK	PTS	AVG
'87-88	LA CLIPPERS	35	857	152	35.6	13	22.4	48	72.7	118	58	29	21	365	10.4
'88-89	LA CLIPPERS	63	1303	260	43.8	30	28.8	92	75.4	179	103	81	29	642	10.2
'89-90	LAC-CLE-SA	47	743	131	38.8	6	16.2	52	76.5	83	53	32	14	320	6.8
'90-91	SA-DEN	73	1896	384	44.9	57	36.3	166	84.3	306	133	113	41	991	13.6
'91-92	DENVER	81	2623	601	47.1	56	35.9	216	80.3	405	235	148	68	1474	18.2
'92-93	DENVER	79	2722	535	45.8	33	27.0	238	80.4	428	295	126	76	1341	17.0
'93-94	DENVER	82	2654	418	41.2	64	27.8	165	73.3	392	300	117	66	1065	13.0
	7 YR TOTALS	460	12798	2481	43.7	259	30.0	977	78.6	1911	1177	646	315	6198	13.5
'93-94	RANK NBA Fs	1	19	27	123	7	43	42	52	53	7	7	22	26	32
'94-95	PROJECTIONS	62	2823	384	39.2	79	27.1	146	69.5	411	348	115	70	993	12.1

PLAYOFFS		G	MIN	FG	FG%	3FG	3PT%	FT	FT%	REB	AST	STL	BLK	PTS	AVG
'89-90	SAN ANTONIO	9	49	9	33.3	0	0.0	2	100.0	11	3	2	0	20	2.2
'93-94	DENVER	12	405	62	41.6	20	40.0	27	77.1	61	42	9	12	171	14.3
	TOTALS	21	454	71	40.3	20	38.5	29	78.4	72	45	11	12	191	9.1

Tom Hammonds   No. 21/F

Full name: Tom Edward Hammonds
HT: 6-9 **WT:** 225
Born: 3/27/67, Fort Walton, FL
High school: Crestview (FL)
College: Georgia Tech

Hammonds gives Denver rebounding off the bench. He was 1 of only 4 Nuggets to shoot 50 percent or better from the field.

REGULAR SEASON		G	MIN	FG	FGx	3FG	3PTx	FT	FTx	REB	AST	STL	BLK	PTS	AVG
'89-90	WASHINGTON	61	805	129	43.7	0	0.0	63	64.3	168	51	11	14	321	5.3
'90-91	WASHINGTON	70	1023	155	46.1	0	0.0	57	72.2	206	43	15	7	367	5.2
'91-92	WASHINGTON	37	984	195	48.8	0	0.0	50	61.0	185	36	22	13	440	11.9
'92-93	CHA-DEN	54	713	105	47.5	0	0.0	38	61.3	127	24	18	12	248	4.6
'93-94	DENVER	74	877	115	50.0	0	---	71	68.3	199	34	20	12	301	4.1
	5 YR TOTALS	296	4402	699	47.2	0	0.0	279	65.6	885	188	86	58	1677	5.7
'93-94	RANK NBA Fs	61	103	103	35	78	78	90	89	98	108	110	113	103	114
'94-95	PROJECTIONS	82	897	102	51.5	0	0.0	85	70.8	222	35	21	12	289	3.5

PLAYOFFS		G	MIN	FG	FGx	3FG	3PTx	FT	FTx	REB	AST	STL	BLK	PTS	AVG
'93-94	DENVER	8	49	2	22.2	0	---	5	83.3	13	2	0	0	9	1.1
	TOTALS	8	49	2	22.2	0	---	5	83.3	13	2	0	0	9	1.1

Robert Pack   No. 14/G

Full name: Robert John Pack, Jr.
HT: 6-2 **WT:** 190
Born: 2/3/69, New Orleans, LA
High school: Lawless (New Orleans)
College: Southern California

Last season, Pack averaged over 20 minutes per game. But he'll be the odd man out if Denver goes to a 3 guard rotation.

REGULAR SEASON		G	MIN	FG	FGx	3FG	3PTx	FT	FTx	REB	AST	STL	BLK	PTS	AVG
'91-92	PORTLAND	72	894	115	42.3	0	0.0	102	80.3	97	140	40	4	332	4.6
'92-93	DENVER	77	1579	285	47.0	1	12.5	239	76.8	160	335	81	10	810	10.5
'93-94	DENVER	66	1382	223	44.3	6	20.7	179	75.8	123	356	81	9	631	9.6
	3 YR TOTALS	215	3855	623	45.1	7	14.9	520	77.2	380	831	202	23	1773	8.2
'93-94	RANK NBA Gs	91	82	95	71	103	111	38	83	90	33	55	78	74	70
'94-95	PROJECTIONS	59	1551	249	43.5	15	30.6	190	74.2	121	474	102	11	703	11.9

PLAYOFFS		G	MIN	FG	FGx	3FG	3PTx	FT	FTx	REB	AST	STL	BLK	PTS	AVG
'91-92	PORTLAND	14	52	4	22.2	0	---	3	75.0	6	7	5	1	11	0.8
'93-94	DENVER	12	332	48	40.7	6	30.0	39	70.9	28	51	18	6	141	11.8
	TOTALS	26	384	52	38.2	6	30.0	42	71.2	34	58	23	7	152	5.8

Rodney Rogers   No. 54/F

Full name: Rodney Ray Rogers, Jr.
HT: 6-7 **WT:** 255
Born: 6/20/71, Durham, NC
High school: Hillside (Durham)
College: Wake Forest
Rogers led the team in scoring 8 times, tops among non-starters. He commits a lot of fouls (5.7 per 40 minutes played).

REGULAR SEASON		G	MIN	FG	FG%	3FG	3PT%	FT	FT%	REB	AST	STL	BLK	PTS	AVG
'93-94	DENVER	79	1406	239	43.9	35	38.0	127	67.2	226	101	63	48	640	8.1
	1 YR TOTALS	79	1406	239	43.9	35	38.0	127	67.2	226	101	63	48	640	8.1
93-94	RANK NBA Fs	25	61	53	85	47	81	20	10	73	47	30	35	52	56

PLAYOFFS		G	MIN	FG	FG%	3FG	3PT%	FT	FT%	REB	AST	STL	BLK	PTS	AVG
'93-94	DENVER	12	190	19	38.8	6	31.6	17	63.0	21	16	7	6	61	5.1
	TOTALS	12	190	19	38.8	6	31.6	17	63.0	21	16	7	6	61	5.1

Jalen Rose   No. 5/F

HT: 6-8 **WT:** 210
Born: 1/20/73, Detroit, MI
College: Michigan
Rose averaged 19.9 points per game at point guard last season. Only 1 other Michigan player had 1,500 points, 400 rebounds, 300 assists and 100 steals. His 1,788 points are sixth on Michigan's all-time list.

REGULAR SEASON	G	MIN	FG	FG%	3FG	3PT%	FT	FT%	REB	AST	STL	BLK	PTS	AVG

ROOKIE -- NO NBA EXPERIENCE

Brian Williams   No. 8/F

Full name: Brian Carson Williams
HT: 6-11 **WT:** 260
Born: 4/6/69, Fresno, CA
High school: Santa Monica (CA)
College: Arizona

Williams is a strong rebounder and shotblocker. He scored in double figures 29 times, and had 8 double-doubles last season.

REGULAR SEASON		G	MIN	FG	FGx	3FG	3PTx	FT	FTx	REB	AST	STL	BLK	PTS	AVG
'91-92	ORLANDO	48	905	171	52.8	0	---	95	66.9	272	33	41	53	437	9.1
'92-93	ORLANDO	21	240	40	51.3	0	0.0	16	80.0	56	5	14	17	96	4.6
'93-94	DENVER	80	1507	251	54.1	0	0.0	137	64.9	446	50	49	87	639	8.0
	3 YR TOTALS	149	2652	462	53.3	0	0.0	248	66.5	774	88	104	157	1172	7.9
'93-94	RANK NBA Fs	23	70	63	10	78		78	53	105	41	96	65	11	63	70
'94-95	PROJECTIONS	82	2197	352	55.9	0	0.0	205	56.8	716	85	36	112	909	11.1
PLAYOFFS		G	MIN	FG	FGx	3FG	3PTx	FT	FTx	REB	AST	STL	BLK	PTS	AVG
'93-94	DENVER	12	289	42	55.3	0	---	27	65.9	89	11	4	11	111	9.3
	TOTALS	12	289	42	55.3	0	---	27	65.9	89	11	4	11	111	9.3

Dan Issel   Head Coach

Full name: Daniel Paul Issel
HT: 6-9 **WT:** 240
Born: 10/25/48, Batavia, IL
High school: Batavia (IL)
College: Kentucky

Last season's 42–40 finish was Denver's first winning campaign since '89–90. The Nuggets were 2,458 the season before Issel took over.

	REGULAR SEASON				PLAYOFFS			
YEAR	TEAM	W	L	PCT	FINISH	W	L	PCT
'92-93	DENVER	36	46	439	4th/Midwest Div.			
'93-94	DENVER	42	40	512	4th/Midwest Div.	6	6	500	lost Western Conf. semifinal to Utah, 4-3
	2 YR TOTALS	78	86	476		6	6	500

Detroit
PISTONS

1994–95 Scouting Report

Frontcourt

Detroit is particularly weak in the frontcourt. The Pistons need a scoring forward, now that Sean Elliott went back to the Spurs, and a center to replace retired Bill Laimbeer. They're hoping Mark West, obtained from Phoenix during the offseason, will fill the hole at center. West is a shotblocking specialist who also rebounds a little. He can score if he gets the ball inside, but he's one of the most foul-prone players in the NBA. Terry Mills plays all forward positions, although power forward is his customary spot. Mills has become a decent scorer, but he's not the kind of rebounder you'd like to see at that position. Greg Anderson emerged as a frontline starter last season. He gave the team a rebounding lift, averaging 8 rebounds a game as a starter. Unfortunately, both he and Pete Chilcutt were unrestricted free agents after last season. Charles Jones, a mid-season pickup last year, is a defensive specialist at center who can rebound, but can't score.

Backcourt

Isiah Thomas' retirement opens a hole at point guard for '93 first-rounder Lindsay Hunter. Hunter started 26 games last year; he's an explosive player who can score, handle the ball, and play defense. Joe Dumars is still one of the most accurate shooting guards in the NBA, as well as one of the best defenders, but he was bothered by soreness in his Achilles heel at the end of last season. Allan Houston will see a lot of time at shooting guard. He's got good shooting range, can create his own shot off the dribble, and is a good passer.

Defense

The Pistons simply don't have the kind of athletes who can force opponents out of their offensive game, and they no longer have a defensive presence in the middle. Teams averaged 104.7 points against the

Pistons, ninth highest in the NBA. Opposing teams shot 47.3 from the floor against Detroit, tenth highest in the league, and grabbed 1,191 offensive rebounds, seventh highest in the league. They also ranked twenty-fifth in the NBA in stealing the ball and twenty-sixth in blocks. On the positive side, they were third in the league in forcing turnovers.

1994–95 Prospects

Last season was Detroit's worst since the 1979–80 campaign, before the Thomas-Laimbeer era began in Detroit, and the second worst finish in team history. Frustrated with injuries and losing, Bill Laimbeer and Isiah Thomas retired, with Laimbeer bailing out one month into the season. They were particularly weak inside their own division, going 4–24 vs. Central Division teams. With no inside game to speak of, the Pistons hoisted 3-pointers like never before, setting a new team record with 358 3-point field goals, third most in the NBA. (Of the top 5 teams in terms of 3-pointers made, only Detroit had a losing record; the other 4 teams, Houston, Orlando, Phoenix and Miami, all made the playoffs and were collectively 206–122, a .628 percentage.) As with most bad teams, Detroit had no home court advantage; they were 10-31 both at home and on the road.

Detroit avoided the Central Division cellar thanks to Milwaukee's dismal season. But the Bucks are poised to make an advance in the standings. The Pistons, sadly, are not. The frontcourt is just too weak to compete in the NBA. Detroit can't rebound (twenty-fourth in the NBA last season), they can't intimidate defensively, and they have no offensive presence down low that opponents are bound to respect. Mark West will help some, but Detroit needs a Chris Webber or a Derrick Coleman for their rebounding hole. Despite a solid ability to hit from the outside (their 34.4 percentage from 3-point range was tenth in the NBA last season), their overall shooting percentage from the field ranked just twenty-third—because they're simply unable to get high percentage shots down low. They don't get many second shots, either, ranking twenty-third in offensive rebounding. After 3 or 4 more lottery picks, Detroit may assemble the frontcourt players to complement Lindsay Hunter and Allan Houston and present a complete team on the court. They'll have a shot at one of those lottery picks after this season.

Team Directory

Managing partner: William Davidson President: Tom Wilson

Executive VP: Dan Hauser Executive VP: John Ciszewski

Player personnel: Billy McKinney Public relations: Matt Dobek

1993–94 Review

EASTERN CONFERENCE								WESTERN CONFERENCE							
ATLANTIC DIV.			CENTRAL DIV.					MIDWEST DIV.				PACIFIC DIV.			
	W	L			W	L			W	L				W	L
NY	0	4		ATL	0	4		HOU	0	2		SEA		1	1
ORL	1	3		CHI	0	5		SAN	1	1		PHO		1	1
NJ	1	3		CLE	2	3		UTAH	0	2		GS		0	2
MIA	2	2		IND	1	4		DEN	0	2		POR		0	2
BOS	1	3		CHA	0	4		MIN	2	0		LAL		0	2
PHI	1	3		DET	–	–		DAL	1	1		SAC		1	1
WAS	2	2		MIL	1	4						LAC		1	1
	8	20			4	24			4	8				4	10

1993-94 finish: 20–62 (10–31 home, 10–31 away), sixth in Central Div.

1994–95 Schedule

11/4	LA Lakers	8:00 pm	1/8	Orlando	7:00 pm	3/4	@ Dallas	8:30 pm
11/5	@ Atlanta	7:30 pm	1/10	New Jersey	7:30 pm	3/7	@ Cleveland	7:30 pm
11/8	Minnesota	7:30 pm	1/11	@ Orlando	7:30 pm	3/8	@ Wash.	7:30 pm
11/10	Indiana	7:30 pm	1/13	@ Minnesota	8:00 pm	3/10	Denver	8:00 pm
11/12	@ Charlotte	7:30 pm	1/14	Wash.	7:30 pm	3/12	Seattle	7:00 pm
11/15	Phila.	7:30 pm	1/16	@ Phila.	2:00 pm	3/14	@ Phoenix	9:00 pm
11/17	@ Denver	9:00 pm	1/18	Utah	7:30 pm	3/15	@ LA Clip.	10:30 pm
11/18	@ Utah	9:00 pm	1/20	Houston	8:00 pm	3/18	@ Seattle	3:30 pm
11/20	@ Portland	10:00 pm	1/21	@ Milwaukee	8:30 pm	3/19	@ Gold. St.	8:00 pm
11/23	Milwaukee	7:30 pm	1/24	Phila.	7:30 pm	3/21	New Jersey	7:30 pm
11/25	Miami	8:00 pm	1/26	Portland	7:30 pm	3/23	Dallas	7:30 pm
11/27	Gold. St.	7:00 pm	1/28	Miami	7:30 pm	3/25	Boston	7:30 pm
11/30	@ Boston	7:30 pm	1/30	LA Clip.	7:30 pm	3/27	San Ant.	7:30 pm
12/2	@ Wash.	7:30 pm	2/1	@ Miami	7:30 pm	3/29	New York	7:30 pm
12/3	Phoenix	7:30 pm	2/2	Cleveland	7:30 pm	4/1	Wash.	7:30 pm
12/6	@ Indiana	7:30 pm	2/4	Atlanta	7:30 pm	4/5	@ Orlando	7:30 pm
12/9	Chicago	8:00 pm	2/6	@ New Jersey	7:30 pm	4/7	Orlando	8:00 pm
12/10	@ Cleveland	7:30 pm	2/8	Charlotte	7:30 pm	4/8	@ New York	8:30 pm
12/13	@ Chicago	8:30 pm	2/14	New York	7:30 pm	4/11	@ Milwaukee	8:30 pm
12/14	Charlotte	7:30 pm	2/15	@ Indiana	7:30 pm	4/12	Chicago	7:30 pm
12/17	@ Phila.	7:30 pm	2/17	@ Chicago	8:30 pm	4/14	Charlotte	8:00 pm
12/21	@ New Jersey	7:30 pm	2/18	@ Charlotte	7:30 pm	4/15	@ Boston	7:30 pm
12/23	Atlanta	8:00 pm	2/20	Sacra.	7:30 pm	4/18	Cleveland	7:30 pm
12/27	Milwaukee	7:30 pm	2/23	@ Houston	8:30 pm	4/20	@ Chicago	8:30 pm
12/28	@ New York	7:30 pm	2/24	@ San Ant.	8:30 pm	4/21	@ Atlanta	7:30 pm
12/30	Boston	8:00 pm	2/27	Milwaukee	7:30 pm	4/23	@ Miami	6:00 pm
1/3	@ LA Lakers	10:30 pm	3/1	Indiana	7:30 pm			
1/5	@ Sacra.	10:30 pm	3/3	@ Atlanta	7:30 pm			

1993–94 Team Stats

NAME	G	MIN	FG	FGA	FG%	3FG	3FGA	3FG%	FT	FTA	FT%	ORB	TRB	AST	PF	STL	BLK	TO	PTS	AVG
Dumars	69	2591	505	1118	45.2	124	320	38.8	276	330	83.6	35	151	261	118	63	4	159	1410	20.4
Mills	80	2773	588	1151	51.1	24	73	32.9	181	227	79.7	193	672	177	309	64	62	153	1381	17.3
Thomas	58	1750	318	763	41.7	39	126	31.0	181	258	70.2	46	159	399	126	68	6	202	856	14.8
Polynice	37	1350	222	406	54.7	0	1	0.0	42	92	45.7	148	456	22	108	24	36	49	486	13.1
Elliott	73	2409	360	791	45.5	26	87	29.9	139	173	80.3	68	263	197	174	54	27	129	885	12.1
Hunter	82	2172	335	893	37.5	69	207	33.3	104	142	73.2	47	189	390	174	121	10	184	843	10.3
Laimbeer	11	248	47	90	52.2	3	9	33.3	11	13	84.6	9	56	14	30	6	4	10	108	9.8
Houston	79	1519	272	671	40.5	35	117	29.9	89	108	82.4	19	120	100	165	34	13	99	668	8.5
Anderson	77	1624	201	370	54.3	1	3	33.3	88	154	57.1	183	571	51	234	55	68	94	491	6.4
Wood	78	1182	119	259	45.9	22	49	44.9	62	82	75.6	104	239	51	201	39	19	35	322	4.1
Chilcutt	30	391	51	120	42.5	3	14	21.4	10	13	76.9	29	100	15	48	10	11	18	115	3.8
Macon	35	370	55	139	39.6	2	7	28.6	15	24	62.5	15	34	40	56	33	0	26	127	3.6
Coleman	9	77	12	25	48.0	0	0	—	4	8	50.0	10	26	0	9	2	2	7	28	3.1
Jones	42	877	36	78	46.2	0	1	0.0	19	34	55.9	89	235	29	136	14	43	12	91	2.2
Murphy	7	57	6	12	50.0	0	0	—	3	6	50.0	4	9	3	8	2	0	1	15	2.1
Moore	3	10	2	3	66.7	0	0	—	2	2	100.0	0	0	0	0	2	0	0	6	2.0
O'Sullivan	13	56	4	12	33.3	0	0	—	9	12	75.0	2	10	3	10	0	0	3	17	1.3
Liberty	35	274	36	116	31.0	10	27	37.0	18	37	48.6	26	56	15	29	11	4	22	100	2.9
Pistons	82	19730	3169	7017	45.2	358	1041	34.4	1253	1715	73.1	1027	3347	1767	1935	602	309	1236	7949	96.9
Opp.	82	19730	3255	6878	47.3	272	814	33.4	1805	2451	73.6	1191	3781	2097	1602	721	368	1169	8587	104.7

HISTORY

TITLES

1954–55 Western Div. champs 1988–89 Central Div. champs
1955–56 Western Div. champs 1988–89 NBA champs
1987–88 Central Div. champs 1989–90 Central Div. champs
1987–88 Eastern Conference champs 1989–90 NBA champs

ALL-TIME TEAM RECORDS

Career

Games played	Isiah Thomas	979	1981–94
Total points	Isiah Thomas	18,822	1981–94
Scoring average	Bob Lanier	22.7	1970–80
Field goals made	Isiah Thomas	7,194	1981–94
Free throws made	Isiah Thomas	4,036	1981–94
Total rebounds	Bill Laimbeer	9,430	1981–94
Assists	Isiah Thomas	9,061	1981–94
Steals	Isiah Thomas	1,861	1981–94

Season

Total points	Dave Bing	2,213	1970–71
Field goals made	Dave Bing	836	1967–68
Free throws made	George Yardley	655	1957–58
Total rebounds	Dennis Rodman	1,530	1991–92
Assists	Isiah Thomas	1,123	1984–85
Steals	Isiah Thomas	204	1983–84

Game

Total points	Kelly Tripucka	56	vs. Chicago, 1/29/83
Field goals made	Dave Bing	22	vs. Chicago, 2/21/71
Free throws made	George Yardley	20	vs. St. Louis, 12/26/57
	Walter Dukes	20	vs. LA Lakers, 1/19/61
	Kelly Tripucka	20	vs. Chicago, 1/29/83
Total rebounds	Dennis Rodman	34	vs. Indiana, 3/4/92
Assists	Kevin Porter	25	vs. Boston, 3/9/79
	Kevin Porter	25	vs. Phoenix, 4/1/79
	Isiah Thomas	25	vs. Dallas, 2/23/85
Steals	Earl Tatum	9	vs LA Lakers, 4/28/78
	Ron Lee	9	vs. Houston, 3/16/80

LEADING COACHES

NAME	YEARS	REGULAR SEASON			PLAYOFFS		
		W	L	PCT	W	L	PCT
Chuck Daly	1983–92	467	271	.633	71	42	.628
Ray Scott	1973–76	147	134	.523	4	6	.400
Dick McGuire	1959–63	122	158	.436	8	13	.321
Scotty Robertson	1980–83	97	149	.394	0	0	—
Bill van Breda Kolff	1969–71	82	92	.471	0	0	—

Detroit Pistons 1994–95 Roster

Head Coach: Don Chaney

No.	Name	Pos.	Ht.	Wt.	Yrs.	Born	College
7	Rafael Addison	F	6-8	233	3	7/22/64	Syracuse
34	Greg Anderson	F-C	6-10	230	7	6/22/64	Houston
34	Pete Chilcutt	F-C	6-10	232	3	9/14/68	North Carolina
0	Jevon Crudup	F	NA	NA	R	4/27/72	Missouri
4	Joe Dumars	G	6-3	195	10	5/24/63	McNeese State
33	Grant Hill	F	6-8	225	R	10/5/72	Duke
20	Allan Houston	G	6-6	200	1	4/4/71	Tennessee
1	Lindsey Hunter	G	6-2	195	1	12/3/70	Jackson State
23	Charles Jones	F	6-9	235	10	4/3/57	Albany State
45	Eric Leckner	C	6-11	265	5	5/27/66	Wyoming
30	Marcus Liberty	F	6-8	225	4	10/27/68	Illinois
2	Mark Macon	G	6-5	200	3	4/14/69	Temple
6	Terry Mills	F	6-10	250	5	12/21/67	Michigan
41	Mark West	C	6-10	246	11	11/5/60	Old Dominion
12	David Wood	F	6-9	230	5	11/30/64	Nevada-Reno

Arena Information

The Palace of Auburn Hills (21,454)
Tickets: 313-377-0100
Ticket prices: $49, $39, $31, $25, $19, $16, $10

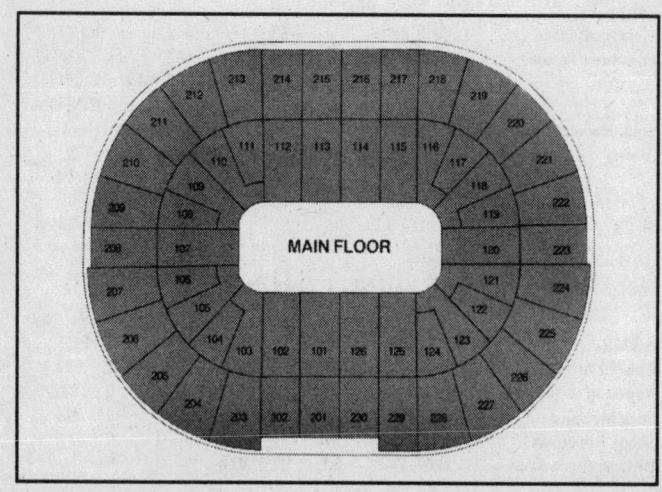

Joe Dumars

No. 4/G

Full name: Joe Dumars III
HT: 6-3 **WT:** 195
Born: 5/24/63, Shreveport, LA
High school: Natchitoches Central (LA)
College: McNeese State

Dumars is one of the most respected players in the NBA. He was a member of Dream Team II, and won the '93–94 J. Walter Kennedy Citizenship Award. Although he's getting older, he's still a dangerous scorer. Dumars' 20.4 points per game average ranked thirteenth in the NBA. That matched his second highest single season scoring mark, set in 1991. He was also nineteenth in the NBA in 3-point FG percentage and free throw percentage. Dumars played better in the second half of the season. He had 20 points or more in 25 of his last 39 games, averaging 22.5 points. And he hit on 90 of 217 3-point FGAs (41 percent) in his last 37 games. He missed Detroit's last 3 games due to Achilles soreness.

REGULAR SEASON		G	MIN	FG	FGx	3FG	3PTx	FT	FTx	REB	AST	STL	BLK	PTS	AVG
'85-86	DETROIT	82	1957	287	48.1	5	31.3	190	79.8	119	390	66	11	769	9.4
'86-87	DETROIT	79	2439	369	49.3	9	40.9	184	74.8	167	352	83	5	931	11.8
'87-88	DETROIT	82	2732	453	47.2	4	21.1	251	81.5	200	387	87	15	1161	14.2
'88-89	DETROIT	69	2408	456	50.5	14	48.3	260	85.0	172	390	63	5	1186	17.2
'89-90	DETROIT	75	2578	508	48.0	22	40.0	297	90.0	212	368	63	2	1335	17.8
'90-91	DETROIT	80	3046	622	48.1	14	31.1	371	89.0	187	443	89	7	1629	20.4
'91-92	DETROIT	82	3192	587	44.8	49	40.8	412	86.7	188	375	71	12	1635	19.9
'92-93	DETROIT	77	3094	677	46.6	112	37.5	343	86.4	148	308	78	7	1809	23.5
'93-94	DETROIT	69	2591	505	45.2	124	38.8	276	83.6	151	261	63	4	1410	20.4
9 YR TOTALS		695	24037	4464	47.3	353	38.2	2584	84.8	1544	3274	663	68	11865	17.1
'93-94	RANK NBA Gs	84	29	14	61	8	28	14	27	77	55	73	102	9	3
'94-95	PROJECTIONS	64	2353	446	44.5	145	39.4	238	81.8	139	218	56	3	1275	19.9

PLAYOFFS		G	MIN	FG	FGx	3FG	3PTx	FT	FTx	REB	AST	STL	BLK	PTS	AVG
'85-86	DETROIT	4	147	25	61.0	0	---	10	66.7	13	25	4	0	60	15.0
'86-87	DETROIT	15	473	78	53.8	2	66.7	32	78.0	19	72	12	1	190	12.7
'87-88	DETROIT	23	804	113	45.7	2	33.3	56	89.3	50	112	13	2	284	12.3
'88-89	DETROIT	17	620	106	45.5	1	8.3	87	86.1	44	96	12	1	300	17.6
'89-90	DETROIT	20	754	130	45.8	5	26.3	99	87.6	44	95	22	0	364	18.2
'90-91	DETROIT	15	588	105	42.9	17	40.5	82	84.5	50	62	16	1	309	20.6
'91-92	DETROIT	5	221	32	47.1	5	50.0	15	78.9	8	16	5	1	84	16.8
TOTALS		99	3607	589	46.6	32	34.8	381	84.9	228	478	84	6	1591	16.1

Grant Hill

No. 33/F

HT: 6-8   **WT:** 225
Born: 10/5/72
College: Duke

Grant Hill did it all in college. Last season's Atlantic Coast Conference Player of the Year, Grant Hill was the first player in ACC history to accumulate 1,900 points, 700 rebounds, 400 assists, 200 steals and 100 blocked shots in a career. Hill was First Team All-ACC in both his junior and senior years, and was a three-time All-America pick during his Duke career, including a unanimous choice as a First Team All-America choice in 1994. Hill was voted the Defensive Player of the Year in his junior year. Perhaps most significantly, during his 4 years at Duke, Hill's Blue Devils appeared in 3 NCAA championship games and won twice. His father is ex-Yale and Dallas Cowboys football star Calvin Hill, and Hillary Rodham Clinton was his mother's roommate in college.

REGULAR SEASON	G	MIN	FG	FG%	3FG	3PT%	FT	FT%	REB	AST	STL	BLK	PTS	AVG
ROOKIE -- NO NBA EXPERIENCE														

Allan Houston

No. 20/G

Full name: Allan Wade Houston
HT: 6-6   **WT:** 200
Born: 4/4/71, Louisville, KY
High school: Ballard (Louisville)
College: Tennessee

Houston was one of Detroit's 2 first-round picks in the '93 draft. He played in 79 games last season, and started 20, splitting time between off guard and small forward. He's a good jumper who finished fourth in the NBA All-Star slam dunk contest. He's not much of a rebounder, but he showed some promise as a scorer, averaging 14.9 points over the season's final 11 games, and putting up 31 points (including 6 for 12 from 3-point range) against Charlotte in the next to last game of the year. He had trouble finding his shot in his rookie season; he was just a 40.5 percent shooter from the field, but was an 82.4 percent shooter from the free throw line.

REGULAR SEASON	G	MIN	FG	FGx	3FG	3PTx	FT	FTx	REB	AST	STL	BLK	PTS	AVG
'93-94 DETROIT	79	1519	272	40.5	35	29.9	89	82.4	120	100	34	13	668	8.5
1 YR TOTALS	79	1519	272	40.5	35	29.9	89	82.4	120	100	34	13	668	8.5
'93-94 RANK NBA Gs	40	78	65	111	57	80	85	42	94	104	107	55	68	79

Lindsey Hunter

No. 1/G

Full name: Lindsey Benson Hunter, Jr.
HT: 6-2   **WT:** 195
Born: 12/3/70, Utica, MS
High school: Murrah (Jackson)
College: Jackson State (MS)
Hunter was a first-round pick in the '93 draft, and made second team All-Rookie after averaging 10.3 points, 4.8 assists, 2.3 rebounds, and 1.5 steals per game. He looks like the point guard of the future, and with Isiah Thomas' retirement, the future is now. Hunter was the only Piston to play in all 82 games. He started 26 games at point guard last season, and averaged 13.6 points in those games. Hunter led the Pistons in steals, and was second on the team in assists. He has to improve his shooting, though; although he was 69 for 207 from 3-point range (33.3 percent), Hunter was a dreadful 37.5 percent from the field.

REGULAR SEASON	G	MIN	FG	FGx	3FG	3PTx	FT	FTx	REB	AST	STL	BLK	PTS	AVG
'93-94 DETROIT	82	2172	335	37.5	69	33.3	104	73.2	189	390	121	10	843	10.3
1 YR TOTALS	82	2172	335	37.5	69	33.3	104	73.2	189	390	121	10	843	10.3
'93-94 RANK NBA Gs	1	53	53	127	28	58	74	99	56	25	24	73	56	64

Mark West

C

Full name: Mark Andre West
HT: 6-10   **WT:** 246
Born: 11/5/60, Petersburg, VA
High school: Petersburg (VA)
College: Old Dominion

West is a veteran rebounder. Although he's foul-prone (6 fouls per 34.7 minutes played), West always shows up to play. He's played in 499 straight games, trailing only A.C. Green for most consecutive games played among active players. West is a rebounder and shotblocker, not a scorer: he scored in double figures 18 times, but broke 20 points just once. But West is a career 59.2 percent shooter from the field, because almost all his points are from putbacks. Still, he's tops in FG percentage among active players, and trails only Artis Gilmore (59.9 percent) on the NBA all-time list. He graduated from the same high school as Moses Malone.

REGULAR SEASON		G	MIN	FG	FGx	3FG	3PTx	FT	FTx	REB	AST	STL	BLK	PTS	AVG
'83-84	DALLAS	34	202	15	35.7	0	---	7	31.8	46	13	1	15	37	1.1
'84-85	MIL-CLE	66	888	106	54.6	0	0.0	43	43.4	251	15	13	49	255	3.9
'85-86	CLEVELAND	67	1172	113	54.1	0	---	54	52.4	322	20	27	62	280	4.2
'86-87	CLEVELAND	78	1333	209	54.3	0	0.0	89	51.4	339	41	22	81	507	6.5
'87-88	CLE-PHE	83	2098	316	55.1	0	0.0	170	59.6	523	74	47	147	802	9.7
'88-89	PHOENIX	82	2019	243	65.3	0	---	108	53.5	551	39	35	187	594	7.2
'89-90	PHOENIX	82	2399	331	62.5	0	---	199	61.1	728	45	36	184	861	10.5
'90-91	PHOENIX	82	1957	247	64.7	0	---	135	65.5	564	37	32	161	629	7.7
'91-92	PHOENIX	82	1436	196	63.2	0	---	109	63.7	372	22	14	81	501	6.1
'92-93	PHOENIX	82	1558	175	61.4	0	---	86	51.8	458	29	16	103	436	5.3
'93-94	PHOENIX	82	1236	162	56.6	0	---	58	50.0	295	33	31	109	382	4.7
	11 YR TOTALS	820	16298	2113	59.2	0	0.0	1058	58.2	4449	368	274	1179	5284	6.4
'93-94	RANK NBA Cs	1	28	27	7	14	14	31	50	28	36	25	12	26	34
'94-95	PROJECTIONS	82	998	133	53.4	0	0.0	39	45.9	214	31	32	99	305	3.7

PLAYOFFS		G	MIN	FG	FGx	3FG	3PTx	FT	FTx	REB	AST	STL	BLK	PTS	AVG
'83-84	DALLAS	4	32	5	55.6	0	---	2	66.7	7	3	0	3	12	3.0
'84-85	CLEVELAND	4	68	3	60.0	0	---	2	40.0	18	4	2	0	8	2.0
'88-89	PHOENIX	12	227	32	64.0	0	---	10	71.4	53	6	7	19	74	6.2
'89-90	PHOENIX	16	544	75	57.7	0	---	27	54.0	164	5	4	41	177	11.1
'90-91	PHOENIX	4	93	9	60.0	0	---	5	71.4	18	2	2	10	23	5.8
'91-92	PHOENIX	8	96	14	73.7	0	---	4	50.0	17	2	2	4	32	4.0
'92-93	PHOENIX	24	469	43	54.4	0	---	28	60.9	99	11	4	33	114	4.8
'93-94	PHOENIX	7	69	5	33.3	0	---	7	70.0	20	0	0	7	17	2.4
	TOTALS	79	1598	186	57.8	0	---	85	59.4	396	33	21	117	457	5.8

Greg Anderson No. 34/F-C

Full name: Gregory Wayne Anderson
HT: 6-10 **WT:** 230
Born: 6/2/64, Houston, TX
High school: E. E. Worthing (Houston)
College: Houston

Anderson started Detroit's last 32 games, connecting on 56 percent of his FGAs in those games.

REGULAR SEASON		G	MIN	FG	FG%	3FG	3PT%	FT	FT%	REB	AST	STL	BLK	PTS	AVG
'87-88	SAN ANTONIO	82	1984	379	50.1	1	20.0	198	60.4	513	79	54	122	957	11.7
'88-89	MILWAUKEE	82	2401	460	50.3	0	0.0	207	51.4	676	61	102	103	1127	13.7
'89-90	MILWAUKEE	60	1291	219	50.7	0	---	91	53.5	373	24	32	54	529	8.8
'90-91	MIL-NJ-DEN	68	924	116	43.0	· 0	0.0	60	52.2	318	16	35	45	292	4.3
'91-92	DENVER	82	2793	389	45.6	0	0.0	167	62.3	941	78	88	65	945	11.5
'93-94	DETROIT	77	1624	201	54.3	1	33.3	88	57.1	571	51	55	68	491	6.4
6 YR TOTALS		451	11017	1764	49.1	2	12.5	811	56.4	3392	309	366	457	4341	9.6
'93-94 RANK NBA Fs		43	63	75	8	69	22	79	123	25	94	56	20	76	88
'94-95 PROJECTIONS		78	1398	149	58.7	2	66.7	66	56.9	511	50	48	64	366	4.7

PLAYOFFS		G	MIN	FG	FG%	3FG	3PT%	FT	FT%	REB	AST	STL	BLK	PTS	AVG
'87-88	SAN ANTONIO	3 ·	95	17	47.2	0	---	4	44.4	21	3	2	4	38	12.7
'89-90	MILWAUKEE	4	101	13	68.4	0	---	7	50.0	24	0	1	4	33	8.3
TOTALS		7	196	30	54.5	0	---	11	47.8	45	3	3	8	71	10.1

Charles Jones No. 23/F

HT: 6-9 **WT:** 235
Born: 4/3/57, McGehee, AR
High school: Delta (Rohwer, AR)
College: Albany State (GA)

CJ averaged 20.9 minutes per game as a defensive specialist at center. He had the rare statistical distinction of having more blocked shots than turnovers.

REGULAR SEASON		G	MIN	FG	FG%	3FG	3PT%	FT	FT%	REB	AST	STL	BLK	PTS	AVG
'87-88	WASHINGTON	69	1313	72	40.7	0	0.0	53	70.7	325	59	67	113	197	2.9
'88-89	WASHINGTON	53	1154	60	48.0	0	0.0	16	64.0	257	42	53	76	136	2.6
'89-90	WASHINGTON	81	2240	94	50.8	0	---	68	64.8	504	139	39	197	256	3.2
'90-91	WASHINGTON	62	1499	67	54.0	0	---	29	58.0	359	48	51	124	163	2.6
'91-92	WASHINGTON	75	1365	33	36.7	0	---	20	50.0	317	62	43	92	86	1.1
'92-93	WASHINGTON	67	1206	33	52.4	0	0.0	22	57.9	277	42	38	77	88	1.3
'93-94	DETROIT	42	877	36	46.2	0	0.0	19	55.9	235	29	14	43	91	2.2
11 YR TOTALS		641	13542	709	48.1	0	0.0	370	62.6	3135	603	406	1099	1788	2.8
'93-94 RANK NBA Fs		122	103	130	75	78	78	129	125	86	116	124	51	130	133
'94-95 PROJECTIONS		28	597	27	44.3	0	0.0	14	56.0	171	18	5	23	68	2.4

PLAYOFFS		G	MIN	FG	FG%	3FG	3PT%	FT	FT%	REB	AST	STL	BLK	PTS	AVG
'86-87	WASHINGTON	3	56	3	60.0	0	---	0	---	8	3	2	5	6	2.0
'87-88	WASHINGTON	5	95	1	20.0	0	---	1	50.0	17	2	2	4	3	0.6
TOTALS		17	333	18	45.0	0	---	14	63.6	60	11	9	21	50	2.9

Marcus Liberty   No. 30/F

HT: 6-8   **WT:** 225
Born: 10/27/68, Chicago, IL
High school: King (Chicago)
College: Illinois

Liberty didn't do much in Detroit after being traded from Denver. He averaged just 2.9 points and 1.6 rebounds for the Pistons.

REGULAR SEASON		G	MIN	FG	FGx	3FG	3PTx	FT	FTx	REB	AST	STL	BLK	PTS	AVG
'90-91	DENVER	76	1171	216	42.1	17	29.8	58	63.0	221	64	48	19	507	6.7
'91-92	DENVER	75	1527	275	44.3	17	34.0	131	72.8	308	58	66	29	698	9.3
'92-93	DENVER	78	1585	252	40.6	22	37.3	102	65.4	335	105	64	21	628	8.1
'93-94	DEN-DET	38	285	40	32.5	10	35.7	19	48.7	61	17	11	4	109	2.9
4 YR TOTALS		267	4568	783	41.7	66	34.0	310	66.4	925	244	189	73	1942	7.3
	RANK NBA Fs	101	108	106	113	106	110	66	77	112	112	112	112	112	112
'94-95 PROJECTIONS		14	0	0	27.0	0	0.0	0	0.0	0	0	0	0	0	0.0

Mark Macon   No. 2/G

Full name: Mark L. Macon
HT: 6-5   **WT:** 200
Born: 4/14/69, Saginaw, MI
High school: Buena Vista (Saginaw)
College: Temple

Macon was Detroit's fifth guard last season. He's a hard worker on defense.

REGULAR SEASON		G	MIN	FG	FGx	3FG	3PTx	FT	FTx	REB	AST	STL	BLK	PTS	AVG
'91-92	DENVER	76	2304	333	37.5	4	13.3	135	73.0	220	168	154	14	805	10.6
'92-93	DENVER	48	1141	158	41.5	0	0.0	42	70.0	103	126	69	3	358	7.5
'93-94	DEN-DET	42	496	69	37.5	2	20.0	23	67.6	41	51	39	1	163	3.9
3 YR TOTALS		166	3941	560	38.5	6	13.0	200	71.7	364	345	262	18	1326	8.0
'93-94 RANK NBA Gs		103	102	100	105	105	100	98	113	103	106	101	103	102	99
'94-95 PROJECTIONS		31	35	5	35.7	0	0.0	2	66.7	3	4	3	0	12	0.4

Terry Mills

No. 6/F

Full name: Terry Richard Mills
HT: 6-10 **WT:** 250
Born: 12/21/67, Romulus, MI
High school: Romulus (MI)
College: Michigan

Mills started 74 games for Detroit last season. He increased his scoring average for the fourth straight year.

REGULAR SEASON		G	MIN	FG	FGx	3FG	3PTx	FT	FTx	REB	AST	STL	BLK	PTS	AVG
'90-91	DEN-NJ	55	819	134	46.5	0	0.0	47	71.2	229	33	35	29	315	5.7
'91-92	NEW JERSEY	82	1714	310	46.3	8	34.8	114	75.0	453	84	48	41	742	9.0
'92-93	DETROIT	81	2183	494	46.1	10	27.8	201	79.1	472	111	44	50	1199	14.8
'93-94	DETROIT	80	2773	588	51.1	24	32.9	181	79.7	672	177	64	62	1381	17.3
4 YR TOTALS		298	7489	1526	48.0	42	30.9	543	77.7	1826	405	191	182	3637	12.2
'93-94	RANK NBA Fs	23	13	8	24	28	26	39	15	17	32	42	24	13	16
'94-95	PROJECTIONS	82	3363	729	54.1	44	38.3	190	81.5	818	246	71	69	1692	20.6

PLAYOFFS		G	MIN	FG	FGx	3FG	3PTx	FT	FTx	REB	AST	STL	BLK	PTS	AVG
'91-92	NEW JERSEY	4	77	10	37.0	0	0.0	7	63.6	24	8	1	2	27	6.8
TOTALS		4	77	10	37.0	0	0.0	7	63.6	24	8	1	2	27	6.8

Don Chaney Head Coach

Full name: Donald John Chaney
HT: 6-5 **WT:** 210
Born: 3/22/46, Baton Rouge, LA
High school: McKinley (Baton Rouge)
College: Houston

Chaney was an assistant coach on Dream Team II. His tenure with the Clippers has prepared him for coaching the Pistons.

	REGULAR SEASON				PLAYOFFS				
YEAR	TEAM	W	L	PCT	FINISH	W	L	PCT	
'84-85	LA CLIPPERS	9	12	.429	T4th/Pacific Div.				
'85-86	LA CLIPPERS	32	50	.390	T3rd/Pacific Div.				
'86-87	LA CLIPPERS	12	70	.146	6th/Pacific Div.				
'88-89	HOUSTON	45	37	.549	2nd/Midwest Div.	1	3	.250	lost Western Conf. first round to Seattle, 3-1
'89-90	HOUSTON	41	41	.500	5th/Midwest Div.	1	3	.250	lost Western Conf. first round to LA Lakers, 3-1
'90-91	HOUSTON	52	30	.634	3rd/Midwest Div.	0	3	.000	lost Western Conf. first round to LA Lakers, 3-0
'91-92	HOUSTON	26	26	.500					
'93-94	DETROIT	20	62	.244	6th/Central Div.				
8 YR TOTALS		237	328	.419		2	9	.182	

Golden State
WARRIORS

1994–95 Scouting Report

Frontcourt

Chris Webber, a natural power forward, was pressed into service at center, and still became the first NBA rookie to post 1,000 points, 500 rebounds, 250 assists, 150 blocks, and 75 steals. (The only other players to have done so are named Abdul-Jabbar, Olajuwon, and David Robinson.) Chris Mullin returns at small forward; plagued by injuries early in the season, he's still the best left-handed spot-up player in the NBA. Billy Owens is a swingman who can rebound as well as score; he led Golden State in rebounding 31 times.

The bench features Victor Alexander and Chris Gatling, who can both play either center or forward. Alexander is more of scorer, while Gatling is the better rebounder; neither is distinguished by his defense. Golden State hopes rookies Clifford Rozier and Carlos Rogers will be able to bolster the frontline. Both Rozier and Rogers can score inside and rebound, but Rogers may be the better shotblocker. If either player can step in at center this season, that would allow Chris Webber to play power forward and let Don Nelson move Billy Owens to a sixth-man role.

Backcourt

In the wake of Tim Hardaway's anterior cruciate ligament tear that sidelined him for the year, Latrell Sprewell turned into one of the best point guards in the NBA. If Hardaway, a three-time All-Star at point, can return to form, Sprewell figures to move back to shooting guard. Golden State added veteran shooter Ricky Pierce, a two-time Sixth Man Award winner, in a trade with Seattle. And if the Warriors can find themselves a center, Billy Owens would see a lot of time at guard coming off the bench.

Defense

Most people don't associate Golden State with defensive prowess, but the Warriors are an underrated defensive team. It's true that teams averaged 106.1 points against the Warriors, fifth highest in the NBA. And they held opponents under 100 points just 25 times. But that's primarily because Golden State plays a fast-paced game that features a lot of shots by both teams; opponents hoisted 7,332 shots from the field last season, fourth highest in the league. Opponents shot 46.8 percent from the floor against Golden State, just fourteenth in the league. And the Warriors ranked fourth in the NBA in steals, blocks, and forced turnovers.

1994–95 Prospects

Last year, Golden State improved 16 games from the previous year, most in the NBA. (That season, they led the NBA in player games lost to injury or illness with 312). Last season they had "only" 209 player games lost to injury or illness, and overcame injuries to key players like All-Star guard Tim Hardaway, Sarunas Marciulonis, and Chris Mullin, as well as squabbling between Coach Don Nelson and Chris Webber. No team was better in winning close games; they were 11–3 in games decided by 3 points or less. They were the worst free throw shooting team in the NBA, shooting just 66 percent from the line. Yet, they were the NBA's second most potent offensive team, averaging 107.9 points per game.

For the Warriors to advance to the next level, they've got to improve their rebounding. Last season, they were the second worst team in preventing offensive rebounds. And of the worst 5 teams in preventing offensive rebounds, Golden State was the only one with a winning record; the other 4 teams (the Clippers, the Lakers, Charlotte, and Philadelphia) had a cumulative record of 126–202, a .384 percentage. Although Webber is a force underneath, when you position yourself to block a shot, as he does, you usually end up in poor rebounding position. If Rozier or Rogers can help out Webber underneath, opponents' offensive rebounds should go way down.

Golden State won 50 games last season, so there isn't much room to improve in the standings (except, of course, avoiding a series split with Minnesota). Still, the Warriors are loaded with young talent (Mullin is the only starter over 30) and are better defensively than some may think. If just one of the draft picks pans out, they will have as good an eight man rotation as anyone in the league. They're definitely a playoff lock for the upcoming season.

Team Directory

Chairman: Jim Fitzgerald
Head coach/GM: Don Nelson

President: Dan Finnane
Dir., media relations: Julie Marvel

1993–94 Review

	WESTERN CONFERENCE					EASTERN CONFERENCE				
MIDWEST DIV.		**PACIFIC DIV.**			**ATLANTIC DIV.**		**CENTRAL DIV.**		
	W	L		W	L		W	L		W	L

MIDWEST	W	L	PACIFIC	W	L	ATLANTIC	W	L	CENTRAL	W	L
HOU	0	4	SEA	1	4	NY	1	1	ATL	2	0
SAN	2	2	PHO	2	3	ORL	1	1	CHI	0	2
UTAH	3	1	GS	–	–	NJ	0	2	CLE	0	2
DEN	3	1	POR	3	2	MIA	2	0	IND	1	1
MIN	2	2	LAL	5	0	BOS	1	1	CHA	2	0
DAL	4	0	SAC	4	1	PHI	1	1	DET	2	0
			LAC	4	1	WAS	2	0	MIL	2	0
	14	10		19	11		8	6		9	5

1993–94 finish: 50–32 (29–12 home, 21–20 away), third in Pacific Div.

1994–95 Schedule

Date	Opponent	Time	Date	Opponent	Time	Date	Opponent	Time
11/4	@ San Ant.	10:00 pm	1/5	Milwaukee	7:30 pm	3/6	@ Seattle	10:30 pm
11/5	@ Denver	10:30 pm	1/10	Seattle	7:30 pm	3/8	LA Clip.	8:30 pm
11/8	Miami	12:00 pm	1/11	@ Portland	10:30 pm	3/10	@ LA Clip.	10:30 pm
11/11	@ Utah	10:30 pm	1/13	@ LA Lakers	10:30 pm	3/12	@ Phoenix	10:30 pm
11/12	LA Lakers	2:30 pm	1/14	Cleveland	8:00 pm	3/13	Dallas	8:30 pm
11/15	Minnesota	3:30 pm	1/16	Denver	8:00 pm	3/15	LA Lakers	8:30 pm
11/17	New York	3:30 pm	1/19	@ Sacra.	10:30 pm	3/17	@ Sacra.	10:30 pm
11/19	Utah	3:30 pm	1/24	New Jersey	8:00 pm	3/19	Detroit	8:30 pm
11/22	@ Charlotte	10:30 pm	1/26	@ Wash.	10:30 pm	3/21	@ Milwaukee	10:30 pm
11/24	@ Indiana	10:30 pm	1/27	@ Boston	10:30 pm	3/22	@ Phila.	10:30 pm
11/26	@ Cleveland	10:30 pm	1/29	@ Chicago	10:30 pm	3/24	@ Miami	10:30 pm
11/27	@ Detroit	10:30 pm	1/31	@ New York	10:30 pm	3/26	@ Orlando	10:30 pm
11/29	LA Clip.	5:00 pm	2/1	@ Atlanta	10:30 pm	3/28	@ New Jersey	10:30 pm
12/1	Houston	7:00 pm	2/3	LA Clip.	8:00 pm	3/30	Atlanta	9:00 pm
12/3	Indiana	7:00 pm	2/5	Chicago	8:00 pm	4/1	Minnesota	9:00 pm
12/6	@ LA Lakers	10:30 pm	2/7	@ Minnesota	10:30 pm	4/4	Phoenix	9:00 pm
12/9	@ Portland	10:30 pm	2/9	@ Denver	10:30 pm	4/6	Houston	9:00 pm
12/10	@ Sacra.	10:30 pm	2/14	@ Seattle	10:30 pm	4/8	San Ant.	9:00 pm
12/12	@ Phoenix	10:30 pm	2/15	Boston	8:00 pm	4/10	@ Dallas	10:30 pm
12/13	Sacra.	7:30 pm	2/17	@ Phoenix	10:30 pm	4/11	@ Minnesota	10:30 pm
12/15	@ LA Clip.	10:30 pm	2/18	Seattle	8:00 pm	4/13	@ Utah	10:30 pm
12/16	Orlando	7:30 pm	2/20	Phila.	8:00 pm	4/15	Seattle	10:00 pm
12/20	Dallas	7:30 pm	2/22	Portland	8:00 pm	4/18	Portland	10:00 pm
12/22	Wash.	7:30 pm	2/25	@ Houston	10:30 pm	4/20	Sacra.	10:00 pm
12/27	LA Lakers	7:30 pm	2/26	@ San Ant.	10:30 pm	4/22	Denver	10:00 pm
12/29	@ Houston	10:30 pm	3/1	Utah	8:00 pm	4/23	@ Portland	10:30 pm
12/30	@ Dallas	10:30 pm	3/3	Charlotte	8:30 pm			
1/3	San Ant.	7:30 pm	3/5	Phoenix	8:30 pm			

1993–94 Team Stats

NAME	G	MIN	FG	FGA	FG%	3FG	3FGA	3FG%	FT	FTA	FT%	ORB	TRB	AST	PF	STL	BLK	TO	PTS	AVG
Sprewell	82	3533	613	1417	43.3	141	391	36.1	353	456	77.4	80	401	385	158	180	76	226	1720	21.0
Webber	76	2438	572	1037	55.2	0	14	0.0	189	355	53.2	305	694	272	247	93	164	206	1333	17.5
Mullin	62	2324	410	869	47.2	55	151	36.4	165	219	75.3	64	345	315	114	107	53	178	1040	16.8
Owens	79	2738	492	971	50.7	3	15	20.0	199	326	61.0	230	640	326	269	83	60	214	1186	15.0
Johnson	82	2332	356	724	49.2	0	12	0.0	178	253	70.4	41	176	433	160	113	8	172	890	10.9
Alexander	69	1318	266	502	53.0	2	13	15.4	68	129	52.7	114	308	66	168	28	32	86	602	8.7
Gatling	82	1296	271	461	58.8	0	1	0.0	129	208	62.0	143	397	41	223	40	63	84	671	8.2
Grayer	67	1096	191	363	52.6	2	12	16.7	71	118	60.2	76	191	62	103	33	13	63	455	6.8
Lichti	5	58	10	28	35.7	2	2	100.0	9	11	81.8	3	10	3	9	0	0	0	31	6.2
Jennings	76	1097	138	342	40.4	56	151	37.1	100	120	83.3	16	89	218	62	65	0	74	432	5.7
Spencer	5	63	9	18	50.0	0	0	—	3	4	75.0	4	12	3	6	1	2	2	21	4.2
Grant	53	382	59	146	40.4	17	61	27.9	22	29	75.9	27	89	24	62	18	8	30	157	3.0
Buechler	36	218	42	84	50.0	12	29	41.4	10	20	50.0	13	32	16	24	8	1	12	106	2.9
Houston	71	866	81	177	45.8	1	7	14.3	33	54	61.1	67	194	32	181	33	31	49	196	2.8
Demps	2	11	2	6	33.3	0	0	—	0	2	0.0	0	0	1	0	2	0	0	4	2.0
Murphy	2	10	0	0	—	0	0	—	0	0	—	0	0	1	2	0	0	0	0	0.0
Warriors	82	19780	3512	7145	49.2	291	859	33.9	1529	2304	66.4	1183	3579	2198	1789	804	511	1433	8844	107.9
Opp.	82	19780	3428	7332	46.8	305	869	35.1	1540	2108	73.1	1324	3732	2184	1870	842	408	1426	8701	106.1

HISTORY

TITLES

1946–47 NBA champs

1955–56 NBA champs

1963–64 NBA Western Div. champs

1966–67 NBA Western Div. champs

1974–75 NBA champs

1975–76 NBA Pacific Div. champs

ALL-TIME TEAM RECORDS

Career

Games played	Nate Thurmond	757	1963–74
Total points	Wilt Chamberlain	17,783	1959–65
Scoring average	Wilt Chamberlain	41.5	1959–65
Field goals made	Wilt Chamberlain	7,216	1959–65
Free throws made	Paul Arizin	5,010	1950–62
Total rebounds	Nate Thurmond	12,771	1963–74
Assists	Guy Rodgers	4,855	1958–66
Steals	Chris Mullin	1,101	1985–94

Season

Total points	Wilt Chamberlain	4,029	1961–62
Scoring average	Wilt Chamberlain	50.4	1961–62
Field goals made	Wilt Chamberlain	1,597	1961–62
Free throws made	Rick Barry	753	1966–67
Total rebounds	Wilt Chamberlain	2,149	1960–61
Assists	Sleepy Floyd	848	1986–87
Steals	Rick Barry	228	1974–75

Games

Total Points	Wilt Chamberlain	100	vs. New York, 3/2/62
Field goals made	Wilt Chamberlain	36	vs. New York, 3/2/62
Free throws made	Wilt Chamberlain	28	vs. New York, 3/2/62
Total rebounds	Wilt Chamberlain	55	vs. Boston, 11/24/60
Assists	Guy Rodgers	28	vs. St. Louis, 3/14/63
Steals	Micheal R. Richardson	9	vs. San Antonio, 2/5/83
	Rick Barry	9	vs. Buffalo, 10/29/74

LEADING COACHES

		REGULAR SEASON			PLAYOFFS		
NAME	YEARS	W	L	PCT	W	L	PCT
Alvin Attles	1970–83	555	516	.518	31	30	.508
Edward Gottlieb	1946–55	263	318	.453	15	17	.469
Don Nelson	1988–94	263	229	.535	9	15	.375
Alex Hannum	1963–66	100	140	.417	5	4	.556
George Senesky	1955–58	119	97	.551	10	10	.500

Golden State Warriors 1994–95 Roster

Head Coach: Don Nelson

No.	Name	Pos.	Ht.	Wt.	Yrs.	Born	College
52	Victor Alexander	C-F	6-9	265	3	8/31/69	Iowa State
25	Chris Gatling	F-C	6-10	225	3	9/3/67	Old Dominion
10	Tim Hardaway	G	6-0	195	5	9/1/66	Texas-El Paso
2	Keith Jennings	G	5-7	160	2	11/2/68	East Tennessee St.
50	Dwayne Morton	G	6-7	195	R	8/10/71	Louisville
17	Chris Mullin	F	6-7	215	9	7/30/63	St. John's
30	Billy Owens	G-F	6-9	220	3	5/1/69	Syracuse
22	Ricky Pierce	G	6-4	215	12	8/19/59	Rice
34	Carlos Rogers	C	6-11	220	R	2/6/71	Tennessee St.
44	Clifford Rozier	F	6-11	245	R	10/31/72	Louisville
15	Latrell Sprewell	G	6-5	190	2	9/8/70	Alabama
4	Chris Webber	F-C	6-10	260	1	3/1/73	Michigan

Arena Information

Oakland Coliseum Arena (15,025)
Tickets: 510-638-6300
Ticket prices: $54, $45.50, $31, $23.50, $18.50, $9.75

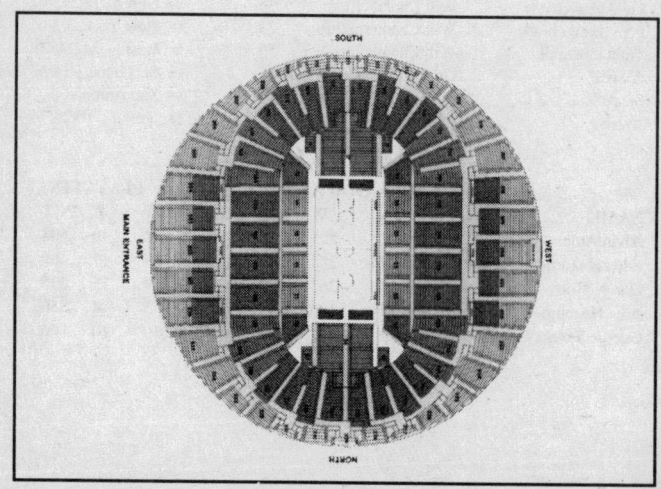

Tim Hardaway

No. 10/G

Full name: Timothy Duane Hardaway
HT: 6-0 **WT:** 195
Born: 9/1/66, Chicago, IL
High school: Carver (Chicago)
College: Texas El-Paso

Hardaway was named a member of Dream Team II, despite spending the entire season on the injured list with a torn anterior cruciate ligament in his left knee. He was coming off a season in which he was named to third team All-NBA. He became the fifth player in league history to average 20 points and 10 assists in consecutive seasons (the others are Oscar Robertson, Magic Johnson, Isiah Thomas and Kevin Johnson). Only Oscar Robertson (who needed 247 games) reached 5,000 points, 2,500 assists faster than Hardaway did in 262 games. His assists-per-game average improved 3 straight seasons from '89–90 to '92–93. He's second on the all-time Warrior leader list in 3-point FGs (Mullin regained the lead last season).

REGULAR SEASON		G	MIN	FG	FG%	3FG	3PT%	FT	FT%	REB	AST	STL	BLK	PTS	AVG
'89-90	GOLDEN STATE	79	2663	464	47.1	23	27.4	211	76.4	310	689	165	12	1162	14.7
'90-91	GOLDEN STATE	82	3215	739	47.6	97	38.5	306	80.3	332	793	214	12	1981	22.9
'91-92	GOLDEN STATE	81	3332	734	46.1	127	33.8	298	76.6	310	807	164	13	1893	23.4
'92-93	GOLDEN STATE	66	2609	522	44.7	102	33.0	273	74.4	263	699	116	12	1419	21.5
'93-94	GOLDEN STATE	did not play -- injured (knee)													
5 YR TOTALS		308	11819	2459	46.4	349	34.2	1088	77.0	1215	2988	659	49	6355	20.6
'93-94	RANK NBA Gs	not ranked -- didn't appear in 25 games in '93-94													
'94-95	PROJECTIONS	57	2261	433	43.5	100	32.4	256	72.3	229	635	84	11	1222	21.4

PLAYOFFS		G	MIN	FG	FG%	3FG	3PT%	FT	FT%	REB	AST	STL	BLK	PTS	AVG
'90-91	GOLDEN STATE	9	396	90	48.6	17	35.4	30	78.9	33	101	28	7	227	25.2
'91-92	GOLDEN STATE	4	176	32	40.0	10	34.5	24	64.9	15	29	13	0	98	24.5
	TOTALS	13	572	122	46.0	27	35.1	54	72.0	48	130	41	7	325	25.0

Chris Mullin

No. 17/

Full name: Christopher Paul Mullin

HT: 6-7   **WT:** 215

Born: 7/30/63, New York, NY

High school: Xaverian (Brookly

College: St. John's

Mullin missed the season's first 2 games due to a torn ligament his right hand; he also misse time due to acute tendinitis in h right shin. As a result, last seaso was the first in 7 years in whic Mullin failed to lead the team scoring. Chris Mullin is in th Warriors' all-time top 10 in 17 d ferent categories. He's alread outscored 28 of the 58 forme NBA players in the Hall of Fam and is the fourth-leading scorer Warriors' history, his 13,767 poin trailing just Wilt Chamberlai (17,783), Rick Barry (16,447) and Paul Arizin (16,266). He's the fir player in Warriors history with 1,000 steals, and the club's all-time leade in 3-point field goals. He's the best left-handed spot-up shooter in th NBA, an excellent passer, and a deceptively good rebounder.

REGULAR SEASON	G	MIN	FG	FG%	3FG	3PT%	FT	FT%	REB	AST	STL	BLK	PTS	AVG
'85-86 GOLDEN STATE	55	1391	287	46.3	5	18.5	189	89.6	115	105	70	23	768	14.0
'86-87 GOLDEN STATE	82	2377	477	51.4	19	30.2	269	82.5	181	261	98	36	1242	15.
'87-88 GOLDEN STATE	60	2033	470	50.8	34	35.1	239	88.5	205	290	113	32	1213	20.
'88-89 GOLDEN STATE	82	3093	830	50.9	23	23.0	493	89.2	483	415	176	39	2176	26.
'89-90 GOLDEN STATE	78	2830	682	53.6	87	37.2	505	88.9	463	319	123	45	1956	25.
'90-91 GOLDEN STATE	82	3315	777	53.6	40	30.1	513	88.4	443	329	173	63	2107	25.
'91-92 GOLDEN STATE	81	3346	830	52.4	64	36.6	350	83.3	450	286	173	62	2074	25.
'92-93 GOLDEN STATE	46	1902	474	51.0	60	45.1	183	81.0	232	166	68	41	1191	25.
'93-94 GOLDEN STATE	62	2324	410	47.2	55	36.4	165	75.3	345	315	107	53	1040	16.
9 YR TOTALS	628	22611	5237	51.3	387	34.8	2906	86.2	2917	2486	1101	394	13767	21.
'93-94 RANK NBA Fs	100	35	29	62	12	16	42	41	62	4	11	31	28	
'94-95 PROJECTIONS	61	2188	315	44.6	50	34.5	110	71.0	344	346	104	53	790	13.0

PLAYOFFS	G	MIN	FG	FG%	3FG	3PT%	FT	FT%	REB	AST	STL	BLK	PTS	AVG
'86-87 GOLDEN STATE	10	262	49	50.0	3	75.0	12	75.0	15	23	9	2	113	11.3
'88-89 GOLDEN STATE	8	341	88	54.0	1	12.5	58	86.6	47	36	14	11	235	29.4
'90-91 GOLDEN STATE	8	366	69	52.7	9	69.2	43	86.0	58	23	15	12	190	23.8
'91-92 GOLDEN STATE	4	168	27	42.9	4	33.3	13	92.9	12	12	5	2	71	17.8
'93-94 GOLDEN STATE	3	135	30	58.8	6	50.0	10	90.9	14	11	0	5	76	25.3
TOTALS	33	1272	263	52.0	23	46.9	136	86.1	146	105	43	32	685	20.8

Billy Owens

No. 30/G-F

Full name: Billy E. Owens
HT: 6-9 **WT:** 220
Born: 5/1/69, Carlisle, PA
High school: Carlisle (PA)
College: Syracuse

Owens was one of only five players to average 15 points, 8 rebounds, and 4 assists per game last season; the others were Charles Barkley, Scottie Pippen, Christian Laettner, and David Robinson. Owens was Golden State's fourth leading scorer, second in rebounds and fourth in assists. He had 20 points or more 18 times, and 10 rebounds or more 26 times. He had 22 rebounds (along with 21 points) at Detroit on November 28, the most by a Warrior since March 28, 1987, when Larry Smith had 24 against Utah. And he scored 20 points in the third quarter against the Clippers, the most points scored in a single quarter by a Warrior last season.

REGULAR SEASON		G	MIN	FG	FG%	3FG	3PT%	FT	FT%	REB	AST	STL	BLK	PTS	AVG
'91-92	GOLDEN STATE	80	2510	468	52.5	1	11.1	204	65.4	639	188	90	65	1141	14.3
'92-93	GOLDEN STATE	37	1201	247	50.1	1	9.1	117	63.9	264	144	35	28	612	16.5
'93-94	GOLDEN STATE	79	2738	492	50.7	3	20.0	199	61.0	640	326	83	60	1186	15.0
	3 YR TOTALS	196	6449	1207	51.3	5	14.3	520	63.3	1543	658	208	153	2939	15.0
'93-94	RANK NBA Gs	40	21	16	7	114	113	29	126	1	42	52	2	27	28
'94-95	PROJECTIONS	82	3593	593	50.5	4	26.7	212	58.4	846	466	106	73	1402	17.1

PLAYOFFS		G	MIN	FG	FG%	3FG	3PT%	FT	FT%	REB	AST	STL	BLK	PTS	AVG
'91-92	GOLDEN STATE	4	157	30	52.6	0	---	17	63.0	33	13	8	2	77	19.3
'93-94	GOLDEN STATE	3	127	25	50.0	0	0.0	9	75.0	30	13	4	2	59	19.7
	TOTALS	7	284	55	51.4	0	0.0	26	66.7	63	26	12	4	136	19.4

Latrell Sprewell   No. 15/

HT: 6-5   **WT:** 190
Born: 9/8/70, Milwaukee, WI
High school: Washington
  (Milwaukee)
College: Alabama

Sprewell led the league in mi
utes, while averaging 21 poir
(eleventh in the NBA), 4
rebounds, 4.7 assists and 2
steals (ninth in the NBA) p
game. He scored 20 or mo
points in a game 50 time
Sprewell, a converted off gua
led the Warriors to a franchi
record for assists (2,198, brea
ing the record of 2,120 assists s
by the 1976–77 Warriors). At 2
he's the youngest player to lea
Golden State in scoring in
years, since 22-year-old Purv
Short averaged 17 points p
game for the 1979–80 Warriors. And Sprewell's 3,533 minutes we
the most by an NBA player since Len Robinson had 3,638 minutes
82 games for the 1977–78 New Orleans Jazz. His 141 3-point FGs s
a Warrior record.

REGULAR SEASON		G	MIN	FG	FG%	3FG	3PT%	FT	FT%	REB	AST	STL	BLK	PTS	AV
'92-93	GOLDEN STATE	77	2741	449	46.4	73	36.9	211	74.6	271	295	126	52	1182	15.
'93-94	GOLDEN STATE	82	3533	613	43.3	141	36.1	353	77.4	401	385	180	76	1720	21.
	2 YR TOTALS	159	6274	1062	44.5	214	36.3	564	76.3	672	680	306	128	2902	18.
'93-94	RANK NBA Gs	1	1	3	83	4	35	4	76	7	27	7	1	2	
'94-95	PROJECTIONS	82	3936	709	40.1	207	35.3	490	80.3	504	434	220	95	2115	25.
PLAYOFFS		G	MIN	FG	FG%	3FG	3PT%	FT	FT%	REB	AST	STL	BLK	PTS	AV
'93-94	GOLDEN STATE	3	122	26	43.3	8	34.8	8	66.7	9	21	2	3	68	22.
	TOTALS	3	122	26	43.3	8	34.8	8	66.7	9	21	2	3	68	22.

Chris Webber

No. 4/F-C

Full name: Mayce Edward
    Christopher Webber III
HT: 6-10   **WT:** 260
Born: 3/1/73, Detroit, MI
High school: Detroit Country
    Day (Birmingham, MI)
College: Michigan

The first player selected in the '93 draft, Webber was everything the Warriors expected of him, and more. Webber was voted Rookie of the Year, even though he played out of position for most of the season. He can simply do it all: score from anywhere on the court, rebound, and intimidate defensively underneath. Webber was second on the team in scoring, and led the Warriors in rebounds and blocked shots. It bears mentioning that, after the '93 draft, Don Nelson was crticized by some for not going after a "true" center—Shawn Bradley. But Webber has shown himself to be a force in the middle, while Bradley has been sidelined with injuries.

REGULAR SEASON	G	MIN	FG	FGx	3FG	3PTx	FT	FTx	REB	AST	STL	BLK	PTS	AVG
'93-94 GOLDEN STATE	76	2438	572	55.2	0	0.0	189	53.2	694	272	93	164	1333	17.5
1 YR TOTALS	76	2438	572	55.2	0	0.0	189	53.2	694	272	93	164	1333	17.5
'93-94 RANK NBA Fs	48	30	10	7	78	78	35	129	15	11	18	2	15	15

PLAYOFFS	G	MIN	FG	FGx	3FG	3PTx	FT	FTx	REB	AST	STL	BLK	PTS	AVG
'93-94 GOLDEN STATE	3	109	22	55.0	0	0.0	3	30.0	26	27	3	9	47	15.7
TOTALS	3	109	22	55.0	0	0.0	3	30.0	26	27	3	9	47	15.7

Chris Gatling   No. 25/F-C

Full name: Chris Raymond Gatling
HT: 6-10 **WT:** 225
Born: 9/3/67, Elizabeth, NJ
High school: Elizabeth (NJ)
College: Old Dominion

Gatling started at center in 23 of his last 2
games. He was 61.7 percent from the floo
over the season's final 48 games.

REGULAR SEASON		G	MIN	FG	FGx	3FG	3PTx	FT	FTx	REB	AST	STL	BLK	PTS	AVG
'91-92	GOLDEN STATE	54	612	117	56.8	0	0.0	72	66.1	182	16	31	36	306	5.7
'92-93	GOLDEN STATE	70	1248	249	53.9	0	0.0	150	72.5	320	40	44	53	648	9.3
'93-94	GOLDEN STATE	82	1296	271	58.8	0	0.0	129	62.0	397	41	40	63	671	8.2
	3 YR TOTALS	206	3156	637	56.4	0	0.0	351	67.0	899	97	115	152	1625	7.9
'93-94	RANK NBA Fs	1	83	60		2	78	78	58	112	52	102	75	23	66
'94-95	PROJECTIONS	82	1570	343	61.8	0	0.0	134	55.6	524	51	37	77	820	10.0

PLAYOFFS		G	MIN	FG	FGx	3FG	3PTx	FT	FTx	REB	AST	STL	BLK	PTS	AVG
'91-92	GOLDEN STATE	4	81	18	62.1	0	---	14	63.6	25	0	2	10	50	12.5
'93-94	GOLDEN STATE	3	54	8	61.5	0	---	10	76.9	17	4	2	1	26	8.7
	TOTALS	7	135	26	61.9	0	---	24	68.6	42	4	4	11	76	10.9

Keith Jennings   No. 2/G

Full name: Keith Russell Jennings
HT: 5-7 **WT:** 160
Born: 11/2/68, Culpepper, VA
High school: Culpepper (VA)
College: East Tennessee State

Coming off a knee injury in '92–93, Jenning
led the team in 3-point shooting percentage
and in assist-to-turnover ratio (2.9 to 1).

REGULAR SEASON		G	MIN	FG	FGx	3FG	3PTx	FT	FTx	REB	AST	STL	BLK	PTS	AVG
'92-93	GOLDEN STATE	8	136	25	59.5	5	55.6	14	77.8	11	23	4	0	69	8.6
'93-94	GOLDEN STATE	76	1097	138	40.4	56	37.1	100	83.3	89	218	65	0	432	5.7
	2 YR TOTALS	84	1233	163	42.4	61	38.1	114	82.6	100	241	69	0	501	6.0
'93-94	RANK NBA Gs	51	79	86	95	63	27	30	33	88	57	80	114	78	85
'94-95	PROJECTIONS	82	2058	137	21.1	80	18.6	158	88.8	167	470	183	0	512	6.2

PLAYOFFS		G	MIN	FG	FGx	3FG	3PTx	FT	FTx	REB	AST	STL	BLK	PTS	AVG
'93-94	GOLDEN STATE	3	39	4	30.8	1	20.0	6	85.7	5	4	1	0	15	5.0
	TOTALS	3	39	4	30.8	1	20.0	6	85.7	5	4	1	0	15	5.0

Ricky Pierce No.22/G

Full name: Ricky Charles Pierce
HT: 6-4 **WT:** 215
Born: 8/19/59, Dallas, TX
High school: South Garland (Garland, TX)
College: Walla Walla Comm. Coll./Rice
Pierce, a two-time Sixth Man award winner, had a variety of injury problems last season, but is still one of the NBA's best shooters.

REGULAR SEASON		G	MIN	FG	FGx	3FG	3PTx	FT	FTx	REB	AST	STL	BLK	PTS	AVG
'90-91	MIL-SEA	78	2167	561	48.5	46	39.7	430	91.3	191	168	60	13	1598	20.5
'91-92	SEATTLE	78	2658	620	47.5	33	26.8	417	91.6	233	241	86	20	1690	21.7
'92-93	SEATTLE	77	2218	524	48.9	42	37.2	313	88.9	192	220	100	7	1403	18.2
'93-94	SEATTLE	51	1022	272	47.1	6	18.8	189	89.6	83	91	42	5	739	14.5
12 YR TOTALS		767	19896	4725	50.0	192	30.1	2940	87.7	1930	1571	652	130	12582	16.4
'93-94	RANK NBA Gs	116	100	65	35	103	120	33	5	111	109	96	97	62	33
'94-95	PROJECTIONS	38	380	105	46.5	1	12.5	75	89.3	29	33	16	2	286	7.5

PLAYOFFS		G	MIN	FG	FGx	3FG	3PTx	FT	FTx	REB	AST	STL	BLK	PTS	AVG
'90-91	SEATTLE	5	112	19	33.3	3	30.0	16	94.1	14	4	4	1	57	11.4
'91-92	SEATTLE	9	316	63	48.1	3	27.3	47	87.0	22	28	5	1	176	19.6
'92-93	SEATTLE	19	578	123	45.6	12	40.0	79	89.8	46	42	12	4	337	17.7
'93-94	SEATTLE	5	74	14	45.2	0	---	12	70.6	5	3	1	0	40	8.0
TOTALS		89	2436	505	47.2	30	38.5	333	86.7	217	168	60	19	1373	15.4

Carlos Rogers No. 34/F-C

HT: 6-11 **WT:** 220
Born: 2/6/71
College: Tennessee State
Ohio Valley Conf. Player of the Year, Rogers was the only NCAA Division I player to rank in the top 15 in scoring (24.5 ppg), rebounding (11.5 rpg), field goal percentage (.614), and blocked shots (3.0 bpg).

REGULAR SEASON	G	MIN	FG	FGx	3FG	3PTx	FT	FTx	REB	AST	STL	BLK	PTS	AVG

ROOKIE -- NO NBA EXPERIENCE

Clifford Rozier No. 44/C-

HT: 6-11 **WT:** 245
Born: 10/31/72
College: Louisville

A deadly shooter, Rozier's .618 field-go
percentage led the Metro Conference ar
was eighth-best in the country. He average
18.1 points and 11.1 rebounds, second
both categories in the conference.

REGULAR SEASON	G	MIN	FG	FGx	3FG	3PTx	FT	FTx	REB	AST	STL	BLK	PTS	AV

ROOKIE -- NO NBA EXPERIENCE

Don Nelson Head Coach

Full name: Donald Arvid Nelson
HT: 6-6 **WT:** 210
Born: 5/15/40, Muskegon, MI
High school: Rock Island (IL)
College: Iowa

Nelson coached Dream Team II to the Worl
Championships this summer; it was only th
third time that the US team won the gold.

	REGULAR SEASON					PLAYOFFS			
YEAR	TEAM	W	L	PCT	FINISH	W	L	PCT	
'78-79	MILWAUKEE	38	44	.463	4th/Midwest Div.				
'79-80	MILWAUKEE	49	33	.598	1st/Midwest Div.	3	4	.429	lost Western Conf. semifinals to Seattle, 4-3
'80-81	MILWAUKEE	60	22	.732	1st/Central Div.	3	4	.429	lost Eastern Conf. semifinals to Philadelphia, 4-3
'81-82	MILWAUKEE	55	27	.671	1st/Central Div.	2	4	.333	lost Eastern Conf. semifinals to Philadelphia, 4-2
'82-83	MILWAUKEE	51	31	.622	1st/Central Div.	5	4	.556	lost Eastern Conf. finals to Philadelphia, 4-1
'83-84	MILWAUKEE	50	32	.610	1st/Central Div.	8	8	.500	lost Eastern Conf. finals to Boston, 4-1
'84-85	MILWAUKEE	59	23	.720	1st/Central Div.	2	5	.286	lost Eastern Conf. semifinals to Philadelphia, 4-0
'85-86	MILWAUKEE	57	25	.695	1st/Central Div.	7	7	.500	lost Eastern Conf. finals to Boston, 4-0
'86-87	MILWAUKEE	50	32	.610	3rd/Central Div.	6	6	.500	lost Eastern Conf. semifinals to Boston, 4-3
'88-89	GOLDEN STATE	43	39	.524	4th/Pacific Div.	4	4	.500	lost Western Conf. semifinals to Phoenix, 4-1
'89-90	GOLDEN STATE	37	45	.451	5th/Pacific Div.				
'90-91	GOLDEN STATE	44	38	.537	4th/Pacific Div.	4	5	.444	lost Western Conf. semifinals to LA Lakers, 4-1
'91-92	GOLDEN STATE	55	27	.671	2nd/Pacific Div.	1	3	.250	lost Western Conf. first round to Seattle, 3-1
'92-93	GOLDEN STATE	34	48	.415	6th/Pacific Div.				
'93-94	GOLDEN STATE	50	32	.610	3rd/Pacific Div.	0	3	.000	lost Western Conf. first round to Phoenix, 3-0
17 YR TOTALS		803	573	.584		50	61	.450	

Houston
ROCKETS

1994–95 Scouting Report

Frontcourt

1993–94 MVP Hakeem Olajuwon is unstoppable inside. He was third in the league in scoring (27.2 points per game), tenth in shooting percentage (53 percent), fourth in rebounding (11.9 per game), and second to Dikembe Mutombo in shotblocking (3.71 per game). At 6–10, small forward Robert Horry creates matchup problems for opponents, plays great defense, and has a variety of low-post moves. Power forward Otis Thorpe attacks the boards and is effective, if unpolished, under the basket. The bench features Mario Elie, a swingman who plays defense, and Carl Herrera, a good rebounder with outstanding leaping ability.

Backcourt

The starting backcourt consists of Vernon Maxwell and Kenny Smith. Maxwell has never been a reliable shooter, and Smith sometimes plays out of control. But Smith is the consistent shooter that Maxwell has never been, while Maxwell is a defensive stopper. Although Maxwell has point guard responsibilities, both men are good passers who can get the ball inside to Olajuwon, and neither is shy about shooting 3-pointers. Sam Cassell was increasingly a favorite of Coach Rudy Tomjanovich for his defense. He flourished in the NBA finals, and will see more playing time this season. Scott Brooks is quick, a good ballhandler, and an accurate shooter, but at 5–11, opponents can post him up and shoot over him.

Defense

Statistically, Houston is one of the best defensive teams in the NBA. The Rockets were fifth in points allowed (96.8) and third in field goal defense, limiting opponents to 44 percent shooting from the field. But the defense turns on Hakeem Olajuwon. He intimidates inside and forces teams to change shots. He's also the reason that Houston was fifth in the NBA in blocking shots. And he covers a lot of ground, so his teammates can go for steals that lead to transition baskets, knowing that they have Olajuwon as a backup. The Rockets aren't skilled at pressuring the ball; Houston ranked fourteenth in the NBA in stealing the ball and only twenty-third in forcing turnovers.

All rebounds are not created equal: Houston was dead last in the NBA in offensive rebounds (behind 25–57 Philadelphia and 20–62 Minnesota). They did lead the league, though, in defensive rebounds. In fact, the top five defensive rebounding teams in the NBA last season (Houston, San Antonio, Denver, New Jersey, and New York) had a collective record of 257–153, a .627 percentage.

1994–95 Prospects

The Rockets opened the season winning 15 in a row, tying the '48–49 Washington Capitols for the all-time best NBA start. They won their fifteenth game at Madison Square Garden, despite the Knicks' determination to thwart Houston's drive for the record. They demonstrated tremendous heart under pressure all season, overcoming a 0–2 deficit to defeat Phoenix in the Western Conference semifinals, and recovering from a 2–3 deficit to win the NBA title over the Knicks.

Houston is far from the most talented team in the league. But they have the NBA's most dominant player in Hakeem Olajuwon. No single player can defend Olajuwon, so Houston spaces the floor to make it difficult for opponents to double-team Olajuwon. If an opponent double-teams Olajuwon down low, someone is left unguarded on the perimeter. Last year, Houston set an NBA record with 429 3-point shots. There are 2 flaws to Houston's strategy. First, if the perimeter shooters are off, and the Rockets can't hit from outside, they'll give up long rebounds that lead to transition opportunities at the opponet's end. Second, with Olajuwon shooting fadeaways and his teammates cruising the perimeter looking for 3-pointers, Houston's offensive style sacrifices offensive rebounds.

Houston is a playoff lock for the upcoming season, but they're not well situated to repeat as NBA champs. They're still looking for consistent guard play. Kenny Smith was having problems at the end of last season, and Sam Cassell was up and down. If they hit a bad skid, they could be knocked off.

Team Directory

Owner: Leslie L. Alexander   President: Tod Leiweke

Vice president: Barry E. Somerstein Mgr., media services: Rose Pietrzak

1993–94 Review

WESTERN CONFERENCE						EASTERN CONFERENCE					
MIDWEST DIV.			PACIFIC DIV.			ATLANTIC DIV.			CENTRAL DIV.		
	W	L		W	L		W	L		W	L
HOU	-	-	SEA	2	2	NY	2	0	ATL	1	1
SAN	2	3	PHO	2	2	ORL	1	1	CHI	1	1
UTAH	3	3	GS	4	0	NJ	2	0	CLE	2	0
DEN	2	3	POR	4	0	MIA	2	0	IND	1	1
MIN	4	1	LAL	3	1	BOS	1	1	CHA	1	1
DAL	4	1	SAC	4	0	PHI	2	0	DET	2	0
			LAC	4	0	WAS	1	1	MIL	1	1
	15	11		23	5		11	3		9	5

1993–94 finish: 58–24 (35–6 home, 23–18 away), first in Midwest Div.

1994–95 Schedule

11/4	New Jersey	8:30 pm	1/5	Dallas	8:30 pm	3/3	@ Minn.	8:00 pm
11/5	@ Minn.	8:00 pm	1/7	Indiana	8:30 pm	3/5	@ San Ant.	1:00 pm
11/8	@ Cleveland	8:00 pm	1/11	Miami	8:30 pm	3/7	Phoenix	8:00 pm
11/9	@ Indiana	6:00 pm	1/13	San Ant.	8:30 pm	3/11	Dallas	8:30 pm
11/11	@ Boston	7:30 pm	1/14	@ Denver	9:00 pm	3/13	@ Atlanta	8:00 pm
11/12	@ New Jersey	8:00 pm	1/16	@ Minn.	8:00 pm	3/14	@ Phila.	7:30 pm
11/15	Sacra.	8:30 pm	1/19	New York	8:00 pm	3/16	Minn.	8:30 pm
11/17	Chicago	8:00 pm	1/20	@ Detroit	8:00 pm	3/19	Phila.	3:30 pm
11/19	@ Denver	9:00 pm	1/22	@ Chicago	1:00 pm	3/21	Seattle	8:30 pm
11/22	Portland	8:30 pm	1/24	@ Milw.	8:30 pm	3/23	Utah	8:30 pm
11/23	@ Orlando	7:30 pm	1/26	@ San Ant.	8:30 pm	3/24	@ Phoenix	9:00 pm
11/26	Seattle	8:30 pm	1/28	Minn.	8:30 pm	3/26	@ LA Lakers	10:00 pm
11/29	Denver	8:30 pm	1/31	Denver	8:30 pm	3/28	LA Lakers	8:30 pm
12/1	@ Gold. St.	10:30 pm	2/2	Utah	8:30 pm	3/30	@ LA Clip.	10:30 pm
12/2	@ LA Lakers	10:30 pm	2/5	@ Phoenix	3:30 pm	4/1	Milw.	8:30 pm
12/6	@ Seattle	8:00 pm	2/6	@ Portland	10:00 pm	4/4	@ Sacra.	10:30 pm
12/8	Charlotte	8:30 pm	2/8	@ Sacra.	10:30 pm	4/6	@ Gold. St.	10:30 pm
12/10	San Ant.	8:30 pm	2/9	@ LA Clip.	10:30 pm	4/7	@ Portland	10:00 pm
12/13	Wash.	8:30 pm	2/14	LA Clip.	8:30 pm	4/9	@ Denver	3:30 pm
12/15	LA Lakers	8:30 pm	2/16	@ Charlotte	8:00 pm	4/11	Dallas	8:30 pm
12/17	Boston	8:30 pm	2/17	@ Wash.	7:30 pm	4/13	Portland	8:30 pm
12/22	Phoenix	8:00 pm	2/19	@ New York	1:00 pm	4/15	Sacra.	8:30 pm
12/23	@ San Ant.	8:30 pm	2/21	San Ant.	8:00 pm	4/17	LA Clip.	8:30 pm
12/26	@ Miami	7:30 pm	2/23	Detroit	8:30 pm	4/19	@ Utah	9:00 pm
12/27	Atlanta	8:30 pm	2/25	Gold. St.	8:30 pm	4/20	@ Seattle	10:00 pm
12/29	Gold. St.	8:30 pm	2/27	Cleveland	8:30 pm	4/23	Utah	3:30 pm
12/30	@ Utah	9:00 pm	2/28	@ Dallas	8:30 pm			
01/3	@ Dallas	8:30 pm	3/2	Orlando	9:30 pm			

1993–94 Team Stats

NAME	G	MIN	FG	FGA	FG%	3FG	3FGA	3FG%	FT	FTA	FT%	ORB	TRB	AST	PF	STL	BLK	TO	PTS	AVG
Olajuwon	80	3277	894	1694	52.8	8	19	42.1	388	542	71.6	229	955	287	289	128	297	271	2184	27.3
Thorpe	82	2909	449	801	56.1	0	2	0.0	251	382	65.7	271	870	189	253	66	28	185	1149	14.0
Maxwell	75	2571	380	976	38.9	120	403	29.8	143	191	74.9	42	229	380	143	125	20	185	1023	13.6
Smith	78	2209	341	711	48.0	89	220	40.5	135	155	87.1	24	138	327	121	59	4	126	906	11.6
Jent	3	78	13	26	50.0	4	11	36.4	1	2	50.0	4	15	7	13	0	0	5	31	10.3
Horry	81	2370	322	702	45.9	44	136	32.4	115	157	73.2	128	440	231	186	119	75	137	803	9.9
Elie	67	1606	208	466	44.6	56	167	33.5	154	179	86.0	28	181	208	124	50	8	109	626	9.3
Cassell	66	1122	162	388	41.8	26	88	29.5	90	107	84.1	25	134	192	136	59	7	94	440	6.7
Brooks	73	1225	142	289	49.1	23	61	37.7	74	85	87.1	10	102	149	98	51	2	55	381	5.2
Herrera	75	1292	142	310	45.8	0	0	—	69	97	71.1	101	285	37	159	32	26	69	353	4.7
Robinson	6	55	10	20	50.0	2	8	25.0	3	8	37.5	4	10	6	8	7	0	10	25	4.2
Bullard	65	725	78	226	34.5	50	154	32.5	20	26	76.9	23	84	64	67	14	6	28	226	3.5
Petruska	22	92	20	46	43.5	7	15	46.7	6	8	75.0	9	31	1	15	2	3	15	53	2.4
Cureton	2	30	2	8	25.0	0	0	—	0	2	0.0	4	12	0	4	0	0	1	4	2.0
Riley	47	219	34	70	48.6	0	1	0.0	20	37	54.1	24	59	9	30	5	9	15	88	1.9
Rockets	82	19780	3197	6733	47.5	429	1285	33.4	1469	1978	74.3	926	3545	2087	1646	717	485	1338	8292	101.1
Opp.	82	19780	3152	7166	44.0	257	841	30.6	1377	1871	73.6	1138	3572	1901	1743	767	312	1221	7938	96.8

HISTORY

TITLES

1976–77 Central Div. champs   1992–93 Midwest Div. champs
1980–81 NBA Western Conf. champs 1993–94 Midwest Div. champs
1985–86 Midwest Div. champs   1993–94 NBA Western Conf. champs
1985–86 NBA Western Conf. champs 1993–94 NBA champs

ALL-TIME TEAM RECORDS

Career

Games	Calvin Murphy	1,002	1970–83
Total points	Calvin Murphy	17,949	1970–83
Field goals made	Calvin Murphy	7,274	1970–83
Field goals attempted	Calvin Murphy	15,030	1970–83
Free throws made	Calvin Murphy	3,445	1970–83
Free throws attempted	Hakeem Olajuwon	5,212	1984–94
Total rebounds	Hakeem Olajuwon	9,464	1984–94
Assists	Calvin Murphy	4,402	1970–83
Steals	Hakeem Olajuwon	1,448	1984–94

Season

Total points	Moses Malone	2,520	1981–82
Field goals made	Elvin Hayes	948	1970–71
Field goals attempted	Elvin Hayes	2,215	1970–71
Free throws made	Moses Malone	630	1981–82
Free throws attempted	Moses Malone	827	1981–82
Total rebounds	Moses Malone	1,444	1978–79
Assists	John Lucas	768	1977–78
Steals	Hakeem Olajuwon	213	1988–89

Game

Total points	Calvin Murphy	57	vs. New Jersey, 3/18/78
Field goals made	Calvin Murphy	24	vs. New Jersey, 3/18/78
Free throws made	Eric Floyd	22	vs. Golden State, 2/3/91
Total rebounds	Moses Malone	37	vs. New Orleans, 2/9/79
Assists	Art Williams	22	vs. Phoenix, 12/28/68
	Art Williams	22	vs. San Francisco, 2/14/70
	Allen Leavell	22	vs. New Jersey, 1/25/83
Steals	Calvin Murphy	9	vs. Boston, 12/14/73

LEADING COACHES

NAME	REGULAR SEASON				PLAYOFFS		
	YEARS	W	L	PCT	W	L	PCT
Bill Fitch	1983–88	216	194	.527	20	15	.571
Don Chaney	1988–92	164	134	.55	2	9	.182
Del Harris	1979–83	141	187	.43	15	16	.484
Rudy Tomjanovich	1992–94	129	65	.665	21	14	.6
John Egan	1973–76	129	152	.459	3	5	.375

Houston Rockets 1994–95 Roster

Head Coach: Rudy Tomjanovich

No.	Name	Pos.	Ht.	Wt.	Yrs.	Born	College
1	Scott Brooks	G	5-11	165	6	7/31/65	Cal-Irvine
50	Matt Bullard	F	6-10	235	5	6/5/67	Iowa
	Albert Burditt	F	6-8	230	R	NA	Texas
10	Sam Cassell	G	6-3	185	1	11/18/69	Florida State
35	Earl Cureton	F-C	6-9	215	14	9/3/57	Robert Morris
17	Mario Elie	F-G	6-5	210	4	11/26/63	Amer. International
7	Carl Herrera	F	6-9	225	3	12/14/66	Houston
25	Robert Horry	F	6-10	220	3	8/25/70	Alabama
21	Chris Jent	F	6-7	220	1	NA	Ohio State
11	Vernon Maxwell	G	6-4	190	6	9/12/65	Florida
34	Hakeem Olajuwon	C	7-0	255	10	1/21/63	Houston
30	Kenny Smith	G	6-3	170	7	3/8/65	North Carolina
33	Otis Thorpe	F	6-10	246	10	8/5/62	Providence

Arena Information

The Summit (16,279)
Tickets: 713-627-3101
Ticket prices: $65.50, $52.50, $37.50, $29.50, $22.50, $16.50, $11

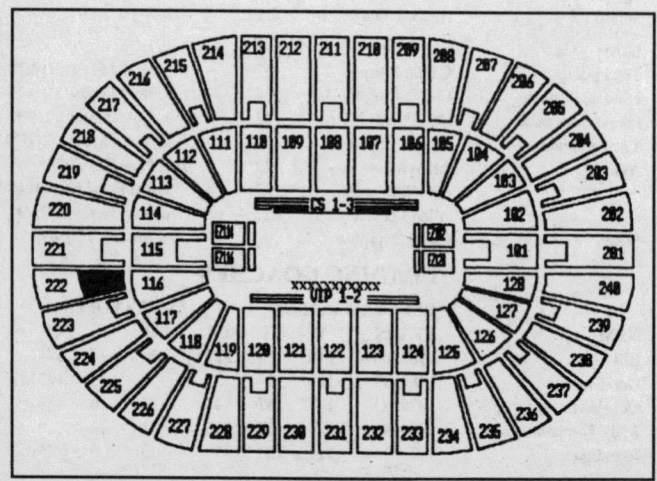

Robert Horry

No. 25/F

Full name: Robert K. Horry
HT: 6-10   **WT:** 220
Born: 8/25/70, Andalusia, AL
High school: Andalusia (AL)
College: Alabama

Robert Horry is destined to become one of the premier small forwards in the NBA. Horry has the same kind of leaping ability, defense, and offensive moves that you see in Scottie Pippen and Larry Nance. He's not the ballhandler that Pippen and Nance are, but he's a better shooter from 3-point range than Nance, and at 6-10 and 220 pounds, he's a better rebounder and shotblocker than Pippen. Opponents have trouble matching up with Horry defensively. Horry was Houston's third-leading rebounder and second leading shotblocker. In '92–93, Horry was the only NBA rookie on a winning team to play and start every game, until tendinitis in his right knee forced him to miss the final 3 games.

REGULAR SEASON		G	MIN	FG	FG%	3FG	3PT%	FT	FT%	REB	AST	STL	BLK	PTS	AVG
'92-93	HOUSTON	79	2330	323	47.4	12	25.5	143	71.5	392	191	80	83	801	10.1
'93-94	HOUSTON	81	2370	322	45.9	44	32.4	115	73.2	440	231	119	75	803	9.9
	2 YR TOTALS	160	4700	645	46.6	56	30.6	258	72.3	832	422	199	158	1604	10.0
'93-94	RANK NBA Fs	15	33	50	80	18	29	65	54	42	17	5	19	50	58
'94-95	PROJECTIONS	82	2410	320	44.3	89	39.0	84	75.0	489	272	159	67	813	9.9

PLAYOFFS		G	MIN	FG	FG%	3FG	3PT%	FT	FT%	REB	AST	STL	BLK	PTS	AVG
'92-93	HOUSTON	12	374	47	46.5	9	30.0	20	74.1	62	38	18	16	123	10.3
'93-94	HOUSTON	23	778	98	43.4	34	38.2	39	76.5	141	82	35	20	269	11.7
	TOTALS	35	1152	145	44.3	43	36.1	59	75.6	203	120	53	36	392	11.2

Vernon Maxwell

No. 11/G

HT: 6-4   **WT:** 190
Born: 9/12/65, Gainesville, FL
High school: Buchholz (Gainesville)
College: Florida

Maxwell led the Rockets in assists and was the team's third-leading scorer. Maxwell has incredible quickness and is a good finisher on transition baskets. He's also fearless driving the to the basket, and he can create his own shots. And he's a prolific 3-point shooter; teams that ignore him on the perimeter to double on Hakeem do so at their own peril. He shoots often, but not well; his career field goal percentage is 41.2 percent, and he was just 38.9 percent from the field last season. Known as one of the league's better defensive guards, Maxwell regularly shuts down the opponent's shooting guard. He victimized Phoenix's Dan Majerle in the Western Conference semifinals.

REGULAR SEASON		G	MIN	FG	FGx	3FG	3PTx	FT	FTx	REB	AST	STL	BLK	PTS	AVG
'88-89	SAN ANTONIO	79	2065	357	43.2	32	24.8	181	74.5	202	301	86	8	927	11.7
'89-90	SA-HOU	79	1987	275	43.9	28	26.7	136	64.5	228	296	84	10	714	9.0
'90-91	HOUSTON	82	2870	504	40.4	172	33.7	217	73.3	238	303	127	15	1397	17.0
'91-92	HOUSTON	80	2700	502	41.3	162	34.2	206	77.2	243	326	104	28	1372	17.2
'92-93	HOUSTON	71	2251	349	40.7	120	33.2	164	71.9	221	297	86	8	982	13.8
'93-94	HOUSTON	75	2571	380	38.9	120	29.8	143	74.9	229	380	125	20	1023	13.6
6 YR TOTALS		466	14444	2367	41.2	634	32.0	1047	72.9	1361	1903	612	89	6415	13.8
'93-94 RANK NBA Gs		65	31	44	123	11	81	55	93	41	29	21	35	41	41
'94-95 PROJECTIONS		75	2646	370	37.8	118	28.2	121	76.1	226	420	141	24	979	13.1

PLAYOFFS		G	MIN	FG	FGx	3FG	3PTx	FT	FTx	REB	AST	STL	BLK	PTS	AVG
'89-90	HOUSTON	4	159	30	37.0	8	30.8	11	52.4	12	17	5	0	79	19.8
'90-91	HOUSTON	3	113	23	41.1	9	33.3	1	50.0	8	9	2	1	56	18.7
'92-93	HOUSTON	9	308	47	40.2	11	23.9	21	87.5	22	32	11	2	126	14.0
'93-94	HOUSTON	23	880	118	37.6	45	32.6	37	68.5	81	96	20	2	318	13.8
TOTALS		39	1460	218	38.4	73	30.8	70	69.3	123	154	38	5	579	14.8

Hakeem Olajuwon

No. 34/C

Full name: Hakeem Abdul Olajuwon
HT: 7-0   **WT:** 255
Born: 1/21/63, Lagos, Nigeria
High school: Moslem Teachers College (Lagos, Nigeria)
College: Houston

The most dominant center in the NBA today, Olajuwon was Mr. Everything last season: MVP, Defensive Player of the Year, first team NBA All-Star, and a unanimous pick as finals MVP. Big, agile, and quick, Olajuwon is a great shotblocker. He's also a tremendous competitor. The Rockets are NBA champions because he outplayed Patrick Ewing in the NBA finals. In game 7, Olajuwon had 25 points, 10 rebounds, 7 assists, and 3 blocked shots. Ewing had 17 points, 10 rebounds, 1 assist, and 2 blocked shots.

REGULAR SEASON		G	MIN	FG	FGx	3FG	3PTx	FT	FTx	REB	AST	STL	BLK	PTS	AVG
'84-85	HOUSTON	82	2914	677	53.8	0	---	338	61.3	974	111	99	220	1692	20.6
'85-86	HOUSTON	68	2467	625	52.6	0	---	347	64.5	781	137	134	231	1597	23.5
'86-87	HOUSTON	75	2760	677	50.8	1	20.0	400	70.2	858	220	140	254	1755	23.4
'87-88	HOUSTON	79	2825	712	51.4	0	0.0	381	69.5	959	163	162	214	1805	22.8
'88-89	HOUSTON	82	3024	790	50.8	0	0.0	454	69.6	1105	149	213	282	2034	24.8
'89-90	HOUSTON	82	3124	806	50.1	1	16.7	382	71.3	1149	234	174	376	1995	24.3
'90-91	HOUSTON	56	2062	487	50.8	0	0.0	213	76.9	770	131	121	221	1187	21.2
'91-92	HOUSTON	70	2636	591	50.2	0	0.0	328	76.6	845	157	127	304	1510	21.6
'92-93	HOUSTON	82	3242	848	52.9	0	0.0	444	77.9	1068	291	150	342	2140	26.1
'93-94	HOUSTON	80	3277	894	52.8	8	42.1	388	71.6	955	287	128	297	2184	27.3
	10 YR TOTALS	756	28331	7107	51.6	10	17.5	3675	70.5	9464	1880	1448	2741	17899	23.7
'93-94	RANK NBA Cs	8	1	2	14	3	3	5	21	3	3	2	2	3	3
'94-95	PROJECTIONS	82	3477	995	53.4	17	63.0	396	68.9	927	325	116	280	2403	29.3

PLAYOFFS		G	MIN	FG	FGx	3FG	3PTx	FT	FTx	REB	AST	STL	BLK	PTS	AVG
'84-85	HOUSTON	5	187	42	47.7	0	---	22	47.8	65	7	7	13	106	21.2
'85-86	HOUSTON	20	766	205	53.0	0	0.0	127	63.8	236	39	40	69	537	26.9
'86-87	HOUSTON	10	389	110	61.5	0	0.0	72	74.2	113	25	13	43	292	29.2
'87-88	HOUSTON	4	162	56	57.1	0	0.0	38	88.4	67	7	9	11	150	37.5
'88-89	HOUSTON	4	162	42	51.9	0	---	17	68.0	52	12	10	11	101	25.3
'89-90	HOUSTON	4	161	31	44.3	0	---	12	70.6	46	8	10	23	74	18.5
'90-91	HOUSTON	3	129	26	57.8	0	0.0	14	82.4	44	6	4	8	66	22.0
'92-93	HOUSTON	12	518	123	51.7	0	0.0	62	82.7	168	57	21	59	308	25.7
'93-94	HOUSTON	23	989	267	51.9	2	50.0	128	79.5	254	98	40	92	664	28.9
	TOTALS	85	3463	902	53.1	2	22.2	492	72.4	1045	259	154	329	2298	27.0

Kenny Smith

No. 30/C

Full name: Kenneth Smith
HT: 6-3   **WT:** 170
Born: 3/8/65, Queens, NY
High school: Archbishop Molloy (Queens)
College: North Carolina

Last season, Kenny Smith was second on the team in assists and tied for the team lead in free throw shooting. Smith can play either guard position. As a point guard, Smith has a talent for distributing the ball without monopolizing the dribble. And he's one of the most accurate shooting guards in the NBA. (He shot 52 percent from the field in '92–93, tops among all NBA guards. He's a good penetrator and a fine leaper. Smith is deadly from 3-point range. He's shot better than 40 percent from 3-point range for 2 straight seasons. He's not a strong defender, and generally switches off on defense to cover the opponent's smaller guard. Smith has also had a problem with playing out of control.

REGULAR SEASON		G	MIN	FG	FGx	3FG	3PTx	FT	FTx	REB	AST	STL	BLK	PTS	AVG
'87-88	SACRAMENTO	61	2170	331	47.7	12	30.8	167	81.9	138	434	92	8	841	13.8
'88-89	SACRAMENTO	81	3145	547	46.2	46	35.9	263	73.7	226	621	102	7	1403	17.3
'89-90	SAC-ATL	79	2421	378	46.6	26	31.3	161	82.1	157	445	79	8	943	11.9
'90-91	HOUSTON	78	2699	522	52.0	49	36.3	287	84.4	163	554	106	11	1380	17.7
'91-92	HOUSTON	81	2735	432	47.5	54	39.4	219	86.6	177	562	104	7	1137	14.0
'92-93	HOUSTON	82	2422	367	52.0	96	43.8	195	87.8	160	446	80	7	1065	13.0
'93-94	HOUSTON	78	2209	341	48.0	89	40.5	135	87.1	138	327	59	4	906	11.6
7 YR TOTALS		540	17801	2938	48.5	372	38.7	1427	82.6	1159	3389	622	52	7675	14.2
'93-94	RANK NBA Gs	48	48	52	27	18	15	62	12	82	41	78	102	50	54
'94-95	PROJECTIONS	77	2036	304	46.8	96	40.5	101	87.8	125	254	45	2	805	10.5

PLAYOFFS		G	MIN	FG	FGx	3FG	3PTx	FT	FTx	REB	AST	STL	BLK	PTS	AVG
'90-91	HOUSTON	3	113	18	47.4	2	50.0	8	88.9	8	24	4	1	46	15.3
'92-93	HOUSTON	12	391	63	49.2	23	50.0	28	77.8	24	50	9	1	177	14.8
'93-94	HOUSTON	23	696	86	45.5	34	44.7	42	80.8	54	94	22	4	248	10.8
TOTALS		38	1200	167	47.0	59	46.8	78	80.4	86	168	35	6	471	12.4

Otis Thorpe

No. 33/F

Full name: Otis Henry Thorpe
HT: 6-10   **WT:** 246
Born: 8/5/62, Boynton Beach, FL
High school: Lake Worth
Community (FL)
College: Providence

Thorpe was Houston's second-leading scorer and rebounder. He was third in the NBA in field goal percentage, and fifteenth in the league in rebounding. In fact, Thorpe's career field goal percentage ranks in the NBA's all-time top 10. He's a hard-working player who rebounds and plays defense. Thorpe moves well on defense and can body up his opponent. Despite his high shooting percentage, Thorpe is not a skilled low-post player. He gets his points from putbacks off the offensive glass, and a one-dribble drive and lefthanded dunk from the right side. He's not much of a shotblocker, despite standing 6–10, because he has relatively short arms. Thorpe also has trouble shooting free throws.

REGULAR SEASON		G	MIN	FG	FG%	3FG	3PT%	FT	FT%	REB	AST	STL	BLK	PTS	AVG
'84-85	KANSAS CITY	82	1918	411	60.0	0	0.0	230	62.0	556	111	34	37	1052	12.8
'85-86	SACRAMENTO	75	1675	289	58.7	0	---	164	66.1	420	84	35	34	742	9.9
'86-87	SACRAMENTO	82	2956	567	54.0	0	0.0	413	76.1	819	201	46	60	1547	18.9
'87-88	SACRAMENTO	82	3072	622	50.7	0	0.0	460	75.5	837	266	62	56	1704	20.8
'88-89	HOUSTON	82	3135	521	54.2	0	0.0	328	72.9	787	202	82	37	1370	16.7
'89-90	HOUSTON	82	2947	547	54.8	0	0.0	307	68.8	734	261	66	24	1401	17.1
'90-91	HOUSTON	82	3039	549	55.6	3	42.9	334	69.6	846	197	73	20	1435	17.5
'91-92	HOUSTON	82	3056	558	59.2	0	0.0	304	65.7	862	250	52	37	1420	17.3
'92-93	HOUSTON	72	2357	385	55.8	0	0.0	153	59.8	589	181	43	19	923	12.8
'93-94	HOUSTON	82	2909	449	56.1	0	0.0	251	65.7	870	189	66	28	1149	14.0
	10 YR TOTALS	803	27064	4898	55.4	3	7.3	2944	69.3	7320	1942	559	352	12743	15.9
'93-94	RANK NBA Fs	1	6	22	5	78	78	17	103	5	27	41	77	23	28
'94-95	PROJECTIONS	82	3015	436	55.9	0	0.0	263	66.6	960	176	74	30	1135	13.8

PLAYOFFS		G	MIN	FG	FG%	3FG	3PT%	FT	FT%	REB	AST	STL	BLK	PTS	AVG
'85-86	SACRAMENTO	3	35	3	23.1	0	---	6	46.2	12	0	1	0	12	4.0
'88-89	HOUSTON	4	152	24	64.9	0	---	16	76.2	20	12	5	1	64	16.0
'89-90	HOUSTON	4	164	27	60.0	0	---	26	68.4	33	7	5	0	80	20.0
'90-91	HOUSTON	3	116	22	57.9	0	---	3	50.0	25	8	2	0	47	15.7
'92-93	HOUSTON	12	419	73	63.5	0	---	28	65.1	103	31	6	1	174	14.5
'93-94	HOUSTON	23	854	111	57.2	1	50.0	38	56.7	228	54	13	10	261	11.3
	TOTALS	49	1740	260	58.8	1	50.0	117	62.2	421	112	31	13	638	13.0

Scott Brooks   No. 1/C

Full name: Scott William Brooks
HT: 5-11 **WT:** 165
Born: 7/31/65, French Camp, CA
High school: East Union (Manteca, CA)
College: Cal-Irvine
Brooks is an intense competitor who thrive
in a running game. He's a good ballhandle
but his size gives him problems on defense.

REGULAR SEASON		G	MIN	FG	FG%	3FG	3PT%	FT	FT%	REB	AST	STL	BLK	PTS	AVG
'90-91	MINNESOTA	80	980	159	43.0	45	33.3	61	84.7	72	204	53	5	424	5.3
'91-92	MINNESOTA	82	1082	167	44.7	32	35.6	51	81.0	99	205	66	7	417	5.1
'92-93	HOUSTON	82	1516	183	47.5	41	41.4	112	83.0	99	243	79	3	519	6.3
'93-94	HOUSTON	73	1225	142	49.1	23	37.7	74	87.1	102	149	51	2	381	5.2
6 YR TOTALS		471	7150	926	44.8	227	36.8	409	85.0	530	1314	365	20	2488	5.3
'93-94	RANK NBA Gs	71	90	101	16	69	31	94	13	102	85	90	115	101	108
'94-95	PROJECTIONS	69	1206	125	51.0	15	38.5	71	88.8	107	109	42	1	336	4.9

PLAYOFFS		G	MIN	FG	FG%	3FG	3PT%	FT	FT%	REB	AST	STL	BLK	PTS	AVG
'92-93	HOUSTON	12	197	16	38.1	5	38.5	10	76.9	10	31	9	0	47	3.9
'93-94	HOUSTON	5	23	5	83.3	1	100.0	0	0.0	2	3	0	0	11	2.2
	TOTALS	29	340	28	38.4	10	43.5	18	72.0	24	55	12	0	84	2.9

Matt Bullard   No. 50/F

Full name: Matthew Gordon Bullard
HT: 6-10 **WT:** 235
Born: 6/5/67, West Des Moines, IA
High school: Valley (West Des Moines)
College: Iowa
Bullard is a big man whose game revolve
around his 3-point shooting accuracy. He ha
problems on defense because he's slow.

REGULAR SEASON		G	MIN	FG	FG%	3FG	3PT%	FT	FT%	REB	AST	STL	BLK	PTS	AVG
'90-91	HOUSTON	18	63	14	45.2	0	0.0	11	64.7	14	2	3	0	39	2.2
'91-92	HOUSTON	80	1278	205	45.9	64	38.6	38	76.0	223	75	26	21	512	6.4
'92-93	HOUSTON	79	1356	213	43.1	91	37.4	58	78.4	222	110	30	11	575	7.3
'93-94	HOUSTON	65	725	78	34.5	50	32.5	20	76.9	84	64	14	6	226	3.5
4 YR TOTALS		242	3422	510	42.6	205	36.2	127	76.0	543	251	73	38	1352	5.6
'93-94	RANK NBA Fs	96	113	115	135	14	28	127	31	126	81	124	130	112	118
'94-95	PROJECTIONS	63	496	38	28.6	42	33.1	2	100.0	39	51	7	4	120	1.9

PLAYOFFS		G	MIN	FG	FG%	3FG	3PT%	FT	FT%	REB	AST	STL	BLK	PTS	AVG
'92-93	HOUSTON	12	169	20	47.6	15	53.6	6	100.0	23	13	4	5	61	5.1
'93-94	HOUSTON	10	55	4	21.1	2	20.0	6	75.0	10	0	1	2	16	1.6
	TOTALS	22	224	24	39.3	17	44.7	12	85.7	33	13	5	7	77	3.5

Sam Cassell No. 10/G

Full name: Samuel James Cassell
HT: 6-3 **WT:** 185
Born: 11/18/69, Baltimore, MD
High school: Dunbar (Baltimore)
College: Florida State

Cassell saw a lot of fourth quarter action last season. He plays tough defense and creates his own shots.

REGULAR SEASON	G	MIN	FG	FGx	3FG	3PTx	FT	FTx	REB	AST	STL	BLK	PTS	AVG
'93-94 HOUSTON	66	1122	162	41.8	26	29.5	90	84.1	134	192	59	7	440	6.7
1 YR TOTALS	66	1122	162	41.8	26	29.5	90	84.1	134	192	59	7	440	6.7
'93-94 RANK NBA Gs	91	94	94	96	66	82	84	22	84	74	78	88	92	94

PLAYOFFS	G	MIN	FG	FGx	3FG	3PTx	FT	FTx	REB	AST	STL	BLK	PTS	AVG
'93-94 HOUSTON	22	478	63	39.4	17	37.8	64	86.5	59	93	21	5	207	9.4
TOTALS	22	478	63	39.4	17	37.8	64	86.5	59	93	21	5	207	9.4

Mario Elie No. 17/F-G

Full name: Mario Antoine Elie
HT: 6-5 **WT:** 210
Born: 11/26/63, New York, NY
High school: Power Memorial (New York)
College: American International

Elie can play shooting guard or small forward. He's a good defender, who can stick the perimeter jumper on offense.

REGULAR SEASON	G	MIN	FG	FGx	3FG	3PTx	FT	FTx	REB	AST	STL	BLK	PTS	AVG
'90-91 PHILA-GS	33	644	79	49.7	4	40.0	75	84.3	110	45	19	10	237	7.2
'91-92 GOLDEN STATE	79	1677	221	52.1	23	32.9	155	85.2	227	174	68	15	620	7.8
'92-93 PORTLAND	82	1757	240	45.8	45	34.9	183	85.5	216	177	74	20	708	8.6
'93-94 HOUSTON	67	1606	208	44.6	56	33.5	154	86.0	181	208	50	8	626	9.3
4 YR TOTALS	261	5684	748	47.6	128	34.0	567	85.4	734	604	211	53	2191	8.4
'93-94 RANK NBA Fs	88	64	69	96	11	21	49	4	107	22	63	124	65	62
'94-95 PROJECTIONS	64	1651	209	42.4	72	32.4	151	86.8	164	248	43	2	641	10.0

PLAYOFFS	G	MIN	FG	FGx	3FG	3PTx	FT	FTx	REB	AST	STL	BLK	PTS	AVG
'90-91 GOLDEN STATE	9	197	28	50.0	4	100.0	27	84.4	32	13	5	1	84	9.3
'91-92 GOLDEN STATE	4	80	23	63.9	2	100.0	2	66.7	22	10	5	.0	50	12.5
'92-93 PORTLAND	4	52	5	50.0	2	100.0	8	88.9	6	4	2	1	20	5.0
'93-94 HOUSTON	23	382	42	39.6	10	31.3	40	85.1	40	38	8	3	134	5.8
TOTALS	40	711	98	47.1	15	40.5	77	84.6	100	65	20	5	288	7.2

Carl Herrera   No. 7/F

Full name: Carl Victor Herrera
HT: 6-9   **WT:** 225
Born: 12/14/66, Trinidad and Tobago
High school: Simon Bolivar (Caracas, Ven.)
College: Houston

Herrera is a tough rebounder who can score when he gets the ball inside. He's also got decent range from the field.

REGULAR SEASON		G	MIN	FG	FG%	3FG	3PT%	FT	FT%	REB	AST	STL	BLK	PTS	AVG
'91-92	HOUSTON	43	566	83	51.6	0	0.0	25	56.8	99	27	16	25	191	4.4
'92-93	HOUSTON	81	1800	240	54.1	0	0.0	125	71.0	454	61	47	35	605	7.5
'93-94	HOUSTON	75	1292	142	45.8	0	---	69	71.1	285	37	32	26	353	4.7
	3 YR TOTALS	199	3658	465	50.8	0	0.0	219	69.1	838	125	95	86	1149	5.8
'93-94	RANK NBA Fs	55	84	94	81	78	78	93	70	73	103	89	82	96	107
'94-95	PROJECTIONS	80	1387	126	40.3	0	0.0	65	74.7	300	29	32	20	317	4.0

PLAYOFFS		G	MIN	FG	FG%	3FG	3PT%	FT	FT%	REB	AST	STL	BLK	PTS	AVG
'92-93	HOUSTON	12	195	22	38.6	0	0.0	12	60.0	45	7	3	2	56	4.7
'93-94	HOUSTON	16	248	31	53.4	0	---	13	81.3	45	3	5	3	75	4.7
	TOTALS	28	443	53	46.1	0	0.0	25	69.4	90	10	8	5	131	4.7

R. Tomjanovich Head Coach

Full name: Rudolph Tomjanovich
HT: 6-8   **WT:** 220
Born: 11/24/48, Hamtramck, MI
High school: Hamtramck (MI)
College: Michigan

If NBA coaching is about motivating players, Tomjanovich is a first-rate NBA coach. Down 0–2 in the West semifinals, his team never quit.

	REGULAR SEASON				PLAYOFFS			
YEAR	TEAM	W	L	PCT	FINISH	W	L	PCT
'91-92	HOUSTON	16	14	.533	3rd/Midwest Div.			
'92-93	HOUSTON	55	27	.671	1st/Midwest Div.	6	6	.500	lost Western Conf. semifinals to Seattle, 4-3
'93-94	HOUSTON	58	24	.707	1st/Midwest Div.	15	8	.652	won NBA Finals over New York, 4-3
	3 YR TOTALS	129	65	.665		21	14	.600

Indiana
PACERS

1994–95 Scouting Report

Frontcourt

Rik Smits had a good season. He's a scorer at center, but he's not good at the other things you look for from a center: rebounding, shot blocking, and defense. Dale Davis starts at power forward; Davis is a rebounding machine (10.9 RPG) who can also block shots and is a dependable, if not flashy, scorer from the low post. Derrick McKey starts at small forward; he played great defense while contributing on offense with 12 points, 5.3 rebounds, and 4.3 assists per game. F-C Antonio Davis was the first big man off the Indiana bench, averaging 14.5 points, 11.7 rebounds and 1.9 blocks per 40 minutes. Sam Mitchell is a good defender off the bench at small forward, without a small forward's outside shot. Scott Haskin ('93's top draft pick) will hope to play more at center and power forward this season. He didn't play much last season, but averaged 11.8 rebounds per 40 minutes. F Greg Minor came over in the Mark Jackson deal; he was a great shooter in college.

Backcourt

Indiana has one of the deepest backcourts in the league. Reggie Miller was one of the best guards in the NBA last year. He was the only player in the league to shoot better than 50 percent from the field, 40 percent from 3-point range, and 90 percent from the foul line. Mark Jackson will take over the point duties for the Pacers this season. Jackson doesn't score much, although he's got a good outside shot, but he's a great playmaker. Byron Scott is also available at shooting guard; a pure offensive player, he averaged 10.4 points per game (fifth on the team), despite averaging less than 18 minutes per game. Vern Fleming is available off the bench to play shooting guard or point guard; he's a much better scorer penetrating than he is shooting from outside. Haywoode Workman will back up Jackson;

he started at point or Indiana last season; he averaged 6.2 assists and only 2.3 turnovers per game.

Defense

Larry Brown came to Indiana stressing defense and rebounding, and the Pacers responded. Indiana plays a rugged brand of defense. Surprisingly, Indiana was eighth in the league in shotblocking, with one more blocked shot than Orlando and Shaquille O'Neal. Teams averaged 97.5 points against the Pacers, eighth lowest in the NBA. Indiana limited opponents to 6,614 FG attempts, fifth lowest in the NBA. Opposing teams shot 45 percent from the floor against Indiana, sixth lowest in the league. They were a so-so team in disrupting their opponents' offenses, ranking fifteenth in the NBA in stealing the ball and eleventh in the league in forcing turnovers. They won't be much different this year; neither Miller nor Jackson is known as a defensive stopper.

1994-95 Prospects

The Pacers were the hottest team in the league at the end of last season, winning their final eight regular season games and going 7-6 in the playoffs. They lost to the Knicks in the Eastern Conference finals, 4 games to 3.

Indiana is in a position to build upon last season's late success. They were just 21-26 vs. playoff teams last season, and should be at least .500 vs. those teams this season. They play good defense and were second in the NBA in shooting percentage from the field (46.8 percent). Their 36.8 percentage from 3-point range was tops among playoff teams. And they're decent rebounders, too; they had just 6 fewer rebounds than tenth place Houston last season. Their biggest hole has been a lack of a scoring forward off the bench, but Greg Minor might develop into the player they need to fill that hole.

Unless Larry Brown leaves town (and with him, that's always a possibility) or Reggie Miller suffers a serious injury, Indiana is a playoff lock. They figure to finish 52-30 this season, and that should be good enough to win the NBA Central Division. And with their brand of defense, they'll be a threat to go to the NBA finals.

Team Directory

Owner: Melvin Simon
President: Donnie Walsh
Dir., player personnel: Billy Knight

Owner: Herbert Simon
VP, basketball oper.: George Irvine
VP, adm. & media rel.: Dale Ratermann

1993–94 Review

EASTERN CONFERENCE						WESTERN CONFERENCE					
ATLANTIC DIV.		CENTRAL DIV.				MIDWEST DIV.			PACIFIC DIV.		
	W	L		W	L		W	L		W	L
NY	0	4	ATL	2	3	HOU	1	1	SEA	1	1
ORL	2	2	CHI	1	4	SAN	0	2	PHO	1	1
NJ	3	1	CLE	3	2	UTAH	1	1	GS	1	1
MIA	3	1	IND	-	-	DEN	1	1	POR	1	1
BOS	4	0	CHA	2	2	MIN	2	0	LAL	0	2
PHI	2	2	DET	4	1	DAL	2	0	SAC	2	0
WAS	3	1	MIL	3	1				LAC	2	0
	17	11		15	13		7	5		8	6

1993–94 finish: 47–35 (29–12 home, 18–23 away), third in Central Div.

1994–95 Team Schedule

11/4	@ Atlanta	7:30 pm	1/6	@ Dallas	8:30 pm	3/4	Boston		7:30 pm
11/5	Boston	7:30 pm	1/7	@ Houston	8:30 pm	3/7	@ San Ant.		8:30 pm
11/9	Houston	6:00 pm	1/10	@ New York	8:00 pm	3/9	@ Sacra.		10:30 pm
11/10	@ Detroit	7:30 pm	1/11	@ Boston	7:30 pm	3/10	@ Phoenix		9:00 pm
11/12	@ Cleveland	7:30 pm	1/13	@ Wash.	7:30 pm	3/13	@ LA Lakers	10:30 pm
11/15	@ Milw.	8:30 pm	1/14	Milw.	7:30 pm	3/15	Milw.		7:30 pm
11/18	Seattle	8:00 pm	1/16	Utah	6:00 pm	3/17	Orlando		7:30 pm
11/19	@ Charlotte	7:30 pm	1/18	LA Lakers	7:30 pm	3/19	Chicago		12:00 pm
11/24	Gold. St.	8:00 pm	1/20	Atlanta	7:30 pm	3/21	@ Miami		7:30 pm
11/25	Milw.	7:30 pm	1/22	San Ant.	2:30 pm	3/22	LA Clip.		7:30 pm
11/27	@ Portland	10:00 pm	1/24	@ Miami	7:30 pm	3/24	Sacra.		7:30 pm
11/28	@ Seattle	10:00 pm	1/26	Phoenix	7:30 pm	3/25	@ Phila.		7:30 pm
12/1	@ LA Clip.	10:30 pm	1/28	Phila.	7:30 pm	3/27	New Jersey		7:30 pm
12/3	@ Gold. St.	10:30 pm	2/1	Cleveland	7:30 pm	3/29	Cleveland		7:30 pm
12/6	Detroit	7:30 pm	2/3	Orlando	7:30 pm	3/31	Denver		7:30 pm
12/9	@ Phila.	7:30 pm	2/4	@ Cleveland	7:30 pm	4/2	Portland		3:30 pm
12/10	Miami	7:30 pm	2/7	@ Charlotte	8:00 pm	4/4	@ New York	7:30 pm
12/13	@ Cleveland	7:30 pm	2/8	New York	7:30 pm	4/5	Wash.		7:30 pm
12/14	Atlanta	7:30 pm	2/14	@ Orlando	7:30 pm	4/7	@ Atlanta		8:00 pm
12/16	Charlotte	7:30 pm	2/15	Detroit	7:30 pm	4/9	Charlotte		1:00 pm
12/20	@ Charlotte	7:30 pm	2/17	@ Minn.	8:00 pm	4/11	@ Chicago		8:30 pm
12/21	Chicago	7:30 pm	2/19	Miami	2:30 pm	4/14	New York		8:00 pm
12/23	@ Chicago	8:00 pm	2/22	@ New Jersey	7:30 pm	4/16	Minn.		3:30 pm
12/27	@ Denver	9:00 pm	2/24	@ Milw.	8:30 pm	4/19	Phila.		8:30 pm
12/28	@ Utah	9:00 pm	2/26	Dallas	2:30 pm	4/21	@ Orlando		8:00 pm
12/30	New Jersey	7:30 pm	2/27	@ Boston	7:30 pm	4/23	Atlanta		3:30 pm
01/3	@ New Jersey	7:30 pm	3/1	@ Detroit	7:30 pm				
01/4	Wash.	7:30 pm	3/3	@ Wash.	7:30 pm				

1993–94 Team Stats

NAME	G	MIN	FG	FGA	FG%	3FG	3FGA	3FG%	FT	FTA	FT%	ORB	TRB	AST	PF	STL	BLK	TO	PTS	AVG
Miller	79	2638	524	1042	50.3	123	292	42.1	403	444	90.8	30	212	248	193	119	24	175	1574	19.9
Smits	78	2113	493	923	53.4	0	1	0.0	238	300	79.3	135	483	156	281	49	82	151	1224	15.7
McKey	76	2613	355	710	50.0	9	31	29.0	192	254	75.6	129	402	327	248	111	49	228	911	12.0
D. Davis	66	2292	308	582	52.9	0	1	0.0	155	294	52.7	280	718	100	214	48	106	102	771	11.7
Scott	67	1197	256	548	46.7	27	74	36.5	157	195	80.5	19	110	133	80	62	9	103	696	10.4
Richardson	37	1022	160	354	45.2	3	12	25.0	47	77	61.0	28	110	237	78	32	3	88	370	10.0
A. Davis	81	1732	216	425	50.8	0	1	0.0	194	302	64.2	190	505	55	189	45	84	107	626	7.7
Workman	65	1714	195	460	42.4	18	56	32.1	93	116	80.2	32	204	404	152	85	4	151	501	7.7
Sealy	43	623	111	274	40.5	4	16	25.0	59	87	67.8	43	118	48	84	31	8	51	285	6.6
Fleming	55	1053	147	318	46.2	0	4	0.0	64	87	73.6	27	123	173	98	40	6	87	358	6.5
Williams	68	982	191	391	48.8	0	4	0.0	45	64	70.3	93	205	52	99	24	49	45	427	6.3
Mitchell	75	1084	140	306	45.8	0	5	0.0	82	110	74.5	71	190	65	152	33	9	50	362	4.8
Conner	11	169	14	38	36.8	0	3	0.0	3	6	50.0	10	24	31	12	14	1	9	31	2.8
Paddio	7	55	9	23	39.1	0	0	—	1	2	50.0	0	5	4	4	2	0	4	19	2.7
Thompson	30	282	27	77	35.1	0	0	—	16	30	53.3	26	75	16	59	10	8	23	70	2.3
Haskin	27	186	21	45	46.7	0	0	—	13	19	68.4	17	55	6	33	2	15	13	55	2.0
Pacers	82	19755	3167	6516	48.6	184	500	36.8	1762	2387	73.8	1130	3539	2055	1974	706	457	1440	8280	101.0
Opp.	82	19755	2978	6614	45.0	273	815	33.5	1768	2422	73.0	1132	3285	1902	1986	826	389	1340	7997	97.5

HISTORY

TITLES

1968–69 NBA Eastern Div. champs
1969–70 ABA champs
1971–72 ABA champs
1972–73 ABA champs
1973–74 ABA Western Div. champs

ALL-TIME TEAM RECORDS

Career

Games played	Vern Fleming	761	1984–94
Total points	Reggie Miller	10,879	1987–94
Scoring average	Mel Daniels	19.5	1968–74
Field goals made	Billy Knight	4,228	1974–83
Free throws made	Reggie Miller	2,803	1987–94
Total rebounds	Mel Daniels	7,622	1968–74
Assists	Vern Fleming	3,929	1984–94
Steals	Don Buse	1,284	1972–77, 1980–82

Season

Total points	George McGinnis	2,353	1974–75
Scoring average	George McGinnis	29.8	1974–75
Field goals made	George McGinnis	868	1972–73
Free throws made	Reggie Miller	551	1990–91
Total rebounds	Mel Daniels	1,475	1970–71
Assists	Don Buse	689	1975–76
Steals	Don Buse	346	1975–76

Games

Total points	George McGinnis	58	vs. Dallas, 11/28/72
Field goals made	Mel Daniels	25	vs. NY Nets, 3/18/69
Free throws made	Detlef Schrempf	22	vs. Golden State, 12/8/92
Total rebounds	George McGinnis	37	vs. Carolina, 1/12/74
Assists	Don Buse	20	vs. Denver, 3/26/76
Steals	Dudley Bradley	9	vs. Cleveland, 11/29/80
	Dudley Bradley	9	vs. Utah, 11/10/80
	Don Buse	9	vs. St. Louis, 2/17/75

LEADING COACHES

	REGULAR SEASON				PLAYOFFS		
NAME	YEARS	W	L	PCT	W	L	PCT
Bob Leonard	1968–80	529	456	.537	69	47	.595
Jack McKinney	1980–84	125	203	.381	0	2	.000
Bob Hill	1990–93	113	108	.511	3	9	.250
Jack Ramsay	1986–88	79	92	.462	1	3	.250
Dick Versace	1989–90	73	87	.456	0	3	.000

Indiana Pacers 1994–95 Roster

Head Coach: Larry Brown

No.	Name	Pos.	Ht.	Wt.	Yrs.	Born	College
	Damon Bailey	G	6-3	201	R	10/21/71	Indiana
12	Lester Conner	G	6-4	180	11	9/17/59	Oregon State
33	Antonio Davis	F-C	6-9	230	1	10/31/68	Texas-El Paso
32	Dale Davis	F	6-11	230	3	3/25/69	Clemson
10	Vern Fleming	G	6-5	185	10	2/4/62	Georgia
43	Scott Haskin	F	6-11	250	1	9/19/70	Oregon State
13	Mark Jackson	G	6-3	192	7	4/1/65	St. John's
9	Derrick McKey	F	6-10	220	7	10/10/66	Alabama
31	Reggie Miller	G	6-7	185	7	8/24/65	UCLA
	Greg Minor	F	6-6	210	R	9/18/71	Louisville
5	Sam Mitchell	F	6-7	210	5	9/2/63	Mercer
	William Njoku	F	6-9	215	R	3/5/72	St. Mary's (Canada)
4	Byron Scott	G	6-3	200	12	3/28/61	Arizona State
45	Rik Smits	C	7-4	265	6	8/23/66	Marist
41	LaSalle Thompson	F	6-10	260	12	6/23/61	Texas
44	Kenny Williams	F	6-9	205	4	6/9/69	Elizabeth City St.
3	Haywoode Workman	G	6-3	180	3	1/23/66	Oral Roberts

Arena Information

Market Square Arena (16,530)
Tickets: 317-263-2100, 317-263-2100 (group sales), 317-239-5151 (Ticketmaster)
Ticket prices: $29, $24, $19, $12, $7

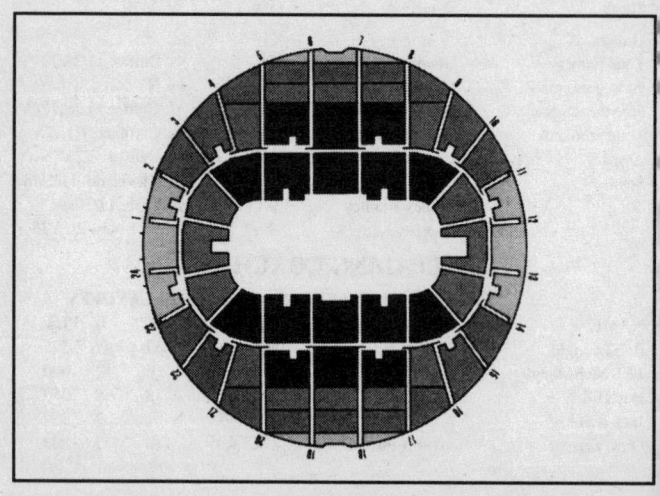

Dale Davis

No. 32/F

Full name: Elliott Lydell Davis
HT: 6-11   **WT:** 230
Born: 3/25/69, Toccoa, GA
High school: Stephens County (Toccoa)
College: Clemson

Davis' role is to guard the other team's power forward and to rebound. Davis led the team in rebounds last season. His 718 rebounds ranked twenty-second in the league last season. And he missed out on qualifying among the league leaders in rebounds per game because he didn't have 70 games last season. But he would've ranked in the NBA's top 20 even if he hadn't snagged one more rebound in the 4 games he needed to qualify. Davis also led the Pacers in blocked shots with 106 (fifth in the league). He was still Indiana's fourth leading scorer. He shot 52.9 per cent from the field, second on the team. Davis' 1,216 rebounds at Clemson trail just Tree Rollins' 1,311, the best in school history.

REGULAR SEASON		G	MIN	FG	FG%	3FG	3PT%	FT	FT%	REB	AST	STL	BLK	PTS	AVG
'91-92	INDIANA	64	1301	154	55.2	0	0.0	87	57.2	410	30	27	74	395	6.2
'92-93	INDIANA	82	2264	304	56.8	0	---	119	52.9	723	69	63	148	727	8.9
'93-94	INDIANA	66	2292	308	52.9	0	0.0	155	52.7	718	100	48	106	771	11.7
3 YR TOTALS		212	5857	766	54.9	0	0.0	361	53.8	1851	199	138	328	1893	8.9
'93-94	RANK NBA Fs	94	38	53	17	78	78	48	130	14	57	66	10	55	4.3
'94-95	PROJECTIONS	59	2721	374	50.4	0	0.0	204	51.5	843	151	48	93	952	16.1

PLAYOFFS		G	MIN	FG	FG%	3FG	3PT%	FT	FT%	REB	AST	STL	BLK	PTS	AVG
'91-92	INDIANA	3	69	4	40.0	0	---	0	---	19	2	0	5	8	2.7
'92-93	INDIANA	4	117	8	66.7	0	---	1	25.0	32	4	4	4	17	4.3
'93-94	INDIANA	16	578	56	52.8	0	0.0	11	30.6	159	11	18	17	123	7.7
TOTALS		23	764	68	53.1	0	0.0	12	30.0	210	17	22	26	148	6.4

Mark Jackson

No. 13/G

Full name: Mark A. Jackson
HT: 6-3   **WT:** 192
Born: 4/1/65, Brooklyn, NY
High school: Bishop Loughlin
  Memorial (Brooklyn)
College: St. John's

Jackson is reunited with his former Clippers' coach, Larry Brown, under whom he had probably his best season as a pro. Jackson was the Clippers' fifth leading scorer last season, as well as team leader in assists with 678 (seventh highest in the NBA). He averaged 8.6 assists per game, eighth in the NBA. He sprained his right wrist in April, snapping a 210-game streak of consecutive games played that dated back to December 28, 1991. Jackson was selected as the eighteenth pick overall in the first round by New York in 1987; he was a near-unanimous choice as the '87–88 Rookie of the Year. His 868 assists that year broke Oscar Robertson's NBA rookie record set in '60–61.

REGULAR SEASON		G	MIN	FG	FGx	3FG	3PTx	FT	FTx	REB	AST	STL	BLK	PTS	AVG
'87-88	NEW YORK	82	3249	438	43.2	32	25.4	206	77.4	396	868	205	6	1114	13.6
'88-89	NEW YORK	72	2477	479	46.7	81	33.8	180	69.8	341	619	139	7	1219	16.9
'89-90	NEW YORK	82	2428	327	43.7	35	26.7	120	72.7	318	604	109	4	809	9.9
'90-91	NEW YORK	72	1595	250	49.2	13	25.5	117	73.1	197	452	60	9	630	8.8
'91-92	NEW YORK	81	2461	367	49.1	11	25.6	171	77.0	305	694	112	13	916	11.3
'92-93	LA CLIPPERS	82	3117	459	48.6	22	26.8	241	80.3	388	724	136	12	1181	14.4
'93-94	LA CLIPPERS	79	2711	331	45.2	36	28.3	167	79.1	348	678	120	6	865	10.9
7 YR TOTALS		550	18038	2651	46.4	230	28.8	1202	76.0	2293	4639	881	57	6734	12.2
'93-94	RANK NBA Gs	40	23	54	59	56	86	45	64	16	7	25	89	52	58
'94-95	PROJECTIONS	78	2751	302	43.7	46	29.7	155	79.3	358	682	123	3	805	10.3

PLAYOFFS		G	MIN	FG	FGx	3FG	3PTx	FT	FTx	REB	AST	STL	BLK	PTS	AVG
'87-88	NEW YORK	4	171	22	36.7	5	41.7	8	72.7	19	39	10	0	57	14.3
'88-89	NEW YORK	9	336	51	51.0	11	39.3	19	67.9	31	91	10	3	132	14.7
'89-90	NEW YORK	9	81	13	41.9	0	0.0	8	72.7	5	21	2	0	34	3.8
'90-91	NEW YORK	3	36	1	33.3	0	---	0	---	0	8	1	1	2	0.7
'91-92	NEW YORK	12	368	37	40.2	4	19.0	22	81.5	27	86	10	0	100	8.3
'92-93	LA CLIPPERS	5	188	28	43.8	1	50.0	19	86.4	29	38	8	1	76	15.2
TOTALS		42	1180	152	43.4	21	32.3	76	76.8	111	283	41	5	401	9.5

Derrick McKey

No. 9/F

Full name: Derrick Wayne McKey
HT: 6-10   **WT:** 220
Born: 10/10/66, Meridian, MS
High school: Meridian (MS)
College: Alabama

McKey came to Indiana last season in the deal that sent Detlef Schrempf to the Sonics. In 6 seasons at Seattle, McKey ranked in the Sonics' top ten of all time in 12 different categories, including points (ninth, with 6,179) and rebounds (tenth, with 2,299). McKey's no superstar, but he is a good all-around player. He plays great defense, has a good shot from the perimeter, and is a very good passer. McKey was Indiana's third leading scorer, fourth on the team in rebounds, and second in steals. The biggest knock on his game is that he sometimes has trouble avoiding turnovers.

REGULAR SEASON		G	MIN	FG	FG%	3FG	3PT%	FT	FT%	REB	AST	STL	BLK	PTS	AVG
'87-88	SEATTLE	82	1706	255	49.1	11	36.7	173	77.2	328	107	70	63	694	8.5
'88-89	SEATTLE	82	2804	487	50.2	30	33.7	301	80.3	464	219	105	70	1305	15.9
'89-90	SEATTLE	80	2748	468	49.3	3	13.0	315	78.2	489	187	87	81	1254	15.7
'90-91	SEATTLE	73	2503	438	51.7	4	21.1	235	84.5	423	169	91	56	1115	15.3
'91-92	SEATTLE	52	1757	285	47.2	19	38.0	188	84.7	268	120	61	47	777	14.9
'92-93	SEATTLE	77	2439	387	49.6	40	35.7	220	74.1	327	197	105	58	1034	13.4
'93-94	INDIANA	76	2613	355	50.0	9	29.0	192	75.6	402	327	111	49	911	12.0
7 YR TOTALS		522	16570	2675	49.7	116	32.8	1624	79.1	2701	1326	630	424	7090	13.6
'93-94 RANK NBA Fs		48	22	41	35	41	37	34	40	49	3	8	39	39	37
'94-95 PROJECTIONS		79	2764	335	50.4	1	20.0	170	73.9	432	419	123	43	841	10.6

PLAYOFFS		G	MIN	FG	FG%	3FG	3PT%	FT	FT%	REB	AST	STL	BLK	PTS	AVG
'87-88	SEATTLE	5	109	24	63.2	2	33.3	10	58.8	20	8	3	5	60	12.0
'89-90	SEATTLE	8	286	44	49.4	1	11.1	17	81.0	52	18	6	15	106	13.3
'90-91	SEATTLE	4	114	16	57.1	0	0.0	6	54.5	23	8	3	0	38	9.5
'91-92	SEATTLE	3	315	52	52.5	5	31.3	28	84.4	44	24	7	12	147	16.3
'92-93	SEATTLE	19	647	83	52.5	2	40.0	46	66.7	98	71	12	17	214	11.3
'93-94	INDIANA	16	587	58	40.8	8	33.3	31	66.0	98	67	26	9	155	9.7
TOTALS		61	2058	277	50.0	18	29.5	148	70.5	335	196	57	58	720	11.8

Reggie Miller

No. 31/G

Full name: Reginald Wayne Miller
HT: 6-7 **WT:** 185
Born: 8/24/65, Riverside, CA
High school: Riverside
Polytechnic (CA)
College: UCLA

Miller is one of the most complete offensive threats in the NBA. He can score from anywhere, and he's deadly from outside. Miller can also pass and play defense. He led the Pacers in scoring last season; his 1,574 points were twelfth highest in the NBA and fourth highest by a guard last season. He also led the team in steals. Miller is the all-time Pacer scoring leader in NBA points. He holds the Pacer record for NBA 3-pointers with 167, set in '92–93. His sister, Cheryl, was a member of the U.S. gold-medal–winning 1984 Olympic basketball team and is the women's basketball head coach at USC. And his brother, Darryl, played baseball with the California Angels in the mid-'80s.

REGULAR SEASON		G	MIN	FG	FG%	3FG	3PT%	FT	FT%	REB	AST	STL	BLK	PTS	AVG
'87-88	INDIANA	82	1840	306	48.8	61	35.5	149	80.1	190	132	53	19	822	10.0
'88-89	INDIANA	74	2536	398	47.9	98	40.2	287	84.4	292	227	93	29	1181	16.0
'89-90	INDIANA	82	3192	661	51.4	150	41.4	544	86.8	295	311	110	18	2016	24.6
'90-91	INDIANA	82	2972	596	51.2	112	34.8	551	91.8	281	331	109	13	1855	22.6
'91-92	INDIANA	82	3120	562	50.1	129	37.8	442	85.8	318	314	105	26	1695	20.7
'92-93	INDIANA	82	2954	571	47.9	167	39.9	427	88.0	258	262	120	26	1736	21.2
'93-94	INDIANA	79	2638	524	50.3	123	42.1	403	90.8	212	248	119	24	1574	19.9
	7 YR TOTALS	563	19252	3618	49.8	840	39.0	2803	87.7	1846	1825	709	155	10879	19.3
'93-94	RANK NBA Gs	40	26	11	9	9	7	2	2	48	57	27	24	4	6
'94-95	PROJECTIONS	77	2436	491	50.8	110	43.8	371	92.3	180	226	119	24	1463	19.0

PLAYOFFS		G	MIN	FG	FG%	3FG	3PT%	FT	FT%	REB	AST	STL	BLK	PTS	AVG
'89-90	INDIANA	3	125	20	57.1	3	42.9	19	90.5	12	6	3	0	62	20.7
'90-91	INDIANA	5	193	34	48.6	8	42.1	32	86.5	16	14	8	2	108	21.6
'91-92	INDIANA	3	130	25	58.1	7	63.6	24	80.0	7	14	4	0	81	27.0
'92-93	INDIANA	4	175	40	53.3	10	52.6	36	94.7	12	11	3	0	126	31.5
'93-94	INDIANA	16	576	121	44.8	35	42.2	94	83.9	48	46	21	4	371	23.2
	TOTALS	31	1199	240	48.7	63	45.3	205	86.1	95	91	39	6	748	24.1

Rik Smits

No. 45/C

HT: 7-4   **WT:** 265
Born: 8/23/66, Eindhoven, Holland
High school: Almonta (Eindhoven, Holland)
College: Marist

Smits has trouble staying in games because he's often on the bench in foul trouble. Last season, Smits fouled out of 11 games; he averaged 5.3 fouls per 40 minutes played. That's a big reason why he averaged only 27 minutes per game last season (and just 25 the season before) despite being Indiana's starting center. Even so, Smits was Indiana's second leading scorer. His 53.4 FG percentage led the Pacers. He was also third on the team in rebounds and blocked shots. He isn't a dominant center, but he works hard and has a nice shooting touch.

REGULAR SEASON		G	MIN	FG	FG%	3FG	3PT%	FT	FT%	REB	AST	STL	BLK	PTS	AVG
'88-89	INDIANA	82	2041	386	51.7	0	0.0	184	72.2	500	70	37	151	956	11.7
'89-90	INDIANA	82	2404	515	53.3	0	0.0	241	81.1	512	142	45	169	1271	15.5
'90-91	INDIANA	76	1690	342	48.5	0	---	144	76.2	357	84	24	111	828	10.9
'91-92	INDIANA	74	1772	436	51.0	0	0.0	152	78.8	417	116	29	100	1024	13.8
'92-93	INDIANA	81	2072	494	48.6	0	---	167	73.2	432	121	27	75	1155	14.3
'93-94	INDIANA	78	2113	493	53.4	0	0.0	238	79.3	483	156	49	82	1224	15.7
6 YR TOTALS		473	12092	2666	51.1	0	0.0	1126	77.0	2701	689	211	688	6458	13.7
'93-94 RANK NBA Cs		14	10	5	11	14	14	9	7	15	7	13	18	6	7
'94-95 PROJECTIONS		78	2183	509	55.3	0	0.0	279	81.1	513	178	60	72	1297	16.6

PLAYOFFS		G	MIN	FG	FG%	3FG	3PT%	FT	FT%	REB	AST	STL	BLK	PTS	AVG
'89-90	INDIANA	3	96	14	50.0	0	---	9	81.8	16	3	2	4	37	12.3
'90-91	INDIANA	5	88	21	56.8	0	---	7	87.5	18	2	1	7	49	9.8
'91-92	INDIANA	3	28	4	36.4	0	---	2	100.0	6	0	2	1	10	3.3
'92-93	INDIANA	4	143	37	57.8	0	0.0	16	72.7	32	7	5	4	90	22.5
'93-94	INDIANA	16	450	103	47.2	0	---	50	80.6	84	31	10	9	256	16.0
TOTALS		31	805	179	50.0	0	0.0	84	80.0	156	43	20	25	442	14.3

Antonio Davis   No. 33/F-C

Full name: Antonio Lee Davis
HT: 6-9   **WT:** 230
Born: 10/31/68, Oakland, CA
High school: McClymonds (Oakland)
College: Texas-El Paso

Antonio Davis provides rebounding and defense off the bench; he was second on the team in rebounds and blocked shots.

REGULAR SEASON	G	MIN	FG	FGx	3FG	3PTx	FT	FTx	REB	AST	STL	BLK	PTS	AVG
'93-94 INDIANA	81	1732	216	50.8	0	0.0	194	64.2	505	55	45	84	626	7.7
1 YR TOTALS	81	1732	216	50.8	0	0.0	194	64.2	505	55	45	84	626	7.7
'93-94 RANK NBA Fs	15	59	67	27	78	78	33	109	30	90	69	13	65	7.

PLAYOFFS	G	MIN	FG	FGx	3FG	3PTx	FT	FTx	REB	AST	STL	BLK	PTS	AVG
'93-94 INDIANA	16	401	48	53.9	1	100.0	37	56.1	106	7	11	18	134	8.4
TOTALS	16	401	48	53.9	1	100.0	37	56.1	106	7	11	18	134	8.4

Vern Fleming   No. 10/C

HT: 6-5   **WT:** 185
Born: 2/4/62, New York, NY
High school: Mater Christi (Long Island, NY)
College: Georgia

Now relegated to a role on the Pacer bench, Fleming has played in more seasons, games, and minutes than any Pacer in team history. He's still a solid playmaker.

REGULAR SEASON	G	MIN	FG	FGx	3FG	3PTx	FT	FTx	REB	AST	STL	BLK	PTS	AVG
'90-91 INDIANA	69	1929	356	53.1	4	22.2	161	72.9	214	369	76	13	877	12.7
'91-92 INDIANA	82	1737	294	48.2	6	22.2	132	73.7	209	266	56	7	726	8.9
'92-93 INDIANA	75	1503	280	50.5	7	19.4	143	72.6	169	224	63	9	710	9.5
'93-94 INDIANA	55	1053	147	46.2	0	0.0	64	73.6	123	173	40	6	358	6.5
10 YR TOTALS	761	22288	3644	50.3	35	20.0	1961	76.6	2096	3929	858	99	9284	12.2
'93-94 RANK NBA Gs	112	97	100	47	131	131	99	96	90	79	99	89	105	97
'94-95 PROJECTIONS	44	668	81	44.3	0	0.0	32	74.4	81	110	25	4	194	4.4

PLAYOFFS	G	MIN	FG	FGx	3FG	3PTx	FT	FTx	REB	AST	STL	BLK	PTS	AVG
'90-91 INDIANA	5	115	18	45.0	0	0.0	11	78.6	17	23	1	3	47	9.4
'91-92 INDIANA	3	51	10	55.6	0	---	1	33.3	2	6	3	0	21	7.0
'92-93 INDIANA	3	80	12	44.4	2	50.0	4	100.0	5	3	2	1	30	10.0
'93-94 INDIANA	16	247	39	51.3	0	0.0	17	85.0	21	38	10	1	95	5.9
TOTALS	34	747	108	46.8	2	15.4	64	80.0	84	112	22	7	282	8.3

Greg Minor F-G

HT: 6-6 **WT:** 210
Born: 9/18/71
College: Louisville
Minor was a first team All-Metro Conference player. He averaged 13.8 points and 6.1 rebounds per game last season, and shot 51 percent for his collegiate career.

REGULAR SEASON	G	MIN	FG	FGx	3FG	3PTx	FT	FTx	REB	AST	STL	BLK	PTS	AVG

ROOKIE -- NO NBA EXPERIENCE

Byron Scott No. 4/G

Full name: Byron Antom Scott
HT: 6-3 **WT:** 200
Born: 3/28/61, Ogden, UT
High school: Morningside (Inglewood, CA)
College: Arizona State
Although he doesn't see the minutes he once did, Scott is still a first-rate scorer. He shot 80.5 percent from the freethrow line.

REGULAR SEASON	G	MIN	FG	FGx	3FG	3PTx	FT	FTx	REB	AST	STL	BLK	PTS	AVG
'90-91 LA LAKERS	82	2630	501	47.7	71	32.4	118	79.7	246	177	95	21	1191	14.5
'91-92 LA LAKERS	82	2679	460	45.8	54	34.4	244	83.8	310	226	105	28	1218	14.9
'92-93 LA LAKERS	58	1677	296	44.9	44	32.6	156	84.8	134	157	55	13	792	13.7
'93-94 INDIANA	67	1197	256	46.7	27	36.5	157	80.5	110	133	62	9	696	10.4
11 YR TOTALS	834	25290	5219	49.1	549	37.1	1963	83.0	2526	2399	1054	225	12950	15.5
'93-94 RANK NBA Gs	88	92	68	44	63	34	48	56	98	91	76	78	65	62
'94-95 PROJECTIONS	66	685	159	47.0	14	37.8	107	79.3	63	84	42	5	439	6.7

PLAYOFFS	G	MIN	FG	FGx	3FG	3PTx	FT	FTx	REB	AST	STL	BLK	PTS	AVG
'90-91 LA LAKERS	18	678	95	51.1	20	52.6	27	79.4	57	29	23	4	237	13.2
'91-92 LA LAKERS	4	148	22	50.0	7	58.3	24	88.9	10	14	6	1	75	18.8
'92-93 LA LAKERS	5	177	21	50.0	8	53.3	18	78.3	11	9	5	0	68	13.6
'93-94 INDIANA	16	239	38	39.6	9	47.4	40	74.4	33	20	12	2	125	7.8
TOTALS	158	4933	887	49.0	121	41.2	402	81.2	499	363	215	29	2297	14.5

Haywoode Workman No. 3/C

HT: 6-3 **WT:** 180
Born: 1/23/66, Charlotte, NC
High school: Myers Park (Charlotte)
College: Oral Roberts
Workman assumed starting point gua
responsibilities last season, and led th
Pacers in assists. His 6.2 assists per gan
was fifteenth in the NBA last season.

REGULAR SEASON	G	MIN	FG	FG%	3FG	3PT%	FT	FT%	REB	AST	STL	BLK	PTS	AVG
'89-90 ATLANTA	6	20	2	66.7	0	---	2	100.0	3	2	3	0	6	1.0
'90-91 WASHINGTON	73	2034	234	45.4	12	24.0	101	75.9	242	353	87	7	581	8.0
'93-94 INDIANA	65	1714	195	42.4	18	32.1	93	80.2	204	404	85	4	501	7.2
3 YR TOTALS	144	3768	431	44.1	30	28.3	196	78.1	449	759	175	11	1088	7.6
'93-94 RANK NBA Gs	78	57	72	74.0	66	52.0	64	70.0	38	21	36	82	72	71.0
'94-95 PROJECTIONS	76	2080	221	34.7	41	44.1	98	77.8	231	625	58	5	581	7.6

PLAYOFFS	G	MIN	FG	FG%	3FG	3PT%	FT	FT%	REB	AST	STL	BLK	PTS	AVG
'93-94 INDIANA	16	511	45	34.4	6	28.6	32	84.2	51	112	28	1	128	8.0
TOTALS	16	511	45	34.4	6	28.6	32	84.2	51	112	28	1	128	8.0

Larry Brown Head Coach

Full name: Lawrence Harvey Brown
HT: 5-9 **WT:** 160
Born: 9/14/40, Brooklyn, NY
High school: Long Beach (NY)
College: North Carolina
Before last season, Indiana had won just fo
playoff games; Brown coached the Pacers
10 wins in 3 series.

	REGULAR SEASON				PLAYOFFS			
YEAR	TEAM	W	L	PCT	FINISH	W	L	PCT	
---	---	---	---	---	---	---	---	---	---
'76-77	DENVER	50	32	610	1st/Midwest Div.	2	4	333	lost Western Conf. semifinals to Portland, 4-2
'77-78	DENVER	48	34	585	1st/Midwest Div.	6	7	462	lost Western Conf. finals to Seattle, 4-2
'78-79	DENVER	28	25	528					
'81-82	NEW JERSEY	44	38	537	3rd/Atlantic Div.	0	2	000	lost Eastern Conf. first round to Washington, 2-0
'82-83	NEW JERSEY	47	29	618					
'88-89	SAN ANTONIO	21	61	256	5th/Midwest Div.				
'89-90	SAN ANTONIO	56	26	683	1st/Midwest Div.	6	4	600	lost Western Conf. semi. to Portland, 4-3
'90-91	SAN ANTONIO	55	27	671	1st/Midwest Div.	1	3	250	lost Western Conf. first round to Golden State, 3-1
'91-92	SAN ANTONIO	21	17	553					
'91-92	LA CLIPPERS	23	12	657	5th/Pacific Div.	2	3	400	lost Western Conf. first round to Utah, 3-2
'92-93	LA CLIPPERS	41	41	500	4th/Pacific Div.	2	3	400	lost Western Conf. first round to Houston, 3-2
'93-94	INDIANA	47	35	573	T3rd/Central Div.	7	6	538	lost Eastern Conf. finals to New York, 4-3
	12 YR TOTALS	481	377	561		26	32	448	

Los Angeles
CLIPPERS

1994–95 Scouting Report

Frontcourt

Stanley Roberts starts at center. He's a big body who can't be moved from under the basket, and is a pretty good shot blocker. Loy Vaught is the starting power forward. He's a decent scorer and rebounds, too. The Clippers, desperately in need of a small forward to replace Danny Manning's replacement, Dominique Wilkins, obtained Malik Sealy from Indiana in a deal that sent Mark Jackson to the Pacers. Draft pick Lamond Murray will get a shot at the starting small forward job. Murray led the Pac-10 in scoring last season, led his team in rebounds, and has a good outside shot. Eric Piatkowski also came to the Clippers in the Mark Jackson deal. He's got a great outside shot, handles and passes the ball well, and is a good rebounder. Elmore Spencer comes off the bench to spell Roberts at center. He's a good shotblocker and passer who will mix it up inside.

Backcourt

Shooting guard Ron Harper is probably the Clippers' best player. He also played nearly 40 minutes per game last season, leaving little time for second string shooting guard Terry Dehere ('93's first pick), who has been a disappointment so far. Clippers management believes he'll thrive if he gets more playing time, and they're looking at deals (such as signing ex-King Waymon Tisdale) that would involve getting rid of Harper. The Clippers traded Mark Jackson for Pooh Richardson, who will take over point guard duties. Reserve point guard Gary Grant can come off the bench to add defensive spark. And Harold Ellis demonstrated that he could score and play aggressive defense, a rarity at shooting guard.

Defense

Defensively, Bob Weiss' 1993–94 Clippers looked a lot like Weiss' '92–93 Atlanta Hawks: one of the weaker defensive squads in the

NBA. Bill Fitch's challenge will be to turn the Clippers around on defense, just like Lenny Wilkens did in Atlanta. Opposing teams shot 47.3 from the floor against the Clippers, ninth highest in the league. On the positive side, the Clippers got good play from the guards; they were third in the NBA in steals and eighth in the league in forcing turnovers. But if you gamble a lot on defense without a defensive intimidator underneath as a backup, you'll get burned for the 108.7 points teams averaged against the Clippers, the highest total in the NBA. The Clippers ranked fifteenth in blocks and allowed more offensive rebounds than any other NBA team, so opponents had an NBA high 7,421 shots from the field.

1994–95 Prospects

Statistically, the Clippers should have been mediocre last season—instead, they were awful. Offensively, they were generally in the middle of the pack. The Clippers shot 46.7 percent from the field last season (thirteenth in the league). The Clippers also ranked fourteenth in rebounding (including tenth in defensive rebounding). And they were third in FGA (although, again, they gave up more shots than any other team). They did shoot just 30.3 percent from 3-point range, fifth worst in the NBA. (The four teams with a poorer record from 3-point range were 131–197, a .399 percentage; only Denver had a winning record.) The problem was that the Clippers played last season with all the intensity of a commuter waiting for a bus. So management fired Coach Bob Weiss and hired Bill Fitch.

Bill Fitch has consistently been able to win in the NBA. Unfortunately, his methods drive his players to mutiny; he's blessed (or cursed) with a sarcastic tongue and a vindictive streak that today's NBA players don't tolerate for long. If Chuck Daly was the ultimate player's coach, Fitch is the anti-Chuck Daly. Larry Bird and Derrick Coleman are just two of Fitch's star players who reportedly begged management for a coaching change. So Fitch's track record of turning teams around will be sorely tested with the Clippers. This is a young team with potential; they could win 35 games and contend for a playoff spot if the young talent pans out. But their confidence needs to be nurtured. If Fitch isn't careful, they could easily go into a season-long sulk—and have another dismal season.

Team Directory

Owner: Donald T. Sterling
Executive VP: Andy Roeser
VP, mktg. & broad.: Mitch Huberman
VP, marketing: Carl Lahr
VP, basketball oper.: Elgin Baylor
VP, communications: Joe Safety

1993–94 Review

WESTERN CONFERENCE					EASTERN CONFERENCE					
MIDWEST DIV.		PACIFIC DIV.			ATLANTIC DIV.			CENTRAL DIV.		
	W	L		W	L		W	L		W	L
HOU	0	4	SEA	1	4	NY	0	2	ATL	1	1
SAN	1	3	PHO	0	5	ORL	1	1	CHI	0	2
UTAH	1	3	GS	1	4	NJ	1	1	CLE	0	2
DEN	1	3	POR	2	3	MIA	1	1	IND	0	2
MIN	1	3	LAL	2	3	BOS	1	1	CHA	1	1
DAL	4	0	SAC	3	2	PHI	1	1	DET	1	1
			LAC	-	-	WAS	1	1	MIL	1	1
	8	16		9	21		6	8		4	10

1993–94 finish: 27–55 (17–24 home, 10–31 away), seventh in Pacific Div.

1994–95 Schedule

11/4	Portland	11:00 pm	12/30	@ Orlando	7:30 pm	2/28	Phoenix	10:30 pm
11/5	@ Portland	10:00 pm	1/5	Phila.	10:30 pm	3/2	Seattle	10:30 pm
11/10	Atlanta	10:30 pm	1/7	San Ant.	10:30 pm	3/4	Denver	10:30 pm
11/12	Phoenix	10:30 pm	1/10	@ San Ant.	8:30 pm	3/6	Minnesota	10:30 pm
11/13	@ Seattle	9:00 pm	1/11	@ Dallas	8:30 pm	3/8	@ Gold. St.	10:30 pm
11/15	LA Lakers	10:30 pm	1/13	@ Seattle	10:00 pm	3/10	Gold. St.	10:30 pm
11/17	@ Charlotte	7:30 pm	1/14	Phoenix	10:30 pm	3/12	Sacra.	6:00 pm
11/18	@ Phila.	7:30 pm	1/16	@ LA Lakers	4:30 pm	3/15	Detroit	10:30 pm
11/20	@ New Jersey	7:00 pm	1/18	Cleveland	10:30 pm	3/17	Miami	10:30 pm
11/22	Chicago	10:30 pm	1/20	Portland	10:30 pm	3/19	@ Minnesota	3:30 pm
11/23	@ Phoenix	9:00 pm	1/21	Sacra.	10:30 pm	3/20	@ Atlanta	7:30 pm
11/25	New Jersey	6:00 pm	1/23	@ Cleveland	7:30 pm	3/22	@ Indiana	7:30 pm
11/29	@ Gold. St.	10:30 pm	1/25	@ Boston	7:30 pm	3/23	@ Milwaukee	8:30 pm
12/1	Indiana	10:30 pm	1/26	@ New York	7:30 pm	3/25	New York	10:30 pm
12/3	Minnesota	10:30 pm	1/28	@ Wash.	7:30 pm	3/27	@ Denver	9:00 pm
12/5	Charlotte	10:30 pm	1/30	@ Detroit	7:30 pm	3/30	Houston	10:30 pm
12/7	Milwaukee	10:30 pm	2/3	@ Gold. St.	10:30 pm	4/1	Utah	10:30 pm
12/9	@ LA Lakers	10:30 pm	2/4	LA Lakers	10:30 pm	4/4	San Ant.	10:30 pm
12/10	Seattle	10:30 pm	2/7	Utah	10:30 pm	4/8	@ Sacra.	10:30 pm
12/14	@ Portland	10:00 pm	2/9	Houston	10:30 pm	4/11	Sacra.	10:30 pm
12/15	Gold. St.	10:30 pm	2/14	@ Houston	8:30 pm	4/13	Denver	10:30 pm
12/17	Dallas	10:30 pm	2/17	Boston	10:30 pm	4/15	@ Utah	9:00 pm
12/20	@ Seattle	10:00 pm	2/18	@ Sacra.	10:30 pm	4/17	@ Houston	8:30 pm
12/21	Orlando	10:30 pm	2/21	@ Denver	9:00 pm	4/18	@ Dallas	8:30 pm
12/23	Wash.	10:30 pm	2/22	@ Utah	9:00 pm	4/21	@ San Ant.	8:30 pm
12/26	@ Minnesota	8:00 pm	2/24	@ Phoenix	9:00 pm	4/23	Dallas	6:00 pm
12/27	@ Chicago	8:30 pm	2/25	LA Lakers	10:30 pm			
12/29	@ Miami	7:30 pm	2/27	@ Portland	10:00 pm			

1993–94 Team Stats

NAME	G	MIN	FG	FGA	FG%	3FG	3FGA	3FG%	FT	FTA	FT%	ORB	TRB	AST	PF	STL	BLK	TO	PTS	AVG
Wilkins	25	948	268	592	45.3	24	97	24.7	167	200	83.5	63	176	55	39	29	8	52	727	29.1
Manning	42	1595	409	829	49.3	2	14	14.3	174	258	67.4	82	296	176	167	53	57	147	994	23.7
Harper	75	2856	569	1335	42.6	71	236	30.1	299	418	71.5	129	460	344	221	144	54	242	1508	20.1
Vaught	75	2118	373	695	53.7	0	5	0.0	131	182	72.0	218	656	74	115	76	22	96	877	11.7
Jackson	79	2711	331	732	45.2	36	127	28.3	167	211	79.1	107	348	678	115	120	6	232	865	10.9
Aguirre	39	859	163	348	46.8	37	93	39.8	50	72	69.4	28	116	104	98	21	8	70	413	10.6
Spencer	76	1930	288	540	53.3	0	2	0.0	97	162	59.9	96	415	75	208	30	127	168	673	8.9
Ellis	49	923	159	292	54.5	0	4	0.0	106	149	71.1	94	153	31	97	73	2	43	424	8.7
Grant	78	1533	253	563	44.9	17	62	27.4	65	76	85.5	42	142	291	139	119	12	136	588	7.5
Roberts	14	350	43	100	43.0	0	0	—	18	44	40.9	27	93	11	54	6	25	24	104	7.4
Outlaw	37	871	98	167	58.7	0	2	0.0	61	103	59.2	81	212	36	94	36	37	31	257	6.9
Williams	34	725	81	188	43.1	5	20	25.0	24	36	66.7	37	127	97	85	25	10	35	191	5.6
Dehere	64	759	129	342	37.7	23	57	40.4	61	81	75.3	25	68	78	69	28	3	61	342	5.3
Tolbert	49	640	74	177	41.8	6	16	37.5	33	45	73.3	36	108	30	61	13	15	39	187	3.8
Woods	40	352	49	133	36.8	27	78	34.6	20	35	57.1	13	29	71	40	24	2	34	145	3.6
James	12	75	16	42	38.1	4	18	22.2	5	5	100.0	6	14	1	9	2	0	2	41	3.4
Martin	53	535	40	88	45.5	0	0	—	31	51	60.8	36	117	17	106	8	33	29	111	2.1
Clippers	82	19780	3343	7163	46.7	252	831	30.3	1509	2128	70.9	1120	3530	2169	1769	807	421	1474	8447	103.0
Opp.	82	19780	3512	7421	47.3	308	882	34.9	1584	2209	71.7	1348	3916	2220	1788	898	476	1364	8916	108.7

HISTORY
ALL-TIME TEAM RECORDS

Career

Games played	Randy Smith	715	1971–79
Total points	Randy Smith	12,735	1971–79
Scoring average	World Free	29.4	1978–80
Field goals made	Randy Smith	5,214	1971–79
Field goals attempted	Randy Smith	11,035	1971–79
Free throws made	Randy Smith	2,203	1971–79
Free throws attempted	Randy Smith	2,869	1971–79
Total rebounds	Bob McAdoo	4,229	1972–76
Assists	Randy Smith	3,498	1971–79
Steals	Randy Smith	1,072	1971–79
Personal fouls	Randy Smith	2,018	1971–79

Season

Total points	Bob McAdoo	2,831	1974–75
Scoring average	Bob McAdoo	34.5	1974–75
Field goals made	Bob McAdoo	1,095	1974–75
Field goals attempted	Bob McAdoo	2,138	1974–75
Free throws made	World Free	654	1979–80
Free throws attempted	World Free	865	1978–79
Total rebounds	Swen Nater	1,216	1979–80
Assists	Norm Nixon	914	1983–84
Steals	Randy Smith	203	1973–74

Game

Total points	Bob McAdoo	52	vs. Seattle, 3/17/76
	Bob McAdoo	52	vs. Boston, 2/22/75
	Charles Smith	52	vs. Denver, 12/1/90
Field goals made	Bob McAdoo	22	vs. Cleveland, 11/20/75
	Bob McAdoo	22	vs. Houston, 3/18/75
	Freeman Williams	22	vs. Phoenix, 1/19/80
Free throws made	World Free	22	vs. Atlanta, 1/13/79
Total rebounds	Swen Nater	32	vs. Denver, 12/14/79
Assists	Ernie DiGregorio	25	vs. Portland, 11/1/74
Steals	Doc Rivers	9	vs. Phoenix, 11/6/91

LEADING COACHES

		REGULAR SEASON			PLAYOFFS		
NAME	YEARS	W	L	PCT	W	L	PCT
Jack Ramsay	1972–76	158	170	.482	9	13	.438
Gene Shue	1978–80, 1987–89	105	179	.348	0	0	—
Paul Silas	1980–83	78	168	.317	0	0	—
Larry Brown	1991–93	64	53	.547	4	6	.400
Don Chaney	1985–87	53	132	.286	0	0	—

Los Angeles Clippers 1994–95 Roster

Head Coach: Bill Fitch

No.	Name	Pos.	Ht.	Wt.	Yrs.	Born	College
24	Terry Dehere	G	6-4	190	1	9/12/71	Seton Hall
30	Harold Ellis	F	6-5	200	1	10/7/70	Morehouse
23	Gary Grant	G	6-3	185	6	4/21/65	Michigan
	Tony Massenburg	F	6-9	245	2	7/31/67	Maryland
6	Lamond Murray	F	6-7	236	R	4/20/73	California
45	Charles Outlaw	F	6-8	210	1	4/13/71	Houston
52	Eric Piatkowski	G-F	6-7	215	R	9/30/70	Nebraska
2	Pooh Richardson	G	6-1	180	5	5/14/66	UCLA
53	Stanley Roberts	C	7-0	290	3	2/7/70	Louisiana State
21	Malik Sealy	F	6-8	190	1	2/1/70	St. John's
27	Elmore Spencer	C	7-0	270	2	12/6/69	Nevada-Las Vegas
35	Loy Vaught	F	6-9	240	4	2/27/68	Michigan
14	Randy Woods	G	6-0	185	2	9/23/70	La Salle

Arena Information

Los Angeles Sports Arena (16,021)
Tickets: 213-745-0500
Ticket prices: $35, $26, $21, $18, $14, $10

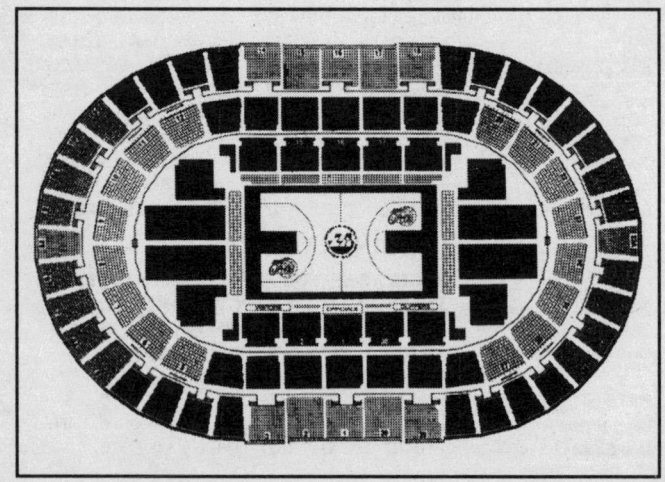

Harold Ellis

No. 30/G

HT: 6-5   **WT:** 200

Born: 10/7/70, Atlanta GA

College: Morehouse

Ellis started 16 games for the Clippers last season (generally at small forward), and they were 5–11 in those games. He played crafty defense for the Clippers, leading the Clippers in steals 12 times in 49 games. In fact, Ellis recorded more steals (73) than turnovers (43). Had Ellis played in enough games to qualify, he would have been among the NBA leaders. Ellis came to the Clippers in January from the CBA's Quad City Thunder, where he was named to the CBA All-Rookie team. When he left Quad City, he was fourth in the CBA in scoring. Ellis played his college ball at Division II Morehouse College, where he was Division II Player of the Year and Morehouse's career scoring leader (2,881 points). He was All-Southern Independent Athletic Conference 4 straight years, and SIAC Player of the Year in 1990 and 1991.

REGULAR SEASON	G	MIN	FG	FG%	3FG	3PT%	FT	FT%	REB	AST	STL	BLK	PTS	AVG
'93-94 LA CLIPPERS	49	923	159	54.5	0	0.0	106	71.1	153	31	73	2	424	8.7
1 YR TOTALS	49	923	159	54.5	0	0.0	106	71.1	153	31	73	2	424	8.7
93-94 RANK NBA Gs	99	89	81	1	59	94	108	131	58	110	97	94	79	63

Gary Grant

No. 23/G

HT: 6-3   **WT:** 195
Born: 4/21/65, Canton, OH
High school: McKinley (Canton)
College: Michigan

Too turnover prone to start at point guard, Grant is a veteran who can come off the bench to play defense. He averaged over 3.1 steals per 40 minutes played last season. Grant led the Clippers in steals 18 times (despite starting just 8 games) and in assists 9 times. Grant's an average scorer, with limited range; he broke 20 points four times, and shot 45 percent from the floor. Last season was Grant's best from the free throw line; his 85.5 percentage led the Clippers. Unfortunately, Grant's offensive game doesn't lead to free throw opportunities; he's not a great penetrator, and he's not a good enough shooter from outside to draw tight defense. That's why Grant had less than 2 free throws per 40 minutes played.

REGULAR SEASON		G	MIN	FG	FGx	3FG	3PTx	FT	FTx	REB	AST	STL	BLK	PTS	AVG
'88-89	LA CLIPPERS	71	1924	361	43.5	5	22.7	119	73.5	238	506	144	9	846	11.9
'89-90	LA CLIPPERS	44	1529	241	46.6	5	23.8	88	77.3	195	442	108	5	575	13.1
'90-91	LA CLIPPERS	68	2105	265	45.1	9	23.1	51	68.9	209	587	103	12	590	8.7
'91-92	LA CLIPPERS	78	2049	275	46.2	15	29.4	44	81.5	184	538	138	14	609	7.8
'92-93	LA CLIPPERS	74	1624	210	44.1	11	26.2	55	74.3	139	353	106	9	486	6.6
'93-94	LA CLIPPERS	78	1533	253	44.9	17	27.4	65	85.5	142	291	119	12	588	7.5
6 YR TOTALS		413	10764	1605	45.0	62	26.2	422	76.3	1107	2717	718	61	3694	8.9
'93-94	RANK NBA Gs	48	76	70	63	77	91	98	19	80	47	27	62	81	87
'94-95	PROJECTIONS	82	1398	254	44.9	19	27.5	67	90.5	129	224	119	13	594	7.2

PLAYOFFS		G	MIN	FG	FGx	3FG	3PTx	FT	FTx	REB	AST	STL	BLK	PTS	AVG
'91-92	LA CLIPPERS	5	77	10	47.6	0	0.0	2	100.0	4	18	3	2	22	4.4
'92-93	LA CLIPPERS	5	101	10	32.3	0	---	1	50.0	2	23	3	0	21	4.2
	TOTALS	10	178	20	38.5	0	0.0	3	75.0	6	41	6	2	43	4.3

Pooh Richardson

No. 2/G

Full name: Jerome Richardson, Jr.
HT: 6-1 **WT:** 180
Born: 5/14/66, Philadelphia, PA
High school: Benjamin Franklin
(Philadelphia)
College: UCLA

Richardson is a solid point guard who doesn't turn over the ball much; his game is questioned less than his attitude. He lost Larry Brown's confidence in Indiana, and lost his starting role to Haywoode Workman. He'd led the Pacers in assists the previous season. Richardson's an average shooter; last season's 45.2 percent from the field was a career low. Richardson is a horrible free throw shooter; last season's 61 percent wasn't far off his career average. Still, he ended up as Indiana's sixth leading scorer. In college, Richardson set a conference career record for assists with 833 (fourteenth best in NCAA history). He also set a UCLA record for steals with 182.

REGULAR SEASON		G	MIN	FG	FG%	3FG	3PT%	FT	FT%	REB	AST	STL	BLK	PTS	AVG
'89-90	MINNESOTA	82	2581	426	46.1	23	27.7	63	58.9	217	554	133	25	938	11.4
'90-91	MINNESOTA	82	3154	635	47.0	42	32.8	89	53.9	286	734	131	13	1401	17.1
'91-92	MINNESOTA	82	2922	587	46.6	53	34.2	123	69.1	301	685	119	25	1350	16.5
'92-93	INDIANA	74	2396	337	47.9	3	10.3	92	74.2	267	573	94	12	769	10.4
'93-94	INDIANA	37	1022	160	45.2	3	25.0	47	61.0	110	237	32	3	370	10
5 YR TOTALS		357	12075	2145	46.7	124	30.5	414	63.6	1181	2783	509	78	4828	13.5
'93-94	RANK NBA Gs	107	83	80	48	94	106	97	95	78	53	67	89	85	55
'94-95	PROJECTIONS	16	166	25	43.9	0	0.0	8	57.1	18	38	4	0	58	3.6

PLAYOFFS		G	MIN	FG	FG%	3FG	3PT%	FT	FT%	REB	AST	STL	BLK	PTS	AVG
'92-93	INDIANA	4	95	6	40.0	1	100.0	4	66.7	11	23	2	0	17	4.3
TOTALS		4	95	6	40.0	1	100.0	4	66.7	11	23	2	0	17	4.3

Stanley Roberts
No. 53/C

Full name: Stanley Corvet Roberts
HT: 7-0   **WT:** 290
Born: 2/7/70, Hopkins, SC
High school: Lower Richland (Hopkins)
College: Louisiana State

This season, Roberts will be trying to return from a ruptured right Achilles tendon that he suffered last December. Before the injury, Roberts had had problems with inconsistency and his weight. He's a good shot blocker, though, gets his share of rebounds, and, with his bulk, can be an offensive force under the basket. He was not off to a great start last season; his scoring was down, he was hitting just 43 percent of his shots from the field, and he had made an atrocious 40.9 percent from the free throw line. He'll turn 25 this season, so he could still improve if he can recover from the Achilles tendon rupture. He's had a history of getting into foul trouble; last season he committed 6.2 fouls per 40 minutes played.

REGULAR SEASON		G	MIN	FG	FG%	3FG	3PT%	FT	FT%	REB	AST	STL	BLK	PTS	AVG
'91-92	ORLANDO	55	1118	236	52.9	0	0	101	51.5	336	39	22	83	573.0	10.4
'92-93	LA CLIPPERS	77	1816	375	52.7	0	---	120	48.8	478	59	34	141	870.0	11.3
'93-94	LA CLIPPERS	14	350	43	43.0	0	---	18	40.9	93	11	6	25	104.0	7.4
3 YR TOTALS		146	3284	654	52	0	0	239	49.2	907	109	62	249	1547.0	10.6
'93-94	RANK NBA C's	not ranked -- didn't appear in 25 games in '93-94													
'94-95	PROJECTIONS	82	2514	507	52.5	0	0.0	111	46.3	568	76	45	204	1125	13.7

Loy Vaught

No. 35/F

Full name: Loy Stephen Vaught
HT: 6-9 **WT:** 240
Born: 2/27/67, Grand Rapids, MI
High school: East Kentwood (MI)
College: Michigan

Vaught is a pretty good scorer, and a strong rebounder. He tied for twenty-second in the NBA in rebounding, and he led Clippers in rebounding 35 times. He doesn't have great low-post moves, but has a decent shot from medium range and gets a lot of points from rebounds. He shot 53.7 percent from the floor (sixth in the NBA). He started 56 games for the Clippers and averaged 13.3 points and 10.0 rebounds per game as a starter. He's turnover prone and doesn't pass well. And because he's not a strong low-post player, he doesn't draw a lot of fouls for someone playing an inside position. Still, last season was Vaught's best as a pro, and he should continue to improve. As a college player, Vaught started on Michigan's 1989 NCAA Championship team.

REGULAR SEASON		G	MIN	FG	FGx	3FG	3PTx	FT	FTx	REB	AST	STL	BLK	PTS	AVG
'90-91	LA CLIPPERS	73	1178	175	48.7	0	0.0	49	66.2	349	40	20	23	399	5.5
'91-92	LA CLIPPERS	79	1687	271	49.2	4	80.0	55	79.7	512	71	37	31	601	7.6
'92-93	LA CLIPPERS	79	1653	313	50.8	1	25.0	116	74.8	492	54	55	39	743	9.4
'93-94	LA CLIPPERS	75	2118	373	53.7	0	0.0	131	72.0	656	74	76	22	877	11.7
4 YR TOTALS		306	6636	1132	51.0	5	31.3	351	73.1	2009	239	188	115	2620	8.6
'93-94	RANK NBA Fs	55	43	33	13	78	78	57	65	18	71	29	91	44	4.2
'94-95	PROJECTIONS	73	2449	433	55.9	-1	-16.7	161	70.3	775	85	101	9	1026	14.1

PLAYOFFS		G	MIN	FG	FGx	3FG	3PTx	FT	FTx	REB	AST	STL	BLK	PTS	AVG
'91-92	LA CLIPPERS	5	36	7	63.6	1	100.0	2	100.0	12	4	1	1	17	3.4
'92-93	LA CLIPPERS	3	50	6	40.0	0	---	4	80.0	18	0	4	1	16	5.3
TOTALS		8	86	13	50.0	1	100.0	6	85.7	30	4	5	2	33	4.1

Terry Dehere   No. 24/G

Full name: Lennox Dominique Dehere
HT: 6-4   **WT:** 190
Born: 9/12/71, New York, NY
High school: St. Anthony's (Jersey City, NJ)
College: Seton Hall
Dehere still has the confidence of Clippers management. They're trying to deal Ron Harper to open up playing time for Dehere.

REGULAR SEASON	G	MIN	FG	FG%	3FG	3PT%	FT	FT%	REB	AST	STL	BLK	PTS	AVG
'93-94 LA CLIPPERS	64	759	129	37.7	23	40.4	61	75.3	68	78	28	3	342	5.3
1 YR TOTALS	64	759	129	37.7	23	40.4	61	75.3	68	78	28	3	342	5.3
'93-94 RANK NBA Gs	99	114	109	125	69	16	102	87	117	114	115	110	106	106

Lamond Murray   F

HT: 6-7   **WT:** 236
Born: 4/20/73, Pasadena, CA
College: California
Playing with Jason Kidd at California, Murray led the Pac-10 in scoring with a 24.3 points per game average. He also led Cal with 7.9 rebounds per game. In 3 years at Cal, he scored 1,688 points, a school record.

REGULAR SEASON	G	MIN	FG	FG%	3FG	3PT%	FT	FT%	REB	AST	STL	BLK	PTS	AVG

ROOKIE -- NO NBA EXPERIENCE

Eric Piatkowski G-F

HT: 6-7 **WT:** 215
Born: 9/30/70, Steubenville, OH
College: Nebraska
Piatkowski was the fifteenth player taken in the draft. He's got a great outside shot, handles and passes the ball well, and is a good rebounder.

REGULAR SEASON	G	MIN	FG	FGx	3FG	3PTx	FT	FTx	REB	AST	STL	BLK	PTS	AVG

ROOKIE -- NO NBA EXPERIENCE

Malik Sealy No. 21/F

HT: 6-8 **WT:** 190
Born: 2/1/70, Bronx, NY
High school: St. Nicholas of Tolentine (Bronx)
College: St. John's
Sealy runs the floor well, but he's not the scorer Manning and Wilkins are, and at 190 lbs., he's a little light to play forward in the NBA.

REGULAR SEASON	G	MIN	FG	FGx	3FG	3PTx	FT	FTx	REB	AST	STL	BLK	PTS	AVG
'92-93 INDIANA	58	672	136	42.6	7	22.6	51	68.9	112	47	36	7	330	5.7
'93-94 INDIANA	43	623	111	40.5	4	25.0	59	67.8	118	48	31	8	285	6.6
2 YR TOTALS	101	1295	247	41.7	11	23.4	110	68.3	230	95	67	15	615	6.1
'93-94 RANK NBA Fs	96	100	86	104	82	77	47	48	95	80	79	100	86	67
'94-95 PROJECTIONS	28	574	89	38.4	1	33.3	65	67.0	122	48	26	9	244	8.7

PLAYOFFS	G	MIN	FG	FGx	3FG	3PTx	FT	FTx	REB	AST	STL	BLK	PTS	AVG
'92-93 INDIANA	3	18	0	0.0	0	0.0	2	100.0	2	0	0	0	2	0.7
TOTALS	3	18	0	0.0	0	0.0	2	100.0	2	0	0	0	2	0.7

Elmore Spencer   No. 27/C

HT: 7-0 **WT:** 270
Born: 12/6/69, Atlanta, GA
High school: Booker T. Washington (Atlanta
College: Nevada-Las Vegas
Spencer started 63 games last season, in th
wake of Stanley Roberts' season-endin
injury. Spencer's primarily a shotblocker; he
an average scorer and rebounder.

REGULAR SEASON		G	MIN	FG	FG%	3FG	3PT%	FT	FT%	REB	AST	STL	BLK	PTS	AVG
'92-93	LA CLIPPERS	44	280	44	53.7	0	---	16	50.0	62	8	8	18	104	2.4
'93-94	LA CLIPPERS	76	1930	288	53.3	0	0.0	97	59.9	415	75	30	127	673	8.9
	2 YR TOTALS	120	2210	332	53.4	0	0.0	113	58.2	477	83	38	145	777	6.5
'93-94	RANK NBA Cs	16	14	13	12	14	14	18	41	20	18	26	9	15	18
'94-95	PROJECTIONS	82	3580	506	53.0	0	0.0	134	69.8	747	176	9	241	1146	14.0

PLAYOFFS		G	MIN	FG	FG%	3FG	3PT%	FT	FT%	REB	AST	STL	BLK	PTS	AVG
'92-93	LA CLIPPERS	2	4	0	0.0	0	---	0	---	1	0	0	0	0	0.0
	TOTALS	2	4	0	0.0	0	---	0	---	1	0	0	0	0	0.0

Bill Fitch   Head Coach

Full name: William Charles Fitch
Born: 5/19/34, Davenport, IA
High school: Cedar Rapids (IA)
College: Coe College (IA)
Fitch coached the Celtics to 3 division title
and an NBA title in 4 seasons. He also too
Houston from 29 wins in his first season t
the NBA finals 2 years later.

	REGULAR SEASON				PLAYOFFS			
YEAR	TEAM	W	L	PCT	FINISH	W	L	PCT
'78-79	CLEVELAND	30	52	366	T4th/Central Div.			
'79-80	BOSTON	61	21	744	1st/Atlantic Div.	5	4	556 lost Eastern Conf. finals to Philadelphia, 4-1
'80-81	BOSTON	62	20	756	T1st/Atlantic Div.	12	5	706 won NBA Finals over Houston, 4-2
'81-82	BOSTON	63	19	768	1st/Atlantic Div.	7	5	583 lost Eastern Conf. finals to Philadelphia, 4-3
'82-83	BOSTON	56	26	683	2nd/Atlantic Div.	2	5	286 lost Eastern Conf. semifinals to Milwaukee, 4-
'83-84	HOUSTON	29	53	354	6th/Midwest Div.			
'84-85	HOUSTON	48	54	471	2nd/Midwest Div.	2	3	400 lost Western Conf. first round to Utah, 3-2
'85-86	HOUSTON	51	31	622	1st/Midwest Div.	13	7	650 lost NBA Finals to Boston, 4-2
'86-87	HOUSTON	42	40	512	3rd/Midwest Div.	5	5	500 lost Western Conf. semifinals to Seattle, 4-2
'87-88	HOUSTON	46	36	561	4th/Midwest Div.			
'89-90	NEW JERSEY	17	65	207	6th/Atlantic Div.			
'90-91	NEW JERSEY	26	56	317	5th/Atlantic Div.			
'91-92	NEW JERSEY	40	42	488	3rd/Atlantic Div.	1	3	250 lost Eastern Conf. first round to Cleveland, 3-1
	21 YR TOTALS	845	897	485		54	48	529

Los Angeles LAKERS

1994–95 Scouting Report

Frontcourt

Center Vlade Divac is the team's leading scorer (despite awful free throw shooting), rebounder, and second leading shotblocker. Starting power forward Elden Campbell led the team in blocks with 146 (nearly two per game), but averaged just 6.8 rebounds per game, despite being second on the team in rebounding. Although not quite the volatile scorer you'd want at small forward, '93 first-round pick George Lynch emerged late last year as the starter, averaging 15.5 points and 9.3 rebounds per 40 minutes played. James Worthy can come off the bench to add offense; he averaged 20.3 points per 40 minutes. Injury-plagued Sam Bowie missed the final 57 games of the season with arthroscopic surgery on his left knee. He's an intelligent player who had done pretty well before the injury, splitting time at center with Divac and averaging 16 points, 9.4 rebounds, and 3.4 assists per 40 minutes played.

Backcourt

The Laker backcourt is loaded with young guards with potential, who are still maturing. Third-year pro Anthony Peeler opened the season as the starting shooting guard before missing the last 47 games due to a stress fracture in his lower left leg. In the wake of Peeler's injury, Doug Christie took over at shooting guard. He also sees some time at small forward, but is really too small for that position. Nick Van Exel, who starts at point guard, had an outstanding rookie year. He's deadly from 3-point range, is a good defender, and should continue to develop as a playmaker. Sedale Threatt is an excellent shooter (fourth in the NBA in free throw percentage) who can play either guard position, although he's better suited to play shooting guard. First-rounder Eddie Jones will compete for time at shooting guard; he can score, rebound, pass and even block shots. If he bulks up, he could be shifted to small forward.

Defense

The Lakers did a lot of things right on defense last season. The were sixth in the NBA in blocked shots. They also ranked ninth in the NBA in stealing the ball and in forcing turnovers. But they had big problem on their defensive boards; opponents snagged 1,28 offensive rebounds against the Lakers, third highest total in the league. With all those second shots, and the Lakers' lack of a defen sive presence in the middle, opponents averaged 104.7 points (nint highest total in the NBA) shooting 47.6 percent from the floor (sev enth highest in the league).

1994–95 Prospects

Their 33–49 record (second worst in Laker history) was 6 game worse than the previous season. In all fairness, the team was devas tated by injuries, losing 216 player games due to injury or illnes Anthony Peeler and Sam Bowie suffered season-ending injurie before last season's halfway mark. As a result, the opening nigh starting lineup started in just 21 games. The Lakers failed to hav even one player appear in all 82 regular season games for the firs time in 19 years. And believe it or not, it could have been worse: th Lakers were 10–7 in games decided by 3 points or less, and 23–42 i other games. One reason is that they don't make many mistake their 14.6 turnovers per game was third lowest in the league.

The Lakers will have major holes up front again this season. The are a woeful rebounding team: seventeenth in overall rebounding twenty-fourth in defensive rebounds. The Lakers also can't scor much inside, which not only means that they don't get high percent age shots, they also don't pick up fouls; only Dallas and Detroi picked up fewer fouls than the Lakers.

There are signs of success in the future: the backcourt is young deep, and promising, and the bench is not bad. The young guard GM Jerry West has drafted are solid players who play good defens and take care of the ball. The Lakers need a couple of big men up front who aren't afraid to bang down low and snag rebounds. A good low-post game from someone wouldn't hurt, either. Th Lakers will probably have another sub-.500 season, but with a cou ple of breaks, they could end up in the playoffs anyway.

Team Directory

Owner/Governor: Dr. Jerry Buss   Pres., Calif. sports: Lou Baumeister
CEO, Calif. sp. mktg.: Frank Mariani   Exec. VP, basketball op.: Jerry West
General manager: Mitch Kupchak   Public relations director: John Black

1993–94 Review

WESTERN CONFERENCE						EASTERN CONFERENCE					
MIDWEST DIV.			PACIFIC DIV.			ATLANTIC DIV.			CENTRAL DIV.		
	W	L		W	L		W	L		W	L
HOU	1	3	SEA	0	5	NY	0	2	ATL	1	1
SAN	0	4	PHO	3	2	ORL	2	0	CHI	1	1
UTAH	2	2	GS	0	5	NJ	0	2	CLE	1	1
DEN	1	3	POR	0	5	MIA	1	1	IND	2	0
MIN	3	1	LAL	–	–	BOS	1	1	CHA	0	2
DAL	4	0	SAC	1	4	PHI	1	1	DET	2	0
			LAC	3	2	WAS	1	1	MIL	2	0
	11	13		7	23		6	8		9	5

1993–94 finish: 33–49 (21–20 home, 12–29 away), fifth in Pacific Div.

1994–95 Schedule

Date	Opponent	Time	Date	Opponent	Time	Date	Opponent	Time
11/4	@ Detroit	8:00 pm	1/8	Miami	10:00 pm	3/7	@ Miami	7:30 pm
11/5	@ Milwaukee	8:30 pm	1/9	@ Portland	10:00 pm	3/8	@ Orlando	7:30 pm
11/8	@ New York	7:30 pm	1/11	Phoenix	10:30 pm	3/10	@ Minnesota	8:00 pm
11/9	@ Minnesota	8:00 pm	1/13	Gold. St.	10:30 pm	3/11	@ Chicago	8:30 pm
11/11	Denver	10:30 pm	1/16	LA Clip.	4:30 pm	3/13	Indiana	10:30 pm
11/12	@ Gold. St.	10:30 pm	1/18	@ Indiana	7:30 pm	3/15	@ Gold. St.	10:30 pm
11/15	@ LA Clip.	10:30 pm	1/20	@ Boston	7:30 pm	3/17	Boston	10:30 pm
11/16	New York	10:30 pm	1/21	@ Phila.	7:30 pm	3/19	Sacra.	10:00 pm
11/18	Cleveland	10:30 pm	1/23	@ Charlotte	7:30 pm	3/22	Portland	10:30 pm
11/23	Dallas	10:30 pm	1/25	New Jersey	10:30 pm	3/24	Wash.	10:30 pm
11/25	@ Atlanta	7:30 pm	1/28	@ Seattle	3:30 pm	3/26	Houston	10:00 pm
11/26	@ Wash.	7:30 pm	1/31	Chicago	10:30 pm	3/28	@ Houston	8:30 pm
11/29	@ New Jersey	7:30 pm	2/1	@ Phoenix	9:00 pm	3/29	@ San Ant.	8:30 pm
11/30	@ Cleveland	7:30 pm	2/3	Denver	10:30 pm	3/31	Atlanta	10:30 pm
12/2	Houston	10:30 pm	2/4	@ LA Clip.	10:30 pm	4/2	Orlando	10:00 pm
12/6	Gold. St.	10:30 pm	2/7	@ Denver	9:00 pm	4/4	@ Denver	9:00 pm
12/9	LA Clip.	10:30 pm	2/8	San Ant.	10:30 pm	4/5	@ Dallas	8:30 pm
12/10	@ Utah	9:00 pm	2/15	Seattle	10:30 pm	4/7	Utah	10:30 pm
12/13	@ Dallas	8:00 pm	2/16	@ Sacra.	10:30 pm	4/9	San Ant.	10:00 pm
12/15	@ Houston	8:30 pm	2/19	Portland	10:00 pm	4/11	@ Sacra.	10:30 pm
12/17	@ San Ant.	8:30 pm	2/20	@ Seattle	10:00 pm	4/11	@ Utah	9:00 pm
12/20	Minnesota	10:30 pm	2/22	Phila.	10:30 pm	4/15	@ Phoenix	10:00 pm
12/23	Sacra.	10:30 pm	2/24	Charlotte	10:30 pm	4/16	Dallas	10:00 pm
12/27	@ Gold. St.	10:30 pm	2/25	@ LA Clip.	10:30 pm	4/18	Seattle	10:30 pm
12/29	Seattle	10:30 pm	2/27	Utah	10:30 pm	4/20	@ Portland	10:00 pm
12/30	@ Phoenix	9:00 pm	3/1	Phoenix	10:30 pm	4/22	Portland	10:30 pm
1/3	Detroit	10:30 pm	3/3	Sacra.	10:30 pm			
1/6	Milwaukee	10:30 pm	3/5	Minnesota	10:00 pm			

1993–94 Team Stats

NAME	G	MIN	FG	FGA	FG%	3FG	3FGA	3%	FT	FTA	FT%	ORB	TRB	AST	PF	STL	BLK	TO	PTS	AVG
Divac	79	2685	453	895	50.6	9	47	19.1	208	303	68.6	282	851	307	288	92	112	191	1123	14.2
Peeler	30	923	176	409	43.0	14	63	22.2	57	71	80.3	48	109	94	93	43	8	59	423	14.1
Van Exel	81	2700	413	1049	39.4	123	364	33.8	150	192	78.1	47	238	466	154	85	8	145	1099	13.6
Campbell	76	2253	373	808	46.2	0	2	0.0	188	273	68.9	167	519	86	241	64	146	98	934	12.3
Threatt	81	2278	411	852	48.2	5	33	15.2	138	155	89.0	28	153	344	186	110	19	106	965	11.9
Christie	65	1515	244	562	43.4	39	119	32.8	145	208	69.7	93	235	136	186	89	28	140	672	10.3
Wilson	5	126	19	39	48.7	0	0	—	13	25	52.0	12	28	12	17	5	1	6	51	10.2
Worthy	80	1597	340	838	40.6	32	111	28.8	100	135	74.1	48	181	154	80	45	18	97	812	10.2
Lynch	71	1762	291	573	50.8	0	5	0.0	99	166	59.6	220	410	96	177	102	27	87	681	9.6
Bowie	25	556	75	172	43.6	1	4	25.0	72	83	86.7	27	131	47	65	4	28	43	223	8.9
Smith	73	1617	272	617	44.1	16	50	32.0	85	119	71.4	106	195	148	128	59	14	76	645	8.8
Jordan	23	259	44	103	42.7	2	4	50.0	35	51	68.6	46	67	26	26	14	5	14	125	5.4
Edwards	45	469	78	168	46.4	0	0	—	54	79	68.4	11	65	22	90	4	3	30	210	4.7
Rambis	50	635	59	114	51.8	0	1	0.0	46	71	64.8	84	189	32	89	22	23	26	164	3.3
Schayes	13	133	14	38	36.8	0	0	—	8	10	80.0	15	34	5	18	5	2	9	36	2.8
Harvey	27	247	29	79	36.7	0	0	—	12	26	46.2	26	59	8	39	8	19	17	70	2.6
Lakers	82	19755	3291	7316	45.0	241	803	30.0	1410	1967	71.7	1260	3464	1983	1877	751	461	1197	8233	100.4
Opp.	82	19755	3337	7008	47.6	228	723	31.5	1683	2346	71.7	1284	3817	2163	1659	664	427	1344	8585	104.7

HISTORY

TITLES

1949–50 NBA champs	1972–73 NBA champs
1950–51 NBA champs	1973–74 Western Conf. champs
1951–52 Western Div. champs	1974–75 Pacific Div. champs
1952–53 NBA champs	1977–78 Pacific Div. champs
1953–54 NBA champs	1980–81 NBA champs
1954–55 NBA champs	1982–83 NBA champs
1959–60 Western Div. champs	1983–84 Western Conf. champs
1962–63 Western Div. champs	1984–85 Western Conf. champs
1963–64 Western Div. champs	1985–86 NBA champs
1965–66 Western Div. champs	1986–87 Pacific Div. champs
1966–67 Western Div. champs	1987–88 NBA champs
1968–69 Western Div. champs	1988–89 NBA champs
1969–70 Western Div. champs	1989–90 Western Conf. champs
1970–71 Western Conf. champs	1990–91 Pacific Div. champs
1971–72 Pacific Div. champs	1991–92 Western Conf. champs

ALL-TIME TEAM RECORDS

Career

Games played	Kareem Abdul-Jabbar	1,093	1976–89
Total points	Jerry West	25,192	1961–74
Total rebounds	Elgin Baylor	11,463	1959–72
Assists	Earvin Johnson	9,921	1980–91

Season

Total points	Elgin Baylor	2,719	1962–63
Total rebounds	Wilt Chamberlain	1,712	1968–69
Assists	Earvin Johnson	989	1990–91

Game

Total points	Elgin Baylor	71	vs. New York, 11/15/60
Field goals made	Wilt Chamberlain	29	vs. Phoenix, 2/9/69
Free throws made	Larry Foust	22	vs. St. Louis, 11/30/57
Total rebounds	Wilt Chamberlain	42	vs. Boston, 3/7/69

LEADING COACHES

NAME	YEARS	REGULAR SEASON			PLAYOFFS		
		W	L	PCT	W	L	PCT
Pat Riley	1981–90	533	194	.733	102	47	.685
John Kundla	1948–57, 1958–59	423	302	.583	60	35	.632
Fred Schaus	1960–67	315	245	.563	33	38	.465
Bill Sharman	1971–76	246	164	.600	22	15	.595
Jerry West	1976–79	145	101	.589	8	14	.364

Los Angeles Lakers 1994–95 Roster

Head Coach: Del Harris

No.	Name	Pos.	Ht.	Wt.	Yrs.	Born	College
31	Sam Bowie	C	7-1	263	9	3/17/61	Kentucky
41	Elden Campbell	F-C	6-11	250	4	7/23/68	Clemson
8	Doug Christie	G-F	6-6	205	2	5/9/70	Pepperdine
12	Vlade Divac	C	7-1	250	5	2/3/68	Yugoslavia
40	Antonio Harvey	C-F	6-11	225	1	7/9/70	Pfeiffer
25	Eddie Jones	G	6-6	190	R	10/20/71	Temple
30	George Lynch	F	6-8	223	1	9/3/70	North Carolina
2	Anthony Miller	F	6-9	255	R	10/22/71	Michigan State
1	Anthony Peeler	G	6-4	212	2	11/25/69	Missouri
5	Trevor Ruffin	G	6-1	199	R	9/26/70	Hawaii
34	Tony Smith	G	6-4	205	4	6/14/68	Marquette
3	Sedale Threatt	G	6-2	185	11	9/10/61	West Virginia Tech
9	Nick Van Exel	G	6-1	170	1	11/27/71	Cincinnati
42	James Worthy	F	6-9	225	12	2/27/61	North Carolina

Arena Information

The Great Western Forum (17,505)
Tickets: 213-480-3232, 714-740-2000, 805-583-8700
Ticket prices: $100, $90, $62.50, $42.50, $28.50, $23.50, $15, $8.50, $2

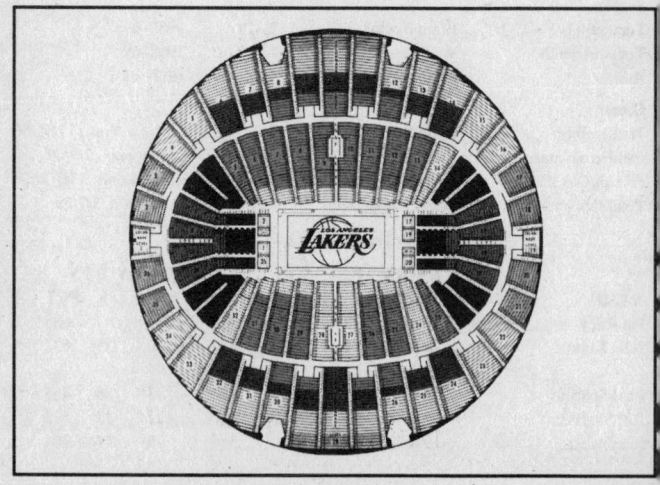

Elden Campbell

No. 41/F-C

Full name: Elden Jerome Campbell
HT: 6-11 **WT:** 250
Born: 7/23/68, Los Angeles, CA
High school: Morningside
(Inglewood, CA)
College: Clemson

Campbell is a good shotblocker and rebounder. He doesn't have a high shooting percentage from the floor for an inside player, and he's not a good free throw shooter. Campbell had the best year of his career last season, posting career high in points per game, rebounds per game, blocked shots per game, and total assists. Campbell also tallied a career high in points with 29 at Houston February 3. Campbell scored in double figures on 51 occasions, and broke 20 points in 9 games, a career high. He was the Lakers' leading scorer 12 times and leading rebounder 19 times.

REGULAR SEASON	G	MIN	FG	FG%	3FG	3PT%	FT	FT%	REB	AST	STL	BLK	PTS	AVG
'90-91 LA LAKERS	52	380	56	45.5	0	---	32	65.3	96	10	11	38	144	2.8
'91-92 LA LAKERS	81	1876	220	44.8	0	0.0	138	61.9	423	59	53	159	578	7.1
'92-93 LA LAKERS	79	1551	238	45.8	0	0.0	130	63.7	332	48	59	100	606	7.7
'93-94 LA LAKERS	76	2253	373	46.2	0	0.0	188	68.9	519	86	64	146	934	12.3
4 YR TOTALS	288	6060	887	45.7	0	0.0	488	65.2	1370	203	187	443	2262	7.9
'93-94 RANK NBA Fs	48	39	33	74	78	78	36	85	29	65	42	3	37	35
'94-95 PROJECTIONS	77	2758	497	46.6	0	0.0	233	72.1	646	119	69	159	1227	15.9

PLAYOFFS	G	MIN	FG	FG%	3FG	3PT%	FT	FT%	REB	AST	STL	BLK	PTS	AVG
'90-91 LA LAKERS	14	138	25	65.8	0	---	7	46.7	29	3	6	8	57	4.1
'91-92 LA LAKERS	4	117	14	37.8	0	---	12	66.7	25	6	3	6	40	10.0
'92-93 LA LAKERS	5	178	29	42.0	0	---	12	50.0	42	7	6	12	70	14.0
TOTALS	23	433	68	47.2	0	---	31	54.4	96	16	15	26	167	7.3

Vlade Divac

No. 12/C

HT: 7-1   **WT:** 250
Born: 2/3/68, Prijepolje, Yugoslavia
High school: Kraljevo (Yugoslavia)
College: None

Divac is one of the best rebounders in the NBA, and is an extraordinary passer. Divac ranked thirteenth in total rebounds and twelfth in rebounding average. Divac also established a career high in assists last season, trailing only David Robinson in total assists among centers. Last season, Divac became the first Laker to lead the team in both scoring and rebounding since Kareem Abdul-Jabbar in '84–85. But Divac's 14.2 points per game was the lowest team-leading average in Los Angeles franchise history. His 40 double-doubles were twelfth in the NBA last season, behind Charles Barkley's 43. He posted a career high in points scored when he tallied 33 points against Denver April 8.

REGULAR SEASON		G	MIN	FG	FGx	3FG	3PTx	FT	FTx	REB	AST	STL	BLK	PTS	AVG
'89-90	LA LAKERS	82	1611	274	49.9	0	0.0	153	70.8	512	75	79	114	701	8.5
'90-91	LA LAKERS	82	2310	360	56.5	5	35.7	196	70.3	666	92	106	127	921	11.2
'91-92	LA LAKERS	36	979	157	49.5	5	26.3	86	76.8	247	60	55	35	405	11.3
'92-93	LA LAKERS	82	2525	397	48.5	21	28.0	235	68.9	729	232	128	140	1050	12.8
'93-94	LA LAKERS	79	2685	453	50.6	9	19.1	208	68.6	851	307	92	112	1123	14.2
5 YR TOTALS		361	10110	1641	51.0	40	25.0	878	70.2	3005	766	460	528	4200	11.6
'93-94	RANK NBA Cs	10	6	6	19	2	11	10	27	6	2	3	11	7	9
'94-95	PROJECTIONS	82	3037	527	50.9	8	16.3	215	67.4	1016	416	78	110	1277	15.6

PLAYOFFS		G	MIN	FG	FGx	3FG	3PTx	FT	FTx	REB	AST	STL	BLK	PTS	AVG
'89-90	LA LAKERS	9	175	32	72.7	1	50.0	17	89.5	48	10	8	15	82	9.1
'90-91	LA LAKERS	19	609	97	56.4	1	16.7	57	80.3	127	21	27	41	252	13.3
'91-92	LA LAKERS	4	143	15	34.9	0	0.0	9	90.0	22	15	5	3	39	9.8
'92-93	LA LAKERS	5	167	37	50.0	4	44.4	12	54.5	47	28	6	12	90	18.0
TOTALS		37	1094	181	54.4	6	31.6	95	77.9	244	74	46	71	463	12.5

George Lynch

No. 24/F

Full name: George DeWitt Lynch III
HT: 6-8   **WT:** 223
Born: 9/3/70, Roanoke, VA
High school: Flint Hill Prep
(Oakton, VA)
College: North Carolina
Lynch is a good rebounder for his size, and a good defender, but he doesn't have a lot of offensive moves; he gets his points on dunks and putbacks. Lynch set a new rookie record for offensive rebounds (breaking Vlade Divac's record of 167 in '89–90) with 220. He had more offensive rebounds (220) than defensive rebounds (190). He became the first Laker rookie since Magic Johnson to score 30 points in a game when he scored 30 against Milwaukee March 27. And his 18 rebounds vs. Detroit January 28 were the most by a Laker rookie since Magic's 18 boards March 7, 1980 against Chicago. Lynch opened the season as a reserve, but moved into the starting lineup after 22 games. He led the Lakers in scoring twice, and in rebounds 10 times.

REGULAR SEASON	G	MIN	FG	FG%	3FG	3PT%	FT	FT%	REB	AST	STL	BLK	PTS	AVG
'93-94 LA LAKERS	71	1762	291	50.8	0	0.0	99	59.6	410	96	102	27	681	9.6
1 YR TOTALS	71	1762	291	50.8	0	0.0	99	59.6	410	96	102	27	681	9.6
'93-94 RANK NBA Fs	74	57	56	28	78	78	72	117	45	60	13	78	59	60

Sedale Threatt   No. 3/G

Full name: Sedale Eugene Threatt
HT: 6-2   **WT:** 185
Born: 9/10/61, Atlanta, GA
High school: Therrell (Atlanta)
College: West Virginia Tech

Threatt is one of the few guards in the NBA who can really play both guard positions: not only is he an outstanding scorer, he's a good playmaker and a terrific ballhandler, with over 3,000 career assists. He's also an excellent free throw shooter. Threatt led the Lakers in FT shooting percentage; his 89 percent mark ranked fourth in the NBA. And he's an outstanding defender, leading the Lakers with 110 steals. Threatt has problems hitting from beyond the arc: he was just 5 for 33 (15.2 percent) last season. Although he had only 20 starts, he was the Lakers' fifth-leading scorer. Threatt scored 20 points or more 18 times, and was the Lakers' leading scorer 11 times.

REGULAR SEASON		G	MIN	FG	FG%	3FG	3PT%	FT	FT%	REB	AST	STL	BLK	PTS	AVG
'84-85	PHILADELPHIA	82	1304	188	45.2	4	18.2	66	73.3	99	175	80	16	446	5.4
'85-86	PHILADELPHIA	70	1754	310	45.3	1	4.2	75	83.3	121	193	30	5	696	9.9
'86-87	PHILA-CHI	68	1446	239	44.8	7	21.9	95	79.8	108	259	74	13	580	8.5
'87-88	CHI-SEA	71	1055	216	50.8	3	11.1	57	80.3	88	160	60	8	492	6.9
'88-89	SEATTLE	63	1220	235	49.4	11	36.7	63	81.8	117	238	83	4	544	8.6
'89-90	SEATTLE	65	1481	303	50.6	8	25.0	130	82.8	115	216	65	8	744	11.4
'90-91	SEATTLE	80	2066	433	51.9	10	28.6	137	79.2	99	273	113	8	1013	12.7
'91-92	LA LAKERS	82	3070	509	48.9	20	32.3	202	83.1	253	593	168	16	1240	15.1
'92-93	LA LAKERS	82	2893	522	50.8	14	26.4	177	82.3	273	564	142	11	1235	15.1
'93-94	LA LAKERS	81	2278	411	48.2	5	15.2	138	89.0	153	344	110	19	965	11.9
11 YR TOTALS		789	19031	3428	48.7	84	23.5	1163	82.0	1466	3056	1001	110	8103	10.3
'93-94	RANK NBA Gs	27	47	38	22	107	124	60	6	75	37	33	39	47	52
'94-95	PROJECTIONS	82	2093	373	47.1	2	8.0	120	93.0	124	286	98	22	868	10.6

PLAYOFFS		G	MIN	FG	FG%	3FG	3PT%	FT	FT%	REB	AST	STL	BLK	PTS	AVG
'84-85	PHILADELPHIA	4	28	2	28.6	0	---	0	---	1	5	1	0	4	1.0
'85-86	PHILADELPHIA	12	312	67	46.9	0	0.0	26	78.8	25	42	23	2	160	13.3
'86-87	CHICAGO	3	70	8	47.1	0	---	4	100.0	5	16	1	0	20	6.7
'87-88	SEATTLE	5	80	14	41.2	0	0.0	4	100.0	1	11	1	0	32	6.4
'88-89	SEATTLE	8	201	39	47.6	1	25.0	17	85.0	13	49	17	0	96	12.0
'90-91	SEATTLE	5	136	30	53.6	4	36.4	9	90.0	8	17	5	0	73	14.6
'91-92	LA LAKERS	4	162	24	52.2	2	66.7	9	75.0	8	17	7	2	59	14.8
'92-93	LA LAKERS	5	205	39	43.8	3	23.1	9	75.0	17	40	13	1	90	18.0
TOTALS		49	1200	224	47.0	10	27.8	78	82.1	90	198	64	3	536	10.9

Nick Van Exel

No. 9/G

Full name: Nickey Maxwell Van Exel
HT: 6-1   **WT:** 170
Born: 11/27/71, Kenosha, WI
High school: St. Joseph's
  (Kenosha)
College: Cincinnati

Van Exel is an outstanding ball-handler and a prolific outside shooter. Van Exel is only the fifth Laker rookie to score 1,000 points. His 13.6 points per game is the highest rookie average ever by a second-round pick. Van Exel was also the first rookie to lead the team in assists since Norm Nixon in '77–78. (Magic Johnson was second to Nixon in his rookie season, '79–80.) Only Anfernee Hardaway posted more assists among NBA rookies last season. Van Exel's 123 3-pointers, which set a new team record, were the second most by a rookie in NBA history. (Dennis Scott had 125 in '90–91.) He put up 16 3-pointers, third most in NBA history, in the Lakers' season finale. (He made only 3 of them.)

REGULAR SEASON	G	MIN	FG	FG%	3FG	3PT%	FT	FT%	REB	AST	STL	BLK	PTS	AVG
'93-94 LA LAKERS	81	2700	413	39.4	123	33.8	150	78.1	238	466	85	8	1099	13.6
1 YR TOTALS	81	2700	413	39.4	123	33.8	150	78.1	238	466	85	8	1099	13.6
'93-94 RANK NBA Gs	27	24	36	120	9	53	50	70	37	17	48	81	35	42

Sam Bowie   No. 31/C

Full name: Samuel Paul Bowie
HT: 7-1 **WT:** 263
Born: 3/17/61, Lebanon, PA
High school: Lebanon (PA)
College: Kentucky

Bowie was second on the Lakers in FT percentage. He shot 51.5 percent from the floor at home, just 38.5 percent on the road.

REGULAR SEASON		G	MIN	FG	FG%	3FG	3PT%	FT	FT%	REB	AST	STL	BLK	PTS	AVG
'88-89	PORTLAND	20	412	69	45.1	5	71.4	28	57.1	106	36	7	33	171	8.6
'89-90	NEW JERSEY	68	2207	347	41.6	10	32.3	294	77.6	690	91	38	121	998	14.7
'90-91	NEW JERSEY	62	1916	314	43.4	4	18.2	169	73.2	480	147	43	90	801	12.9
'91-92	NEW JERSEY	71	2179	421	44.5	8	32.0	212	75.7	578	186	41	120	1062	15.0
'92-93	NEW JERSEY	79	2092	287	45.0	2	33.3	141	77.9	556	127	32	128	717	9.1
'93-94	LA LAKERS	25	556	75	43.6	1	25.0	72	86.7	131	47	4	28	223	8.9
9 YR TOTALS		444	12873	2009	45.3	30	31.6	1210	74.7	3557	957	242	829	5258	11.8
'93-94	RANK NBA Cs	55	39	38	42	8	6	27	3	39	26	50	35	37	17
'94-95	PROJECTIONS	0	-247	-30	42.9	0	0.0	-39	92.9	-54	-23	0	-12	-99	---

PLAYOFFS		G	MIN	FG	FG%	3FG	3PT%	FT	FT%	REB	AST	STL	BLK	PTS	AVG
'88-89	PORTLAND	3	67	12	42.9	1	50.0	6	75.0	20	3	0	7	31	10.3
'91-92	NEW JERSEY	4	112	14	42.4	1	50.0	8	66.7	19	9	3	3	37	9.3
'92-93	NEW JERSEY	3	71	4	44.4	0	---	2	100.0	12	2	6	1	10	3.3
TOTALS		19	509	56	43.4	2	50.0	30	63.8	127	35	13	32	144	7.6

Doug Christie   No. 8/G-F

Full name: Douglas Dale Christie
HT: 6-6 **WT:** 205
Born: 5/9/70, Seattle, WA
High school: Rainier Beach (Seattle)
College: Pepperdine

Christie was second on the team in 3-point accuracy, but was inconsistent as a shooter, averaging just 43.4 percent from the field.

REGULAR SEASON		G	MIN	FG	FG%	3FG	3PT%	FT	FT%	REB	AST	STL	BLK	PTS	AVG
'92-93	LA LAKERS	23	332	45	42.5	2	16.7	50	75.8	51	53	22	5	142	6.2
'93-94	LA LAKERS	65	1515	244	43.4	39	32.8	145	69.7	235	136	89	28	672	10.3
2 YR TOTALS		88	1847	289	43.3	41	31.3	195	71.2	286	189	111	33	814	9.3
'93-94	RANK NBA Gs	94	79	72	81	49	65	53	114	38	90	45	18	67	63
'94-95	PROJECTIONS	82	2698	506	44.4	159	48.8	130	63.7	423	54	138	59	1301	15.9

PLAYOFFS		G	MIN	FG	FG%	3FG	3PT%	FT	FT%	REB	AST	STL	BLK	PTS	AVG
'92-93	LA LAKERS	5	39	4	36.4	1	33.3	0	---	4	6	2	2	9	1.8
TOTALS		5	39	4	36.4	1	33.3	0	---	4	6	2	2	9	1.8

Eddie Jones   No. 25/G-F

HT: 6-6   **WT:** 190
Born: 10/20/71, Pompano Beach, FL
College: Temple
Last season's Atlantic-10 Player of the Year, Jones averaged 19.2 points, 6.8 rebounds and 2.3 steals per game. He became the first player in school history to accumulate 100 assists and 100 blocked shots in a career.

REGULAR SEASON	G	MIN	FG	FGx	3FG	3PTx	FT	FTx	REB	AST	STL	BLK	PTS	AVG
ROOKIE -- NO NBA EXPERIENCE														

Anthony Peeler   No. 1/G

Full name: Anthony Eugene Peeler
HT: 6-4   **WT:** 212
Born: 11/25/69, Kansas City, MO
High school: Paseo (Kansas City)
College: Missouri
Known as a perimeter scorer, Peeler's 3-point shooting dropped from 39.0 percent in '92–93 to just 22.2 percent last season.

REGULAR SEASON		G	MIN	FG	FGx	3FG	3PTx	FT	FTx	REB	AST	STL	BLK	PTS	AVG
'92-93	LA LAKERS	77	1656	297	46.8	46	39.0	162	78.6	179	166	60	14	802	10.4
'93-94	LA LAKERS	30	923	176	43.0	14	22.2	57	80.3	109	94	43	8	423	14.1
	2 YR TOTALS	107	2579	473	45.3	60	33.1	219	79.1	288	260	103	22	1225	11.4
'93-94	RANK NBA Gs	134	108	92	85	82	103	104	58	100	106	95	81	97	36
'94-95	PROJECTIONS	54	1290	237	45.3	30	33.1	110	79.1	144	130	52	11	613	11

James Worthy   No. 42/F

Full name: James Ager Worthy
HT: 6-9   **WT:** 225
Born: 2/27/61, Gastonia, NC
High school: Ashbrook (Gastonia)
College: North Carolina
Although Worthy can still provide an offensive threat off the bench, age is taking a toll on his defensive capability.

REGULAR SEASON		G	MIN	FG	FG%	3FG	3PT%	FT	FT%	REB	AST	STL	BLK	PTS	AVG
'89-90	LA LAKERS	80	2960	711	54.8	15	30.6	248	78.2	478	288	99	49	1685	21.1
'90-91	LA LAKERS	78	3008	716	49.2	26	28.9	212	79.7	356	275	104	35	1670	21.4
'91-92	LA LAKERS	54	2108	450	44.7	9	20.9	166	81.4	305	252	76	23	1075	19.9
'92-93	LA LAKERS	82	2359	510	44.7	30	27.0	171	81.0	247	278	92	27	1221	14.9
'93-94	LA LAKERS	80	1597	340	40.6	32	28.8	100	74.1	181	154	45	18	812	10.2
12 YR TOTALS		926	30001	6878	52.1	117	24.1	2447	76.9	4708	2791	1041	624	16320	17.6
'93-94	RANK NBA Fs	23	67	45	126	25	38	71	47	107	39	69	98	49	57
'94-95	PROJECTIONS	82	1140	235	37.5	30	30.0	64	70.3	123	101	27	12	564	6.9

PLAYOFFS		G	MIN	FG	FG%	3FG	3PT%	FT	FT%	REB	AST	STL	BLK	PTS	AVG
'89-90	LA LAKERS	9	366	90	49.7	2	25.0	36	83.7	50	27	14	3	218	24.2
'90-91	LA LAKERS	18	733	161	46.5	4	16.7	53	73.6	73	70	19	2	379	21.1
'92-93	LA LAKERS	5	148	32	37.2	2	25.0	3	60.0	17	13	5	0	69	13.8
TOTALS		143	5297	1267	54.4	14	20.9	474	72.7	747	463	177	96	3022	21.1

Del Harris   Head Coach

Full name: Delmer W. Harris
Born: 6/18/37, Plainfield, IN
College: Milligan
Harris comes to the Lakers after serving as a basketball consultant to the Sacramento Kings. In 6 seasons, his teams went to the playoffs 5 times and the NBA finals once.

	REGULAR SEASON				PLAYOFFS			
YEAR	TEAM	W	L	PCT	FINISH	W	L	PCT	
'79-80	HOUSTON	41	41	500	2nd/Central Div.	2	5	286	lost Eastern Conf. semifinals to Boston, 4-0
'80-81	HOUSTON	40	42	488	3rd/Central Div.	12	9	571	lost NBA Finals to Boston, 4-2
'81-82	HOUSTON	46	36	561	3rd/Midwest Div.	1	2	333	lost Western Conf. first round to Seattle, 2-1
'82-83	HOUSTON	14	68	171	6th/Midwest Div.				
'87-88	MILWAUKEE	42	40	512	4th/Central Div.	2	3	400	lost Eastern Conf. first round to Atlanta, 3-2
'88-89	MILWAUKEE	49	33	598	4th/Central Div.	3	6	333	lost Eastern Conf. semifinals to Detroit, 4-0
'89-90	MILWAUKEE	44	38	537	3rd/Central Div.	1	3	250	lost Eastern Conf. first round to Chicago, 3-1
'90-91	MILWAUKEE	48	34	585	3rd/Central Div.	0	3	000	lost Eastern Conf. first round to Philadelphia, 3-0
'91-92	MILWAUKEE	8	9	471					
9 YR TOTALS		332	341	493		21	31	404	

Miami
HEAT

994–95 Scouting Report

rontcourt

lthough not in the top rank of NBA centers, Rony Seikaly can ore and rebound. He's one of the key players on the team; Miami ffers greatly when he's out of the lineup. Glen Rice, the starter at nall forward, had a great season last season, ranking tenth in the ague in scoring. If you shut down Glen Rice, you shut down the eat; they were 34–12 when Rice got his 20 points, 8–27 when he dn't. Grant Long starts at power forward. He's an average bounder and scorer. Salley comes off the bench to play power for-ard and center. He's a good defender and a very good shotblocker. orward Keith Askins doesn't play much offense, but contributes on efense and averaged 10.3 rebounds per 40 minutes played. Matt eiger improved dramatically in his second year, coming off the ench to back up Seikaly, and averaged 17.4 points and 10.1 bounds per 40 minutes played.

ackcourt

he starting backcourt of 6-6 Brian Shaw and 6-8 Steve Smith is one f the biggest in the NBA. Smith starts at point guard, although he an also play at shooting guard and small forward. He can shoot and bound well for a guard. Brian Shaw can defend either guard posi-on and can rebound. He's not much of a scorer, but he's a better laymaker than Smith. Harold Miner plays shooting guard. He's not favorite of coach Kevin Loughery because his defense is shaky, he ommits a lot of turnovers, and he doesn't pass the ball much. imbo Coles also sees time at point, although he's more of a shoot-g guard in a point guard's body. First-rounder Khalid Reeves adds the Heat's depth at guard. He'll probably be moved to point. 'illie Burton is a swingman who provides offense (but not much D) f the bench; he averaged 21.3 points and 7.8 rebounds per 40 min-es played.

Defense

Miami is one of the NBA's better defensive teams, primarily because they play big on the defensive boards, ranking fifth in the league in limiting offensive rebounds. Of course, when your guards are 6-6 and 6-8, you're going to get more than your share of rebounds. Limiting opponents' offensive rebounds is a big reason why opponents managed just 6,641 shots from the field, eighth fewest in the league. Teams averaged 100.7 points against the Heat, eleventh fewest in the NBA. And opponents shot 45.7 percent from the floor against Miami, ninth lowest in the league. The Heat plays solid fundamental defense but they're not particularly athletic defenders; Miami ranked twenty-fourth in the NBA in stealing the ball, twentieth in blocked shots, and fourteenth in the league in forcing turnovers.

1994–95 Prospects

The Heat rebounded from an injury-filled '92–93 season to improve by 6 games; their 42 wins was a franchise record. But the Heat slumped late, finishing the season just 5–13, and barely holding on to a playoff spot. (A sprained ankle by Rony Seikaly was a big reason for the slump.) They were about as good at home (22–19) as on the road (20–21). In fact, they were the only NBA team to sweep a 5-game road trip last season. They had trouble in close games, with a record of 1–3 in overtime games, and 2–6 in games decided by points or less.

The Heat aren't an easy team to figure out. The Heat can hit from outside; Miami's 337 3-pointers were fifth most in the league last year. (Of the top 5 teams in this category, only Detroit failed to make the playoffs.) They have an above average frontcourt, with Rice and Seikaly, although they could use improvement at power forward. The challenge for Coach Kevin Loughery is to assemble a productive backcourt. None of his prospective starters, for instance, is particularly gifted defensively. And none of his guards is presently a first-rate point guard. Before the Heat can advance, they need either a stud at shooting guard who can play 35 minutes a game and give Miami a third scoring option, or a first-rate point guard who can play 35 minutes a game and average 8 assists a game. The Heat will probably be a .500 team again this season. But this time, that might not be good enough to make the playoffs.

Team Directory

Managing partner: Lewis Schaffel   Exec. VP: Pauline Winick
VP, finance: Sammy Schulman   VP, broadcasting: Kip Hunter-Epstein
VP, sponsor rel.: Joy Behrman   Dir. of public relations: Mark Pray

1993–94 Review

EASTERN CONFERENCE						WESTERN CONFERENCE					
ATLANTIC DIV.		CENTRAL DIV.			MIDWEST DIV.			PACIFIC DIV.			
	W	L		W	L		W	L		W	L
NY	2	2	ATL	1	3	HOU	0	2	SEA	1	1
ORL	2	3	CHI	2	2	SAN	0	2	PHO	0	2
NJ	2	3	CLE	3	1	UTAH	1	1	GS	0	2
MIA	–	–	IND	1	3	DEN	1	1	POR	0	2
BOS	3	2	CHA	3	1	MIN	2	0	LAL	1	1
PHI	4	1	DET	2	2	DAL	2	0	SAC	1	1
WAS	3	1	MIL	4	0				LAC	1	1
	16	12		16	12		6	6		4	10

1993–94 finish: 42–40 (22–19 home, 20–21 away), fourth in Atlantic Div.

1994–95 Schedule

1/4	@ Utah	9:00 pm	1/5	Minnesota	7:30 pm	3/5	Wash.	1:00 pm
1/6	@ Phoenix	9:00 pm	1/7	@ Sacra.	10:30 pm	3/7	LA Lakers	7:30 pm
1/8	@ Gold. St.	10:30 pm	1/8	@ LA Lakers	10:00 pm	3/9	Portland	7:30 pm
1/12	Wash.	8:00 pm	1/11	@ Houston	8:30 pm	3/11	@ Charlotte	7:30 pm
1/15	Dallas	7:30 pm	1/12	@ San Ant.	8:00 pm	3/12	Utah	6:00 pm
1/16	@ Phila.	7:30 pm	1/14	@ Dallas	8:30 pm	3/14	@ Portland	10:00 pm
1/18	Boston	7:30 pm	1/16	@ Atlanta	3:30 pm	3/16	@ Seattle	10:00 pm
1/21	@ Orlando	7:30 pm	1/18	Boston	7:30 pm	3/17	@ LA Clip.	10:30 pm
1/23	Cleveland	7:30 pm	1/20	San Ant.	7:30 pm	3/19	Phoenix	6:00 pm
1/25	@ Detroit	8:00 pm	1/22	New York	7:30 pm	3/21	Indiana	7:30 pm
1/29	Sacra.	7:30 pm	1/24	Indiana	7:30 pm	3/22	@ Atlanta	7:30 pm
1/30	@ Charlotte	7:30 pm	1/27	@ Milwaukee	8:30 pm	3/24	Gold. St.	7:30 pm
2/2	New Jersey	7:30 pm	1/28	@ Detroit	7:30 pm	3/25	New Jersey	7:30 pm
2/7	Phila.	7:30 pm	1/30	Atlanta	7:30 pm	3/28	Boston	7:30 pm
2/9	Orlando	7:30 pm	2/1	Detroit	7:30 pm	3/29	@ Wash.	7:30 pm
2/10	@ Indiana	7:30 pm	2/3	@ Wash.	7:30 pm	3/31	@ Boston	7:30 pm
2/12	@ New York	7:30 pm	2/5	Seattle	1:00 pm	4/2	Charlotte	6:00 pm
2/13	@ Phila.	7:30 pm	2/8	Wash.	7:30 pm	4/4	Phila.	7:30 pm
2/15	Denver	8:00 pm	2/14	Milwaukee	7:30 pm	4/8	@ New Jersey	7:30 pm
2/17	Atlanta	7:30 pm	2/16	New York	7:30 pm	4/11	@ New York	7:30 pm
2/18	@ New Jersey	7:00 pm	2/17	@ New York	7:30 pm	4/13	Cleveland	7:30 pm
2/21	Milwaukee	7:30 pm	2/19	@ Indiana	2:30 pm	4/15	Orlando	3:30 pm
2/23	Charlotte	7:30 pm	2/20	@ Cleveland	6:00 pm	4/17	Chicago	7:30 pm
2/26	Houston	7:30 pm	2/24	Chicago	8:00 pm	4/19	@ Cleveland	7:30 pm
2/27	@ Orlando	7:30 pm	2/26	@ Minnesota	3:30 pm	4/21	@ Phila.	7:30 pm
2/29	LA Clip.	7:30 pm	2/28	@ Milwaukee	8:30 pm	4/23	Detroit	6:00 pm
2/30	@ Chicago	8:30 pm	3/1	@ Chicago	8:30 pm			
3/4	@ Boston	7:30 pm	3/3	@ Denver	9:00 pm			

1993–94 Team Stats

NAME	G	MIN	FG	FGA	FG%	3FG	3FGA	3FG%	FT	FTA	FT%	ORB	TRB	AST	PF	STL	BLK	TO	PTS	AVG
Rice	81	2999	663	1421	46.7	132	346	38.2	250	284	88.0	76	434	184	186	110	32	130	1708	21.1
Smith	78	2776	491	1076	45.6	91	262	34.7	273	327	83.5	156	352	394	217	84	35	202	1346	17.3
Seikaly	72	2410	392	803	48.8	0	2	0.0	304	422	72.0	244	740	136	279	59	100	195	1088	15.1
Long	69	2201	300	672	44.6	1	6	16.7	187	238	78.6	190	495	170	244	89	26	125	788	11.4
Miner	63	1358	254	532	47.7	4	6	66.7	149	180	82.8	75	156	95	132	31	13	95	661	10.5
Shaw	77	2037	278	667	41.7	73	216	33.8	64	89	71.9	104	350	385	195	71	21	173	693	9.0
Coles	76	1726	233	519	44.9	20	99	20.2	102	131	77.9	50	159	263	132	75	12	107	588	7.7
Salley	76	1910	208	436	47.7	2	3	66.7	164	225	72.9	132	407	135	260	56	78	94	582	7.7
Geiger	72	1199	202	352	57.4	1	5	20.0	116	149	77.9	119	303	32	201	36	29	61	521	7.2
Burton	53	697	124	283	43.8	3	15	20.0	120	158	75.9	50	136	39	96	18	20	54	371	7.0
Askins	37	319	36	88	40.9	4	21	19.0	9	10	90.0	33	82	13	57	11	1	21	85	2.3
Kessler	15	66	11	25	44.0	5	9	55.6	6	8	75.0	4	10	2	14	1	0	5	33	2.2
Wiley	4	34	3	8	37.5	1	4	25.0	0	0	—	0	3	7	4	2	0	6	7	1.8
Alexander	4	12	1	2	50.0	0	0	—	0	2	0.0	0	3	1	3	0	0	1	2	0.5
Bol	8	61	1	12	8.3	0	0	0.0	0	0	—	1	11	0	4	0	6	5	2	0.3
Heat	82	19805	3197	6896	46.4	337	997	33.8	1744	2223	78.5	1235	3642	1856	2024	643	374	1315	8475	103.4
Opp.	82	19805	3036	6641	45.7	295	892	33.1	1889	2527	74.8	1074	3340	1821	1946	689	438	1314	8256	100.7

HISTORY
ALL-TIME TEAM RECORDS

Career

Games played	Grant Long	470	1988–94
Total points	Glen Rice	7,417	1988–94
Field goals made	Glen Rice	2,937	1989–94
Field goals attempted	Glen Rice	6,441	1989–94
Free throws made	Rony Seikaly	1,766	1988–94
Free throws attempted	Rony Seikaly	2,669	1988–94
Total rebounds	Rony Seikaly	4,544	1988–94
Assists	Sherman Douglas	1,262	1989–92
Steals	Grant Long	664	1988–94
Personal fouls	Grant Long	1,688	1988–94
Blocked shots	Rony Seikaly	610	1988–94

Season

Total points	Glen Rice	1,765	1991–92
Field goals made	Glen Rice	672	1991–92
Field goals attempted	Glen Rice	1,432	1991–92
Free throws made	Rony Seikaly	397	1992–93
Total rebounds	Rony Seikaly	934	1991–92
Assists	Sherman Douglas	624	1990–91
Steals	Sherman Douglas	145	1989–90
Personal fouls	Grant Long	337	1988–89
Blocked shots	Rony Seikaly	124	1989–90

Game

Total points	Glen Rice	46	vs. Orlando, 4/11/92
Field goals made	Glen Rice	19	vs. Orlando, 4/11/92
Free throws made	Rony Seikaly	16	vs. Boston, 3/13/94
Total rebounds	Rony Seikaly	34	vs. Washington, 3/3/93
Assists	Sherman Douglas	17	vs. Atlanta, 2/26/90
Steals	ten players	6	—
Blocked shots	Rony Seikaly	8	vs. New Jersey, 11/7/89

LEADING COACHES

	REGULAR SEASON				PLAYOFFS		
NAME	YEARS	W	L	PCT	W	L	PCT
Kevin Loughery	1991–94	116	130	.472	2	6	.250
Ron Rothstein	1988–91	57	189	.232	0	0	—

Miami Heat 1994–95 Roster

Head Coach: Kevin Loughery

No.	Name	Pos.	Ht.	Wt.	Yrs.	Born	College
2	Keith Askins	G-F	6-8	223	4	12/15/67	Alabama
34	Willie Burton	G-F	6-8	219	4	5/26/68	Minnesota
12	Bimbo Coles	G	6-2	185	4	4/22/68	Virginia Tech
52	Matt Geiger	C	7-0	245	2	9/10/69	Georgia Tech
33	Alec Kessler	F-C	6-11	240	4	1/13/67	Georgia
43	Grant Long	F	6-9	248	6	3/12/66	Eastern Michigan
32	Harold Miner	G	6-5	215	2	5/5/71	Southern California
	Khalid Reeves	G	6-3	207	R	7/15/72	Arizona
41	Glen Rice	F	6-8	220	5	5/28/67	Michigan
22	John Salley	F-C	6-11	250	8	5/16/64	Georgia Tech
4	Rony Seikaly	C	6-11	252	6	5/10/65	Syracuse
20	Brian Shaw	G	6-6	194	5	3/22/66	Cal-Santa Barbara
3	Steve Smith	G	6-8	213	3	3/31/69	Michigan State
	Jeff Webster	F	6-8	232	R	2/19/71	Oklahoma

Arena Information

Miami Arena (15,200)
Tickets: 305-577-HEAT
Ticket prices: $34, Lower level; $23, Upper level; $17, Upper level; $10.50, Upper level

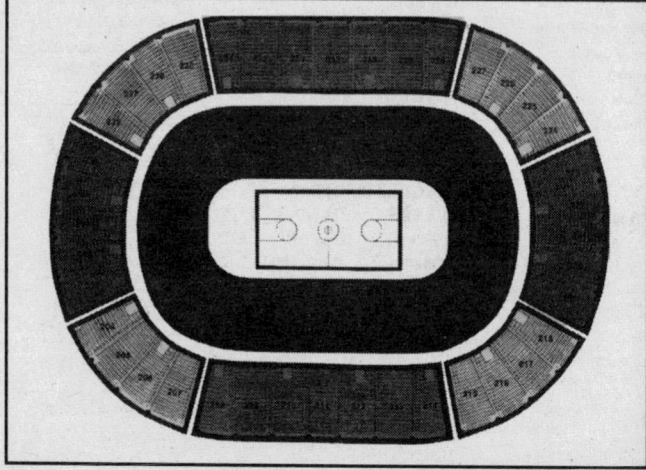

Grant Long

No. 43/F

Full name: Grant Andrew Long
HT: 6-9   **WT:** 248
Born: 3/12/66, Wayne, MI
High school: Romulus (MI)
College: Eastern Michigan

In 6 seasons played with the Heat, Long is Miami's all-time leader in games played, with 470 games, and in steals, with 664. Long and Rony Seikaly are the only players on the current rosters who have been members of the Heat all 6 seasons of the franchise's existence. Last season, Long was second on the Heat in steals and rebounds. Long missed the first 13 games of last season due to a fractured bone in his right hand, suffered in a preseason contest vs. the Lakers. As a result, he played in only 69 games, a career low, and came off the bench in his first 10 games. He grabbed 17 rebounds against New York on April 5, the most by a Heat player this season.

REGULAR SEASON	G	MIN	FG	FGx	3FG	3PTx	FT	FTx	REB	AST	STL	BLK	PTS	AVG
'88-89 MIAMI	82	2435	336	48.6	0	0.0	304	74.9	546	149	122	48	976	11.9
'89-90 MIAMI	81	1856	257	48.3	0	0.0	172	71.4	402	96	91	38	686	8.5
'90-91 MIAMI	80	2514	276	49.2	1	16.7	181	78.7	568	176	119	43	734	9.2
'91-92 MIAMI	82	3063	440	49.4	6	27.3	326	80.7	691	225	139	40	1212	14.8
'92-93 MIAMI	76	2728	397	46.9	6	23.1	261	76.5	568	182	104	31	1061	14.0
'93-94 MIAMI	69	2201	300	44.6	1	16.7	187	78.6	495	170	89	26	788	11.4
6 YR TOTALS	470	14797	2006	47.8	14	20.6	1431	76.9	3270	998	664	226	5457	11.6
'93-94 RANK NBA Fs	83	40	54	95	69	69	37	18	34	33	20	82	52	46
'94-95 PROJECTIONS	64	1957	263	42.8	0	0.0	157	79.3	419	162	77	21	683	10.7

PLAYOFFS	G	MIN	FG	FGx	3FG	3PTx	FT	FTx	REB	AST	STL	BLK	PTS	AVG
'91-92 MIAMI	3	120	15	41.7	0	0.0	7	70.0	15	8	5	0	37	12.3
'93-94 MIAMI	4	110	14	38.9	0	---	21	77.8	18	7	3	2	49	12.3
TOTALS	7	230	29	40.3	0	0.0	28	75.7	33	15	8	2	86	12.3

Glen Rice

No. 41/F

Full name: Glen Anthony Rice
HT: 6-8　　**WT:** 220
Born: 5/28/67, Flint, MI
High school: Northwestern Community (Flint)
College: Michigan

As a scorer, Rice can do it all. He can score from anywhere on the floor, he can hit from outside, and he's deadly from the free throw line. The Heat's leading scorer for the third straight season, Rice was tenth in the NBA in scoring and fourth in the Eastern Conference. He was fourth in the league (and second among forwards) in 3-point FGM. He averaged 21.2 points, 5.4 rebounds, 2.3 assists, and 1.4 steals, shooting 46.7 percent from the field, 38.2 from 3-point range, and 88 percent from the free throw line. His rebounding, assists and free throw percentages were the best of his career. He put up 36 shots vs. New Jersey in an OT game December 13, setting a franchise record.

REGULAR SEASON		G	MIN	FG	FGx	3FG	3PTx	FT	FTx	REB	AST	STL	BLK	PTS	AVG
'89-90	MIAMI	77	2311	470	43.9	17	24.6	91	73.4	352	138	67	27	1048	13.6
'90-91	MIAMI	77	2646	550	46.1	71	38.6	171	81.8	381	189	101	26	1342	17.4
'91-92	MIAMI	79	3007	672	46.9	155	39.1	266	83.6	394	184	90	35	1765	22.3
'92-93	MIAMI	82	3082	582	44.0	148	38.3	242	82.0	424	180	92	25	1554	19.0
'93-94	MIAMI	81	2999	663	46.7	132	38.2	250	88.0	434	184	110	32	1708	21.1
5 YR TOTALS		396	14045	2937	45.6	523	37.9	1020	82.9	1985	875	460	145	7417	18.7
'93-94	RANK NBA Fs	15	3	3	72	1	9	19	3	43	29	9	68	3	5
'94-95	PROJECTIONS	82	3050	706	47.5	142	38.8	271	91.6	451	187	121	34	1825	22.3

PLAYOFFS		G	MIN	FG	FGx	3FG	3PTx	FT	FTx	REB	AST	STL	BLK	PTS	AVG
'91-92	MIAMI	3	119	24	37.5	3	25.0	6	85.7	10	5	2	0	57	19.0
'93-94	MIAMI	5	195	26	38.2	7	30.4	6	75.0	36	10	11	2	65	13.0
TOTALS		8	314	50	37.9	10	28.6	12	80.0	46	15	13	2	122	15.3

Rony Seikaly

No. 4/C

Full name: Ronald F. Seikaly
HT: 6-11 **WT:** 252
Born: 5/10/65, Beirut, Lebanon
High school: American School
(Athens, Greece)
College: Syracuse

Seikaly gives the Heat a strong presence inside: he's a good rebounder and shotblocker. He pulled down double figures in rebounds 42 times; Miami was 27–15 in those games, but was 12–18 when he didn't rebound in double figures, and 3–7 when Seikaly did not play. Seikaly's 60 starts were the second fewest total of his career. He missed 8 straight games after spraining his ankle March 26. Nevertheless he posted 136 assists, a career high, and led the team in rebounds and blocked shots. He averaged 17.4 points, 13.0 rebounds before the injury, 10 points and 7.7 rebounds after. Seikaly set a Miami team record when he hit 16 free throws (out of 17 shots) against Boston on March 13.

REGULAR SEASON		G	MIN	FG	FGx	3FG	3PT%	FT	FT%	REB	AST	STL	BLK	PTS	AVG
'88-89	MIAMI	78	1962	333	44.8	1	25.0	161	51.1	549	55	46	96	848	10.9
'89-90	MIAMI	74	2409	486	50.2	0	0.0	256	59.4	766	79	78	124	1228	16.6
'90-91	MIAMI	64	2171	395	48.1	2	33.3	258	61.9	709	95	51	86	1050	16.4
'91-92	MIAMI	79	2800	463	48.9	0	0.0	370	73.3	934	109	40	121	1296	16.4
'92-93	MIAMI	72	2456	417	48.0	1	12.5	397	73.5	546	100	38	83	1232	17.1
'93-94	MIAMI	72	2410	392	48.8	0	0.0	304	72.0	740	136	59	100	1088	15.1
6 YR TOTALS		439	14208	2486	48.3	4	16.7	1766	66.2	4244	573	312	610	6742	15.4
'93-94 RANK NBA Cs		21	7	8	29	14	14	6	18	8	9	10	13	8	8
'94-95 PROJECTIONS		72	2370	371	49.0	0	0.0	280	73.1	765	154	65	101	1022	14.2

PLAYOFFS		G	MIN	FG	FGx	3FG	3PT%	FT	FT%	REB	AST	STL	BLK	PTS	AVG
'91-92	MIAMI	3	117	19	54.3	0	---	24	75.0	30	4	1	5	62	20.7
'93-94	MIAMI	5	165	14	43.8	0	---	13	56.5	47	8	4	7	41	8.2
TOTALS		8	282	33	49.3	0	---	37	67.3	77	12	5	12	103	12.9

Brian Shaw

No. 20/G

HT: 6-6   **WT:** 194
Born: 3/22/66, Oakland, CA
High school: Bishop O'Dowd (Oakland)
College: Cal-Santa Barbara

Shaw is a good playmaker, takes care of the ball, and is one of the best rebounding guards in the NBA. He's steadily improving his outside shot; last season's 33.8 percentage from 3-point range was a career high, and marked the fourth straight year that he's improved in that category. (He was 47 for 118—39.8 percent—in the last 31 games.) In fact, Shaw set the NBA record for most 3-point FGM in one game when he hit 10 at Milwaukee on April 8, 1993. The knock on Shaw is that he's not a strong defensive player. He also needs to work on his halfcourt offensive game; last year's 41.7 percentage from the floor was his best in the past three seasons. Shaw started 52 games for the Heat last season.

REGULAR SEASON		G	MIN	FG	FGx	3FG	3PTx	FT	FTx	REB	AST	STL	BLK	PTS	AVG
'88-89	BOSTON	82	2301	297	43.3	0	0.0	109	82.6	376	472	78	27	703	8.6
'90-91	BOSTON	79	2772	442	46.9	3	11.1	204	81.9	370	602	105	34	1091	13.8
'91-92	BOS-MIA	63	1423	209	40.7	5	21.7	72	79.1	204	250	57	22	495	7.9
'92-93	MIAMI	68	1603	197	39.3	43	33.1	61	78.2	257	235	48	19	498	7.3
'93-94	MIAMI	77	2037	278	41.7	73	33.8	64	71.9	350	385	71	21	693	9.0
5 YR TOTALS		369	10136	1423	43.0	124	30.3	510	79.8	1557	1944	359	123	3480	9.4
'93-94	RANK NBA Gs	53	58	62	99	23	52	99	105	13	27	64	34	66	73
'94-95	PROJECTIONS	81	2145	294	41.8	117	39.5	52	68.4	390	425	76	19	757	9.3

PLAYOFFS		G	MIN	FG	FGx	3FG	3PTx	FT	FTx	REB	AST	STL	BLK	PTS	AVG
'88-89	BOSTON	3	124	22	51.2	0	0.0	7	77.8	17	19	3	0	51	17.0
'90-91	BOSTON	11	316	47	47.0	1	33.3	26	86.7	38	51	10	1	121	11.0
'91-92	MIAMI	3	85	14	46.7	3	60.0	5	62.5	13	12	2	0	36	12.0
'93-94	MIAMI	5	112	16	39.0	0	0.0	7	58.3	20	9	4	1	39	7.8
TOTALS		22	637	99	46.3	4	18.2	45	76.3	88	91	19	2	247	11.2

Steve Smith

No. 3/G

Full name: Steven Delano Smith
HT: 6-8   **WT:** 213
Born: 3/31/69, Highland Park, MI
High school: Pershing (Detroit, MI)
College: Michigan State

Smith is big enough to post up most guards in the NBA. He won't be mistaken for Magic Johnson, but he's a decent playmaker, although he turns the ball over more than you'd like. Smith was Miami's second-leading scorer last season. He avoided the injury problems that had dogged him during his first 2 seasons, started in 77 of 78 games, and had career highs in virtually every statistical category, including games played, games started, minutes, scoring, rebounding, steals, FG percentage, FT percentage, and 3-point FGs made and attempted. Smith was the team's sixth-leading rebounder, and led the team in assists. He's a good defensive player, ranking third on the team in steals.

REGULAR SEASON		G	MIN	FG	FGx	3FG	3PTx	FT	FTx	REB	AST	STL	BLK	PTS	AVG
'91-92	MIAMI	61	1806	297	45.4	40	32.0	95	74.8	188	278	59	19	729	12.0
'92-93	MIAMI	48	1610	279	45.1	53	40.2	155	78.7	197	267	50	16	766	16.0
'93-94	MIAMI	78	2776	491	45.6	91	34.7	273	83.5	352	394	84	35	1346	17.3
3 YR TOTALS		187	6192	1067	45.4	184	35.5	523	80.3	737	939	193	70	2841	15.2
'93-94	RANK NBA Gs	48	17	17	55	17	49	15	29	12	24	50	12	11	14
'94-95	PROJECTIONS	82	3635	661	46.0	127	32.7	408	88.1	490	462	106	53	1857	22.6
PLAYOFFS		G	MIN	FG	FGx	3FG	3PTx	FT	FTx	REB	AST	STL	BLK	PTS	AVG
'91-92	MIAMI	3	100	18	52.9	7	63.6	5	83.3	6	15	4	1	48	16.0
'93-94	MIAMI	5	192	33	41.3	9	40.9	21	84.0	30	11	4	2	96	19.2
	TOTALS	8	292	51	44.7	16	48.5	26	83.9	36	26	8	3	144	18.0

Bimbo Coles No. 12/G

Full name: Vernell E. Coles
HT: 6-2 **WT:** 185
Born: 4/22/68, Covington, VA
High school: Greenbriar E. (Lewisburg, WV)
College: Virginia Tech

Coles is a good defender who can drive to the basket. He's a pretty good playmaker who could improve his perimeter shooting.

REGULAR SEASON		G	MIN	FG	FGx	3FG	3PTx	FT	FTx	REB	AST	STL	BLK	PTS	AVG
'90-91	MIAMI	82	1355	162	41.2	6	17.6	71	74.7	153	232	65	12	401	4.9
'91-92	MIAMI	81	1976	295	45.5	10	19.2	216	82.4	189	366	73	13	816	10.1
'92-93	MIAMI	81	2232	318	46.4	42	30.7	177	80.5	166	373	80	11	855	10.6
'93-94	MIAMI	76	1726	233	44.9	20	20.2	102	77.9	159	263	75	12	588	7.7
4 YR TOTALS		320	7289	1008	44.9	78	24.2	566	79.9	667	1234	293	48	2660	8.3
'93-94	RANK NBA Gs	61	68	75	64	74	112	77	71	69	53	60	62	81	85
'94-95	PROJECTIONS	73	1557	205	44.7	17	16.8	71	76.3	148	218	73	12	498	6.8

PLAYOFFS		G	MIN	FG	FGx	3FG	3PTx	FT	FTx	REB	AST	STL	BLK	PTS	AVG
'91-92	MIAMI	3	45	7	70.0	1	100.0	8	80.0	7	6	3	0	23	7.7
'93-94	MIAMI	5	140	25	53.2	1	25.0	18	78.3	14	17	7	1	69	13.8
	TOTALS	8	185	32	56.1	2	40.0	26	78.8	21	23	10	1	92	11.5

Matt Geiger No. 52/C

HT: 7-0 **WT:** 245
Born: 9/10/69, Salem, MA
High school: Countyside (Clearwater, FL)
College: Georgia Tech

Geiger has provided points and rebounds off the bench. He would probably thrive as a starter, but he won't get many minutes in Miami behind Rony Seikaly.

REGULAR SEASON		G	MIN	FG	FGx	3FG	3PTx	FT	FTx	REB	AST	STL	BLK	PTS	AVG
'92-93	MIAMI	48	554	76	52.4	0	0.0	62	67.4	120	14	15	18	214	4.5
'93-94	MIAMI	72	1199	202	57.4	1	20.0	116	77.9	303	32	36	29	521	7.2
2 YR TOTALS		120	1753	278	55.9	1	11.1	178	73.9	423	46	51	47	735	6.1
'93-94	RANK NBA Cs	21	29	21	5	8	9	15	9	27	37	23	32	21	23
'94-95	PROJECTIONS	82	1844	374	62.3	1	50.0	134	88.2	533	52	61	29	883	10.8

PLAYOFFS		G	MIN	FG	FGx	3FG	3PTx	FT	FTx	REB	AST	STL	BLK	PTS	AVG
'93-94	MIAMI	2	11	0	0.0	0	---	1	50.0	4	0	0	0	1	0.5
	TOTALS	2	11	0	0.0	0	---	1	50.0	4	0	0	0	1	0.5

Harold Miner   No. 32/G

Full name: Harold David Miner
HT: 6-5   **WT:** 215
Born: 5/5/71, Inglewood, CA
High school: Inglewood (CA)
College: Southern California
Miner is a scorer who averaged 19.5 points per 40 minutes played coming off the bench. Miner is a spectacular leaper and dunker.

REGULAR SEASON		G	MIN	FG	FGx	3FG	3PTx	FT	FTx	REB	AST	STL	BLK	PTS	AVG
'92-93	MIAMI	73	1383	292	47.5	3	33.3	163	76.2	147	73	34	8	750	10.3
'93-94	MIAMI	63	1358	254	47.7	4	66.7	149	82.8	156	95	31	13	661	10.5
	2 YR TOTALS	136	2741	546	47.6	7	46.7	312	79.2	303	168	65	21	1411	10.4
'93-94	RANK NBA Gs	100	83	69	31	110	1	51	39	74	105	112	55	69	61
'94-95	PROJECTIONS	53	1333	217	48.0	3	100.0	131	89.1	165	116	28	18	568	10.7

PLAYOFFS		G	MIN	FG	FGx	3FG	3PTx	FT	FTx	REB	AST	STL	BLK	PTS	AVG
'93-94	MIAMI	4	57	12	46.2	0	---	8	72.7	8	2	1	0	32	8.0
	TOTALS	4	57	12	46.2	0	---	8	72.7	8	2	1	0	32	8.0

Khalid Reeves   G

Full name: Khalid Reeves
HT: 6–3   **WT:** 207
Born: 7/15/72, Queens, NY
College: Arizona
Although primarily a shooting guard as a senior, Reeves played both guard spots at Arizona, and may play point guard as a pro. Reeves averaged 24.2 points per game.

REGULAR SEASON	G	MIN	FG	FGx	3FG	3PTx	FT	FTx	REB	AST	STL	BLK	PTS	AVG

ROOKIE -- NO NBA EXPERIENCE

John Salley No. 22/F-C

Full name: John Thomas Salley
HT: 6-11 **WT:** 250
Born: 5/16/64, Brooklyn, NY
High school: Canarsie (Brooklyn)
College: Georgia Tech
Salley provides shotblocking, defense, and rebounding off the bench. He started 45 games at power forward and center.

REGULAR SEASON		G	MIN	FG	FG%	3FG	3PT%	FT	FT%	REB	AST	STL	BLK	PTS	AVG
'89-90	DETROIT	82	1914	209	51.2	1	25.0	174	71.3	439	67	51	153	593	7.2
'90-91	DETROIT	74	1649	179	47.5	0	0.0	186	72.7	327	70	52	112	544	7.4
'91-92	DETROIT	72	1774	249	51.2	0	0.0	186	71.5	296	116	43	110	684	9.5
'92-93	MIAMI	51	1422	154	50.2	0	---	115	79.9	313	93	32	70	423	8.3
'93-94	MIAMI	76	1910	208	47.7	2	66.7	164	72.9	407	135	56	78	582	7.7
8 YR TOTALS		586	13593	1586	51.3	3	21.4	1250	71.2	2815	713	377	857	4425	7.6
'93-94	RANK NBA Fs	48	52	69	60	62	1	44	57	46	45	55	18	70	74
'94-95	PROJECTIONS	82	2071	218	46.5	4	100.0	169	71.3	450	164	65	65	609	7.4

PLAYOFFS		G	MIN	FG	FG%	3FG	3PT%	FT	FT%	REB	AST	STL	BLK	PTS	AVG
'89-90	DETROIT	20	547	58	47.5	0	---	74	75.5	117	20	9	33	190	9.5
'90-91	DETROIT	15	308	38	54.3	0	---	36	60.0	62	11	6	20	112	7.5
'91-92	DETROIT	5	149	20	45.5	0	0.0	23	82.1	30	14	3	14	63	12.6
'93-94	MIAMI	5	201	22	38.6	0	---	11	68.8	40	8	2	5	55	11.0
	TOTALS	100	2531	285	50.7	0	0.0	256	69.8	555	94	47	151	826	8.3

Kevin Loughery Head Coach

Full name: Kevin Michael Loughery
HT: 6-3 **WT:** 190
Born: 3/28/40, Brooklyn, NY
High school: Cardinal Hayes (Bronx, NY)
College: St. John's
Loughery recently signed a new contract to coach the Heat. He's the winningest coach in NJ Nets franchise history.

	REGULAR SEASON					PLAYOFFS				
YEAR	TEAM	W	L	PCT	FINISH	W	L	PCT		
'77-78	NEW JERSEY	24	58	293	5th/Atlantic Div.					
'78-79	NEW JERSEY	37	45	451	3rd/Atlantic Div.	0	2	000	lost Eastern Conf. first round to Philadelphia, 2-0
'79-80	NEW JERSEY	34	48	415	5th/Atlantic Div.				
'80-81	NEW JERSEY	12	23	343					
'81-82	ATLANTA	42	40	512	2nd/Central Div.	0	2	000	lost Eastern Conf. first round to Philadelphia, 2-0
'82-83	ATLANTA	43	39	524	2nd/Central Div.	1	2	333	lost Eastern Conf. first round to Boston, 2-1
'83-84	CHICAGO	27	55	329	5th/Central Div.				
'84-85	CHICAGO	38	44	463	3rd/Central Div.	1	3	250	lost Eastern Conf. first round to Milwaukee, 3-1
'85-86	WASHINGTON	7	6	538	T3rd/Atlantic Div.	2	3	400	lost Eastern Conf. first round to Philadelphia, 3-2
'86-87	WASHINGTON	42	40	512	3rd/Atlantic Div.	0	3	000	lost Eastern Conf. first round to Detroit, 3-0
'87-88	WASHINGTON	8	19	296					
'91-92	MIAMI	38	44	463	4th/Atlantic Div.	0	3	000	lost Eastern Conf. first round to Chicago, 3-0
'92-93	MIAMI	36	46	439	5th/Atlantic Div.				
'93-94	MIAMI	42	40	512	4th/Atlantic Div.	2	3	400	lost Eastern Conf. first round to Atlanta, 3-2
16 YR TOTALS		457	633	419		6	21	222	

Milwaukee *BUCKS*

1994–95 Scouting Report

Frontcourt

6-11 Vin Baker was the lone bright spot in the Milwaukee front-court last season. A first-team All-Rookie selection, Baker is an excellent shotblocker, a good ballhandler, and has a good jump hook. Although he's a little light (234 pounds) to play power forward, by the end of last season the Bucks had pressed him into service as the starting center. Glenn Robinson, the number one pick in the '94 draft, will start at small forward. Consensus College Player of the Year, he averaged 30.3 points (best in the nation) and 10.1 rebounds per game. The Bucks lack a strong inside player who can play defense at center. Joe Courtney can rebound a little; he was claimed by Milwaukee after being waived by Phoenix. Ed Pinckney came over in the Blue Edwards deal. (The Bucks also obtained the rights to Andrei Fetisov, but he's not expected to play for Milwaukee this season). Pinckney can give Milwaukee much-needed rebounding and defense, but he's best used as a reserve forward. Anthony Cook spells at power forward and even center; he's a modest rebounder and a decent shotblocker, with a pretty good low-post game. Veteran Roy Hinson hasn't played since 1991 due to an injury to his knee.

Backcourt

With Blue Edwards' departure, swingman Todd Day should take over the starting role at shooting guard. Day needs to improve his shot selection; he was only 41.5 percent from the field last season. Eric Murdock led the team in scoring, assists, and steals. Lee Mayberry backs up Murdock; he's not as good a defender, scorer, or playmaker as Murdock. Jon Barry averaged over 17 minutes a game last season coming off the Milwaukee bench, even though his skills are limited.

Defense

Teams averaged 103.4 points against the Bucks, fourteenth in the NBA. But that number is a result of Milwaukee doing some things on defense pretty well, and other things not so well. Milwaukee was successful at holding down opponents' shots from the field. Opponents had trouble turning possessions into shots. Milwaukee was fifth in the NBA in steals and sixth in forcing turnovers. As a result, the Bucks limited opponents to 6,625 shots last season, sixth lowest in the NBA. And they allowed few second shots; the Bucks held opponents to 1,086 offensive rebounds, seventh fewest in the NBA. Unfortunately for Milwaukee, when the other team was able to get off a shot, they were able to hit at a 49.1 percent clip, third highest in the league. The Bucks ranked just seventeenth in blocking opponents' shots.

1994–95 Prospects

Milwaukee's '93–94 season was a classic season for a rebuilding team. The Bucks' problems in '93–94 included weak rebounding (twenty-sixth in NBA last season, in front of Washington) and little offense (twenty-sixth in points scored, ahead of Dallas). They go together, because if you don't rebound, you don't get fast break opportunities on defense or second shots on offense. They played pretty good defense, considering the holes they had in the frontcourt. But there wasn't enough talent on this team to compete in the NBA, as last season's record showed.

Milwaukee is a young team with potential, but with no competitive center and virtually no depth. There isn't much reason to think the Bucks will be better this season. Milwaukee took a big step forward by drafting Glenn Robinson. Robinson will definitely upgrade Milwaukee's offense, and he should improve their rebounding, but at small forward he won't have the impact on rebounding that Milwaukee needs to see for a major step up.

The Bucks have missed out on the playoffs for three straight seasons, and they'll be watching this season's playoffs on TV, too. In fact, they could lose as many as 65 games this season, three more than last season.

Team Directory

President: Herbert Kohl
bus. oper: John Steinmiller
, finance: Jim Woloszyk

VP, basketball oper.: Mike Dunleavy
VP, player personnel: Lee Rose
Dir., publicity: Bill King II

1993–94 Review

EASTERN CONFERENCE				WESTERN CONFERENCE					
ATLANTIC DIV.		CENTRAL DIV.		MIDWEST DIV.		PACIFIC DIV.			
W	L		W	L		W	L		W	L
0	4	ATL	0	5	HOU	1	1	SEA	0	2
1	3	CHI	0	4	SAN	0	2	PHO	0	2
1	3	CLE	2	3	UTAH	0	2	GS	0	2
0	4	IND	1	3	DEN	0	2	POR	1	1
1	3	CHA	2	3	MIN	0	2	LAL	0	2
1	3	DET	4	1	DAL	2	0	SAC	1	1
1	3	MIL	–	–				LAC	1	1
5	23		9	19		3	9		3	11

93–94 finish: 20–62 (11–30 home, 9–32 away), seventh in Central Div.

1994–95 Schedule

	Opponent	Time	Date	Opponent	Time	Date	Opponent	Time
	@ Phila.	7:30 pm	1/5	@ Gold. St.	10:30 pm	3/2	Atlanta	8:30 pm
	LA Lakers	8:30 pm	1/6	@ LA Lakers	10:30 pm	3/3	@ Boston	7:30 pm
0	@ Cleveland	7:30 pm	1/8	@ Denver	9:00 pm	3/5	@ New Jersey	1:00 pm
1	Charlotte	8:00 pm	1/9	@ Phoenix	9:00 pm	3/7	Portland	8:30 pm
5	Indiana	8:30 pm	1/11	Sacra.	8:30 pm	3/10	@ Wash.	7:30 pm
8	@ Atlanta	7:30 pm	1/13	New York	8:30 pm	3/12	Denver	2:30 pm
9	Seattle	8:30 pm	1/14	@ Indiana	7:30 pm	3/14	Charlotte	8:30 pm
2	@ Boston	7:30 pm	1/18	@ Chicago	8:30 pm	3/15	@ Indiana	7:30 pm
3	@ Detroit	7:30 pm	1/19	Wash.	8:30 pm	3/17	@ Chicago	8:30 pm
5	@ Indiana	7:30 pm	1/21	Detroit	8:30 pm	3/19	Boston	2:30 pm
6	Orlando	8:30 pm	1/24	Houston	8:30 pm	3/21	Gold. St.	8:30 pm
9	Phoenix	8:30 pm	1/25	@ Phila.	7:30 pm	3/23	LA Clip.	8:30 pm
	Cleveland	8:30 pm	1/27	Miami	8:30 pm	3/25	San Ant.	8:30 pm
3	@ Seattle	10:00 pm	1/28	@ Orlando	7:30 pm	3/28	@ Dallas	8:30 pm
4	@ Portland	10:00 pm	1/31	Dallas	8:30 pm	3/31	@ San Ant.	8:30 pm
5	@ Sacra.	10:30 pm	2/1	@ New Jersey	7:30 pm	4/1	@ Houston	8:30 pm
7	@ LA Clip.	10:30 pm	2/3	@ Charlotte	7:30 pm	4/5	New York	8:30 pm
0	Chicago	8:30 pm	2/4	Phila.	8:30 pm	4/7	New Jersey	8:30 pm
3	@ Charlotte	7:30 pm	2/7	@ New York	7:30 pm	4/9	Atlanta	1:00 pm
4	Phila.	8:30 pm	2/8	Minnesota	8:30 pm	4/11	Detroit	8:30 pm
8	Utah	7:00 pm	2/14	@ Miami	7:30 pm	4/14	@ Minnesota	8:00 pm
0	@ Atlanta	7:30 pm	2/16	Cleveland	8:30 pm	4/15	@ Wash.	7:30 pm
1	@ Miami	7:30 pm	2/18	Chicago	8:30 pm	4/17	@ New York	7:30 pm
3	@ Orlando	7:30 pm	2/20	Orlando	8:30 pm	4/19	Boston	8:30 pm
6	New Jersey	8:30 pm	2/22	Wash.	8:30 pm	4/21	@ Cleveland	7:30 pm
7	@ Detroit	7:30 pm	2/24	Indiana	8:30 pm	4/23	Chicago	2:30 pm
0	Charlotte	8:30 pm	2/27	@ Detroit	7:30 pm			
	@ Utah	9:00 pm	2/28	Miami	8:30 pm			

1993–94 Team Stats

NAME	G	MIN	FG	FGA	FG%	3FG	3FGA	3FG%	FT	FTA	FT%	ORB	TRB	AST	PF	STL	BLK	TO	PTS	AVG
Murdock	82	2533	477	1019	46.8	69	168	41.1	234	288	81.3	91	261	546	189	197	12	206	1257	15.3
Brickowski	43	1441	251	521	48.2	3	18	16.7	148	191	77.5	53	279	165	165	52	16	125	653	15.2
Baker	82	2560	435	869	50.1	1	5	20.0	234	411	56.9	277	621	163	231	60	114	162	1105	13.5
Day	76	2127	351	845	41.5	33	148	22.3	231	331	69.8	115	310	138	221	103	52	129	966	12.7
Norman	82	2539	412	919	44.8	63	189	33.3	92	183	50.3	169	500	222	209	58	46	150	979	11.9
Edwards	82	2322	382	800	47.8	38	106	35.8	151	189	79.9	104	329	171	235	83	27	146	953	11.6
Avent	33	695	92	228	40.4	0	0	—	61	79	77.2	60	154	33	60	20	20	43	245	7.4
Strong	67	1131	141	341	41.3	3	13	23.1	159	206	77.2	109	281	48	69	38	14	61	444	6.6
Barry	72	1242	158	382	41.4	32	115	27.8	97	122	79.5	36	146	168	110	102	17	83	445	6.2
Mayberry	82	1472	167	402	41.5	41	119	34.5	58	84	69.0	26	101	215	114	46	4	97	433	5.3
Lohaus	67	962	102	281	36.3	46	134	34.3	20	29	69.0	33	150	62	142	30	55	58	270	4.0
Courtney	19	177	27	70	38.6	2	3	66.7	9	15	60.0	14	29	6	21	7	0	11	65	3.4
Foster	3	19	4	7	57.1	0	0	—	2	2	100.0	0	3	0	3	0	1	1	10	3.3
Cook	23	201	26	53	49.1	0	1	0.0	10	25	40.0	20	56	4	22	3	12	11	62	2.7
Schayes	23	230	14	46	30.4	0	0	—	21	22	95.5	16	45	5	27	5	8	14	49	2.1
Gminski	8	54	5	24	20.8	0	0	—	3	4	75.0	3	15	0	3	0	0	2	13	1.6
Bucks	82	19705	3044	6807	44.7	331	1019	32.5	1530	2181	70.2	1126	3280	1946	1821	800	407	1343	7949	96.9
Opp.	82	19705	3255	6625	49.1	286	789	36.2	1684	2284	73.7	1086	3581	2092	1777	768	420	1416	8480	103.4

HISTORY

TITLES

70–71 NBA champs	1980–81 Central Div. champs
71–72 NBA Midwest Div. champs	1981–82 Central Div. champs
72–73 NBA Midwest Div. champs	1982–83 Central Div. champs
73–74 NBA Western Conf. champs	1983–84 Central Div. champs
75–76 NBA Midwest Div. champs	1984–85 Central Div. champs
79–80 Midwest Div. champs	1985–86 Central Div. champs

ALL-TIME TEAM RECORDS

Career

games played	Junior Bridgeman	711	1975–87
total points	Kareem Abdul-Jabbar	14,211	1969–75
scoring average	Kareem Abdul-Jabbar	30.4	1969–75
field goals made	Kareem Abdul-Jabbar	5902	1969–75
free throws made	Sidney Moncrief	3505	1979–89
total rebounds	Kareem Abdul-Jabbar	7,161	1969–75
assists	Paul Pressey	3,272	1982–90
steals	Quinn Buckner	1,042	1976–82

Season

total points	Kareem Abdul-Jabbar	2,822	1971–72
scoring average	Kareem Abdul-Jabbar	34.8	1971–72
field goals made	Kareem Abdul-Jabbar	1159	1971–72
free throws made	Sidney Moncrief	529	1983–84
total rebounds	Kareem Abdul-Jabbar	1,346	1971–72
assists	Oscar Robertson	668	1970–71
steals	Alvin Robertson	246	1990–91

Game

total points	Kareem Abdul-Jabbar	55	vs. Boston, 12/10/71
field goals made	Kareem Abdul-Jabbar	24	vs. Houston, 1/25/73
free throws made	Flynn Robinson	21	vs. Atlanta, 2/17/69
total rebounds	Swen Natar	33	vs. Atlanta, 12/19/76
assists	Guy Rodgers	22	vs. Detroit, 11/30/68
steals	Alvin Robertson	10	vs. Utah, 11/19/90

LEADING COACHES

NAME	REGULAR SEASON				PLAYOFFS		
	YEARS	W	L	PCT	W	L	PCT
Don Nelson	1976–87	540	344	.611	41	46	.471
Larry Costello	1968–76	410	264	.608	37	23	.617
Del Harris	1987–91	191	154	.554	6	15	.286
Mike Dunleavy	1992–94	48	116	.293	0	0	—
Frank Hamblen	1991–92	23	42	.354	0	0	—

Milwaukee Bucks 1994–95 Roster

Head Coach: Mike Dunleavy

No.	Name	Pos.	Ht.	Wt.	Yrs.	Born	College
42	Vin Baker	F	6-10	250	1	11/23/71	Hartford
17	Jon Barry	G	6-5	204	2	7/25/69	Georgia Tech
50	Marty Conlon	C	6-11	245	4	1/19/68	Providence
0	Anthony Cook	F-C	6-9	240	4	3/19/67	Arizona
40	Joe Courtney	F	6-9	235	2	10/17/69	So. Mississippi
10	Todd Day	G-F	6-6	188	2	1/7/70	Arkansas
	Andrei Fetisov	F-C	NA	NA	R	NA	Russia/Spanish Lg.
	Roy Hinson	F	6-9	215	11	5/2/61	Rutgers
54	Brad Lohaus	F-C	6-11	238	7	9/29/64	Iowa
11	Lee Mayberry	G	6-1	172	2	6/12/70	Arkansas
52	Eric Mobley	C	6-11	250	R	2/1/70	Pittsburgh
5	Eric Murdock	G	6-1	200	3	6/14/68	Providence
	Ed Pinckney	F	6-9	215	9	3/27/63	Villanova
13	Glenn Robinson	F	6-7	240	R	1/10/73	Purdue

Arena Information

The Bradley Center (18,633)
Tickets: 414-276-4545, 608-255-4646, 312-559-1212
Ticket prices: $37, $34, $26, $24, $20, $17*, $12*, $9* (*20 bonus nights)

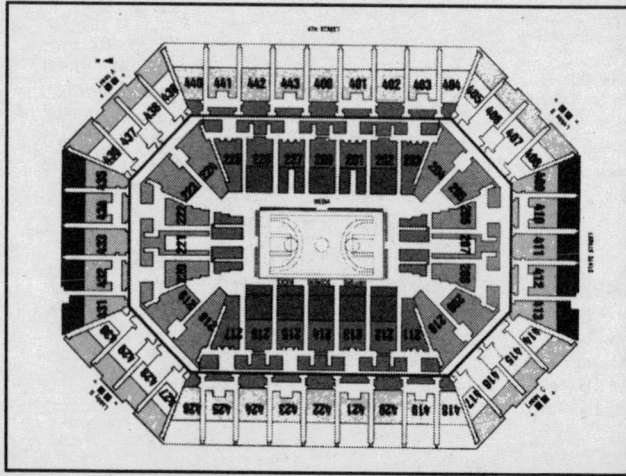

in Baker

No. 42/F-C

Full name: Vincent Lamont Baker
HT: 6-10   **WT:** 250
Born: 11/23/71, Lake Wales, FL
High school: Old Saybrook (CT)
College: Hartford

Baker is an excellent shotblocker, a good ballhandler, and has a good jump hook. He was first-team All-Rookie; the other Bucks to do so were Kareem Abdul-Jabbar ('69–70), Bob Dandridge ('69–70), and Marques Johnson ('77–78). He was second in rebounding among NBA rookies at 7.6 per game third in blocks with 114, and fourth in minutes with 2,560. His 13.5 points per game ranked seventh among rookies. Baker led Milwaukee in rebounding, minutes played, blocked shots and FG percent-

je, and was the team's second-leading scorer. Baker started lwaukee's final 33 games at center.

EGULAR SEASON	G	MIN	FG	FG%	3FG	3PT%	FT	FT%	REB	AST	STL	BLK	PTS	AVG
4-94 MILWAUKEE	82	2560	435	50.1	1	20.0	234	56.9	621	163	60	114	1105	13.5
1 YR TOTALS	82	2560	435	50.1	1	20.0	234	56.9	621	163	60	114	1105	13.5
93-94 RANK NBA Fs	1	25	25	34	69	64	22	124	20	36	48	8	25	30

Todd Day

No. 10/G-

Full name: Todd Fitzgerald Day
HT: 6-6 **WT:** 188
Born: 1/7/70, Decatur, IL
High school: Hamilton
(Memphis, TN)
College: Arkansas

Day started in 39 games. H
should be a regular in the upcon
ing season; he started 27 of h
final 30 games last season. Da
led Milwaukee in scoring 1
times, rebounding 3 times. H
had one double-double, scoring
season-best 27 points an
career-high 11 rebounds v
Golden State on February 2.
Day's 3-point shooting improve
as the season went on: he wa
18–142 (12.7 percent) in his fir
51 games, but was 15 for 4
(32.6 percent) in his final 2
games. Day could stand to pass the ball a little more; he averaged ju
1.8 assists last season. One of the best defenders on the team, Da
led the Bucks in steals 21 times. He had three or more steals in a si
gle game 16 times.

REGULAR SEASON		G	MIN	FG	FG%	3FG	3PT%	FT	FT%	REB	AST	STL	BLK	PTS	AVG
'92-93	MILWAUKEE	71	1931	358	43.2	54	29.3	213	71.7	291	117	75	48	983	13.8
'93-94	MILWAUKEE	76	2127	351	41.5	33	22.3	231	69.8	310	138	103	52	966	12.7
2 YR TOTALS		147	4058	709	42.4	87	26.2	444	70.7	601	255	178	100	1949	13.3
'93-94 RANK NBA Gs		61	55	50	104	59	102	21	113	21	89	36	4	46	48
'94-95 PROJECTIONS		81	2323	339	39.9	16	15.7	248	67.8	327	161	135	56	942	11.6

ric Murdock

No. 5/G

Full name: Eric Lloyd Murdock
HT: 6-1   **WT:** 200
Born: 6/14/68, Somerville, NJ
High school: Bridgewater
  (Raritan, NJ)
College: Providence

Murdock is an outstanding play-maker. Murdock led Milwaukee in scoring, assists and steals. He played particularly well in the second half of last season, averaging 17.7 points and 3.1 steals per game in Milwaukee's final 22 contests. His 2.4 steals per game was fifth best in the NBA. He was sixth in the league in 3FG percentage, and his 6.7 assists per game tied for twelfth in the league. He established career highs for games played, minutes, FGM, FGA, 3FGM, 3FGA, 3FG%, eals, blocked shots, points, and scoring average. He was the Bucks ading scorer 20 times, hit for 20 points 21 times and for 30 points 3 nes.

EGULAR SEASON	G	MIN	FG	FG%	3FG	3PT%	FT	FT%	REB	AST	STL	BLK	PTS	AVG
1-92 UTAH	50	478	76	41.5	5	19.2	46	75.4	54	92	30	7	203	4.1
2-93 MILWAUKEE	79	2437	438	46.8	31	26.1	231	78.0	284	603	174	7	1138	14.4
3-94 MILWAUKEE	82	2533	477	46.8	69	41.1	234	81.3	261	546	197	12	1257	15.3
3 YR TOTALS	211	5448	991	46.4	105	33.5	511	79.2	599	1241	401	26	2598	12.3
'93-94 RANK NBA Gs	1	34	22	43	28	11	20	51	33	10	4	62	22	25
'94-95 PROJECTIONS	82	3189	639	48.2	135	54.2	286	84.4	299	655	270	10	1699	20.7

LAYOFFS	G	MIN	FG	FG%	3FG	3PT%	FT	FT%	REB	AST	STL	BLK	PTS	AVG
1-92 UTAH	3	11	3	60.0	0	0.0	2	100.0	3	1	1	1	8	2.7
TOTALS	3	11	3	60.0	0	0.0	2	100.0	3	1	1	1	8	2.7

Ed Pinckney

Full name: Edward Lewis Pinckne
HT: 6-9 **WT:** 215
Born: 3/27/63, Bronx, NY
High school: Stevenson (Bronx
College: Villanova

Pinckney is an above-averag
rebounder who plays goo
defense. Last season, Pinckne
was Boston's third-leadin
rebounder. He can convert offe
sive rebounds into baskets; pu
backs are a big reason that h
shot 52.2 percent from the fie
last season. Too slight to b
effective inside, he's not know
for his low-post moves, but h
has a good mid-range jumpe
Pinckney's a competitor who
not afraid to match up defensive
with opposing centers, and he
given Patrick Ewing fits throug
out their Big East and pro careers. He played on the '85 Villanova tea
that upset Ewing's Georgetown Hoyas to win the NCA
Championship.

REGULAR SEASON		G	MIN	FG	FG%	3FG	3PT%	FT	FT%	REB	AST	STL	BLK	PTS	AVG
'85-86	PHOENIX	80	1602	255	55.8	0	0.0	171	67.3	308	90	71	37	681	8.5
'86-87	PHOENIX	80	2250	290	58.4	0	0.0	257	73.9	580	116	86	54	837	10.5
'87-88	SACRAMENTO	79	1177	179	52.2	0	0.0	133	74.7	230	66	39	32	491	6.2
'88-89	SAC-BOS	80	2012	319	51.3	0	0.0	280	80.0	448	118	83	66	918	11.5
'89-90	BOSTON	77	1082	135	54.2	0	0.0	92	77.3	225	68	34	42	362	4.7
'90-91	BOSTON	70	1165	131	53.9	0	0.0	104	89.7	341	45	61	43	366	5.2
'91-92	BOSTON	81	1917	203	53.7	0	0.0	207	81.2	564	62	70	56	613	7.6
'92-93	BOSTON	7	151	10	41.7	0	---	12	92.3	43	1	4	7	32	4.6
'93-94	BOSTON	76	1524	151	52.2	0	---	92	73.6	478	62	58	44	394	5.2
	9 YR TOTALS	630	12880	1673	53.9	0	0.0	1348	76.7	3218	628	506	381	4694	7.5
'93-94	RANK NBA Fs	48	69	89	20	78	78	75	50	36	82	52	50	89	91
'94-95	PROJECTIONS	82	1876	197	54.6	0	0.0	89	66.4	622	92	76	43	483	5.9

PLAYOFFS		G	MIN	FG	FG%	3FG	3PT%	FT	FT%	REB	AST	STL	BLK	PTS	AVG
'88-89	BOSTON	3	45	3	25.0	0	---	2	100.0	5	1	1	1	8	2.7
'89-90	BOSTON	4	25	6	85.7	0	---	7	77.8	6	0	0	0	19	4.8
'90-91	BOSTON	11	170	16	76.2	0	---	17	81.0	40	2	6	2	49	4.5
'91-92	BOSTON	10	314	35	60.3	0	0.0	26	83.9	84	7	12	9	96	9.6
	TOTALS	28	554	60	61.2	0	0.0	52	82.5	135	10	19	12	172	6.1

Glenn Robinson

Full name: Glenn Robinson
HT: 6-8   **WT:** 225
Born: 1/10/73
College: Purdue

Last season's Wooden Award winner and consensus collegiate Player of the Year, Robinson is the biggest draft pick to arrive in Milwaukee since Lew Alcindor in 1969. His 30.3 points per game average was tops in the nation last year, and he averaged 10.1 rebounds per game. He was the first player to lead the Big Ten in both scoring and rebounding in a single season since Minnesota's Mychal Thompson in 1978. He became the fifteenth player in NCAA history to score over 1,000 points in a season last year (1,030) and scored 30 or more points in a game 18 times. In fact, Robinson was Purdue's leading scorer 56 times in his 62 career collegiate games.

REGULAR SEASON	G	MIN	FG	FG%	3FG	3PT%	FT	FT%	REB	AST	STL	BLK	PTS	AVG
ROOKIE -- NO NBA EXPERIENCE														

Jon Barry   No. 17/G

Full name: Jon Alan Barry
HT: 6-5   **WT:** 204
Born: 7/25/69, Oakland, CA
High school: De La Salle Catholic (Concord, CA)
College: Georgia Tech

Barry is a fair offensive and defensive player who may be called on more this season to help out in the backcourt.

REGULAR SEASON		G	MIN	FG	FG%	3FG	3PT%	FT	FT%	REB	AST	STL	BLK	PTS	AVG
'92-93	MILWAUKEE	47	552	76	36.9	21	33.3	33	67.3	43	68	35	3	206	4.4
'93-94	MILWAUKEE	72	1242	158	41.4	32	27.8	97	79.5	146	168	102	17	445	6.2
	2 YR TOTALS	119	1794	234	39.8	53	29.8	130	76.0	189	236	137	20	651	5.5
'93-94	RANK NBA Gs	75	89	99	105	60	88	79	63	78	82	39	44	91	99
'94-95	PROJECTIONS	82	1932	214	45.8	31	22.6	191	91.8	304	285	195	42	650	7.9

Joe Courtney   No. 40/F

Full name: Joseph Pierre Courtney
HT: 6-9   **WT:** 235
Born: 10/17/69, Jackson, MS
High school: Callaway (Jackson, MS)
College: So. Mississippi

Courtney has played for 4 NBA teams in the past 2 seasons. His game is rebounding; he's never been a big scorer.

REGULAR SEASON		G	MIN	FG	FG%	3FG	3PT%	FT	FT%	REB	AST	STL	BLK	PTS	AVG
'92-93	CHI-GS	12	104	13	40.6	0	---	7	77.8	19	3	5	5	33	2.8
'93-94	PHE-MIL	52	345	67	45.3	2	66.7	32	68.1	56	15	10	12	168	3.2
	2 YR TOTALS	64	449	80	44.4	2	66.7	39	69.6	75	18	15	17	201	3.1
'93-94	RANK NBA Fs	109	129	122	89	62	1	119	90	130	127	130	113	123	121
'94-95	PROJECTIONS	82	586	161	50.0	13	130.0	64	58.7	83	34	6	13	399	4.9

Brad Lohaus   No. 54/F-C

Full name: Brad Allen Lohaus
HT: 6-11 **WT:** 238
Born: 9/29/64, New Ulm, MN
High school: Greenway (Phoenix, AZ)
College: Iowa

Lohaus is Milwaukee's all-time leader in 3-point FGM with 267. He led the team in assists twice and steals 3 times.

REGULAR SEASON		G	MIN	FG	FGx	3FG	3PT%	FT	FT%	REB	AST	STL	BLK	PTS	AVG
'88-89	BOS-SAC	77	1214	210	43.2	1	9.1	81	78.6	256	66	30	56	502	6.5
'89-90	MIN-MIL	80	1943	305	46.0	47	34.3	75	72.8	398	168	58	88	732	9.2
'90-91	MILWAUKEE	81	1219	179	43.1	33	27.7	37	68.5	217	75	50	74	428	5.3
'91-92	MILWAUKEE	70	1081	162	45.0	57	39.6	27	65.9	249	74	40	71	408	5.8
'92-93	MILWAUKEE	80	1766	283	46.1	85	37.0	73	72.3	276	127	47	74	724	9.1
'93-94	MILWAUKEE	67	962	102	36.3	46	34.3	20	69.0	150	62	30	55	270	4.0
7 YR TOTALS		525	8903	1363	44.5	272	34.5	363	73.6	1684	621	275	459	3361	6.4
'93-94	RANK NBA Fs	88	100	106	133	17	20	127	83	113	82	95	30	106	115
'94-95 PROJECTIONS		61	663	56	31.8	34	34.0	9	69.2	94	40	20	40	155	2.5

PLAYOFFS		G	MIN	FG	FGx	3FG	3PT%	FT	FT%	REB	AST	STL	BLK	PTS	AVG
'89-90	MILWAUKEE	4	147	16	40.0	6	37.5	0	---	27	5	8	9	38	9.5
'90-91	MILWAUKEE	3	41	5	31.3	3	37.5	1	50.0	9	1	0	0	14	4.7
TOTALS		16	214	29	43.3	9	34.6	1	50.0	40	6	8	10	68	4.3

Lee Mayberry   No. 11/G

Full name: Orva Lee Mayberry, Jr.
HT: 6-1 **WT:** 172
Born: 6/12/70, Tulsa, OK
High school: Rogers (Tulsa)
College: Arkansas

Mayberry averaged 11.8 points and 5.8 assists per 40 minutes played. He was 41 for 119 (34.5 percent) from 3-point range.

REGULAR SEASON		G	MIN	FG	FGx	3FG	3PT%	FT	FT%	REB	AST	STL	BLK	PTS	AVG
'92-93	MILWAUKEE	82	1503	171	45.6	43	39.1	39	57.4	118	273	59	7	424	5.2
'93-94	MILWAUKEE	82	1472	167	41.5	41	34.5	58	69.0	101	215	46	4	433	5.3
2 YR TOTALS		164	2975	338	43.5	84	36.7	97	63.8	219	488	105	11	857	5.2
'93-94	RANK NBA Gs	1	80	93	103	47	51	103	115	103	66	94	102	94	107
'94-95 PROJECTIONS		82	1441	160	37.4	38	29.7	80	80.8	85	159	33	1	438	5.3

Eric Mobley   No. 52/F

HT: 6-11 **WT:** 250
Born: 2/1/70
College: Pittsburgh
Mobley averaged 13.7 points, 8.8 rebounds and 2.8 blocks per game at Pitt last season. He shot 57 percent from the field, but really made his mark as a shotblocker, rejecting 184 shots in just 88 games.

REGULAR SEASON	G	MIN	FG	FGx	3FG	3PTx	FT	FTx	REB	AST	STL	BLK	PTS	AVG

ROOKIE -- NO NBA EXPERIENCE

Mike Dunleavy   Head Coach

Full name: Michael Joseph Dunleavy
HT: 6-3 **WT:** 180
Born: 3/21/54, Brooklyn, NY
High school: Nazareth Regional (Brooklyn)
College: South Carolina
Dunleavy knew rebuilding would take time; his contract as Milwaukee's basketball boss runs through the 1999–2000 season.

	REGULAR SEASON					PLAYOFFS				
YEAR	TEAM	W	L	PCT	FINISH	W	L	PCT	
'90-91	LA LAKERS	58	24	707	2nd/Pacific Div.	12	7	632	lost NBA finals to Chicago, 4-1
'91-92	LA LAKERS	43	39	524	6th/Pacific Div.	1	3	250	lost Western Conf. first round to Portland, 3-1
'92-93	MILWAUKEE	28	54	341	7th/Central Div.				
'93-94	MILWAUKEE	20	62	244	7th/Central Div.				
	4 YR TOTALS	149	179	454		13	10	565	

Minnesota
TIMBERWOLVES

994–95 Scouting Report

rontcourt

hristian Laettner is the T-wolves' leading scorer and rebounder. onyell Marshall should move in as the starting small forward. Iarshall is a great scorer who can hit the short jumper or drive to the oop. The T-wolves are thin at center. Mike Brown and Stacey King btained from Chicago in exchange for Luc Longley) will compete start at center, provided King can come back from a fractured right nee that caused him to miss Minnesota's last 11 games. King's no orse than Longley, and showed signs of being an improvement, but either King nor Brown are the long term answer at center. Thurl ailey is a veteran who comes off the bench to play power forward. Iarlon Maxey is the kind of inside presence Minnesota needs. Indersized to play power forward, but a hard worker, he could be a aluable role player for years to come.

Backcourt

wingman Isaiah Rider should play mainly at shooting guard this eason, thanks to Minnesota's drafting of F Donyell Marshall. Iinnesota's second leading scorer, Rider is a tremendously skilled ffensive player, with great leaping ability and the talent to drive to e hoop or post up defenders. Last year's starter at shooting guard, Ooug West, will probably move to a reserve role. West was the eam's third-leading scorer behind Laettner and Rider. Michael Villiams starts at point guard. Chris Smith comes off the bench to ack Williams up at point guard. He's a good ballhandler who led he team in assist to turnover ratio (3.94 to 1), but he can't match Villiams' quality of defense.

Defense

Iinnesota is mediocre defensively. Teams averaged 103.6 points gainst the Timberwolves, sixteenth in the NBA. And they held

opponents under 100 points only 31 times. Opposing teams shot 47.
percent from the floor against Minnesota, seventeenth in the league
Minnesota has little athleticism on defense. The Timberwolves wer
pretty good at blocking shots, ranking twelfth in the NBA, but place
twenty-sixth in stealing the ball and in forcing turnovers.

1994–95 Prospects

Minnesota didn't do much right last season. The T-Wolves ranke
twenty-sixth in points scored (only Dallas was worse), nineteenth in
FG percentage, and twenty-fifth in rebounding. They were also a
middle of the pack team defensively. The T-Wolves were 12–18 vs.
lottery teams last season, including a remarkable 1–5 vs. Dallas. The
T-Wolves stayed fairly healthy last season, losing only 68 playe
games to injury or illness. The team was awful when either Michae
Williams or Stacey King was sidelined (2–20).

Minnesota goes into this season with a multitude of holes. They're
still a bad rebounding team. They need to find a center who can play
defense. They have one of the weakest benches in the NBA. And a
small forward off the bench who can score would help, too. The
T-Wolves need to upgrade themselves at point guard, and sign a
defensive stopper at big guard. Minnesota will open the season with
yet another head coach, Bill Blair (their fourth head coach in 5 seasons). However, by drafting Donyell Marshall, and putting him in
the starting lineup with Laettner and Rider, Minnesota will soon
have one of the prerequisites to NBA success: three viable offensive
threats in the lineup.

Minnesota has been the least successful of the NBA's four most
recent expansion teams. Only the T-Wolves have failed to make the
playoffs. In fact, Minnesota won more games in each of their first
two seasons than they did last season. Because most of the lottery
teams have improved, the T-Wolves are in for another difficult season. But the good news for T-Wolves fans is that this team will be a
lot more interesting to watch, and being a lottery team again this
season will give them a shot at the defensive stud at center or defensive stopper that could allow Minnesota to make a major improvement in '95–96.

Team Directory

wner: Glen Taylor

P/CFO: Joe Petirossi

neral manager: Jack McCloskey

President: Bob Stein

VP, mktg. & sales: Chris Wright

Dir., media services: Kent Wipf

1993–94 Review

ESTERN CONFERENCE						EASTERN CONFERENCE					
IDWEST DIV.		PACIFIC DIV.				ATLANTIC DIV.			CENTRAL DIV.		
	W	L		W	L		W	L		W	L
OU	1	4	SEA	0	4	NY	0	2	ATL	0	2
AN	1	4	PHO	0	4	ORL	1	1	CHI	0	2
TAH	1	4	GS	2	2	NJ	1	1	CLE	0	2
EN	1	4	POR	0	4	MIA	0	2	IND	0	2
IN	-	-	LAL	1	3	BOS	1	1	CHA	0	2
AL	1	5	SAC	2	2	PHI	2	0	DET	0	2
			LAC	3	1	WAS	0	2	MIL	2	0
	5	21		8	20		5	9		2	12

993–94 finish: 20–62 (13–28 home, 7–34 away), fifth in Midwest Div.

1994–95 Schedule

1/4	@ Denver	9:00 pm	1/6	@ Orlando	7:30 pm	3/3	Houston	8:00 pm
1/5	Houston	8:00 pm	1/8	@ New York	6:00 pm	3/5	@ LA Lakers	10:00 pm
1/8	@ Detroit	7:30 pm	1/10	Sacra.	8:00 pm	3/6	@ LA Clip.	10:30 pm
1/9	LA Lakers	8:00 pm	1/11	@ Charlotte	7:30 pm	3/8	Seattle	8:00 pm
1/11	Chicago	8:00 pm	1/13	Detroit	8:00 pm	3/10	LA Lakers	8:00 pm
1/12	Boston	8:00 pm	1/14	@ New Jersey	7:30 pm	3/12	Portland	3:30 pm
1/15	@ Gold. St.	10:30 pm	1/16	Houston	8:00 pm	3/14	@ San Ant.	8:30 pm
1/16	@ Phoenix	9:00 pm	1/19	Seattle	8:00 pm	3/16	@ Houston	8:30 pm
1/19	San Ant.	8:00 pm	1/20	@ Chicago	8:30 pm	3/17	Cleveland	8:00 pm
1/22	@ Cleveland	7:30 pm	1/22	Charlotte	3:30 pm	3/19	LA Clip.	3:30 pm
1/23	Atlanta	8:00 pm	1/24	Phoenix	8:00 pm	3/22	Dallas	8:00 pm
1/25	Phila.	8:00 pm	1/27	@ Dallas	8:30 pm	3/24	San Ant.	8:00 pm
1/28	@ San Ant.	8:30 pm	1/28	@ Houston	8:30 pm	3/26	Sacra.	3:30 pm
1/29	@ Dallas	8:30 pm	1/30	@ Utah	9:00 pm	3/29	@ Seattle	10:00 pm
2/1	@ Utah	9:00 pm	2/1	Dallas	8:00 pm	3/31	@ Phoenix	9:00 pm
2/3	@ LA Clip.	10:30 pm	2/3	Portland	8:00 pm	4/1	@ Gold. St.	10:30 pm
2/6	Denver	8:00 pm	2/5	@ Boston	7:00 pm	4/4	@ Portland	10:00 pm
2/10	Phoenix	8:00 pm	2/7	Gold. St.	8:00 pm	4/7	@ Dallas	8:30 pm
2/13	@ Atlanta	7:30 pm	2/8	@ Milwaukee	8:30 pm	4/10	Denver	8:00 pm
2/14	Utah	8:00 pm	2/14	Wash.	8:00 pm	4/11	Gold. St.	8:00 pm
2/16	New Jersey	8:00 pm	2/15	@ Phila.	7:30 pm	4/14	Milwaukee	8:00 pm
2/17	@ Wash.	7:30 pm	2/17	Indiana	8:00 pm	4/16	@ Indiana	3:30 pm
2/20	@ LA Lakers	10:30 pm	2/19	Orlando	3:30 pm	4/18	Utah	8:00 pm
2/22	@ Sacra.	10:30 pm	2/21	@ Portland	10:00 pm	4/19	@ Denver	9:00 pm
2/26	LA Clip.	8:00 pm	2/22	@ Seattle	10:00 pm	4/21	@ Utah	9:00 pm
2/30	New York	8:00 pm	2/26	Miami	3:30 pm	4/23	San Ant.	3:30 pm
3/3	Denver	8:00 pm	2/28	@ Denver	9:00 pm			
3/5	@ Miami	7:30 pm	3/1	@ Sacra.	10:30 pm			

1993–94 Team Stats

NAME	G	MIN	FG	FGA	FG%	3FG	3FGA	3FG%	FT	FTA	FT%	ORB	TRB	AST	PF	STL	BLK	TO	PTS	AVG
Laettner	70	2428	396	883	44.8	6	25	24.0	375	479	78.3	160	602	307	264	87	86	259	1173	16.8
Rider	79	2415	522	1115	46.8	54	150	36.0	215	265	81.1	118	315	202	194	54	28	218	1313	16.6
West	72	2182	434	891	48.7	1	8	12.5	187	231	81.0	61	231	172	236	65	24	137	1056	14.7
M. Williams	71	2206	314	687	45.7	10	45	22.2	333	397	83.9	67	221	512	193	118	24	203	971	13.7
King	18	516	78	170	45.9	0	0	—	57	83	68.7	40	109	19	57	13	30	40	213	11.8
Person	77	2029	356	843	42.2	100	272	36.8	82	108	75.9	55	253	185	164	45	12	121	894	11.6
Bailey	79	1297	232	455	51.0	0	2	0.0	119	149	79.9	66	215	54	93	20	58	58	583	7.4
Longley	49	989	134	289	46.4	0	1	0.0	56	80	70.0	87	295	46	131	35	58	79	324	6.6
Smith	80	1617	184	423	43.5	10	39	25.6	95	141	67.4	15	122	285	131	38	18	101	473	5.9
Maxey	55	626	89	167	53.3	0	2	0.0	70	98	71.4	75	199	10	113	16	33	40	248	4.5
Brown	82	1921	111	260	42.7	0	2	0.0	77	118	65.3	119	447	72	218	51	29	75	299	3.6
Guibert	5	33	6	20	30.0	0	0	—	3	6	50.0	10	16	2	6	0	1	6	15	3.0
Frank	67	959	67	160	41.9	0	2	0.0	54	76	71.1	83	220	57	163	35	35	49	188	2.8
C. Williams	4	46	5	13	38.5	0	1	0.0	1	1	100.0	1	6	6	6	2	0	2	11	2.8
Jackson	17	92	17	33	51.5	5	5	20.0	3	3	100.0	12	27	16	13	5	0	10	38	2.2
Davis	68	374	40	126	31.7	1	3	33.3	50	68	73.5	21	55	22	34	16	4	19	131	1.9
T-wolves	82	19730	2985	6535	45.7	183	557	32.9	1777	2303	77.2	990	3333	1967	2016	600	440	1478	7930	96.7
Opp.	82	19730	3244	6874	47.2	227	738	30.8	1783	2451	72.7	1102	3398	2108	1855	824	549	1164	8498	103.6

HISTORY
ALL-TIME TEAM RECORDS

Career

Games played	Doug West	359	1989–94
Total points	Tony Campbell	4,888	1989–92
Field goals made	Tony Campbell	1,902	1989–92
Field goals attempted	Tony Campbell	4,220	1989–92
Free throws made	Tony Campbell	1,046	1989–92
Free throws attempted	Tony Campbell	1,314	1989–92
Total rebounds	Sam Mitchell	1,455	1989–90, 1991–93
Assists	Pooh Richardson	1,973	1989–92
Steals	Pooh Richardson	383	1989–92
Personal fouls	Sam Mitchell	869	1989–90, 1991–93
Blocked shots	Felton Spencer	266	1990–93

Season

Total points	Tony Campbell	1,903	1989–90
Field goals made	Tony Campbell	723	1989–90
Field goals attempted	Tony Campbell	1,581	1989–90
Free throws made	Christian Laettner	462	1992–93
Free throws attempted	Tony Campbell	569	1989–90
Total rebounds	Christian Laettner	708	1992–93
Assists	Pooh Richardson	734	1990–91
Steals	Tyrone Corbin	175	1989–90
Personal fouls	Sam Mitchell	338	1990–91
Blocked shots	Felton Spencer	121	1990–91

Game

Total points	Tony Campbell	44	vs. Boston, 2/2/90
Field goals made	Pooh Richardson	16	vs. Golden State, 1/19/91
	Doug West	16	vs. Gold. St.(OT), 12/19/92
Free throws made	Christian Laettner	18	vs. Sacramento, 2/18/93
Total rebounds	Tod Murphy	20	vs. LA Clippers, 1/2/90
Assists	Michael Williams	17	vs. LA Clippers, 12/10/93
	Pooh Richardson	17	vs. Washington, 3/13/92
	Sidney Lowe	17	vs. Golden State, 3/20/90
Steals	Tyrone Corbin	8	vs. Dallas, 3/30/90
Blocked shots	Randy Breuer	9	vs. Orlando, 4/13/90

LEADING COACHES
REGULAR SEASON

NAME	YEARS	W	L	PCT
Bill Musselman	1989–91	51	113	.311
Sidney Lowe	1992–94	33	102	.244
Jimmy Rodgers	1991–93	21	90	.189

Minnesota Timberwolves 1994–95 Roster

Head Coach: Bill Blair

No.	Name	Pos.	Ht.	Wt.	Yrs.	Born	College
41	Thurl Bailey	F	6-11	247	10	4/7/61	North Carolina State
40	Mike Brown	C-F	6-10	260	9	7/19/63	George Washington
23	Brian Davis	G-F	6-7	195	1	6/21/70	Duke
30	Tellis Frank	F-C	6-10	225	5	4/26/65	Western Kentucky
	Andres Guibert	C	6-10	242	1	10/28/68	Cuba
7	Stanley Jackson	G	6-3	185	1	10/14/70	Ala.-Birmingham
21	Stacey King	F-C	6-11	250	5	1/29/67	Oklahoma
32	Christian Laettner	F	6-11	235	2	8/17/69	Duke
	Donyell Marshall	F	6-9	218	R	5/18/73	Connecticut
25	Marlon Maxey	F	6-8	250	3	2/19/69	Texas-El Paso
	Zeljko Rebraca	C	NA	NA	R	NA	Yugoslavia
34	Isaiah Rider	G-F	6-5	215	1	3/12/71	Nevada-Las Vegas
3	Chris Smith	G	6-3	191	2	5/17/70	Connecticut
5	Doug West	G	6-6	200	5	5/27/67	Villanova
24	Michael Williams	G	6-2	175	6	7/23/66	Baylor

Arena Information

Target Center (19,006)
Tickets: 612-339-HOWL, 612-989-5151 (Ticketmaster),
    612-673-1645 (group orders)
Ticket prices: $32.50, $27.50, $21.50, $16.50, $12.50, $8.50

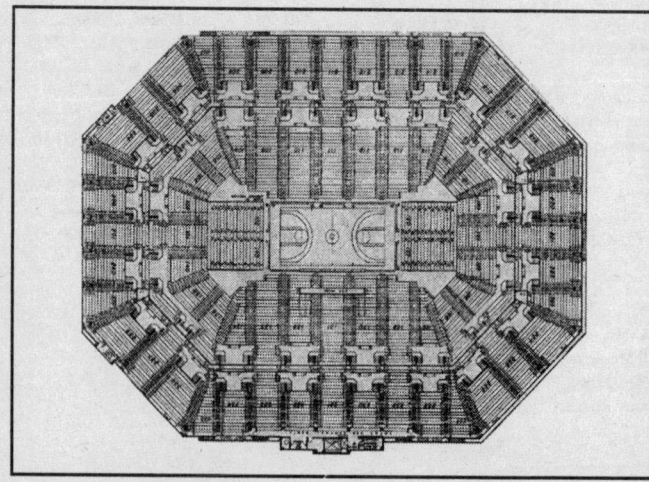

Thurl Bailey

No. 41/F

Full name: Thurl Lee Bailey
HT: 6-11   **WT:** 247
Born: 4/7/61, Washington, DC
High school: Bladensburg
   School (MD)
College: North Carolina State

A well-liked player, Bailey is amazingly durable: he's only missed 19 games over his 11-year NBA career. Bailey is a good low-post player and free throw shooter, but a remarkably poor rebounder (6.6 rebounds per 40 minutes played) despite standing 6-11 and weighing 247 pounds. Although he scored in double figures 21 times, he had his first point/rebound double-double since the '91–92 season when he scored 13 points and grabbed 10 rebounds against Sacramento on December 1. Last season, he shot 51 percent from the field (and 57.8 percent over the final 21 games), but only averaged 7.4 points per game.

REGULAR SEASON		G	MIN	FG	FG%	3FG	3PT%	FT	FT%	REB	AST	STL	BLK	PTS	AVG
'83-84	UTAH	81	2009	302	51.2	0	---	88	75.2	464	129	38	122	692	8.5
'84-85	UTAH	80	2481	507	49.0	1	100.0	197	84.2	525	138	51	105	1212	15.2
'85-86	UTAH	82	2358	483	44.8	0	0.0	230	83.0	493	153	42	114	1196	14.6
'86-87	UTAH	81	2155	463	44.7	0	0.0	190	80.5	432	102	38	88	1116	13.8
'87-88	UTAH	82	2804	633	49.2	1	33.3	337	82.6	531	158	49	125	1604	19.6
'88-89	UTAH	82	2777	615	48.3	2	40.0	363	82.5	447	138	48	91	1595	19.5
'89-90	UTAH	82	2583	470	48.1	0	0.0	222	77.9	410	137	32	100	1162	14.2
'90-91	UTAH	82	2486	399	45.8	0	0.0	219	80.8	407	124	53	91	1017	12.4
'91-92	UTAH-MINN	84	2104	368	44.0	0	0.0	215	79.6	485	78	35	117	951	11.3
'92-93	MINNESOTA	70	1276	203	45.5	0	---	119	83.8	215	61	20	47	525	7.5
'93-94	MINNESOTA	79	1297	232	51.0	0	0.0	119	79.3	215	54	20	58	583	7.4
11 YR TOTALS		895	24330	4675	47.3	4	12.1	2299	81.3	4624	1272	426	1058	11653	13.2
'93-94	RANK NBA Fs	30	82	66	26	78	78	62	14	94	91	110	27	69	76
'94-95	PROJECTIONS	80	1022	189	53.8	0	0.0	92	78.6	161	40	15	47	470	5.9

PLAYOFFS		G	MIN	FG	FG%	3FG	3PT%	FT	FT%	REB	AST	STL	BLK	PTS	AVG
'83-84	UTAH	11	340	50	51.5	0	0.0	17	81.0	61	10	2	11	117	10.6
'84-85	UTAH	10	375	62	40.8	0	---	45	81.8	92	27	5	18	169	16.9
'85-86	UTAH	4	147	28	36.4	0	0.0	8	72.7	32	13	2	2	64	16.0
'86-87	UTAH	5	151	30	47.6	0	---	18	100.0	30	9	3	6	78	15.6
'87-88	UTAH	11	449	99	48.8	0	0.0	57	83.8	63	18	6	23	255	23.2
'88-89	UTAH	3	122	12	35.3	0	---	12	80.0	25	3	1	4	36	12.0
'89-90	UTAH	5	190	43	48.9	0	---	19	79.2	32	7	5	6	105	21.0
'90-91	UTAH	9	228	23	35.9	0	---	22	88.0	32	9	3	6	68	7.6
	TOTALS	58	2002	347	44.6	0	0.0	198	83.5	367	96	27	76	892	15.4

Stacey King

No. 21/F-C

Full name: Ronald Stacey King
HT: 6-11 **WT:** 250
Born: 1/29/67, Lawton, OK
High school: Lawton (OK)
College: Oklahoma

King's game might flourish in Minnesota, where he stands to get the minutes he never saw as a reserve in Chicago. King came to Minnesota in exchange for Luc Longley in February. Before a fractured right knee ended his season, King started 15 games for the T-Wolves, and averaged 11.8 points and 6.1 rebounds. He led Minnesota in rebounds 5 times and in scoring 3 times, and had 3 double-doubles. King's inside play is soft, which is why he doesn't grab many rebounds or intimidate defensively. But he did have 30 blocks in his 18 games with Minnesota, after recording just 12 blocks in 31 games with Chicago.

REGULAR SEASON		G	MIN	FG	FG%	3FG	3PT%	FT	FT%	REB	AST	STL	BLK	PTS	AVG
'89-90	CHICAGO	82	1777	267	50.4	0	0.0	194	72.7	384	87	38	58	728	8.9
'90-91	CHICAGO	76	1198	156	46.7	0	0.0	107	70.4	208	65	24	42	419	5.5
'91-92	CHICAGO	79	1268	215	50.6	2	40.0	119	75.3	205	77	21	25	551	7.0
'92-93	CHICAGO	76	1059	160	47.1	2	33.3	86	70.5	207	71	26	20	408	5.4
'93-94	CHI-MIN	49	1053	146	42.8	0	0.0	93	69.4	241	58	31	42	385	7.9
5 YR TOTALS		362	6355	944	47.9	4	25.0	599	71.7	1245	358	140	187	2491	6.9
'93-94	RANK NBA Fs	116	97	93	114	78	78	74	88	84	87	91	53	91	71
'94-95	PROJECTIONS	34	967	127	33.9	0	0.0	85	66.4	243	50	32	47	339	10.0

PLAYOFFS		G	MIN	FG	FG%	3FG	3PT%	FT	FT%	REB	AST	STL	BLK	PTS	AVG
'89-90	CHICAGO	16	281	37	40.7	0	0.0	36	76.6	51	9	6	8	110	6.9
'90-91	CHICAGO	11	86	8	29.6	0	0.0	7	63.6	22	2	1	1	23	2.1
'91-92	CHICAGO	14	111	18	45.0	2	100.0	15	65.2	20	5	5	2	53	3.8
'92-93	CHICAGO	19	229	26	39.4	0	---	25	80.6	40	14	9	4	77	4.1
TOTALS		60	707	89	39.7	2	50.0	83	74.1	133	30	21	15	263	4.4

Christian Laettner

No. 32/F

Full name: Christian Donald Laettner

HT: 6-11   **WT:** 235

Born: 8/17/69, Angola, NY

High school: Nichols School (Buffalo, NY)

College: Duke

Laettner led Minnesota in scoring, rebounding, and blocked shots. Although his clashes with his teammates have obscured his game, Laettner is one of the most skilled and complete players in basketball. He has a nice shooting touch, but is strong enough to score inside and rebound, and athletic enough to dunk and block shots. Laettner's been frustrated with his team's lack of success after playing on back-to-back NCAA champions at Duke, but that situation should improve as his supporting cast is upgraded. Laettner was 1 of only 5 players to average 15 points, 8 rebounds, and 4 assists per game last season; the others were Charles Barkley, Scottie Pippen, Billy Owens, and David Robinson.

REGULAR SEASON		G	MIN	FG	FG%	3FG	3PT%	FT	FT%	REB	AST	STL	BLK	PTS	AVG
'92-93	MINNESOTA	81	2823	503	47.4	4	10.0	462	83.5	708	223	105	83	1472	18.2
'93-94	MINNESOTA	70	2428	396	44.8	6	24.0	375	78.3	602	307	87	86	1173	16.8
	2 YR TOTALS	151	5251	899	46.2	10	15.4	837	81.1	1310	530	192	169	2645	17.5
'93-94	RANK NBA Fs	77	31	30	91	47	55	4	20	22	5	22	12	22	19
'94-95	PROJECTIONS	59	2033	302	42.2	5	38.5	295	73.0	498	354	70	84	904	15.3

Isaiah Rider

No. 34/G-F

Full name: Isaiah Rider, Jr.
HT: 6-5   **WT:** 215
Born: 3/12/71, Oakland, CA
High school: Encinal (Alameda, CA)
College: Nevada-Las Vegas

Rider is a gifted athlete who looks like he'll be a first-rate NBA scorer. He won the slam-dunk championship during All-Star weekend last season, and even blocked a Patrick Ewing dunk attempt. Rider also set franchise rookie records for FGM and 3-pointers. Not known for his passing ability, he improved as the season developed. He has only a passing acquaintance with defense, although he's athletic enough to become a good defender. Rider was Minnesota's second-leading scorer and led his team in scoring 28 times. He had one point/rebound double-double last season, when he scored 30 points and had 12 reounds on December 30 against Houston.

REGULAR SEASON	G	MIN	FG	FGx	3FG	3PTx	FT	FTx	REB	AST	STL	BLK	PTS	AVG
'93-94 MINNESOTA	79	2415	522	46.8	54	36.0	215	81.1	315	202	54	28	1313	16.6
1 YR TOTALS	79	2415	522	46.8	54	36.0	215	81.1	315	202	54	28	1313	16.6
'93-94 RANK NBA Gs	40	39	12	42	36	36	24	52	19	70	86	18	16	16

Micheal Williams

No. 24/G

Full name: Micheal Douglas Williams
HT: 6-2   **WT:** 175
Born: 7/23/66, Dallas, TX
High school: David Carter (Dallas)
College: Baylor

Williams is an excellent free throw shooter. He set an NBA record with 97 straight free throws over the past two seasons, and ended the season having made his final 34 from the line. He's a good playmaker who averaged 7.2 assists per game last season. But his play fell off sharply after he suffered a sprained wrist vs. Houston on February 6 (he averaged 16.8 points, 8.1 assists through the end of January, 9.7 points and 6.0 assists after). Williams broke 20 points 18 times, and led Minnesota in scoring 10 times. Williams takes a lot of chances on defense; he gets his share of steals, but also gives up easy baskets. He commits a lot of turnovers (203 last season, third most on the team).

REGULAR SEASON	G	MIN	FG	FGx	3FG	3PTx	FT	FTx	REB	AST	STL	BLK	PTS	AVG
'88-89 DETROIT	49	358	47	36.4	2	22.2	31	66.0	27	70	13	3	127	2.6
'89-90 PHE-CHA	28	329	60	50.4	0	0.0	36	78.3	32	81	22	1	156	5.6
'90-91 INDIANA	73	1706	261	43.9	1	14.3	290	87.9	176	348	150	17	813	11.1
'91-92 INDIANA	79	2750	404	49.0	8	24.2	372	87.1	282	647	233	22	1188	15.0
'92-93 MINNESOTA	76	2661	353	44.6	26	24.3	419	90.7	273	661	165	23	1151	15.1
'93-94 MINNESOTA	71	2206	314	45.7	10	22.2	333	83.9	221	512	118	24	971	13.7
6 YR TOTALS	376	10010	1439	46.8	47	23.0	1481	86.7	1011	2319	701	90	4406	11.7
'93-94 RANK NBA Gs	79	49	57	54	90	103	, 7	25	45	13	29	24	45	40
'84-95 PROJECTIONS	71	2183	308	45.0	10	24.4	332	81.8	217	500	96	27	958	13.5

PLAYOFFS	G	MIN	FG	FGx	3FG	3PTx	FT	FTx	REB	AST	STL	BLK	PTS	AVG
'88-89 DETROIT	4	6	0	---	0	---	2	100.0	2	2	1	0	2	0.5
'90-91 INDIANA	5	183	30	46.2	0	0.0	43	89.6	16	42	14	0	103	20.6
'91-92 INDIANA	3	106	18	41.9	3	33.3	11	73.3	8	24	9	0	50	16.7
TOTALS	12	295	48	44.4	3	30.0	56	86.2	26	68	24	0	155	12.9

Mike Brown

No. 40/C-F

Full name: Michael Brown
HT: 6-10 **WT:** 260
Born: 7/19/63, Newark, NJ
High school: C. J. Scott (East Orange, NJ)
College: George Washington
Brown was the only T-Wolf to appear in all 82 games. He was Minnesota's second-leading rebounder.

REGULAR SEASON		G	MIN	FG	FG%	3FG	3PT%	FT	FT%	REB	AST	STL	BLK	PTS	AVG
'89-90	UTAH	82	1397	177	51.5	1	50.0	157	78.9	373	47	32	28	512	6.2
'90-91	UTAH	82	1391	129	45.4	0	---	132	74.2	337	49	29	24	390	4.8
'91-92	UTAH	82	1783	221	45.3	0	0.0	190	66.7	476	81	42	34	632	7.7
'92-93	UTAH	82	1551	176	43.0	0	0.0	113	68.9	391	64	32	23	465	5.7
'93-94	MINNESOTA	82	1921	111	42.7	0	0.0	77	65.3	447	72	51	29	299	3.6
	8 YR TOTALS	584	10503	1102	45.8	1	14.3	848	69.7	2655	406	242	166	3053	5.2
'93-94	RANK NBA C.s	1	15	33	44	14	14	25	33	17	19	12	32	31	39
'94-95	PROJECTIONS	82	2108	64	41.3	0	0.0	38	62.1	465	76	61	30	164	2.0

PLAYOFFS		G	MIN	FG	FG%	3FG	3PT%	FT	FT%	REB	AST	STL	BLK	PTS	AVG
'89-90	UTAH	5	67	7	46.7	0	---	4	80.0	10	3	1	1	18	3.6
'90-91	UTAH	9	223	27	48.2	0	---	32	84.2	66	5	3	1	86	9.6
'91-92	UTAH	16	274	30	40.0	0	---	32	78.0	65	11	2	2	92	5.8
'92-93	UTAH	5	93	13	52.0	0	---	7	63.6	16	2	0	1	33	6.6
	TOTALS	39	675	77	44.3	0	---	76	78.4	159	22	8	5	230	5.9

Donyell Marshall

F

HT: 6-9 **WT:** 218
Born: 5/18/73, Reading, PA
College: Connecticut
Runner-up to Glenn Robinson for Player of the Year honors, Marshall was the unanimous Big East Player of the Year. He set a Big East season record with 462 points. He blocked 245 shots during his college career.

REGULAR SEASON	G	MIN	FG	FG%	3FG	3PT%	FT	FT%	REB	AST	STL	BLK	PTS	AVG

ROOKIE -- NO NBA EXPERIENCE

Marlon Maxey   No. 25/F

Full name: Marlon Lee Maxey
HT: 6-8 **WT:** 250
Born: 2/19/69, Chicago, IL
High school: Percy L. Julian (Chicago)
College: Texas–El Paso

He's a good rebounder off the bench (12.7 rebounds per 40 minutes), shoots for a high percentage, and blocks his share of shots.

REGULAR SEASON		G	MIN	FG	FGx	3FG	3PTx	FT	FTx	REB	AST	STL	BLK	PTS	AVG
'92-93	MINNESOTA	43	520	93	55.0	0	0.0	45	64.3	164	12	11	18	231	5.4
'93-94	MINNESOTA	55	626	89	53.3	0	0.0	70	71.4	199	10	16	33	248	4.5
	2 YR TOTALS	98	1146	182	54.2	0	0.0	115	68.5	363	22	27	51	479	4.9
'93-94	RANK NBA Fs	104	122	111	16	78	78	91	67	98	131	122	65	108	110
'94-95	PROJECTIONS	67	732	79	51.6	0	0.0	103	78.6	235	6	22	52	261	3.9

Chris Smith   No. 3/G

Full name: Chris G. Smith
HT: 6-3 **WT:** 191
Born: 5/17/70, Bridgeport, CT
High school: Kolbe Cathedral (Bridgeport)
College: Connecticut

Smith averaged 6.6 assists per game in the 16 games he started at point; he averaged 7.1 assists per 40 minutes for the season.

REGULAR SEASON		G	MIN	FG	FGx	3FG	3PTx	FT	FTx	REB	AST	STL	BLK	PTS	AVG
'92-93	MINNESOTA	80	1266	125	43.3	2	14.3	95	79.2	96	196	48	16	347	4.3
'93-94	MINNESOTA	80	1617	184	43.5	10	25.6	95	67.4	122	295	38	18	473	5.9
	2 YR TOTALS	160	2883	309	43.4	12	22.6	190	72.8	218	481	86	34	820	5.1
'93-94	RANK NBA Gs	33	72	89	80	90	94	80	119	93	48	105	42	89	102
'94-95	PROJECTIONS	80	1968	254	43.8	27	37.0	87	55.4	148	389	18	19	622	7.8

Doug West   No. 5/G

Full name: Jeffery Douglas West
HT: 6-6   **WT:** 200
Born: 5/27/67, Altoona, PA
High school: Altoona Area (PA)
College: Villanova
West is effective going to the hoop or shooting jumpers from medium range. He's a better defender than the starter, Isaiah Rider.

REGULAR SEASON		G	MIN	FG	FGx	3FG	3PTx	FT	FTx	REB	AST	STL	BLK	PTS	AVG
'89-90	MINNESOTA	52	378	53	39.3	3	27.3	26	81.3	70	18	10	6	135	2.6
'90-91	MINNESOTA	75	824	118	48.0	0	0.0	58	69.0	136	48	35	23	294	3.9
'91-92	MINNESOTA	80	2540	463	51.8	4	17.4	186	80.5	257	281	66	26	1116	14.0
'92-93	MINNESOTA	80	3104	646	51.7	2	8.7	249	84.1	247	235	85	21	1543	19.3
'93-94	MINNESOTA	72	2182	434	48.7	1	12.5	187	81.0	231	172	65	24	1056	14.7
	5 YR TOTALS	359	9028	1714	50.2	10	15.2	706	80.8	941	754	261	100	4144	11.5
'93-94	RANK NBA Gs	75	51	32	18	124	126	34	54	40	80	69	24	38	32
'94-95	PROJECTIONS	70	2133	442	48.3	0	0.0	194	81.2	220	169	64	22	1078	15.4

Bill Blair   Head Coach

College: Virginia Military Institute
Bill Blair is known as a defensive specialist. He served as an assistant under Larry Brown at New Jersey and at Indiana. He also spent 7 seasons as an assistant with the Washington Bullets and Chicago Bulls. Blair also served as head coach at VMI and Colorado.

	REGULAR SEASON				PLAYOFFS			
YEAR	TEAM	W	L	PCT	FINISH	W	L	PCT

no prior NBA head-coaching experience

New Jersey
NETS

1994–95 Scouting Report

Frontcourt

Derrick Coleman is the star of the team and a formidable player at power forward. He led the Nets in scoring, rebounding and blocks. 6-11 P.J. Brown emerged as a regular starter at small forward, supplanting injured (and inconsistent) Chris Morris. Morris isn't much of a rebounder (1.7 RPG), defender, or ballhandler (1.6 assists per turnover), and he hasn't shown a great outside shot, but he can score driving to the hoop. Armon Gilliam played well coming off the bench, finishing the season as the club's fourth leading scorer (11.8 per game) and rebounder (6.1). Center was a glaring hole for New Jersey last season; Benoit Benjamin's concentration was an issue. His game tended to fade after the first quarter, and he averaged less than 24 minutes per game. Top draft choice Yinka Dare is being counted on to become the team's starting center, although Dare will probably use his debut season to learn the ropes of the NBA. Center Dwayne Schintzius comes off the bench to provide rebounding and shot blocking. Jayson Williams also saw time at center off the bench although he plays better at his natural position, power forward. He's a better scorer and rebounder than Schintzius. Rick Mahorn has a reputation as a rebounder and defensive intimidator, but injuries limited him to just 28 games last season. He looks like he's nearing the end of his career.

Backcourt

Kenny Anderson is developing into the point guard senior Nets management hoped for when they overruled GM Willis Reed and drafted Anderson as the team's top draft choice in '91. But the team still hasn't recovered from the loss of Drazen Petrovic at shooting guard. Kevin Edwards starts at shooting guard, but he's only an average scorer (14 points per game). '93 first-rounder Rex Walters was drafted as a shooting guard but saw most his time backing up Anderson at point. He's an excellent shooter from outside, and he should assume a more significant role this season. Ex-Knick Johnny Newman returned to the New York area to take a role as a scorer off the bench.

Defense

Opposing teams shot 45.8 percent from the floor against New Jersey, eleventh in the league. Teams averaged 101 points against the Nets, twelfth fewest in the NBA. They held opponents under 100 points only 34 times. They played smart defense; only 5 other NBA teams committed fewer fouls. And thanks to Derrick Coleman, the Nets ranked second in the NBA in blocks, despite lacking a first-rate center. The Nets could have gotten better play from their guards; they were just eighteenth in the NBA in stealing the ball and only twentieth in the league in forcing turnovers.

1994–95 Prospects

Despite losing Drazen Petrovic and Chris Dudley, the Nets actually improved their record last season by two wins. New Jersey was one of the worst shooting teams in the NBA (twenty-sixth in FG%), but was one of the best at not turning the ball over (third in the NBA). And they led the NBA in rebounds (including second in offensive rebounds, and fourth in defensive rebounds). As a result, the Nets ranked eighth in points scored.

The Nets are a pretty solid team. They play tough defense, don't turn over the ball, and they rebound well. They're set at point guard and power forward. They need a scorer at shooting guard, and at small forward. New Jersey has never had a first-rate NBA center. They'll be better if Dare turns into an NBA-level rebounder and shotblocker to take some of the burden off Derrick Coleman. There's also no telling how much Coach Chuck Daly's retirement will hurt the Nets. They improved after he took over from Bill Fitch in 1992, and you have to wonder whether New Jersey, one of the more emotionally fragile teams in the NBA, will take to new coach Butch Beard.

The Nets are definitely good enough to be a playoff team again. But to make it to the next level, they've got to come up with a third offensive option, and they've got to improve their bench.

Team Directory

Chairman: Alan L. Aufzien   Vice chair./Treas.: David B. Gerstein

Vice chair./Secretary: Jerry L. Cohen   President & CEO: Jon Spoelstra

Exec. VP/GM: Willis Reed   Dir., public relations: John Mertz

1993–94 Review

EASTERN CONFERENCE					WESTERN CONFERENCE					
ATLANTIC DIV.		CENTRAL DIV.			MIDWEST DIV.			PACIFIC DIV.		
	W	L		W	L		W	L		W	L
NY	4	1	ATL	3	1	HOU	0	2	SEA	1	1
ORL	0	5	CHI	1	3	SAN	1	1	PHO	0	2
NJ	-	-	CLE	2	2	UTAH	1	1	GS	2	0
MIA	3	2	IND	1	3	DEN	1	1	POR	0	2
BOS	4	1	CHA	2	2	MIN	1	1	LAL	2	0
PHI	3	1	DET	3	1	DAL	2	0	SAC	1	1
WAS	3	1	MIL	3	1				LAC	1	1
	17	11		15	13		6	6		7	7

1993–94 finish: 45–37 (29–12 home, 16–25 Away), third in Atlantic Div.

1994–95 Schedule

1/4	@ Houston	8:30 pm	12/26	@ Milwaukee	8:30 pm	2/27	@ Chicago	8:30 pm
1/5	@ Dallas	8:30 pm	12/27	New York	7:30 pm	3/3	Phila.	7:30 pm
1/7	@ San Ant.	8:30 pm	12/30	@ Indiana	7:30 pm	3/5	Milwaukee	1:00 pm
1/9	Chicago	7:30 pm	1/3	Indiana	7:30 pm	3/8	@ Phila.	7:30 pm
1/11	@ Wash.	7:30 pm	1/4	@ Orlando	7:30 pm	3/10	@ Boston	7:30 pm
1/12	Houston	8:00 pm	1/6	Charlotte	7:30 pm	3/11	@ Wash.	7:30 pm
1/15	Seattle	7:30 pm	1/7	@ Atlanta	7:30 pm	3/15	Orlando	7:30 pm
1/17	Wash.	7:30 pm	1/10	@ Detroit	7:30 pm	3/17	Utah	7:30 pm
1/18	@ Orlando	7:30 pm	1/13	@ Phila.	7:30 pm	3/18	@ New York	7:30 pm
1/20	LA Clip.	7:00 pm	1/14	Minnesota	7:30 pm	3/21	@ Detroit	7:30 pm
1/22	@ Seattle	10:00 pm	1/16	@ New York	1:00 pm	3/22	San Ant.	7:30 pm
1/23	@ Sacra.	10:30 pm	1/20	@ Charlotte	7:30 pm	3/25	@ Miami	7:30 pm
1/25	@ LA Clip.	6:00 pm	1/22	Wash.	2:00 pm	3/27	@ Indiana	7:30 pm
1/27	@ Phoenix	9:00 pm	1/24	@ Gold. St.	10:30 pm	3/28	Gold. St.	7:30 pm
1/29	LA Lakers	7:30 pm	1/25	@ LA Lakers	10:30 pm	3/30	Portland	7:30 pm
2/2	@ Miami	7:30 pm	1/27	@ Denver	9:00 pm	4/2	New York	1:30 pm
2/3	Sacra.	8:00 pm	1/28	@ Utah	9:00 pm	4/5	Chicago	7:30 pm
2/5	@ Chicago	8:30 pm	1/30	@ Portland	10:00 pm	4/7	@ Milwaukee	8:30 pm
2/6	Atlanta	7:30 pm	2/1	Milwaukee	7:30 pm	4/8	Miami	7:30 pm
2/8	Phoenix	7:30 pm	2/4	Boston	8:00 pm	4/11	@ Charlotte	7:30 pm
2/10	Boston	7:30 pm	2/6	Detroit	7:30 pm	4/13	@ Phila.	7:30 pm
2/12	Orlando	7:30 pm	2/8	@ Atlanta	7:30 pm	4/15	Phila.	7:30 pm
2/14	Cleveland	7:30 pm	2/14	Charlotte	7:30 pm	4/17	@ Boston	7:30 pm
2/16	@ Minnesota	8:00 pm	2/16	Denver	7:30 pm	4/19	Atlanta	7:30 pm
2/18	Miami	7:00 pm	2/18	Cleveland	7:30 pm	4/21	Wash.	7:30 pm
2/20	@ New York	8:00 pm	2/22	Indiana	7:30 pm	4/23	Boston	6:00 pm
2/21	Detroit	7:30 pm	2/24	Dallas	7:30 pm			
2/23	@ Cleveland	7:30 pm	2/25	@ Cleveland	7:30 pm			

1993–94 Team Stats

NAME	G	MIN	FG	FGA	FG%	3FG	3FGA	3FG%	FT	FTA	FT%	ORB	TRB	AST	PF	STL	BLK	TO	PTS	AVG
Coleman	77	2778	541	1209	44.7	38	121	31.4	439	567	77.4	262	870	262	209	68	142	208	1559	20.2
K. Anderson	82	3135	576	1381	41.7	40	132	30.3	346	423	81.8	89	322	784	201	158	15	266	1538	18.8
Edwards	82	2727	471	1028	45.8	35	99	35.4	167	217	77.0	94	281	232	150	120	34	135	1144	14.0
Gilliam	82	1969	348	682	51.0	0	1	0.0	274	361	75.9	197	500	69	129	38	61	106	970	11.8
Morris	50	1349	203	454	44.7	53	147	36.1	85	118	72.0	91	228	83	120	55	49	52	544	10.9
Newman	63	1268	222	490	45.3	20	74	27.0	134	166	80.7	65	122	43	152	51	22	62	598	9.5
Benjamin	77	1817	283	589	48.0	0	0	—	152	214	71.0	135	499	44	198	35	90	97	718	9.3
Robinson	17	301	42	119	35.3	7	15	46.7	10	20	50.0	4	24	45	33	15	3	25	101	5.9
Brown	79	1950	167	402	41.5	1	6	16.7	115	152	75.7	188	493	93	177	71	93	72	450	5.7
Williams	70	877	125	293	42.7	0	0	—	72	119	60.5	109	263	26	140	17	36	35	322	4.6
R. Anderson	11	176	15	43	34.9	4	12	33.3	10	12	83.3	8	26	6	9	5	2	1	44	4.0
Walters	48	386	60	115	52.2	14	28	50.0	28	34	82.4	6	38	71	41	15	3	30	162	3.4
Wesley	60	542	64	174	36.8	11	47	23.4	44	53	83.0	10	44	123	47	38	4	52	183	3.1
Schintzius	30	319	29	84	34.5	0	0	0.0	10	17	58.8	26	89	13	49	7	17	13	68	2.3
Mahorn	28	226	23	47	48.9	0	0	0.0	13	20	65.0	16	54	5	38	3	5	7	59	2.1
Jamerson	4	10	0	5	0.0	0	0	—	1	2	50.0	0	3	1					1	0.3
Nets	82	19830	3169	7115	44.5	223	683	32.7	1900	2495	76.2	1300	3856	1900	1693	696	576	1196	8461	103.2
Opp.	82	19830	3266	7125	45.8	235	739	31.8	1514	2038	74.3	1142	3670	1919	1901	715	582	1248	8281	101.0

HISTORY

TITLES

1971–72 ABA Eastern Conference champs
1973–74 ABA champs
1975–76 ABA champs

ALL-TIME TEAM RECORDS

Career

Games	Buck Williams	635	1981–89
Total points	Buck Williams	10,440	1981–89
Scoring average	Julius Erving	28.1	1973–76
Field goals made	Buck Williams	3,981	1981–89
Field goals attempted	Buck Williams	7,234	1981–89
Free throws made	Buck Williams	2,476	1981–89
Free throws attempted	Buck Williams	3,818	1981–89
Total rebounds	Buck Williams	7,576	1981–89
Assists	Bill Melchionni	2,778	1969–75
Steals	Darwin Cook	875	1980–86
Blocked shots	George Johnson	863	1977–80, 1984–85

Season

Total points	Rick Barry	2,518	1971–72
Scoring average	Rick Barry	31.5	1971–72
Field goals made	Julius Erving	949	1975–76
Free throws made	Rick Barry	641	1971–72
Total rebounds	Billy Paultz	1,035	1971–72
Assists	Kevin Porter	801	1977–78
Steals	Micheal R. Richardson	243	1984–85
Blocked shots	Geroge Johnson	274	1977–78

Game

Total points	Julius Erving	63	vs. San Diego, 2/14/75
Field goals made	Julius Erving	25	vs. San Diego, 2/14/75
Free throws made	Tony Jackson	24	vs. Kentucky, 11/27/67
Total rebounds	Billy Paultz	33	vs. Dallas, 12/17/71
Assists	Kevin Porter	29	vs. Houston, 2/24/78
Steals	Ed Jordan	10	vs. Philadelphia, 3/23/79
Blocked shots	Darryl Dawkins	13	vs. Philadelphia, 11/5/83

LEADING COACHES

	REGULAR SEASON				PLAYOFFS		
NAME	YEARS	W	L	PCT	W	L	PCT
Kevin Loughery	1973–81	297	318	.483	21	13	.618
Lou Carnesecca	1970–73	114	138	.452	13	17	.433
Larry Brown	1981–83	91	67	.576	0	2	.000
Chuck Daly	1992–94	88	76	.537	3	6	.333
Stan Albeck	1983–85	87	77	.530	5	9	.357

New Jersey Nets 1994–95 Roster

Head Coach: Butch Beard

No.	Name	Pos.	Ht.	Wt.	Yrs.	Born	College
7	Kenny Anderson	G	6-1	168	3	10/9/70	Georgia Tech
0	Benoit Benjamin	C	7-0	265	9	11/22/64	Creighton
42	P.J. Brown	C-F	6-11	240	1	10/14/69	Louisiana Tech
44	Derrick Coleman	F	6-10	258	4	6/21/67	Syracuse
11	Yinka Dare	C	7-0	265	R	10/10/72	George Washington
21	Kevin Edwards	G	6-3	210	6	10/30/65	DePaul
43	Armon Gilliam	F	6-9	245	7	5/28/64	Nevada-Las Vegas
22	Sean Higgins	G-F	6-9	215	4	12/30/68	Michigan
4	Rick Mahorn	F	6-10	260	13	9/21/58	Hampton Institute
34	Chris Morris	F	6-8	220	6	1/20/66	Auburn
22	Johnny Newman	F	6-7	198	8	11/28/63	Richmond
33	Dwayne Schintzius	C	7-2	285	4	10/14/68	Florida
2	Rex Walters	G	6-4	190	1	3/12/70	Kansas
55	Jayson Williams	F	6-10	245	4	2/22/68	St. John's

Arena Information

Meadowlands Arena (20,049)
Tickets: 201-935-8888
Ticket prices: $49.50, $39.50, $20, $16

Kenny Anderson

No. 7/G

Full name: Kenneth Anderson
HT: 6-1 **WT:** 168
Born: 10/9/70, Queens, NY
High school: Archbishop Molloy (Queens)
College: Georgia Tech

Anderson is on his way to a great career in the NBA. He's a fine playmaker who can drive the lane, and he's improving his outside shot. Last season, Anderson had career highs in all categories. He started every game during the season, averaging 18.8 points per game (second on the Nets, tops among NBA point guards) and 9.6 assists (fourth in the NBA). Already second on the all-time Nets' assist list, Anderson could become the all-time leader by the end of his fourth season.

Anderson led the Nets in assists in 74 games. He was the club's second leading scorer; his 45 points against Detroit April 15 was the second highest total in Nets history. Fans voted him the Nets' MVP, and he was elected to start in the 1994 NBA All-Star Game.

REGULAR SEASON	G	MIN	FG	FG%	3FG	3PT%	FT	FT%	REB	AST	STL	BLK	PTS	AVG
'91-92 NEW JERSEY	64	1086	187	39.0	3	23.1	73	74.5	127	203	67	9	450	7.0
'92-93 NEW JERSEY	55	2010	370	43.5	7	28.0	180	77.6	226	449	96	11	927	16.9
'93-94 NEW JERSEY	82	3135	576	41.7	40	30.3	346	81.8	322	784	158	15	1538	18.8
3 YR TOTALS	201	6231	1133	41.8	50	29.4	599	79.5	675	1436	321	35	2915	14.5
'93-94 RANK NBA Gs	1	3	6	98	48	77	6	47	18	3	9	49	5	10
'94-95 PROJECTIONS	82	3936	733	41.5	84	33.1	526	85.8	371	1099	192	14	2076	25.3

PLAYOFFS	G	MIN	FG	FG%	3FG	3PT%	FT	FT%	REB	AST	STL	BLK	PTS	AVG
'91-92 NEW JERSEY	3	24	3	33.3	0	---	2	100.0	3	3	1	0	8	2.7
'93-94 NEW JERSEY	4	181	19	35.2	3	30.0	22	66.7	12	27	9	0	63	15.8
TOTALS	7	205	22	34.9	3	30.0	24	68.6	15	30	10	0	71	10.1

Benoit Benjamin

No. 0/C

Full name: Lenard Benoit Benjamin
HT: 7-0   **WT:** 265
Born: 11/22/64, Monroe, LA
High school: Carroll (Monroe)
College: Creighton

Benjamin is a decent rebounder and shotblocking specialist whose dedication has been questioned throughout his career. He's turnover prone, he doesn't pass the ball (just 44 assists in over 1,800 minutes played). He averaged under 24 minutes per game, despite starting 74 of 77 games. He shot 48 percent from the field (third on the team) and was also third in rebounds. Benjamin came to the Nets in a deal engineered by GM Willis Reed, Benjamin's former college coach. Benjamin averaged 4.6 rebounds per game in college and was the third player chosen in the 1985 draft.

REGULAR SEASON		G	MIN	FG	FG%	3FG	3PT%	FT	FT%	REB	AST	STL	BLK	PTS	AVG
'85-86	LA CLIPPERS	79	2088	324	49.0	1	33.3	229	74.6	600	79	64	206	878	11.1
'86-87	LA CLIPPERS	72	2230	320	44.9	0	0.0	188	71.5	586	135	60	187	828	11.5
'87-88	LA CLIPPERS	66	2171	340	49.1	0	0.0	180	70.6	530	172	50	225	860	13.0
'88-89	LA CLIPPERS	79	2585	491	54.1	0	0.0	317	74.4	636	157	57	221	1299	16.4
'89-90	LA CLIPPERS	71	2313	362	52.6	0	0.0	235	73.2	657	159	59	187	959	13.5
'90-91	LAC-SEA	70	2236	386	99.41	0	0	210	141.8	723	119	54	145	982	27.83
'91-92	SEATTLE	63	1941	354	47.8	0	0.0	171	68.7	513	76	39	118	879	14.0
'92-93	SEA-LAL	59	754	133	49.1	0	---	69	66.3	209	22	31	48	335	5.7
'93-94	NEW JERSEY	77	1817	283	48.0	0	---	152	71.0	499	44	35	90	718	9.3
9 YR TOTALS		636	18135	2993	49.6	1	5.6	1751	71.9	5013	963	449	1427	7738	12.2
'93-94	RANK NBA Cs	15	18	14	34	14	14	13	25	13	29	24	16	13	15
'94-95	PROJECTIONS	82	2001	266	43.2	0	0.0	145	66.5	542	32	26	83	677	8.3

PLAYOFFS		G	MIN	FG	FG%	3FG	3PT%	FT	FT%	REB	AST	STL	BLK	PTS	AVG
'90-91	SEATTLE	5	163	20	48.8	0	---	29	90.6	33	1	3	13	69	13.8
'91-92	SEATTLE	9	161	23	56.1	0	0.0	9	50.0	46	5	5	13	55	6.1
'93-94	NEW JERSEY	4	108	7	41.2	0	---	7	87.5	21	1	2	8	21	5.3
	TOTALS	18	432	50	50.5	0	0.0	45	77.6	100	7	10	34	145	8.1

P.J. Brown

No. 42/C-F

Full name: Collier Brown, Jr.
HT: 6-11   **WT:** 240
Born: 10/14/68, Detroit, MI
High school: Winnfield Sr. (LA)
College: Louisiana Tech

Brown was a great surprise last season. As a second-round pick he emerged as the starting small forward in his rookie season. He has long arms that make him an effective shotblocker, and he runs the court well. Brown isn't the scorer the Nets want at small forward, but he was a consistent contributor on defense, often shutting down some of the league's best small forwards. Brown was among the leading rookies in rebounds (6.2 per game) and blocks (1.18 per game). Brown was the Nets' third leading rebounder and second leading shotblocker. He led New Jersey in rebounds 9 times.

REGULAR SEASON	G	MIN	FG	FGx	3FG	3PTx	FT	FTx	REB	AST	STL	BLK	PTS	AVG
'93-94 NEW JERSEY	79	1950	167	415	1	16.7	115	75.7	493	93	71	93	450	5.7
1 YR TOTALS	79	1950	167	415	1	16.7	115	75.7	493	93	71	93	450	5.7
'93-94 RANK NBA Cs	10	13	26	47	8	12	16	15	14	14	8	15	25	28

PLAYOFFS	G	MIN	FG	FGx	3FG	3PTx	FT	FTx	REB	AST	STL	BLK	PTS	AVG
'93-94 NEW JERSEY	4	56	2	22.2	0	---	8	100.0	8	3	0	2	12	3.0
TOTALS	4	56	2	22.2	0	---	8	100.0	8	3	0	2	12	3.0

Derrick Coleman

No. 44/F

Full name: Derrick D. Coleman
HT: 6-10   **WT:** 258
Born: 6/21/67, Mobile, AL
High school: Northern (Detroit, MI)
College: Syracuse

Coleman is a rebounding, shot-blocking stud who can score driving to the hoop or posting up his opponent. The one drawback to his game is that he commits a lot of turnovers; Coleman has averaged 200 turnovers a season as a pro. Coleman was a top 20 scorer and rebounder last season, and scored over 1500 points and 800 rebounds for the second straight year. He was voted to start in his first All-Star Game in 1994 (an overdue honor). The Nets' leading scorer, rebounder, and shotblocker, Coleman led the Nets in rebounds 55 times and in scoring 34 times. In just 4 seasons, Coleman's accumulated over 5,000 points and 3,000 rebounds.

REGULAR SEASON		G	MIN	FG	FG%	3FG	3PT%	FT	FT%	REB	AST	STL	BLK	PTS	AVG
'90-91	NEW JERSEY	74	2602	514	46.7	13	34.2	323	73.1	759	163	71	99	1364	18.4
'91-92	NEW JERSEY	65	2207	483	50.4	23	30.3	300	76.3	618	205	54	98	1289	19.8
'92-93	NEW JERSEY	76	2759	564	46.0	23	23.2	421	80.8	852	276	92	126	1572	20.7
'93-94	NEW JERSEY	77	2778	541	44.7	38	31.4	439	77.4	870	262	68	142	1559	20.2
4 YR TOTALS		292	10346	2102	46.8	97	29.0	1483	77.1	3099	906	285	465	5784	19.8
'93-94	RANK NBA Fs	43	12	13	93	20	32	3	27	5	13	38	4	6	7
'94-95	PROJECTIONS	80	2899	543	43.2	50	34.0	485	77.0	905	279	61	161	1621	20.3

PLAYOFFS		G	MIN	FG	FG%	3FG	3PT%	FT	FT%	REB	AST	STL	BLK	PTS	AVG
'91-92	NEW JERSEY	4	162	36	48.6	1	16.7	16	76.2	45	21	7	4	89	22.3
'92-93	NEW JERSEY	5	225	50	53.2	5	41.7	29	80.6	67	23	6	13	134	26.8
'93-94	NEW JERSEY	4	173	27	39.7	5	55.6	39	78.0	57	10	2	5	98	24.5
TOTALS		13	560	113	47.9	11	40.7	84	78.5	169	54	15	22	321	24.7

Kevin Edwards

No. 21/G

Full name: Kevin Durell Edwards
HT: 6-3   **WT:** 210
Born: 10/30/65, Cleveland
   Heights, OH
High school: St. Joseph Academy
   (Cleveland)
College: DePaul

Edwards has a quick first step and is an effective scorer driving the lane. He's also a tenacious defender. Edwards came to New Jersey with a reputation for inconsistency. But given an opportunity to start, Edwards responded with the best year of his career. He started every game last season, and posted career highs in minutes, points, scoring average and rebounds. He improved from 3-point range last season (35.4 percent, second–best on the team), and he plays good defense. His 1.46 steals per game was second on the club.

REGULAR SEASON		G	MIN	FG	FGx	3FG	3PTx	FT	FTx	REB	AST	STL	BLK	PTS	AVG
'88-89	MIAMI	79	2349	470	42.5	10	27.0	144	74.6	262	349	139	27	1094	13.8
'89-90	MIAMI	78	2211	395	41.2	9	30.0	139	76.0	282	252	125	33	938	12.0
'90-91	MIAMI	79	2000	380	41.0	24	28.6	171	80.3	205	240	129	46	955	12.1
'91-92	MIAMI	81	1840	325	45.4	7	21.9	162	84.8	211	170	99	20	819	10.1
'92-93	MIAMI	40	1134	216	46.8	5	29.4	119	84.4	121	120	68	12	556	13.9
'93-94	NEW JERSEY	82	2727	471	45.8	35	35.4	167	77.0	281	232	120	34	1144	14.0
6 YR TOTALS		439	12261	2257	43.4	90	30.1	902	79.3	1362	1363	680	172	5506	12.5
'93-94	RANK NBA Gs	1	22	27	51	57	41	45	79	27	60	25	13	31	38
'94-95	PROJECTIONS	82	3329	551	46.3	59	39.3	154	73.7	330	247	121	40	1315	16.0

PLAYOFFS		G	MIN	FG	FGx	3FG	3PTx	FT	FTx	REB	AST	STL	BLK	PTS	AVG
'91-92	MIAMI	3	55	5	38.5	0	---	5	62.5	7	7	2	0	15	5.0
'93-94	NEW JERSEY	4	148	18	36.0	0	0.0	13	92.9	16	9	5	1	49	12.3
	TOTALS	7	203	23	36.5	0	0.0	18	81.8	23	16	7	1	64	9.1

Yinka Dare   No. 11/C

HT: 6-11 **WT:** 265
Born: 10/10/72, Kabba, Nigeria
College: George Washington
Before attending college, Dare had played only 1 year of organized basketball. But in just 2 seasons, Dare became GW's all-time leader in blocked shots with 140 in 60 games.

REGULAR SEASON	G	MIN	FG	FGx	3FG	3PTx	FT	FTx	REB	AST	STL	BLK	PTS	AVG

ROOKIE -- NO NBA EXPERIENCE

Armon Gilliam   No. 43/F

Full name: Armon Louis Gilliam
HT: 6-9 **WT:** 245
Born: 5/28/64, Pittsburgh, PA
High school: Bethel Park Senior (PA)
College: Nevada-Las Vegas
Gilliam is a physical player who is a great scorer from the low post. He was 1 of only 3 Nets to play in all 82 games.

REGULAR SEASON	G	MIN	FG	FGx	3FG	3PTx	FT	FTx	REB	AST	STL	BLK	PTS	AVG
'88-89	PHOENIX	74	2120	468	50.3	0	---	240	74.3	541	52	54	27	1176	15.9
'89-90	PHE-CHA	76	2426	484	49.32	0	0	303	95.72	599	39	69	51	1271	16.7
'90-91	CHA-PHL	75	2644	487	98.34	0	0	268	162.8	598	105	69	53	1242	16.6
'91-92	PHILADELPHIA	81	2771	512	51.1	0	0.0	343	80.7	660	118	51	85	1367	16.9
'92-93	PHILADELPHIA	80	1742	359	46.4	0	0.0	274	84.3	472	116	37	54	992	12.4
'93-94	NEW JERSEY	82	1969	348	51.0	0	0.0	274	75.9	500	69	38	61	970	11.9
7 YR TOTALS		523	15479	3000	49.6	0	0.0	1833	77.2	3804	631	376	360	7833	15.0
'93-94	RANK NBA Fs	1	50	42	25	78	78	12	36	31	77	78	25	33	40
'94-95	PROJECTIONS	82	1841	280	48.4	0	0.0	228	64.6	468	47	33	60	788	9.6

PLAYOFFS	G	MIN	FG	FGx	3FG	3PTx	FT	FTx	REB	AST	STL	BLK	PTS	AVG
'88-89	PHOENIX	9	126	27	52.9	0	---	19	86.4	45	2	1	2	73	8.1
'90-91	PHILADELPHIA	8	287	48	46.2	0	---	39	84.8	52	10	5	6	135	16.9
'93-94	NEW JERSEY	4	112	15	44.1	0	0.0	12	75.0	25	1	2	7	42	10.5
TOTALS		21	525	90	47.6	0	0.0	70	83.3	122	13	8	15	250	11.9

Chris Morris   No. 34/F

Full name: Christopher Vernard Morris
HT: 6-8 **WT:** 220
Born: 1/20/66, Atlanta, GA
High school: Douglass (Atlanta)
College: Auburn

Morris was 23 of 39 from 3-point range before he broke his thumb; the injury cost him his starting slot.

REGULAR SEASON		G	MIN	FG	FGx	3FG	3PTx	FT	FTx	REB	AST	STL	BLK	PTS	AVG
'88-89	NEW JERSEY	76	2096	414	45.7	64	36.6	182	71.7	397	119	102	60	1074	14.1
'89-90	NEW JERSEY	80	2449	449	42.2	61	31.6	228	72.2	422	143	130	79	1187	14.8
'90-91	NEW JERSEY	79	2553	409	42.5	45	25.1	179	73.4	521	220	138	96	1042	13.2
'91-92	NEW JERSEY	77	2394	346	47.7	22	20.0	165	71.4	494	197	129	81	879	11.4
'92-93	NEW JERSEY	77	2302	436	48.1	17	22.4	197	79.4	454	106	144	52	1086	14.1
'93-94	NEW JERSEY	50	1349	203	44.7	53	36.1	85	72.0	228	83	55	49	544	10.9
6 YR TOTALS		439	13143	2257	45.0	262	29.8	1036	73.4	2516	868	698	417	5812	13.2
'93-94	RANK NBA Fs	112	80	72	94	13	17	82	64	88	67	56	39	72	49
'94-95	PROJECTIONS	36	811	113	44.0	49	43.0	44	69.8	125	49	26	33	319	8.9

PLAYOFFS		G	MIN	FG	FGx	3FG	3PTx	FT	FTx	REB	AST	STL	BLK	PTS	AVG
'91-92	NEW JERSEY	4	135	32	55.2	4	40.0	7	77.8	20	5	7	7	75	18.8
'92-93	NEW JERSEY	5	163	34	55.7	6	37.5	11	91.7	32	7	8	6	85	17.0
'93-94	NEW JERSEY	4	98	12	27.9	3	15.0	10	100.0	22	7	5	5	37	9.3
TOTALS		13	396	78	48.1	13	28.3	28	90.3	74	19	20	18	197	15.2

Johnny Newman No. 22/F

Full name: John Sylvester Newman, Jr.
HT: 6-7 **WT:** 198
Born: 11/28/63, Danville, VA
High school: George Washington (Danville)
College: Richmond

This swingman averaged 19.6 points per 40 minutes. He can play tough defense against an opponent's shooting guard.

REGULAR SEASON		G	MIN	FG	FGx	3FG	3PTx	FT	FTx	REB	AST	STL	BLK	PTS	AVG
'89-90	NEW YORK	80	2277	374	47.6	45	31.7	239	79.9	191	180	95	22	1032	12.9
'90-91	CHARLOTTE	81	2477	478	47.0	30	35.7	385	80.9	254	188	100	17	1371	16.9
'91-92	CHARLOTTE	55	1651	295	47.7	13	28.3	236	76.6	179	146	70	14	839	15.3
'92-93	CHARLOTTE	64	1471	279	52.2	12	26.7	194	80.8	143	117	45	19	764	11.9
'93-94	CHA-NJ	81	1697	313	47.1	24	26.7	182	80.9	180	72	69	27	832	10.3
8 YR TOTALS		578	14128	2577	47.1	248	30.7	1795	80.8	1382	954	582	140	7197	12.5
'93-94	RANK NBA Fs	15	60	51	63	28	48	38	10	110	74	37	78	47	56
'94-95	PROJECTIONS	82	1658	305	45.8	26	25.0	153	81.4	182	37	71	31	789	9.6

PLAYOFFS		G	MIN	FG	FGx	3FG	3PTx	FT	FTx	REB	AST	STL	BLK	PTS	AVG
'89-90	NEW YORK	10	231	38	44.7	4	40.0	37	75.5	21	10	9	3	117	11.7
'92-93	CHARLOTTE	9	173	28	50.9	1	20.0	11	68.8	19	18	10	1	68	7.6
'93-94	NEW JERSEY	4	54	3	23.1	1	25.0	5	71.4	5	2	2	2	12	3.0
TOTALS		36	829	150	45.7	13	23.2	105	76.6	81	54	35	8	418	11.6

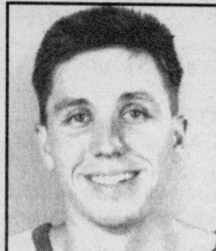

Rex Walters   No. 2/G

Full name: Rex Andrew Walters
HT: 6-4   **WT:** 190
Born: 3/12/70, Omaha, NE
College: Kansas

Walters led the team in shooting percentage and 3-point accuracy (50 percent, going 14 for 28). He's also a good ballhandler, passer, defender, and shot creator.

REGULAR SEASON		G	MIN	FG	FGx	3FG	3PTx	FT	FTx	REB	AST	STL	BLK	PTS	AVG
'93-94	NEW JERSEY	48	386	60	52.2	14	50.0	28	82.4	38	71	15	3	162	3.4
1 YR TOTALS		48	386	60	52.2	14	50.0	28	82.4	38	71	15	3	162	3.4
'93-94	RANK NBA Gs	121	127	124	4	82	3	122	43	128	118	128	110	123	125

PLAYOFFS		G	MIN	FG	FGx	3FG	3PTx	FT	FTx	REB	AST	STL	BLK	PTS	AVG
'93-94	NEW JERSEY	1	1	1	100.0	0	---	0	---	0	0	0	0	2	2.0
TOTALS		1	1	1	100.0	0	---	0	---	0	0	0	0	2	2.0

Butch Beard   Head Coach

Full name: Alfred Beard, Jr.
HT: 6-3   **WT:** 185
Born: 5/4/47, Hardinburg, KY
College: Louisville

Beard was 45–69 at Howard University. An NBA assistant for 6 seasons, he was a Net assistant coach under present GM Willis Reed in the '88–89 season.

	REGULAR SEASON				PLAYOFFS			
YEAR	TEAM	W	L PCT	FINISH		W	L PCT	

no prior NBA head-coaching experience

New York
KNICKS

1994–95 Scouting Report

Frontcourt

Patrick Ewing is coming off one of his best seasons. He averaged 24.5 points, 11.2 rebounds and 2.75 blocked shots per game. Charles Oakley is the board banger and defensive stud the Knicks ask him to be, with 11.8 rebounds per game. Charles Smith has failed to become the scorer at small forward the Knicks hoped for; fans didn't let him live down his four straight misses against Chicago in the '93 Eastern finals. Anthony Bonner ended up as the Knicks' starting small forward. Anthony Mason is one of the best sixth men in the NBA, and another tough defender. Herb Williams backs up Ewing at center. He's a fan favorite who provides some defense, rebounding and shot blocking off the bench. New York hopes first round pick Monty Williams will develop into a big-league scorer at small forward.

Backcourt

New York has to develop a perimeter shooter to complement the streaky John Starks. The Knicks gave up on Rolando Blackmon filling that role, but they have high hopes for Hubert Davis. Davis is scary from long-range (40.2 percent from 3-point range, ninth in the league), and a pretty good ballhandler. (At press time, the Knicks are looking at the Clippers' Ron Harper; player and team are fed up with each other.) At point guard, the Knicks brought in Derek Harper to replace injured Doc Rivers. Both are experienced floor leaders, but both will be 33 when the season begins. Rivers is a better playmaker and a much better ballhandler than Harper. Harper is the superior shooter, and he isn't coming off of a serious knee injury. Both players are tough defenders. Greg Anthony, the understudy at point, still needs to mature as a player. He may lose his spot to first-round pick Charlie Ward.

Defense

The Knicks are the best defensive team in the NBA. They allowed just 91.5 points per game and limited opponents to 43.1 percent shooting from the field, both tops in the league. They held opponents under 100 points 62 times (one short of the all-time post-clock NBA record), and under 90 points 39 times. They also led the league in limiting field goal attempts; thanks to Patrick Ewing and Charles Oakley cleaning the glass, New York tied for second in limiting opponents' offensive rebounds. (One surprising fact: despite having Patrick Ewing, the Knicks ranked just nineteenth in the NBA in blocks.) The Knicks got good play from their guards; they were seventh in the NBA in stealing the ball and fifth in the league in forcing turnovers.

1994–95 Prospects

Last season, New York dominated a weak Atlantic Division. They played consistently throughout the season, going 31–5 against lottery teams (including just 1–3 against Alonzo Mourning's Charlotte Hornets) and were 14–0 in March. They finally beat Chicago in the playoffs and went on to the NBA finals, only to lose to Houston in seven games.

The Knicks are a defense-first team; they shot only 46 percent from the field, despite centering their offense around Patrick Ewing's inside game. But they force their opponents to shoot even worse. Their physical defensive style forces opponents to run down the 24-second clock and force bad shots. That strategy does send opponents to the line a lot; the Knicks were fourth in committing personal fouls last season. As a result, teams that shoot well from the line can give the Knicks problems. Against the 5 best free throw shooting teams, the Knicks were 10–9: 2–2 vs. Miami, 2–0 vs. Minnesota, 4–0 vs. Cleveland, 1–3 vs. Charlotte, and 1–4 vs. New Jersey. Against the other 21 teams, the Knicks were 47–16.

The Knicks should return to the Eastern Conference finals once again; even with Horace Grant, Orlando is a year away from challenging the Knicks for the Atlantic Division title. The Knicks aren't young by any means, but the key players (Ewing, Oakley, and Starks) have several more years left at the top of their game.

Team Directory

President: David W. Checketts   VP/Gen. counsel: Kenneth W. Munoz
VP/Business mgr: Francis P. Murphy   VP/General manager: Ernie Grunfeld
Dir., marketing: Pam Harris   VP/Public relations: John Cirillo

1993–94 Review

EASTERN CONFERENCE						WESTERN CONFERENCE					
ATLANTIC DIV.		CENTRAL DIV.				MIDWEST DIV.			PACIFIC DIV.		
	W	L		W	L		W	L		W	L
NY	-	-	ATL	2	2	HOU	0	2	SEA	1	1
ORL	3	2	CHI	3	1	SAN	1	1	PHO	1	1
NJ	1	4	CLE	4	0	UTAH	0	2	GS	1	1
MIA	2	2	IND	4	0	DEN	1	1	POR	2	0
BOS	4	0	CHA	1	3	MIN	2	0	LAL	2	0
PHI	3	2	DET	4	0	DAL	2	0	SAC	2	0
WAS	5	0	MIL	4	0				LAC	2	0
	18	10		22	6		6	6		11	3

1993–94 finish: 57–25 (32–9 home, 25–16 away), first in Atlantic Div.

1994–95 Schedule

11/4	@ Boston	7:30 pm	1/6	@ Cleveland	7:30 pm	3/7	Boston	7:30 pm
11/8	LA Lakers	7:30 pm	1/8	Minnesota	6:00 pm	3/8	@ Boston	7:30 pm
11/10	Orlando	8:00 pm	1/10	Indiana	8:00 pm	3/10	@ Atlanta	7:30 pm
11/12	@ San Ant.	8:30 pm	1/13	@ Milwaukee	8:30 pm	3/11	Seattle	8:30 pm
11/14	@ Utah	9:00 pm	1/14	Utah	7:30 pm	3/14	Denver	8:00 pm
11/16	@ LA Lakers	10:30 pm	1/16	New Jersey	1:00 pm	3/17	@ Wash.	7:30 pm
11/17	@ Gold. St.	10:30 pm	1/19	@ Houston	8:00 pm	3/18	New Jersey	7:30 pm
11/19	Atlanta	8:30 pm	1/20	@ Dallas	8:30 pm	3/21	Charlotte	7:30 pm
11/21	San Ant.	7:30 pm	1/22	@ Miami	7:30 pm	3/23	@ Denver	9:00 pm
11/26	Charlotte	1:00 pm	1/24	Portland	7:30 pm	3/25	@ LA Clip.	10:30 pm
11/29	@ Wash.	7:30 pm	1/26	LA Clip.	7:30 pm	3/26	@ Seattle	9:00 pm
12/2	@ Orlando	8:00 pm	1/27	@ Charlotte	8:00 pm	3/28	Chicago	8:00 pm
12/3	Wash.	7:30 pm	1/29	Phoenix	12:00 pm	3/29	@ Detroit	7:30 pm
12/5	@ Phila.	7:30 pm	1/31	Gold. St.	7:30 pm	3/31	Dallas	7:30 pm
12/6	Boston	7:30 pm	2/3	@ Phila.	7:30 pm	4/2	@ New Jersey	1:30 pm
12/9	@ Atlanta	7:30 pm	2/5	@ Orlando	1:00 pm	4/4	Indiana	7:30 pm
12/10	Phila.	7:30 pm	2/7	Milwaukee	7:30 pm	4/5	@ Milwaukee	8:30 pm
12/12	Miami	7:30 pm	2/8	@ Indiana	7:30 pm	4/8	Detroit	8:30 pm
12/15	@ Sacra.	10:30 pm	2/14	@ Detroit	7:30 pm	4/11	Miami	7:30 pm
12/16	@ Phoenix	8:00 pm	2/16	@ Miami	7:30 pm	4/13	Wash.	7:30 pm
12/18	@ Portland	8:00 pm	2/17	Miami	7:30 pm	4/14	@ Indiana	8:00 pm
12/20	New Jersey	8:00 pm	2/19	Houston	1:00 pm	4/16	@ Chicago	5:30 pm
12/22	Cleveland	7:30 pm	2/21	Cleveland	7:30 pm	4/17	Milwaukee	7:30 pm
12/25	@ Chicago	6:30 pm	2/23	Sacra.	7:30 pm	4/20	@ Charlotte	8:00 pm
12/27	@ New Jersey	7:30 pm	2/26	Phila.	6:00 pm	4/21	@ Boston	7:30 pm
12/28	Detroit	7:30 pm	2/28	@ Orlando	8:00 pm	4/23	Orlando	1:00 pm
12/30	@ Minnesota	8:00 pm	3/2	Chicago	7:30 pm			
1/4	Atlanta	7:30 pm	3/4	@ Cleveland	7:30 pm			

1993–94 Team Stats

NAME	G	MIN	FG	FGA	FG%	3FG	3FGA	3FG%	FT	FTA	FT%	ORB	TRB	AST	PF	STL	BLK	TO	PTS	AVG
Ewing	79	2972	745	1503	49.6	4	14	28.6	445	582	76.5	219	885	179	275	90	217	260	1939	24.5
Starks	59	2057	410	977	42.0	113	337	33.5	187	248	75.4	37	185	348	191	95	6	184	1120	19.0
Oakley	82	2932	363	760	47.8	0	3	0.0	243	313	77.6	349	965	218	293	110	18	193	969	11.8
Davis	56	1333	238	505	47.1	53	132	40.2	85	103	82.5	23	67	165	118	40	4	76	614	11.0
Smith	43	1105	176	397	44.3	8	16	50.0	87	121	71.9	66	165	50	144	26	45	64	447	10.4
Harper	54	1311	173	402	43.0	36	98	36.7	84	113	74.3	10	86	236	117	80	4	81	466	8.6
Anthony	80	1994	225	571	39.4	48	160	30.0	130	168	77.4	43	189	365	163	114	13	127	628	7.9
Rivers	19	499	55	127	43.3	19	52	36.5	14	22	63.6	4	39	100	44	25	5	29	143	7.5
Blackman	55	969	161	369	43.6	30	84	35.7	48	53	90.6	23	93	76	100	25	6	44	400	7.3
Mason	73	1903	206	433	47.6	0	1	0.0	116	161	72.0	158	427	151	190	31	9	107	528	7.2
Campbell	22	379	63	128	49.2	1	3	33.3	30	37	81.1	28	60	31	59	20	1	29	157	7.1
Bonner	73	1402	162	288	56.3	0	0	—	50	105	47.6	150	344	88	175	76	13	89	374	5.1
Williams	70	774	103	233	44.2	0	1	0.0	27	42	64.3	56	182	28	108	18	43	39	233	3.3
Anderson	11	39	7	17	41.2	2	2	100.0	5	14	35.7	6	17	9	9	0	1	2	21	1.9
Gaines	18	78	9	20	45.0	2	5	40.0	13	15	86.7	3	13	30	12	2	0	5	33	1.8
Paddio	3	8	2	5	40.0	0	0	—	0	0	—	0	0	0	3	0	0	0	4	1.3
Knicks	82	19755	3098	6735	46.0	316	908	34.8	1564	2097	74.6	1175	3717	2067	2001	752	385	1360	8076	98.5
Opp.	82	19755	2783	6451	43.1	253	825	30.7	1684	2341	71.9	1016	3261	1677	1897	677	333	1420	7503	91.5

HISTORY

TITLES

1950–51 Eastern Div. champs	1972–73 Eastern Conf. champs
1951–52 Eastern Div. champs	1972–73 NBA champs
1952–53 Eastern Div. champs	1988–89 Atlantic Div. champs
1969–70 Eastern Div. champs	1991–92 Atlantic Div. champs
1969–70 NBA champs	1992–93 Atlantic Div. champs
1970–71 Atlantic Div. champs	1993–94 Atlantic Div. champs
1971–72 Eastern Conf. champs	1993–94 Eastern Conf. champs

ALL-TIME TEAM RECORDS

Career

Games played	Walt Frazier	759	1967–77
Total points	Patrick Ewing	16,191	1985–94
Total rebounds	Willis Reed	8,414	1964–74
Assists	Walt Frazier	4,791	1967–77
Steals	Micheal R. Richardson	810	1978–82

Season

Total points	Patrick Ewing	2,347	1989–90
Field goals made	Patrick Ewing	922	1989–90
Free throws made	Richie Guerin	625	1961–62
Assists	Mark Jackson	868	1987–88
Steals	Micheal R. Richardson	265	1979–80

Game

Total points	Bernard King	60	vs. New Jersey, 12/25/84
Field goals made	Richie Guerin	23	vs. Boston, 2/14/62
	Willie Naulls	23	vs. Detroit, 2/7/61
Free throws made	Bernard King	22	vs. New Jersey, 12/25/84
	Richie Guerin	22	vs. Boston, 2/11/61
Total rebounds	Willis Reed	33	vs. Cincinnati, 2/2/71
	Harry Gallatin	33	vs. Ft. Wayne, 3/15/53
Assists	Richie Guerin	21	vs. St. Louis, 12/12/58

LEADING COACHES

	REGULAR SEASON				PLAYOFFS		
NAME	**YEARS**	**W**	**L**	**PCT**	**W**	**L**	**PCT**
Red Holzman	1967–77, 1978–82	613	484	.559	53	43	.552
Joe Lapchick	1947–56	326	247	.569	30	30	.500
Hubie Brown	1982–87	142	202	.413	8	10	.444
Rick Pitino	1987–89	90	74	.549	6	7	.462
Pat Riley	1991–94	168	78	.683	29	23	.558

New York Knicks 1994–95 Roster

Head Coach: Pat Riley

No.	Name	Pos.	Ht.	Wt.	Yrs.	Born	College
50	Greg Anthony	G	6-2	185	3	11/15/67	Nevada-Las Vegas
4	Anthony Bonner	F	6-8	225	4	6/8/68	Saint Louis
44	Hubert Davis	G	6-5	183	2	5/17/70	North Carolina
33	Patrick Ewing	C	7-0	240	9	8/5/62	Georgetown
11	Derek Harper	G	6-4	206	12	10/13/61	Illinois
14	Anthony Mason	F	6-7	250	5	12/14/66	Tennessee State
40	Tim McCormick	C	7-0	240	10	3/10/62	Michigan
34	Charles Oakley	F	6-9	245	9	12/18/63	Virginia Union
25	Doc Rivers	G	6-4	185	11	10/13/61	Marquette
54	Charles Smith	F	6-10	244	6	7/16/65	Pittsburgh
3	John Starks	G	6-5	185	5	8/10/65	Oklahoma State
21	Charlie Ward	G	6-0	190	R	10/12/70	Florida State
32	Herb Williams	F-C	6-11	260	13	2/16/58	Ohio State
2	Monty Williams	F	6-8	225	R	10/8/71	Notre Dame

Arena Information

Madison Square Garden (19,763)
Tickets: 212-465-6073, 212-465-6080 (group tickets)
Ticket prices: $75, $50, $44, $39, $32, $24, $16, $12

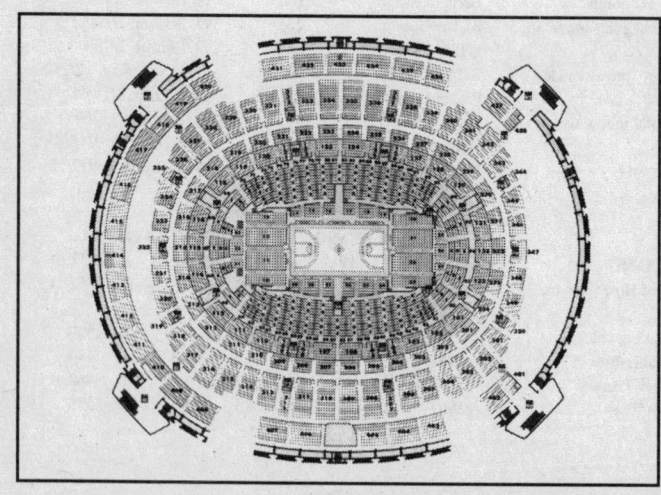

Anthony Bonner

No. 4/F

HT: 6-8   **WT:** 225
Born: 6/8/68, St. Louis, MO
High school: Vashon (St. Louis)
College: St. Louis

Bonner is a quick and fearless defender whose game fits right in with the Knicks' defensive philosophy. He opened the season as a reserve but ended up starting in each of his last 29 games. Bonner started in 38 games last season, and the Knicks were 29–9 when he started. Bonner's not much of a scorer: although he shot for an impressive 56.3 percent, he's not a good ballhandler, he's a sub-.500 free throw shooter, and he can't hit from outside. He gets his points off offensive rebounds and transition baskets. His high game came November 13 against Milwaukee when he scored 17 points, along with 9 rebounds.

REGULAR SEASON		G	MIN	FG	FG%	3FG	3PT%	FT	FT%	REB	AST	STL	BLK	PTS	AVG
'90-91	SACRAMENTO	34	750	103	44.8	0	---	44	57.9	161	49	39	5	250	7.4
'91-92	SACRAMENTO	79	2287	294	44.7	1	25.0	151	62.7	485	125	94	26	740	9.4
'92-93	SACRAMENTO	70	1764	229	46.1	0	0.0	143	59.3	455	96	86	17	601	8.6
'93-94	NEW YORK	73	1402	162	56.3	0	---	50	47.6	344	88	76	13	374	5.1
4 YR TOTALS		256	6203	788	47.1	1	9.1	388	58.5	1445	358	295	61	1965	7.7
'93-94	RANK NBA Fs	67	75	87	4	78	78	103	134	63	64	29	110	92	100
'94-95	PROJECTIONS	77	1206	118	63.1	0	0.0	22	39.3	302	80	70	11	258	3.4

PLAYOFFS		G	MIN	FG	FG%	3FG	3PT%	FT	FT%	REB	AST	STL	BLK	PTS	AVG
'93-94	NEW YORK	13	118	10	45.5	0	---	7	53.8	28	2	5	0	27	2.1
TOTALS		13	118	10	45.5	0	---	7	53.8	28	2	5	0	27	2.1

Patrick Ewing

No. 33/C

Full name: Patrick Aloysius Ewing
HT: 7-0   **WT:** 240
Born: 8/5/62, Kingston, Jamaica
High school: Cambridge Rindge & Latin (MA)
College: Georgetown

Ewing is the Knicks' all-time leader in virtually every offensive category, including points (16,191), FGM (6,386), FGA (12,228), FTM (3,412), FTA (4,601) and blocks (1,984). His 7,006 career rebounds trails only Willis Reed's 8,414. He was sixth in the NBA in scoring, tenth in rebounding (11.2 per game) and seventh in blocks (2.75 per game). He averaged 37.6 minutes per game last season. Ewing was named to the All-Star team for the eighth time, and seventh straight year. He led the Knicks in scoring 58 times and recorded 49 double-doubles. In January, he averaged 29.4 points per game, 12.6 rebounds per game and shot 50.1 percent from the field on the way to NBA Player of the Month honors.

REGULAR SEASON		G	MIN	FG	FG%	3FG	3PT%	FT	FT%	REB	AST	STL	BLK	PTS	AVG
'85-86	NEW YORK	50	1771	386	47.4	0	0.0	226	73.9	451	102	54	103	998	20.0
'86-87	NEW YORK	63	2206	530	50.3	0	0.0	296	71.3	555	104	89	147	1356	21.5
'87-88	NEW YORK	82	2546	656	55.5	0	0.0	341	71.6	676	125	104	245	1653	20.2
'88-89	NEW YORK	80	2896	727	56.7	0	0.0	361	74.6	740	188	117	281	1815	22.7
'89-90	NEW YORK	82	3165	922	55.1	1	25.0	502	77.5	893	182	78	327	2347	28.6
'90-91	NEW YORK	81	3104	845	51.4	0	0.0	464	74.5	905	244	80	258	2154	26.6
'91-92	NEW YORK	82	3150	796	52.2	1	16.7	377	73.8	921	156	88	245	1970	24.0
'92-93	NEW YORK	81	3003	779	50.3	1	14.3	400	71.9	980	151	74	161	1959	24.2
'93-94	NEW YORK	79	2972	745	49.6	4	28.6	445	76.5	885	179	90	217	1939	24.5
9 YR TOTALS		680	24813	6386	52.2	7	12.1	3412	74.2	7006	1431	774	1984	16191	23.8
'93-94	RANK NBA Cs	10	4	4	24	5	5	3	13	4	6	4	5	4	4
'94-95	PROJECTIONS	78	2919	712	48.6	7	38.9	460	78.1	855	183	95	218	1891	24.2

PLAYOFFS		G	MIN	FG	FG%	3FG	3PT%	FT	FT%	REB	AST	STL	BLK	PTS	AVG
'87-88	NEW YORK	4	153	28	49.1	0	0.0	19	86.4	51	10	6	13	75	18.8
'88-89	NEW YORK	9	340	70	48.6	1	50.0	39	75.0	90	20	9	18	179	19.9
'89-90	NEW YORK	10	395	114	52.1	0	---	65	82.3	105	31	13	20	294	29.4
'90-91	NEW YORK	3	110	18	40.0	0	---	14	77.8	30	6	1	5	50	16.7
'91-92	NEW YORK	12	482	109	45.6	0	0.0	54	74.0	133	27	7	31	272	22.7
'92-93	NEW YORK	15	604	165	51.2	1	100.0	51	63.8	164	36	17	31	382	25.5
'93-94	NEW YORK	25	1032	210	43.7	4	36.4	123	75.5	293	65	32	76	547	21.9
TOTALS		78	3116	714	47.4	6	37.5	365	74.9	866	195	85	194	1799	23.1

Charles Oakley

No. 34/F

HT: 6-9 **WT:** 245
Born: 12/18/63, Cleveland, OH
High school: John Hay
(Cleveland)
College: Virginia Union

Oakley tied for sixth in the NBA with 11.8 rebounds per game, and was named to the All-Star team for the first time. He led the Knicks in rebounding 47 times, and put up 43 double-doubles. Oakley broke his own team record of 343 offensive rebounds (set in '88–89) with 349 last season. He's now in fourth place on the all-time Knicks' rebounding list with 4,881. Last season's 11.8 scoring average was his highest since he had 14.6 in '89–90. The only Knick to play in all 82 games (all starts), he had three complete 48 minute games: against Washington December 30, against Minnesota January 17, and against Indiana March 25. Oakley was named Knick of the Month in November, December, and February.

REGULAR SEASON		G	MIN	FG	FGx	3FG	3PTx	FT	FTx	REB	AST	STL	BLK	PTS	AVG
'85-86	CHICAGO	77	1772	281	51.9	0	0.0	178	66.2	664	133	68	30	740	9.6
'86-87	CHICAGO	82	2980	468	44.5	11	36.7	245	68.6	1074	296	85	36	1192	14.5
'87-88	CHICAGO	82	2816	375	48.3	3	25.0	261	72.7	1066	248	68	28	1014	12.4
'88-89	NEW YORK	82	2604	426	51.0	12	25.0	197	77.3	861	187	104	14	1061	12.9
'89-90	NEW YORK	61	2196	336	52.4	0	0.0	217	76.1	727	146	64	16	889	14.6
'90-91	NEW YORK	76	2739	307	51.6	0	0.0	239	78.4	920	204	62	17	853	11.2
'91-92	NEW YORK	82	2309	210	52.2	0	0.0	86	73.5	700	133	67	15	506	6.2
'92-93	NEW YORK	82	2230	219	50.8	0	0.0	127	72.2	708	126	85	15	565	6.9
'93-94	NEW YORK	82	2932	363	47.8	0	0.0	243	77.6	965	218	110	18	969	11.8
	9 YR TOTALS	706	22578	2985	49.5	26	24.8	7685	73.6	7685	1691	713	189	7789	11.0
'93-94	RANK NBA FₛS	1	5	37	58	78	78	20	26	2	20	9	98	34	41
'94-95	PROJECTIONS	82	3247	428	45.8	0	0.0	307	79.5	1086	264	131	19	1163	14.2

PLAYOFFS		G	MIN	FG	FGx	3FG	3PTx	FT	FTx	REB	AST	STL	BLK	PTS	AVG
'85-86	CHICAGO	3	88	11	52.4	0	---	8	61.5	30	3	6	2	30	10.0
'86-87	CHICAGO	3	129	19	38.0	2	50.0	20	83.3	46	6	4	1	60	20.0
'87-88	CHICAGO	10	373	40	44.0	0	0.0	21	87.5	128	32	6	4	101	10.1
'88-89	NEW YORK	9	299	35	47.9	1	50.0	16	66.7	101	11	12	1	87	9.7
'89-90	NEW YORK	10	336	43	51.2	1	100.0	34	65.4	110	27	11	2	121	12.1
'90-91	NEW YORK	3	100	10	47.6	0	---	3	50.0	31	3	2	1	23	7.7
'91-92	NEW YORK	12	354	22	37.9	0	---	20	74.1	108	8	8	5	64	5.3
'92-93	NEW YORK	15	507	63	48.1	0	---	40	72.7	165	17	16	2	166	11.1
'93-94	NEW YORK	25	992	125	47.7	0	---	79	77.5	292	59	35	5	329	13.2
	TOTALS	90	3178	368	46.5	4	44.4	241	73.7	1011	166	100	23	981	10.9

Doc Rivers

No. 25/G

Full name: Glenn Anton Rivers
HT: 6-4 **WT:** 185
Born: 10/13/61, Chicago, IL
High school: Proviso East
(Maywood, IL)
College: Marquette

Rivers is an outstanding ballhandler and playmaker. He's not the offensive threat he was earlier in his career, but he's still a tenacious defender. Rivers is a veteran who has demonstrated amazing toughness throughout his career. He'll need that toughness to bounce back from last season's knee injury. Rivers suffered a torn anterior cruciate ligament and torn medial meniscus of his left knee on December 16 against the Lakers. The injury ended his season, although he was approaching playing condition by season's end. He was the starting point guard at the time, and led the Knicks in 10 of his 19 games. Former Baltimore Oriole outfielder Ken Singleton is his cousin.

REGULAR SEASON		G	MIN	FG	FGx	3FG	3PTx	FT	FTx	REB	AST	STL	BLK	PTS	AVG
'83-84	ATLANTA	81	1938	250	46.2	2	16.7	255	78.5	220	314	127	30	757	9.3
'84-85	ATLANTA	69	2126	334	47.6	15	41.7	291	77.0	214	410	163	53	974	14.1
'85-86	ATLANTA	53	1571	220	47.4	0	0.0	172	60.8	162	443	120	13	612	11.5
'86-87	ATLANTA	82	2590	342	45.1	4	19.0	365	82.8	299	823	171	30	1053	12.8
'87-88	ATLANTA	80	2502	403	45.3	9	27.3	319	75.8.	366	747	140	42	1134	14.2
'88-89	ATLANTA	76	2462	371	45.5	43	34.7	247	86.1	286	525	181	40	1032	13.6
'89-90	ATLANTA	48	1526	218	45.4	24	36.4	138	81.2	200	264	116	22	598	12.5
'90-91	ATLANTA	79	2586	444	43.5	98	33.6	221	84.4	253	340	148	47	1197	15.2
'91-92	LA CLIPPERS	59	1657	226	42.4	26	28.3	163	83.2	147	233	111	19	641	10.9
'92-93	NEW YORK	77	1886	216	43.7	39	31.7	133	82.1	192	405	123	9	604	7.8
'93-94	NEW YORK	19	499	55	43.3	19	36.5	14	63.6	39	100	25	5	143	7.5
11 YR TOTALS		723	21343	3079	45.1	269	32.1	2318	78.7	2378	4604	1425	309	8745	12.1
'93-94 RANK NBA Gs		not ranked -- didn't appear in 25 games in '93-94													
'94-95 PROJECTIONS		82	1850	180	43.9	39	32.0	108	81.2	189	457	119	0	507	6.2

PLAYOFFS		G	MIN	FG	FGx	3FG	3PTx	FT	FTx	REB	AST	STL	BLK	PTS	AVG
'83-84	ATLANTA	5	130	16	50.0	0	0.0	36	87.8	10	16	12	4	68	13.6
'85-86	ATLANTA	9	262	40	43.5	3	50.0	31	73.8	42	78	18	0	114	12.7
'86-87	ATLANTA	8	245	18	38.3	0	---	26	50.0	27	90	9	3	62	7.8
'87-88	ATLANTA	12	409	71	51.1	7	31.8	39	90.7	59	115	25	2	188	15.7
'88-89	ATLANTA	5	191	22	38.6	6	31.6	17	70.8	24	34	7	2	67	13.4
'90-91	ATLANTA	5	173	30	46.9	1	9.1	17	89.5	20	15	5	2	79	15.6
'91-92	LA CLIPPERS	5	187	25	44.6	4	50.0	22	81.5	13	21	6	0	76	15.2
'92-93	NEW YORK	15	458	48	45.3	11	35.5	46	76.7	39	86	29	1	153	10.2
TOTALS		64	2055	270	45.5	32	32.0	234	76.0	240	455	111	14	806	12.6

John Starks

No. 3/G

Full name: John Levell Starks
HT: 6-5   **WT:** 185
Born: 8/10/65, Tulsa, OK
High school: Tulsa Central (OK)
College: Oklahoma State

Starks too often plays out of control. He's an athletically gifted, often brilliant, shooter who's not afraid of the ball in crunch time, as he demonstrated in game 6 of the Eastern Conference finals vs. Indiana. Playing on the road in a game where the Knicks faced playoff elimination, Starks tied his own club playoff record with five 3-point FGs on the way to a team-high 26 points that led New York to a 98–91 triumph. Starks is also a decent playmaker for a shooting guard, a good ballhandler and a fearless defender. He was selected by the coaches to the East All-Star team.

REGULAR SEASON		G	MIN	FG	FG%	3FG	3PT%	FT	FT%	REB	AST	STL	BLK	PTS	AVG
'88-89	GOLDEN STATE	36	316	51	40.8	10	38.5	34	65.4	41	27	23	3	146	4.1
'90-91	NEW YORK	61	1173	180	43.9	27	29.0	79	75.2	131	204	59	17	466	7.6
'91-92	NEW YORK	82	2118	405	44.9	94	34.8	235	77.8	191	276	103	18	1139	13.9
'92-93	NEW YORK	80	2477	513	42.8	108	32.1	263	79.5	204	404	91	12	1397	17.5
'93-94	NEW YORK	59	2057	410	42.0	113	33.5	187	75.4	185	348	95	6	1120	19.0
	5 YR TOTALS	318	8141	1559	43.1	352	33.1	798	76.9	752	1259	371	56	4268	13.4
'93-94	RANK NBA Gs	106	57	39	93	14	56	34	86	60	34	43	89	32	9
'94-95	PROJECTIONS	52	2127	434	41.3	135	33.8	182	74.9	186	384	98	1	1185	22.8

PLAYOFFS		G	MIN	FG	FG%	3FG	3PT%	FT	FT%	REB	AST	STL	BLK	PTS	AVG
'90-91	NEW YORK	3	28	2	40.0	0	---	2	100.0	3	6	0	0	6	2.0
'91-92	NEW YORK	12	295	46	37.4	11	23.9	42	80.8	30	38	17	0	145	12.1
'92-93	NEW YORK	15	575	88	44.0	28	37.3	43	71.7	52	96	15	3	247	16.5
'93-94	NEW YORK	25	840	110	38.1	47	35.6	97	77.0	58	114	35	2	364	14.6
	TOTALS	55	1738	246	39.9	86	34.0	184	76.7	143	254	67	5	762	13.9

Hubert Davis   No. 44/G

Full name: Hubert Ira Davis, Jr.
HT: 6-5   **WT:** 183
Born: 5/17/70, Winston-Salem, NC
High school: Lake Braddock (Burke, VA)
College: North Carolina

Davis started New York's final 27 games; the Knicks went 21–6 in those games, while Davis shot 42.1 percent from 3-point range.

REGULAR SEASON		G	MIN	FG	FGx	3FG	3PTx	FT	FTx	REB	AST	STL	BLK	PTS	AVG
'92-93	NEW YORK	50	815	110	43.8	6	31.6	43	79.6	56	83	22	4	269	5.4
'93-94	NEW YORK	56	1333	238	47.1	53	40.2	85	82.5	67	165	40	4	614	11.0
2 YR TOTALS		106	2148	348	46.0	59	39.1	128	81.5	123	248	62	8	883	8.3
'93-94 RANK NBA Gs		110	86	74	37	37	18	87	41	118	83	99	102	76	57
'94-95 PROJECTIONS		62	1851	420	50.5	157	46.5	139	85.3	59	270	61	2	1136	18.3

PLAYOFFS		G	MIN	FG	FGx	3FG	3PTx	FT	FTx	REB	AST	STL	BLK	PTS	AVG
'92-93	NEW YORK	7	96	14	56.0	1	50.0	2	66.7	6	5	6	0	31	4.4
'93-94	NEW YORK	23	396	44	36.4	10	28.6	23	71.9	21	26	5	3	121	5.3
TOTALS		30	492	58	39.7	11	29.7	25	71.4	27	31	11	3	152	5.1

Anthony Mason   No. 14/F

Full name: Anthony George Douglas Mason
HT: 6-7   **WT:** 250
Born: 12/14/66, Miami, FL
High school: Springfield Gardens (NY)
College: Tennessee State

Mason started 12 games, averaging 10.3 points, 6.2 rebounds, and 31 minutes per game on 52 percent shooting.

REGULAR SEASON		G	MIN	FG	FGx	3FG	3PTx	FT	FTx	REB	AST	STL	BLK	PTS	AVG
'89-90	NEW JERSEY	21	108	14	35.0	0	---	9	60.0	34	7	2	2	37	1.8
'90-91	DENVER	3	21	2	50.0	0	---	6	75.0	5	0	1	0	10	3.3
'91-92	NEW YORK	82	2199	203	50.9	0	---	167	64.2	573	106	46	20	573	7.0
'92-93	NEW YORK	81	2482	316	50.2	0	---	199	68.2	640	170	43	19	831	10.3
'93-94	NEW YORK	73	1903	206	47.6	0	0.0	116	72.0	427	151	31	9	528	7.2
5 YR TOTALS		260	6712	741	49.2	0	0.0	497	67.5	1679	434	123	50	1979	7.6
'93-94 RANK NBA Fs		67	53	71	61	78	78	64	63	44	40	91	120	73	79
'94-95 PROJECTIONS		79	1990	207	47.0	0	0.0	66	75.0	407	186	25	6	480	6.1

PLAYOFFS		G	MIN	FG	FGx	3FG	3PTx	FT	FTx	REB	AST	STL	BLK	PTS	AVG
'91-92	NEW YORK	12	288	19	44.2	0	---	22	78.6	76	10	2	8	60	5.0
'92-93	NEW YORK	15	510	72	59.0	0	---	43	63.2	109	41	10	6	187	12.5
'93-94	NEW YORK	25	660	67	48.9	0	---	55	71.4	146	46	15	5	189	7.6
TOTALS		52	1458	158	52.3	0	---	120	69.4	331	97	27	19	436	8.4

Charles Smith No. 54/F

Full name: Charles Daniel Smith
HT: 6-10 **WT:** 244
Born: 7/16/65, Bridgeport, CT
High school: Warren Harding (Bridgeport)
College: Pittsburgh
Dogged by a knee injury and angry fans who remembered his play against Chicago in the '93 playoffs, Smith lost his starting spot.

REGULAR SEASON	G	MIN	FG	FGx	3FG	3PTx	FT	FTx	REB	AST	STL	BLK	PTS	AVG
'88-89 LA CLIPPERS	71	2161	435	49.5	0	0.0	285	72.5	465	103	68	89	1155	16.3
'89-90 LA CLIPPERS	78	2732	595	52.0	1	8.3	454	79.4	524	114	86	119	1645	21.1
'90-91 LA CLIPPERS	74	2703	548	46.9	0	0.0	384	79.3	608	134	81	145	1480	20.0
'91-92 LA CLIPPERS	49	1310	251	46.6	0	0.0	212	78.5	301	56	41	98	714	14.6
'92-93 NEW YORK	81	2172	358	46.9	0	0.0	287	78.2	432	142	48	96	1003	12.4
'93-94 NEW YORK	43	1105	176	44.3	8	50.0	87	71.9	165	50	26	45	447	10.4
6 YR TOTALS	396	12183	2363	48.3	9	19.6	1709	77.4	2495	599	350	592	6444	16.3
'93-94 RANK NBA Fs	119	94	83	99	43	3	90	66	112	96	98	49	81	54
'94-95 PROJECTIONS	28	578	85	42.7	9	75.0	28	68.3	68	23	13	20	207	7.4

PLAYOFFS	G	MIN	FG	FGx	3FG	3PTx	FT	FTx	REB	AST	STL	BLK	PTS	AVG
'91-92 LA CLIPPERS	5	148	22	39.3	0	---	14	93.3	28	9	4	12	58	11.6
'92-93 NEW YORK	15	388	65	47.1	0	---	37	74.0	60	20	9	14	167	11.1
'93-94 NEW YORK	25	612	85	48.0	0	0.0	51	72.9	95	25	12	24	221	8.8
TOTALS	45	1148	172	46.4	0	0.0	102	75.6	183	54	25	50	446	9.9

Charlie Ward No. 21/G

HT: 6-0 **WT:** 183
Born: 10/12/70, Thomasville, GA
College: Florida State
Florida State's all-time leader in steals with 236, Ward averaged 10.5 points, 4.9 assists, and an ACC-leading 2.7 steals per game last season. Bob Dandridge compares him to Lenny Wilkens and Maurice Cheeks.

REGULAR SEASON	G	MIN	FG	FGx	3FG	3PTx	FT	FTx	REB	AST	STL	BLK	PTS	AVG

ROOKIE -- NO NBA EXPERIENCE

Monty Williams   No. 2/F

HT: 6-8   **WT:** 225
Born: 10/8/71, Fredericksburg, VA
College: Notre Dame
Williams shot 51 percent from the field last season, averaging 22.4 points and 8.2 rebounds. He averaged 18.5 points and 9.3 rebounds as a junior. A heart ailment sidelined Williams between 1990 and 1992.

REGULAR SEASON	G	MIN	FG	FGx	3FG	3PTx	FT	FTx	REB	AST	STL	BLK	PTS	AVG
ROOKIE -- NO NBA EXPERIENCE														

Pat Riley   Head Coach

Full name: Patrick James Riley
HT: 6-4   **WT:** 205
Born: 3/20/45, Rome, NY
High school: Linton (Schenectady, NY)
College: Kentucky
Every team Riley has coached has finished first in their division. He's won more playoff games than any coach in NBA history.

	REGULAR SEASON				PLAYOFFS			
YEAR	TEAM	W	L	PCT	FINISH	W	L	PCT
'81-82	LA LAKERS	50	21	.704	1st/Pacific Div.	12	2	.857 won NBA Finals over Philadelphia, 4-2
'82-83	LA LAKERS	58	24	.707	1st/Pacific Div.	8	7	.533 lost NBA Finals to Philadelphia, 4-0
'83-84	LA LAKERS	54	28	.659	1st/Pacific Div.	14	7	.667 lost NBA Finals to Boston, 4-3
'84-85	LA LAKERS	62	20	.756	1st/Pacific Div.	15	4	.789 won NBA Finals over Boston, 4-2
'85-86	LA LAKERS	62	20	.756	1st/Pacific Div.	8	6	.571 lost Western Conf. finals to Houston, 4-1
'86-87	LA LAKERS	65	17	.793	1st/Pacific Div.	15	3	.833 won NBA Finals over Boston, 4-2
'87-88	LA LAKERS	62	20	.756	1st/Pacific Div.	15	9	.625 won NBA Finals over Detroit, 4-3
'88-89	LA LAKERS	57	25	.695	1st/Pacific Div.	11	4	.733 lost NBA Finals to Detroit, 4-0
'89-90	LA LAKERS	63	19	.768	1st/Pacific Div.	4	5	.444 lost Western Conf. semifinals to Phoenix, 4-1
'91-92	NEW YORK	51	31	.622	T1st/Atlantic Div.	6	6	.500 lost Eastern Conf. semifinals to Chicago, 4-3
'92-93	NEW YORK	60	22	.732	1st/Atlantic Div.	9	6	.600 lost Eastern Conf. finals to Chicago, 4-2
'93-94	NEW YORK	57	25	.695	1st/Atlantic Div.	14	11	.560 lost NBA Finals to Houston, 4-3
	12 YR TOTALS	701	272	.720		131	70	.652

Orlando
MAGIC

1994–95 Scouting Report

Frontcourt

Shaquille O'Neal is often maligned for having a one-dimensional offensive game, but he was second in scoring with 29.3 points per game, and tops in shooting percentage, hitting 59.9 percent. The Magic had a hole at power forward all last season, so Orlando acquired free agent power forward Horace Grant from the Bulls to take some of the rebounding burden off Shaquille O'Neal. Swingman Dennis Scott emerged as the starter at small forward late last season. Greg Kite was Shaquille's backup, but he tore a muscle in his right calf that ended his season. Assistant coach Tree Rollins was pressed into service as a backup center; he can't shoot, pass, or ball-handle, but he can still block shots and rebound. Anthony Avent comes off the bench to play power forward. Donald Royal is a reserve at small forward. Rookie Rodney Dent and Jeff Turner are both good shooters who are trying to come back from knee injuries to fill the gap at forward.

Backcourt

With Scott Skiles' trade to Washington, the point guard responsibilities rest with Anfernee Hardaway. He's coming off a strong rookie campaign in which he averaged 16 points and 2.32 steals (sixth in the NBA) per game. Nick Anderson, who's really a shooting guard, opened last season at small forward; he'll now move back to guard. Anthony Bowie is a backup at shooting guard and also small forward. Rookie guard Brooks Thompson has an outstanding shot from the perimeter.

Defense

Orlando's defense figures to improve with Horace Grant's arrival. Last year, teams averaged 101.8 points against the Magic, thirteenth in the NBA. Opponents shot 45.8 percent from the floor against

Orlando, tenth lowest in the league. That's because Shaquille O'Neal was underneath to block shots and change shots; Orlando ranked ninth in blocks. But Shaquille needed help underneath; Orlando ranked just twenty-second in keeping opponents from grabbing offensive rebounds. As a result of giving up so may second shots, the Magic were twentieth in allowing opponents' field goal attempts. Those numbers should improve with Horace Grant's addition, but the Magic also need better defensive play from their guards. They ranked only nineteenth in the NBA in stealing the ball and twenty-second in the league in forcing turnovers.

1994–95 Prospects

Last season, the Magic improved to 50 wins, considered the prerequisite for membership in the NBA elite. But when Indiana ignominiously bounced the Magic out of the playoffs in the first round, the muttering about Shaquille O'Neal being an overrated player grew to a crescendo. It mattered little that underrated Indiana subsequently eliminated East top seed Atlanta, and took second seed New York to a seventh game in the Eastern finals.

Basketball at the NBA level is not a one-man game (or even a two- or three-man game). Michael Jordan couldn't do it alone, Patrick Ewing hasn't done it yet, and Hakeem Olajuwon had help when his Rockets finally won. Shaquille O'Neal is an impact player; his game's not perfect, but it's one of the most effective in the league.

The Magic will continue to improve in '94–95. With Horace Grant at power forward and Nick Anderson back at shooting guard, Orlando should feast on the lottery teams (last season, they were a modest 24–11 vs. the NBA's weakest), and they'll play tougher against the better teams in the league. They still have too many holes to challenge for the NBA title, or even for the Atlantic Division. They were twenty-sixth in the league in free throw shooting (just ahead of Golden State at 67.8 percent), they need a small forward who can score going to the basket, and their bench could be better. But they should win around 54 games this season, good enough for home court advantage in the first round of the playoffs.

Team Directory

Chairman: Rich DeVos   Exec. V. chair.: Cheri Vander Weide

General manager/COO: Pat Williams   Exec. VP/Asst. GM: Jack Swope

Basketball oper.: Bob Vander Weide   Publicity/Media rel.: Alex Martins

1993–94 Review

EASTERN CONFERENCE						WESTERN CONFERENCE					
ATLANTIC DIV.			CENTRAL DIV.			MIDWEST DIV.			PACIFIC DIV.		
	W	L		W	L		W	L		W	L
NY	2	3	ATL	1	3	HOU	1	1	SEA	1	1
ORL	–	–	CHI	2	2	SAN	0	2	PHO	1	1
NJ	5	0	CLE	2	2	UTAH	2	0	GS	1	1
MIA	3	2	IND	2	2	DEN	1	1	POR	2	0
BOS	2	2	CHA	2	2	MIN	1	1	LAL	0	2
PHI	4	0	DET	3	1	DAL	2	0	SAC	2	0
WAS	4	1	MIL	3	1				LAC	1	1
	20	8		15	13		7	5		8	6

1993–94 finish: 50–32 (31–10 home, 19–22 away), second in Atlantic Div.

1994–95 Schedule

1/4	@ Wash.	7:30 pm	12/30	LA Clip.	7:30 pm	3/2	@ Houston	9:30 pm
1/5	Phila.	7:30 pm	1/4	New Jersey	7:30 pm	3/3	@ San Ant.	8:30 pm
1/9	@ Charlotte	7:30 pm	1/6	Minnesota	7:30 pm	3/5	Atlanta	7:30 pm
1/10	@ New York	8:00 pm	1/8	@ Detroit	7:00 pm	3/8	LA Lakers	7:30 pm
1/12	@ Phila.	7:30 pm	1/10	@ Chicago	8:30 pm	3/10	Portland	7:30 pm
1/15	Wash.	7:30 pm	1/11	Detroit	7:30 pm	3/12	San Ant.	12:00 pm
1/18	New Jersey	7:30 pm	1/13	@ Atlanta	7:30 pm	3/14	Utah	7:30 pm
1/21	Miami	7:30 pm	1/14	Phila.	7:30 pm	3/15	@ New Jersey	7:30 pm
1/23	Houston	7:30 pm	1/17	Charlotte	7:30 pm	3/17	@ Indiana	7:30 pm
1/25	@ Boston	7:30 pm	1/18	@ Dallas	8:30 pm	3/21	Phoenix	8:00 pm
1/26	@ Milwaukee	8:30 pm	1/20	@ Denver	8:00 pm	3/23	Charlotte	8:00 pm
1/30	Sacra.	7:30 pm	1/22	@ Phoenix	3:30 pm	3/24	@ Chicago	8:30 pm
2/2	New York	8:00 pm	1/24	Boston	7:30 pm	3/26	Gold. St.	12:00 pm
2/3	@ Atlanta	7:30 pm	1/26	Chicago	8:00 pm	3/28	@ Sacra.	10:30 pm
2/6	@ Cleveland	7:30 pm	1/28	Milwaukee	7:30 pm	3/31	@ Utah	8:00 pm
2/7	Cleveland	7:30 pm	2/2	Seattle	8:00 pm	4/2	@ LA Lakers	10:00 pm
2/9	@ Miami	7:30 pm	2/3	@ Indiana	7:30 pm	4/5	Detroit	7:30 pm
2/10	Atlanta	7:30 pm	2/5	New York	1:00 pm	4/7	@ Detroit	8:00 pm
2/12	@ New Jersey	7:30 pm	2/8	Dallas	7:30 pm	4/8	@ Phila.	7:30 pm
2/14	Denver	7:30 pm	2/14	Indiana	7:30 pm	4/11	Cleveland	7:30 pm
2/16	@ Gold. St.	10:30 pm	2/15	@ Cleveland	7:30 pm	4/13	@ Boston	7:30 pm
2/17	@ Seattle	10:00 pm	2/17	Phila.	7:30 pm	4/15	@ Miami	3:30 pm
2/20	@ Portland	10:00 pm	2/19	@ Minnesota	3:30 pm	4/17	Wash.	7:30 pm
2/21	@ LA Clip.	10:30 pm	2/20	@ Milwaukee	8:30 pm	4/19	@ Wash.	7:30 pm
2/23	Milwaukee	7:30 pm	2/23	@ Boston	7:30 pm	4/21	Indiana	8:00 pm
2/26	@ Wash.	7:30 pm	2/24	Boston	7:30 pm	4/23	@ New York	1:00 pm
2/27	Miami	7:30 pm	2/26	Chicago	1:00 pm			
2/29	@ Charlotte	8:00 pm	2/28	New York	8:00 pm			

1993–94 Team Stats

NAME	G	MIN	FG	FGA	FG%	3FG	3FGA	3FG%	FT	FTA	FT%	ORB	TRB	AST	PF	STL	BLK	TO	PTS	AVG
O'Neal	81	3224	953	1591	59.9	0	2	0.0	471	850	55.4	384	1072	195	281	76	231	222	2377	29.3
Hardaway	82	3015	509	1092	46.6	50	187	26.7	245	330	74.2	192	439	544	205	190	51	292	1313	16.0
Anderson	81	2811	504	1054	47.8	101	314	32.2	168	250	67.2	113	476	294	148	134	33	165	1277	15.8
Scott	82	2283	384	949	40.5	155	388	39.9	123	159	77.4	54	218	216	161	81	32	93	1046	12.8
Skiles	82	2303	276	644	42.9	68	165	41.2	195	222	87.8	42	189	503	171	47	2	193	815	9.9
Royal	74	1357	174	347	50.1	0	2	0.0	199	269	74.0	94	248	61	121	50	16	76	547	7.4
Turner	68	1536	199	426	46.7	18	55	32.7	35	45	77.8	79	271	60	239	23	11	75	451	6.6
Krystkowiak	34	682	71	148	48.0	0	1	0.0	31	39	79.5	38	123	35	74	14	4	29	173	5.1
Bowie	70	948	139	289	48.1	1	18	5.6	41	49	83.7	29	120	102	81	32	12	58	320	4.6
Avent	41	676	58	170	34.1	0	0	—	28	44	63.6	84	184	32	87	17	11	42	144	3.5
Green	29	126	22	57	38.6	1	4	25.0	28	37	75.7	6	12	9	16	6	1	13	73	2.5
Lichti	4	20	4	9	44.4	0	0	—	0	0	—	3	4	2	3	2	0	0	8	2.0
Hammink	1	3	1	3	33.3	0	0	—	0	0	—	1	4	1	1	0	0	2	2	2.0
Rollins	45	384	29	53	54.7	0	0	—	18	30	60.0	33	96	9	55	7	35	13	76	1.7
Kite	29	309	13	35	37.1	0	0	—	8	22	36.4	22	70	4	61	12	12	17	34	1.2
Tower	11	32	4	9	44.4	0	0	—	0	0	—	0	6	1	6	0	0	0	8	0.7
Williams	3	19	1	6	16.7	0	1	0.0	0	0	—	3	4	0	3	2	0	0	8	0.7
Cook	2	2	0	10	0.0	0	0	—	0	0	—	0	0	0	2	2	0	1	0	0.0
Magic	82	19730	3341	6883	48.5	394	1137	34.7	1590	2346	67.8	1177	3533	2070	1713	683	456	1327	8666	105.7
Opp.	82	19730	3263	7125	45.8	296	847	34.9	1525	2047	74.5	1197	3502	2103	1844	756	442	1228	8347	101.8

HISTORY

ALL-TIME TEAM RECORDS

Career

Total points	Nick Anderson	5,968	1989–94
Field goals made	Scott Skiles	1,703	1989–94
Field goals attempted	Scott Skiles	1,319	1989–94
Free throws made	Nick Anderson	1,027	1989–94
Free throws attempted	Shaquille O'Neal	1,571	1992–94
Total rebounds	Shaquille O'Neal	2,194	1992–94
Assists	Scott Skiles	2,776	1989–94
Steals	Nick Anderson	502	1989–94
Personal Fouls	Jeff Turner	1,055	1989–94
Blocked Shots	Shaquille O'Neal	517	1992–94

Season

Total points	Shaquille O'Neal	2,377	1993–94
Field goals made	Shaquille O'Neal	953	1993–94
Field goals attempted	Shaquille O'Neal	1,591	1993–94
Free throws made	Shaquille O'Neal	471	1993–94
Free throws attempted	Shaquille O'Neal	850	1993–94
Total rebounds	Shaquille O'Neal	1,122	1992–93
Assists	Scott Skiles	735	1992–93
Steals	Anfernee Hardaway	190	1993–94
Personal Fouls	Shaquille O'Neal	381	1992–93
Blocked Shots	Shaquille O'Neal	286	1992–93

Game

Total points	Shaquille O'Neal	53	vs. Minnesota, 04/20/94
Field goals made	Shaquille O'Neal	22	vs. Minnesota, 4/20/94
Free throws made	Sam Vincent	17	vs. Seattle, 1/8/92
Total rebounds	Shaquille O'Neal	28	vs. New Jersey, 11/20/93
Assists	Scott Skiles	30	vs. Denver, 12/30/90
Steals	Nick Anderson	8	vs. Washington, 11/21/91
Blocked Shots	Shaquille O'Neal	15	vs. New Jersey, 11/20/93

LEADING COACHES

NAME	REGULAR SEASON				PLAYOFFS		
	YEARS	W	L	PCT	W	L	PCT
Brian Hill	1993–94	50	32	.610	0	3	.000
Matt Guokas	1989–93	111	217	.338	0	0	—

Orlando Magic 1994–95 Roster

Head Coach: Brian Hill

No.	Name	Pos.	Ht.	Wt.	Yrs.	Born	College
25	Nick Anderson	G-F	6-6	220	5	1/20/68	Illinois
0	Anthony Avent	F	6-9	235	2	10/18/69	Seton Hall
14	Anthony Bowie	G	6-6	200	5	11/9/63	Oklahoma
24	Rodney Dent	F	6-9	256	R	12/25/70	Kentucky
54	Horace Grant	F	6-10	235	8	7/4/65	Clemson
43	Geert Hammink	F-C	7-0	262	1	4/12/69	Louisiana St.
1	Anfernee Hardaway	G	6-7	200	1	7/18/72	Memphis State
34	Greg Kite	C-F	6-11	263	11	8/5/61	Brigham Young
32	Shaquille O'Neal	C	7-1	301	2	3/6/72	Louisiana State
30	Tree Rollins	C	7-1	255	17	9/16/55	Clemson
5	Donald Royal	F	6-8	210	4	5/22/66	Notre Dame
3	Dennis Scott	G-F	6-8	229	4	9/5/68	Georgia Tech
22	Brooks Thompson	G	6-4	193	R	7/19/70	Oklahoma State
55	Keith Tower	F-C	6-11	250	1	5/15/70	Notre Dame
31	Jeff Turner	F	6-9	244	8	4/9/62	Vanderbilt

Arena Information

Orlando Arena (15,077)
Tickets: 800-338-0005
Ticket prices:$32, $25, $18

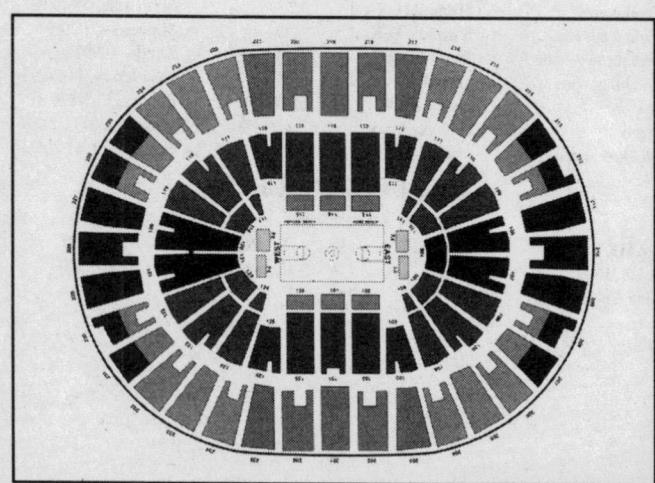

Nick Anderson

No. 25/G-F

Full name: Nelison Anderson
HT: 6-6   **WT:** 220
Born: 1/20/68, Chicago, IL
High school: Neal F. Simeon (Chicago)
College: Illinois

Anderson is an excellent offensive ballplayer. He can post up opponents, has developed a good shot from 3-point range, passes well and can rebound. Anderson scored 20 points or more 25 times, but he only led the Magic in scoring 9 times. He led the team in rebounds 6 times. Anderson also holds the Magic record for career points scored, free throws made, and steals. But Anderson has problems defensively. Although he ranked twenty-fourth in the league in steals, Anderson is shorter than his listed 6-6, and he's had problems defending taller forwards like Billy Owens, Dominique Wilkins, and Shawn Kemp.

REGULAR SEASON		G	MIN	FG	FGx	3FG	3PTx	FT	FTx	REB	AST	STL	BLK	PTS	AVG
'89-90	ORLANDO	81	1785	372	43.4	1	5.9	186	70.5	316	124	69	34	931	11.5
'90-91	ORLANDO	70	1971	400	46.7	17	29.3	173	66.8	386	106	74	44	990	14.1
'91-92	ORLANDO	60	2203	482	46.3	30	35.3	202	66.7	384	163	97	33	1196	19.9
'92-93	ORLANDO	79	2920	594	44.9	88	35.3	298	74.1	477	265	128	56	1574	19.9
'93-94	ORLANDO	81	2811	504	47.8	101	32.2	168	67.2	476	294	134	33	1277	15.8
5 YR TOTALS		371	11690	2352	46.8	237	32.8	1027	69.5	2039	952	502	200	5968	16.1
'93-94	RANK NBA Gs	27	15	15	28	16	69	43	120	2	46	17	15	19	23
'94-95	PROJECTIONS	82	2994	489	48.8	138	32.8	124	65.3	502	354	151	24	1240	15.1

PLAYOFFS		G	MIN	FG	FGx	3FG	3PTx	FT	FTx	REB	AST	STL	BLK	PTS	AVG
'93-94	ORLANDO	3	120	13	38.2	8	40.0	9	75.0	10	10	5	2	43	14.3
	TOTALS	3	120	13	38.2	8	40.0	9	75.0	10	10	5	2	43	14.3

Horace Grant

No. 54/F

Full name: Horace Junior Grant
HT: 6-10 **WT:** 235
Born: 7/4/65, Augusta, GA
High school: Hancock Central
(Sparta, GA)
College: Clemson

Grant is one of the best—and most underrated—power forwards in the NBA. A key member of three NBA championship teams in Chicago, Grant was named to the All-Star team for the first time last season. Predominantly a rebounder and defensive stud, Grant ranked eleventh in the NBA in rebounding, and led the Bulls in blocked shots. Grant has an underrecognized low-post offensive game, and was the Bulls' second-leading scorer. He's shot better than 50 percent from the field in each of his seven NBA seasons. He scored in double figures in 62 games, and had 42 double-doubles in '93-94. The Bulls were 8-2 in the 10 games he led the team in scoring.

REGULAR SEASON		G	MIN	FG	FG%	3FG	3PT%	FT	FT%	REB	AST	STL	BLK	PTS	AVG
'87-88	CHICAGO	81	1827	254	50.1	0	0.0	114	62.6	447	89	51	53	622	7.7
'88-89	CHICAGO	79	2809	405	51.9	0	0.0	140	70.4	681	168	86	62	950	12.0
'89-90	CHICAGO	80	2753	446	52.3	0	—	179	69.9	629	227	92	84	1071	13.4
'90-91	CHICAGO	78	2641	401	54.7	1	16.7	197	71.1	659	178	95	69	1000	12.8
'91-92	CHICAGO	81	2859	457	57.8	0	0.0	235	74.1	807	217	100	131	1149	14.2
'92-93	CHICAGO	77	2745	421	50.8	1	20.0	174	61.9	729	201	89	96	1017	13.2
'93-94	CHICAGO	70	2570	460	52.4	0	0.0	137	59.6	769	236	74	84	1057	15.1
	7 YR TOTALS	546	18204	2844	53.0	2	7.7	1176	67.5	4721	1316	587	579	6866	12.6
'93-94	RANK NBA Fs	77	24	21	18	78	78	53	118	10	16	31	13	27	23
'94-95	PROJECTIONS	66	2473	471	51.9	0	0.0	113	55.7	787	250	65	77	1055	16.0

PLAYOFFS		G	MIN	FG	FG%	3FG	3PT%	FT	FT%	REB	AST	STL	BLK	PTS	AVG
'87-88	CHICAGO	10	299	46	56.9	0	0.0	9	60.0	70	16	14	2	101	10.1
'88-89	CHICAGO	17	625	72	51.9	0	0.0	40	80.0	167	35	11	16	184	10.8
'89-90	CHICAGO	16	616	81	50.9	0	0.0	33	62.3	159	40	18	18	195	12.2
'90-91	CHICAGO	17	666	91	58.3	0	—	44	73.3	138	38	15	6	226	13.3
'91-92	CHICAGO	22	856	99	54.1	0	0.0	51	67.1	194	66	24	39	249	11.3
'92-93	CHICAGO	19	651	83	54.6	0	—	37	68.5	156	44	23	23	203	10.7
'93-94	CHICAGO	10	393	65	54.2	1	100.0	31	73.8	74	26	10	18	162	16.2
	TOTALS	111	4106	537	54.2	1	16.7	245	70.0	958	265	115	122	1320	11.9

nfernee Hardaway   No. 1/G

Full name: Anfernee Deon
Hardaway
HT: 6-7   **WT:** 195
Born: 7/18/72, Memphis, TN
High school: Treadwell
(Memphis)
College: Memphis State

Of all the tall guards who are called "the next Magic Johnson," Hardaway may be the closest to fulfilling that promise. Hardaway is a versatile player who can bring the ball up the court, score, rebound and play good defense. He's still developing as a play-maker. He averaged 6.6 assists per game, but he split time between point guard (sharing duties with Scott Skiles) and shooting guard. Hardaway set a Magic rookie record with 15 ssists at Golden State March 22. He was sixth in the NBA in steals, urteenth in assists and thirty-ninth in scoring. He also averaged 36.8 inutes per game, and was Orlando's second-leading scorer behind haquille O'Neal.

REGULAR SEASON	G	MIN	FG	FGx	3FG	3PTx	FT	FTx	REB	AST	STL	BLK	PTS	AVG
'93-94 ORLANDO	82	3015	509	46.6	50	26.7	245	74.2	439	544	190	51	1313	16.0
1 YR TOTALS	82	3015	509	46.6	50	26.7	245	74.2	439	544	190	51	1313	16.0
'93-94 RANK NBA Gs	1	5	13	45	41	92	18	94	5	11	5	5	16	21

PLAYOFFS	G	MIN	FG	FGx	3FG	3PTx	FT	FTx	REB	AST	STL	BLK	PTS	AVG
'93-94 ORLANDO	3	133	22	44.0	5	45.5	7	70.0	20	21	5	6	56	18.7
TOTALS	3	133	22	44.0	5	45.5	7	70.0	20	21	5	6	56	18.7

Shaquille O'Neal

No. 32/C

Full name: Shaquille Rashaun
  O'Neal
HT: 7-1   **WT:** 301
Born: 3/6/72, Newark, NJ
High school: Cole (San Antonio,
  TX)
College: Louisiana State

O'Neal is big and strong, but he's also quick, with good hands and footwork. He's a great rebounder, and a shotblocking intimidator. He can't shoot free throws, and his range may be limited to within 6 feet of the basket. On the other hand, at 7-1, 301 pounds, it's hard to keep Shaq from setting up down low. O'Neal was second in the NBA in scoring with 29.3 points per game, and tops in shooting percentage, hitting 59.9 percent. He also averaged 13.2 rebounds (second in the NBA), and 2.85 blocks (sixth), making him the only NBA player to finish in the top 6 in 4 different categories. He has his critics, but the bottom line is that Orlando won 20 more games in Shaq's first season, and another 9 (and a playoff berth) in his second.

REGULAR SEASON		G	MIN	FG	FG%	3FG	3PT%	FT	FT%	REB	AST	STL	BLK	PTS	AVG
'92-93	ORLANDO	81	3071	733	56.2	0	0.0	427	59.2	1122	152	60	286	1893	23.4
'93-94	ORLANDO	81	3224	953	59.9	0	0.0	471	55.4	1072	195	76	231	2377	29.3
	2 YR TOTALS	162	6295	1686	58.2	0	0.0	898	57.2	2194	347	136	517	4270	26.4
'93-94	RANK NBA Cs	7	3	1	3	14	14	2	46	1	5	7	4	2	2
'94-95	PROJECTIONS	81	3377	1208	63.6	0	0.0	510	51.6	1012	241	93	169	2926	36.1

PLAYOFFS		G	MIN	FG	FG%	3FG	3PT%	FT	FT%	REB	AST	STL	BLK	PTS	AVG
'93-94	ORLANDO	3	126	23	51.1	0	---	16	47.1	40	7	2	9	62	20.7
	TOTALS	3	126	23	51.1	0	---	16	47.1	40	7	2	9	62	20.7

Dennis Scott

Full name: Dennis Eugene Scott
HT: 6-8   **WT:** 229
Born: 9/5/68, Hagerstown, MD
High school: Flint Hill Prep
  (Oakton, VA)
College: Georgia Tech

Scott doesn't like to drive the lane, so his career FG percentage is just 41.8, and he's often out of position to rebound. Fortunately, he's a good passer and has a great outside shot, so he can make teams that double up on Shaq pay the price. His FG percentage (40.5 percent) just topped his percentage from 3-point range (39.9 percent). His 155 3-pointers were second most made in the NBA last season, behind Dan Majerle's 192. Scott was one of three Orlando players to appear in all 82 games, and he started in 37. He scored 20 points or more 18 times. Scott also had career highs in assists and steals.

REGULAR SEASON		G	MIN	FG	FGx	3FG	3PTx	FT	FTx	REB	AST	STL	BLK	PTS	AVG
'90-91	ORLANDO	82	2336	503	42.5	125	37.4	153	75.0	235	134	62	25	1284	15.7
'91-92	ORLANDO	18	608	133	40.2	29	32.6	64	90.1	66	35	20	9	359	19.9
'92-93	ORLANDO	54	1759	329	43.1	108	40.3	92	78.6	186	136	57	18	858	15.9
'93-94	ORLANDO	82	2283	384	40.5	155	39.9	123	77.4	218	216	81	32	1046	12.8
4 YR TOTALS		236	6986	1349	41.8	417	38.6	432	78.4	705	521	220	84	3547	15.0
'93-94	RANK NBA Gs	1	46	42	113	2	20	65	78	46	64	55	16	39	46
'94-95	PROJECTIONS	82	2731	407	39.4	206	41.3	125	75.3	244	302	104	42	1145	14.0

PLAYOFFS		G	MIN	FG	FGx	3FG	3PTx	FT	FTx	REB	AST	STL	BLK	PTS	AVG
'93-94	ORLANDO	3	99	14	34.1	7	31.8	8	80.0	6	3	2	3	43	14.3
TOTALS		3	99	14	34.1	7	31.8	8	80.0	6	3	2	3	43	14.3

Anthony Avent   No. 0/F

HT: 6-9 **WT:** 235
Born: 10/18/69, Rocky Mount, NC
High school: M. X. Shabazz (Newark, NJ)
College: Seton Hall

Avent contributes rebounding and defensive ability. He can score off offensive rebounds, but his low post game is tentative, and he has little range.

REGULAR SEASON		G	MIN	FG	FG%	3FG	3PT%	FT	FT%	REB	AST	STL	BLK	PTS	AVG
'92-93	MILWAUKEE	82	2285	347	43.3	0	0.0	112	65.1	512	91	57	73	806	9.8
'93-94	MIL-ORL	74	1371	150	37.7	0	---	89	72.4	338	65	33	31	389	5.3
	2 YR TOTALS	156	3656	497	41.4	0	0.0	201	68.1	850	156	90	104	1195	7.7
'93-94	RANK NBA Fs	61	77	91	131	78	78	78	61	65	78	96	71	90	98
'94-95	PROJECTIONS	66	457	34	32.4	0	0.0	38	79.2	123	25	11	6	106	1.6

PLAYOFFS		G	MIN	FG	FG%	3FG	3PT%	FT	FT%	REB	AST	STL	BLK	PTS	AVG
'93-94	ORLANDO	2	40	6	46.2	0	---	7	87.5	11	1	0	0	19	9.5
	TOTALS	2	40	6	46.2	0	---	7	87.5	11	1	0	0	19	9.5

Anthony Bowie No. 14/G-F

Full name: Anthony Lee Bowie
HT: 6-6 **WT:** 200
Born: 11/9/63, Tulsa, OK
High school: East Central (Tulsa)
College: Oklahoma

Bowie doesn't handle the ball as well as you'd like from a guard, and he's not a defensive stopper, but he can penetrate and pass.

REGULAR SEASON		G	MIN	FG	FG%	3FG	3PT%	FT	FT%	REB	AST	STL	BLK	PTS	AVG
'88-89	SAN ANTONIO	18	438	72	50.0	1	20.0	10	66.7	56	29	18	4	155	8.6
'89-90	HOUSTON	66	918	119	40.6	6	28.6	40	74.1	118	96	42	5	284	4.3
'91-92	ORLANDO	52	1721	312	49.3	17	38.6	117	86.0	245	163	55	38	758	14.6
'92-93	ORLANDO	77	1761	268	47.1	15	31.3	67	79.8	194	175	54	14	618	8.0
'93-94	ORLANDO	70	948	139	48.1	1	5.6	41	83.7	120	102	32	12	320	4.6
	5 YR TOTALS	283	5786	910	47.2	40	29.4	275	81.4	733	565	201	73	2135	7.5
'93-94	RANK NBA Gs	80	107	104	24	124	130	117	26	94	102	110	62	111	114
'94-95	PROJECTIONS	74	683	96	48.5	-1	-3.1	29	85.3	88	78	23	9	220	3.0

PLAYOFFS		G	MIN	FG	FG%	3FG	3PT%	FT	FT%	REB	AST	STL	BLK	PTS	AVG
'89-90	HOUSTON	2	4	0	0.0	0	---	0	---	0	0	0	0	0	0.0
'93-94	ORLANDO	2	13	0	0.0	0	---	0	---	0	0	0	0	0	0.0
	TOTALS	4	17	0	0.0	0	---	0	---	0	0	0	0	0	0.0

Rodney Dent

No. 24/F

HT: 6–9 **WT:** 256
Born: 12/25/70
College: Kentucky

Dent is coming back from suffering a torn anterior cruciate ligament and torn medial collateral ligament in his left knee, both suffered last January. He was a 68 percent shooter in the eleven games he played as a senior.

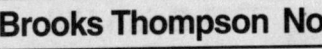

REGULAR SEASON	G	MIN	FG	FGx	3FG	3PTx	FT	FTx	REB	AST	STL	BLK	PTS	AVG
ROOKIE -- NO NBA EXPERIENCE														

Brooks Thompson No. 22/G

HT: 6-4 **WT:** 195
College: Oklahoma State

Thompson averaged 16.9 points and 5.7 assists per game as a senior. He shot 47 per cent from three-point range, scoring 110 3-pointers in 30 games. Thompson was first team All-Big Eight last year. He played well at the Phoenix Desert Classic in April.

REGULAR SEASON	G	MIN	FG	FGx	3FG	3PTx	FT	FTx	REB	AST	STL	BLK	PTS	AVG
ROOKIE -- NO NBA EXPERIENCE														

Jeff Turner   No. 31/F

Full name: Jeffrey Steven Turner
HT: 6-9 **WT:** 240
Born: 4/9/62, Bangor, ME
High school: Brandon (FL)
College: Vanderbilt

Turner is attempting to return from a torn ligament in his left knee. He's a decent rebounder and has a good 3-point shot.

REGULAR SEASON		G	MIN	FG	FGx	3FG	3PTx	FT	FTx	REB	AST	STL	BLK	PTS	AVG
'85-86	NEW JERSEY	53	650	84	49.1	0	0.0	58	74.4	137	14	21	3	226	4.3
'86-87	NEW JERSEY	76	1003	151	46.5	0	0.0	76	73.1	197	60	33	13	378	5.0
'89-90	ORLANDO	60	1105	132	42.9	2	20.0	42	77.8	227	53	23	12	308	5.1
'90-91	ORLANDO	71	1683	259	48.7	6	40.0	85	75.9	363	97	29	10	609	8.6
'91-92	ORLANDO	75	1591	225	45.1	1	12.5	79	69.3	246	92	24	16	530	7.1
'92-93	ORLANDO	75	1479	231	52.9	10	58.8	56	80.0	252	107	19	9	528	7.0
'93-94	ORLANDO	68	1536	199	46.7	18	32.7	35	77.8	271	60	23	11	451	6.6
8 YR TOTALS		550	10476	1452	47.2	37	33.6	510	76.2	1911	591	201	81	3451	6.3
'93-94	RANK NBA Fs	69	55	60	55	96	21	29	26	63	71	62	93	64	66
'94-95	PROJECTIONS	66	1558	188	45.5	22	28.6	19	79.2	274	41	23	11	417	6.3

PLAYOFFS		G	MIN	FG	FGx	3FG	3PTx	FT	FTx	REB	AST	STL	BLK	PTS	AVG
'85-86	NEW JERSEY	3	18	1	33.3	0	...	1	100.0	3	3	0	0	3	1.0
TOTALS		6	39	3	37.5	0	...	1	100.0	7	5	0	0	7	1.2

Brian Hill   Head Coach

Full name: Brian Hill
HT: 5-9 **WT:** 175
Born: 9/19/47, East Orange, NJ
High school: Our Lady of the Valley (East Orange)
College: Kennedy (NE)

Hill is only the Magic's second head coach. He had served as Matt Guokas' top assistant.

	REGULAR SEASON					PLAYOFFS				
YEAR	TEAM	W	L	PCT	FINISH	W	L	PCT		
'93-94	ORLANDO	50	32	.610	2nd/Atlantic Div.	0	3	.000	lost Eastern Conf. first round to Indiana, 3-0
1 YR TOTALS		50	32	.610		0	3	.000		

Philadelphia
76ERS

1994–95 Scouting Report

Frontcourt

The Sixers are Shawn Bradley's team. Bradley has 3 things going for him: he's young (just 22), he's 7-6, and he's a monster shot-blocker. Philly needs to pair him with a power forward who can rebound and score inside. Tim Perry starts as the Sixers' power forward. He doesn't pass, he's soft on defense, doesn't rebound well, and shot just 43.5 percent from the floor (and only 58 percent from the free throw line).The Sixers will look for frontline help from first-round pick Sharone Wright. He entered the NBA draft after averaging 15.4 points, 10.6 rebounds, and 2.9 blocked shots per game as a junior, and the Sixers took him with the sixth pick overall. The Sixers' starting small forward, Clarence Weatherspoon, was their leading scorer and rebounder last season. Spoon is a wide-body bruiser who can score down low or from medium range, and he'll block shots and play good defense without committing a lot of fouls. Philadelphia signed free agent ex-Bull Scott Williams for additional help up front. Rookie power forward Derrick Alston is a good scorer who can block shots, too.

Backcourt

Jeff Malone came to Philadelphia to replace Jeff Hornacek as the starting shooting guard. Malone has a good shot from mid-range and outside. Dana Barros starts at point guard. At 5-11, he's too small to play shooting guard as he did in college, but he's not the quality playmaker you want to see at point. Johnny Dawkins is available off the bench to play point. But he doesn't drive the lane as well as he did before the knee injury that cost him his '90–91 season, and he shot just 41.8 percent from the field. First-round pick B.J. Tyler will challenge for playing time at the point. Tyler was the Southwest Conference Player of the Year, leading the conference in scoring (22.8 ppg), steals (87) and 3-pointers (99).

Defense

The Sixers played some of the softest D in the NBA; it's no accident they committed fewer fouls than any other team. With Shawn Bradley in the middle, the Sixers ranked third in blocked shots. But that was the Sixers' lone defensive bright spot; teams averaged 105.6 points against the Sixers, sixth highest in the NBA. And opponents shot 48.4 percent from the floor against Philadelphia, fourth highest in the league. Philadelphia's defensive problems included giving up too many second shots and an inability to disrupt the other teams' offenses. Only 4 other teams gave up more offensive rebounds. And only 2 other teams allowed their opponents more shots than Philadelphia. The Sixers were just twenty-third in the NBA in stealing the ball and twenty-fourth in the league in forcing turnovers.

1994–95 Prospects

The Sixers were a bad basketball team last year. Philadelphia ranked twenty-third in total points scored, twentieth in FG percentage, and twenty-second in rebounding (but fourteenth in defensive rebounding). But the Sixers were capable of surprising teams on occasion; they were 19–12 in games in which they held the other team under 100 points, 6–45 in other games.

When you're rebuilding a basketball team, you have to focus on the positives and build around them. The negatives are too easy to see. Philadelphia is competititve at small forward. Draft picks Wright and Tyler could develop into an NBA-level power forward and point guard. And Philadelphia's shooting guard is on a par with most in the NBA. The big question mark is at center. Their starting center needs to develop his low-post game and the rebounding.

This is a team that could move up—after 2 or 3 more years in the lottery. But Red Auerbach in his prime couldn't turn this team around in a year. The Sixers may have less depth than any team in the NBA, their starting power forward couldn't make half the teams in the NBA at all, and their center is unproven. They'll improve as the season goes on, but they'll return to the lottery after another losing season.

Team Directory

Owner: Harold Katz

Vice president: David Katz

GM/Head coach: John Lucas

Business manager: Gerry Ryan

Dir., player pers.: Gene Shue

Dir., public relations: Joe Favorito

1993–94 Review

EASTERN CONFERENCE				WESTERN CONFERENCE					
ATLANTIC DIV.		CENTRAL DIV.		MIDWEST DIV.			PACIFIC DIV.		
	W	L		W	L		W	L	
NY	2	3	ATL	0	4	HOU	0	2	SEA	0	2
ORL	0	4	CHI	1	3	SAN	0	2	PHO	0	2
NJ	1	3	CLE	0	4	UTAH	1	1	GS	1	1
MIA	1	4	IND	2	2	DEN	2	0	POR	0	2
BOS	1	4	CHA	1	3	MIN	0	2	LAL	1	1
PHI	-	-	DET	3	1	DAL	2	0	SAC	0	2
WAS	2	3	MIL	3	1				LAC	1	1
	7	21		10	18		5	7		3	11

1993–94 finish: 25–57 (15–26 home, 10–31 away), sixth in Atlantic Div.

1994–95 Schedule

1/4	Milwaukee	7:30 pm	1/4	@ Phoenix	9:00 pm	3/3	@ New Jersey	7:30 pm
1/5	@ Orlando	7:30 pm	1/5	@ LA Clip.	10:30 pm	3/4	Chicago	7:30 pm
1/7	@ Chicago	8:30 pm	1/7	@ Utah	9:00 pm	3/8	New Jersey	7:30 pm
1/9	Wash.	7:30 pm	1/11	Chicago	7:30 pm	3/10	San Ant.	7:30 pm
1/11	Dallas	7:30 pm	1/13	New Jersey	7:30 pm	3/12	Cleveland	1:00 pm
1/12	Orlando	7:30 pm	1/14	@ Orlando	7:30 pm	3/14	Houston	7:30 pm
1/15	@ Detroit	7:30 pm	1/16	Detroit	2:00 pm	3/16	@ San Ant.	8:30 pm
1/16	Miami	7:30 pm	1/18	@ Atlanta	7:30 pm	3/17	@ Dallas	8:30 pm
1/18	LA Clip.	7:30 pm	1/20	@ Wash.	7:30 pm	3/19	@ Houston	3:30 pm
1/22	@ Atlanta	7:30 pm	1/21	LA Lakers	7:30 pm	3/22	Gold. St.	7:30 pm
1/25	@ Minnesota	8:00 pm	1/24	@ Detroit	7:30 pm	3/24	Boston	7:30 pm
1/26	Boston	7:30 pm	1/25	Milwaukee	7:30 pm	3/25	Indiana	7:30 pm
2/2	Sacra.	7:30 pm	1/27	Phoenix	7:30 pm	3/29	Charlotte	7:30 pm
2/3	@ Cleveland	7:30 pm	1/28	@ Indiana	7:30 pm	3/31	Portland	7:30 pm
2/5	New York	7:30 pm	1/30	Seattle	7:30 pm	4/1	@ Chicago	8:30 pm
2/7	@ Miami	7:30 pm	2/1	Wash.	7:30 pm	4/4	@ Miami	7:30 pm
2/9	Indiana	7:30 pm	2/3	New York	7:30 pm	4/5	@ Charlotte	7:30 pm
2/10	@ New York	7:30 pm	2/4	@ Milwaukee	8:30 pm	4/7	@ Boston	7:30 pm
2/13	Miami	7:30 pm	2/6	Atlanta	7:30 pm	4/8	Orlando	7:30 pm
2/14	@ Milwaukee	8:30 pm	2/7	@ Cleveland	7:30 pm	4/11	Atlanta	7:30 pm
2/16	Cleveland	7:30 pm	2/15	Minnesota	7:30 pm	4/13	New Jersey	7:30 pm
2/17	Detroit	7:30 pm	2/17	@ Orlando	7:30 pm	4/15	@ New Jersey	7:30 pm
2/20	Utah	7:30 pm	2/18	Denver	7:30 pm	4/17	Charlotte	7:30 pm
2/22	@ Charlotte	7:30 pm	2/20	@ Gold. St.	10:30 pm	4/19	@ Indiana	8:30 pm
2/23	@ Boston	7:30 pm	2/22	@ LA Lakers	10:30 pm	4/21	Miami	7:30 pm
2/26	@ Portland	10:00 pm	2/23	@ Denver	8:00 pm	4/23	@ Wash.	1:00 pm
2/28	@ Seattle	10:00 pm	2/26	@ New York	6:00 pm			
2/30	@ Sacra.	10:30 pm	2/28	@ Wash.	7:30 pm			

1993–94 Team Stats

NAME	G	MIN	FG	FGA	FG%	3FG	3FGA	3FG%	FT	FTA	FT%	ORB	TRB	AST	PF	STL	BLK	TO	PTS	AVG
Weathrspn.	82	3147	602	1246	48.3	4	17	23.5	298	430	69.3	254	832	192	152	100	116	195	1506	18.4
J. Malone	27	903	187	389	48.1	4	6	66.7	76	94	80.9	23	84	59	46	14	10	28	454	16.8
Hornacek	53	1994	325	715	45.5	52	166	31.3	178	204	87.3	41	212	315	115	95	10	138	880	16.6
Barros	81	2519	412	878	46.9	135	354	38.1	116	145	80.0	28	196	424	96	107	5	167	1075	13.3
Woolridge	74	1955	364	773	47.1	1	14	7.1	208	302	68.9	103	298	139	186	41	56	142	937	12.7
Bradley	49	1385	201	491	40.9	0	3	0.0	102	168	60.7	98	306	98	170	45	147	148	504	10.3
Perry	80	2336	272	625	43.5	73	200	36.5	102	176	58.0	117	404	94	154	60	82	80	719	9.0
Dawkins	72	1343	177	423	41.8	37	105	35.2	84	100	84.0	28	123	263	74	63	5	111	475	6.6
M. Malone	55	618	102	232	44.0	0	1	0.0	90	117	76.9	106	226	34	52	11	17	59	294	5.3
Austin	14	201	29	66	43.9	0	1	0.0	14	23	60.9	25	69	17	29	5	10	17	72	5.1
Leckner	71	1163	139	286	48.6	0	2	0.0	84	130	64.6	75	282	86	190	18	34	86	362	5.1
Graham	70	889	122	305	40.0	2	25	8.0	92	110	83.6	21	86	66	54	61	4	65	338	4.8
Green	35	332	63	182	34.6	10	41	24.4	13	18	72.2	10	34	16	21	18	6	27	149	4.3
Kidd	68	884	100	169	59.2	0	0	—	47	86	54.7	76	233	19	129	19	23	44	247	3.6
Edwards	3	44	2	18	11.1	0	5	0.0	2	5	40.0	5	14	4	6	3	1	4	6	2.0
Bol	4	49	3	7	42.9	0	0	—	0	0		2	6	0	8	2	9	0	6	1.5
Curry	10	43	3	14	21.4	0	2	0.0	3	4	75.0	0	0	6	6	1	0	3	9	0.9
76ers	82	19805	3103	6819	45.5	318	942	33.8	1509	2112	71.4	1012	3406	1827	1488	663	525	1368	8033	98.0
Opp.	82	19805	3549	7338	48.4	263	795	33.1	1297	1744	74.4	1202	3809	2357	1729	806	385	1190	8658	105.6

HISTORY

TITLES

1949–50 Eastern Div. champs

1953–54 Eastern Div. champs

1954–55 Eastern Div. champs

1954–55 NBA champs

1966–67 Eastern Div. champs

1966–67 NBA champs

1976–77 Atlantic Div. champs

1976–77 Eastern Conf. champs

1977–78 Atlantic Div. champs

1979–80 Eastern Conf. champs

1981–82 Eastern Conf. champs

1982–83 Atlantic Div. champs

1982–83 Eastern Conf. champs

1982–83 NBA champs

1989–90 Atlantic Div. champs

ALL-TIME TEAM RECORDS

Career

Games played	Hal Greer	1,122	1963–73
Total points	Hal Greer	21,586	1963–73
Field goals made	Hal Greer	8,504	1963–73
Free throws made	Dolph Schayes	6,979	1948–64
Total rebounds	Dolph Schayes	6,638	1948–64
Assists	Maurice Cheeks	6,212	1978–89
Steals	Maurice Cheeks	1,942	1978–89

Season

Total points	Wilt Chamberlain	3,836	1965–66
Field goals made	Wilt Chamberlain	1,074	1965–66
Free throws made	Moses Malone	737	1984–85
Total rebounds	Wilt Chamberlain	1,957	1965–66
Assists	Maurice Cheeks	753	1985–86
Steals	Steve Mix	212	1973–74

Game

Total points	Wilt Chamberlain	68	vs. Chicago, 12/16/87
Field goals made	Wilt Chamberlain	30	vs. Chicago, 12/16/87
Free throws made	Dolph Schayes	23	vs. Minneapolis, 1/17/52
Total rebounds	Wilt Chamberlain	43	vs. Boston, 3/6/69
Assists	Maurice Cheeks	21	vs. New Jersey, 10/30/82
	Wilt Chamberlain	21	vs. Detroit, 2/2/68

LEADING COACHES

	REGULAR SEASON				PLAYOFFS		
NAME	YEARS	W	L	PCT	W	L	PCT
Billy Cunningham	1977–85	454	196	.698	66	39	.629
Al Cervi	1948–56	334	224	.599	35	29	.547
Jim Lynam	1987–92	194	173	.529	8	13	.381
Gene Shue	1973–77	157	177	.470	11	11	.500
Paul Seymour	1956–60	155	124	.556	9	11	.450

Philadelphia 76ers 1994–95 Roster

Head Coach: John Lucas

No.	Name	Pos.	Ht.	Wt.	Yrs.	Born	College
	Derrick Alston	F	6-11	225	R	8/20/72	Duquesne
3	Dana Barros	G	5-11	163	5	4/13/67	Boston College
76	Shawn Bradley	C	7-6	248	1	3/22/72	Brigham Young
12	Johnny Dawkins	G	6-2	170	8	9/28/63	Duke
20	Greg Graham	G	6-4	215	1	11/26/70	Indiana
25	Jeff Malone	G	6-4	256	11	6/28/61	Mississippi State
23	Tim Perry	F	6-9	220	6	6/4/65	Temple
	B.J. Tyler	G	6-1	185	R	4/30/71	Texas
35	Clarence Weatherspoon	F	6-7	240	2	9/8/70	So. Mississippi
42	Scott Williams	C	6-10	230	5	3/21/68	North Carolina
	Sharone Wright	C	6-11	260	R	1/30/73	Clemson

Arena Information

The Spectrum (18,168)
Tickets: 215-339-7676
Ticket prices: $45, $33, $24, $18, $10

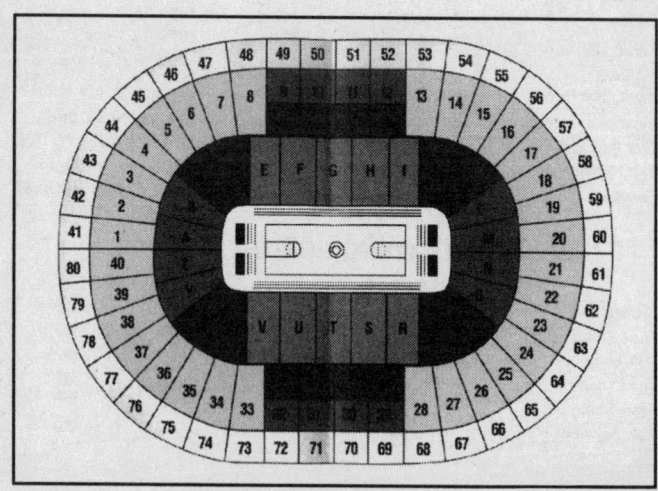

Dana Barros

No. 3/G

Full name: Dana Bruce Barros
HT: 5-11   **WT:** 163
Born: 4/13/67, Boston, MA
High school: Xaverian Brothers
  (Westwood, MA)
College: Boston College

Barros is a good ballhandler who doesn't turn over the ball a lot. He's quick, accurate from the free throw line, and he's got a good outside shot. In fact, Barros set Sixers' season records for 3-point FGs made (135) and attempted (354). '93–94 was Barros' best year, as he posted career highs in every statistical category. He also led the Sixers in assists and steals. But Barros seemed to wear down as the season went on: he averaged only 10 points per game in Philadelphia's last 22 games, shooting only 40 percent from the field. His size will always be an issue. Although he works hard on defense, bigger guards can get a good look at the basket when they have the ball.

REGULAR SEASON	G	MIN	FG	FGx	3FG	3PTx	FT	FTx	REB	AST	STL	BLK	PTS	AVG
'89-90 SEATTLE	81	1630	299	40.5	95	39.9	89	80.9	132	205	53	1	782	9.7
'90-91 SEATTLE	66	750	154	49.5	32	39.5	78	91.8	71	111	23	1	418	6.3
'91-92 SEATTLE	75	1331	238	48.3	83	44.6	60	75.9	81	125	51	4	619	8.3
'92-93 SEATTLE	69	1243	214	45.1	64	37.9	49	83.1	107	151	63	3	541	7.8
'93-94 PHILADELPHIA	81	2519	412	46.9	135	38.1	116	80.0	196	424	107	5	1075	13.3
5 YR TOTALS	372	7473	1317	45.5	409	39.8	392	82.0	587	1016	297	14	3435	9.2
'93-94 RANK NBA Gs	27	35	37	41	5	30	68	60	52	19	34	97	37	44
'94-95 PROJECTIONS	82	3189	492	47.4	171	37.2	137	78.7	243	618	136	6	1292	15.8

PLAYOFFS	G	MIN	FG	FGx	3FG	3PTx	FT	FTx	REB	AST	STL	BLK	PTS	AVG
'90-91 SEATTLE	3	25	9	69.2	2	40.0	3	75.0	4	5	3	0	23	7.7
'91-92 SEATTLE	7	96	21	52.5	10	58.8	0	---	7	8	4	0	52	7.4
'92-93 SEATTLE	16	136	22	46.8	5	31.3	6	75.0	12	12	5	0	55	3.4
TOTALS	26	257	52	52.0	17	44.7	9	75.0	23	25	12	0	130	5.0

Shawn Bradley   No. 76/C

Full name: Shawn Paul Bradley
HT: 7-6   **WT:** 248
Born: 3/22/72, Landstuhl, West
  Germany
High school: Emery County
  (Castle Dale, UT)
College: Brigham Young

Bradley's rookie season showed that he needed work in his low-post game. He needs to develop as a rebounder, too. Bradley's concentrating on blocking shots can leave him out of position for rebounding. Other times, he simply gets outmuscled under the basket. He was touted to have excellent hands and body control. But he wasn't a good ballhandler last season, and despite a reputation for having a good jumper, he demonstrated little range as a pro. It could be that he was simply overwhelmed by his first NBA season. Or that he lost his shooting touch after being out of basketball for 2 years. Bradley will doubtless be a better player than in his rookie year, but his long-term prospects at center are up in the air.

REGULAR SEASON	G	MIN	FG	FGx	3FG	3PTx	FT	FTx	REB	AST	STL	BLK	PTS	AVG
'93-94 PHILADELPHIA	49	1385	201	40.9	0	0.0	102	60.7	306	98	45	147	504	10.3
1 YR TOTALS	49	1385	201	40.9	0	0.0	102	60.7	306	98	45	147	504	10.3
'93-94 RANK NBA Cs	34	24	22	49	14	14	17	38	26	13	14	8	22	14

Jeff Malone

No. 25/G

Full name: Jeffrey Nigel Malone
HT: 6-4 **WT:** 256
Born: 6/28/61, Mobile, AL
High school: Southwest
(Macon, GA)
College: Mississippi State

Although critics claim he can only score off a pick and can't create his own shot, Malone is one of the best pure shooters in the NBA. Malone fit right in with Philadelphia on offense after his trade from Utah last season. In his 27 games for the Sixers, he led Philadelphia in scoring in 10 games, shot 50 percent or better in 16 games, and scored 20 points or more 12 times. Malone's not known as an unselfish player, and he won't be mistaken for Michael Jordan on defense. And he'll only take a 3-point shot if he's totally unguarded. Malone is fourteenth among active NBA scorers with 16,695 points and tenth all-time in free throw percentage (.870).

REGULAR SEASON		G	MIN	FG	FG%	3FG	3PT%	FT	FT%	REB	AST	STL	BLK	PTS	AVG
'83-84	WASHINGTON	81	1976	408	44.4	24	32.4	142	82.6	155	151	23	13	982	12.1
'84-85	WASHINGTON	76	2613	605	49.9	15	20.8	211	84.4	206	184	52	9	1436	18.9
'85-86	WASHINGTON	80	2992	735	48.3	3	17.6	322	86.8	289	191	70	12	1795	22.4
'86-87	WASHINGTON	80	2763	689	45.7	4	15.4	376	88.5	218	298	75	13	1758	22.0
'87-88	WASHINGTON	80	2655	648	47.6	10	41.7	335	88.2	206	237	51	13	1641	20.5
'88-89	WASHINGTON	76	2418	677	48.0	1	5.3	296	87.1	179	219	39	14	1651	21.7
'89-90	WASHINGTON	75	2567	781	49.1	1	16.7	257	87.7	206	243	48	6	1820	24.3
'90-91	UTAH	69	2466	525	50.8	1	16.7	231	91.7	206	143	50	6	1282	18.6
'91-92	UTAH	81	2922	691	51.1	1	8.3	256	89.8	233	180	56	5	1639	20.2
'92-93	UTAH	79	2558	595	49.4	3	33.3	236	85.2	173	126	42	4	1429	18.1
'93-94	UTAH-PHILA	77	2560	525	48.6	7	58.3	205	83.0	199	125	40	5	1262	16.4
11 YR TOTALS		854	28490	6879	48.5	70	25.3	2867	87.1	2269	2099	546	100	16695	19.5
'93-94	RANK NBA G's	53	33	10		20	99	2	26	34	51	95	99	97	21	19
'94-95	PROJECTIONS	77	2523	474	47.8	11	78.6	187	80.6	200	109	36	5	1146	14.9

PLAYOFFS		G	MIN	FG	FG%	3FG	3PT%	FT	FT%	REB	AST	STL	BLK	PTS	AVG
'83-84	WASHINGTON	4	71	12	46.2	0	0.0	0	---	5	2	1	0	24	6.0
'84-85	WASHINGTON	4	126	27	48.2	1	33.3	10	76.9	6	8	5	0	65	16.3
'85-86	WASHINGTON	5	197	42	40.8	0	---	26	89.7	16	17	7	3	110	22.0
'86-87	WASHINGTON	3	105	17	37.0	0	0.0	11	100.0	7	9	1	0	45	15.0
'87-88	WASHINGTON	5	199	50	51.5	0	0.0	28	75.7	17	11	5	5	128	25.6
'90-91	UTAH	9	351	71	49.3	0	0.0	44	91.7	35	29	9	1	186	20.7
'91-92	UTAH	16	610	134	48.7	1	33.3	62	86.1	39	31	8	2	331	20.7
'92-93	UTAH	5	150	29	44.6	0	---	9	69.2	16	3	3	1	67	13.4
TOTALS		51	1809	382	47.0	2	16.7	190	85.2	141	110	39	12	956	18.7

Tim Perry
No. 23/F

Full name: Timothy D. Perry
HT: 6-9   **WT:** 220
Born: 6/4/65, Freehold, NJ
High school: Freehold (NJ)
College: Temple

Perry is primarily known as a defensive force. He's an outstanding shotblocker and rebounder. But although his offense in the past was limited to dunks and putbacks, Perry became an aggressive shooter from the perimeter. He was a 36.5 percent shooter from 3-point range last season, and shot 200 3-point FGAs, over 3 times as many as he'd tried in his first 5 seasons in the NBA. Perry set records for 3-point FGs made and attempted when he was 7 for 15 from beyond the arc against Charlotte February 7. Perry also went 9 for 9 from the field on December 20 against Detroit, tying with 3 other players for the best effort in the NBA last season.

REGULAR SEASON		G	MIN	FG	FG%	3FG	3PT%	FT	FT%	REB	AST	STL	BLK	PTS	AVG
'88-89	PHOENIX	62	614	108	53.7	1	25.0	40	61.5	132	18	19	32	257	4.1
'89-90	PHOENIX	60	612	100	51.3	1	100.0	53	58.9	152	17	21	22	254	4.2
'90-91	PHOENIX	48	587	75	52.1	0	0.0	43	61.4	126	27	23	43	193	4.0
'91-92	PHOENIX	80	2483	413	52.3	3	37.5	153	71.2	551	134	44	116	982	12.3
'92-93	PHILADELPHIA	81	2104	287	46.8	10	20.4	147	71.0	409	126	40	91	731	9.0
'93-94	PHILADELPHIA	80	2336	272	43.5	73	36.5	102	58.0	404	94	60	82	719	9.0
6 YR TOTALS		411	8736	1255	48.9	88	33.0	538	65.4	1774	416	207	386	3136	7.6
'93-94 RANK NBA Fs		23	34	59	109	6	15	69	122	47	62	48	15	57	6.3
'94-95 PROJECTIONS		82	2629	270	40.4	128	39.5	83	52.5	403	89	70	75	751	9.2

PLAYOFFS		G	MIN	FG	FG%	3FG	3PT%	FT	FT%	REB	AST	STL	BLK	PTS	AVG
'88-89	PHOENIX	4	17	2	50.0	0	---	0	0.0	2	0	2	1	4	1.0
'89-90	PHOENIX	11	100	13	52.0	0	---	8	44.4	21	2	3	6	34	3.1
'91-92	PHOENIX	8	185	38	60.3	0	---	23	71.9	39	11	3	6	99	12.4
TOTALS		23	302	53	57.6	0	---	31	59.6	62	13	8	13	137	6.0

Clarence Weatherspoon

No. 35/F

HT: 6-7   **WT:** 240
Born: 9/8/70, Crawford, MS
High school: Motley (Columbus, MS)
College: Southern Mississippi

Weatherspoon is an offensive force, thanks to his ability to run the floor and his impressive leaping ability. He followed his Sixer record–setting rookie year of 1,280 points with 1,504 points last season. He was 1 of only 5 players to record 100 points, rebounds, steals, blocks and assists last season. Weatherspoon was virtually the only inside offensive threat the Sixers had last season. He led the team in virtually every offensive category, including minutes played, scoring, points, FGM, FGA, FTM, FTA, and rebounds. He was also second on the team in blocked shots and steals, and fourth in assists. Weatherspoon put up 45 double-doubles, seventh highest in the NBA and eighth highest for a Sixer in a season.

REGULAR SEASON		G	MIN	FG	FGx	3FG	3PTx	FT	FTx	REB	AST	STL	BLK	PTS	AVG
'92-93	PHILADELPHIA	82	2654	494	46.9	1	25.0	291	71.3	589	147	85	67	1280	15.6
'93-94	PHILADELPHIA	82	3147	602	48.3	4	23.5	298	69.3	832	192	100	116	1506	18.4
2 YR TOTALS		164	5801	1096	47.7	5	23.8	589	70.3	1421	339	185	183	2786	17.0
'93-94	RANK NBA Fs	1	2	7	51	54	57	11	81	9	26	15	7	9	12
'94-95	PROJECTIONS	82	3640	715	49.7	8	23.5	293	67.4	1117	243	115	176	1731	21.1

Derrick Alston   F

HT: 6-11 **WT:** 225
Born: 8/20/72, Hoboken, NJ
College: Duquesne

Alston averaged 21.3 points per game last season, and became the first person in Atlantic-10 history to lead the conference in scoring and field goal percentage (.578). He played well in postseason tournaments.

REGULAR SEASON	G	MIN	FG	FG%	3FG	3PT%	FT	FT%	REB	AST	STL	BLK	PTS	AVG
ROOKIE -- NO NBA EXPERIENCE														

Johnny Dawkins No. 12/G

Full name: Johnny Earl Dawkins, Jr.
HT: 6-2 **WT:** 170
Born: 9/28/63, Washington, DC
High school: Mackin (Washington, DC)
College: Duke

Dawkins is a pretty good ballhandler and playmaker, and is an accurate shooter from the free throw line and from outside.

REGULAR SEASON		G	MIN	FG	FG%	3FG	3PT%	FT	FT%	REB	AST	STL	BLK	PTS	AVG
'87-88	SAN ANTONIO	65	2179	405	48.5	19	31.1	198	89.6	204	480	88	2	1027	15.8
'88-89	SAN ANTONIO	32	1083	177	44.3	0	0.0	100	89.3	101	224	55	0	454	14.2
'89-90	PHILADELPHIA	81	2865	465	48.9	22	33.3	210	86.1	247	601	121	9	1162	14.3
'90-91	PHILADELPHIA	4	124	26	63.4	1	25.0	10	90.9	16	28	3	0	63	15.8
'91-92	PHILADELPHIA	82	2815	394	43.7	36	35.6	164	88.2	227	567	89	5	988	12.0
'92-93	PHILADELPHIA	74	1598	258	43.7	26	31.0	113	79.6	136	339	80	4	655	8.9
'93-94	PHILADELPHIA	72	1343	177	41.8	37	35.2	84	84.0	123	263	63	5	475	6.6
8 YR TOTALS		491	13689	2236	45.6	155	32.8	1032	85.5	1223	2792	566	28	5659	11.5
'93-94	RANK NBA Gs	75	85	90	94	55	42	89	24	90	53	73	97	88	96
'94-95	PROJECTIONS	75	1102	128	38.9	40	37.4	65	84.4	101	207	55	5	361	4.8

PLAYOFFS		G	MIN	FG	FG%	3FG	3PT%	FT	FT%	REB	AST	STL	BLK	PTS	AVG
'87-88	SAN ANTONIO	3	53	6	26.1	0	0.0	3	75.0	3	5	2	0	15	5.0
'89-90	PHILADELPHIA	10	386	53	46.1	0	0.0	36	83.7	22	93	17	2	142	14.2
TOTALS		13	439	59	42.8	0	0.0	39	83.0	25	98	19	2	157	12.1

B.J. Tyler G

HT: 6-1 **WT:** 185
Born: 4/30/71, Port Arthur, TX
College: Texas
Tyler had 480 assists and 202 steals in just 76 games at Texas. Last season's Southwest Conference Player of the Year, he led the conference in scoring (22.8 ppg), steals (87), and 3-pointers (99) as a senior.

REGULAR SEASON	G	MIN	FG	FGx	3FG	3PTx	FT	FTx	REB	AST	STL	BLK	PTS	AVG

ROOKIE -- NO NBA EXPERIENCE

Scott Williams No. 42/C

Full name: Scott Christopher Williams
HT: 6-10 **WT:** 230
Born: 3/21/68, Hacienda Heights, CA
High school: Wilson (Los Angeles, CA)
College: North Carolina
Williams adds a sorely needed defensive presence inside. He didn't play much in Chicago, but he'll get minutes in Philly.

REGULAR SEASON	G	MIN	FG	FGx	3FG	3PTx	FT	FTx	REB	AST	STL	BLK	PTS	AVG
'90-91 CHICAGO	51	337	53	51.0	1	50.0	20	71.4	98	16	12	13	127	2.5
'91-92 CHICAGO	63	690	83	48.3	0	0.0	48	64.9	247	50	13	36	214	3.4
'92-93 CHICAGO	71	1369	166	46.6	0	0.0	90	71.4	451	68	55	66	422	5.9
'93-94 CHICAGO	38	638	114	48.3	1	20.0	60	61.2	181	39	16	21	289	7.6
4 YR TOTALS	223	3034	416	47.9	2	11.8	218	66.9	977	173	96	136	1052	4.7
'93-94 RANK NBA Cs	39	32	29	31	27	34	7	9	31	28	29	34	29	21
'94-95 PROJECTIONS	21	419	88	48.4	1	25.0	44	55.7	107	27	8	10	221	10.5

PLAYOFFS	G	MIN	FG	FGx	3FG	3PTx	FT	FTx	REB	AST	STL	BLK	PTS	AVG
'90-91 CHICAGO	12	72	6	46.2	0	0.0	11	55.0	20	3	1	3	23	1.9
'91-92 CHICAGO	22	321	34	48.6	0	0.0	20	71.4	95	7	6	18	88	4.0
'92-93 CHICAGO	19	395	44	50.6	0	0.0	16	55.2	111	26	7	17	104	5.5
'93-94 CHICAGO	10	151	24	42.1	0	---	15	71.4	39	7	7	3	63	6.3
TOTALS	63	939	108	47.6	0	0.0	62	63.3	265	43	21	41	278	4.4

Sharone Wright C

HT: 6-11 **WT:** 260
Born: 1/30/73, Macon, GA
College: Clemson
His 901 career rebounds in 3 seasons is fourth in school history, behind Tree Rollins, Dale Davis, and Horace Grant (who all played 4 seasons). He was also one of the best shotblockers in college hoops.

REGULAR SEASON	G	MIN	FG	FG%	3FG	3PT%	FT	FT%	REB	AST	STL	BLK	PTS	AVG

ROOKIE -- NO NBA EXPERIENCE

John Lucas Head Coach

Full name: John Harding Lucas, Jr.
HT: 6-3 **WT:** 185
Born: 10/31/53, Durham, NC
High school: Hillside (Durham)
College: Maryland
Lucas left San Antonio to take over rebuilding the Sixers, who gave him a long-term contract as coach and GM.

YEAR	REGULAR SEASON TEAM	W	L	PCT	FINISH	PLAYOFFS W	L	PCT	
'92-93	SAN ANTONIO	39	22	.639	2nd/Midwest Div	5	5	.500	lost Western Conf. semifinals to Phoenix, 4-2
'93-94	SAN ANTONIO	55	27	.671	2nd/Midwest Div	1	3	.250	lost Western Conf. first round to Utah, 3-1
	2 YR TOTALS	94	49	.657		6	8	.429	

1994–95 Scouting Report

Frontcourt

Phoenix is loaded at forward, so they're able to rotate their frontline players. Charles Barkley always starts, when he's healthy. He's unstoppable under the basket, and he's still one of the better defensive players at his poistion. He is still hampered by back problems; he changed his mind about retiring last season, but this year looks like his last. A.C. Green plays power forward for Phoenix; he started 55 games last season and is a tough defender. He's also a solid rebounder, gets more than his share of points from putbacks of offensive rebounds, and is a decent outside shooter. Oliver Miller takes over at center for the departed Mark West. Miller, a second-year pro last season, improved his low-post game; his 60.9 shooting percentage led the team last season. Wide-body Joe Kleine will backup Miller at center. Cedric Ceballos is a tremendous baseline player who became a phenomenal scorer; he was third on the team in scoring. Richard Dumas' drug problems caused him to miss last season. He may return this season. A great open-court player, Dumas has a typical gunner's mentality: he's not much of a defender, and he won't pass the ball.

By the time you read this, the Suns may have added free agents Danny Manning and Waymon Tisdale. Danny Manning said he'd sign with Phoenix after a summer visit. He can post up or drive to the basket, plays aggressive defense, passes as well as many point guards, and rebounds well for a small forward. And Waymon Tisdale expressed interest in Phoenix, too.

Backcourt

Dan Majerle is one of the NBA's best 3-point shooters, leading the league in 3-pointers made (192) and attempted (503). He's also a great defender. Danny Ainge plays shooting guard off the bench.

He's still a threat from 3-point range, shoots free throws better than anyone on the team, and is a pretty good playmaker who can handle the ball. Kevin Johnson starts at point guard; he's the second best playmaker in the league, after John Stockton. He can penetrate or hit the jumper from mid-range, and he's great from the free throw line. Frank Johnson, a good playmaker off the bench, is a veteran who backs up Kevin Johnson at point.

Defense

Teams averaged 103.4 points against the Suns, tied for fourteenth in the NBA with Milwaukee. Defensively, Phoenix's frontcourt is pretty good. They more than held their own on the defensive glass, ranking eighth in limiting offensive rebounds. And the Suns were seventh in blocked shots. Phoenix also ranked tenth in the NBA in stealing the ball. But although Phoenix has a group of talented athletes, they play pretty soft on defense. That's why they were just nineteenth in the league in forcing turnovers, and why only two other NBA teams committed fewer fouls. And that's why opposing teams shot 47.4 percent from the floor against Phoenix, eighth highest in the league.

1994–95 Prospects

Phoenix is an offensive club that outscores their opponents. They led the league in points per game (108.2) and in assists with 27.6 per game. They're also a tough rebounding team, ranking sixth in total rebounding and eighth in defensive rebounding. They may be the most talented club in the NBA.

Phoenix stands to be an even better team this season. They lost 211 player games to injury or illness last season, one of the higher figures in the league. They'll probably get more production from Charles Barkley. And Oliver Miller is developing rapidly.

The Suns will fight it out with Seattle and Golden State for the Pacific Division title. In the competitive Western Conference, Phoenix could be eliminated in the first round as easily as they could end up in the NBA finals. But they have to be considered one of the favorites for the NBA title. They match up well against the best teams in the East, and they've been there before.

Team Directory

President/CEO: Jerry Colangelo
VP, player pers.: Dick Van Arsdale
VP/Asst. GM: Bryan Colangelo

Sr. exec. VP: Lowell Fitzsimmons
VP/CEO: Richard H. Dozer
Dir., media relations: Julie Fie

1993–94 Review

WESTERN CONFERENCE						EASTERN CONFERENCE					
MIDWEST DIV.			PACIFIC DIV.			ATLANTIC DIV.			CENTRAL DIV.		
	W	L		W	L		W	L		W	L
HOU	2	2	SEA	2	3	NY	1	1	ATL	1	1
SAN	3	1	PHO	–	–	ORL	1	1	CHI	1	1
UTAH	2	2	GS	3	2	NJ	2	0	CLE	2	0
DEN	3	1	POR	3	2	MIA	2	0	IND	1	1
MIN	4	0	LAL	2	3	BOS	1	1	CHA	0	2
DAL	4	0	SAC	4	1	PHI	2	0	DET	1	1
			LAC	5	0	WAS	2	0	MIL	2	0
	18	6		19	11		11	3		8	6

1993–94 finish: 56–26 (36–5, home, 20–21 away), second in Pacific Div.

1994–95 Schedule

11/4	@ Sacra.	10:30 pm	12/30	LA Lakers	9:00 pm	2/28	@ LA Clip.	10:30 pm
11/6	Miami	9:00 pm	1/3	@ Sacra.	10:30 pm	3/1	@ LA Lakers	10:30 pm
11/9	Atlanta	9:00 pm	1/4	Phila.	9:00 pm	3/3	Seattle	8:00 pm
11/11	@ Seattle	10:00 pm	1/7	@ Denver	9:00 pm	3/5	@ Gold. St.	3:30 pm
11/12	@ LA Clip.	10:30 pm	1/9	Milw.	9:00 pm	3/7	@ Houston	8:00 pm
11/15	@ Portland	10:00 pm	1/11	@ LA Lakers	10:30 pm	3/10	Indiana	9:00 pm
11/16	Minn.	9:00 pm	1/12	Cleveland	9:00 pm	3/12	Gold. St.	9:00 pm
11/18	Portland	9:00 pm	1/14	@ LA Clip.	10:30 pm	3/14	Detroit	9:00 pm
11/21	@ Utah	9:00 pm	1/17	Denver	9:00 pm	3/16	@ Charlotte	8:00 pm
11/23	LA Clip.	9:00 pm	1/19	@ Portland	10:00 pm	3/18	@ Atlanta	7:30 pm
11/26	San Ant.	9:00 pm	1/22	Orlando	3:30 pm	3/19	@ Miami	6:00 pm
11/27	New Jersey	9:00 pm	1/24	@ Minn.	8:00 pm	3/21	@ Orlando	8:00 pm
11/29	@ Milw.	8:30 pm	1/26	@ Indiana	7:30 pm	3/24	Houston	9:00 pm
11/30	@ Chicago	8:00 pm	1/27	@ Phila.	7:30 pm	3/28	Utah	9:00 pm
12/2	@ Boston	7:30 pm	1/29	@ New York	12:00 pm	3/30	@ Sacra.	10:30 pm
12/3	@ Detroit	7:30 pm	1/30	@ Cleveland	7:30 pm	3/31	Minn.	9:00 pm
12/6	@ Wash.	7:30 pm	2/1	LA Lakers	9:00 pm	4/2	@ San Ant.	1:30 pm
12/8	@ New Jersey	7:30 pm	2/3	Chicago	9:30 pm	4/4	@ Gold. St.	9:00 pm
12/10	@ Minn.	8:00 pm	2/5	Houston	3:30 pm	4/9	@ Portland	3:30 pm
12/12	Gold. St.	9:00 pm	2/7	@ Dallas	8:30 pm	4/11	@ Seattle	9:00 pm
12/14	Seattle	9:00 pm	2/8	@ Utah	9:00 pm	4/12	San Ant.	10:00 pm
12/16	New York	8:00 pm	2/15	Portland	9:00 pm	4/14	@ Denver	9:00 pm
12/17	Sacra.	10:00 pm	2/17	Gold. St.	8:00 pm	4/15	LA Lakers	10:00 pm
12/19	Wash.	9:00 pm	2/19	Utah	9:00 pm	4/18	Sacra.	10:00 pm
12/22	@ Houston	8:00 pm	2/21	Boston	9:00 pm	4/21	Dallas	10:00 pm
12/23	Denver	9:00 pm	2/22	@ San Ant.	8:30 pm	4/23	Seattle	3:30 pm
12/26	Dallas	9:00 pm	2/24	LA Clip.	9:00 pm			
12/27	@ Dallas	8:30 pm	2/26	Charlotte	3:30 pm			

1993–94 Team Stats

NAME	G	MIN	FG	FGA	FG%	3FG	3FGA	3FG%	FT	FTA	FT%	ORB	TRB	AST	PF	STL	BLK	TO	PTS	AVG
Barkley	65	2298	518	1046	49.5	48	178	27.0	318	452	70.4	198	727	296	160	101	37	206	1402	21.6
K. Johnson	67	2449	477	980	48.7	6	27	22.2	380	464	81.9	55	167	637	127	125	10	235	1340	20.0
Ceballos	53	1602	425	795	53.5	0	9	0.0	160	221	72.4	153	344	91	124	59	23	93	1010	19.1
Majerle	80	3207	476	1138	41.8	192	503	38.2	176	238	73.9	120	349	275	153	129	43	137	1320	16.5
Green	82	2825	465	926	50.2	8	35	22.9	266	362	73.5	275	753	137	142	70	38	100	1204	14.7
Miller	69	1786	277	455	60.9	2	9	22.2	80	137	58.4	140	476	244	230	83	156	164	636	9.2
Ainge	68	1555	224	537	41.7	80	244	32.8	78	94	83.0	28	131	180	140	57	8	81	606	8.9
West	82	1236	162	286	56.6	0	—	—	58	116	50.0	112	295	33	214	31	109	74	382	4.7
F. Johnson	70	875	134	299	44.8	2	12	16.7	54	69	78.3	29	82	148	120	41	1	65	324	4.6
Perry	27	432	42	113	37.2	0	3	0.0	21	28	75.0	12	39	125	36	25	1	43	105	3.9
Kleine	74	848	125	256	48.8	5	11	45.5	30	39	76.9	50	193	45	118	14	19	35	285	3.9
Courtney	33	168	40	78	51.3	0	0	—	23	32	71.9	14	27	9	23	3	6	10	103	3.1
Mustaf	33	196	30	84	35.7	0	0	—	13	22	59.1	20	55	8	29	4	5	10	73	2.2
Cooper	23	136	18	41	43.9	1	7	14.3	11	15	73.3	2	9	28	12	3	0	20	48	2.1
Knight	1	8	1	4	25.0	0	0	—	0	0	—	0	0	1	—	0	—	0	2	2.0
Mackey	22	69	14	37	37.8	0	2	0.0	4	8	50.0	12	24	0	9	0	3	2	32	1.5
Henry	4	15	1	5	20.0	0	2	0.0	2	4	50.0	0	2	4	—	0	0	1	4	1.0
Suns	82	19705	3429	7080	48.4	344	1042	33.0	1674	2301	72.8	1220	3673	2261	1639	745	460	1305	8876	108.2
Opp.	82	19705	3379	7135	47.4	283	863	32.8	1438	1998	72.0	1086	3333	2154	1870	748	437	1254	8479	103.4

HISTORY

TITLES

1975–76 NBA Western Conf. champs
1980–81 Pacific Div. champs
1992–93 Pacific Div. champs
1992–93 NBA Western Conf. champs

ALL-TIME TEAM RECORDS

Career

Games played	Alvan Adams	988	1975–88
Total points	Walter Davis	15,666	1977–88
Scoring average	Charlie Scott	25	1972–75
Field goals made	Walter Davis	6,497	1977–88
Field goals attempted	Walter Davis	12,497	1977–88
Free throws made	Dick Van Arsdale	3,404	1968–77
Free throws attempted	Dick Van Arsdale	4,186	1968–77
Total rebounds	Alvan Adams	6,937	1975–88
Assists	Kevin Johnson	4,674	1988–94
Steals	Alvan Adams	1,289	1975–88

Season

Total points	Tom Chambers	2,201	1989–90
Scoring average	Tom Chambers	27	1989–90
Field goals made	Tom Chambers	810	1989–90
Free throws made	Connie Hawkins	577	1969–70
Total rebounds	Paul Silas	1,015	1970–71
Assists	Kevin Johnson	991	1988–89
Steals	Ron Lee	225	1977–78

Game

Total points	Tom Chambers	60	vs. Seattle, 3/24/90
Field goals made	Tom Chambers	22	vs. Seattle, 3/24/90
Free throws made	Kevin Johnson	23	vs. Utah (OT), 4/9/90
Total rebounds	Paul Silas	27	vs. Cincinnati, 1/18/71
Assists	Kevin Johnson	25	vs. San Antonio, 4/6/94
Steals	Kevin Johnson	10	vs. Washington, 12/9/93

LEADING COACHES

NAME	REGULAR SEASON				PLAYOFFS		
	YEARS	W	L	PCT	W	L	PCT
John MacLeod	1973–87	579	543	.516	37	44	.457
Cotton Fitzsimmons	1970–72, 1988–92	314	178	.638	21	19	.525
Paul Westphal	1992–94	118	46	.720	19	15	.559
Jerry Colangelo	1970, 1972–73	59	60	.496	3	4	.429
Johnny Kerr	1968–70	31	89	.258	0	0	—

Phoenix Suns 1994–95 Roster

Head Coach: Paul Westphal

No.	Name	Pos.	Ht.	Wt.	Yrs.	Born	College
22	Danny Ainge	G	6-5	185	13	3/17/59	Brigham Young
34	Charles Barkley	F	6-6	252	10	2/20/63	Auburn
23	Cedric Ceballos	F	6-7	225	4	8/2/69	Fullerton State
11	Duane Cooper	G	6-1	185	2	6/25/69	USC
	Anthony Goldwire	G	6-1	182	R	9/6/71	Houston
45	A.C. Green	F	6-9	225	9	10/4/63	Oregon State
3	Frank Johnson	G	6-3	185	10	11/23/59	Wake Forest
7	Kevin Johnson	G	6-1	190	7	3/4/66	California
35	Joe Kleine	C	7-0	271	9	1/4/62	Arkansas
	Antonio Lang	F	6-8	205	R	5/15/72	Duke
9	Dan Majerle	G-F	6-6	220	6	9/9/65	Central Michigan
25	Oliver Miller	C	6-9	280	2	4/6/70	Arkansas
2	Elliot Perry	G	6-0	160	2	3/28/69	Memphis State
	Wesley Person	G	6-6	195	R	3/28/71	Auburn

Arena Information

America West Arena (19,023)
Tickets: 602-379-SUNS
Ticket prices: $200, $70, $44, $38, $34, $25, $19, $16, $10

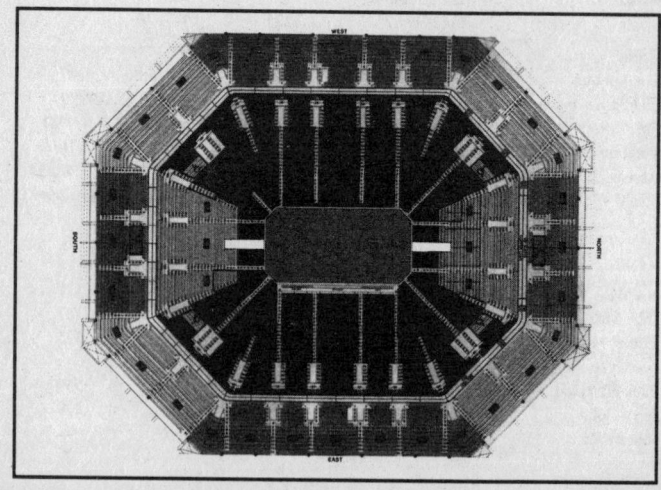

Charles Barkley

No. 34/F

Full name: Charles Wade Barkley
HT: 6-6   **WT:** 252
Born: 2/20/63, Leeds, AL
High school: Leeds (AL)
College: Auburn

Barkley is one of the best scorers and rebounders in the league. He ranks second among active players in field goal accuracy. But back problems and a torn tendon in his right knee made last season one of his worst. Playing in a career-low 65 games, Barkley shot only 49.5 percent from the field (a career-low), and averaged only 21.6 points, his lowest average in eight years. On the other hand, even a bad year for Charles Barkley is a great year for most other forwards. He would've been tenth in the league in rebounds, but he lacked the league minimums of 70 games or 800 boards needed to qualify. Even with his nagging back problems and limited games, he still scored 30 points or more 10 times, and 20 rebounds or more 5 times last season.

REGULAR SEASON		G	MIN	FG	FGx	3FG	3PTx	FT	FTx	REB	AST	STL	BLK	PTS	AVG
'84-85	PHILADELPHIA	82	2347	427	54.5	1	16.7	293	73.3	703	155	95	80	1148	14.0
'85-86	PHILADELPHIA	80	2952	595	57.2	17	22.7	396	68.5	1026	312	173	125	1603	20.0
'86-87	PHILADELPHIA	68	2740	557	59.4	21	20.2	429	76.1	994	331	119	104	1564	23.0
'87-88	PHILADELPHIA	80	3170	753	58.7	44	28.0	714	75.1	951	254	100	103	2264	28.3
'88-89	PHILADELPHIA	79	3088	700	57.9	35	21.6	602	75.3	986	325	126	67	2037	25.8
'89-90	PHILADELPHIA	79	3085	706	60.0	20	21.7	557	74.9	909	307	148	50	1989	25.2
'90-91	PHILADELPHIA	67	2498	665	57.0	44	28.4	475	72.2	680	284	110	33	1849	27.6
'91-92	PHILADELPHIA	75	2881	622	55.2	32	23.4	454	69.5	830	308	136	44	1730	23.1
'92-93	PHOENIX	76	2859	716	52.0	67	30.5	445	76.5	928	385	119	74	1944	25.6
'93-94	PHOENIX	65	2298	518	49.5	48	27.0	318	70.4	727	296	101	37	1402	21.6
10 YR TOTALS		751	27918	6259	56.2	329	25.6	4683	73.4	8734	2957	1227	717	17530	23.3
'93-94	RANK NBA Fs	96	37	16	39	16	47	8	72	13	8	14	59	12	4
'94-95	PROJECTIONS	60	2019	436	46.9	46	26.6	253	68.6	652	269	89	28	1171	19.5

PLAYOFFS		G	MIN	FG	FGx	3FG	3PTx	FT	FTx	REB	AST	STL	BLK	PTS	AVG
'84-85	PHILADELPHIA	13	408	75	54.0	4	66.7	40	63.5	144	26	23	15	194	14.9
'85-86	PHILADELPHIA	12	497	104	57.8	1	6.7	91	69.5	189	67	27	15	300	25.0
'86-87	PHILADELPHIA	5	210	43	57.3	0	---	36	80.0	63	12	4	8	123	24.6
'88-89	PHILADELPHIA	3	135	29	64.4	1	20.0	22	71.0	35	16	5	2	81	27.0
'89-90	PHILADELPHIA	10	419	88	54.3	6	33.3	65	60.2	155	43	8	7	247	24.7
'90-91	PHILADELPHIA	8	326	74	59.2	2	10.0	49	65.3	84	48	15	3	199	24.9
'92-93	PHOENIX	24	1026	230	47.7	10	22.2	168	77.1	325	102	39	25	638	26.6
'93-94	PHOENIX	10	425	110	50.9	14	35.0	42	76.4	130	48	25	9	276	27.6
TOTALS		85	3446	753	52.9	38	25.5	513	70.7	1128	362	146	84	2058	24.2

A.C. Green

No. 45/F

Full name: A.C. Green, Jr.
HT: 6-9   **WT:** 225
Born: 10/4/63, Portland, OR
High school: Benson Polytechnic (Portland)
College: Oregon State

Green had a career-high in scoring average last season, his first in Phoenix. Green scored in double figures in 66 games, broke 20 points 14 times, and broke 30 points twice. He also had the second-highest rebounding total of his career, and was Phoenix's leading rebounder last season. Green was a starter for the Suns' first 56 games, but moved to a reserve role for the final 26 games of the regular season. Green is one of the all-time Iron Men in the league; he's played in 82 games for the seventh straight season. His string of 649 consecutive regular season games is sixth-longest in NBA history, and leads all active players.

REGULAR SEASON		G	MIN	FG	FGx	3FG	3PTx	FT	FTx	REB	AST	STL	BLK	PTS	AVG
'85-86	LA LAKERS	82	1542	209	53.9	1	16.7	102	61.1	381	54	49	49	521	6.4
'86-87	LA LAKERS	79	2240	316	53.8	0	0.0	220	78.0	615	84	70	80	852	10.8
'87-88	LA LAKERS	82	2636	322	50.3	0	0.0	293	77.3	710	93	87	45	937	11.4
'88-89	LA LAKERS	82	2510	401	52.9	4	23.5	282	78.6	739	103	94	55	1088	13.3
'89-90	LA LAKERS	82	2709	385	47.8	13	28.3	278	75.1	712	90	66	50	1061	12.9
'90-91	LA LAKERS	82	2164	258	47.6	11	20.0	223	73.8	516	71	59	23	750	9.1
'91-92	LA LAKERS	82	2902	382	47.6	12	21.4	340	74.4	762	117	91	36	1116	13.6
'92-93	LA LAKERS	82	2819	379	53.7	16	34.8	277	73.9	711	116	88	39	1051	12.8
'93-94	PHOENIX	82	2825	465	50.2	8	22.9	266	73.5	753	137	70	38	1204	14.7
9 YR TOTALS		735	22347	3117	50.6	65	24.3	2281	74.7	5899	865	674	415	8590	11.7
'93-94	RANK NBA Fs	1	10	20	29	43	59	15	51	11	44	34	56	21	27
'94-95	PROJECTIONS	82	2879	522	50.1	5	19.2	257	73.2	787	154	64	39	1306	15.9

PLAYOFFS		G	MIN	FG	FGx	3FG	3PTx	FT	FTx	REB	AST	STL	BLK	PTS	AVG
'85-86	LA LAKERS	9	106	9	52.9	0	---	4	44.4	16	0	1	3	22	2.4
'86-87	LA LAKERS	18	505	71	54.6	0	---	65	74.7	142	11	9	8	207	11.5
'87-88	LA LAKERS	24	726	92	54.4	0	---	55	75.3	175	20	11	12	239	10.0
'88-89	LA LAKERS	15	502	47	41.2	0	0.0	58	76.3	137	18	16	6	152	10.1
'89-90	LA LAKERS	9	252	41	51.9	0	---	24	75.0	81	9	5	4	106	11.8
'90-91	LA LAKERS	19	400	41	42.3	4	50.0	38	70.4	102	9	12	3	124	6.5
'91-92	LA LAKERS	4	153	16	41.0	0	---	19	82.6	36	7	7	0	51	12.8
'92-93	LA LAKERS	5	220	18	42.9	0	0.0	13	61.9	73	13	7	3	49	9.8
'93-94	PHOENIX	10	350	40	48.2	7	41.2	38	61.3	84	13	10	2	125	12.5
TOTALS		113	3214	375	48.7	11	33.3	314	71.9	846	100	78	41	1075	9.5

Kevin Johnson

No. 7/G

Full name: Kevin Maurice Johnson
HT: 6-1   **WT:** 190
Born: 3/4/66, Sacramento, CA
High school: Sacramento (CA)
College: California

Johnson is one of the best point guards in the NBA. He can score (although 3-point shooting isn't his strength), he can dish assists, and he plays great defense, too. Not only did Johnson lead Phoenix in assists, he was the Suns' second-leading scorer. Johnson was also second on the team in steals, and had the Suns' second-best free throw average. Johnson set an all-time team single-game record for assists when he dished out 25 against San Antonio April 6. He's also the Suns' all-time assists leader with 4,674. Last season, Johnson had 26 double-doubles and the tenth triple-double of his career (17 points, 13 assists and 10 steals vs. Washington December 9). And Johnson made the All-Star team last season for the third time.

REGULAR SEASON		G	MIN	FG	FG%	3FG	3PT%	FT	FT%	REB	AST	STL	BLK	PTS	AVG
'87-88	CLE-PHE	80	1917	275	46.1	5	20.8	177	83.9	191	437	103	24	732	9.2
'88-89	PHOENIX	81	3179	570	50.5	2	9.1	508	88.2	340	991	135	24	1650	20.4
'89-90	PHOENIX	74	2782	578	49.9	8	19.5	501	83.8	270	846	95	14	1665	22.5
'90-91	PHOENIX	77	2772	591	51.6	9	20.5	519	84.3	271	781	163	11	1710	22.2
'91-92	PHOENIX	78	2899	539	47.9	10	21.7	448	80.7	292	836	116	23	1536	19.7
'92-93	PHOENIX	49	1643	282	49.9	1	12.5	226	81.9	104	384	85	20	791	16.1
'93-94	PHOENIX	67	2449	477	48.7	6	22.2	380	81.9	167	637	125	10	1340	20.0
7 YR TOTALS		506	17641	3312	49.4	41	19.3	2759	83.7	1635	4912	822	126	9424	18.6
'93-94	RANK NBA Gs	88	37	22	19	103	103	3	46	67	8	21	73	12	5
'94-95	PROJECTIONS	69	2547	507	48.1	7	24.1	396	81.6	156	659	134	4	1417	20.5

PLAYOFFS		G	MIN	FG	FG%	3FG	3PT%	FT	FT%	REB	AST	STL	BLK	PTS	AVG
'88-89	PHOENIX	12	494	90	49.5	3	30.0	102	92.7	51	147	19	5	285	23.8
'89-90	PHOENIX	16	582	123	47.9	2	19.2	92	82.1	53	170	25	0	340	21.3
'90-91	PHOENIX	4	146	16	30.2	1	14.3	18	60.0	13	39	2	1	51	12.8
'91-92	PHOENIX	8	335	62	48.4	3	50.0	62	86.1	33	93	12	2	189	23.6
'92-93	PHOENIX	23	914	143	48.0	0	0.0	124	79.5	62	182	35	13	410	17.8
'93-94	PHOENIX	10	427	97	45.8	3	30.0	69	85.2	35	96	10	1	266	26.6
TOTALS		73	2898	531	47.0	12	25.5	467	83.2	247	727	103	22	1541	21.1

Dan Majerle

No. 9/G-F

Full name: Daniel Lewis Majerle
HT: 6-6   **WT:** 220
Born: 9/9/65, Traverse City, MI
High school: Traverse City Senior (MI)
College: Central Michigan

Majerle, a member of Dream Team II, is a complete offensive threat. He can go inside when he wants, and is a good ballhandler and passer. As a shooting guard, Majerle was third on the team in assists, and had twice as many assists as turnovers. Majerle has tremendous shooting range; his 192 3-pointers set a new NBA record. But Majerle's 41.8 shooting percentage from the floor was the lowest of any Suns starter, and Majerle's lowest since his rookie season. Majerle's an Iron Man: he averaged 40.1 minutes per game, fifth highest in Suns' history.

REGULAR SEASON		G	MIN	FG	FGx	3FG	3PTx	FT	FTx	REB	AST	STL	BLK	PTS	AVG
'88-89	PHOENIX	54	1354	181	41.9	27	32.9	78	61.4	209	130	63	14	467	8.6
'89-90	PHOENIX	73	2244	296	42.4	19	23.8	198	76.2	430	188	100	32	809	11.1
'90-91	PHOENIX	77	2281	397	48.4	30	34.9	227	76.2	418	216	106	40	1051	13.6
'91-92	PHOENIX	82	2853	551	47.8	87	38.2	229	75.6	483	274	131	43	1418	17.3
'92-93	PHOENIX	82	3199	509	46.4	167	38.1	203	77.8	383	311	138	33	1388	16.9
'93-94	PHOENIX	80	3207	476	41.8	192	38.2	176	73.9	349	275	129	43	1320	16.5
6 YR TOTALS		448	15138	2410	45.1	522	36.8	1111	74.7	2272	1394	667	205	6453	14.4
'93-94 RANK NBA Gs		33	2	24	95	1	29	41	95	14	50	19	10	14	17
'94-95 PROJECTIONS		80	3391	473	39.4	252	39.3	150	72.5	296	275	129	46	1348	16.9

PLAYOFFS		G	MIN	FG	FGx	3FG	3PTx	FT	FTx	REB	AST	STL	BLK	PTS	AVG
'88-89	PHOENIX	12	352	63	43.8	8	28.6	38	79.2	57	14	13	4	172	14.3
'89-90	PHOENIX	16	479	73	48.7	4	33.3	51	78.5	81	34	20	2	201	12.6
'90-91	PHOENIX	4	110	12	37.5	4	36.4	14	73.7	15	7	5	1	42	10.5
'91-92	PHOENIX	7	266	48	43.2	9	27.3	25	96.2	44	20	10	0	130	18.6
'92-93	PHOENIX	24	1071	134	43.1	54	39.4	48	69.6	140	88	33	28	370	15.4
'93-94	PHOENIX	10	410	46	36.2	20	33.9	11	68.8	43	24	11	4	123	12.3
TOTALS		73	2688	376	43.0	99	35.4	187	77.0	380	187	92	39	1038	14.2

Oliver Miller

No. 25/C

Full name: Oliver J. Miller
HT: 6-9   **WT:** 280
Born: 4/6/70, Fort Worth, TX
High school: Southwest (Fort Worth)
College: Arkansas

Miller's a good passer, defender, shotblocker and rebounder. He was eighth in the league in blocked shots. He had trouble with committing fouls last season. He would have led the NBA in field goal accuracy but he lacked the league minimum of 300 FGs. Miller was second on the Suns in rebounds and fourth on the team in assists. Miller's one of the few big men who will have more assists than turnovers. He started in 30 games and averaged 11 points, 9.1 rebounds, and 2.4 blocks per game, shooting 57.3 percent from the field. Miller had 10 double-doubles last season, including one with points/assists. He looks like he will be one of the league's best centers before he's through.

REGULAR SEASON		G	MIN	FG	FGx	3FG	3PTx	FT	FTx	REB	AST	STL	BLK	PTS	AVG
'92-93	PHOENIX	56	1069	121	47.5	0	0.0	71	71.0	275	118	38	100	313	5.6
'93-94	PHOENIX	69	1786	277	60.9	2	22.2	80	58.4	476	244	83	156	636	9.2
	2 YR TOTALS	125	2855	398	56.1	2	16.7	151	63.7	751	362	121	256	949	7.6
'93-94	RANK NBA Cs	24	19	15	1	6	8	24	44	16	4	5	7	16	16
'94-95	PROJECTIONS	82	2503	504	74.3	8	44.4	89	46.0	690	408	144	203	1085	13.2

PLAYOFFS		G	MIN	FG	FGx	3FG	3PTx	FT	FTx	REB	AST	STL	BLK	PTS	AVG
'92-93	PHOENIX	24	513	71	58.7	0	0.0	31	58.4	124	51	21	59	173	7.2
'93-94	PHOENIX	10	146	16	59.3	0	...	3	42.9	44	13	6	12	35	3.5
	TOTALS	34	659	87	58.8	0	0.0	34	54.8	168	64	27	71	208	6.1

Danny Ainge　　No. 22/G

Full name: Daniel Ray Ainge
HT: 6-5　**WT:** 185
Born: 3/17/59, Eugene, OR
High school: North Eugene (OR)
College: Brigham Young
Ainge still has one of the best outside shots in the NBA. But as he gets older, he can't penetrate as well as he used to.

REGULAR SEASON		G	MIN	FG	FG%	3FG	3PT%	FT	FT%	REB	AST	STL	BLK	PTS	AVG
'90-91	PORTLAND	80	1710	337	47.2	102	40.6	114	82.6	205	285	63	13	890	11.1
'91-92	PORTLAND	81	1595	299	44.2	78	33.9	108	82.4	148	202	73	13	784	9.7
'92-93	PHOENIX	80	2163	337	46.2	150	40.3	123	84.8	214	260	69	8	947	11.8
'93-94	PHOENIX	68	1555	224	41.7	80	32.8	78	83.0	131	180	57	8	606	8.9
13 YR TOTALS		968	26381	4449	46.9	924	37.9	1571	84.9	2659	3989	1087	125	11393	11.8
'93-94 RANK NBA Gs		85	74	84	97	20	64	92	35	86	78	83	81	77	74
'94-95 PROJECTIONS		62	1312	170	39.6	62	29.8	56	82.4	98	139	48	6	458	7.4

PLAYOFFS		G	MIN	FG	FG%	3FG	3PT%	FT	FT%	REB	AST	STL	BLK	PTS	AVG
'90-91	PORTLAND	16	277	47	44.8	11	30.6	23	82.1	28	31	12	4	128	8.0
'91-92	PORTLAND	21	449	81	47.9	21	40.4	39	83.0	40	49	15	1	222	10.6
'92-93	PHOENIX	24	591	64	37.6	33	41.3	34	87.2	60	56	12	2	195	8.1
'93-94	PHOENIX	10	230	27	45.8	17	42.5	15	71.4	23	21	6	1	86	8.6
TOTALS		183	4901	698	45.5	160	39.3	286	82.7	433	646	167	19	1842	10.1

Cedric Ceballos　　No. 23/F

Full name: Cedric Z. Ceballos
HT: 6-7　**WT:** 225
Born: 8/2/69, Maui, HI
High school: Dominguez (Compton, CA)
College: Fullerton State
Ceballos is one of the best driving to the basket. He has good hands and is a decent rebounder, but he will not pass the ball.

REGULAR SEASON		G	MIN	FG	FG%	3FG	3PT%	FT	FT%	REB	AST	STL	BLK	PTS	AVG
'90-91	PHOENIX	63	730	204	48.7	1	16.7	110	66.3	150	35	22	5	519	8.2
'91-92	PHOENIX	64	725	176	48.2	1	16.7	109	73.6	152	50	16	11	462	7.2
'92-93	PHOENIX	74	1607	381	57.6	0	0.0	187	72.5	408	77	54	28	949	12.8
'93-94	PHOENIX	53	1602	425	53.5	0	0.0	160	72.4	344	91	59	23	1010	19.1
4 YR TOTALS		254	4684	1186	52.9	2	8.7	566	71.4	1054	253	151	67	2940	11.6
'93-94 RANK NBA Fs		107	66	26	14	78	78	45	60	63	63	50	88	30	11
'94-95 PROJECTIONS		43	1843	507	53.5	-1	-8.3	147	72.8	375	108	76	26	1160	27.0

PLAYOFFS		G	MIN	FG	FG%	3FG	3PT%	FT	FT%	REB	AST	STL	BLK	PTS	AVG
'90-91	PHOENIX	3	24	7	58.3	0	---	2	33.3	5	2	2	0	16	5.3
'91-92	PHOENIX	8	188	44	55.0	0	---	20	66.7	51	12	6	6	108	13.5
'92-93	PHOENIX	16	185	40	57.1	0	---	16	72.7	37	13	5	7	96	6.0
'93-94	PHOENIX	10	212	43	46.2	0	0.0	15	83.3	44	8	8	2	101	10.1
TOTALS		37	609	134	52.5	0	0.0	53	68.7	137	35	21	15	321	8.7

Frank Johnson No. 3/G

Full name: Franklin Lenard Johnson
HT: 6-1 **WT:** 185
Born: 11/23/58, Weirsdale, FL
High school: Lake Weir (Summersdale, FL)
College: Wake Forest

Johnson is a veteran playmaker. He's never been much of a scorer, but he won't make mistakes that cost points.

REGULAR SEASON	G	MIN	FG	FGx	3FG	3PTx	FT	FTx	REB	AST	STL	BLK	PTS	AVG
'88-89 HOUSTON	67	879	109	44.3	1	16.7	75	80.6	79	181	42	0	294	4.4
'92-93 PHOENIX	77	1122	136	43.6	1	8.3	59	77.6	113	186	60	7	332	4.3
'93-94 PHOENIX	70	875	134	44.8	2	16.7	54	78.3	82	148	41	1	324	4.6
10 YR TOTALS	596	12897	1947	43.9	53	21.8	990	76.0	1025	2476	570	35	4937	8.3
'93-94 RANK NBA Gs	80	112	107	65	117	121	106	67	112	87	98	125	110	113
'94-95 PROJECTIONS	71	811	133	45.2	3	23.1	46	78.0	76	137	36	0	315	4.4

PLAYOFFS	G	MIN	FG	FGx	3FG	3PTx	FT	FTx	REB	AST	STL	BLK	PTS	AVG
'88-89 HOUSTON	4	36	2	33.3	0	0.0	6	60.0	5	7	1	0	10	2.5
'92-93 PHOENIX	22	172	22	44.0	1	33.3	25	86.2	11	17	6	0	70	3.2
'93-94 PHOENIX	7	46	1	8.3	0	0.0	1	50.0	4	5	2	0	3	0.4
TOTALS	54	801	102	39.7	8	27.6	78	85.7	63	126	31	0	290	5.4

Joe Kleine No. 35/C

Full name: Joseph William Kleine
HT: 7-0 **WT:** 271
Born: 1/14/62, Colorado Springs, CO
High school: Slater (MO)
College: Arkansas

Kleine started 4 games for Phoenix; he averaged 4.8 points and 3.8 rebounds per game.

REGULAR SEASON	G	MIN	FG	FGx	3FG	3PTx	FT	FTx	REB	AST	STL	BLK	PTS	AVG
'90-91 BOSTON	72	850	102	46.8	0	0.0	54	78.3	244	21	15	14	258	3.6
'91-92 BOSTON	70	991	144	49.1	4	50.0	34	70.8	296	32	23	14	326	4.7
'92-93 BOSTON	78	1129	108	40.4	0	0.0	41	70.7	346	39	17	17	257	3.3
'93-94 PHOENIX	74	848	125	48.8	5	45.5	30	76.9	193	45	14	19	285	3.9
9 YR TOTALS	691	11431	1570	46.1	8	26.5	733	79.3	3247	460	204	237	3882	5.6
'93-94 RANK NBA Cs	19	31	31	28	4	2	39	11	32	27	35	39	34	38
'94-95 PROJECTIONS	73	727	121	51.3	8	66.7	23	79.3	140	46	12	19	273	3.7

PLAYOFFS	G	MIN	FG	FGx	3FG	3PTx	FT	FTx	REB	AST	STL	BLK	PTS	AVG
'90-91 BOSTON	5	31	4	44.4	0	---	0	---	11	1	0	0	8	1.6
'91-92 BOSTON	9	82	9	40.9	0	0.0	2	100.0	22	1	0	1	20	2.2
'92-93 BOSTON	4	29	3	60.0	0	---	0	---	5	0	0	1	6	1.5
'93-94 PHOENIX	8	81	12	42.9	0	---	4	66.7	17	3	1	4	28	3.5
TOTALS	37	412	52	49.5	0	0.0	23	79.3	100	10	4	11	127	3.4

Wesley Person   G

HT: 6-6 **WT:** 195
Born: 3/28/71, Crenshaw, AL
College: Auburn
Person is Auburn's third all-time scorer with 2,066 points, behind brother Chuck Person and former NBA star Mike Mitchell. He averaged 22.2 points per game as a senior, ranking twenty-eighth in the nation in scoring.

REGULAR SEASON	G	MIN	FG	FG%	3FG	3PT%	FT	FT%	REB	AST	STL	BLK	PTS	AVG
ROOKIE -- NO NBA EXPERIENCE														

Paul Westphal Head Coach

Full name: Paul Douglas Westphal
HT: 6-4 **WT:** 195
Born: 11/30/50, Torrance, CA
High school: Aviation (Redondo Beach, CA)
College: Southern California
It took Westphal 140 games to win 100 games, fourth fastest head coach behind Red Auerbach, Pat Riley, and Bill Russell.

	REGULAR SEASON				PLAYOFFS				
YEAR	TEAM	W	L	PCT	FINISH	W	L	PCT	
'92-93	PHOENIX	62	20	.756	1st/Pacific Div.	13	11	.542	lost NBA Finals to Chicago, 4-2
'93-94	PHOENIX	56	26	.683	2nd/Pacific Div.	6	4	.600	lost Western Conf. semifinal to Houston, 4-3
	2 YR TOTALS	118	46	.720		19	15	.559	

Portland
TRAIL BLAZERS ⊚ *BLAZERS*

1994–95 Scouting Report

Frontcourt

Cliff Robinson is Portland's best frontcourt player. At 6-10 and 225 pounds, he can play all three frontcourt positions. Robinson was Portland's leading scorer and second-leading rebounder. Buck Williams starts at power forward. Williams led Portland in rebounding, and only takes high percentage shots. He's a tough defensive player, although he's not a good free throw shooter. Portland needs a first-rate defensive center. They're hoping they will get a contribution from Chris Dudley, who's a good rebounder. Unfortunately, Dudley is not a threat from the floor, and simply cannot shoot free throws. If Portland needs offense at center, they'll either play Robinson there or put in Mark Bryant. Harvey Grant was expected to be a scorer at forward, but is attempting to bounce back from a disappointing '93–94 season. Reserves include Jerome Kersey and Tracy Murray, who led the NBA in 3-point shooting last season, going 50 for 10 for a 45.9 percentage.

Backcourt

Rod Strickland returns from an excellent '93–94 campaign. He averaged 9 assists per game (sixth in the NBA), along with 17.2 points per game, both career highs. Shooting guard Clyde Drexler has been injury prone over the past 2 seasons and is starting to show signs of age. He shot only 42.8 percent from the floor while averaging 19.2 points per game. Terry Porter comes off the bench. Porter lost his starting job to Strickland, but he's still a fine playmaker. Porter can play both guard positions, and has a great shot from outside. Reserves include rookie Aaron McKie, swingman Jaren Jackson, and reserve point guard James Robinson. McKie was one of the draft's top prospects at shooting guard, and Jackson scores a lot of points for his limited minutes in a reserve role. Robinson is an explosive scorer who turns the ball over too much for a point guard.

Defense

Portland is an offensive team, not a defensive team. They're a good rebounding team that tied for second in limiting offensive rebounds. But thanks to their torrid offensive pace, they still allowed 7,057 shots from the field, ninth highest total in the league. Opposing teams averaged 104.6 points against the Blazers, 18th in the NBA, and shot 46.9 percent from the floor against Portland, 15th in the league. Portland gets good defensive play from their guard, so the Blazers ranked eleventh in the NBA in stealing the ball and seventh in the league in forcing turnovers.

1994–95 Prospects

Last season, the Blazers averaged 107.2 points per game, third highest in the NBA. Portland also ranked third in rebounding (seventh in defensive rebounding). But they were only twenty-first in field goal percentage, hitting only 45.4 percent; the only winning team that shot worse from the field was New Jersey. They went 27–8 vs. lottery teams (including just 2–3 against Washington and ex-Blazer Kevin Duckworth).

New coach P.J. Carlesimo knows that Portland needs to retool for the rest of the '90s. Portland is a team of gunners that tries to outscore the opposition. That can be successful against Eastern teams used to walking the ball up on offense. But athletic teams that can play Portland's game can wear them out. And Portland should tire more easily than ever this season. Key players like Clyde Drexler and Buck Williams are over 30, and it's tough to play at a wide-open pace for extended minutes at their age. But Portland doesn't have enough physical athletes to play successfully at a slower pace.

The Blazers may make the playoffs virtually by default; 8 teams go, and the other competition for the last playoff spot include the Clippers, Lakers, Kings, Minnesota, and Dallas. The Blazers are getting old and tired, but they'll be superior to these pretenders for one more season. Unfortunately, though, they match up really poorly against the West's top teams (going 4–14 against Seattle, Houston, Phoenix, and San Antonio). So they'll probably have an early playoff exit once again.

Team Directory

Chairman: Paul Allen   Vice chairman: Jody Patton
Pres., bus. affairs: Marshall Glickman   Pres./GM: Bob Whitsitt
VP, player pers.: Brad Greenberg   Dir., media services: John Lashway

1993–94 Review

WESTERN CONFERENCE							EASTERN CONFERENCE						
MIDWEST DIV.			PACIFIC DIV.				ATLANTIC DIV.			CENTRAL DIV.			
	W	L		W	L			W	L			W	L
HOU	0	4	SEA	1	4		NY	0	2	ATL	1	1	
SAN	1	3	PHO	2	3		ORL	0	2	CHI	2	0	
UTAH	1	3	GS	2	3		NJ	2	0	CLE	0	2	
DEN	3	1	POR	–	–		MIA	2	0	IND	1	1	
MIN	4	0	LAL	5	0		BOS	1	1	CHA	2	0	
DAL	3	1	SAC	4	1		PHI	2	0	DET	2	0	
			LAC	3	2		WAS	2	0	MIL	1	1	
	12	12		17	13			9	5			9	5

1993–94 finish: 47–35 (30–11 home, 17–24 away), fourth in Pacific Div.

1994–95 Schedule

11/4	@ LA Clip.	11:00 pm	1/6	@ Boston	7:30 pm	3/7	@ Milw.	8:30 pm
11/5	LA Clip.	10:00 pm	1/7	@ Wash.	7:30 pm	3/9	@ Miami	7:30 pm
11/10	@ Sacra.	10:30 pm	1/9	LA Lakers	10:00 pm	3/10	@ Orlando	7:30 pm
11/15	Phoenix	10:00 pm	1/11	Gold. St.	10:00 pm	3/12	@ Minn.	3:30 pm
11/17	Cleveland	10:00 pm	1/15	@ Seattle	9:00 pm	3/14	Miami	10:00 pm
11/18	@ Phoenix	9:00 pm	1/17	@ Sacra.	10:30 pm	3/16	Boston	10:00 pm
11/20	Detroit	10:00 pm	1/19	Phoenix	10:00 pm	3/18	@ Denver	9:00 pm
11/22	@ Houston	8:30 pm	1/20	@ LA Clip.	10:30 pm	3/21	Wash.	10:00 pm
11/23	@ San Ant.	8:30 pm	1/22	Sacra.	10:00 pm	3/22	@ LA Lakers	10:30 pm
11/25	@ Dallas	8:30 pm	1/24	@ New York	7:30 pm	3/24	Seattle	10:00 pm
11/27	Indiana	10:00 pm	1/26	@ Detroit	7:30 pm	3/26	Denver	8:00 pm
11/29	Utah	10:00 pm	1/27	@ Cleveland	7:30 pm	3/28	Atlanta	10:00 pm
12/2	San Ant.	10:00 pm	1/30	New Jersey	10:00 pm	3/30	@ New Jersey	7:30 pm
12/4	Milw.	10:00 pm	2/1	San Ant.	10:00 pm	3/31	@ Phila.	7:30 pm
12/9	Gold. St.	10:00 pm	2/3	@ Minn.	8:00 pm	4/2	@ Indiana	3:30 pm
12/11	Sacra.	10:00 pm	2/6	Houston	10:00 pm	4/4	Minn.	10:00 pm
12/12	@ Utah	9:00 pm	2/8	Chicago	10:00 pm	4/7	Houston	10:00 pm
12/14	LA Clip.	10:00 pm	2/14	@ Dallas	8:30 pm	4/9	Phoenix	3:30 pm
12/15	@ Seattle	10:00 pm	2/15	@ Phoenix	9:00 pm	4/11	@ San Ant.	8:30 pm
12/18	New York	8:00 pm	2/17	Seattle	10:00 pm	4/13	@ Houston	8:30 pm
12/20	Orlando	10:00 pm	2/19	@ LA Lakers	10:00 pm	4/15	Dallas	10:00 pm
12/23	Dallas	10:00 pm	2/21	Minn.	10:00 pm	4/17	@ Seattle	10:00 pm
12/26	Phila.	10:00 pm	2/22	@ Gold. St.	10:30 pm	4/18	Gold. St.	10:30 pm
12/27	@ Sacra.	10:30 pm	2/24	Utah	10:00 pm	4/20	LA Lakers	10:00 pm
12/29	Denver	10:00 pm	2/27	LA Clip.	10:00 pm	4/22	@ LA Lakers	10:30 pm
12/30	@ Denver	9:00 pm	3/2	Charlotte	10:00 pm	4/23	Gold. St.	10:00 pm
01/3	@ Atlanta	7:30 pm	3/4	@ Utah	3:30 pm			
01/4	@ Charlotte	7:30 pm	3/6	@ Chicago	8:30 pm			

1993–94 Team Stats

NAME	G	MIN	FG	FGA	FG%	3FG	3FGA	3FG%	FT	FTA	FT%	ORB	TRB	AST	PF	STL	BLK	TO	PTS	AVG
C. Robinson	82	2853	641	1404	45.7	13	53	24.5	352	460	76.5	164	550	159	263	118	111	169	1647	20.1
Drexler	68	2334	473	1105	42.8	71	219	32.4	286	368	77.7	154	445	333	202	98	34	167	1303	19.2
Strickland	82	2889	528	1093	48.3	2	10	20.0	353	471	74.9	122	370	740	171	147	24	257	1411	17.2
Porter	77	2074	348	836	41.6	110	282	39.0	204	234	87.2	45	215	401	132	79	18	166	1010	13.1
Grant	77	2112	356	774	46.0	2	7	28.6	84	131	64.1	109	351	107	179	70	49	56	798	10.4
Williams	81	2636	291	524	55.5	0	1	0.0	201	296	67.9	315	843	80	239	58	47	111	783	9.7
Murray	66	820	167	355	47.0	50	109	45.9	50	72	69.4	43	111	31	76	21	20	37	434	6.6
Kersey	78	1276	203	469	43.3	1	8	12.5	101	135	74.8	130	331	75	213	71	49	63	508	6.5
Bryant	79	1441	185	384	48.2	0	0	0.0	72	104	69.2	117	315	37	187	32	29	66	442	5.6
J. Robinson	58	673	104	285	36.5	23	73	31.5	45	67	67.2	34	78	68	69	30	15	52	276	4.8
Jackson	29	187	34	87	39.1	0	6	0.0	12	14	85.7	6	17	27	20	4	2	14	80	2.8
Dudley	6	86	6	25	24.0	0	0	—	2	4	50.0	16	24	5	18	4	3	2	14	2.3
Smith	43	316	29	72	40.3	0	0	—	18	38	47.4	40	99	4	47	12	6	12	76	1.8
Thompson	14	58	6	14	42.9	0	1	0.0	1	2	50.0	7	13	3	11	0	2	5	13	0.9
Blazers	82	19755	3371	7427	45.4	272	770	35.3	1781	2396	74.3	1302	3762	2070	1827	744	409	1210	8795	107.3
Opp.	82	19755	3311	7057	46.9	296	830	35.7	1661	2216	75.0	1016	3497	2094	1944	654	393	1391	8579	104.6

HISTORY

TITLES

1976–77 Western Conf. champs
1976–77 NBA champs
1977–78 Pacific Div. champs
1989–90 Western Conf. champs

1990–91 Pacific Div. champs
1991–92 Pacific Div. champs
1991–92 Western Conf. champs

ALL-TIME TEAM RECORDS

Career

Games played	Clyde Drexler	826	1983–94
Total points	Clyde Drexler	17,136	1983–94
Field goals made	Clyde Drexler	6,584	1983–94
Free throws made	Clyde Drexler	3,591	1983–94
Total rebounds	Clyde Drexler	5,105	1983–94
Assists	Terry Porter	5,186	1985–94
Steals	Clyde Drexler	1,721	1983–94

Season

Total points	Clyde Drexler	2,185	1987–88
Field goals made	Clyde Drexler	849	1987–88
Free throws made	Kiki Vandeweghe	523	1985–86
Total rebounds	Lloyd Neal	967	1972–73
Assists	Terry Porter	831	1987–88
Steals	Larry Steele	217	1973–74

Game

Points	Geoff Petrie	51	vs. Houston, 3/16/73
	Geoff Petrie	51	vs. Houston, 1/20/73
Field goals made	Clyde Drexler	20	vs. New York, 1/22/89
	Lionel Hollins	20	vs. Boston, 2/22/77
	Geoff Petrie	20	vs. Philadelphia, 3/20/74
	Geoff Petrie	20	vs. Golden State, 2/8/73
Free throws made	Kiki Vandeweghe	18	vs. Seattle, 3/21/86
	Geoff Petrie	18	vs. Seattle, 3/19/71
Rebounds	Sidney Wicks	27	vs. Los Angeles, 2/26/75
Assists	Terry Porter	19	vs. Utah, 2/26/75
Steals	Clyde Drexler	10	vs. Milwaukee, 1/10/86
	Larry Steele	10	vs. LA Lakers, 11/16/74

LEADING COACHES

		REGULAR SEASON				PLAYOFFS	
NAME	YEARS	W	L	PCT	W	L	PCT
Jack Ramsay	1976–86	453	367	.552	29	30	.492
Rick Adelman	1989–94	291	154	.654	36	33	.522
Mike Schuler	1986–89	127	84	.602	2	6	.250
Lenny Wilkens	1974–76	75	89	.457	0	0	—
Jack McCloskey	1972–74	48	116	.293	0	0	—

Portland Trail Blazers 1994–95 Roster

Head Coach: P.J. Carlesimo

No.	Name	Pos.	Ht.	Wt.	Yrs.	Born	College
2	Mark Bryant	F	6-9	245	6	4/25/65	Seton Hall
22	Clyde Drexler	G	6-7	222	11	6/22/62	Houston
24	Chris Dudley	C	6-11	240	7	2/22/65	Yale
44	Harvey Grant	F	6-9	235	6	7/4/65	Oklahoma
21	Jaren Jackson	G-F	6-6	200	4	10/27/67	Georgetown
25	Jerome Kersey	F	6-7	225	10	6/26/62	Longwood
23	Aaron McKie	G	6-5	209	R	10/2/72	Temple
31	Tracy Murray	F	6-7	228	2	7/25/71	UCLA
30	Terry Porter	G	6-3	195	9	4/8/63	Wis.-Stevens Point
3	Clifford Robinson	F	6-10	225	5	12/16/66	Connecticut
26	James Robinson	G	6-2	180	1	8/31/70	Alabama
43	Shawnelle Scott	C	6-10	250	R	6/16/72	St. John's
1	Rod Strickland	G	6-3	185	6	7/11/66	DePaul
35	Kevin Thompson	C	6-11	260	1	2/7/71	NC State
52	Buck Williams	F	6-8	225	13	3/8/60	Maryland

Arena Information

Memorial Coliseum (12,888)
Tickets: 503-234-9291 (Portland home games have been sold out for
17 straight seasons.)

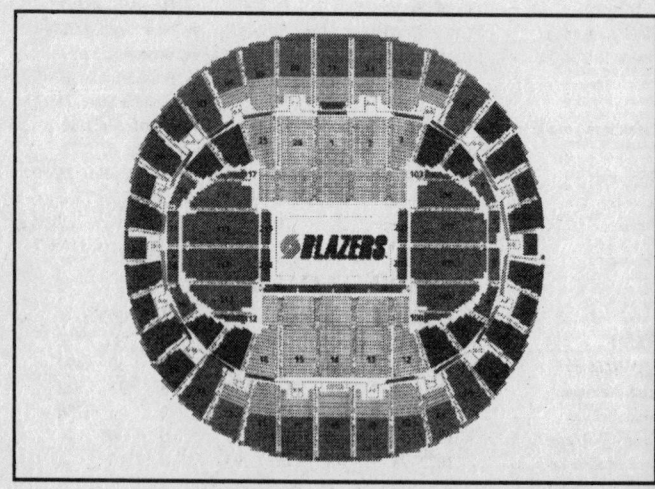

Clyde Drexler

No. 22/G

HT: 6-7   **WT:** 222
Born: 11/7/63, New Orleans, LA
High school: Sterling (Houston, TX)
College: Houston

Drexler has been one of the best shooting guards in the NBA. He ranks first or second in 17 different all-time Portland statistical categories. And among active players, he's one of the 15 best active scorers and one of the 10 career assist leaders. But age and injuries are taking their toll on his game. He's had knee and hamstring problems the past 2 seasons that have kept him from being the same "Clyde the Glide" who once drove the lane for layups and dunks. Last season, Drexler shot just 42.8 percent from the field, a new career low. (His previous low was 42.9 percent in '92–93.) He's relying more on shots from the perimeter. Still, Drexler is an all-around player. He was Portland's second-leading scorer, and was third on the team in rebounds, assists, and steals.

REGULAR SEASON		G	MIN	FG	FG%	3FG	3PT%	FT	FT%	REB	AST	STL	BLK	PTS	AVG
'85-86	PORTLAND	75	2576	542	47.5	12	20.0	293	76.9	421	600	197	46	1389	18.5
'86-87	PORTLAND	82	3114	707	50.2	11	23.4	357	78.0	518	566	204	71	1782	21.7
'87-88	PORTLAND	81	3060	849	50.6	11	21.2	476	81.1	533	467	203	52	2185	27.0
'88-89	PORTLAND	78	3064	829	49.6	27	26.0	438	79.9	615	450	213	54	2123	27.2
'89-90	PORTLAND	73	2683	670	49.4	30	28.3	333	77.4	507	432	145	51	1703	23.3
'90-91	PORTLAND	82	2852	645	48.2	61	31.9	416	79.4	546	493	144	60	1767	21.5
'91-92	PORTLAND	76	2751	694	47.0	114	33.7	401	79.4	500	512	138	70	1903	25.0
'92-93	PORTLAND	49	1671	350	42.9	31	23.3	245	83.9	309	278	95	37	976	19.9
'93-94	PORTLAND	68	2334	473	42.8	71	32.4	286	77.7	445	333	98	34	1303	19.2
11 YR TOTALS		826	28068	6584	48.0	377	29.2	3591	78.6	5105	4725	1721	572	17136	20.7
'93-94 RANK NBA Gs		85	42	25	87	25	66	12	72	4	40	40	13	18	8
'94-95 PROJECTIONS		70	2383	454	41.4	83	35.0	267	75.9	461	304	85	25	1258	18.0

PLAYOFFS		G	MIN	FG	FG%	3FG	3PT%	FT	FT%	REB	AST	STL	BLK	PTS	AVG
'85-86	PORTLAND	4	145	26	45.6	2	40.0	18	78.3	25	26	6	3	72	18.0
'86-87	PORTLAND	4	153	36	45.6	1	25.0	23	79.3	30	15	7	3	96	24.0
'87-88	PORTLAND	4	170	32	38.6	3	50.0	21	72.4	28	21	12	2	88	22.0
'88-89	PORTLAND	3	128	35	49.3	0	0.0	13	76.5	20	25	6	2	83	27.7
'89-90	PORTLAND	21	853	172	44.1	9	22.0	96	77.4	151	150	53	16	449	21.4
'90-91	PORTLAND	16	633	128	47.6	15	26.8	76	77.6	129	129	34	16	347	21.7
'91-92	PORTLAND	21	847	198	46.6	19	23.5	139	80.7	155	147	31	20	553	26.3
'92-93	PORTLAND	3	116	18	41.9	5	41.7	16	80.0	19	14	5	3	57	19.0
'93-94	PORTLAND	4	157	31	42.5	3	23.1	19	82.6	41	22	8	2	84	21.0
TOTALS		94	3626	746	45.0	59	25.9	464	79.2	670	640	190	79	2015	21.4

Harvey Grant

No. 44/F

HT: 6-9   **WT:** 235
Born: 7/4/65, Augusta, GA
High school: Hancock Central
   (Sparta, GA)
College: Oklahoma

Harvey Grant is Horace Grant's twin brother, but he's not strong enough to be the same kind of inside player. He's a good defensive player, but he'll only grab 5 rebounds a game. He makes a bigger contribution on offense. Grant runs the court, is a fine passer and ballhandler, and has a good mid-range jumper. Last season was an off-year for Grant; he'd averaged over 18 points per game in his last 3 seasons with the Bullets, but managed only 10.4 points per game as a starter in his first season with Portland. He struggled all season to find his shot: he shot just 46 percent from the field, a career low, and his 64.1 percent from the free throw line was his worst since his rookie year. Grant's a scorer at the prime of his career, and he could come back strong this season.

REGULAR SEASON		G	MIN	FG	FG%	3FG	3PT%	FT	FT%	REB	AST	STL	BLK	PTS	AVG
'88-89	WASHINGTON	71	1193	181	46.4	0	0.0	34	59.6	163	79	35	29	396	5.6
'89-90	WASHINGTON	81	1846	284	47.3	0	0.0	96	70.1	342	131	52	43	664	8.2
'90-91	WASHINGTON	77	2842	609	49.8	2	13.3	185	74.3	557	204	91	61	1405	18.2
'91-92	WASHINGTON	64	2398	489	47.8	1	12.5	176	80.0	432	170	74	27	1155	18.0
'92-93	WASHINGTON	72	2667	560	48.7	1	10.0	218	72.7	412	205	72	44	1339	18.6
'93-94	PORTLAND	77	2112	356	46.0	2	28.6	84	64.1	351	107	70	49	798	10.4
6 YR TOTALS		442	13048	2479	48.0	6	12.2	793	72.5	2257	896	394	253	5757	13.0
'93-94 RANK NBA Fs		43	44	39	77	62	40	83	110	60	54	34	39	51	55
'94-95 PROJECTIONS		80	1895	288	44.7	2	33.3	48	59.3	310	73	67	50	626	7.8

PLAYOFFS		G	MIN	FG	FG%	3FG	3PT%	FT	FT%	REB	AST	STL	BLK	PTS	AVG
'93-94	PORTLAND	4	76	17	51.5	0	---	0	---	9	3	1	2	34	8.5
TOTALS		4	76	17	51.5	0	---	0	---	9	3	1	2	34	8.5

Clifford Robinson

No. 3/F

Full name: Clifford Ralph Robinson
HT: 6-10   **WT:** 225
Born: 12/16/66, Buffalo, NY
High school: Riverside (Buffalo)
College: Connecticut

This second-round pick in the '89 draft has become one of the best all-around players in the NBA. He can run the floor, score driving to the hoop or popping mid-range jumpers, rebounds and block shots. '92–93's Sixth Man of the Year, Robinson assumed starting responsibilities last season and responded with the best season of his career. Portland's leading scorer and second leading rebounder, Robinson ranked sixteenth in the NBA in scoring and thirty-eighth in rebounds. His 1.44 steals per game ranked thirty-eighth in the NBA, and his 1.35 blocks per game ranked twenty-second. He's now fifth on Portland's all-time career blocked shots list.

REGULAR SEASON		G	MIN	FG	FG%	3FG	3PT%	FT	FT%	REB	AST	STL	BLK	PTS	AVG
'89-90	PORTLAND	82	1565	298	39.7	12	27.3	138	55.0	308	72	53	53	746	9.1
'90-91	PORTLAND	82	1940	373	46.3	6	31.6	205	65.3	349	151	78	76	957	11.7
'91-92	PORTLAND	82	2124	398	46.6	1	9.1	219	66.4	416	137	95	107	1016	12.4
'92-93	PORTLAND	82	2575	632	47.3	19	24.7	287	69.0	542	182	98	163	1570	19.1
'93-94	PORTLAND	82	2853	641	45.7	13	24.5	352	76.5	550	159	118	111	1647	20.1
5 YR TOTALS		410	11057	2342	45.5	51	25.0	1201	67.8	2165	701	432	510	5936	14.5
'93-94	RANK NBA F:	1	9	4	84	37	53	6	34	28	39	6	9	4	8
'94-95	PROJECTIONS	82	3170	726	45.5	14	25.0	420	81.9	598	157	136	100	1886	23.0

PLAYOFFS		G	MIN	FG	FG%	3FG	3PT%	FT	FT%	REB	AST	STL	BLK	PTS	AVG
'89-90	PORTLAND	21	391	54	35.8	0	0.0	29	55.8	87	23	19	24	137	6.5
'90-91	PORTLAND	16	354	63	53.8	1	33.3	38	55.1	63	18	7	16	165	10.3
'91-92	PORTLAND	21	522	91	46.2	1	16.7	44	57.1	88	43	22	21	227	10.8
'92-93	PORTLAND	4	131	16	26.2	0	0.0	9	40.9	17	6	6	7	41	10.3
'93-94	PORTLAND	4	149	28	41.2	2	22.2	7	87.5	25	10	3	6	65	16.3
TOTALS		66	1547	252	42.4	4	17.4	127	55.7	280	100	57	74	635	9.6

Rod Strickland

No. 1/G

Full name: Rodney Strickland
HT: 6-3   **WT:** 185
Born: 7/11/66, Bronx, NY
High school: Oak Hill Academy (Mouth of Wilson, VA)
College: DePaul

Strickland may be the most underrated point guard in the NBA. He can score, rebound, and control the pace. Last season was Strickland's best. He led Portland in assists and steals, and was their third leading scorer. Strickland's 9.0 assists per game ranked sixth in the NBA, and his 1.79 steals per game ranked eighteenth. And his 740 assists (a new career-high) were the second most ever by a Blazer in a single season, behind Terry Porter's 831 in '87–88. He's not a great shooter from outside, but he had the good judgment to attempt just 10 shots from 3-point range. Strickland has improved every season, and has thrived since his arrival in Portland.

REGULAR SEASON		G	MIN	FG	FGx	3FG	3PTx	FT	FTx	REB	AST	STL	BLK	PTS	AVG
'88-89	NEW YORK	81	1358	265	46.7	19	32.2	172	74.5	160	319	98	3	721	8.9
'89-90	NY-SAC	82	2140	343	45.4	8	26.7	174	62.6	259	468	127	14	868	10.6
'90-91	SAN ANTONIO	58	2076	314	48.2	11	33.3	161	76.3	219	463	117	11	800	13.8
'91-92	SAN ANTONIO	57	2053	300	45.5	5	33.3	182	68.7	265	491	118	17	787	13.8
'92-93	PORTLAND	78	2474	396	48.5	4	13.3	273	71.7	337	559	131	24	1069	13.7
'93-94	PORTLAND	82	2889	528	48.3	2	20.0	353	74.9	370	740	147	24	1411	17.2
6 YR TOTALS		438	12990	2146	47.2	49	27.7	1315	71.6	1610	3040	738	93	5656	12.9
'93-94	RANK NBA Gs	1	9	9	21	117	113	4	92	11	5	13	24	8	15
'94-95	PROJECTIONS	82	3212	634	48.8	-1	33.3	439	77.3	412	870	156	27	1706	20.8

PLAYOFFS		G	MIN	FG	FGx	3FG	3PTx	FT	FTx	REB	AST	STL	BLK	PTS	AVG
'88-89	NEW YORK	9	111	22	44.9	1	100.0	9	52.9	13	25	4	1	54	6.0
'89-90	SAN ANTONIO	10	384	54	42.5	0	0.0	15	55.6	53	112	14	0	123	12.3
'90-91	SAN ANTONIO	4	168	29	43.3	0	0.0	17	81.0	21	35	9	0	75	18.8
'91-92	SAN ANTONIO	2	80	13	59.1	0	---	5	62.5	7	19	3	2	31	15.5
'92-93	PORTLAND	4	156	22	42.3	0	0.0	10	83.3	26	37	5	2	54	13.5
'93-94	PORTLAND	4	154	36	50.0	0	0.0	22	81.5	16	39	4	2	94	23.5
TOTALS		33	1053	176	45.2	1	6.3	78	69.6	136	267	39	7	431	13.1

Buck Williams

No. 52/F

Full name: Charles Linwood Williams

HT: 6-8   **WT:** 225

Born: 3/8/60, Rocky Mount, NC

High school: Rocky Mount (NC)

College: Maryland

Williams is one of 20 players to post 10,000 points and 10,000 rebounds in his career. Williams is a terrific rebounder and plays good defense down low. He always takes shots from close in, so he always shoots for a high percentage. Last season's 55.5 percentage from the field was tops on the Trail Blazers, and would have been fourth in the NBA had he had enough games to qualify. Williams also led the team in rebounds and was Portland's sixth-leading scorer. His 10.4 rebounds per game ranked sixteenth in the NBA. The biggest knock on his game is that he's never been a very good free throw shooter. But he's a hard-working, solid citizen who plays within his abilities and is always a team player.

REGULAR SEASON		G	MIN	FG	FGx	3FG	3PTx	FT	FTx	REB	AST	STL	BLK	PTS	AVG
'83-84	NEW JERSEY	81	3003	495	53.5	0	0.0	284	57.0	1000	130	81	125	1274	15.7
'84-85	NEW JERSEY	82	3182	577	53.0	1	25.0	336	62.5	1005	167	63	110	1491	18.2
'85-86	NEW JERSEY	82	3070	500	52.3	0	0.0	301	67.6	986	131	73	96	1301	15.9
'86-87	NEW JERSEY	82	2976	521	55.7	0	0.0	430	73.1	1023	129	78	91	1472	18.0
'87-88	NEW JERSEY	70	2637	466	56.0	1	100.0	346	66.8	834	109	68	44	1279	18.3
'88-89	NEW JERSEY	74	2446	373	53.1	0	0.0	213	66.6	696	78	61	36	959	13.0
'89-90	PORTLAND	82	2801	413	54.8	0	0.0	288	70.6	800	116	69	39	1114	13.6
'90-91	PORTLAND	80	2582	358	60.2	0	---	217	70.5	751	97	47	47	933	11.7
'91-92	PORTLAND	80	2519	340	60.4	0	0.0	221	75.4	704	108	62	41	901	11.3
'92-93	PORTLAND	82	2498	270	51.1	0	0.0	138	64.5	690	81	61	61	678	8.3
'93-94	PORTLAND	81	2636	291	55.5	0	0.0	201	67.9	843	80	58	47	793	9.7
13 YR TOTALS		1040	36136	5653	55.4	2	8.3	3541	66.3	11364	1452	916	931	14849	14.3
'93-94	RANK NBA Fs	15	20	56	6	78	78	30	91	8	68	52	45	53	59
'94-95	PROJECTIONS	81	2679	277	55.7	0	0.0	209	67.4	912	74	51	44	763	9.4

PLAYOFFS		G	MIN	FG	FGx	3FG	3PTx	FT	FTx	REB	AST	STL	BLK	PTS	AVG
'83-84	NEW JERSEY	11	473	63	48.5	0	---	45	55.6	155	16	15	17	171	15.5
'84-85	NEW JERSEY	3	123	26	65.0	0	---	22	73.3	32	1	3	5	74	24.7
'85-86	NEW JERSEY	3	126	21	72.4	0	---	20	76.9	31	2	6	1	62	20.7
'89-90	PORTLAND	21	776	101	50.8	0	---	71	67.6	193	39	13	6	273	13.0
'90-91	PORTLAND	16	572	65	50.0	0	---	35	60.3	143	14	10	4	165	10.3
'91-92	PORTLAND	21	758	66	50.8	0	---	69	75.8	179	22	27	17	201	9.6
'92-93	PORTLAND	4	119	11	47.8	0	---	13	68.4	29	1	1	3	35	8.8
'93-94	PORTLAND	4	125	19	67.9	0	---	13	86.7	35	2	4	2	51	12.8
TOTALS		87	3236	397	52.4	0	---	311	67.6	841	104	82	59	1105	12.7

Mark Bryant   No. 2/F

Full name: Mark Craig Bryant
HT: 6-9   **WT:** 245
Born: 4/25/65, Glen Ridge, NJ
High school: Columbia (Maplewood, NJ)
College: Seton Hall

Bryant is a good rebounder who's not afraid to mix it up. His shooting range is limited; he's only tried 6 3-pointers in 6 years.

REGULAR SEASON		G	MIN	FG	FG%	3FG	3PT%	FT	FT%	REB	AST	STL	BLK	PTS	AVG
'90-91	PORTLAND	53	781	99	48.8	0	0.0	74	73.3	190	27	15	12	272	5.1
'91-92	PORTLAND	56	800	95	48.0	0	0.0	40	66.7	201	41	26	8	230	4.1
'92-93	PORTLAND	80	1396	186	50.3	0	0.0	104	70.3	324	41	37	23	476	6.0
'93-94	PORTLAND	79	1441	185	48.2	0	0.0	72	69.2	315	37	32	29	442	5.6
	6 YR TOTALS	382	5783	755	48.6	0	0.0	358	67.3	1355	192	148	88	1868	4.9
'93-94	RANK NBA Fs	30	73	80	53	78	78	82	41	68	103	89	76	83	95
'94-95	PROJECTIONS	82	1642	211	47.7	0	0.0	66	70.2	339	34	32	38	488	6.0

PLAYOFFS		G	MIN	FG	FG%	3FG	3PT%	FT	FT%	REB	AST	STL	BLK	PTS	AVG
'90-91	PORTLAND	14	137	10	45.5	0	---	14	87.5	32	2	2	1	34	2.4
'91-92	PORTLAND	12	116	10	34.5	0	---	3	75.0	29	1	3	0	23	1.9
'92-93	PORTLAND	4	83	17	45.9	0	---	5	100.0	18	0	0	3	39	9.8
'93-94	PORTLAND	4	64	5	29.4	0	0.0	0	---	12	2	2	2	10	2.5
	TOTALS	47	560	60	43.5	0	0.0	28	84.8	120	8	10	8	148	3.1

Chris Dudley   No. 24/C

Full name: Christen Guilford Dudley
HT: 6-11   **WT:** 240
Born: 2/22/65, Stamford, CT
High school: Torrey Pines (Encinitas, CA)
College: Yale

Portland signed Dudley to give them rebounding help. He's not a scorer and may be the worst free throw shooter in the NBA.

REGULAR SEASON		G	MIN	FG	FG%	3FG	3PT%	FT	FT%	REB	AST	STL	BLK	PTS	AVG
'88-89	CLEVELAND	61	544	73	43.5	0	0.0	39	36.4	157	21	9	23	185	3.0
'89-90	CLE-NJ	64	1356	146	83	0	0	58	64.24	423	39	41	72	350	5.5
'90-91	NEW JERSEY	61	1560	170	40.8	0	---	94	53.4	511	37	39	153	434	7.1
'91-92	NEW JERSEY	82	1902	190	40.3	0	---	80	46.8	739	58	38	179	460	5.6
'92-93	NEW JERSEY	71	1398	94	35.3	0	---	57	51.8	513	16	17	103	245	3.5
'93-94	PORTLAND	6	86	6	24.0	0	---	2	50.0	24	5	4	3	14	2.3
	7 YR TOTALS	400	7359	744	40.4	0	0.0	370	45.1	2511	199	161	552	1858	4.6
'93-94	RANK NBA Cs	not ranked -- didn't appear in 25 games in '93-94													
'94-95	PROJECTIONS	71	1309	58	29.0	0	---	41	52.6	492	3	9	91	157	2.2

PLAYOFFS		G	MIN	FG	FG%	3FG	3PT%	FT	FT%	REB	AST	STL	BLK	PTS	AVG
'88-89	CLEVELAND	1	4	0	0.0	0	---	0	---	0	0	0	0	0	0.0
'91-92	NEW JERSEY	4	77	5	35.7	0	---	4	50.0	25	3	2	10	14	3.5
'93-94	PORTLAND	4	81	4	40.0	0	---	1	50.0	15	0	6	0	9	2.3
	TOTALS	13	186	11	37.9	0	---	6	50.0	46	5	8	10	28	2.2

Jerome Kersey   No. 25/F

HT: 6-7   **WT:** 225
Born: 6/26/62, Clarksville, VA
High school: Bluestone Sr. (Skipwith, VA)
College: Longwood
Kersey's 43.3 percent field goal shooting percentage was a career-low. He was particularly foul-prone last season, averaging 6.7 fouls per 40 minutes.

REGULAR SEASON		G	MIN	FG	FGx	3FG	3PTx	FT	FTx	REB	AST	STL	BLK	PTS	AVG
'90-91	PORTLAND	73	2359	424	47.8	4	30.8	232	70.9	481	227	101	76	1084	14.8
'91-92	PORTLAND	77	2553	398	46.7	1	12.5	174	66.4	633	243	114	71	971	12.6
'92-93	PORTLAND	65	1719	281	43.8	8	28.6	116	63.4	406	121	80	41	686	10.6
'93-94	PORTLAND	78	1276	203	43.3	1	12.5	101	74.8	331	75	71	49	508	6.5
10 YR TOTALS		768	20617	3778	48.0	27	19.6	1976	69.6	4822	1680	1007	587	9559	12.4
'93-94	RANK NBA Fs	40	85	72	111	69	73	70	43	66	70	33	39	75	86
'94-95	PROJECTIONS	82	817	127	42.2	0	0.0	66	79.5	222	39	50	37	320	3.9

PLAYOFFS		G	MIN	FG	FGx	3FG	3PTx	FT	FTx	REB	AST	STL	BLK	PTS	AVG
'90-91	PORTLAND	16	588	105	46.5	0	---	76	75.2	111	49	28	7	286	17.9
'91-92	PORTLAND	21	756	131	51.0	0	0.0	79	69.3	162	75	41	19	341	16.2
'92-93	PORTLAND	4	98	22	52.4	1	100.0	12	70.6	34	4	4	2	57	14.3
'93-94	PORTLAND	3	38	5	31.3	0	---	1	20.0	9	0	1	1	11	3.7
TOTALS		88	2731	519	47.5	1	9.1	315	72.1	587	202	138	61	1354	15.4

Aaron McKie   G

HT: 6-5   **WT:** 209
Born: 10/2/72, Philadelphia, PA
College: Temple
One of the draft's top shooting guard prospects, McKie averaged 18.8 points and 7.2 rebounds as a senior. He was Atlantic-10 Conference Player of the Year as a junior.

REGULAR SEASON	G	MIN	FG	FGx	3FG	3PTx	FT	FTx	REB	AST	STL	BLK	PTS	AVG

ROOKIE -- NO NBA EXPERIENCE

Terry Porter　　No. 30/G

HT: 6-3　**WT:** 195
Born: 4/8/63, Milwaukee, WI
High school: South Division (Milwaukee)
College: Wisconsin-Stevens Point

Even though he's a reserve, Porter was among the NBA leaders in free throw shooting, 3-point shooting, and assists.

REGULAR SEASON		G	MIN	FG	FGx	3FG	3PTx	FT	FTx	REB	AST	STL	BLK	PTS	AVG
'90-91	PORTLAND	81	2665	486	51.5	130	41.5	279	82.3	282	649	158	12	1381	17.0
'91-92	PORTLAND	82	2784	521	46.1	128	39.5	315	85.6	255	477	127	12	1485	18.1
'92-93	PORTLAND	81	2883	503	45.4	143	41.4	327	84.3	316	419	101	10	1476	18.2
'93-94	PORTLAND	77	2074	348	41.6	110	39.0	204	87.2	215	401	79	18	1010	13.1
	9 YR TOTALS	723	23208	3896	47.3	722	38.2	2497	85.0	2539	5186	1152	90	11018	15.2
'93-94	RANK NBA Gs	53	56	51	101	15	26	27	11	47	22	58	42	43	45
'94-95	PROJECTIONS	75	1690	273	38.9	95	39.2	149	88.2	176	337	59	19	790	10.5

PLAYOFFS		G	MIN	FG	FGx	3FG	3PTx	FT	FTx	REB	AST	STL	BLK	PTS	AVG
'90-91	PORTLAND	16	595	102	50.0	17	36.2	68	86.1	44	105	24	1	289	18.1
'91-92	PORTLAND	21	870	147	51.6	37	47.4	119	83.2	97	141	22	3	450	21.4
'92-93	PORTLAND	4	152	27	39.7	3	15.8	9	81.8	20	8	4	0	66	16.5
'93-94	PORTLAND	4	76	12	34.3	6	42.9	11	78.6	12	9	4	0	41	10.3
	TOTALS	81	2999	506	48.3	111	38.9	385	83.5	288	523	106	12	1508	18.6

P.J. Carlesimo　Head Coach

Carlesimo left the head coaching job at Seton Hall to take over the reins with Portland. His '89 team came within seconds of capturing the NCAA Championship. Carlesimo's professional coaching experience includes a stint as an assistant with the Dream Team under Chuck Daly. He reportedly has a five-year, $7.8 million contract at Portland.

		REGULAR SEASON			PLAYOFFS			
YEAR	TEAM	W	L	PCT	FINISH	W	L	PCT

no prior NBA head-coaching experience

Sacramento
KINGS

1994–95 Scouting Report

Frontcourt

Small forward Lionel Simmons is Sacramento's best frontcourt player. He can score, rebound, pass, and play strong defense. Olden Polynice filled a gaping void at center, becoming a top rebounder and improving as a scorer. Trevor Wilson is a reserve who can rebound and play defense. Center Duane Causwell, a shotblocking specialist who never distinguished himself as a starter, will play in a reserve role this season. The Kings needed a power forward who can bang under the boards, so they signed free agent Frank Brickowski as a short-term fix. They also loaded up on power forwards in the draft, selecting Lawrence Funderburke, Michael Smith, and Brian Grant. Funderburke had 131 blocked shots during his college career, Smith is the only player to lead the Big East Conference in rebounding 3 straight years, and Grant was Midwestern Collegiate Conference Player of the Year his junior and senior years.

Backcourt

Mitch Richmond is perhaps the best shooting guard in the NBA. He's an all-around scoring talent, although he has problems with turnovers and plays lackluster defense. Spud Webb will probably start at point guard again this season. Webb is known for his fearless drives to the basket, and he's not afraid to take shots at crunch time. Bobby Hurley is Sacramento's future at point, and he'll get as much playing time as he can handle. But he'll have to overcome his size (6-0, 165), his lack of speed, and any lingering effects from the auto accident that wiped out most of his '93–94 season. The Kings lacked a perimeter shooter off the bench; if he gains some consistency, it could be Walt Williams, a swingman who can hit the 3-pointer or drive to the basket. Randy Brown can contribute defense off the bench. And LaBradford Smith is also available to play point guard.

His scoring has improved, but he's never been a first-rate NBA playmaker.

Defense

Sacramento simply couldn't keep opponents from doing what they wanted on offense. Sacramento ranked just twenty-third in blocked shots and twenty-second in the NBA in stealing the ball. The Kings were also weak on the defensive glass; they were just twentieth in preventing offensive rebounds. If you can't disrupt your opponents offense, and give up a lot of high-percentage second shots, you'll allow a lot of points. Last season, opposing teams shot 47.9 percent from the floor against Sacramento, fifth highest in the league. And they averaged 106.9 points against the Kings, third highest in the NBA. Not only did the Kings play soft D, they also committed a lot of fouls: their 1,979 personal fouls were the sixth highest total in the NBA last year.

1994–95 Prospects

The Kings lost 54 games last season for the same reason they lost 57 the season before: serious injuries to key players, and no depth. Sacramento lost a total of 226 games due to player illness or injury. When you don't have a lot of quality players, and you lose key ones to injury, you end up having to search for players who can compete. That's what Coach Gary St. Jean did, going through 20 different starting lineups last season. Still, the Kings improved by 3 games. In fact, last season's 28–54 record is the fourth best in team history since they moved to Sacramento. And by beating the Clippers by one game, the Kings avoided last place in the division for the first time since '88–89. They were 18–12 vs. lottery teams, and occasionally surprised the league's better teams at home on an off-night.

Sacramento has several problems to overcome: they have too many players who can't shoot (last season's 45.2 percent was twenty-second in the league and worst by a Kings team in 19 seasons). They have far too many players on the bench who have never proven that they can be consistent NBA players. But the Kings will be a tougher team on the blocks this season (barring injury), and that will improve their woeful defense. They don't shape up to as a playoff threat, but they'll probably surprise more than a few teams this year.

Team Directory

Managing gen. partner: Jim Thomas   President: Rick Benner

VP, basketball oper.: Geoff Petrie   VP, arena operations: Mike Duncan

VP, mktg.: Michael A. McCullough   Dir., media rel.: Travis Stanley

1994–94 Review

WESTERN CONFERENCE						EASTERN CONFERENCE					
MIDWEST DIV.		PACIFIC DIV.				ATLANTIC DIV.			CENTRAL DIV.		
W	L		W	L			W	L		W	L
HOU	0	4	SEA	0	5	NY	0	2	ATL	0	2
SAN	1	3	PHO	1	4	ORL	0	2	CHI	1	1
UTAH	1	3	GS	1	4	NJ	1	1	CLE	0	2
DEN	2	2	POR	1	4	MIA	1	1	IND	0	2
MIN	2	2	LAL	4	1	BOS	1	1	CHA	1	1
DAL	2	2	SAC	–	–	PHI	2	0	DET	1	1
			LAC	2	3	WAS	2	0	MIL	1	1
	8	16		9	21		7	7		4	10

1993–94 finish: 28–54 (20–21 home, 8–33 away), sixth in Pacific Div.

1994–95 Schedule

1/4	Phoenix	10:30 pm	1/5	Detroit	10:30 pm	3/7	Utah	10:30 pm	
1/9	@ Seattle	10:00 pm	1/7	Miami	10:30 pm	3/9	Indiana	10:30 pm	
1/10	Portland	10:30 pm	1/10	@ Minn.	8:00 pm	3/10	@ Utah	9:00 pm	
1/12	Atlanta	10:30 pm	1/11	@ Milw.	8:30 pm	3/12	@ LA Clip.	6:00 pm	
1/15	@ Houston	8:30 pm	1/13	@ Chicago	8:30 pm	3/14	Dallas	10:30 pm	
1/17	@ Dallas	8:30 pm	1/15	@ Boston	7:00 pm	3/16	@ Denver	9:00 pm	
1/20	Cleveland	9:00 pm	1/17	Portland	10:30 pm	3/17	Gold. St.	10:30 pm	
1/23	New Jersey	10:30 pm	1/19	Gold. St.	10:30 pm	3/19	@ LA Lakers	10:00 pm	
1/25	Denver	10:30 pm	1/21	@ LA Clip.	10:30 pm	3/20	Denver	10:30 pm	
1/27	Utah	9:00 pm	1/22	@ Portland	10:00 pm	3/22	@ Cleveland	7:30 pm	
1/29	@ Miami	7:30 pm	1/24	Dallas	10:30 pm	3/24	@ Indiana	7:30 pm	
1/30	@ Orlando	7:30 pm	1/25	@ Utah	9:00 pm	3/26	@ Minn.	3:30 pm	
2/2	@ Phila.	7:30 pm	1/28	@ Dallas	8:30 pm	3/28	Orlando	10:30 pm	
2/3	@ New Jersey	8:00 pm	1/31	San Ant.	10:30 pm	3/30	Phoenix	10:30 pm	
2/6	Milw.	10:30 pm	2/2	Chicago	10:30 pm	3/31	@ Seattle	10:00 pm	
2/8	Seattle	8:00 pm	2/4	@ San Ant.	8:30 pm	4/4	Houston	10:30 pm	
2/10	Gold. St.	10:30 pm	2/8	Houston	10:30 pm	4/6	San Ant.	10:30 pm	
2/11	@ Portland	10:00 pm	2/14	Boston	10:30 pm	4/8	LA Clip.	10:30 pm	
2/13	@ Gold. St.	10:30 pm	2/16	LA Lakers	10:30 pm	4/11	@ LA Clip.	10:30 pm	
2/15	New York	10:30 pm	2/18	LA Clip.	10:30 pm	4/12	LA Lakers	10:30 pm	
2/17	@ Phoenix	10:00 pm	2/20	@ Detroit	7:30 pm	4/14	@ San Ant.	8:30 pm	
2/20	Wash.	10:30 pm	2/22	@ Charlotte	7:30 pm	4/15	@ Houston	8:30 pm	
2/22	Minn.	10:30 pm	2/23	@ New York	7:30 pm	4/18	@ Phoenix	10:00 pm	
2/23	@ LA Lakers	10:30 pm	2/25	@ Wash.	7:30 pm	4/20	Gold. St.	10:30 pm	
2/26	@ Seattle	10:00 pm	2/27	@ Atlanta	7:30 pm	4/21	Seattle	10:30 pm	
2/27	Portland	10:30 pm	3/1	Minn.	10:30 pm	4/23	@ Denver	9:00 pm	
2/30	Phila.	10:30 pm	3/3	@ LA Lakers	10:30 pm				
3/3	Phoenix	10:30 pm	3/5	Charlotte	9:00 pm				

1993–94 Team Stats

NAME	G	MIN	FG	FGA	FG%	3FG	3FGA	3FG%	FT	FTA	FT%	ORB	TRB	AST	PF	STL	BLK	TO	PTS	AVG
Richmond	78	2897	635	1428	44.5	127	312	40.7	426	511	83.4	70	286	313	211	103	17	216	1823	23.4
Tisdale	79	2557	552	1102	50.1	0	0	—	215	266	80.8	159	560	139	290	37	52	124	1319	16.7
Simmons	75	2702	436	996	43.8	6	17	35.3	251	323	77.7	168	562	305	189	104	50	183	1129	15.1
Webb	79	2567	373	810	46.0	55	164	33.5	204	251	81.3	44	222	528	182	93	23	168	1005	12.7
Williams	57	1356	226	580	39.0	38	132	28.8	148	233	63.5	71	235	132	200	52	23	145	638	11.2
Polynice	31	1052	124	256	48.4	0	1	0.0	55	99	55.6	151	353	19	81	18	31	29	303	9.8
Wilson	52	1095	168	349	48.1	0	2	0.0	79	141	56.0	108	245	60	106	33	10	87	415	8.0
Chilcutt	46	974	152	328	46.3	0	1	0.0	31	52	59.6	100	271	71	116	43	28	56	335	7.3
Hurley	19	499	54	146	37.0	2	16	12.5	24	30	80.0	6	34	115	28	13	1	48	134	7.1
Spencer	23	286	43	100	43.0	0	0	—	52	73	71.2	26	61	19	37	18	5	19	138	6.0
Smith	59	829	116	288	40.3	21	60	35.0	48	64	75.0	29	76	104	88	37	4	49	301	5.1
Brown	61	1041	110	251	43.8	0	4	0.0	53	87	60.9	40	112	133	132	63	14	75	273	4.5
Causwell	41	674	71	137	51.8	0	0	—	40	68	58.8	68	186	11	109	19	49	33	182	4.4
Peplowski	55	667	76	141	53.9	0	1	0.0	24	44	54.5	49	169	24	131	17	25	34	176	3.2
Les	18	169	13	34	38.2	8	18	44.4	11	13	84.6	5	13	39	16	7	1	11	45	2.5
Burns	23	143	22	55	40.0	0	0	—	12	23	52.2	13	30	9	33	6	3	7	56	2.4
Breuer	26	247	8	26	30.8	0	1	0.0	3	14	21.4	15	56	8	30	6	19	9	19	0.7
Kings	82	19755	3179	7027	45.2	257	729	35.3	1676	2292	73.1	1122	3471	2029	1979	669	355	1333	8291	101.1
Opp.	82	19755	3360	7017	47.9	277	771	35.9	1767	2448	72.2	1189	3763	2052	1895	746	498	1341	8764	106.9

HISTORY

TITLES

950–51 Western Div. champs
950–51 NBA champs

ALL-TIME TEAM RECORDS

Career

Games played	Sam Lacey	888	1970–82
Total points	Oscar Robertson	22,009	1960–70
Field goals made	Oscar Robertson	7,713	1960–70
Free throws made	Oscar Robertson	6,583	1960–70
Total rebounds	Sam Lacey	9,353	1970–82
Assists	Oscar Robertson	7,731	1960–70
Steals	Sam Lacey	950	1970–82

Season

Total points	Nate Archibald	2,719	1972–73
Field goals made	Nate Archibald	1,028	1972–73
Free throws made	Oscar Robertson	800	1963–64
Total rebounds	Jerry Lucas	1,668	1965–66
Assists	Nate Archibald	910	1972–73
Steals	Brian Taylor	199	1976–77

Game

Total points	Jack Twyman	59	vs. Minneapolis, 1/15/60
Field goals made	Mike Woodson	22	vs. Houston, 2/20/83
	Nate Archibald	22	vs. Houston, 2/13/73
	Jack Twyman	22	vs. St. Louis, 2/28/59
Free throws made	Nate Archibald	23	vs. Portland, 1/21/75
	Nate Archibald	23	vs. Detroit, 2/5/72
Rebounds	Jerry Lucas	40	vs. Philadelphia, 2/29/64
Assists	Phil Ford	22	vs. Milwaukee, 2/21/79
	Oscar Robertson	22	vs. New York, 3/5/66
	Oscar Robertson	22	vs. Syracuse, 10/29/61
Steals	Danny Ainge	8	vs. LA Clippers, 4/22/89
	Sam Lacey	8	vs. Portland, 2/5/75

LEADING COACHES

	REGULAR SEASON				PLAYOFFS		
NAME	**YEARS**	**W**	**L**	**PCT**	**W**	**L**	**PCT**
Les Harrison	1948–55	295	181	.620	19	20	.487
Cotton Fitzsimmons	1978–84	248	244	.504	9	17	.346
Phil Johnson	1973–78	236	305	.436	2	7	.222
Jack McMahon	1963–67	187	134	.583	8	15	.348
ob Cousy	1969–73	141	209	.403	0	0	—

Sacramento Kings 1994–95 Roster

Head Coach: Garry St. Jean

No.	Name	Pos.	Ht.	Wt.	Yrs.	Born	College
40	Frank Brickowski	F-C	6-9	248	10	8/14/59	Penn State
3	Randy Brown	G	6-3	190	3	5/22/68	New Mexico State
31	Duane Causwell	C	7-0	240	4	5/31/68	Temple
	L. Funderburke	F	6-9	230	R	12/15/70	Ohio State
	Brian Grant	F	6-9	254	R	3/5/72	Xavier
7	Bobby Hurley	G	6-0	165	1	6/28/71	Duke
54	Mike Peplowski	F-C	6-10	270	1	10/15/70	Michigan State
0	Olden Polynice	C	7-0	250	7	11/21/64	Virginia
2	Mitch Richmond	G	6-5	215	6	6/30/65	Kansas State
22	Lionel Simmons	F	6-7	210	4	11/14/68	La Salle
15	LaBradford Smith	G	6-3	205	3	4/3/69	Louisville
	Michael Smith	F	6-8	230	R	3/28/72	Providence
4	Spud Webb	G	5-7	133	9	7/13/63	North Carolina St.
42	Walt Williams	G-F	6-8	230	2	4/16/70	Maryland
21	Trevor Wilson	F	6-8	215	2	3/16/68	UCLA

Arena Information

Arco Arena II (17,317)
Tickets: 916-928-6900, 916-923-BASS, 916-928-TIXX
Ticket prices: $42, $41, $40, $39, $38, $34, $29.50, $26,$21, $20, $17,
$16, $13, $8

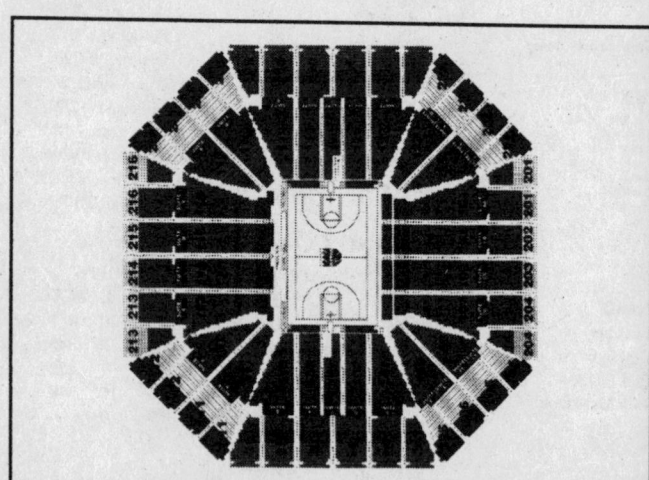

Frank Brickowski

No. 40/F-C

Full name: Francis Anthony Brickowski

HT: 6-9   **WT:** 248

Born: 8/15/59, Bayville, NY

High school: Locust Valley (NY)

College: Penn State

Free-agent signee Frank Brickowski is a well-traveled veteran who is a strong inside player. He gets his share of points and rebounds, and he's a pretty good passer for a big man. Last season, his 222 assists ranked second among Eastern Conference centers. Brickowski isn't very fast, but he's surprisingly quick. He's got a strong move to the basket, shoots for a high percentage, and plays solid defense. Last season, he averaged 17.9 points, 7.7 rebounds, 4.2 assists, and 1.5 steals per 40 minutes played. Brickowski will be 35 this season, and he's played in the slower-paced Eastern Conference for the past 4 seasons. It remains to be seen if he'll be up to playing a full season in the faster-paced Western Conference.

REGULAR SEASON		G	MIN	FG	FG%	3FG	3PT%	FT	FT%	REB	AST	STL	BLK	PTS	AVG
'84-85	SEATTLE	78	1115	150	49.2	0	0.0	85	66.9	260	100	34	15	385	4.9
'85-86	SEATTLE	40	311	30	51.7	0	—	18	66.7	54	21	11	7	78	2.0
'86-87	LAL-SA	44	487	63	89.72	6	8.333	50	158.7	116	17	20	6	176	8.2
'87-88	SAN ANTONIO	70	2227	425	52.8	1	20.0	268	76.8	483	266	74	36	1119	16.0
'88-89	SAN ANTONIO	64	1822	337	51.5	0	0.0	201	71.5	406	131	102	35	875	13.7
'89-90	SAN ANTONIO	78	1438	211	54.5	0	0.0	95	67.4	327	105	66	37	517	6.6
'90-91	MILWAUKEE	75	1912	372	52.7	0	0.0	198	79.8	426	131	86	43	942	12.6
'91-92	MILWAUKEE	65	1556	306	52.4	3	50.0	125	76.7	344	122	60	23	740	11.4
'92-93	MILWAUKEE	66	2075	456	54.5	8	30.8	195	72.8	405	196	80	27	1115	16.9
'93-94	MIL-CHA	71	2094	368	48.8	4	20.0	195	76.8	404	222	80	20	935	13.2
	10 YR TOTALS	651	15037	2718	52.1	16	22.5	1430	74.2	3225	1311	613	273	6882	10.6
'93-94	RANK NBA Fs	74	46	35	45	54	64	32	33	47	18	26	78	36	31
'94-95	PROJECTIONS	72	2222	362	46.2	4	16.7	212	78.2	409	261	82	20	940	13.1

PLAYOFFS		G	MIN	FG	FG%	3FG	3PT%	FT	FT%	REB	AST	STL	BLK	PTS	AVG
'87-88	SAN ANTONIO	3	113	22	50.0	1	100.0	13	68.4	22	14	6	2	58	19.3
'88-89	SAN ANTONIO	10	161	31	57.4	0	—	17	65.4	44	11	8	1	79	7.9
'90-91	MILWAUKEE	3	110	24	53.3	0	0.0	7	50.0	26	3	1	2	55	18.3
	TOTALS	16	384	77	53.8	1	33.3	37	62.7	92	28	15	5	192	12.0

Olden Polynice

No. 0/C

HT: 7-0   **WT:** 250
Born: 11/21/64, Port-au-Prince, Haiti
High school: All Hallows Institute
   (Bronx, NY)
College: Virginia

The Kings are Polynice's fourth team, but he appears to have found a home in Sacramento. Polynice came to the Kings from Detroit in exchange for Pete Chilcutt, a conditional first-round pick, and the Kings's second round pick in the '94 draft. Polynice averaged 11.9 rebounds per game last season, ranking fifth in the NBA in rebounding. That was the highest rebounding average by a Kings player since Sam Lacey's 12.6 in '75–76. Polynice was also thirteenth in the league in field goal percentage. He led the Kings in rebounding 23 times and pulled down double-figure rebounds 46 times. Polynice had 33 double-doubles, including 12 in a Sacramento uniform.

REGULAR SEASON		G	MIN	FG	FGx	3FG	3PTx	FT	FTx	REB	AST	STL	BLK	PTS	AVG
'87-88	SEATTLE	82	1080	118	46.5	0	0.0	101	63.9	330	33	32	26	337	4.1
'88-89	SEATTLE	80	835	91	50.6	0	0.0	51	59.3	206	21	37	30	233	2.9
'89-90	SEATTLE	79	1085	156	54.0	1	50.0	47	47.5	300	15	25	21	360	4.6
'90-91	SEA-LAC	79	2092	316	56.0	0	0.0	146	57.9	553	42	43	32	778	9.8
'91-92	LA CLIPPERS	76	1834	244	51.9	0	0.0	125	62.2	536	46	45	20	613	8.1
'92-93	DETROIT	67	1299	210	49.0	0	0.0	66	46.5	418	29	31	21	486	7.3
'93-94	DET-SAC	68	2402	346	52.3	0	0.0	97	50.8	809	41	42	67	789	11.6
7 YR TOTALS		531	10627	1481	52.0	1	9.1	633	56.1	3152	227	255	217	3596	6.8
'93-94	RANK NBA Cs	27	8	11	15	14	14	18	49	7	31	17	20	12	12
'94-95	PROJECTIONS	66	2857	400	52.8	0	0.0	92	50.3	1017	42	41	99	892	13.5

PLAYOFFS		G	MIN	FG	FGx	3FG	3PTx	FT	FTx	REB	AST	STL	BLK	PTS	AVG
'87-88	SEATTLE	5	44	5	45.5	0	---	0	0.0	8	0	3	0	10	2.0
'88-89	SEATTLE	8	162	25	61.0	0	---	7	53.8	62	1	6	4	57	7.1
'91-92	LA CLIPPERS	5	63	7	58.3	0	---	2	33.3	18	2	1	1	16	3.2
TOTALS		18	269	37	57.8	0	---	9	42.9	88	3	10	5	83	4.6

Mitch Richmond

No. 2/G

Full name: Mitchell James Richmond
HT: 6-5   **WT:** 215
Born: 6/30/65, Fort Lauderdale, FL
High school: Boyd Anderson (Fort Lauderdale)
College: Kansas State

Richmond can score from anywhere. He can stick jumpers from outside, and can score driving to the hoop or from the low-post. Richmond is eighth among all active players in career scoring average. His 23.4 point average was the nineteenth best in club history, and the best by a King since Otis Birdsong's 24.6 in '80–81. Among all NBA players, Richmond was seventh in scoring and in 3-point percentage. He's the franchise's all-time leader in 3-pointers made (278) and attempted (710), and is third all-time in 3-point percentage. The biggest drawback to his game are the turnovers he commits. He committed more turnovers last season than anyone on the team, and had just a 1.45 assists-to-turnovers ratio.

REGULAR SEASON		G	MIN	FG	FG%	3FG	3PT%	FT	FT%	REB	AST	STL	BLK	PTS	AVG
'88-89	GOLDEN STATE	79	2717	649	46.8	33	36.7	410	81.0	468	334	82	13	1741	22.0
'89-90	GOLDEN STATE	78	2799	640	49.7	34	35.8	406	86.6	360	223	98	24	1720	22.1
'90-91	GOLDEN STATE	77	3027	703	49.4	40	34.8	394	84.7	452	238	126	34	1840	23.9
'91-92	SACRAMENTO	80	3095	685	46.8	103	38.4	330	81.3	319	411	92	34	1803	22.5
'92-93	SACRAMENTO	45	1728	371	47.4	48	36.9	197	84.5	154	221	53	9	987	21.9
'93-94	SACRAMENTO	78	2897	635	44.5	127	40.7	426	83.4	286	313	103	17	1823	23.4
6 YR TOTALS		437	16263	3683	47.4	385	38.1	2163	83.5	2039	1740	554	131	9914	22.7
'93-94	RANK NBA Gs	128	100	97	60	114	95	112	127	98	59	110	110	103	67
'94-95	PROJECTIONS	82	3160	687	42.7	174	42.8	511	83.0	299	329	117	15	2059	25.1

PLAYOFFS		G	MIN	FG	FG%	3FG	3PT%	FT	FT%	REB	AST	STL	BLK	PTS	AVG
'88-89	GOLDEN STATE	8	314	62	45.9	3	18.8	34	89.5	58	35	14	1	161	20.1
'90-91	GOLDEN STATE	9	372	85	50.3	8	33.3	23	95.8	47	22	5	6	201	22.3
TOTALS		17	686	147	48.4	11	27.5	57	91.9	105	57	19	7	362	21.3

Lionel Simmons

No. 22/F

Full name: Lionel James Simmons
HT: 6-7   **WT:** 210
Born: 11/14/68, Philadephia, PA
High school: South Philadephia (PA)
College: La Salle

Although he's had problems with consistency throughout his career, Simmons would be a star if he played for anyone other than the Kings. The "L Train" is as versatile a player on offense as anyone in the league. And he even plays defense, stealing the ball and blocking shots. Simmons is one of only 8 players in franchise history to compile 5,000 points, 2,000 rebounds, and 1,000 assists over their career. Last season, Simmons led the Kings in steals and was the team's second-leading rebounder and third-leading scorer. He was also third in assists. He had 19 games of 20 or more points, pulled down double-figure rebounds 16 times, and had 16 point/rebound double-doubles.

REGULAR SEASON	G	MIN	FG	FGx	3FG	3PTx	FT	FTx	REB	AST	STL	BLK	PTS	AVG
'90-91 SACRAMENTO	79	2978	549	42.2	3	27.3	320	73.6	697	315	113	85	1421	18.0
'91-92 SACRAMENTO	78	2895	527	45.4	1	20.0	281	77.0	634	337	135	132	1336	17.1
'92-93 SACRAMENTO	69	2502	468	44.4	1	9.1	298	81.9	495	312	95	38	1235	17.9
'93-94 SACRAMENTO	75	2702	436	43.8	6	35.3	251	77.7	562	305	104	50	1129	15.1
4 YR TOTALS	301	11077	1980	43.9	11	25.0	1150	77.3	2388	1269	447	305	5121	17.0
'93-94 RANK NBA Fs	55	16	24	105	47	19	17	25	26	6	12	36	24	25
'94-95 PROJECTIONS	76	2706	398	43.5	10	45.5	222	76.8	559	295	101	38	1028	13.5

Spud Webb

No. 4/G

Full name: Anthony Jerome Webb
HT: 5-7 **WT:** 133
Born: 7/13/63, Dallas, TX
High school: Wilmer-Hutchins (Dallas)
College: North Carolina State
Webb is fast and quick, a fearless competitor who sacrifices his body on drives against players who are twice his weight. He regained his starting point guard job after Bobby Hurley's auto accident. Webb averaged 13.2 points, 2.8 rebounds, 7.3 assists, 1.19 steals, and 34.8 minutes per game as a starter. Webb was twelfth in the NBA in assists, thirty-fourth in free throw percentage, and thirty-eighth in 3-point shooting. He led Sacramento in scoring 5 times and assists 48 times. Webb scored 20 points or more 10 times, posted 10 or more assists 12 times, and had 10 point/assist double-doubles. Webb finished strong; he had 10 or more asists in 21 of his last 22 games, and had 20 points or more in 5 of his last 6 games.

REGULAR SEASON		G	MIN	FG	FG%	3FG	3PT%	FT	FT%	REB	AST	STL	BLK	PTS	AVG
'85-86	ATLANTA	79	1229	199	48.3	2	18.2	216	78.5	123	337	82	5	616	7.8
'86-87	ATLANTA	33	532	71	43.8	1	16.7	80	76.2	60	167	34	2	223	6.8
'87-88	ATLANTA	82	1347	191	47.5	1	5.3	107	81.7	146	337	63	11	490	6.0
'88-89	ATLANTA	81	1219	133	45.9	1	4.5	52	86.7	123	284	70	6	319	3.9
'89-90	ATLANTA	82	2184	294	47.7	1	5.3	162	87.1	201	477	105	12	751	9.2
'90-91	ATLANTA	75	2197	359	44.7	54	32.1	231	86.8	174	417	118	6	1003	13.4
'91-92	SACRAMENTO	77	2724	448	44.5	73	36.7	262	85.9	223	547	125	24	1231	16.0
'92-93	SACRAMENTO	69	2335	342	43.3	37	27.4	279	85.1	193	481	104	6	1000	14.5
'93-94	SACRAMENTO	79	2567	373	46.0	55	33.5	204	81.3	222	528	93	23	1005	12.7
9 YR TOTALS		657	16334	2410	45.6	225	30.3	1593	83.5	1465	3575	794	95	6638	10.1
'93-94	RANK NBA Gs	40	32	45	48	34	55	27	50	44	12	44	28	44	47
'94-95	PROJECTIONS	82	2660	376	46.9	65	36.7	177	79.0	235	550	82	30	994	12.1

PLAYOFFS		G	MIN	FG	FG%	3FG	3PT%	FT	FT%	REB	AST	STL	BLK	PTS	AVG
'85-86	ATLANTA	9	183	42	51.9	0	0.0	26	78.8	31	65	4	1	110	12.2
'86-87	ATLANTA	8	122	9	47.4	0	0.0	13	76.5	8	38	6	0	31	3.9
'87-88	ATLANTA	12	211	35	43.2	2	25.0	34	91.9	20	56	9	0	106	8.8
'88-89	ATLANTA	5	55	3	27.3	0	---	2	100.0	4	15	4	0	8	1.6
'90-91	ATLANTA	5	154	25	43.9	5	41.7	11	68.8	22	24	7	1	66	13.2
TOTALS		39	725	114	45.8	7	30.4	86	81.9	85	198	30	2	321	8.2

Randy Brown   No. 3/G

HT: 6-3 **WT:** 190
Born: 5/22/68, Chicago, IL
High school: Collins (Chicago)
College: New Mexico State
Brown averaged 2.42 steals per 40 minutes played last season. Brown plays defense with a relentless approach and has been dogged with injuries while in Sacramento.

REGULAR SEASON		G	MIN	FG	FGx	3FG	3PTx	FT	FTx	REB	AST	STL	BLK	PTS	AVG
'91-92	SACRAMENTO	56	535	77	45.6	0	0.0	38	65.5	69	59	35	12	192	3.4
'92-93	SACRAMENTO	75	1726	225	46.3	2	33.3	115	73.2	212	196	108	34	567	7.6
'93-94	SACRAMENTO	61	1041	110	43.8	0	0.0	53	60.9	112	133	63	14	273	4.5
	3 YR TOTALS	192	3302	412	45.5	2	12.5	206	68.2	393	388	206	60	1032	5.4
'93-94	RANK NBA Gs	102	98	114	75	131	131	107	128	96	91	73	53	115	115
'94-95	PROJECTIONS	55	1013	86	42.0	0	0.0	40	53.3	96	141	59	8	212	3.9

Bobby Hurley   No. 7/G

Full name: Robert Matthew Hurley
HT: 6-0 **WT:** 165
Born: 6/28/71, Jersey City, NJ
High school: St. Anthony's (Jersey City)
College: Duke
Known for his great court vision, Hurley is a superb passer who can penetrate the lane or hit from outside.

REGULAR SEASON		G	MIN	FG	FGx	3FG	3PTx	FT	FTx	REB	AST	STL	BLK	PTS	AVG
'93-94	SACRAMENTO	19	499	54	37.0	2	12.5	24	80.0	34	115	13	1	134	7.1
	1 YR TOTALS	19	499	54	37.0	2	12.5	24	80.0	34	115	13	1	134	7.1
'93-94	RANK NBA Gs	not ranked -- didn't appear in 25 games in '93-94													

LaBradford Smith   No. 15/G

Full name: LaBradford Corvey Smith
HT: 6-3   **WT:** 205
Born: 4/3/69, Bay City, TX
High school: Bay City (TX)
College: Louisville
Smith had a career-night on 3/19/93, scoring 37 points against Michael Jordan. The next night, Jordan put up 46 points on Smith

REGULAR SEASON	G	MIN	FG	FG%	3FG	3PT%	FT	FT%	REB	AST	STL	BLK	PTS	AVG
'91-92 WASHINGTON	48	708	100	40.7	2	9.5	45	80.4	81	99	44	1	247	5.1
'92-93 WASHINGTON	69	1546	261	45.8	8	34.8	109	95.8	106	186	58	9	639	9.3
'93-94 WAS-SAC	66	877	124	40.5	21	35.0	63	75.0	84	109	40	5	332	5.0
3 YR TOTALS	183	3131	485	43.2	31	29.8	217	81.3	271	394	142	15	1218	6.7
'93-94 RANK NBA Gs	91	111	110	112	73	46	101	89	110	99	99	97	109	109
'94-95 PROJECTIONS	69	780	100	37.7	34	41.5	57	68.7	82	95	36	5	291	4.2

Walt Williams   No. 42/G-F

Full name: Walter Ander Williams
HT: 6-8   **WT:** 230
Born: 4/16/70, Washington, DC
High school: Crossland (Temple Hills, MD)
College: Maryland
Williams primarily plays as Sacramento's sixth man. He's had trouble with injuries, and he needs minutes to play his best.

REGULAR SEASON	G	MIN	FG	FG%	3FG	3PT%	FT	FT%	REB	AST	STL	BLK	PTS	AVG
'92-93 SACRAMENTO	59	1673	358	43.5	61	31.9	224	74.2	265	178	66	29	1001	17.0
'93-94 SACRAMENTO	57	1356	226	39.0	38	26.8	148	63.5	235	132	52	23	638	11.2
2 YR TOTALS	116	3029	584	41.6	99	30.7	372	69.5	500	310	118	52	1639	14.1
'93-94 RANK NBA Gs	109	84	81	122	51	95	52	125	38	94	88	28	73	56
'94-95 PROJECTIONS	55	1039	130	34.4	22	26.2	90	52.9	196	92	39	17	372	6.8

Trevor Wilson   No. 21/F

HT: 6-8 **WT:** 215
Born: 3/16/68, Los Angeles, CA
High school: G. Cleveland (Los Angeles)
College: UCLA

A free-agent acquisition last December, Wilson concentrates mainly on defense and rebounding, but scored in double figures 21 times and had 8 double-doubles.

REGULAR SEASON	G	MIN	FG	FG%	3FG	3PT%	FT	FT%	REB	AST	STL	BLK	PTS	AVG
'93-94 LAL-SAC	57	1221	187	48.2	0	0.0	92	55.4	273	72	38	11	466	8.2
1 YR TOTALS	57	1221	187	48.2	0	0.0	92	55.4	273	72	38	11	466	8.2
'93-94 RANK NBA Fs	102	86	79	52	78	78	75	126	75	74	78	116	78	67

Garry St. Jean   Head Coach

HT: 6-4 **WT:** 210
Born: 2/10/42, Chicopee, MA
High school: Chicopee (MA)
College: Springfield (MA)

St. Jean spent 11 seasons as an assistant to Don Nelson. Not surprisingly, he prefers to play an up-tempo style that features fast-breaks and pressure defense.

	REGULAR SEASON				PLAYOFFS			
YEAR	TEAM	W	L	PCT	FINISH	W	L	PCT
'92-93	SACRAMENTO	25	57	.305	7th/Pacific Div.			
'93-94	SACRAMENTO	28	54	.341	6th/Pacific Div.			
	2 YR TOTALS	53	111	.323				

San Antonio
SPURS

1994–95 Scouting Report

Frontcourt

With David Robinson and Dennis Rodman, the Spurs have one of the best frontcourt combinations in the NBA. Robinson led the NBA in scoring and Rodman led the league in rebounding, the first time in NBA history that different players on the same team have led in those categories. Robinson was among the league leaders in rebounding, blocked shots, and field goal percentage. He's also an excellent defensive center and passer, and he led the league in free throw attempts last season. When you look up "Players who can contribute without scoring," you find Dennis Rodman's picture. San Antonio went 8–4 in the 12 games that Rodman failed to score a point, but led the team in rebounding. Sean Elliott is a scorer who plays defense, too, and he'll get a lot of minutes this season. In his prime, Terry Cummings blended power and quickness at power forward, but he's getting old and injuries are taking their toll. Chuck Person is an explosive scorer and a threat from outside, but he's a poor defender. The big question is how this temperamental player will respond if asked to take a reserve role. Other frontcourt reserves include low-post scorers Antoine Carr and J.R. Reid, and veteran Moses Malone. The only active NBA player to have played in the ABA, Malone is far past his prime, doesn't work hard on defense, and has had back problems for the past 2 seasons.

Backcourt

Willie Anderson seems to have gotten over the leg ailments that had ruined 2 seasons. When he's healthy, he's an outstanding offensive threat, at his best reminiscent of Spurs' great George Gervin. Dale Ellis is a good perimeter shooter, but he doesn't play much defense. Vinny Del Negro starts at point guard, largely by default. Del Negro isn't flashy, but he is consistent. Lloyd Daniels, who can play either guard position, is a brilliant passer, but he's inconsistent. Backup point guard Chris Whitney has solid skills, but his 6-0 height creates problems on defense. Negele Knight, another reserve at point, is improving as a shooter, but he's not Del Negro's equal as a playmaker. Veteran Sleepy Floyd seems to have lost his shot, and after 12 years, he may not be long for the NBA.

Defense

San Antonio ranked second in the NBA in fewest points allowed, holding opponents to just 94.8 points per game. And opponents shot just 44.6 percent against the Spurs, fourth lowest in the league. With Robinson and Rodman up front, San Antonio was second in defensive rebounds and fourth in defensive rebounding percentage. The Spurs were also tenth in blocking shots. But thanks to weak defensive play from the guards, they only snagged 12.4 turnovers per game, lowest in the league. The Spurs were also dead last in steals.

1994–95 Prospects

San Antonio won 23 games on the road, a club record, and their 55 wins, just 1 win shy of the team record set by the '89–90 team, represented a 6 game improvement. The Spurs were one of the NBA's hottest teams throughout January, February, and March, going 33–9 during that time. But they slumped in April with a 4–7 mark, and bowed out in 4 games against Utah in the first round of the playoffs.

There was a major shakeup in San Antonio during the off-season, and head coach John Lucas bailed out to run the Sixers' rebuilding effort. New coach Bob Hill will need to get his players to deliver the defensive and rebounding effort they gave Lucas. San Antonio ranked just twentieth in total points, twenty-first in assists, and twenty-third in turnovers, so they need to play tough defense and crash the boards to win.

You have to wonder which San Antonio team will show up this season: the squad that dominated the league for most of the season, or the crew that staggered badly in the stretch and bowed quickly in the playoffs. They were just 13–19 last season against Western Conference playoff teams. The Spurs have the inside game, offensively and defensively, to go far, but they need better play from both guard positions to win in the playoffs.

Team Directory

Chairman: Gen. Robert F. McDermott   President /CEO: Jack Diller
VP, basketball oper.: Gregg Popovich   VP, adm. & comm.: Larry Alexander
Dir., media services: Tom James

1993–94 Review

WESTERN CONFERENCE						EASTERN CONFERENCE					
MIDWEST DIV.		PACIFIC DIV.				ATLANTIC DIV.			CENTRAL DIV.		
	W	L		W	L		W	L		W	L
HOU	3	2	SEA	0	4	NY	1	1	ATL	1	1
SAN	-	-	PHO	1	3	ORL	2	0	CHI	1	1
UTAH	0	5	GS	2	2	NJ	1	1	CLE	2	0
DEN	4	2	POR	3	1	MIA	2	0	IND	2	0
MIN	4	1	LAL	4	0	BOS	2	0	CHA	2	0
DAL	5	0	SAC	3	1	PHI	2	0	DET	1	1
			LAC	3	1	WAS	2	0	MIL	2	0
	16	10		16	12		12	2		11	3

1993–94 finish: 55–27 (32–9 home, 23–18 away), second in Midwest Div.

1994–95 Schedule

11/4	Gold. St.	8:30 pm	1/10	LA Clip.	8:30 pm	3/9	@ Cleveland	8:00 pm
11/7	New Jersey	8:30 pm	1/12	Miami	8:00 pm	3/10	@ Phila.	7:30 pm
11/9	Utah	8:30 pm	1/13	@ Houston	8:30 pm	3/12	@ Orlando	12:00 pm
11/12	New York	8:30 pm	1/15	Dallas	7:00 pm	3/14	Minn.	8:30 pm
11/15	@ Denver	8:00 pm	1/17	@ Boston	7:30 pm	3/16	Phila.	8:30 pm
11/16	Chicago	8:30 pm	1/18	@ Charlotte	7:30 pm	3/18	Dallas	8:30 pm
11/19	@ Minn.	8:00 pm	1/20	@ Miami	7:30 pm	3/20	Seattle	8:30 pm
11/21	@ New York	7:30 pm	1/22	@ Indiana	2:30 pm	3/22	@ New Jersey	7:30 pm
11/23	Portland	8:30 pm	1/24	@ Chicago	8:00 pm	3/24	@ Minn.	8:00 pm
11/25	Seattle	8:30 pm	1/26	Houston	8:30 pm	3/25	@ Milw.	8:30 pm
11/26	@ Phoenix	9:00 pm	1/28	Denver	8:30 pm	3/27	@ Detroit	7:30 pm
11/28	Minn.	8:30 pm	1/31	@ Sacra.	10:30 pm	3/29	LA Lakers	8:30 pm
11/30	@ Seattle	10:00 pm	2/1	@ Portland	10:00 pm	3/31	Milw.	8:30 pm
12/2	@ Portland	10:00 pm	2/3	@ Dallas	8:30 pm	4/2	Phoenix	1:30 pm
12/6	Dallas	8:30 pm	2/4	Sacra.	8:30 pm	4/4	@ LA Clip.	10:30 pm
12/8	Utah	8:30 pm	2/7	@ Seattle	10:00 pm	4/6	@ Sacra.	10:30 pm
12/10	@ Houston	8:30 pm	2/8	@ LA Lakers	10:30 pm	4/8	@ Gold. St.	10:30 pm
12/12	Wash.	8:30 pm	2/14	Utah	8:00 pm	4/9	@ LA Lakers	10:00 pm
12/14	Boston	8:30 pm	2/16	@ Utah	9:00 pm	4/11	Portland	8:30 pm
12/17	LA Lakers	8:30 pm	2/18	Atlanta	8:30 pm	4/12	@ Phoenix	10:00 pm
12/21	@ Denver	9:00 pm	2/21	@ Houston	8:00 pm	4/14	Sacra.	8:30 pm
12/23	Houston	8:30 pm	2/22	Phoenix	8:30 pm	4/16	@ Denver	3:00 pm
12/27	Charlotte	8:30 pm	2/24	Detroit	8:30 pm	4/18	Denver	8:00 pm
12/29	@ Atlanta	7:30 pm	2/26	Gold. St.	7:00 pm	4/20	@ Dallas	8:30 pm
12/30	@ Wash.	7:30 pm	2/28	Cleveland	8:30 pm	4/21	LA Clip.	8:30 pm
01/3	@ Gold. St.	10:30 pm	3/3	Orlando	8:30 pm	4/23	@ Minn.	3:30 pm
01/5	@ Utah	8:00 pm	3/5	Houston	1:00 pm			
01/7	@ LA Clip.	10:30 pm	3/7	Indiana	8:30 pm			

1993–94 Team Stats

NAME	G	MIN	FG	FGA	FG%	3FG	3FGA	3FG%	FT	FTA	FT%	ORB	TRB	AST	PF	STL	BLK	TO	PTS	AVG
Robinson	80	3241	840	1658	50.7	10	29	34.5	693	925	74.9	241	855	381	228	139	265	253	2383	29.8
Ellis	77	2590	478	967	49.4	131	332	39.5	83	107	77.6	70	255	80	141	66	11	75	1170	15.2
Anderson	80	2488	394	837	47.1	22	68	32.4	145	171	84.8	68	242	347	187	71	46	153	955	11.9
Del Negro	77	1949	309	634	48.7	15	43	34.9	140	170	82.4	27	161	320	168	64	1	102	773	10.0
Knight	64	1430	224	471	47.6	4	21	19.0	141	174	81.0	28	103	197	120	34	10	94	593	9.3
Reid	70	1344	260	530	49.1	0	3	0.0	107	153	69.9	91	220	73	165	43	25	84	627	9.0
Cummings	59	1133	183	428	42.8	0	2	0.0	63	107	58.9	132	297	50	137	31	13	59	429	7.3
Carr	34	465	78	160	48.8	1	1	0.0	42	58	72.4	12	51	15	75	9	22	15	198	5.8
Daniels	65	980	140	372	37.6	44	125	35.2	46	64	71.9	45	111	94	69	29	16	60	370	5.7
Rodman	79	2989	156	292	53.4	5	24	20.8	53	102	52.0	453	1367	184	229	52	32	138	370	4.7
Floyd	53	737	70	209	33.5	8	36	22.2	52	78	66.7	10	70	101	71	12	8	61	200	3.8
Nevitt	1	1	0	0	—	0	0	—	3	6	50.0	1	1	0	1	0	0	1	3	3.0
Haley	28	94	21	48	43.8	0	0	—	17	21	81.0	6	24	1	18	0	0	10	59	2.1
Whitney	40	339	25	82	30.5	10	30	33.3	12	15	80.0	5	29	53	53	11	1	37	72	1.8
Spurs	82	19780	3178	6688	47.5	249	714	34.9	1597	2151	74.2	1189	3786	1896	1662	561	450	1198	8202	100.0
Opp.	82	19780	3066	6880	44.6	290	871	33.3	1349	1875	71.9	1089	3242	1769	1791	632	346	1020	7771	94.8

HISTORY

TITLES

1977–78 Central Div. champs
1978–79 Central Div. champs
1980–81 Midwest Div. champs
1981–82 Midwest Div. champs

1982–83 Midwest Div. champs
1989–90 Midwest Div. champs
1990–91 Midwest Div. champs

ALL-TIME TEAM RECORDS

Career

Total points	George Gervin	19,383	1976–85
Field goals made	George Gervin	7,599	1976–85
Field goals attempted	George Gervin	14,900	1976–85
Free throws made	George Gervin	4,258	1976–85
Free throws attempted	George Gervin	5,061	1976–85
Total rebounds	David Robinson	4,686	1989–94
Assists	Johnny Moore	3,772	1980–87, 1989–90
Steals	Alvin Robertson	1,128	1984–89

Season

Total points	George Gervin	2,585	1979–80
Field goals made	George Gervin	1,024	1979–80
Field goals attempted	George Gervin	1,987	1981–82
Free throws made	David Robinson	693	1993–94
Free throws attempted	David Robinson	925	1993–94
Total rebounds	Dennis Rodman	1,367	1993–94
Assists	Johnny Moore	816	1984–85
Steals	Alvin Robertson	301	1985–86

Game

Total points	David Robinson	71	vs. LA Clippers, 4/24/94
Field goals made	David Robinson	26	vs. LA Clippers, 4/24/94
Free throws made	David Robinson	18	vs. LA Clippers, 4/24/94
Total rebounds	Dennis Rodman	32	vs. Dallas, 1/22/94
Assists	John Lucas	24	vs. Denver, 4/15/84
Steals	Larry Kenon	11	vs. Kansas City, 12/26/76

LEADING COACHES

	REGULAR SEASON				PLAYOFFS		
NAME	**YEARS**	**W**	**L**	**PCT**	**W**	**L**	**PCT**
Doug Moe	1976–80	177	135	.567	9	13	.409
Stan Albeck	1980–83	153	93	.622	13	14	.481
Bob Bass	1974–76, 1980, 1984, 1992	144	108	.569	6	13	.316
Cliff Hagan	1967–70	109	90	.548	9	12	.429
Tom Nissalke	1971–72, 1973–74	104	91	.533	3	8	.273

San Antonio Spurs 1994–95 Roster

Head Coach: Bob Hill

No.	Name	Pos.	Ht.	Wt.	Yrs.	Born	College
40	Willie Anderson	G-F	6-8	205	6	1/8/67	Georgia
35	Antoine Carr	F	6-9	255	10	7/23/61	Wichita State
34	Terry Cummings	F	6-9	250	12	3/15/61	DePaul
24	Lloyd Daniels	G-F	6-7	205	2	9/4/67	None
15	Vinny Del Negro	G	6-4	200	4	8/9/66	North Carolina State
32	Sean Elliott	F	6-8	215	6	2/2/68	Arizona
3	Dale Ellis	G	6-7	215	11	8/6/60	Tennessee
21	Sleepy Floyd	G	6-3	185	12	3/6/60	Georgetown
54	Jack Haley	C	6-10	250	6	1/27/64	UCLA
32	Negele Knight	G	6-1	182	4	3/6/67	Dayton
2	Moses Malone	C	6-10	255	17	3/23/55	None
45	Chuck Person	F	6-8	225	9	6/27/64	Auburn
7	J.R. Reid	F-C	6-9	260	5	3/31/68	North Carolina
50	David Robinson	C	7-1	225	5	8/6/65	Navy
10	Dennis Rodman	F	6-8	210	8	5/13/61	SE Oklahoma St.
20	Chris Whitney	G	6-0	170	1	10/5/71	Clemson

Arena Information

Alamodome (21,372)
Tickets: 210-554-7787
Ticket prices: $31, $22, $17, $10, $8, $5

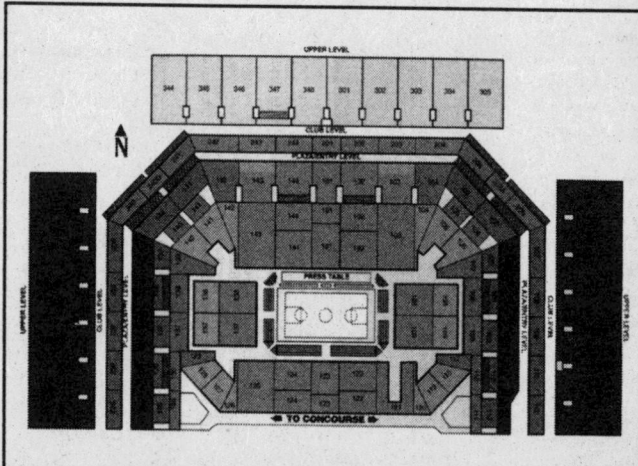

Willie Anderson

No. 40/G-F

Full name: Willie Lloyd Anderson
HT: 6-8 **WT:** 205
Born: 1/8/67, Greenville, SC
High school: East Atlanta (GA)
College: Georgia

Anderson has bounced back from a series of leg injuries that plagued him for the better part of 2 seasons. Anderson has size, terrific lateral quickness, and great offensive skills at shooting guard. He can shoot over anyone, can back in against smaller guards, and he's too quick for bigger defenders. Anderson is best in transition, where he can use his athletic ability. His modest jump shooting skills become exposed in a half-court game. Last season, Anderson was San Antonio's third-leading scorer, and was second on the team in assists in steals. His 84.8 FT percentage ranked fifteenth in the NBA. Defense is not his strength. He has the physical gifts to play good defense, but lacks the size to fight through picks.

REGULAR SEASON		G	MIN	FG	FG%	3FG	3PT%	FT	FT%	REB	AST	STL	BLK	PTS	AVG
'88-89	SAN ANTONIO	81	2738	640	49.8	4	19.0	224	77.5	417	372	150	62	1508	18.6
'89-90	SAN ANTONIO	82	2788	532	49.2	7	26.9	217	74.8	372	364	111	58	1288	15.7
'90-91	SAN ANTONIO	75	2592	453	45.7	7	20.0	170	79.8	351	358	79	46	1083	14.4
'91-92	SAN ANTONIO	57	1889	312	45.5	13	23.2	107	77.5	300	302	54	51	744	13.1
'92-93	SAN ANTONIO	38	560	80	43.0	1	12.5	22	78.6	57	79	14	6	183	4.8
'93-94	SAN ANTONIO	80	2488	394	47.1	22	32.4	145	84.8	242	347	71	46	955	11.9
6 YR TOTALS		413	13055	2411	47.6	54	25.2	885	78.4	1739	1822	479	269	5761	13.9
'93-94	RANK NBA Gs	33	36	41	39	72	67	53	21	36	35	64	7	48	51
'94-95	PROJECTIONS	82	3017	476	48.2	39	39.8	185	88.1	250	414	86	58	1176	14.3

PLAYOFFS		G	MIN	FG	FG%	3FG	3PT%	FT	FT%	REB	AST	STL	BLK	PTS	AVG
'89-90	SAN ANTONIO	10	375	87	51.8	2	40.0	29	80.6	54	52	9	4	205	20.5
'90-91	SAN ANTONIO	4	159	33	48.5	2	20.0	8	61.5	19	19	6	2	76	19.0
'92-93	SAN ANTONIO	10	219	37	45.1	6	54.5	15	88.2	23	28	9	2	95	9.5
'93-94	SAN ANTONIO	4	106	14	37.8	1	100.0	4	57.1	8	12	5	2	33	8.3
TOTALS		28	859	171	48.2	11	40.7	56	76.7	104	111	29	10	409	14.6

Vinny Del Negro

No. 15/C

Full name: Vincent Joseph Del Negro

HT: 6-4   **WT:** 200

Born: 8/9/66, Springfield, MA

High school: Suffield Academy (Suffield, MA)

College: North Carolina State

Del Negro makes the most of his limited physical gifts. He may be slow, but he's a great shooter and he doesn't turn over the ball. San Antonio was 40–16 (.714) when he started, 15–11 (.577) when he didn't. Last season, Del Negro made 50 consecutive free throws, a new team record. Even so, his 82.9 FT percentage was a career low, although it ranked twenty-ninth in the NBA. He had career highs in scoring average and assists. An underrated play maker, Del Negro has one of the highest assist-to-turnover ratios (3.13) in the game. Previously not much of a shooter from 3-point range, he had his best season ever last season.

REGULAR SEASON		G	MIN	FG	FGx	3FG	3PTx	FT	FTx	REB	AST	STL	BLK	PTS	AVG
'88-89	SACRAMENTO	80	1556	239	47.5	6	30.0	85	85.0	171	206	65	14	569	7.1
'89-90	SACRAMENTO	76	1858	297	46.2	10	31.3	135	87.1	198	250	64	10	739	9.7
'92-93	SAN ANTONIO	73	1526	218	50.7	6	25.0	101	86.3	163	231	44	1	543	7.4
'93-94	SAN ANTONIO	77	1949	309	48.7	15	34.9	140	82.4	161	320	64	1	773	10.0
	4 YR TOTALS	306	6889	1063	48.1	37	31.1	461	85.1	693	1067	237	26	2624	8.6
'93-94	RANK NBA Gs	53	63	58	17	80	47	58	43	68	44	72	125	61	65
'94-95	PROJECTIONS	78	2149	352	48.7	22	39.3	161	79.7	145	352	71	0	887	11.4

PLAYOFFS		G	MIN	FG	FGx	3FG	3PTx	FT	FTx	REB	AST	STL	BLK	PTS	AVG
'92-93	SAN ANTONIO	8	112	17	44.7	2	22.2	4	100.0	19	24	1	1	40	5.0
'93-94	SAN ANTONIO	4	93	12	44.4	2	50.0	3	60.0	7	18	1	0	29	7.3
	TOTALS	12	205	29	44.6	4	30.8	7	77.8	26	42	2	1	69	5.8

Sean Elliott
F

Full name: Sean Michael Elliott
HT: 6-8   **WT:** 215
Born: 2/2/68, Tucson, AZ
High school: Cholla (Tucson)
College: Arizona

Elliott is a versatile player who can also play shooting guard. He can shoot, pass, drive, create off the dribble, and is a good rebounder. Few players of Elliott's caliber have been involved in so many transactions in the space of one year. The Spurs traded Elliott to Detroit on October 1, 1993 for Dennis Rodman. Detroit tried to trade him to Houston in February for Robert Horry, Matt Bullard, and two second-round draft choices, but the trade was nullified by Houston after Elliott failed his physical due to a kidney condition. Elliott returned to the Pistons after doctors at the University of Arizona cleared him to play, and came back to San Antonio in a trade with Detroit after the season.

REGULAR SEASON		G	MIN	FG	FG%	3FG	3PT%	FT	FT%	REB	AST	STL	BLK	PTS	AVG
'89-90	SAN ANTONIO	81	2032	311	48.1	1	11.1	187	86.6	297	154	45	14	810	10.0
'90-91	SAN ANTONIO	82	3044	478	49.0	20	31.3	325	80.8	456	238	69	33	1301	15.9
'91-92	SAN ANTONIO	82	3120	514	49.4	25	30.5	285	86.1	439	214	84	29	1338	16.3
'92-93	SAN ANTONIO	70	2604	451	49.1	37	35.6	268	79.5	322	265	68	28	1207	17.2
'93-94	DETROIT	73	2409	360	45.5	26	29.3	139	80.3	263	197	54	27	885	12.1
5 YR TOTALS		388	13209	2114	48.4	109	31.5	1204	82.5	1777	1068	320	131	5541	14.3
'93-94	RANK NBA Fs	67	32	38	87	27	36	52	12	77	24	58	78	43	36
'94-95	PROJECTIONS	71	2242	316	43.6	26	29.2	82	79.6	215	177	47	27	740	10.4

PLAYOFFS		G	MIN	FG	FG%	3FG	3PT%	FT	FT%	REB	AST	STL	BLK	PTS	AVG
'89-90	SAN ANTONIO	10	291	53	55.2	0	0.0	21	72.4	41	18	9	6	127	12.7
'90-91	SAN ANTONIO	4	132	17	42.5	0	0.0	25	78.1	22	16	4	1	59	14.8
'91-92	SAN ANTONIO	3	137	19	47.5	5	62.5	16	88.9	13	8	3	4	59	19.7
'92-93	SAN ANTONIO	10	381	59	47.2	3	21.4	37	92.5	48	36	8	3	158	15.8
TOTALS		27	941	148	49.2	8	30.8	99	83.2	124	78	24	14	403	14.9

David Robinson

No. 50/C

Full name: David Maurice
  Robinson
HT: 7-1   **WT:** 225
Born: 8/6/65, Key West, FL
High school: Osbourn Park
  (Manassas, VA)
College: Navy

Robinson was the only player
rank in the top 30 in all 6 major sta
tistical categories: points (first
rebounds (fourteenth), assist
(twenty-eighth), blocks (third
steals (nineteenth) and FG pe
centage (twentieth). Only 3 othe
players have accomplished thi
feat: Larry Bird, Bob Lanier an
Kareem Abdul-Jabbar. Robinson
quadruple-double against Detro
February 17 (34 points, 10 re
bounds, 10 assists, and 10 blocks
was only the fourth quadruple-dou
ble in NBA history. He became only the fourth player to score 70 points
an NBA game with his 71 points in the season finale in Los Angele
against the Clippers. That was the most points scored in a game by a sin
gle player in over 16 years.

REGULAR SEASON		G	MIN	FG	FGx	3FG	3PTx	FT	FTx	REB	AST	STL	BLK	PTS	AVG
'87-88	SAN ANTONIO	did not play -- in military service													
'88-89	SAN ANTONIO	did not play -- in military service													
'89-90	SAN ANTONIO	82	3002	690	53.1	0	0.0	613	73.2	983	164	138	319	1993	24.3
'90-91	SAN ANTONIO	82	3095	754	55.2	1	14.3	592	76.2	1063	208	127	320	2101	25.6
'91-92	SAN ANTONIO	68	2564	592	55.1	1	12.5	393	70.1	829	181	158	305	1578	23.2
'92-93	SAN ANTONIO	82	3211	676	50.1	3	17.6	561	73.2	956	301	127	264	1916	23.4
'93-94	SAN ANTONIO	80	3241	840	50.7	10	34.5	693	74.9	855	381	139	265	2383	29.8
5 YR TOTALS		394	15113	3552	52.7	15	23.8	2852	73.8	4686	1235	689	1473	9971	25.3
'93-94	RANK NBA Cs	8	2	3	18	1	4	1	16	5	1	1	3	1	1
'94-95	PROJECTIONS	81	3360	930	49.7	18	46.2	788	76.0	797	462	139	248	2666	32.9

PLAYOFFS		G	MIN	FG	FGx	3FG	3PTx	FT	FTx	REB	AST	STL	BLK	PTS	AVG
'89-90	SAN ANTONIO	10	375	99	53.2	0	---	65	67.7	120	23	11	40	243	24.3
'90-91	SAN ANTONIO	4	166	35	68.6	0	0.0	33	86.8	54	8	6	15	103	25.8
'92-93	SAN ANTONIO	10	421	79	46.5	0	0.0	73	66.4	126	40	10	36	231	23.1
'93-94	SAN ANTONIO	4	146	30	41.1	0	0.0	20	74.1	40	14	3	10	80	20.0
TOTALS		28	1108	233	50.5	0	0.0	191	70.5	340	85	30	101	657	23.5

Dennis Rodman

Full name: Dennis Keith Rodman
HT: 6-8   **WT:** 210
Born: 5/13/61, Trenton, NJ
High school: South Oak Cliff (Dallas, TX)
College: Southeastern Oklahoma State

Rodman is a physically gifted talent who has the tools to match up defensively with anyone in the NBA: great leaping ability, quick feet, and agility. A tremendous competitor, a superb defender, and a brilliant rebounder, Rodman is also an erratic personality. He set single-season team records for total rebounds (1,367), offensive rebounds, defensive rebounds, and most 20-plus rebound games (27), but also set Spurs' records for most ejections (5), most technical fouls (32), and most suspensions in a season (2). He's particularly tough on the offensive boards; Rodman helped San Antonio improve from the worst offensive rebounding team in '92–93 to the best in '93–94.

REGULAR SEASON		G	MIN	FG	FGx	3FG	3PTx	FT	FTx	REB	AST	STL	BLK	PTS	AVG
'86-87	DETROIT	77	1155	213	54.5	0	0.0	74	58.7	332	56	38	48	500	6.5
'87-88	DETROIT	82	2147	398	56.1	5	29.4	152	53.5	715	110	75	45	953	11.6
'88-89	DETROIT	82	2208	316	59.5	6	23.1	97	62.6	772	99	55	76	735	9.0
'89-90	DETROIT	82	2377	288	58.1	1	11.1	142	65.4	792	72	52	60	719	8.8
'90-91	DETROIT	82	2747	276	49.3	6	20.0	111	63.1	1026	85	65	55	669	8.2
'91-92	DETROIT	82	3301	342	53.9	32	31.7	84	60.0	1530	191	68	70	800	9.8
'92-93	DETROIT	62	2410	183	42.7	15	20.5	87	53.4	1132	102	48	45	468	7.5
'93-94	SAN ANTONIO	79	2989	156	53.4	5	20.8	53	52.0	1367	184	52	32	370	4.7
8 YR TOTALS		628	19334	2172	53.7	70	24.9	800	58.7	7666	899	453	431	5214	8.3
'93-94 RANK NBA Fs		30	4	88	15	51	61	102	131	1	29	62	68	93	108
'94-95 PROJECTIONS		82	3153	89	56.3	0	0.0	29	49.2	1476	225	49	18	207	2.5

PLAYOFFS		G	MIN	FG	FGx	3FG	3PTx	FT	FTx	REB	AST	STL	BLK	PTS	AVG
'86-87	DETROIT	15	245	40	54.1	0	---	18	56.3	71	3	6	17	98	6.5
'87-88	DETROIT	23	474	71	52.2	0	0.0	22	40.7	136	21	14	14	164	7.1
'88-89	DETROIT	17	409	37	52.9	0	0.0	24	68.6	170	16	6	12	98	5.8
'89-90	DETROIT	19	560	54	56.8	0	---	18	51.4	161	17	9	13	126	6.6
'90-91	DETROIT	15	495	41	45.1	2	22.2	10	41.7	177	14	11	10	94	6.3
'91-92	DETROIT	5	156	16	59.3	0	0.0	4	50.0	51	9	4	2	36	7.2
'93-94	SAN ANTONIO	3	114	12	50.0	0	0.0	1	16.7	48	2	6	4	25	8.3
TOTALS		97	2453	271	52.4	2	9.1	97	50.0	814	82	56	72	641	6.6

Terry Cummings   No. 34/

Full name: Robert Terrell Cummings
HT: 6-9   **WT:** 250
Born: 3/15/61, Chicago, IL
High school: Carver (Chicago)
College: DePaul

Cummings has played tentatively since com
ing back from the torn ligaments he suffere
in his right knee before the '92–93 season.

REGULAR SEASON		G	MIN	FG	FG%	3FG	3PT%	FT	FT%	REB	AST	STL	BLK	PTS	AVG
'90-91	SAN ANTONIO	67	2195	503	48.4	7	21.2	164	68.3	521	157	61	30	1177	17.6
'91-92	SAN ANTONIO	70	2149	514	48.8	5	38.5	177	71.1	631	102	58	34	1210	17.3
'92-93	SAN ANTONIO	8	76	11	37.9	0	—	5	50.0	19	4	1	1	27	3.4
'93-94	SAN ANTONIO	59	1133	183	42.8	0	0.0	63	58.9	297	50	31	13	429	7.3
12 YR TOTALS		835	27426	6934	48.7	39	28.9	2913	71.1	6979	1877	1033	566	16820	20.1
'93-94	RANK NBA Fs	101	91	82	115	76	78	95	121	70	96	91	110	85	7·
'94-95	PROJECTIONS	68	1076	157	42.3	0	0.0	48	57.8	285	40	32	11	362	5.3

PLAYOFFS		G	MIN	FG	FG%	3FG	3PT%	FT	FT%	REB	AST	STL	BLK	PTS	AVG
'90-91	SAN ANTONIO	4	124	25	51.0	0	0.0	9	50.0	37	4	3	2	59	14.8
'91-92	SAN ANTONIO	3	122	34	51.5	0	0.0	10	50.0	34	7	4	4	78	26.0
'92-93	SAN ANTONIO	10	138	31	44.3	0	0.0	5	62.5	39	5	3	1	67	6.7
'93-94	SAN ANTONIO	4	72	11	50.0	0	—	10	83.3	25	2	5	3	32	8.0
	TOTALS	75	2412	600	51.0	1	10.0	267	71.6	604	150	78	53	1468	19.6

Lloyd Daniels   No. 24/G-

HT: 6-7   **WT:** 205
Born: 9/4/67, Brooklyn, NY
High school: Andrew Jackson (Queens, NY
College: Mount San Antonio (CA)

An outstanding passer, Daniels needs to pla
more consistently to start at point guard. He
had problems finding the range with h
jumper, and he needs to improve defensively

REGULAR SEASON		G	MIN	FG	FG%	3FG	3PT%	FT	FT%	REB	AST	STL	BLK	PTS	AVG
'92-93	SAN ANTONIO	77	1573	295	44.3	59	33.3	72	72.7	216	148	38	30	701	9.1
'93-94	SAN ANTONIO	65	980	140	37.6	44	35.2	46	71.9	111	94	29	16	370	5.7
2 YR TOTALS		142	2553	425	41.8	103	34.1	118	72.4	327	242	67	46	1071	7.5
'93-94	RANK NBA Gs	94	105	103	126	45	43	113	106	97	106	114	46	103	10·
'94-95	PROJECTIONS	53	387	42	31.1	20	36.4	18	69.2	35	38	14	5	122	2.3

PLAYOFFS		G	MIN	FG	FG%	3FG	3PT%	FT	FT%	REB	AST	STL	BLK	PTS	AVG
'92-93	SAN ANTONIO	8	74	11	36.7	1	14.3	5	83.3	15	2	3	0	28	3.5
'93-94	SAN ANTONIO	4	66	8	40.0	4	50.0	2	100.0	9	3	0	1	22	5.5
	TOTALS	12	140	19	38.0	5	33.3	7	87.5	24	5	3	1	50	4.2

Dale Ellis   No. 3/G

HT: 6-7   **WT:** 215
Born: 8/6/60, Marietta, GA
High school: Marietta (GA)
College: Tennessee

The first player to score 1,000 3-pointers in his career, Ellis has a terrific jump shot, especially off a pick. Ellis made 131 3-pointers last season, setting a team record.

REGULAR SEASON		G	MIN	FG	FG%	3FG	3PT%	FT	FT%	REB	AST	STL	BLK	PTS	AVG
'89-90	SEATTLE	55	2033	502	49.7	96	37.5	193	81.8	238	110	59	7	1293	23.5
'90-91	SEA-MIL	51	1424	340	94.92	57	74.45	120	144.5	173	95	49	8	857	16.8
'91-92	MILWAUKEE	81	2191	485	46.9	138	41.9	164	77.4	253	104	57	18	1272	15.7
'92-93	SAN ANTONIO	82	2731	545	43.9	119	40.1	157	79.7	312	107	78	18	1366	16.7
'93-94	SAN ANTONIO	77	2590	478	49.4	131	39.5	83	77.8	255	80	66	11	1170	15.2
11 YR TOTALS		796	23481	5448	48.9	1013	40.2	-2005	78.0	3016	1244	722	152	13914	17.5
'93-94	RANK NBA G/s	53	30	21	14	6	24	90	74	35	113	68	68	29	26
'94-95	PROJECTIONS	79	2737	421	45.8	131	36.3	31	72.1	244	61	65	8	1004	12.7

PLAYOFFS		G	MIN	FG	FG%	3FG	3PT%	FT	FT%	REB	AST	STL	BLK	PTS	AVG
'92-93	SAN ANTONIO	10	305	51	45.1	10	31.3	13	81.3	35	11	4	0	125	12.5
'93-94	SAN ANTONIO	4	114	17	39.5	5	29.4	3	60.0	10	1	3	0	42	10.5
	TOTALS	60	1738	373	45.0	56	34.4	117	77.9	246	83	47	13	919	15.3

Negele Knight   No. 32/G

Full name: Negele Oscar Knight
HT: 6-1   **WT:** 182
Born: 3/6/67, Detroit, MI
High school: St. Martin De Porres (Detroit)
College: Dayton

Knight is a passer, and a tough defender. He improved markedly as a shooter last season, increasing his FG percentage by 83 points.

REGULAR SEASON		G	MIN	FG	FG%	3FG	3PT%	FT	FT%	REB	AST	STL	BLK	PTS	AVG
'90-91	PHOENIX	64	792	131	42.5	6	24.0	71	60.2	71	191	20	7	339	5.3
'91-92	PHOENIX	42	631	103	47.5	4	30.8	33	68.8	46	112	24	3	243	5.8
'92-93	PHOENIX	52	888	124	39.1	0	0.0	67	77.9	64	145	23	4	315	6.1
'93-94	PHE-SA	65	1438	225	47.4	4	19.0	141	81.0	103	197	34	11	595	9.2
4 YR TOTALS		223	3749	583	44.3	14	21.2	312	73.2	284	645	101	25	1492	6.7
'93-94	RANK NBA G/s	94	81	82	34	110	118	57	53	101	72	107	68	80	71
'94-95	PROJECTIONS	73	1828	290	50.7	6	23.1	211	86.5	127	201	37	17	797	10.9

PLAYOFFS		G	MIN	FG	FG%	3FG	3PT%	FT	FT%	REB	AST	STL	BLK	PTS	AVG
'90-91	PHOENIX	4	56	13	50.0	1	33.3	5	71.4	4	9	1	0	32	8.0
'92-93	PHOENIX	9	34	9	56.3	0	---	0	---	3*	7	0	1	18	2.0
'93-94	SAN ANTONIO	4	108	13	31.7	0	0.0	11	91.7	6	12	3	0	37	9.3
	TOTALS	17	198	35	42.2	1	16.7	16	84.2	13	28	4	1	87	5.1

J. R. Reid No. 7/F-C

Full name: Herman Reid, Jr.
HT: 6-9 **WT:** 260
Born: 3/31/68, Virginia Beach, VA
High school: Kempsville (Virginia Beach)
College: North Carolina

Reid can play with his back to the basket. Bu he doesn't shoot well outside the paint, and he's too short to be effective at center.

REGULAR SEASON		G	MIN	FG	FGx	3FG	3PTx	FT	FTx	REB	AST	STL	BLK	PTS	AVG
'89-90	CHARLOTTE	82	2757	358	44.0	0	0.0	192	66.4	691	101	92	54	908	11.1
'90-91	CHARLOTTE	80	2467	360	46.6	0	0.0	182	70.3	502	89	87	47	902	11.3
'91-92	CHARLOTTE	51	1257	213	49.0	0	0.0	134	70.5	317	81	49	23	560	11.0
'92-93	CHA-SA	83	1887	283	47.6	0	0.0	214	76.4	456	80	47	31	780	9.4
'93-94	SAN ANTONIO	70	1344	260	49.1	0	0.0	107	69.9	220	73	43	25	627	9.0
5 YR TOTALS		366	9712	1474	46.8	0	0.0	829	70.8	2186	424	318	180	3777	10.3
'93-94	RANK NBA Fs	77	81	62	42	78	78	67	74	91	73	73	84	64	64
'94-95	PROJECTIONS	68	1037	224	49.9	0	0.0	73	68.9	129	61	34	20	521	7.7

PLAYOFFS		G	MIN	FG	FGx	3FG	3PTx	FT	FTx	REB	AST	STL	BLK	PTS	AVG
'92-93	SAN ANTONIO	10	220	29	48.3	0	0.0	27	77.1	50	15	8	8	85	8.5
'93-94	SAN ANTONIO	4	56	6	28.6	0	---	3	60.0	12	3	1	2	15	3.8
TOTALS		14	276	35	43.2	0	0.0	30	75.0	62	18	9	10	100	7.1

Bob Hill Head Coach

Full name: Robert W. Hill
HT: 6-5 **WT:** 200
Born: 11/24/48, Columbus, OH
High school: Worthington (OH)
College: Bowling Green State University

Hill has coached the Knicks and Pacers, and served as an assistant with Hubie Brown in New York, and Larry Brown at Kansas.

	REGULAR SEASON				PLAYOFFS			
YEAR	TEAM	W	L	PCT	FINISH	W	L	PCT	
'86-87	NEW YORK	20	46	.303	T4th/Atlantic Div.				
'90-91	INDIANA	32	25	.561	5th/Central Div.	2	3	.400	lost Eastern Conference first round to Boston, 3-2
'91-92	INDIANA	40	42	.488	4th/Central Div.	0	3	.000	lost Eastern Conference first round to Boston, 3-0
'92-93	INDIANA	41	41	.500	5th/Central Div.	1	3	.250	lost Eastern Conference first round to New York 3-1
		133	154	.463		3	9	.250	

Seattle
SUPERSONICS

SEATTLE
SUPERSONICS

1994–95 Scouting Report

Frontcourt

All-Star Shawn Kemp starts at power forward. Kemp is strong, quick, agile, runs the floor well, and has great hands. Detlef Schrempf plays small forward. With Michael Cage's departure, backup Sam Perkins will take over at center. He led the team in 3-point shooting (99 for 270, 36.7 percent). Perkins is an intelligent player with a good post-up game and adds defense off the bench. Steve Scheffler and '93 first round pick Ervin Johnson are also available to play center. Johnson has good speed, and can block shots and rebound, but needs work on his offense and defense. Seattle could use a scoring forward to come off the bench. That could be first round pick Dontonio Wingfield, who joins the Sonics after just one year in college. Foul-prone rebounding ace Byron Houston, obtained from Golden State in a trade is also available.

Backcourt

No team in the NBA is deeper at guard than Seattle, with Gary Payton, Kendall Gill, Nate McMillan, Vincent Askew, and Sarunas Marciulionis. Gary Payton, the starting point guard, may be the best pressure defender in the NBA. Kendall Gill starts at shooting guard. Nate McMillan can play both guard positions and small forward. A great defensive player, he led the league in steals. He's also the team's best playmaker. Vincent Askew also plays defense, and is a clutch scorer, too. Guard Sarunas Marciulionis came from Golden State. He's a tremendous scorer when healthy, but he's coming off a knee injury and has been injury-prone.

Defense

Seattle plays a swarming, switching, 48 minutes of pressure defense, going for steals on the perimeter that can lead to easy baskets on the other end. Seattle led the league in forcing turnovers (20.3 per game) and steals. In fact, Seattle's 1,053 steals were just 6 off the NBA record. They can do that because they're versatile and deep, loaded with athletes who can guard anyone anywhere on the floor. And because they force so many turnovers, they limit the number of shots that opponents get. Last season, Seattle was second in allowing shots from the floor. Opponents shot just 45.3 percent against the Sonics, seventh lowest in the NBA. They were sixth in allowing opponents to score, giving up 96.9 points per game. That's one reason Seattle had the best point differential in the NBA (9.1). They also clean the defensive glass very well, ranking sixth last year in preventing offensive rebounds.

1994–95 Prospects

The SuperSonics were the best team in the NBA during the regular season. They were the only team in the league not to lose a season series, and they won 43 games by 10 points or more, tops in the NBA. Seattle's defensive system of forcing turnovers lets them match up extremely well against the NBA's less talented (and more turnover prone) teams; they were a dominating 33–2 vs. the lottery teams last season.

Seattle should win around 60 games again, and are still the team to beat in the Pacific Division. The assortment of talented athletes on the team gives Coach George Karl a variety of options. Last year, nine players averaged 20 minutes or more per game. Because they have so many weapons, they really don't have one go-to guy, and that can hurt them in crunch time. On the other hand, they win so many blowouts, they're not in crunch time situations all that often.

Seattle is the ultimate Western Conference team, loaded with athletes who can shoot, playing at a frenetic pace. They have trouble with teams that play the slower paced Eastern Conference style that features intimdiating defense and scores in the 90s. They were just 8–8 vs. Eastern Conference playoff teams, and 4–4 against Houston and Denver, who play a physical style. And in games where both teams were held under 100 points, the Sonics were 13–10. Unfortunately for Seattle, that's the kind of game you see in the playoffs. Seattle will do well against a Utah, or a San Antonio, or a Phoenix in the playoffs. But inevitaby they'll encounter a team like the Rockets, Nuggets, or Knicks that will give them trouble.

Team Directory

Owner/Chairman: Barry Ackerley   President/GM: Wally Walker

Exec. VP: John Dresel   VP, mktg. & prom.: Kim Cleworth

VP, finance: Brian Dixon   Dir., media relations: Cheri White

1993–94 Review

WESTERN CONFERENCE					EASTERN CONFERENCE					
MIDWEST DIV.		PACIFIC DIV.			ATLANTIC DIV.			CENTRAL DIV.		
	W	L		W	L		W	L		W	L
HOU	2	2	SEA	-	-	NY	1	1	ATL	1	1
SAN	4	0	PHO	3	2	ORL	1	1	CHI	1	1
UTAH	3	1	GS	4	1	NJ	1	1	CLE	1	1
DEN	2	2	POR	4	1	MIA	1	1	IND	1	1
MIN	4	0	LAL	5	0	BOS	2	0	CHA	2	0
DAL	4	0	SAC	5	0	PHI	2	0	DET	1	1
			LAC	4	1	WAS	2	0	MIL	2	0
	19	5		25	5		10	4		9	5

1993–94 finish: 63–19 (37–4, home, 26–15 away), first in Pacific Div.

1994–95 Team Schedule

11/5	Utah	10:00 pm	1/4	@ Cleveland	7:30 pm	3/8	@ Minn.	8:00 pm
11/9	Sacra.	10:00 pm	1/6	@ Chicago	8:00 pm	3/9	@ Charlotte	7:30 pm
11/11	Phoenix	10:00 pm	1/10	@ Gold. St.	10:30 pm	3/11	@ New York	8:30 pm
11/13	LA Clip.	9:00 pm	1/13	LA Clip.	10:00 pm	3/12	@ Detroit	7:00 pm
11/15	@ New Jersey	7:30 pm	1/15	Portland	9:00 pm	3/14	Boston	10:00 pm
11/16	@ Boston	7:30 pm	1/17	Cleveland	10:00 pm	3/16	Miami	10:00 pm
11/18	@ Indiana	8:00 pm	1/19	@ Minn.	8:00 pm	3/18	Detroit	3:30 pm
11/19	@ Milw.	8:30 pm	1/21	@ Dallas	8:30 pm	3/20	@ San Ant.	8:30 pm
11/22	New Jersey	10:00 pm	1/24	Denver	10:00 pm	3/21	@ Houston	8:30 pm
11/23	@ Utah	9:00 pm	1/26	Utah	10:00 pm	3/23	Wash.	10:00 pm
11/25	@ San Ant.	8:30 pm	1/28	LA Lakers	3:30 pm	3/24	@ Portland	10:00 pm
11/26	@ Houston	8:30 pm	1/30	@ Phila.	7:30 pm	3/26	New York	9:00 pm
11/28	Indiana	10:00 pm	2/2	@ Orlando	8:00 pm	3/29	Minn.	10:00 pm
11/30	San Ant.	10:00 pm	2/3	@ Atlanta	8:00 pm	3/31	Sacra.	10:00 pm
12/3	Milw.	10:00 pm	2/5	@ Miami	1:00 pm	4/2	Atlanta	4:00 pm
12/6	Houston	8:00 pm	2/7	San Ant.	10:00 pm	4/4	@ Utah	9:00 pm
12/8	@ Sacra.	8:00 pm	2/9	Chicago	10:00 pm	4/6	@ Denver	8:00 pm
12/10	@ LA Clip.	10:30 pm	2/14	Gold. St.	10:00 pm	4/8	@ Dallas	8:30 pm
12/14	@ Phoenix	9:00 pm	2/15	@ LA Lakers	10:30 pm	4/11	Phoenix	9:00 pm
12/15	Portland	10:00 pm	2/17	@ Portland	10:00 pm	4/13	Dallas	10:00 pm
12/17	Orlando	10:00 pm	2/18	@ Gold. St.	10:30 pm	4/15	@ Gold. St.	3:30 pm
12/20	LA Clip.	10:00 pm	2/20	LA Lakers	10:00 pm	4/17	Portland	10:00 pm
12/22	Dallas	10:30 pm	2/22	Minn.	10:00 pm	4/18	@ LA Lakers	10:30 pm
12/25	@ Denver	4:00 pm	2/24	Denver	10:00 pm	4/20	Houston	10:00 pm
12/26	Sacra.	10:00 pm	2/27	Charlotte	10:00 pm	4/21	@ Sacra.	10:30 pm
12/28	Phila.	10:00 pm	3/2	@ LA Clip.	10:30 pm	4/23	@ Phoenix	3:30 pm
12/29	@ LA Lakers	10:30 pm	3/3	@ Phoenix	8:00 pm			
01/3	@ Wash.	7:30 pm	3/6	Gold. St.	10:00 pm			

1993–94 Team Stats

NAME	G	MIN	FG	FGA	FG%	3FG	3FGA	3FG%	FT	FTA	FT%	ORB	TRB	AST	PF	STL	BLK	TO	PTS	AVG
Kemp	79	2597	533	990	53.8	1	4	25.0	364	491	74.1	312	851	207	312	142	166	259	1431	18.1
Payton	82	2881	584	1159	50.4	15	54	27.8	166	279	59.5	105	269	494	227	188	19	173	1349	16.5
Schrempf	81	2728	445	903	49.3	22	68	32.4	300	390	76.9	144	454	275	273	73	9	173	1212	15.0
Pierce	51	1022	272	577	47.1	6	32	18.8	189	211	89.6	29	83	91	194	42	5	64	739	14.5
Gill	79	2435	429	969	44.3	38	120	31.7	215	275	78.2	91	268	275	194	151	32	143	1111	14.1
Perkins	81	2170	341	779	43.8	99	270	36.7	218	272	80.1	120	366	111	197	67	31	103	999	12.3
Askew	80	1690	273	567	48.1	6	31	19.4	175	211	82.9	60	184	194	145	73	19	70	727	9.1
McMillan	73	1887	177	396	44.7	52	133	39.1	31	55	56.4	50	283	387	201	216	22	126	437	6.0
Cage	82	1708	171	314	54.5	0	1	0.0	36	74	48.6	164	444	45	179	77	38	51	378	4.6
King	15	86	19	48	39.6	2	7	28.6	15	26	57.7	5	15	11	12	4	0	12	55	3.7
Ford	6	16	7	13	53.8	1	1	100.0	1	2	50.0	0	0	0	2	2	0	1	16	2.7
Johnson	45	280	44	106	41.5	0	0	—	29	46	63.0	48	118	7	45	10	22	24	117	2.6
Scheffler	35	152	28	46	60.9	0	0	—	19	20	95.0	11	26	6	25	7	0	8	75	2.1
King	27	78	15	34	44.1	0	1	0.0	11	22	50.0	9	20	8	18	1	2	7	41	1.5
Sonics	82	19730	3338	6901	48.4	242	722	33.5	1769	2374	74.5	1148	3381	2112	1914	1053	365	1262	8687	105.9
Opp.	82	19730	2928	6459	45.3	326	946	34.5	1760	2374	74.1	1084	3275	1808	1884	686	421	1666	7942	96.9

HISTORY

TITLES

1977–78 NBA Western Conf. champs
1978–79 Pacific Div. champs
1978–79 NBA Western Conf. champs
1978–79 NBA champs
1993–94 Pacific Div. champs

ALL-TIME TEAM RECORDS

Career

Games played	Fred Brown	963	1971–84
Total points	Fred Brown	14,018	1971–84
Field goals made	Fred Brown	6,006	1971–84
Field goals attempted	Fred Brown	12,568	1971–84
Free throws made	Jack Sikma	3,044	1977–86
Free throws attempted	Jack Sikma	3,641	1977–86
Total rebounds	Jack Sikma	7,729	1977–86
Assists	Nate McMillan	4,080	1986–94
Steals	Nate McMillan	1,212	1986–94

Season

Total points	Dale Ellis	2,253	1986–87
Field goals made	Spencer Haywood	889	1972–73
Free throws made	Lenny Wilkens	547	1968–69
Total rebounds	Jack Sikma	1,038	1981–82
Assists	Lenny Wilkens	766	1971–72
Steals	Slick Watts	261	1975–76

Game

Total points	Fred Brown	58	vs. Golden State, 3/23/74
Field goals made	Fred Brown	24	vs. Golden State, 3/23/74
Free throws made	Lenny Wilkens	21	vs. Philadelphia, 11/8/69
	Jack Sikma	21	vs. Kansas City, 11/14/80
	Spencer Haywood	21	vs. Kansas City, 1/3/73
Total rebounds	Jim Fox	30	vs. LA Lakers, 12/26/73
Assists	Nate McMillan	25	vs. LA Clippers, 2/23/87
Steals	Gus Williams	10	vs. New Jersey, 2/22/78

LEADING COACHES

NAME	REGULAR SEASON				PLAYOFFS		
	YEARS	W	L	PCT	W	L	PCT
Lenny Wilkens	1969–72, 1977–85	478	402	.543	37	32	.536
Bernie Bickerstaff	1985–90	202	208	.493	12	15	.444
Bill Russell	1973–77	162	166	.494	6	9	.400
George Karl	1992–94	145	61	.704	16	17	.485
K.C. Jones	1990–92	59	59	.500	2	3	.400

Seattle SuperSonics 1994–95 Roster

Head Coach: George Karl

No.	Name	Pos.	Ht.	Wt.	Yrs.	Born	College
17	Vincent Askew	G-F	6-6	235	5	2/28/66	Memphis State
13	Kendall Gill	G	6-5	200	4	5/25/68	Illinois
21	Byron Houston	F	6-5	250	2	11/22/69	Oklahoma State
50	Ervin Johnson	C	6-11	245	1	12/21/67	New Orleans
40	Shawn Kemp	F	6-10	245	5	11/26/69	Trinity JC
45	Rich King	C	7-2	265	3	4/4/69	Nebraska
35	Chris King	F	6-8	215	1	7/24/69	Wake Forest
30	S. Marciulionis	G	6-5	215	4	6/13/64	Lithuania
10	Nate McMillan	G-F	6-5	200	8	8/3/64	North Carolina State
20	Gary Payton	G	6-4	190	4	7/23/68	Oregon State
14	Sam Perkins	F-C	6-9	255	10	6/14/61	North Carolina
55	Steve Scheffler	C	6-9	250	4	9/3/67	Purdue
11	Detlef Schrempf	F	6-10	235	9	1/21/63	Washington
34	D. Wingfield	F	6-8	256	R	6/23/74	Cincinnati

Arena Information

Tacoma Dome (16,296)
Tickets: 206-283-DUNK, 206-628-0888 (Ticketmaster/single game tickets)
Ticket prices: $60, $33, $25, $20, $12, $7

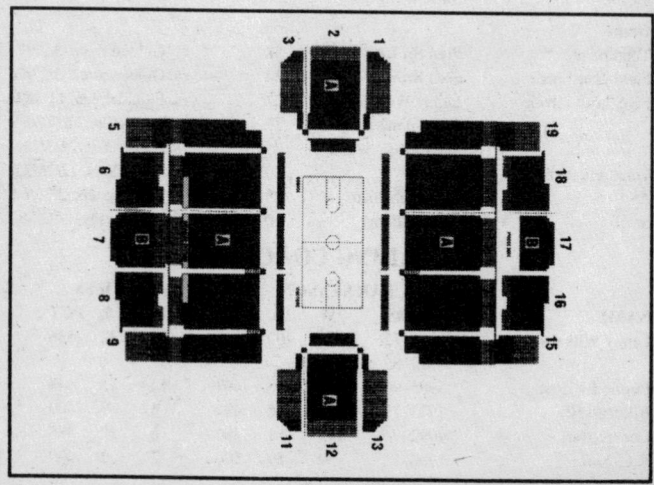

Kendall Gill

No. 13/G

Full name: Kendall Cedric Gill
HT: 6-5 **WT:** 200
Born: 5/25/68, Chicago, IL
High school: Rich Central
(Olympia Fields, IL)
College: Illinois

Gill is a future All-Star guard. He's a terrific leaper who can score and play defense. The only drawback to his offense is his shooting range; he's a career 45 percent shooter from the field. He's also had trouble from 3-point range: he entered last season a 24.8 percent shooter from 3-point range, but shot 31.7 percent from beyond the arc, a career-high. A point guard who was moved to shooting guard at Charlotte, Gill can dish out assists as well as score. He tied for third on the Sonics in assists, and was Seattle's fourth-leading scorer. Gill finished fourteenth in the NBA in steals, averaging 1.91 per game. Seattle was 14–2 when he scored at least 20 points. He had two double-doubles.

REGULAR SEASON		G	MIN	FG	FGx	3FG	3PTx	FT	FTx	REB	AST	STL	BLK	PTS	AVG
'90-91	CHARLOTTE	82	1944	376	45.0	2	14.3	152	83.5	263	303	104	39	906	11.0
'91-92	CHARLOTTE	79	2906	666	46.7	6	24.0	284	74.5	402	329	154	46	1622	20.5
'92-93	CHARLOTTE	69	2430	463	44.9	17	27.4	224	77.2	340	268	98	36	1167	16.9
'93-94	SEATTLE	79	2435	429	44.3	38	31.7	215	78.2	268	275	151	32	1111	14.1
4 YR TOTALS		309	9715	1934	45.4	63	28.5	875	77.6	1273	1175	507	153	4806	15.6
'93-94	RANK NBA Gs	40	38	34	72	51	72	24	68	31	50	11	16	34	37
'94-95	PROJECTIONS	82	2413	389	43.6	60	36.1	208	78.5	223	263	173	27	1046	12.8

PLAYOFFS		G	MIN	FG	FGx	3FG	3PTx	FT	FTx	REB	AST	STL	BLK	PTS	AVG
'92-93	CHARLOTTE	9	353	65	40.1	1	16.7	25	71.4	46	26	21	6	156	17.3
'93-94	SEATTLE	5	153	26	43.3	2	22.2	13	61.9	24	10	6	1	67	13.4
TOTALS		14	506	91	41.0	3	20.0	38	67.9	70	36	27	7	223	15.9

Shawn Kemp

No. 40/F

Full name: Shawn T. Kemp
HT: 6-10   **WT:** 245
Born: 11/26/69, Elkhart, IN
High school: Concord (Elkhart)
College: Trinity Valley
   Community (TX)

Kemp has good low-post moves, is unstoppable inside, and has a nice outside shot. He averaged 18.1 points, 10.8 rebounds, and 2.1 blocks per game, shooting 54 percent from the field. Kemp led the team in scoring, rebounding, blocked shots and shooting percentage. He was the Sonics' leading scorer 22 times, its leading rebounder 60 times. He had 47 double-doubles, as well as his first career triple-double against Charlotte March 20, with 15 points, 11 rebounds and a career high 12 assists. A spectacular athlete, Kemp finished third in the slam-dunk contest on All-Star weekend. He's one of the better defensive small forwards, but he has a tendency to get into foul trouble.

REGULAR SEASON		G	MIN	FG	FGx	3FG	3PTx	FT	FTx	REB	AST	STL	BLK	PTS	AVG
'89-90	SEATTLE	81	1120	203	47.9	2	16.7	117	73.6	346	26	47	70	525	6.5
'90-91	SEATTLE	81	2442	462	50.8	2	16.7	288	66.1	679	144	77	123	1214	15.0
'91-92	SEATTLE	64	1808	362	50.4	0	0.0	270	74.8	665	86	70	124	994	15.5
'92-93	SEATTLE	78	2582	515	49.2	0	0.0	358	71.2	833	155	119	146	1388	17.8
'93-94	SEATTLE	79	2597	533	53.8	1	25.0	364	74.1	851	207	142	166	1431	18.1
5 YR TOTALS		383	10549	2075	50.8	5	14.3	1397	71.6	3374	618	455	629	5552	14.5
'93-94	RANK NBA Fs	30	23	15	12	63	49	5	46	7	23	3	1	10	14
'94-95	PROJECTIONS	81	2805	588	56.1	1	50.0	402	75.4	924	263	173	186	1579	19.5

PLAYOFFS		G	MIN	FG	FGx	3FG	3PTx	FT	FTx	REB	AST	STL	BLK	PTS	AVG
'90-91	SEATTLE	5	149	22	38.6	0	0.0	22	81.5	36	6	3	4	66	13.2
'91-92	SEATTLE	9	338	48	47.5	0	---	61	76.3	110	4	5	14	157	17.4
'92-93	SEATTLE	19	663	110	51.2	0	---	93	80.9	190	49	29	40	313	16.5
'93-94	SEATTLE	5	206	26	37.1	0	---	22	66.7	49	17	10	12	74	14.8
TOTALS		38	1356	206	46.5	0	0.0	198	77.6	385	76	47	70	610	16.1

Gary Payton

No. 20/G

Full name: Gary Dwayne Payton
HT: 6-4   **WT:** 190
Born: 7/23/68, Oakland, CA
High school: Skyline (Oakland)
College: Oregon State

Payton is considered the best defensive point guard in the NBA. He was named to the West All-Star team as a replacement for Charles Barkley. He's also a good playmaker. Payton led the Sonics in assists and was Seattle's second-leading scorer. Payton doesn't have outstanding shooting range and gets most of his points cutting to the basket. He runs the floor as well as anyone in the NBA. His 50.4 FG percentage was first among NBA point guards. He scored 20 or more points 24 times; the Sonics were 21–3 in those games. He had problems from the free throw line last season, hitting less than 60 percent of his attempts. He's only missed 1 game in 4 years as a pro.

REGULAR SEASON		G	MIN	FG	FGx	3FG	3PTx	FT	FTx	REB	AST	STL	BLK	PTS	AVG
'90-91	SEATTLE	82	2244	259	45.0	1	7.7	69	71.1	243	528	165	15	588	7.2
'91-92	SEATTLE	81	2549	331	45.1	3	13.0	99	66.9	295	506	147	21	764	9.4
'92-93	SEATTLE	82	2548	476	49.4	7	20.6	151	77.0	281	399	177	21	1110	13.5
'93-94	SEATTLE	82	2881	584	50.4	15	27.8	166	59.5	269	494	188	19	1349	16.5
4 YR TOTALS		327	10222	1650	48.1	26	21.0	485	67.4	1088	1927	677	76	3811	11.7
'93-94 RANK NBA Gs		1	10	5	8	80	89	47	130	30	15	6	39	10	18
'94-95 PROJECTIONS		82	3118	725	52.2	26	35.1	185	51.2	257	514	200	18	1661	20.3
PLAYOFFS		G	MIN	FG	FGx	3FG	3PTx	FT	FTx	REB	AST	STL	BLK	PTS	AVG
'90-91	SEATTLE	5	135	11	40.7	0	0.0	2	100.0	13	32	8	1	24	4.8
'91-92	SEATTLE	8	221	27	46.6	0	0.0	7	58.3	21	38	8	2	61	7.6
'92-93	SEATTLE	19	605	104	44.3	1	16.7	25	67.6	63	70	34	3	234	12.3
'93-94	SEATTLE	5	181	34	49.3	3	33.3	8	42.1	17	28	8	2	79	15.8
TOTALS		37	1142	176	45.2	4	22.2	42	60.0	114	168	58	8	398	10.8

Sam Perkins

No. 14/F-C

Full name: Samuel Bruce Perkins
HT: 6-9 **WT:** 255
Born: 6/14/61, Brooklyn, NY
High school: Shaker (Latham, NY)
College: North Carolina

Perkins is one of the most under-rated centers in the league. He plays good defense, gets his share of rebounds, and is one of the most versatile offensive players at his position in the NBA. Perkins combines a strong post-up game with a deadly touch from outside. He tied the NBA record for most 3-pointers without a miss in a single game when he went 7 for 7 from 3-point range on November 9 vs. Denver. His 99 3-point FGM were the most by a Sonic since Dale Ellis' 162 in the '88–89 season. He scored 20 points or more 9 times, and Seattle was 8–1 in those games.

REGULAR SEASON		G	MIN	FG	FGx	3FG	3PT%	FT	FT%	REB	AST	STL	BLK	PTS	AVG
'84-85	DALLAS	82	2317	347	47.1	9	25.0	200	82.0	605	135	63	63	903	11.0
'85-86	DALLAS	80	2626	458	50.3	11	33.3	307	81.4	685	153	75	94	1234	15.4
'86-87	DALLAS	80	2687	461	48.2	19	35.2	245	82.8	616	146	109	77	1186	14.8
'87-88	DALLAS	75	2439	394	45.0	5	16.7	273	82.2	601	118	74	54	1066	14.2
'88-89	DALLAS	78	2860	445	46.4	7	18.4	274	83.3	688	127	76	54	1171	15.0
'89-90	DALLAS	76	2668	435	49.3	6	21.4	330	77.8	572	175	88	64	1206	15.9
'90-91	LA LAKERS	73	2504	368	49.5	18	28.1	229	82.1	538	108	64	78	983	13.5
'91-92	LA LAKERS	63	2332	361	45.0	15	21.7	304	81.7	556	141	64	62	1041	16.5
'92-93	LAL-SEA	79	2351	381	47.7	24	33.8	250	82.0	524	156	60	82	1036	13.1
'93-94	SEATTLE	81	2170	341	43.8	99	36.7	218	80.1	366	111	67	31	999	12.3
10 YR TOTALS		767	25014	3991	47.3	213	30.7	2630	81.4	5751	1370	740	697	10825	14.1
'93-94	RANK NBA Fs	15	41	44	106	3	14	26	13	56	53	40	71	31	34
'94-95	PROJECTIONS	82	2046	319	41.9	146	40.8	194	79.5	286	94	67	11	978	11.9

PLAYOFFS		G	MIN	FG	FGx	3FG	3PT%	FT	FT%	REB	AST	STL	BLK	PTS	AVG
'84-85	DALLAS	4	169	24	43.0	1	25.0	26	76.5	51	11	2	1	75	18.8
'85-86	DALLAS	10	347	57	42.9	2	25.0	33	76.7	83	24	9	14	149	14.9
'86-87	DALLAS	4	133	26	50.0	0	0.0	16	69.6	34	5	4	1	68	17.0
'87-88	DALLAS	17	572	88	45.1	1	14.3	53	80.3	112	31	25	17	230	13.5
'89-90	DALLAS	3	118	16	44.4	0	0.0	13	76.5	22	8	3	2	45	15.0
'90-91	LA LAKERS	19	752	121	54.8	11	36.7	83	76.1	157	33	15	27	336	17.7
'92-93	SEATTLE	19	626	98	43.6	30	38.0	48	87.3	133	37	19	25	274	14.4
'93-94	SEATTLE	5	141	14	33.3	6	42.9	15	88.2	36	4	4	2	49	9.8
TOTALS		81	2858	444	46.6	51	34.7	287	78.8	628	153	81	89	1226	15.1

Detlef Schrempf

No. 11/F

HT: 6-10   **WT:** 235
Born: 1/21/63, Leverkusen, West
    Germany
High school: Centralia (WA)
College: Washington

A two-time winner of the NBA
Sixth Man Award, Schrempf can
do virtually anything on a basketball court. He's one of the few
players capable of being among
the league leaders in points,
rebounding and assists. And
thanks to his size and athleticism,
he generally matches up well on
defense with opposing small forwards. Last season, Schrempf
was third on the team in scoring,
second in rebounds, and tied for
third in assists. He was also second on the team in turnovers and
personal fouls. He had 10 double-
doubles. He scored 20 points or more 11 times; Seattle was 10–1
when did. He led the Sonics in scoring 15 times and in rebounding 8
times.

REGULAR SEASON		G	MIN	FG	FG%	3FG	3PT%	FT	FT%	REB	AST	STL	BLK	PTS	AVG
'85-86	DALLAS	64	969	142	45.1	3	42.9	110	72.4	198	88	23	10	397	6.2
'86-87	DALLAS	81	1711	265	47.2	33	47.8	193	74.2	303	161	50	16	756	9.3
'87-88	DALLAS	82	1587	246	45.6	5	15.6	201	75.6	279	159	42	32	698	8.5
'88-89	DAL-IND	69	1850	274	47.4	7	20.0	273	78.0	395	179	53	19	828	12.0
'89-90	INDIANA	78	2573	424	51.6	17	35.4	402	82.0	620	247	59	16	1267	16.2
'90-91	INDIANA	82	2632	432	52.0	15	37.5	441	81.8	660	301	58	22	1320	16.1
'91-92	INDIANA	80	2605	496	53.6	23	32.4	365	82.8	770	312	62	37	1380	17.3
'92-93	INDIANA	82	3098	517	47.6	8	15.4	525	80.4	780	493	79	27	1567	19.1
'93-94	SEATTLE	81	2728	445	49.3	22	32.4	300	76.9	454	275	73	9	1212	15.0
9 YR TOTALS		699	19753	3241	49.4	133	31.5	2810	79.4	4459	2215	499	188	9425	13.5
'93-94 RANK NBA Fs		15	15	23	40	30	29	10	31	39	10	32	120	19	26
'94-95 PROJECTIONS		81	2669	423	48.7	27	36.5	228	74.5	313	222	75	0	1101	13.6

PLAYOFFS		G	MIN	FG	FG%	3FG	3PT%	FT	FT%	REB	AST	STL	BLK	PTS	AVG
'85-86	DALLAS	10	120	13	46.4	0	0.0	11	64.7	23	14	2	1	37	3.7
'86-87	DALLAS	4	97	13	37.1	0	0.0	5	45.5	12	6	3	2	31	7.8
'87-88	DALLAS	15	274	40	46.5	1	33.3	36	70.6	55	24	8	7	117	7.8
'88-90	INDIANA	3	125	23	48.9	0	0.0	15	93.8	22	5	2	1	61	20.3
'90-91	INDIANA	5	179	27	47.4	0	0.0	25	83.3	36	11	2	0	79	15.8
'91-92	INDIANA	3	120	18	38.3	2	50.0	25	89.3	39	7	2	1	63	21.0
'92-93	INDIANA	4	165	25	39.1	0	0.0	28	77.8	23	29	1	-2	78	19.5
'93-94	SEATTLE	5	174	26	52.0	2	33.3	39	86.7	27	10	1	3	93	18.6
TOTALS		49	1254	185	44.7	5	19.2	184	78.6	237	106	21	17	559	11.4

Vincent Askew   No. 17/G-F

Full name: Vincent Jerome Askew
HT: 6-6   **WT:** 235
Born: 2/28/66, Memphis, TN
High school: Frayser (Memphis)
College: Memphis State

A defensive force at forward, Askew can also score in the clutch. He had career highs in nearly every major category last season.

REGULAR SEASON		G	MIN	FG	FGx	3FG	3PTx	FT	FTx	REB	AST	STL	BLK	PTS	AVG
'90-91	GOLDEN STATE	7	85	12	48.0	0	---	9	81.8	11	13	2	0	33	4.7
'91-92	GOLDEN STATE	80	1496	193	50.9	1	10.0	111	69.4	233	198	47	23	498	6.2
'92-93	SAC-SEA	73	1129	152	49.2	2	33.3	105	70.5	161	122	40	19	411	5.6
'93-94	SEATTLE	80	1690	273	48.1	6	19.4	175	82.9	184	194	73	19	727	9.1
5 YR TOTALS		254	4634	652	48.2	9	19.1	408	75.3	611	550	172	67	1721	6.8
'93-94	RANK NBA Gs	33	70	64	23	103	117	42	37	61	73	62	39	63	72
'94-95	PROJECTIONS	82	2079	371	48.8	11	20.8	239	88.5	195	229	100	19	992	12.1

PLAYOFFS		G	MIN	FG	FGx	3FG	3PTx	FT	FTx	REB	AST	STL	BLK	PTS	AVG
'90-91	GOLDEN STATE	6	41	6	40.0	0	---	3	50.0	11	2	2	0	15	2.5
'91-92	GOLDEN STATE	4	30	1	12.5	0	---	0	---	4	5	0	0	2	0.5
'92-93	SEATTLE	12	103	23	56.1	0	---	16	69.6	19	9	1	1	62	5.2
'93-94	SEATTLE	5	95	10	35.7	0	0.0	16	84.2	6	9	2	0	36	7.2
TOTALS		27	269	40	43.5	0	0.0	35	72.9	40	25	5	1	115	4.3

Ervin Johnson   No. 50/C

Full name: Ervin Johnson, Jr.
HT: 6-11 **WT:** 245
Born: 12/21/67, New Orleans, LA
High school: Block (Jonesville, LA)
College: New Orleans

Johnson is hardworking, coachable, and a strong leaper and rebounder. He was a tremendous shotblocker in college.

REGULAR SEASON		G	MIN	FG	FGx	3FG	3PTx	FT	FTx	REB	AST	STL	BLK	PTS	AVG
'93-94	SEATTLE	45	280	44	41.5	0	---	29	63.0	118	7	10	22	117	2.6
1 YR TOTALS		45	280	44	41.5	0	---	29	63.0	118	7	10	22	117	2.6
'93-94	RANK NBA Cs	37	48	42	48	14	14	40	35	41	50	38	37	41	42

PLAYOFFS		G	MIN	FG	FGx	3FG	3PTx	FT	FTx	REB	AST	STL	BLK	PTS	AVG
'93-94	SEATTLE	2	8	0	0.0	0	---	0	---	4	0	0	0	0	0.0
TOTALS		2	8	0	0.0	0	---	0	---	4	0	0	0	0	0.0

S. Marciulionis   No.30/G

Full name: Raimondas Sarunas Marciulionis
HT: 6-5   **WT:** 215
Born: 6/13/64, Kaunas, U.S.S.R.
College: State Univ. of Vilnius (Lithuania)

When healthy, Marciulionis is one of the best scorers in the game. He can drive to the basket, or he can pop jumpers from outside.

REGULAR SEASON		G	MIN	FG	FG%	3FG	3PT%	FT	FT%	REB	AST	STL	BLK	PTS	AVG
'89-90	GOLDEN STATE	75	1695	289	51.9	10	25.6	317	78.7	221	121	94	7	905	12.1
'90-91	GOLDEN STATE	50	987	183	50.1	1	16.7	178	72.4	118	85	62	4	545	10.9
'91-92	GOLDEN STATE	72	2117	491	53.8	3	30.0	376	78.8	208	243	116	10	1361	18.9
'92-93	GOLDEN STATE	30	836	178	54.3	3	20.0	162	76.1	97	105	51	2	521	17.4
'93-94	GOLDEN STATE	did not play -- injured (knee)													
5 YR TOTALS		227	5635	1141	52.8	17	24.3	1033	77.1	644	554	323	23	3332	14.7
'93-94	RANK NBA Gs	not ranked -- didn't appear in 25 games in '93-94													
'94-95	PROJECTIONS	8	288	62	55.4	1	14.3	58	75.3	34	41	18	0	183	22.9

PLAYOFFS		G	MIN	FG	FG%	3FG	3PT%	FT	FT%	REB	AST	STL	BLK	PTS	AVG
'90-91	GOLDEN STATE	9	206	42	50.0	0	0.0	35	89.7	23	27	11	1	119	13.2
'91-92	GOLDEN STATE	4	133	25	53.2	1	50.0	34	82.9	9	20	3	1	85	21.3
TOTALS		13	339	67	51.1	1	33.3	69	86.3	32	47	14	2	204	15.7

Nate McMillan   No. 10/G-F

Full name: Nathaniel McMillan
HT: 6-5   **WT:** 200
Born: 8/3/64, Raleigh, NC
High school: Enloe (Raleigh)
College: North Carolina State

McMillan is a defensive stud when matched up against guards or small forwards. He plays particularly well in a pressing defense.

REGULAR SEASON		G	MIN	FG	FG%	3FG	3PT%	FT	FT%	REB	AST	STL	BLK	PTS	AVG
'89-90	SEATTLE	82	2338	207	47.3	11	35.5	98	64.1	403	598	140	37	523	6.4
'90-91	SEATTLE	78	1434	132	43.3	17	35.4	57	61.3	251	371	104	20	338	4.3
'91-92	SEATTLE	72	1652	177	43.7	27	27.6	54	64.3	252	359	129	29	435	6.0
'92-93	SEATTLE	73	1977	213	46.4	25	38.5	95	70.9	306	384	173	33	546	7.5
'93-94	SEATTLE	73	1887	177	44.7	52	39.1	31	56.4	283	387	216	22	437	6.0
8 YR TOTALS		606	16054	1483	45.1	156	32.8	686	65.1	2552	4080	1212	275	3808	6.3
'93-94	RANK NBA Gs	71	65	90	66	38	25	119	133	25	26	1	30	93	101
'94-95	PROJECTIONS	72	1903	170	44	69	41.3	11	50.0	276	378	252	18	420	5.8

PLAYOFFS		G	MIN	FG	FG%	3FG	3PT%	FT	FT%	REB	AST	STL	BLK	PTS	AVG
'90-91	SEATTLE	5	95	6	26.1	0	0.0	2	50.0	18	22	6	1	14	2.8
'91-92	SEATTLE	9	246	35	42.2	6	23.1	10	71.4	33	63	16	3	86	9.6
'92-93	SEATTLE	19	415	35	34.0	5	20.8	16	53.3	67	103	40	11	91	4.8
'93-94	SEATTLE	5	109	8	32.0	4	36.4	1	25.0	16	10	6	1	21	4.2
TOTALS		65	1548	142	38.3	15	22.7	71	61.7	234	406	94	34	370	5.7

Dontonio Wingfield   No. 34/F

SEATTLE SUPERSONICS

HT: 6-8   **WT:** 256
Born: 6/23/74, Albany, GA
College: Cincinnati
Wingfield played just one season in college. He averaged 16 points and 9 rebounds per game while being named Great Midwest Conference Newcomer of the Year and Second Team All-Conference.

REGULAR SEASON	G	MIN	FG	FG%	3FG	3PT%	FT	FT%	REB	AST	STL	BLK	PTS	AVG
ROOKIE -- NO NBA EXPERIENCE														

George Karl   Head Coach

Full name: George Matthew Karl
HT: 6-2   **WT:** 190
Born: 5/12/51, Penn Hills, PA
High school: Penn Hills (PA)
College: North Carolina
He's been called the Billy Martin of the NBA. Karl has the highest winning percentage (.703) of any coach in Seattle's history.

	REGULAR SEASON				PLAYOFFS			
YEAR	TEAM	W	L	PCT	FINISH	W	L	PCT	
'84-85	CLEVELAND	36	46	.439	4th/Central Div.	1	3	.250	lost Eastern Conf. first round to Boston,
'85-86	CLEVELAND	25	42	.373					
'86-87	GOLDEN STATE	42	40	.512	3rd/Pacific Div.	4	6	.400	lost Western Conf. semifinals to LA Lakers, 4-1
'87-88	GOLDEN STATE	16	48	.250					
'91-92	SEATTLE	27	15	.643	4th/Pacific Div.	4	5	.444	lost Western Conf. to Utah, 4-1
'92-93	SEATTLE	55	27	.671	2nd/Pacific Div.	10	9	.526	lost Western Conf. finals to Phoenix, 4-3
'93-94	SEATTLE	63	19	.768	1st/Pacific Div.	2	3	.400	lost Western Conf. first round to Denver, 3-2
	7 YR TOTALS	264	237	.527		21	26	.447	

Utah
JAZZ

1994–95 Scouting Report

Frontcourt

Utah has one of the most physical frontcourts this side of New York. Power forward Karl Malone is big enough to go through smaller forwards, and quick enough to go around bigger ones. He's got the best perimeter shot among power forwards in the NBA, and he's unstoppable in the low post. He's also a very good defensive player. Felton Spencer is a big, strong center who doesn't shy away from contact and is a good rebounder and shotblocker. His biggest problem is that his slow feet can cause him to get into foul trouble. Tyrone Corbin plays small forward like a power forward, concentrating on defense, rebounds, and an inside game on offense. Center Luther Wright, Utah's top pick in the '93 draft, is a good rebounder and shotblocker. He needs to develop more low-post moves. He had trouble maintaining intensity, but was diagnosed last season as suffering from Attention Deficit Disorder. The Utah bench also features David Benoit, Bryon Russell, and Stephen Howard. Benoit plays small forward; he's got talent as an offensive threat and shotblocker, but he's had trouble with consistency. Russell plays like a younger version of Tyrone Corbin. Howard played in Europe most of last season, where he scored 21.5 points per game and averaged 11.1 rebounds.

Backcourt

John Stockton is still the best point guard in the league. He led the league in assists (12.6 per game), shot 53 percent from the field, (leading all NBA guards), and is a scrappy defender. At shooting guard, Jeff Hornacek can score from the perimeter or create off the dribble. Reserves include Jay Humphries and John Crotty. Humphries can play either guard position, and is a talented penetrator. Crotty is a good playmaker, with a great shot from 3-point range.

Defense

The Jazz held opponents to just 97.7 points per game, ninth lowest in the NBA. Opponents averaged 44.8 percent shooting from the field, fifth lowest in the NBA. The Jazz frontline isn't particularly agile (Utah was just twenty-second in blocked shots), but they can body up on defense. They get their share of rebounds off the defensive glass. And they employ double-teams to force opponents to use up the shot clock. As a result, opponents attempted just 6,641 shots from the field, seventh fewest in the league. Utah ranked ninth in the NBA in stealing the ball and fifteenth in the league in forcing turnovers. But Utah's style of D comes at a price; the Jazz collected the fifth highest number of fouls in the league last season.

1994–95 Prospects

The Jazz rode a franchise-record 20 road wins to a 53–29 record—a 6 game improvement over the previous year. They swept the season series against San Antonio, and were fortunate enough to draw the Spurs in the first round of the playoffs. Utah matches up well with the Spurs because San Antonio has trouble with Utah's defensive pressure. In fact, going back to the '92–93 season, Utah has won 10 out of 11 from the Spurs (including the '93–94 playoffs). However, fast, athletic teams like Seattle and Golden State give the Jazz problems. (And, of course, Denver took the Jazz to the brink in the Western semifinals last season.)

Utah ranked tenth in total points in the NBA. Because the Jazz have so many big, slow-footed players, they don't have the running game that can create transition baskets. Their half-court offense combines Karl Malone's low-post game with John Stockton and Jeff Hornacek's ability to score from anywhere. The other players on the court rely on putbacks and shots from the paint. That's why Utah ranked sixth in field goal percentage.

Utah will return to the playoffs once again. Although Malone will be 31 years old and Stockton 32, they should be effective for several more seasons. And remember, this is not a running team. Utah projects to a 49–33 season. But Utah could advance in the playoffs if they draw the right pairings and avoid teams like Seattle, Phoenix, and Golden State, who can wear Utah down with their fast-paced styles.

Team Directory

Owner: Larry H. Miller   President: Frank Layden

Dir. of basketball oper.: Scott Layden   General manager: R. Tim Howells

VP, public rel.: David Allred   Dir., media services: Kim Turner

1993–94 Review

WESTERN CONFERENCE						EASTERN CONFERENCE					
MIDWEST DIV.		PACIFIC DIV.				ATLANTIC DIV.			CENTRAL DIV.		
	W	L		W	L		W	L		W	L
HOU	3	3	SEA	1	3	NY	2	0	ATL	1	1
SAN	5	0	PHO	2	2	ORL	0	2	CHI	0	2
UTAH	–	–	GS	1	3	NJ	1	1	CLE	1	1
DEN	4	1	POR	3	1	MIA	1	1	IND	1	1
MIN	4	1	LAL	2	2	BOS	2	0	CHA	1	1
DAL	5	0	SAC	3	1	PHI	1	1	DET	2	0
			LAC	3	1	WAS	2	0	MIL	2	0
	21	5		15	13		9	5		8	6

1993–94 finish: 53–29 (33–8 home, 20–21 away), third in Midwest Div.

1994–95 Schedule

11/4	Miami	9:00 pm	1/3	Milw.	9:00 pm	3/1	@ Gold. St.	10:30 pm
11/5	@ Seattle	10:00 pm	1/5	San Ant.	8:00 pm	3/4	Portland	3:30 pm
11/7	Atlanta	9:00 pm	1/7	Phila.	9:00 pm	3/7	@ Sacra.	10:30 pm
11/9	@ San Ant.	8:30 pm	1/9	Dallas	9:00 pm	3/8	Dallas	9:00 pm
11/11	Gold. St.	9:00 pm	1/11	Denver	9:00 pm	3/10	Sacra.	9:00 pm
11/12	@ Denver	9:00 pm	1/13	@ Boston	8:00 pm	3/12	@ Miami	6:00 pm
11/14	New York	9:00 pm	1/14	@ New York	7:30 pm	3/14	@ Orlando	7:30 pm
11/18	Detroit	9:00 pm	1/16	@ Indiana	6:00 pm	3/16	@ Cleveland	7:30 pm
11/19	@ Gold. St.	10:30 pm	1/18	@ Detroit	7:30 pm	3/17	@ New Jersey	7:30 pm
11/21	Phoenix	9:00 pm	1/20	Cleveland	9:00 pm	3/19	@ Charlotte	12:00 pm
11/23	Seattle	9:00 pm	1/23	Dallas	9:00 pm	3/22	Denver	9:00 pm
11/25	Chicago	9:00 pm	1/25	Sacra.	9:00 pm	3/23	@ Houston	8:30 pm
11/27	@ Sacra.	9:00 pm	1/26	@ Seattle	10:00 pm	3/25	@ Dallas	8:30 pm
11/29	@ Portland	10:00 pm	1/28	New Jersey	9:00 pm	3/27	Wash.	9:00 pm
12/1	Minn.	9:00 pm	1/30	Minn.	9:00 pm	3/28	@ Phoenix	9:00 pm
12/3	@ Dallas	8:30 pm	2/1	Denver	9:00 pm	3/31	Orlando	8:00 pm
12/6	Charlotte	9:00 pm	2/2	@ Houston	8:30 pm	4/1	@ LA Clip.	10:30 pm
12/8	@ San Ant.	8:30 pm	2/4	@ Dallas	8:30 pm	4/4	Seattle	9:00 pm
12/10	LA Lakers	9:00 pm	2/7	@ LA Clip.	10:30 pm	4/7	@ LA Lakers	10:30 pm
12/12	Portland	9:00 pm	2/8	Phoenix	9:00 pm	4/11	LA Lakers	9:00 pm
12/14	@ Minn.	8:00 pm	2/14	@ San Ant.	8:00 pm	4/13	Gold. St.	8:00 pm
12/15	@ Wash.	7:30 pm	2/16	San Ant.	9:00 pm	4/15	LA Clip.	9:00 pm
12/17	@ Chicago	8:30 pm	2/18	Boston	9:00 pm	4/18	@ Minn.	8:00 pm
12/18	@ Milw.	7:00 pm	2/19	@ Phoenix	9:00 pm	4/19	Houston	9:00 pm
12/20	@ Phila.	7:30 pm	2/22	LA Clip.	9:00 pm	4/21	Minn.	9:00 pm
12/22	@ Atlanta	7:30 pm	2/24	@ Portland	10:00 pm	4/23	@ Houston	3:30 pm
12/28	Indiana	9:00 pm	2/26	@ Denver	3:30 pm			
12/30	Houston	9:00 pm	2/27	@ LA Lakers	10:30 pm			

364 Street & Smith's Guide to Pro Basketball 1994

1993–94 Team Stats

NAME	G	MIN	FG	FGA	FG%	3FG	3FGA	3FG%	FT	FTA	FT%	ORB	TRB	AST	PF	STL	BLK	TO	PTS	AVG
K. Malone	82	3329	772	1552	49.7	8	32	25.0	511	736	69.4	235	940	328	268	125	126	234	2063	25.2
J. Malone	50	1657	338	692	48.8	3	6	50.0	129	153	84.3	66	115	66	77	26	5	57	808	16.2
Stockton	82	2969	458	868	52.8	48	149	32.2	272	338	80.5	72	258	1031	236	199	22	266	1236	15.1
Hornacek	27	826	147	289	50.9	18	42	42.9	82	92	89.1	19	67	104	71	32	3	33	394	14.6
Chambers	80	1838	329	748	44.0	14	45	31.1	221	281	78.6	87	326	79	232	40	32	89	893	11.2
Spencer	79	2210	256	507	50.5	0	0	—	165	272	60.7	235	658	43	304	41	67	127	677	8.6
Corbin	82	2149	268	588	45.6	6	29	20.7	117	144	81.3	150	389	122	212	99	24	92	659	8.0
Humphries	75	1619	233	535	43.6	38	96	39.6	57	76	75.0	35	127	219	168	65	11	95	561	7.5
Benoit	55	1070	139	361	38.5	12	59	20.3	68	88	77.3	89	260	23	115	23	37	37	358	6.5
Russell	67	1121	135	279	48.4	2	22	9.1	62	101	61.4	61	181	54	138	68	19	55	334	5.0
Howard	9	53	10	17	58.8	0	0	—	11	16	68.8	10	16	0	13	1	3	6	31	3.4
Bond	56	559	63	156	40.4	19	54	35.2	31	40	77.5	20	61	31	90	16	12	17	176	3.1
Gallagher	2	3	3	3	100.0	0	0	—	0	0	—	0	0	0	2	0	0	0	6	3.0
Crotty	45	313	45	99	45.5	11	24	45.8	31	36	86.1	11	31	77	36	15	1	27	132	2.9
Morningstar	1	4	1	1	100.0	0	1	0.0	0	0	—	0	0	0	0	0	0	0	2	2.0
Wright	15	92	8	23	34.8	0	0	—	3	4	75.0	6	10	0	21	1	2	6	19	1.3
Jamerson	4	4	0	2	0.0	0	0	—	1	1	100.0	0	1	0	0	0	0	0	4	1.0
Williams	6	12	2	8	25.0	0	0	—	0	0	0.0	1	3	0	4	0	0	1	4	0.7
Green	1	2	0	0	—	0	0	—	0	0	—	0	0	0	0	0	0	0	0	0.0
Jazz	82	19830	3207	6729	47.7	179	559	32.0	1761	2379	74.0	1059	3444	2179	1988	751	364	1191	8354	101.9
Opp.	82	19830	2973	6641	44.8	289	967	29.9	1773	2444	72.5	1100	3427	1806	1922	593	459	1318	8008	97.7

HISTORY

TITLES

1988–89 Midwest Div. champs
1983–84 Midwest Div. champs

1988–89 Midwest Div. champs
1991–92 Midwest Div. champs

ALL-TIME TEAM RECORDS

Career

Games played	Mark Eaton	875	1982–93
Total points	Karl Malone	19,050	1985–94
Field goals made	Karl Malone	7,027	1985–94
Free throws made	Karl Malone	4,956	1985–94
Total rebounds	Karl Malone	8,058	1985–94
Assists	John Stockton	9,383	1984–94
Steals	John Stockton	2,031	1984–94

Season

Total points	Karl Malone	2,540	1989–90
Scoring average	Pete Maravich	31	1976–77
Field goals made	Karl Malone	914	1989–90
Free throws made	Adrian Dantley	813	1983–84
Total rebounds	Len "Truck" Robinson	1,288	1977–78
Assists	John Stockton	1,164	1990–91
Steals	John Stockton	263	1988–89

Game

Total points	Pete Maravich	68	vs. New York, 2/25/77
Field goals made	Pete Maravich	26	vs. New York, 2/25/77
Free throws made	Adrian Dantley	28	vs. Houston, 1/4/84
Total rebounds	Len "Truck" Robinson	27	vs. Indiana, 12/7/77
	Len "Truck" Robinson	27	vs. LA Lakers, 11/11/77
Assists	John Stockton	28	vs. San Antonio, 1/15/91
Steals	Rickey Green	9	vs. Denver, 11/10/82
	Rickey Green	9	vs. Philadelphia, 11/27/82
	John Stockton	9	vs. Houston, 2/12/91

LEADING COACHES

		REGULAR SEASON			PLAYOFFS		
NAME	YEARS	W	L	PCT	W	L	PCT
Richie Guerin	1964–72	327	291	.529	26	34	.433
Mike Fratello	1983–90	324	250	.564	18	22	.450
Hubie Brown	1976–81	199	208	.489	6	10	.375
Cotton Fitzsimmons	1972–76	140	180	.438	2	4	.333
Bob Weiss	1990–93	124	122	.504	2	6	.250

Utah Jazz 1994–95 Roster

Head Coach: Jerry Sloan

No.	Name	Pos.	Ht.	Wt.	Yrs.	Born	College
21	David Benoit	F	6-8	220	3	5/9/68	Alabama
20	Walter Bond	G	6-5	200	2	2/1/69	Minnesota
23	Tyrone Corbin	F	6-6	222	9	12/31/62	DePaul
25	John Crotty	G	6-1	185	2	7/15/69	Virginia
14	Jeff Hornacek	G	6-4	190	8	5/3/63	Iowa State
43	Stephen Howard	F	6-9	230	2	7/15/70	DePaul
6	Jay Humphries	G	6-3	185	10	10/17/62	Colorado
32	Karl Malone	F	6-9	256	9	7/24/63	Louisiana Tech
34	Bryon Russell	F	6-7	225	1	12/31/70	Long Beach State
50	Felton Spencer	C	7-0	265	4	1/5/68	Louisville
12	John Stockton	G	6-1	175	10	3/26/62	Gonzaga
15	Jamie Watson	F	6-7	190	R	2/23/72	South Carolina
44	Luther Wright	C	7-2	270	1	9/22/71	Seton Hall

Arena Information

Delta Center (19,911)
Tickets: 801-355-3865
Ticket prices: $47, $42, $37, $34, $22, $17, $12, $9

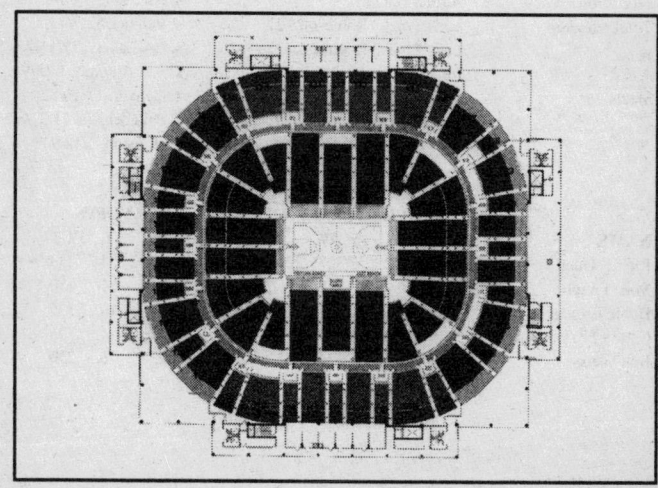

Tyrone Corbin

No. 23/F

Full name: Tyrone Kennedy Corbin
HT: 6-6 **WT:** 222
Born: 12/31/62, Columbia, SC
High school: A.C. Flora (Columbia)
College: DePaul

Corbin brings a blue-collar approach to small forward. He's a rugged inside player who plays tough defense and is willing to work in the paint for rebounds. Offensively, he's not flashy: he can't pop the 20-foot jumper, and he can't create a shot off the dribble, but he's got a nice touch around the hoop and can score on putbacks or jump hooks. He's also very accurate from the free throw line. Corbin was one of three Utah players to play in all 82 games last season. He has now played in 410 consecutive games, the NBA's fourth longest streak. He scored in double figures 30 times; his season high was 20 points against the Clippers on April 9.

REGULAR SEASON		G	MIN	FG	FGx	3FG	3PTx	FT	FTx	REB	AST	STL	BLK	PTS	AVG
'85-86	SAN ANTONIO	16	174	27	42.2	0	0.0	10	71.4	25	11	11	2	64	4.0
'86-87	SA-CLE	63	1170	156	79.56	1	25	91	146.8	215	97	55	5	404	6.4
'87-88	CLE-PHE	84	1739	257	97.84	1	33.33	110	161.1	350	115	72	18	625	7.4
'88-89	PHOENIX	77	1655	245	54.0	0	0.0	141	78.8	398	118	82	13	631	8.2
'89-90	MINNESOTA	82	3011	521	48.1	0	0.0	161	77.0	604	216	175	41	1203	14.7
'90-91	MINNESOTA	82	3196	587	44.8	2	20.0	296	79.8	589	347	162	53	1472	18.0
'91-92	MIN-UTAH	80	2207	303	48.1	0	0.0	174	86.6	472	140	82	20	780	9.8
'92-93	UTAH	82	2555	385	50.3	0	0.0	180	82.6	519	173	108	32	950	11.6
'93-94	UTAH	82	2149	268	45.6	6	20.7	117	81.3	389	122	99	24	659	8.0
	9 YR TOTALS	648	17856	2749	47.4	10	13.9	1280	80.1	3561	1339	846	208	6788	10.5
'93-94	RANK NBA Fs	1	42	61	85	47	62	63	9	54	50	16	87	61	69
'94-95	PROJECTIONS	82	1899	208	44.0	11	29.7	85	81.0	323	91	89	20	512	6.2

PLAYOFFS		G	MIN	FG	FGx	3FG	3PTx	FT	FTx	REB	AST	STL	BLK	PTS	AVG
'85-86	SAN ANTONIO	1	14	0	0.0	0	---	0	---	1	1	0	0	0	0.0
'88-89	PHOENIX	12	310	45	52.3	0	---	19	76.0	85	26	24	4	109	9.1
'91-92	UTAH	16	447	69	50.4	0	0.0	42	77.8	88	17	12	3	180	11.3
'92-93	UTAH	5	161	24	48.0	0	---	11	64.7	38	9	3	1	59	11.8
'93-94	UTAH	16	413	41	38.7	4	33.3	14	93.3	79	15	21	3	100	6.3
	TOTALS	50	1345	179	46.7	4	28.6	86	77.5	291	68	60	11	448	9.0

Jeff Hornacek

No. 14/G

Full name: Jeffrey John Hornacek
HT: 6-4   **WT:** 190
Born: 5/3/63, Elmhurst, IL
High school: Lyons Township
  (La Grange, IL)
College: Iowa State

Hornacek's name doesn't spring to mind when the casual fan thinks of shooting guards, but he is one of the league's top offensive threats at that position. Hornacek can hit jumpers from the perimeter all day. He can also create off the dribble and use his deceptive quickness to score on a variety of driving layups. He's also an effective finisher in transition. He finished the season as Utah's third-leading scorer, averaging 14.6 points, and 3.9 assists in 30.6 minutes per game with the Jazz. But it is his accuracy that's so impressive: he shot 50.9 percent from the field, an impressive 42.9 percent from 3-point range, and 89.1 percent from the free throw line.

REGULAR SEASON		G	MIN	FG	FGx	3FG	3PTx	FT	FTx	REB	AST	STL	BLK	PTS	AVG
'86-87	PHOENIX	80	1561	159	45.4	12	27.9	94	77.7	184	361	70	5	424	5.3
'87-88	PHOENIX	82	2243	306	50.6	17	29.3	152	82.2	262	540	107	10	781	9.5
'88-89	PHOENIX	78	2487	440	49.5	27	33.3	147	82.6	266	465	129	8	1054	13.5
'89-90	PHOENIX	67	2278	483	53.6	40	40.8	173	85.6	313	337	117	14	1179	17.6
'90-91	PHOENIX	80	2733	544	51.8	61	41.8	201	89.7	321	409	111	16	1350	16.9
'91-92	PHOENIX	81	3078	635	51.2	83	43.9	279	88.6	407	411	158	31	1632	20.1
'92-93	PHILADELPHIA	79	2860	582	47.0	97	39.0	250	86.5	342	548	131	21	1511	19.1
'93-94	PHILA-UTAH	80	2820	472	47.0	70	33.7	260	87.8	279	419	127	13	1274	15.9
8 YR TOTALS		627	20060	3621	49.7	407	38.0	1556	86.0	2374	3490	950	118	9205	14.7
'93-94	RANK NBA Gs	33	14	26	40	27	54	17	8	28	20	20	55	20	22
'94-95	PROJECTIONS	81	2819	420	45.7	64	30.0	271	88.0	241	394	124	9	1175	14.5

PLAYOFFS		G	MIN	FG	FGx	3FG	3PTx	FT	FTx	REB	AST	STL	BLK	PTS	AVG
'88-89	PHOENIX	12	374	74	49.7	0	0.0	21	84.0	69	62	16	3	169	14.1
'89-90	PHOENIX	16	583	112	51.1	6	25.0	68	93.2	62	73	24	0	298	18.6
'90-91	PHOENIX	4	145	22	43.1	3	50.0	26	92.9	25	8	3	2	73	18.3
'91-92	PHOENIX	8	343	62	48.4	8	47.1	31	91.2	51	42	14	2	163	20.4
'93-94	UTAH	16	558	85	47.5	15	44.1	62	91.2	39	64	24	6	247	15.4
	TOTALS	56	2003	355	48.9	32	36.4	208	91.2	246	249	81	13	950	17.0

Karl Malone

No. 32/F

HT: 6-9   **WT:** 256
Born: 7/24/63, Summerfield, LA
High school: Summerfield (LA)
College: Louisiana Tech

What do Keith Lee, Joe Kleine, Jon Koncak and Kenny Green all have in common? They were all drafted ahead of Karl Malone in the '85 draft. Malone is the Jazz's best inside player, unstoppable in the low post. He's the Jazz all-time leading scorer and rebounder, and ranks third in assists. Malone is one of the best at getting in position to rebound. He was the fifth leading scorer in the NBA last season, as well as the eighth leading rebounder. He led the team in scoring and rebounding, and was third in assists and steals. Malone scored 20 points or more in 70 games, and had 10 or more rebounds in 60. He's been playing more around the perimeter, taking advantage of his outside shot. Malone has only missed 4 games in his career.

REGULAR SEASON		G	MIN	FG	FGx	3FG	3PTx	FT	FTx	REB	AST	STL	BLK	PTS	AVG
'85-86	UTAH	81	2475	504	49.6	0	0.0	195	48.1	718	236	105	44	1203	14.9
'86-87	UTAH	82	2857	728	51.2	0	0.0	323	59.8	855	158	104	60	1779	21.7
'87-88	UTAH	82	3198	858	52.0	0	0.0	552	70.0	986	199	117	50	2268	27.7
'88-89	UTAH	80	3126	809	51.9	5	31.3	703	76.6	853	219	144	70	2326	29.1
'89-90	UTAH	82	3122	914	56.2	16	37.2	696	76.2	911	226	121	50	2540	31.0
'90-91	UTAH	82	3302	847	52.7	4	28.6	684	77.0	967	270	89	79	2382	29.0
'91-92	UTAH	81	3054	798	52.6	3	17.6	673	77.8	909	241	108	51	2272	28.0
'92-93	UTAH	82	3099	797	55.2	4	20.0	619	74.0	919	308	124	85	2217	27.0
'93-94	UTAH	82	3329	772	49.7	8	25.0	511	69.4	940	328	125	126	2063	25.2
9 YR TOTALS		734	27562	7027	52.5	40	25.6	4956	71.9	8058	2185	1037	615	19050	26.0
'93-94	RANK NBA Fs	1	1	1	38	43	49	1	80	4	2	4	6	1	2
'94-95	PROJECTIONS	82	3436	745	47.4	10	26.3	438	66.2	946	357	131	157	1938	23.6

PLAYOFFS		G	MIN	FG	FGx	3FG	3PTx	FT	FTx	REB	AST	STL	BLK	PTS	AVG
'85-86	UTAH	4	144	38	52.8	0	---	11	42.3	30	4	8	0	87	21.8
'86-87	UTAH	5	200	37	42.0	0	---	26	72.2	48	6	11	4	100	20.0
'87-88	UTAH	11	494	123	48.2	0	0.0	81	72.3	130	17	13	7	327	29.7
'88-89	UTAH	3	136	33	50.0	0	---	26	81.3	49	4	3	1	92	30.7
'89-90	UTAH	5	203	46	43.8	0	0.0	34	75.6	51	11	11	5	126	25.2
'90-91	UTAH	9	383	95	45.5	0	0.0	77	84.6	120	29	9	11	267	29.7
'91-92	UTAH	16	688	149	52.1	0	0.0	169	80.5	181	42	22	19	465	29.1
'92-93	UTAH	5	216	44	45.4	1	50.0	31	81.6	52	10	6	2	120	24.0
'93-94	UTAH	16	703	158	46.7	0	0.0	118	73.8	198	54	23	13	434	27.1
	TOTALS	74	3167	722	47.7	1	5.6	573	76.4	859	177	106	62	2018	27.3

Felton Spencer

No. 50/C

Full name: Felton LaFrance Spencer
HT: 7-0   **WT:** 265
Born: 1/5/68, Louisville, KY
High school: Eastern (Middletown, KY)
College: Louisville

Spencer inherited the starting center role from Mark Eaton last season. He's a poor free-throw shooter, and his shooting range is very limited. Spencer is too slow to be an offensive force, but he's certainly not afraid to throw his considerable bulk around at the defensive end. Spencer tied for the team shotblocking lead with Karl Malone and was second on the Jazz in rebounding. But Spencer's physical style of defense, and his slow foot speed, get him into foul trouble. He had 304 fouls last season, averaging 5.5 fouls per 40 minutes played. Spencer's season highs included scoring 22 points twice last season, and grabbing 18 rebounds against Sacramento February 18.

REGULAR SEASON		G	MIN	FG	FGx	3FG	3PTx	FT	FTx	REB	AST	STL	BLK	PTS	AVG
'90-91	MINNESOTA	81	2099	195	51.2	0	0.0	182	72.2	641	25	48	121	572	7.1
'91-92	MINNESOTA	61	1481	141	42.6	0	---	123	69.1	435	53	27	79	405	6.6
'92-93	MINNESOTA	71	1296	105	46.5	0	---	83	65.4	324	17	23	66	293	4.1
'93-94	UTAH	79	2210	256	50.5	0	---	165	60.7	658	43	41	67	677	8.6
4 YR TOTALS		292	7086	697	48.2	0	0.0	553	66.7	2058	138	139	333	1947	6.7
'93-94	RANK NBA C's	10	9	17	21	14	14	11	39	9	30	19	20	14	20
'94-95	PROJECTIONS	82	2649	357	53.0	0	0.0	197	56.3	830	52	49	44	911	11.1

PLAYOFFS		G	MIN	FG	FGx	3FG	3PTx	FT	FTx	REB	AST	STL	BLK	PTS	AVG
'93-94	UTAH	16	492	47	44.8	0	---	33	66.0	135	7	3	20	127	7.9
TOTALS		16	492	47	44.8	0	---	33	66.0	135	7	3	20	127	7.9

John Stockton

No. 12/G

Full name: John Houston Stockton
HT: 6-1 **WT:** 175
Born: 3/26/62, Spokane, WA
High school: Gonzaga Prep
(Spokane)
College: Gonzaga

Stockton was Utah's second-leading scorer last season. For all of Karl Malone's ability, the Jazz are John Stockton's team. His leadership makes the Jazz what they are. Stockton is the best playmaker since Magic Johnson, has a fine shot from the perimeter, can score penetrating to the basket, and plays scrappy defense. Stockton has recorded 9,000 career assists; only 3 other players have recorded as many. He posted 1,000 assists in a single season for a record sixth time, and won his seventh consecutive assists title. He was also fourth in the NBA in steals with 2.43 per game. In fact, Stockton is second on the NBA all-time steals list; his 2,031 steals trails only Maurice Cheeks' 2,310.

REGULAR SEASON		G	MIN	FG	FGx	3FG	3PTx	FT	FTx	REB	AST	STL	BLK	PTS	AVG
'85-86	UTAH	82	1935	228	48.9	2	13.3	172	83.9	179	610	157	10	630	7.7
'86-87	UTAH	82	1858	231	49.9	7	18.4	179	78.2	151	670	177	14	648	7.9
'87-88	UTAH	82	2842	454	57.4	24	35.8	272	84.0	237	1128	242	16	1204	14.7
'88-89	UTAH	82	3171	497	53.8	16	24.2	390	86.3	248	1118	263	14	1400	17.1
'89-90	UTAH	78	2915	472	51.4	47	41.6	354	81.9	206	1134	207	18	1345	17.2
'90-91	UTAH	82	3103	496	50.7	58	34.5	363	83.6	237	1164	234	16	1413	17.2
'91-92	UTAH	82	3002	453	48.2	83	40.7	308	84.2	270	1126	244	22	1297	15.8
'92-93	UTAH	82	2863	437	48.6	72	38.5	293	79.8	237	987	199	21	1239	15.1
'93-94	UTAH	82	2969	458	52.8	48	32.2	272	80.5	258	1031	199	22	1236	15.1
10 YR TOTALS		816	26148	3883	51.2	359	35.3	2745	82.2	2128	9383	2031	164	10870	13.3
'93-94 RANK NBA Gs		1	6	28	2	43	68	16	57	34	1	3	30	23	2.7
'94-95 PROJECTIONS		82	2984	458	54.6	38	28.6	250	79.9	267	1013	190	23	1204	14.7

PLAYOFFS		G	MIN	FG	FGx	3FG	3PTx	FT	FTx	REB	AST	STL	BLK	PTS	AVG
'85-86	UTAH	4	73	9	52.9	1	88.9	6	14	5	0	27	6.8		
'86-87	UTAH	5	157	18	62.1	4	80.0	10	76.9	11	40	15	1	50	10.0
'87-88	UTAH	11	478	68	50.7	4	28.6	75	82.4	45	163	37	3	215	19.5
'88-89	UTAH	3	139	30	50.8	3	75.0	19	90.5	10	41	11	5	82	27.3
'89-90	UTAH	5	194	29	42.0	1	7.7	16	80.0	16	75	6	0	75	15.0
'90-91	UTAH	9	373	58	53.7	11	40.7	37	84.1	42	124	20	2	164	18.2
'91-92	UTAH	16	623	77	42.3	18	31.0	65	83.3	47	217	34	5	237	14.8
'92-93	UTAH	5	193	23	45.1	5	38.5	15	83.3	12	55	12	0	66	13.2
'93-94	UTAH	16	597	88	45.6	4	16.7	51	81.0	52	157	27	8	231	14.4
TOTALS		84	3013	421	47.5	51	31.7	322	82.1	269	929	178	26	1215	14.5

David Benoit   No. 21/F

HT: 6-8 **WT:** 220
Born: 5/9/68, Lafayette, LA
High school: Lafayette (LA)
College: Alabama

Benoit was sidelined by a hamstring injury early in the season, and his game never recovered. Last season was Benoit's worst; his 38.5 FG percentage was a career low.

REGULAR SEASON		G	MIN	FG	FG%	3FG	3PT%	FT	FT%	REB	AST	STL	BLK	PTS	AVG
'91-92	UTAH	77	1161	175	46.7	3	21.4	81	81.0	296	34	19	44	434	5.6
'92-93	UTAH	82	1712	258	43.6	34	34.7	114	75.0	392	43	45	43	664	8.1
'93-94	UTAH	55	1070	139	38.5	12	20.3	68	77.3	260	23	23	37	358	6.5
3 YR TOTALS		214	3943	572	43.1	49	28.7	263	77.4	948	100	87	124	1456	6.8
'93-94 RANK NBA Fs		104	96	97	130	38	63	94	28	79	123	105	59	95	87
'94-95 PROJECTIONS		36	960	110	34.1	8	12.9	58	77.3	237	17	20	37	286	7.9

PLAYOFFS		G	MIN	FG	FG%	3FG	3PT%	FT	FT%	REB	AST	STL	BLK	PTS	AVG
'91-92	UTAH	13	257	36	42.9	6	46.2	11	100.0	50	6	6	5	89	6.8
'92-93	UTAH	5	136	13	31.7	2	22.2	9	69.2	24	5	3	6	37	7.4
'93-94	UTAH	16	357	48	39.3	3	18.8	16	64.0	67	10	7	11	115	7.2
TOTALS		34	750	97	39.3	11	28.9	36	73.5	141	21	16	22	241	7.1

Walter Bond   No. 20/G

HT: 6-5 **WT:** 200
Born: 2/1/69, Chicago, IL
High school: Collins (Chicago)
College: Minnesota

Bond is a good perimeter shooter, and he gets a lot of rebounds for a guard whose minutes are limited. He's not a good penetrator, and that holds down his FG percentage.

REGULAR SEASON		G	MIN	FG	FG%	3FG	3PT%	FT	FT%	REB	AST	STL	BLK	PTS	AVG
'92-93	DALLAS	74	1578	227	40.2	7	16.7	129	77.2	196	122	75	18	590	8.0
'93-94	UTAH	56	559	63	40.4	19	35.2	31	77.5	61	31	16	12	176	3.1
2 YR TOTALS		130	2137	290	40.2	26	27.1	160	77.3	257	153	91	30	766	5.9
'93-94 RANK NBA Gs		110	119	122	114	75	44	119	75	119	130	125	62	121	127

PLAYOFFS		G	MIN	FG	FG%	3FG	3PT%	FT	FT%	REB	AST	STL	BLK	PTS	AVG
'93-94	UTAH	4	13	0	0.0	0	0.0	1	50.0	1	0	1	0	1	0.3
TOTALS		4	13	0	0.0	0	0.0	1	50.0	1	0	1	0	1	0.3

Jay Humphries   No. 6/G

Full name: John Jay Humphries
HT: 6-3 **WT:** 185
Born: 10/17/62, Los Angeles, CA
High school: Inglewood (CA)
College: Colorado

Humphries is one of the first players off the bench for Utah. He's a good shooter from the perimeter and from the line.

REGULAR SEASON		G	MIN	FG	FG%	3FG	3PT%	FT	FT%	REB	AST	STL	BLK	PTS	AVG
'90-91	MILWAUKEE	80	2726	482	50.2	60	37.3	191	79.9	220	538	129	7	1215	15.2
'91-92	MILWAUKEE	71	2261	377	46.9	42	29.2	195	78.3	184	466	119	13	991	14.0
'92-93	UTAH	78	2034	287	43.6	15	20.0	101	77.7	143	317	101	11	690	8.8
'93-94	UTAH	75	1619	233	43.6	38	39.6	57	75.0	127	219	65	11	561	7.5
10 YR TOTALS		770	22861	3494	47.7	217	29.6	1547	78.2	1990	4320	1144	89	8752	11.4
'93-94 RANK NBA Gs		65	71	75	79	51	23	104	89	89	62	69	68	83	88
'94-95 PROJECTIONS		74	1268	174	42.1	39	46.4	26	72.2	100	145	44	10	413	5.6

PLAYOFFS		G	MIN	FG	FG%	3FG	3PT%	FT	FT%	REB	AST	STL	BLK	PTS	AVG
'90-91	MILWAUKEE	3	123	17	53.1	2	40.0	9	90.0	6	25	2	0	45	15.0
'92-93	UTAH	5	115	11	33.3	2	25.0	2	50.0	10	17	3	3	26	5.2
'93-94	UTAH	16	356	46	42.6	7	31.8	19	67.9	37	39	13	2	118	7.4
TOTALS		41	1104	151	46.7	15	26.8	79	78.2	93	187	32	5	396	9.7

Bryon Russell   No. 34/F

Full name: Bryon Demetrise Russell
HT: 6-7 **WT:** 225
Born: 12/31/70, San Bernardino, CA
High school: San Bernardino (CA)
College: Long Beach State

A second-round pick in the '93 draft, Russell started 48 games last season. He gives Utah a rebounding and defensive boost.

REGULAR SEASON		G	MIN	FG	FG%	3FG	3PT%	FT	FT%	REB	AST	STL	BLK	PTS	AVG
'93-94	UTAH	67	1121	135	48.4	2	9.1	62	61.4	181	54	68	19	334	5.0
1 YR TOTALS		67	1121	135	48.4	2	9.1	62	61.4	181	54	68	19	334	5.0
'93-94 RANK NBA Fs		88	93	99	49	62	75	96	113	107	91	38	96	100	103

PLAYOFFS		G	MIN	FG	FG%	3FG	3PT%	FT	FT%	REB	AST	STL	BLK	PTS	AVG
'93-94	UTAH	6	36	4	40.0	2	66.7	6	100.0	9	3	0	0	16	2.7
TOTALS		6	36	4	40.0	2	66.7	6	100.0	9	3	0	0	16	2.7

Luther Wright   No. 44/C

Full name: Luther A. Wright
HT: 7-2   **WT:** 270
Born: 9/22/71, Jersey City, NJ
High school: Elizabeth (NJ)
College: Seton Hall
Wright was sidelined for the season in late
January after doctors determined he required
treatment for Attention Deficit Disorder.

REGULAR SEASON	G	MIN	FG	FG%	3FG	3PT%	FT	FT%	REB	AST	STL	BLK	PTS	AVG
'93-94 UTAH	15	92	8	34.8	0	0.0	3	75.0	10	0	1	2	19	1.3
1 YR TOTALS	15	92	8	34.8	0	0.0	3	75.0	10	0	1	2	19	1.3
93-94 RANK NBA C s	not ranked -- didn't appear in 25 games in '93-94													

Jerry Sloan   Head Coach

Full name: Gerald Eugene Sloan
HT: 6-5   **WT:** 200
Born: 3/28/42, McLeansboro, IL
High school: McLeansboro (IL)
College: Evansville
Sloan has averaged 52 wins per season as a
head coach. He's second in tenure with one
team behind Don Nelson among coaches.

	REGULAR SEASON				PLAYOFFS			
YEAR	TEAM	W	L	PCT	FINISH	W	L	PCT
'79-80	CHICAGO	30	52	.366	4th/Midwest Div.			
'80-81	CHICAGO	45	37	.549	2nd/Central Div.	2	4	.333	lost Eastern Conf. semifinals to Boston, 4-0
'81-82	CHICAGO	19	32	.373				
'88-89	UTAH	40	25	.615	1st/Midwest Div.	0	3	.000	lost Western Conf. first round to Golden State, 3-0
'89-90	UTAH	55	27	.671	2nd/Midwest Div.	2	3	.400	lost Western Conf. first round to Phoenix, 3-2
'90-91	UTAH	54	28	.659	2nd/Midwest Div.	4	5	.444	lost Western Conf. semifinals to Portland, 4-1
'91-92	UTAH	55	27	.671	1st/Midwest Div.	9	7	.563	lost Western Conf. finals to Portland, 4-2
'92-93	UTAH	47	35	.573	3rd/Midwest Div.	2	3	.400	lost Western Conf. first round to Seattle, 3-2
'93-94	UTAH	53	29	.646	3rd/Midwest Div.	8	8	.500	lost Western Conf. finals to Houston, 4-1
	9 YR TOTALS	398	292	.577		27	33	.450	

Washington *BULLETS*

1994–95 Scouting Report

Frontcourt

Washington is deepest at small forward. Last year's leading scorer, Don MacLean, and versatile Tom Gugliotta are candidates to start. MacLean is a scorer, but Gugliotta is more versatile (he led Washington in rebounding last season). Gugliotta can play either forward spot, but is more of a threat at small forward. First-round pick Juwan Howard will get an opportunity to play power forward. Washington needs to find a starting center to replace the departed Pervis Ellison. The candidates include underachieving veteran Kevin Duckworth, 7-7 Gheorghe Muresan, and second round pick Jim McIlvaine. Duckworth, a big body at center who plays a lot shorter on defense, was a big disappointment last season. Muresan is a second-year pro with only one year of American basketball experience. He has a decent low-post game, but has trouble with teams that run, is not a good shotblocker, and picks up fouls quickly. Although he's just a rookie, McIlvaine might be the best candidate. His 399 blocked shots as a collegian rank fifth in Division I history, and he improved as a scorer and rebounder every season. The bench includes veteran Kenny Walker, who played well last season in a reserve role (fourth on the team in rebounds), and Larry Stewart.

Backcourt

Rex Chapman starts at shooting guard; he's coming off the best season of his short pro career. He needs to improve on defense and remain injury-free. Swingman Calbert Cheaney will see time at shooting guard and small forward. Cheaney is an all-around talent who can score, defend, and rebound. Scott Skiles will be the starting point guard this season. He's a good playmaker and 3-point shooter. Doug Overton is a good defender who was second on the team in free throw shooting percentage. Brent Price, the backup point guard, is improving as a shooter and playmaker.

Defense

Washington was one of the worst defensive teams in the NBA.
Opponents were able to go inside at will. Washington ranked just
twenty-fifth in blocks, and opponents shot 50.8 percent from the
floor against Washington, highest in the league. In fact, Washington
was the only NBA team to allow opponents to shoot better than 50
percent. So even though opponents attempted 7,026 shots from the
field, seventeenth in the league, they averaged 107.7 points against
the Bullets, second highest in the NBA. Washington ranked seventeenth in the NBA in steals, and sixteenth in forcing turnovers.

1994–95 Prospects

The Bullets have been one of the smallest teams in the league. They
had real problems against the bigger teams in the league last season,
going 7–43 against playoff teams. Washington wasn't bad offensively, ranking twelfth in FG shooting and seventh in FT shooting.
They would have finished better than eighteenth place in total points
if they hadn't been the worst rebounding team in the league (twenty-
fifth in defensive rebounds).

The Bullets should be a better team this season. With Juwan Howard
and Jim McIlvaine, they should be a better rebounding team, and
their young shooters will have another year of development. Defense
will be the Bullets' weakness once again. They should be a little
tougher underneath, but they'll have to rely on two rookies, Juwan
Howard and Jim McIlvaine. And neither Chapman nor Skiles are
regarded as accomplished defenders, so Washington will have trouble disrupting their opponents' offenses again.

Washington is building around a nucleus of Juwan Howard, Rex
Chapman, Tom Gugliotta, Calbert Cheaney, and Don MacLean. In
Scott Skiles, they have the first-rate point guard they've lacked for
years. If the Bullets can come up with a first-rate center, they could
contend for a playoff spot.

Team Directory

Chairman of the board: Abe Pollin   Vice chairman: Jerry Sachs
President: Susan O'Malley   Vice president: Wes Unseld
VP/General manager: John Nash   Public rel./Broadcast.: Matt Williams

1993–94 Review

EASTERN CONFERENCE						WESTERN CONFERENCE					
ATLANTIC DIV.			CENTRAL DIV.			MIDWEST DIV.			PACIFIC DIV.		
	W	L		W	L		W	L		W	L
NY	0	5	ATL	0	4	HOU	1	1	SEA	0	2
ORL	1	4	CHI	0	4	SAN	0	2	PHO	0	2
NJ	1	3	CLE	1	3	UTAH	0	2	GS.	0	2
MIA	1	3	IND	1	3	DEN	1	1	POR	0	2
BOS	2	3	CHA	2	2	MIN	2	0	LAL	1	1
PHI	3	2	DET	2	2	DAL	1	1	SAC	0	2
WAS	-	-	MIL	3	1				LAC	1	1
	8	20		9	19		5	7		2	12

1993–94 finish: 24–58 (17–4 home, 7–34 away), seventh in Atlantic Div.

1994–95 Schedule

11/4	Orlando	7:30 pm	1/4	@ Indiana	7:30 pm	3/3	Indiana	7:30 pm
11/5	@ Chicago	8:30 pm	1/6	@ Atlanta	7:30 pm	3/5	@ Miami	1:00 pm
11/9	@ Phila.	7:30 pm	1/7	Portland	7:30 pm	3/8	Detroit	7:30 pm
11/11	New Jersey	7:30 pm	1/9	@ Boston	7:30 pm	3/10	Milw.	7:30 pm
11/12	@ Miami	8:00 pm	1/10	Atlanta	7:30 pm	3/11	New Jersey	7:30 pm
11/15	@ Orlando	7:30 pm	1/13	Indiana	7:30 pm	3/13	@ Charlotte	7:30 pm
11/17	@ New Jersey	7:30 pm	1/14	@ Detroit	7:30 pm	3/14	Chicago	7:30 pm
11/19	Boston	7:30 pm	1/16	Chicago	1:00 pm	3/17	New York	7:30 pm
11/25	Cleveland	7:30 pm	1/19	@ Milw.	8:30 pm	3/19	Cleveland	1:00 pm
11/26	LA Lakers	7:30 pm	1/20	Phila.	7:30 pm	3/21	@ Portland	10:00 pm
11/29	New York	7:30 pm	1/22	@ New Jersey	2:00 pm	3/23	@ Seattle	10:00 pm
12/2	Detroit	7:30 pm	1/26	Gold. St.	7:30 pm	3/24	@ LA Lakers	10:30 pm
12/3	@ New York	7:30 pm	1/28	LA Clip.	7:30 pm	3/27	@ Utah	9:00 pm
12/6	Phoenix	7:30 pm	1/31	Charlotte	8:00 pm	3/29	Miami	7:30 pm
12/8	@ Dallas	8:30 pm	2/1	@ Phila.	7:30 pm	3/31	@ Cleveland	7:30 pm
12/10	@ Denver	9:00 pm	2/3	Miami	7:30 pm	4/1	@ Detroit	7:30 pm
12/12	@ San Ant.	8:30 pm	2/5	@ Charlotte	2:00 pm	4/5	@ Indiana	7:30 pm
12/13	@ Houston	8:30 pm	2/8	@ Miami	7:30 pm	4/7	Charlotte	7:30 pm
12/15	Utah	7:30 pm	2/14	@ Minn.	8:00 pm	4/9	Boston	1:00 pm
12/17	Minn.	7:30 pm	2/15	@ Chicago	8:30 pm	4/11	@ Atlanta	7:30 pm
12/19	@ Phoenix	9:00 pm	2/17	Houston	7:30 pm	4/13	@ New York	7:30 pm
12/20	@ Sacra.	10:30 pm	2/19	Denver	6:00 pm	4/15	Milw.	7:30 pm
12/22	@ Gold. St.	10:30 pm	2/21	Dallas	7:30 pm	4/17	@ Orlando	7:30 pm
12/23	@ LA Clip.	10:30 pm	2/22	@ Milw.	8:30 pm	4/19	Orlando	7:30 pm
12/26	Orlando	7:30 pm	2/24	Atlanta	7:30 pm	4/21	@ New Jersey	7:30 pm
12/28	@ Cleveland	7:30 pm	2/25	Sacra.	7:30 pm	4/23	Phila.	1:00 pm
12/30	San Ant.	7:30 pm	2/28	Phila.	7:30 pm			
01/3	Seattle	7:30 pm	3/1	@ Boston	7:30 pm			

1993–94 Team Stats

NAME	G	MIN	FG	FGA	FG%	3FG	3FGA	3FG%	FT	FTA	FT%	ORB	TRB	AST	PF	STL	BLK	TO	PTS	AVG
Chapman	60	2025	431	865	49.8	64	165	38.8	168	206	81.6	57	146	185	83	59	8	117	1094	18.2
MacLean	75	2487	517	1030	50.2	3	21	14.3	328	398	82.4	140	467	160	169	47	22	152	1365	18.2
Gugliotta	78	2795	540	1159	46.6	40	148	27.0	213	311	68.5	189	728	276	174	172	51	247	1333	17.1
Adams	70	2337	285	698	40.8	55	191	28.8	224	270	83.0	37	183	480	140	96	6	167	849	12.1
Cheaney	65	1604	327	696	47.0	1	23	4.3	124	161	77.0	88	190	126	148	63	10	108	779	12.0
Ellison	47	1178	137	292	46.9	0	3	0.0	70	97	72.2	77	242	70	140	25	50	73	344	7.3
Butler	75	1321	207	418	49.5	0	5	0.0	104	180	57.8	106	225	77	131	54	20	87	518	6.9
Duckworth	69	1485	184	441	41.7	0	0	—	88	132	66.7	103	325	56	223	37	35	101	456	6.6
Price	65	1035	141	326	43.3	50	150	33.3	68	87	78.2	31	90	213	114	55		119	400	6.2
Muresan	54	650	128	235	54.5	0	0	—	48	71	67.6	66	192	18	120	28	48	54	304	5.6
Anderson	10	180	20	43	46.5	3	14	21.4	9	11	81.8	8	27	11	7	3	1	9	52	5.2
Conlon	14	201	29	56	51.8	0	1	0.0	12	15	80.0	19	50	6	33	4		10	70	5.0
Walker	73	1397	132	274	48.2	0	3	0.0	87	125	69.6	118	289	33	156	26	59	44	351	4.8
Smith	7	48	8	18	44.4	0	0	—	15	20	75.0	5	8	5	8	3		1	31	4.4
Stewart	3	35	3	8	37.5	0	0	—	7	10	70.0	5	7	2	4	2		2	13	4.3
Paddio	8	74	11	32	34.4	0	0	0.0	8	14	57.1	5	11	7	4	3	1	2	30	3.8
Overton	61	749	87	216	40.3	1	11	9.1	43	52	82.7	19	69	92	48	21		54	218	3.6
Gaze	7	70	8	17	47.1	4	8	50.0	2	2	100.0	7	7	5	9	2		3	22	3.1
Bol	2	6	0	0	0.0	0	0	—	0	0	—	1	1	1	1	0	3	0	0	0.0
Horford	3	28	0	2	0.0	0	0	—	0	0	—	3	3	0	3	0		1	0	0.0
Bullets	82	19705	3195	6826	46.8	221	744	29.7	1618	2162	74.8	1071	3260	1823	1715	701	321	1403	8229	100.4
Opp.	82	19705	3569	7026	50.8	252	723	34.9	1444	1996	72.3	1119	3481	2113	1823	815	470	1291	8834	107.7

HISTORY

TITLES

1970–71 Central Div. champs
1970–71 NBA Eastern Conf. champs
1971–72 Central Div. champs
1972–73 Central Div. champs
1973–74 Central Div. champs
1974–75 Central Div. champs

1974–75 NBA Eastern Conf. champs
1977–78 NBA champs
1977–78 NBA Eastern Conf. champs
1978–79 Central Div. champs
1978–79 NBA Eastern Conf. champs

ALL-TIME TEAM RECORDS

Career

Games played	Wes Unseld	984	1968–81
Total points	Elvin Hayes	15,551	1972–81
Field goals made	Elvin Hayes	6,251	1972–81
Free throws made	Elvin Hayes	3,046	1972–81
Total rebounds	Wes Unseld	13,769	1968–81
Assists	Wes Unseld	3,822	1968–81
Steals	Greg Ballard	762	1977–85

Season

Total points	Walt Bellamy	2,495	1961–62
Field goals made	Walt Bellamy	973	1961–62
Free throws made	Moses Malone	570	1986–87
Total rebounds	Walt Bellamy	1,500	1961–62
Assists	Kevin Porter	734	1980–81
Steals	Gus Williams	178	1984–85

Game

Total points	Earl Monroe	56	vs. LA Lakers, 2/3/68
Field goals made	Phil Chenier	22	vs. Portland, 12/6/72
	Walt Bellamy	22	vs. Philadelphia, 1/21/64
Free throws made	Moses Malone	21	vs. Golden State, 12/29/86
Total rebounds	Walt Bellamy	37	vs. St. Louis, 12/4/64
Assists	Kevin Porter	24	vs. Detroit, 3/23/80
Steals	Gus Williams	9	vs. Atlanta, 10/30/84
	Michael Adams	9	vs. Indiana, 2/26/87

LEADING COACHES

NAME	REGULAR SEASON				PLAYOFFS		
	YEARS	W	L	PCT	W	L	PCT
Gene Shue	1966–73, 1980–86	522	505	.510	19	41	.317
Dick Motta	1976–80	185	143	.564	27	24	.529
Wes Unseld	1988–94	202	345	.369	2	3	.400
K.C. Jones	1973–76	155	91	.630	14	17	.452
Kevin Loughery	1986–88	57	65	.432	2	6	.250

Washington Bullets 1994–95 Roster

Head Coach: Jim Lynam

No.	Name	Pos.	Ht.	Wt.	Yrs.	Born	College
32	Mitchell Butler	G	6-5	210	1	12/15/70	UCLA
3	Rex Chapman	G	6-4	205	6	10/5/67	Kentucky
40	Calbert Cheaney	F-G	6-7	215	1	7/17/71	Indiana
0	Kevin Duckworth	C	7-0	275	8	4/1/64	Eastern Illinois
24	Tom Gugliotta	F	6-10	240	2	12/19/69	North Carolina State
	Juwan Howard	F	6-9	250	R	2/7/73	Michigan
34	Don MacLean	F	6-10	225	2	1/16/70	UCLA
	Jim McIlvaine	C	7-1	240	R	7/30/72	Marquette
77	Gheorghe Muresan	C	7-7	315	1	2/14/71	Cluj (Romania)
14	Doug Overton	G	6-3	190	2	8/3/69	La Salle
20	Brent Price	G	6-1	185	2	12/9/68	Oklahoma
4	Scott Skiles	G	6-1	180	8	3/5/64	Michigan State
33	Larry Stewart	F	6-8	230	3	8/21/68	Coppin State
15	Kenny Walker	F	6-8	220	6	8/18/64	Kentucky

Arena Information

USAir Arena (18,756)
Tickets: 301-NBA-DUNK
Ticket prices: $35, $33, $30, $22, $15, $11

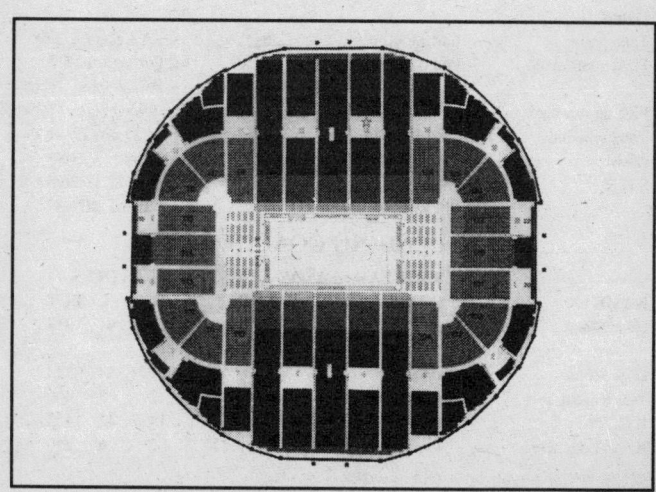

Rex Chapman

No. 3/G

Full name: Rex Everett Chapman
HT: 6-4   **WT:** 205
Born: 10/5/67, Bowling Green, KY
High school: Apollo
  (Owensboro, KY)
College: Kentucky

Chapman is a tremendous athlete with a 42-inch vertical leap and a terrific outside shot. Last season, for the first time as a pro, Chapman displayed the shooting touch that he had in college. Chapman was a vastly improved shooter last season as he tied for the team scoring lead with Don MacLean; his 9.8 field goal percentage was a career-high. He's also a threat from 3-point range; he's tops on the Bullets' all-time list in career 3-point percentage (107 for 283, 37.8 percent).

Dogged with injuries throughout his career, Chapman averaged 33.8 minutes per game, second on the Bullets. Chapman needs to improve his defense before he can attain All-Star recognition.

REGULAR SEASON		G	MIN	FG	FG%	3FG	3PT%	FT	FT%	REB	AST	STL	BLK	PTS	AVG
'88-89	CHARLOTTE	75	2219	526	41.4	60	31.4	155	79.5	187	176	70	25	1267	16.9
'89-90	CHARLOTTE	54	1762	377	40.8	47	33.1	144	75.0	179	132	46	6	945	17.5
'90-91	CHARLOTTE	70	2100	410	44.5	48	32.4	234	83.0	191	250	73	16	1102	15.7
'91-92	CHA-WAS	22	567	113	44.8	8	27.6	36	67.9	58	89	15	8	270	12.3
'92-93	WASHINGTON	60	1300	287	47.7	43	37.1	132	81.0	88	116	38	10	749	12.5
'93-94	WASHINGTON	60	2025	431	49.8	64	38.8	168	81.6	146	185	59	8	1094	18.2
6 YR TOTALS		341	9973	2144	44.3	270	34.1	869	79.7	849	948	301	73	5427	15.9
'93-94	RANK NBA Gs	104	61	33	11	31	27	43	49	78	76	78	81	36	11
'94-95	PROJECTIONS	64	2399	510	52.0	84	41.6	188	83.6	158	198	70	4	1292	20.2

Kevin Duckworth

No. 0/C

Full name: Kevin Jerome Duckworth
HT: 7-0   **WT:** 275
Born: 4/1/64, Harvey, IL
High school: Thornridge (Dolton)
College: Eastern Illinois

Duckworth combines a strong low-post game with a soft shooting touch from mid-range. Duckworth is primarily an offensve threat at center; he's never been much of a rebounder or shot-blocker, and he has been criticized for his soft play. (Duckworth was only third on the Bullets in rebounds, behind 6-10 forwards Tom Gugliotta and Don MacLean, and four other Bullets had more blocks.) Duckworth was a major disappointment in his first year as a Bullet. He showed up nearly 30 pounds overweight, and was the Bullets' third center by March. But he regained his starting job and played better by season's end.

REGULAR SEASON		G	MIN	FG	FGx	3FG	3PTx	FT	FTx	REB	AST	STL	BLK	PTS	AVG
'86-87	SA-PTL	65	875	130	89.12	0	0	92	133.5	223	29	21	21	352	5.4
'87-88	PORTLAND	78	2223	450	49.6	0	—	331	77.0	576	66	31	32	1231	15.8
'88-89	PORTLAND	79	2662	554	47.7	0	0.0	324	75.7	635	60	56	49	1432	18.1
'89-90	PORTLAND	82	2462	548	47.8	0	—	231	74.0	509	91	36	34	1327	16.2
'90-91	PORTLAND	81	2511	521	48.1	0	0.0	240	77.2	531	.89	33	34	1282	15.8
'91-92	PORTLAND	82	2222	362	46.1	0	0.0	156	69.0	497	99	38	37	880	10.7
'92-93	PORTLAND	74	1762	301	43.8	0	0.0	127	73.0	387	70	45	39	729	9.9
'93-94	WASHINGTON	69	1495	184	41.7	0	—	88	66.7	325	56	37	35	456	6.6
8 YR TOTALS		610	16202	3050	47.0	0	0.0	1589	74.0	3683	560	297	281	7689	12.6
'93-94	RANK NBA Cs	24	23	24	46	14	14	22	31	23	23	22	27	24	26
'94-95	PROJECTIONS	64	1177	115	39.9	0	0.0	60	63.8	258	43	32	31	290	4.5

PLAYOFFS		G	MIN	FG	FGx	3FG	3PTx	FT	FTx	REB	AST	STL	BLK	PTS	AVG
'86-87	PORTLAND	4	53	6	50.0	0	—	2	40.0	8	1	4	1	14	3.5
'87-88	PORTLAND	4	151	34	48.6	0	0.0	18	78.3	44	7	1	2	86	21.5
'88-89	PORTLAND	3	83	14	40.0	0	—	6	54.5	17	2	1	1	34	11.3
'89-90	PORTLAND	15	453	82	43.9	0	—	33	71.7	87	16	5	9	197	13.1
'90-91	PORTLAND	16	511	73	40.1	0	—	41	73.2	107	14	8	8	187	11.7
'91-92	PORTLAND	21	647	107	49.5	0	—	35	66.0	117	41	11	12	249	11.9
'92-93	PORTLAND	4	58	7	33.3	0	—	4	100.0	13	3	0	1	18	4.5
TOTALS		67	1956	323	44.7	0	0.0	139	70.2	393	84	30	34	785	11.7

Tom Gugliotta
No. 24/F

Full name: Thomas James Gugliotta
HT: 6-10   **WT:** 240
Born: 12/19/69, Huntington
   Station, NY
High school: Walt Whitman
   (Huntington Station)
College: North Carolina State
Gugliotta is a skilled shooter, passer, and rebounder who can play all three frontcourt positions, although he generally starts at small forward. He's an outstanding ballhandler, and has a nice shooting touch from outside. Pat Riley has compared the way he shoots, dribbles, runs the break, and shoots, 3-pointers to Larry Bird. Last season, Gugliotta was Washington's third-leading scorer, and was second in assists. He was also the team's leading rebounder, and second-leading shotblocker. After an outstanding rookie season, Gugliotta found his shots being challenged on the perimeter; he needs to develop more of an inside game so that he can take adavntage of smaller defenders.

REGULAR SEASON		G	MIN	FG	FG%	3FG	3PT%	FT	FT%	REB	AST	STL	BLK	PTS	AVG
'92-93	WASHINGTON	81	2795	484	42.6	38	28.1	181	64.4	781	306	134	35	1187	14.7
'93-94	WASHINGTON	78	2795	540	46.6	40	27.0	213	68.5	728	276	172	51	1333	17.1
2 YR TOTALS		159	5590	1024	44.6	78	27.6	394	66.6	1509	582	306	86	2520	15.8
'93-94 RANK NBA Fs		40	11	14	73	19	46	28	86	12	9	2	35	15	17
'94-95 PROJECTIONS		75	2795	598	50.5	42	26.1	247	72.4	675	246	210	67	1485	19.8

Don MacLean

No. 34/F

Full name: Donald James MacLean
HT: 6-10   **WT:** 225
Born: 1/16/70, Palo Alto, CA
High school: Simi Valley (CA)
College: UCLA

MacLean was one of the most improved players in the league last season. As a rookie, MacLean came off the bench. Moving to a starting role in his second year, MacLean led the team in scoring and was second in minutes played. He scored 20 points or more 32 times, and broke 30 points scored 6 times. He was also second on the team in rebounds per game and free throw percentage. MacLean does a good job of going to the basket and drawing fouls, averaging over 5 free throws a game. He still needs to improve as a rebounder and defender, and he needs to be more consistent coming off screens. He's got to cut down on turnovers (he's got 199 career assists and 194 turnovers). MacLean is the all-time scoring leader in the Pac-10.

REGULAR SEASON		G	MIN	FG	FGx	3FG	3PTx	FT	FTx	REB	AST	STL	BLK	PTS	AVG
'92-93	WASHINGTON	62	674	157	43.5	3	50.0	90	81.1	122	39	11	4	407	6.6
'93-94	WASHINGTON	75	2487	517	50.2	3	14.3	328	82.4	467	160	47	22	1365	18.2
	2 YR TOTALS	137	3161	674	48.5	6	22.2	418	82.1	589	199	58	26	1772	12.9
'93-94	RANK NBA Fs	55	29	17	30	58	70	7	8	37	37	68	91	14	13
'94-95	PROJECTIONS	82	3936	655	56.9	-7	-22.6	513	83.8	766	279	85	46	1816	22.1

Scott Skiles

No. 4/G

Full name: Scott Allen Skiles
HT: 6-1 **WT:** 180
Born: 3/5/64, LaPorte, IN
High school: Plymouth (IN)
College: Michigan State

Skiles is an excellent playmaker who doesn't make mistakes. His 30 assists vs. Denver December 30, 1990, is an NBA record. Skiles is also an excellent free throw shooter; he's currently third on the all-time NBA free throw percentage list at 87.8 percent, behind Rick Barry's 90 percent and Mark Price's 88.8 percent. Skiles also put together a career-high streak of 40 consecutive free throws last season. He lost his starting spot in Orlando to Anfernee Hardaway, but as a starter, Skiles averaged 12.6 points, 8.2 assists, and 2.9 rebounds per game. His size and lack of speed contribute to his troubles on defense; bigger guards can post him up or drive to the hoop.

REGULAR SEASON		G	MIN	FG	FGx	3FG	3PTx	FT	FTx	REB	AST	STL	BLK	PTS	AVG
'86-87	MILWAUKEE	13	205	18	29.0	3	21.4	10	83.3	26	45	5	1	49	3.8
'87-88	INDIANA	51	760	86	41.1	6	30.0	45	83.3	66	180	22	3	223	4.4
'88-89	INDIANA	80	1571	198	44.8	20	29.9	130	90.3	149	390	64	2	546	6.8
'89-90	ORLANDO	70	1460	190	40.9	52	39.4	104	87.4	159	334	36	4	536	7.7
'90-91	ORLANDO	79	2714	462	44.5	93	40.8	340	90.2	270	660	89	4	1357	17.2
'91-92	ORLANDO	75	2377	359	41.4	91	36.4	248	89.5	202	544	74	5	1057	14.1
'92-93	ORLANDO	78	3086	416	46.7	80	34.0	289	89.2	290	735	86	2	1201	15.4
'93-94	ORLANDO	82	2303	276	42.9	68	41.2	195	87.8	189	503	47	2	815	9.9
8 YR TOTALS		528	14476	2005	43.4	413	37.2	1361	89.0	1351	3391	423	23	5784	11.0
'93-94	RANK NBA Gs	1	45	63	86	30	10	30	8	56	14	93	115	59	68
'94-95	PROJECTIONS	82	2116	228	42.1	60	44.1	165	87.3	160	443	34	1	681	8.3

PLAYOFFS		G	MIN	FG	FGx	3FG	3PTx	FT	FTx	REB	AST	STL	BLK	PTS	AVG
'93-94	ORLANDO	2	23	4	50.0	0	0.0	1	100.0	1	3	0	0	9	4.5
	TOTALS	2	23	4	50.0	0	0.0	1	100.0	1	3	0	0	9	4.5

Mitchell Butler   No. 32/G

HT: 6-5 **WT:** 210
Born: 12/15/70, Los Angeles, CA
High school: Oakwood (CA)
College: UCLA
Butler was ignored in the '93 NBA draft but
was invited to Washington's training camp
and made the team. He started in 19 games
and improved as the season progressed.

REGULAR SEASON	G	MIN	FG	FG%	3FG	3PT%	FT	FT%	REB	AST	STL	BLK	PTS	AVG
'93-94 WASHINGTON	75	1321	207	49.5	0	0.0	104	57.8	225	77	54	20	518	6.9
1 YR TOTALS	75	1321	207	49.5	0	0.0	104	57.8	225	77	54	20	518	6.9
'93-94 RANK NBA Gs	65	88	86	13	131	131	74	131	43	115	86	35	86	91

Calbert Cheaney No. 40/F-G

Full name: Calbert N. Cheaney
HT: 6-7   **WT:** 215
Born: 7/17/71, Evansville, IN
High school: Harrison (Evansville)
College: Indiana
Cheaney started 21 games for Washington
when Rex Chapman was injured, averaging
15.8 points and 3.7 rebounds as a starter.

REGULAR SEASON	G	MIN	FG	FG%	3FG	3PT%	FT	FT%	REB	AST	STL	BLK	PTS	AVG
'93-94 WASHINGTON	65	1604	327	47.0	1	4.3	124	77.0	190	126	63	10	779	12.0
1 YR TOTALS	65	1604	327	47.0	1	4.3	124	77.0	190	126	63	10	779	12.0
'93-94 RANK NBA Fs	96	65	49	66	69	77	61	30	102	47	44	118	54	38

Juwan Howard C

HT: 6-9 **WT:** 250
Born: 2/7/73, Chicago, IL
College: Michigan

Howard, the starting center for Michigan's "Fab Five," averaged 20.8 points as a senior. He was named Most Outstanding Player of the NCAA Midwest Regional after averaging 29 points and 12.8 rebounds in 4 games.

REGULAR SEASON	G	MIN	FG	FG%	3FG	3PT%	FT	FT%	REB	AST	STL	BLK	PTS	AVG

ROOKIE -- NO NBA EXPERIENCE

Brent Price No. 20/G

Full name: Hartley Brent Price
HT: 6-1 **WT:** 185
Born: 12/9/68, Shawnee, OK
High school: Enid (OK)
College: Oklahoma

Mark Price's younger brother, Brent Price has improved his field goal and 3-point percentages.

REGULAR SEASON		G	MIN	FG	FG%	3FG	3PT%	FT	FT%	REB	AST	STL	BLK	PTS	AVG
'92-93	WASHINGTON	68	859	100	35.8	8	16.7	54	79.4	103	154	56	.3	262	3.9
'93-94	WASHINGTON	65	1035	141	43.3	50	33.3	68	78.2	90	213	55	2	400	6.2
	2 YR TOTALS	133	1894	241	39.8	58	29.3	122	78.7	193	367	111	5	662	5.0
'93-94	RANK NBA Gs	94	99	102	84	41	58	97	69	106	67	95	115	99	100
'94-95	PROJECTIONS	62	1211	187	50.5	142	50.2	83	76.3	65	281	50	0	599	9.7

Kenny Walker   No. 15/F

Full name: Kenneth Walker
HT: 6-8 **WT:** 220
Born: 8/18/64, Roberta, GA
High school: Crawford County (GA)
College: Kentucky
Walker is a fierce defender who is willing to crash
the boards. He played overseas for 2 years
before returning to the NBA with Washington.

REGULAR SEASON		G	MIN	FG	FG%	3FG	3PT%	FT	FT%	REB	AST	STL	BLK	PTS	AVG
'88-89	NEW YORK	79	1163	174	48.9	5	25.0	66	77.6	230	36	41	45	419	5.3
'89-90	NEW YORK	68	1595	204	53.1	2	40.0	125	72.3	343	49	33	52	535	7.9
'90-91	NEW YORK	54	771	83	43.5	0	0.0	64	78.0	157	13	18	30	230	4.3
'93-94	WASHINGTON	73	1397	132	48.2	0	0.0	87	69.6	289	33	26	59	351	4.8
6 YR TOTALS		424	8784	1222	48.6	7	20.6	620	74.9	1746	292	230	294	3071	7.2
'93-94	RANK NBA Fs	67	76	100	54	78	78	80	76	72	110	98	26	97	105
'94-95	PROJECTIONS	77	1502	117	48.8	0	0.0	84	66.1	314	34	23	68	318	4.1

PLAYOFFS		G	MIN	FG	FG%	3FG	3PT%	FT	FT%	REB	AST	STL	BLK	PTS	AVG
'88-89	NEW YORK	9	90	3	23.1	0	---	14	73.7	16	2	1	3	20	2.2
'89-90	NEW YORK	10	154	16	55.2	0	---	9	64.3	25	6	0	4	41	4.1
'90-91	NEW YORK	3	31	4	50.0	0	---	2	100.0	7	2	1	1	10	3.3
TOTALS		26	355	31	41.9	0	0.0	27	73.0	57	15	4	11	89	3.4

Jim Lynam   Head Coach

Born: 9/15/41
College: St. Joseph's (Philadelphia, PA)
The third-winningest coach in Sixer history,
Lynam was head coach at Philadelphia when
Bullets' GM John Nash was the Sixers' GM
there. He's a disciple of Jack Ramsay, having
played for Ramsay at St. Joseph's and having
served as Ramsay's assistant at Portland.

	REGULAR SEASON				PLAYOFFS			
YEAR	TEAM	W	L	PCT	FINISH	W	L	PCT
'83-84	SAN DIEGO	30	52	.366	6th/Pacific Div.			
'84-95	LA CLIPPERS	22	39	.361				
'87-88	PHILADELPHIA	36	46	.439	4th/Atlantic Div.			
'88-89	PHILADELPHIA	46	36	.561	2nd/Atlantic Div.	0	3	.000	lost Eastern Conf. first round to New York, 3-0
'89-90	PHILADELPHIA	53	29	.646	1st/Atlantic Div.	4	6	.400	lost Eastern Conf. seminfinals to Chicago, 4-1
'90-91	PHILADELPHIA	44	38	.537	2nd/Atlantic Div.	4	4	.500	lost Eastern Conf. seminfinals to Chicago, 4-1
'91-92	PHILADELPHIA	35	47	.427	5th/Atlantic Div.			
		266	287	.481		8	13	.381

1993 NBA DRAFT

SELECTION/TEAM	NAME	POS	COLLEGE	HT/WT
FIRST ROUND				
1. Milwaukee	Glenn Robinson	F	Purdue	6-7, 240
2. Dallas	Jason Kidd	G	California	6-4, 205
3. Detroit	Grant Hill	F	Duke	6-8, 225
4. Minnesota	Donyell Marshall	F	Connecticut	6-9, 218
5. Washington	Juwan Howard	C	Michigan	6-9, 250
6. Philadelphia	Sharone Wright	C	Clemson	6-11, 260
7. Los Angeles Clippers	Lamond Murray	F	California	6-7, 220
8. Sacramento	Brian Grant	F	Xavier-Ohio	6-9, 254
9. Boston	Eric Montross	C	North Carolina	7-0, 275
10. Los Angeles Lakers	Eddie Jones	G	Temple	6-6, 190
11. Seattle (from Charlotte)	Carlos Rogers	C	Tennessee State	6-11, 220
12. Miami	Khalid Reeves	G	Arizona	6-3, 207
13. Denver	Jalen Rose	G	Michigan	6-8, 210
14. New Jersey	Yinka Dare	C	George Washington	7-0, 265
15. Indiana	Eric Piatkowski	G	Nebraska	6-6, 215
16. Golden State (from Cleve.)	Clifford Rozier	F	Louisville	6-11, 245
17. Portland	Aaron McKie	G	Temple	6-5, 209
18. Milwaukee (from Orlando)	Eric Mobley	F	Pittsburgh	6-11, 250
19. Dallas (from Golden State)	Tony Dumas	G	Missouri-K.C.	6-6, 190
20. Philadelphia (from Utah)	B.J. Tyler	G	Texas	6-1, 185
21. Chicago	Dickie Simpkins	F	Providence	6-9, 248
22. San Antonio	Bill Curley	F	Boston College	6-9, 245
23. Phoenix	Wesley Person	G	Auburn	6-6, 195
24. New York	Monty Williams	F	Notre Dame	6-8, 225
25. LA Clippers (from Atl.)	Greg Minor	F	Louisville	6-6, 210
26. NY (from Hou. via Atl.)	Charlie Ward	G	Florida State	6-0, 190
27. Orl. (from Sea. via LA Clip.)	Brooks Thompson	G	Oklahoma State	6-4, 193
SECOND ROUND				
28. Dallas	Deon Thomas	F	Illinois	6-9, 238
29. Phoenix (from Det. via SA)	Antonio Lang	F	Duke	6-8, 205
30. Minnesota	Howard Eisley	G	Boston College	6-3, 180
31. Orl. (from Mil.via Den.and Was.)	Rodney Dent	C	Kentucky	6-9, 256
32. Washington	Jim McIlvaine	C	Marquette	7-1, 240
33. Philadelphia	Derrick Alston	F	Duquesne	6-11, 225
34. Atlanta (from LA Clippers)	Gaylon Nickerson	G	NW Oklahoma St.	6-3, 190
35. Sacramento	Michael Smith	F	Providence	6-8, 230
36. Boston	Andrei Fetisov	F-C	Russia/Spanish Lg.	6-10, NA
37. Seattle (from LA Lakers)	Dontonio Wingfield	F	Cincinnati	6-9, 235
38. Charlotte	Darrin Hancock	G	Kansas/France	6-7, 205
39. Golden State (from Denver)	Anthony Miller	F	Michigan State	NA
40. Miami	Jeff Webster	F	Oklahoma	6-8, 232
41. Indiana (from NJ via Phila.)	William Njoku	F	St. Mary's (Canada)	6-9, 215
42. Cleveland	Gary Collier	G	Tulsa	6-4, 195
43. Portland	Shawnelle Scott	C	St. John's	6-10, 250
44. Indiana	Damon Bailey	G	Indiana	6-3, 201
45. Golden State	Dwayne Morton	G	Louisville	6-7, 195
46. Milwaukee (from Orlando)	Voshon Lenard	G	Minnesota	6-4, 205
47. Utah	Jamie Watson	F	South Carolina	6-7, 190
48. Detroit (from SA via Sacra.)	Jevon Crudup	F	Missouri	6-6, 252
49. Chicago	Kris Bruton	G	Benedict	6-6, 210
50. Phoenix	Charles Claxton	C	Georgia	7-0, 265
51. Sacramento (from Atlanta)	Lawrence Funderburke	F	Ohio State	6-9, 230
52. Phoenix (from New York)	Anthony Goldwire	G	Houston	6-1, 182
53. Houston	Albert Burditt	F	Texas	6-8, 230
54. Seattle	Zeljko Rebraca	C	Yugoslavia	NA

TOP 1993—94 INDIVIDUAL PERFORMANCES

POINTS

PLAYER	TEAM	OPPONENT	TOTAL	DATE
David Robinson	S.A.	at LA Clippers	71	4/24/94
Shaquille O'Neal	Orl.	vs. Minnesota	53	4/20/94
David Robinson	S.A.	at Minnesota	50	2/21/94
Shaquille O'Neal	Orl.	at Indiana	49	12/10/93
David Robinson	S.A.	vs. Sacramento	48	3/19/94

REBOUNDS

PLAYER	TEAM	OPPONENT	TOTAL	DATE
Dennis Rodman	S.A.	vs. Dallas	32	1/22/94
Dennis Rodman	S.A.	vs. Minnesota	29	11/9/93
Dennis Rodman	S.A.	at Charlotte	28	12/1/93
Shaquille O'Neal	Orl.	at New Jersey	28	11/20/93
Dennis Rodman	S.A.	vs. Houston	26	2/19/94

ASSISTS

PLAYER	TEAM	OPPONENT	TOTAL	DATE
Kevin Johnson	Pho.	vs. San Antonio	25	4/6/94
Sherman Douglas	Bos.	at Philadelphia	22	4/3/94
Sherman Douglas	Bos.	vs. Sacramento	21	12/8/93

1993-94 TRIPLE-DOUBLES

1.	David Robinson	S.A. vs. Min.	11/9	43 pts 11 rbs 10 blocks	10th career
2.	Kenny Anderson	N.J. vs. Hou.	11/16	24 pts 13 rbs 12 ast	3rd career
3.	Shaquille O'Neal	Orl. at N.J.	11/20	24 pts 28 rbs 15 blocks	1st career
4.	Dikembe Mutombo	Den. vs. Por.	11/26	17 pts 13 rbs 11 blocks	3rd career
5.	Mookie Blaylock	ATL vs. Phi.	11/27	15 pts 10 rbs 10 ast	1st career
6.	David Robinson	S.A. at Orl.	12/3	23 pts 11 rbs 10 ast	2nd sea.,11th car.
7.	Kevin Johnson	Pho. vs. Was.	12/9	17 pts 13 ast 10 stl	10th career
8.	Kenny Anderson	N.J. vs. Mia.	12/13	32 pts 10 rbs 11 ast	2nd sea.,4th car.
9.	Scottie Pippen	Chi. vs. Cha.	12/20	22 pts 11 rbs 10 ast	12th career
10.	Danny Manning	LAC. vs. Was.	12/22	12 pts 12 rbs 10 ast	1st career
11.	Scottie Pippen	Chi. at Det.	12/23	16 pts 10 rbs 10 ast	2nd sea., 13th. car.
12.	Chris Webber	G.S. vs. LAC	12/23	22 pts 12 rbs 12 ast	1st career
13.	Larry Johnson	Cha. at Det.	12/27	29 pts 20 rbs 11 ast	3rd career
14.	Charles Barkley	Pho. vs. Phi.	12/30	22 pts 14 rbs 12 ast	18th career
15.	Lionel Simmons	Sac. at Sea.	1/7	14 pts 12 rbs 13 ast	2nd career
16.	David Robinson	S.A. vs. Min.	1/11	27 pts 12 rbs 10 ast	3rd sea., 12th car.
17.	Chris Mullin	G.S. vs. Sea.	1/14	18 pts 12 rbs 10 ast	1st sea., 2nd car.
18.	Kenny Anderson	N.J. vs. G.S.	1/22	20 pts 10 rbs 10 ast	3rd sea., 5th car.
19.	Ron Harper	LAC vs. Sac.	2/5	24 pts 10 rbs 10 ast	1st sea., 3rd car.
20.	C. Weatherspoon	Phi. vs. Cha.	2/7	15 pts 15 rbs 13 ast	1st career
21.	David Robinson	Was. at S.A.	2/8	31 pts 14 rbs 10 ast	4th sea., 13th car.
22.	Oliver Miller	Pho. vs. Min.	2/9	14 pts 15 rbs 11 ast	1st career
23.	Vlade Divac	LAL vs. LAC	2/15	14 pts 16 rbs 12 ast	1st career
24.	Mitch Richmond	Sac. vs. Phi.	2/16	31 pts 12 rbs 10 ast	1st sea., 2nd car.
25.	David Robinson	S.A. vs. Det.	2/17	34 pts 10 rbs 10 as/10 bl	5th sea., 15th car.
26.	Derrick Coleman	N.J. vs. Phi.	3/6	13 pts 12 rbs 10 ast	1st sea., 2nd car.
27.	Vlade Divac	LAL vs. Dal.	3/10	22 pts 17 rbs 12 ast	2nd sea., 2nd car.
28.	Ron Harper	LAC vs. Dal.	3/11	26 pts 10 rbs 10 ast	2nd sea., 4th car.
29.	Mark Jackson	LAC vs. G.S.	3/13	11 pts 13 rbs 17 ast	1st sea., 10th car.
30.	Shawn Kemp	Sea. at Cha.	3/20	15 pts 11 rbs 12 ast	1st career
31.	Mookie Blaylock	Atl. vs. Mia.	3/26	17 pts 14 rbs 14 ast	2nd sea., 2nd car.
32.	Dikembe Mutombo	Den. vs. LAC	4/5	11 pts 16 rbs 10 blk	2nd sea., 4th car.
33.	Dikembe Mutombo	Den. vs. Sea.	4/7	13 pts 13 rbs 11 blk	3rd sea., 5th car.
34.	Hakeem Olajuwon	Hou. vs. G.S.	4/7	26 pts 13 rbs 10 ast	1st sea., 8th car.
35.	Anfernee Hardaway	Orl. at Bos.	4/15	14 pts 11 rbs 12 ast	1st career
36.	Derrick Coleman	N.J. at Phi.	4/19	31 pts 12 rbs 10 ast	2nd sea., 3rd car.

INDIVIDUAL LEADERS

SCORING AVERAGE
Minimum 70 games or 1400 points

		G	FG	FT	PTS	AVG
1. Robinson	S.A.	80	840	693	2383	29.8
2. O'Neal	Orl.	81	953	471	2377	29.3
3. Olajuwon	Hou.	80	894	388	2184	27.3
4. Wilkins	Atl.-LAC	74	698	442	1923	26.0
5. K. Malone	Utah	82	772	511	2063	25.2
6. Ewing	N.Y.	79	745	445	1939	24.5
7. Richmond	Sac.	78	635	426	1823	23.4
8. Pippen	Chi.	72	627	270	1587	22.0
9. Barkley	Pho.	65	518	318	1402	21.6
10. Rice	Mia.	81	663	250	1708	21.1
11. Sprewell	G.S.	82	613	353	1720	21.0
12. Manning	LAC-Atl.	68	586	228	1403	20.6
13. Dumars	Det.	69	505	276	1410	20.4
14. Coleman	N.J.	77	541	439	1559	20.2
15. Harper	LAC	75	569	299	1508	20.1
16. C. Robinson	Por.	82	641	352	1647	20.1
17. Miller	Ind.	79	524	403	1574	19.9
18. Jackson	Dal.	82	637	285	1576	19.2
19. Mashburn	Dal.	79	561	306	1513	19.2
20. Willis	Atl.	80	627	268	1531	19.1
21. K. Anderson	N.J.	82	576	346	1538	18.8
22. Weatherspoon	Phi.	82	602	298	1506	18.4
23. MacLean	Was.	75	517	328	1365	18.2
24. Kemp	Sea.	79	533	364	1431	18.1
25. Abdul-Rauf	Den.	80	588	219	1437	18.0

REBOUNDS PER GAME
Minimum 70 games or 1400 points

		G	OFF	DEF	TOT	AVG
1. Rodman	S.A.	79	453	914	1367	17.3
2. O'Neal	Orl.	81	384	688	1072	13.2
3. Willis	Atl.	80	335	628	963	12.0
4. Olajuwon	Hou.	80	229	726	955	11.9
5. Polynice	Det.-Sac.	68	299	510	809	11.9
6. Mutombo	Den.	82	286	685	971	11.8
7. Oakley	N.Y.	82	349	616	965	11.8
8. K. Malone	Utah	82	235	705	940	11.5
9. Coleman	N.J.	77	262	608	870	11.3
10. Ewing	N.Y.	79	219	666	885	11.2
11. Grant	Chi.	70	306	463	769	11.0
12. Divac	LA-L	79	282	569	851	10.8
13. Kemp	Sea.	79	312	539	851	10.8
14. Robinson	S.A.	80	241	614	855	10.7
15. Thorpe	Hou.	82	271	599	870	10.6
16. Williams	Por.	81	315	528	843	10.4
17. Seikaly	Mia.	72	244	496	740	10.3
18. Weatherspoon	Phi.	82	254	578	832	10.1
19. Gugliotta	Was.	78	189	539	728	9.3
20. Green	Pho.	82	275	478	753	9.2
21. Webber	G.S.	76	305	389	694	9.1
22. Vaught	LAC	75	218	438	656	8.7
23. Pippen	Chi.	72	173	456	629	8.7
24. Ellis	Den.	79	220	462	682	8.6
25. Laettner	Min.	70	160	442	602	8.6

FIELD GOAL PCT.
Minimum 300 FG made

		FG	FGA	PCT
1. O'Neal	Orl.	953	1591	.599
2. Mutombo	Den.	365	642	.569
3. Thorpe	Hou.	449	801	.561
4. Webber	G.S.	572	1037	.552
5. Kemp	Sea.	533	990	.538
6. Vaught	LAC	373	695	.537
7. Ceballos	Pho.	425	795	.535
8. Smits	Ind.	493	923	.534
9. D. Davis	Ind.	308	582	.529
10. Olajuwon	Hou.	894	1694	.528
11. Stockton	Utah	458	868	.528
12. Grant	Chi.	460	878	.524
13. Polynice	Dt-Sac	346	662	.523
14. Radja	Bos.	491	942	.521
15. L. Johnson	Cha.	346	672	.515
16. Mills	Det.	588	1151	.511
17. Gilliam	N.J.	348	682	.510
18. Augmon	Atl.	439	861	.510
19. Owens	G.S.	492	971	.507
20. Robinson	S.A.	840	1658	.507

3-PT FIELD GOAL PCT.
Minimum 50 made

		3FG	3GA	PCT
Murray	Por.	50	109	.459
Armstrong	Chi.	60	135	.444
Miller	Ind.	123	292	.421
Kerr	Chi.	52	124	.419
Skiles	Orl.	68	165	.412
Murdock	Mil.	69	168	.411
Richmond	Sac.	127	312	.407
Smith	Hou.	89	220	.405
Curry	Cha.	152	378	.402
Davis	N.Y.	53	132	.402
Scott	Orl.	155	388	.399
Price	Cle.	118	297	.397
Wilkins	Cle.	84	212	.396
Ellis	S.A.	131	332	.395
E. Johnson	Cha.	59	150	.393
McMillan	Sea.	52	133	.391
Porter	Por.	110	282	.390
Chapman	Was.	64	165	.388
Dumars	Det.	124	320	.388
Majerle	Pho.	192	503	.382

FREE THROW PCT.
Minimum 125 made

		FT	FTA	PCT
1. Abdul-Rauf	Den.	219	229	.956
2. Miller	Ind.	403	444	.908
3. Pierce	Sea.	189	211	.896
4. Threatt	LAL	138	155	.890
5. Price	Cle.	238	268	.888
6. Rice	Mia.	250	284	.880
7. Hornacek	Phi-Ut	260	296	.878
8. Skiles	Orl.	195	222	.878
9. Porter	Por.	204	234	.872
10. Smith	Hou.	135	155	.871
11. Hawkins	Cha.	312	362	.862
12. Elie	Hou.	154	179	.860
13. Brandon	Cle.	139	162	.858
14. Armstrong	Chi.	194	227	.855
15. Anderson	S.A.	145	171	.848
16. Wilkins	Atl-LAC	442	522	.847
17. Legler	Dal.	142	169	.840
18. M. Williams	Min.	333	397	.839
19. Dumars	Det.	276	330	.836
20. Smith	Mia.	273	327	.835

ASSISTS PER GAME
Minimum 70 games or 400 assists

		G	AST	AVG
Stockton	Utah	82	1031	12.6
Bogues	Cha.	77	780	10.1
Blaylock	Atl.	81	789	9.7
K. Anderson	N.J.	82	784	9.6
K. Johnson	Pho.	67	637	9.5
Strickland	Por.	82	740	9.0
Douglas	Bos.	78	683	8.8
Jackson	LAC	79	678	8.6
Price	Cle.	76	589	7.8
M. Williams	Min.	71	512	7.2
Adams	Was.	70	480	6.9
Webb	Sac.	79	528	6.7
Murdock	Mil.	82	546	6.7
Hardaway	Orl.	82	544	6.6
Workman	Ind.	65	404	6.2
Skiles	Orl.	82	503	6.1
Payton	Sea.	82	494	6.0
Van Exel	LAL	81	466	5.8
Pippen	Chi.	72	403	5.6
McMillan	Sea.	73	387	5.3

STEALS PER GAME
Minimum 70 games or 125 steals

		G	STL	AVG
1. McMillan	Sea.	73	216	2.96
2. Pippen	Chi.	72	211	2.93
3. Blaylock	Atl.	81	212	2.62
4. Stockton	Utah	82	199	2.43
5. Murdock	Mil.	82	197	2.40
6. Hardaway	Orl.	82	190	2.32
7. Payton	Sea.	82	188	2.29
8. Gugliotta	Was.	78	172	2.21
9. Sprewell	G.S.	82	180	2.20
10. Brown	Bos.	77	156	2.03

BLOCKS PER GAME
Minimum 70 games or 100 blocked shots

		G	BLK	AVG
Mutombo	Den.	82	336	4.10
Olajuwon	Hou.	80	297	3.71
Robinson	S.A.	80	265	3.31
Mourning	Cha.	60	188	3.13
Bradley	Phi.	49	147	3.00
O'Neal	Orl.	81	231	2.85
Ewing	N.Y.	79	217	2.75
Miller	Pho.	69	156	2.26
Webber	G.S.	76	164	2.16
Kemp	Sea.	79	166	2.10

NBA Team Stats
Offensive stats

	G	FIELD GOALS			3-PT. FGS			FREE THROWS			REBOUNDS			AST	MISCELLANEOUS			TO	BLK	SCORING	
		MADE	ATT.	PCT.	MADE	ATT.	PCT.	MADE	ATT.	PCT.	OFF.	DEF.	TOT.		PF	DQ	STL			PTS	AVG.
Phoe.	82	3429	7060	48.6	344	1042	33.0	1674	2301	72.8	1220	2453	3673	2261	1639	8	745	1305	460	8876	108.2
G.S.	82	3512	7145	49.2	291	859	33.9	1529	2304	66.4	1183	2396	3579	2198	1769	18	804	1433	511	8844	107.9
Port.	82	3371	7427	45.4	272	770	35.3	1781	2395	74.3	1302	2460	3762	2070	1827	5	744	1210	409	8795	107.3
Cha.	82	3362	7100	47.5	335	916	36.7	1632	2135	76.4	1019	2475	3494	2214	1747	17	724	1265	394	8732	106.5
Sea.	82	3336	6901	48.4	242	722	33.5	1769	2374	74.5	1148	2233	3381	2112	1914	16	1053	1262	365	8687	105.9
Orl.	82	3341	6883	48.5	394	1137	34.7	1590	2346	67.8	1177	2356	3533	2070	1713	10	683	1327	455	8666	105.7
Miami	82	3197	6895	46.4	337	997	33.8	1744	2223	78.5	1235	2407	3642	1855	2024	26	643	1315	374	8475	103.4
N.J.	82	3169	7115	44.5	223	683	32.7	1900	2495	76.2	1190	2555	3855	1900	1693	9	696	1196	576	8461	103.2
LAC	82	3343	7163	46.7	252	831	30.3	1909	2128	70.9	1120	2410	3530	2169	1769	18	807	1474	421	8447	103.0
Utah	82	3207	6729	47.7	179	559	32.0	1761	2379	74.0	1069	2385	3444	2179	1988	13	751	1191	364	8354	101.9
Atl.	82	3247	7039	46.1	268	830	32.3	1595	2070	75.2	1290	2423	3673	2095	1625	5	915	1252	449	8318	101.4
Clev.	82	3133	6731	46.5	294	813	36.2	1756	2284	77.0	1090	2353	3443	2049	1701	15	705	1135	426	8256	101.2
Sac.	82	3179	7027	45.2	257	729	35.3	1676	2292	73.1	1122	2349	3471	2029	1979	27	669	1338	355	8291	101.1
Hou.	82	3197	6733	47.5	429	1285	33.4	1469	1978	74.3	925	2619	3545	2067	1646	7	717	1402	485	8292	101.1
Ind.	82	3167	6516	48.6	184	500	36.8	1762	2387	73.8	1130	2409	3539	2055	1974	19	705	1440	457	8280	101.0
Bos.	82	3333	7057	47.2	138	477	28.9	1463	2000	73.0	1037	2380	3417	1928	1849	19	674	1400	440	8257	100.8
Wash.	82	3195	6826	46.8	221	744	29.7	1618	2162	74.8	1071	2189	3260	1823	1715	19	701	1403	321	8229	100.4
LAL	82	3291	7316	45.0	241	800	30.0	1410	1967	71.7	1260	2204	3464	1983	1877	13	751	1197	461	8233	100.4
Den.	82	3155	6781	46.5	170	597	28.5	1739	2423	71.8	1105	2557	3652	1763	1925	19	679	1360	686	8221	100.3
S.A.	82	3178	6810	46.7	249	714	34.9	1597	2151	74.2	1189	2597	3786	1896	1662	4	561	1198	450	8202	100.0
N.Y.	82	3058	6735	45.0	316	908	34.8	1564	2097	74.6	1175	2542	3717	2057	2001	23	752	1360	385	8076	98.5
Chi.	82	3245	6815	47.6	233	659	35.4	1310	1859	70.5	1143	2391	3533	2102	1750	11	740	1305	354	8033	98.0
Phil.	82	3103	6819	45.5	318	942	33.8	1509	2112	71.4	1012	2394	3405	1827	1488	7	683	1368	525	8033	98.0
Det.	82	3169	7017	45.2	358	1041	34.4	1253	1715	73.1	1027	2320	3347	1757	1935	23	602	1236	309	7949	96.9
Milw.	82	3044	6807	44.7	331	1019	32.5	1530	2181	70.2	1126	2154	3280	1946	1821	19	800	1343	407	7949	96.9
Minn.	82	2985	6535	45.7	183	557	32.9	1777	2303	77.2	990	2343	3333	1957	2016	20	600	1478	440	7930	96.7
Dall.	82	3055	7070	43.2	241	773	31.2	1450	1942	74.7	1271	2150	3421	1629	2007	13	767	1393	299	7801	95.1

NBA Team Stats
Defensive stats

| | FIELD GOALS | | | 3-PT. FGS | | | FREE THROWS | | | REBOUNDS | | | AST | PF | MISCELLANEOUS | | | | PTS | SCORING | |
	MADE	ATT	PCT	MADE	ATT	PCT	MADE	ATT	PCT	OFF	DEF	TOT			DQ	STL	TO	BLK		AVG	DIFF
N.Y.	2783	6451	43.1	263	825	30.7	1684	2341	71.9	1015	2245	3251	1671	1697	22	677	1420	333	7503	91.5	7.0
S.A.	3065	6880	44.6	290	871	33.3	1349	1875	71.9	1089	2153	3242	1769	1791	15	632	1020	346	7771	94.8	5.3
Chi.	3029	6542	46.3	262	780	33.3	1470	1987	74.0	985	2240	3225	1840	1725	13	730	1335	374	7790	94.9	5.3
Atl.	3163	6954	45.5	275	872	31.5	1285	1752	74.2	1157	2358	3515	1697	1722	13	641	1465	338	7866	95.2	3.1
Hou.	3152	7165	44.0	267	841	30.5	1377	1871	73.5	1138	2434	3572	1901	1743	13	767	1221	312	7938	95.8	4.3
Sea.	2928	6459	45.3	325	946	34.5	1760	2374	74.1	1084	2191	3275	1808	1884	8	695	1665	421	7942	95.9	9.1
Clev.	3131	6741	46.4	268	729	35.4	1446	1967	73.5	1069	2325	3394	2005	1797	12	638	1293	461	7955	97.1	4.0
Ind.	2976	6514	45.0	273	815	33.5	1768	2422	73.0	1100	2153	3427	1902	1986	15	626	1340	389	7997	97.5	3.5
Utah	2973	6641	44.8	289	967	29.9	1773	2444	72.5	1027	2027	3427	1806	1922	15	593	1318	469	8006	97.7	4.2
Den.	3065	7000	43.8	208	717	29.0	1761	2349	75.0	1116	2331	3449	1746	1957	18	725	1245	502	8099	98.8	1.5
Miami	3006	6541	45.7	235	892	33.1	1889	2527	74.8	1074	2295	3340	1821	1946	25	689	1314	438	8255	101.0	2.7
N.J.	3265	7125	45.8	235	739	31.8	1514	2036	74.3	1142	2528	3670	1919	1901	20	715	1246	582	8261	101.0	2.2
Orl.	3265	7125	45.8	295	847	34.9	1525	2047	74.5	1197	2305	3502	2103	1844	16	755	1228	442	8347	101.8	-3.9
Milw.	3255	6525	49.1	286	789	36.2	1684	2284	73.7	1065	2495	3581	2092	1777	15	768	1416	437	8480	103.4	-6.5
Phoe.	3379	7135	47.4	263	863	32.8	1438	1998	72.0	1086	2247	3333	2154	1870	16	746	1254	457	8479	103.4	4.8
Minn.	3244	6874	47.2	227	738	30.8	1783	2451	72.7	1101	2295	3396	2108	1855	21	824	1164	549	8498	103.5	-6.9
Dall.	3212	6508	49.4	249	686	36.2	1841	2498	73.7	1015	2600	3604	1970	1649	7	782	1428	507	8514	103.8	-8.7
Port.	3311	7057	46.9	295	830	35.7	1651	2216	74.5	1016	2481	3497	2094	1944	15	654	1391	390	8579	104.6	2.6
LAL	3337	7006	47.6	272	723	31.5	1693	2046	71.7	1284	2603	3817	2163	1669	10	664	1344	427	8585	104.7	-4.3
Det.	3255	6878	47.3	272	814	33.4	1805	2451	73.5	1191	2590	3781	2097	1602	9	721	1169	368	8587	104.7	-7.8
Bos.	3357	7034	47.7	231	665	34.7	1673	2218	75.4	1131	2508	3639	2089	1738	12	690	1273	414	8618	105.1	-4.3
Phil.	3549	7338	48.4	263	795	33.1	1297	1744	74.4	1202	2607	3809	2357	1729	10	806	1190	385	8658	105.6	-7.6
G.S.	3426	7332	46.8	305	869	35.1	1540	2108	73.1	1324	2408	3732	2184	1870	18	842	1250	406	8701	106.1	1.7
Cha.	3463	7359	47.1	277	916	34.5	1507	2035	74.0	1217	2467	3684	2116	1761	12	629	1250	430	8750	106.7	-0.2
Sac.	3360	7017	47.9	317	771	35.9	1767	2446	72.2	1189	2674	3763	2052	1895	14	746	1341	498	8764	106.9	-5.8
Wash.	3569	7025	50.8	262	723	34.9	1444	1995	72.3	1119	2362	3481	2113	1823	8	815	1470	393	8834	107.7	-7.4
LAC	3512	7421	47.3	308	882	34.9	1584	2209	71.7	1348	2568	3916	2220	1768	11	898	1354	476	8915	108.7	-5.7

Composite Statistics

TEAM	POINTS PER GAME OWN	OPP.	FIELD GOAL PERCENTAGE OWN	OPP.	TURNOVERS PER GAME OWN	OPP.	REBOUND PERCENTAGES OFF.	DEF.	TOT	BELOW 100 PTS. OWN	OPP.	OVERTIME GAMES W	L	3 PTS. OR LESS W	L	10 PTS. OR MORE W	L
Atlanta	101.4	96.2	.461	.455	15.3	17.9	.346	.677	.512	37	57	1	2	8	5	28	10
Boston	100.8	105.1	.472	.477	15.1	15.5	.293	.678	.485	40	22	5	2	4	7	10	25
Charlotte	106.5	106.7	.476	.471	15.4	15.4	.292	.670	.481	28	28	3	3	8	3	20	21
Chicago	98.0	94.9	.476	.463	15.9	16.3	.338	.708	.523	48	60	1	3	13	4	25	16
Cleveland	101.2	97.1	.465	.464	13.9*	15.8	.318	.690	.504	39	49	4	3	1	10	27	16
Dallas	95.1	103.8	.432	.494	17.0	17.4	.337	.661	.499	56	23	1	1	3	8	5	38
Denver	100.3	98.8	.465	.438	17.3	15.2	.322	.696	.509	42	48	1	1	4	8	21	16
Detroit	96.9	104.7	.452	.473	15.1	14.3	.284	.661	.472	51	32	3	1	11	3	5	33
Golden State	107.9	106.1	.492*	.468	17.5	17.4	.329	.644	.487	22	25	3	1	8	9	28	16
Houston	101.1	96.8	.475	.440	16.3	14.9	.276	.697	.486	40	51	2	1	5	9	28	10
Indiana	101.0	97.5	.486	.450	17.6	16.3	.344	.680	.512	34	48	1	2	10	7	10	28
L.A. Clippers	103.0	108.7	.467	.473	18.0	16.6	.304	.641	.472	34	19	1	2	8	7	7	28
L.A. Lakers	100.4	104.7	.450	.476	14.6	16.4	.332	.632	.482	42	26	2	0	6	9	26	14
Miami	103.4	100.7	.464	.457	16.0	16.0	.353	.691	.522	29	38	3	0	6	9	5	28
Milwaukee	96.9	103.4	.447	.491	16.4	17.3	.311	.665	.488	51	29	1	3	5	6	23	18
Minnesota	96.7	103.6	.457	.472	18.0	14.2	.301	.680	.491	50	31	0	2	6	5	35	11
New Jersey	103.2	101.0	.445	.458	14.6	15.2	.340	.691	.515	32	34	3	3	6	9	29	10
New York	98.5	91.5*	.460	.431*	16.6	17.3	.344	.714*	.529	47	62	2	1	5	6	12	32
Orlando	105.7	101.8	.485	.458	16.7	15.0	.338	.663	.501	25	36	0	1	6	5	30	12
Philadelphia	98.0	105.5	.455	.484	16.7	14.5	.280	.666	.473	47	31	2	3	5	7	25	16
Phoenix	108.2*	103.4	.484	.474	15.9	15.3	.352	.693	.523	18	29	1	0	8	7	10	35
Portland	107.3	104.6	.454	.469	14.8	17.0	.344	.708	.526	19	25	2	1	7	6	33	12
Sacramento	101.1	106.9	.452	.479	16.3	16.4	.304	.664	.484	33	23	1	2	6	6	43	5
San Antonio	100.0	94.8	.475	.446	14.6	12.4	.356*	.705	.530*	37	55	2	0	3	6	30	9
Seattle	105.9	96.9	.484	.453	15.4	20.3*	.344	.673	.509	27	52	2	3	9	5	43	5
Utah	101.9	97.7	.477	.448	14.5	16.1	.313	.684	.499	32	50	2	0	9	6	30	9
Washington	100.4	107.7	.468	.508	17.1	15.7	.312	.662	.487	43	20	0	3	4	5	9	39
Composite: 2214 games	101.5		.466		16.0		.322	.678		1003	1003	43		175		554	

*—League Leader

REBOUND PERCENTAGES: OFF.—Percentage of a given team's missed shots which that team rebounds; DEF.—Percentage of opponents' missed shots which a given team rebounds; TOT.—Average of offensive and defensive rebound percentages.

MOST VALUABLE PLAYER

Year	Player	Team	PPG	RPG	APG
1955–56	Bob Pettit	St. Louis Hawks	25.7	16.2	2.6
1956–57	Bob Cousy	Boston Celtics	20.6	4.8	7.5
1957–58	Bill Russell	Boston Celtics	16.6	22.7	2.9
1958–59	Bob Pettit	St. Louis Hawks	29.2	16.4	3
1959–60	Wilt Chamberlain	Philadelphia Warriors	37.6	27.0	2.3
1960–61	Bill Russell	Boston Celtics	16.9	23.9	3.4
1961–62	Bill Russell	Boston Celtics	18.9	24.9	4.5
1962–63	Bill Russell	Boston Celtics	16.8	23.6	4.5
1963–64	Oscar Robertson	Cincinnati Royals	31.4	9.9	10.9
1964–65	Bill Russell	Boston Celtics	14.1	24.1	5.3
1965–66	Wilt Chamberlain	Philadelphia 76ers	33.5	24.6	5.2
1966–67	Wilt Chamberlain	Philadelphia 76ers	24.1	24.1	7.8
1967–68	Wilt Chamberlain	Philadelphia 76ers	24.3	23.8	8.6
1968–69	Wes Unseld	Baltimore Bullets	13.8	18.2	2.6
1969–70	Willis Reed	New York Knicks	21.7	13.9	2.0
1970–71	Lew Alcindor	Milwaukee Bucks	31.7	16.0	3.3
1971–72	K. Abdul-Jabbar	Milwaukee Bucks	34.8	16.6	4.6
1972–73	Dave Cowens	Boston Celtics	20.5	16.0	4.1
1973–74	K. Abdul-Jabbar	Milwaukee Bucks	27.0	14.5	4.8
1974–75	Bob McAdoo	Buffalo Braves	34.5	14.1	2.2
1975–76	K. Abdul-Jabbar	Los Angeles Lakers	27.7	16.9	5.0
1976–77	K. Abdul-Jabbar	Los Angeles Lakers	26.2	13.3	3.9
1977–78	Bill Walton	Portland Trail Blazers	18.9	13.2	5.0
1978–79	Moses Malone	Houston Rockets	24.8	17.6	1.8
1979–80	K. Abdul-Jabbar	Los Angeles Lakers	24.8	10.8	4.5
1980–81	Julius Erving	Philadelphia 76ers	24.6	8.0	4.4
1981–82	Moses Malone	Houston Rockets	31.1	14.7	1.8
1982–83	Moses Malone	Philadelphia 76ers	24.5	15.3	1.3
1983–84	Larry Bird	Boston Celtics	24.2	10.1	6.6
1984–85	Larry Bird	Boston Celtics	28.7	10.5	6.6
1985–86	Larry Bird	Boston Celtics	25.8	9.8	6.8
1986–87	Magic Johnson	Los Angeles Lakers	23.9	6.3	12.2
1987–88	Michael Jordan	Chicago Bulls	35.0	5.5	5.9
1988–89	Magic Johnson	Los Angeles Lakers	22.5	7.9	12.8
1989–90	Magic Johnson	Los Angeles Lakers	22.3	6.6	11.2
1990–91	Michael Jordan	Chicago Bulls	31.5	6.0	5.5
1991–92	Michael Jordan	Chicago Bulls	30.1	6.4	6.1
1992–93	Charles Barkley	Phoenix Suns	25.6	12.2	5.1
1993–94	Hakeem Olajuwon	Houston Rockets	27.3	11.9	3.6

ROOKIE OF THE YEAR

Year	Player	Team	PPG	RPG	APG
1952–53	Don Meineke	Fort Wayne Pistons	10.7	6.9	2.2
1953–54	Ray Felix	Baltimore Bullets	17.6	13.3	1.1
1954–55	Bob Pettit	Milwaukee Hawks	20.4	13.8	3.2
1955–56	Maurice Stokes	Rochester Royals	16.8	16.3	4.9
1956–57	Tom Heinsohn	Boston Celtics	16.2	9.8	1.6
1957–58	Woody Sauldsberry	Philadelphia Warriors	12.8	10.3	0.8
1958–59	Elgin Baylor	Minneapolis Lakers	24.9	15.0	4.1
1959–60	Wilt Chamberlain	Philadelphia Warriors	37.6	27.0	2.3
1960–61	Oscar Robertson	Cincinnati Royals	30.5	10.1	9.7
1961–62	Walt Bellamy	Chicago Packers	31.6	19.0	2.7
1962–63	Terry Dischinger	Chicago Zephyrs	25.5	8.0	3.1
1963–64	Jerry Lucas	Cincinnati Royals	17.7	17.4	2.6
1964–65	Willis Reed	New York Knicks	19.5	14.7	1.7
1965–66	Rick Barry	SF Warriors	25.7	10.6	2.2
1966–67	Dave Bing	Detroit Pistons	20.0	4.5	4.1
1967–68	Earl Monroe	Baltimore Bullets	24.3	5.7	4.3
1968–69	Wes Unseld	Baltimore Bullets	13.8	18.2	2.6
1969–70	Lew Alcindor	Milwaukee Bucks	28.8	14.5	4.1
1970–71	Dave Cowens	Boston Celtics	17.0	15.0	2.8
1970–71	Geoff Petrie	Portland Trail Blazers	24.8	3.4	4.8
1971–72	Sidney Wicks	Portland Trail Blazers	24.5	11.5	4.3
1972–73	Bob McAdoo	Buffalo Braves	18.0	9.1	1.7
1973–74	Ernie DiGregorio	Buffalo Braves	15.2	2.7	8.2
1974–75	Keith Wilkes	Golden State Warriors	14.2	8.2	2.2
1975–76	Alvan Adams	Phoenix Suns	19.0	9.1	5.6
1976–77	Adrian Dantley	Buffalo Braves	20.3	7.6	1.9
1977–78	Walter Davis	Phoenix Suns	24.2	6.0	3.4
1978–79	Phil Ford	Kans.a. City Kings	15.9	2.3	8.6
1979–80	Larry Bird	Boston Celtics	21.3	10.4	4.5
1980–81	Darrell Griffith	Utah Jazz	20.6	3.6	2.4
1981–82	Buck Williams	New Jersey Nets	15.5	12.3	1.3
1982–83	Terry Cummings	San Diego Clippers	23.7	10.6	2.5
1983–84	Ralph Sampson	Houston Rockets	21.0	11.1	2.0
1984–85	Michael Jordan	Chicago Bulls	28.2	6.5	5.8
1985–86	Patrick Ewing	New York Knicks	20.0	9.0	2.0
1986–87	Chuck Person	Indiana Pacers	18.8	8.3	3.6
1987–88	Mark Jackson	New York Knicks	13.6	4.8	10.6
1988–89	Mitch Richmond	Golden State Warriors	22.0	5.9	4.2
1989–90	David Robinson	San Antonio Spurs	24.3	12.0	2.0
1990–91	Derrick Coleman	New Jersey Nets	18.4	10.3	2.2
1991–92	Larry Johnson	Charlotte Hornets	19.2	11.0	3.6
1992–93	Shaquille O'Neal	Orlando Magic	23.4	13.9	1.9
1993–94	Chris Webber	Golden State Warriors	17.5	9.1	3.6

FINALS MVP

Year	Player	Team	Year	Player	Team
1969	Jerry West	Los Angeles	1982	Magic Johnson	LA Lakers
1970	Willis Reed	New York	1983	Moses Malone	Philadelphia
1971	K. Abdul-Jabbar	Milwaukee	1984	Larry Bird	Boston
1972	Wilt Chamberlain	Los Angeles	1985	K. Abdul-Jabbar	LA Lakers
1973	Willis Reed	New York	1986	Larry Bird	Boston
1974	John Havlicek	Boston	1987	Magic Johnson	LA Lakers
1975	Rick Barry	Golden State	1988	James Worthy	LA Lakers
1976	Jo Jo White	Boston	1989	Joe Dumars	Detroit
1977	Bill Walton	Portland	1990	Isiah Thomas	Detroit
1978	Wes Unseld	Washington	1991	Michael Jordan	Chicago
1979	Dennis Johnson	Seattle	1992	Michael Jordan	Chicago
1980	Magic Johnson	Los Angeles	1993	Michael Jordan	Chicago
1981	Cedric Maxwell	Boston	1994	Hakeem Olajuwon	Houston

DEFENSIVE PLAYER OF THE YEAR

Season	Player	Team	Season	Player	Team
1982–83	Sidney Moncrief	Milwaukee	1988–89	Mark Eaton	Utah Jazz
1983–84	Sidney Moncrief	Milwaukee	1989–90	Dennis Rodman	Detroit
1984–85	Mark Eaton	Utah	1990–91	Dennis Rodman	Detroit
1985–86	Alvin Robertson	San Antonio	1991–92	David Robinson	San Antonio
1986–87	Michael Cooper	LA Lakers	1992–93	Hakeem Olajuwon	Houston
1987–88	Michael Jordan	Chicago	1993–94	Hakeem Olajuwon	Houston

COACH OF THE YEAR

Season	Coach	Team	Season	Coach	Team
1962–63	Harry Gallatin	St. Louis	1978–79	Cotton Fitsimmons	Kansas. City
1963–64	Alex Hannum	San Francisco	1979–80	Bill Fitch	Boston
1964–65	Red Auerbach	Boston	1980–81	Jack McKinney	Boston
1965–66	Dolph Schayes	Philadelphia	1981–82	Gene Shue	Washington
1966–67	Johnny Kerr	Chicago	1982–83	Don Nelson	Milwaukee
1967–68	Richie Guerin	St. Louis	1983–84	Frank Layden	Utah
1968–69	Gene Shue	Baltimore	1984–85	Don Nelson	Milwaukee
1969–70	Red Holzman	New York	1985–86	Mike Fratello	Atlanta
1970–71	Dick Motta	Chicago	1986–87	Mike Schuler	Portland
1971–72	Bill Sharman	Los Angeles	1987–88	Doug Moe	Denver
1972–73	Tom Heinsohn	Boston	1988–89	Cotton Fitsimmons	Phoenix
1973–74	Ray Scott	Detroit	1989–90	Pat Riley	LA Lakers
1974–75	Phil Johnson	KC-Omaha	1990–91	Don Chaney	Houston
1975–76	Bill Fitch	Cleveland	1991–92	Don Nelson	Golden State
1976–77	Tom Nissalke	Houston	1992–93	Pat Riley	New York
1977–78	Hubie Brown	Atlanta	1993–94	Lenny Wilkens	Atlanta

NBA ALL-STAR GAME

1994 ALL-STAR GAME ROSTERS & BOX SCORE

Sunday, February 13, 1994

EASTERN CONFERENCE

NO.	NAME	TEAM	POS	HT.	WT.
7	(X) Kenny Anderson	New Jersey	G	6-1	168
10	(X) B.J. Armstrong	Chicago	G	6-2	185
11	Mookie Blaylock	Atlanta	G	6-1	185
44	(X) Derrick Coleman	New Jersey	F	6-10	258
33	Patrick Ewing	New York	C	7-0	240
54	Horace Grant	Chicago	F	6-10	235
45	(I) Alonzo Mourning	Charlotte	C	6-10	240
32	(X) Shaquille O'Neal	Orlando	C	7-1	301
34	Charles Oakley	New York	F	6-9	245
30	(X) Scottie Pippen	Chicago	G/F	6-7	225
25	Mark Price	Cleveland	G	6-0	178
3	John Starks	New York	G	6-5	185
21	Dominique Wilkins	Atlanta	F	6-8	215

Head Coach: Lenny Wilkens, Atlanta

WESTERN CONFERENCE

NO.	NAME	TEAM	POS	HT.	WT.
8	(X) Charles Barkley (I)	Phoenix	F	6-6	252
22	(X) Clyde Drexler	Portland	G	6-7	222
7	Kevin Johnson	Phoenix	G	6-1	190
40	(X) Shawn Kemp	Seattle	F	6-10	245
32	Karl Malone	Utah	F	6-9	256
25	Danny Manning	LA Clippers	F	6-10	234
34	(X) Hakeem Olajuwon	Houston	C	7-0	255
20	Gary Payton	Seattle	G	6-4	190
2	(X) Mitch Richmond	Sacramento	G	6-5	215
50	Clifford Robinson	Portland	F	6-10	225
50	David Robinson	San Antonio	C	7-1	235
15	Latrell Sprewell	Golden St.	G	6-5	190
12	John Stockton	Utah	G	6-1	175

Head Coach: George Karl, Seattle

X - selected to starting lineup in All-Star fan balloting
I - injured, did not play

EAST (127)

	min	fg m-a	ft m-a	rb o-t	a	pf	tp
Pippen	31	9-15	6-10	0-11	2	2	29
Coleman	18	1-6	0-0	1-3	1	3	2
O'Neal	26	2-12	4-11	4-10	0	2	8
Armstrong	22	5-9	0-0	1-1	4	1	11
Anderson	16	3-10,	0-0	0-0	3	2	6
Starks	20	4-9	0-0	1-3	3	1	9
Price	22	8-10	2-2	0-2	5	1	20
Ewing	24	7-15	6-7	4-8	1	2	20
Oakley	11	1-3	0-0	1-3	3	2	2
Wilkins	17	4-9	3-6	2-2	4	1	11
Blaylock	16	2-5	0-0	0-1	2	3	5
Grant	17	2-8	0-0	6-8	2	0	4
TOTALS	240	48-111	21-36	21-56	30	21	127

Percentages: FG-.432, FT-.583. 3-Point Goals: 10-24, .417 (Pippen 5-9, Coleman 0-2, Armstrong 1-2, Anderson 0-1, Starks 1-3, Price 2-3, Wilkins 0-2, Blaylock 1-2). Team rebounds: 16. Blocked shots: 10 (O'Neal 4, Grant 3, Pippen, Coleman, Price). Turnovers: 13 (Anderson 4, Pippen 2, Starks 2, Armstrong, Blaylock, Ewing, Grant, O'Neal). Steals: 11 (Pippen 4, Blaylock 2, Coleman, Grant, O'Neal, Price, Starks).

WEST (118)

	min	fg m-a	ft m-a	rb o-t	a	pf	tp
Kemp	22	3-11	0-0	6-12	4	4	6
Malone	21	3-9	0-0	3-7	2	2	6
Olajuwon	30	8-15	3-6	4-11	2	4	19
Drexler	15	3-7	0-0	0-3	1	1	6
Richmond	24	5-16	0-0	0-2	3	0	10
Stockton	26	6-10	0-0	1-5	10	2	13
D Robinson	21	6-13	7-10	3-5	0	2	19
Johnson	14	3-6	0-1	0-1	2	1	6
C Robinson	18	5-8	0-0	1-2	5	0	10
Manning	17	4-7	0-0	0-4	2	4	8
Payton	17	3-4	0-0	2-6	9	2	6
Sprewell	15	3-8	3-7	4-7	1	1	9
TOTALS	240	52-114	13-24	24-65	41	23	118

Percentages: FG-.456, FT-.542. 3-Point Goals: 1-6, .167 (Drexler 0-2, Stockton 1-1, C Robinson 0-1, Sprewell 0-2). Team rebounds: 14. Blocked shots: 12 (Olajuwon 5, Kemp 3, D Robinson 2, Drexler, Manning). Turnovers: 22 (Kemp 6, Stockton 4, Olajuwon 3, Johnson 2, Richmond 2, Sprewell 2, D Robinson, Drexler, Malone). Steals: 7 (Olajuwon 2, C Robinson, Drexler, Johnson, Malone, Stockton).

East	33	39	29	26	- 127
West	28	36	26	28	- 118

Technical fouls: None. Flagrant fouls: None. A: 17,096. T: 2:13. Officials: J O'Donnell, Kersey, D. Crawford.

1993-94 ALL-NBA TEAM

FIRST TEAM
Player/Pos/Team
Scottie Pippen, F, Chicago
Karl Malone, F, Utah
Hakeem Olajuwon, C, Houston
John Stockton, G, Utah
Latrell Sprewell, G, Golden State

SECOND TEAM
Player/Pos/Team
Shawn Kemp, F, Seattle
Charles Barkley, F, Phoenix
David Robinson, C, San Antonio
Mitch Richmond, G, Sacramento
Kevin Johnson, G, Phoenix

THIRD TEAM
Player/Pos/Team
Derrick Coleman, F, New Jersey
Dominique Wilkins, F, LA Clippers
Shaquille O'Neal, C, Orlando
Mark Price, G, Cleveland
Gary Payton, G, Seattle

1993-94 NBA ALL-ROOKIE TEAM

FIRST TEAM
Player/Team
Chris Webber, Golden State
Anfernee Hardaway, Orlando
Vin Baker, Milwaukee
Jamal Mashburn, Dallas
Isaiah Rider, Minnesota

SECOND TEAM
Player/Team
Dino Radja, Boston
Nick Van Exel, LA Lakers
Shawn Bradley, Philadelphia
Toni Kukoc, Chicago
Lindsey Hunter, Detroit

1993-94 NBA ALL-DEFENSIVE TEAM

FIRST TEAM
Pos Player/Team
G   Mookie Blaylock, Atlanta
G   Gary Payton, Seattle
F   Scottie Pippen, Chicago
F   Charles Oakley, New York
C   Hakeem Olajuwon

SECOND TEAM
Pos Player/Team
G   Nate McMillan, Seattle
G   Latrell Sprewell, Golden St.
F   Dennis Rodman, San Antonio
F   Horace Grant, Chicago
C   David Robinson, San Antonio

NBA TITLE WINNERS

Year	Champion	Games W-L	Eastern Div./Conf. W-L	Coach	Western Div./Conf. W-L	Coach
1946–47	Philadelphia	4-1	Philadelphia 35-25	E. Gottlieb	Chicago 39-22	H. Olsen
1947–48	Baltimore	4-2	Philadelphia 27-21	E. Gottlieb	Baltimore 28-20	B. Jeannette
1948–49	Minneapolis	4-2	Washington 38-22	R. Auerbach	Minneapolis 44-16	J. Kundla
1949–50	Minneapolis	4-2	Syracuse 51-13	A. Cervi	Minneapolis 51-17	J. Kundla
1950–51	Rochester	4-3	New York 36-30	J. Lapchick	Rochester 41-27	L. Harrison
1951–52	Minneapolis	4-3	New York 37-29	J. Lapchick	Minneapolis 40-26	J. Kundla
1952–53	Minneapolis	4-1	New York 47-23	J. Lapchick	Minneapolis 48-22	J. Kundla
1953–54	Minneapolis	4-3	Syracuse 42-30	A. Cervi	Minneapolis 46-26	J. Kundla
1954–55	Syracuse	4-3	Syracuse 43-29	A. Cervi	Ft. Wayne 43-29	C. Eckman
1955–56	Philadelphia	4-1	Philadelphia 45-27	G. Senesky	Ft. Wayne 37-35	C. Eckman
1956–57	Boston	4-3	Boston 44-28	R. Auerbach	St. Louis 34-38	A. Hannum
1957–58	St. Louis	4-2	Boston 49-23	R. Auerbach	St. Louis 41-31	A. Hannum
1958–59	Boston	4-0	Boston 52-20	R. Auerbach	Minneapolis 33-39	J. Kundla
1959–60	Boston	4-3	Boston 59-16	R. Auerbach	St. Louis 46-29	E. Macauley
1960–61	Boston	4-1	Boston 57-22	R. Auerbach	St. Louis 51-28	P. Seymour
1961–62	Boston	4-3	Boston 60-20	R. Auerbach	Los Angeles 54-26	F. Schaus
1962–63	Boston	4-2	Boston 58-22	R. Auerbach	Los Angeles 53-27	F. Schaus
1963–64	Boston	4-1	Boston 59-21	R. Auerbach	San Fran. 48-32	A. Hannum
1964–65	Boston	4-1	Boston 62-18	R. Auerbach	Los Angeles 49-31	F. Schaus
1965–66	Boston	4-3	Boston 54-26	R. Auerbach	Los Angeles 45-35	F. Schaus
1966–67	Philadelphia	4-2	Philadelphia 68-13	A. Hannum	San Fran. 44-37	B. Sharman
1967–68	Boston	4-2	Boston 54-28	B. Russell	Los Angeles 52-30	van B. Kolff
1968–69	Boston	4-3	Boston 48-34	B. Russell	Los Angeles 55-27	van B. Kolff
1969–70	New York	4-3	New York 60-22	R. Holzman	Los Angeles 46-36	J. Mullaney
1970–71	Milwaukee	4-0	Baltimore 42-40	G. Shue	Milwaukee 66-16	L. Costello
1971–72	Los Angeles	4-1	New York 48-34	R. Holzman	Los Angeles 69-13	B. Sharman
1972–73	New York	4-1	New York 57-25	R. Holzman	Los Angeles 60-22	B. Sharman
1973–74	Boston	4-3	Boston 56-26	T. Heinsohn	Milwaukee 59-23	L. Costello
1974–75	Golden St.	4-0	Washington 60-22	K.C. Jones	Golden St. 48-34	A. Attles
1975–76	Boston	4-2	Boston 54-28	T. Heinsohn	Phoenix 42-40	J. MacLeod
1976–77	Portland	4-2	Philadelphia 50-32	G. Shue	Portland 49-33	J. Ramsay
1977–78	Washington	4-3	Washington 44-38	D. Motta	Seattle 47-35	L. Wilkens
1978–79	Seattle	4-1	Washington 54-28	D. Motta	Seattle 52-30	L. Wilkens
1979–80	Los Angeles	4-2	Philadelphia 59-23	Cunningham	Los Angeles 60-22	P. Westhead
1980–81	Boston	4-2	Boston 62-20	B. Fitch	Houston 40-42	D. Harris
1981–82	Los Angeles	4-2	Philadelphia 58-24	Cunningham	Los Angeles 57-25	P. Riley
1982–83	Philadelphia	4-0	Philadelphia 65-17	Cunningham	Los Angeles 58-24	P. Riley
1983–84	Boston	4-3	Boston 62-20	K.C. Jones	Los Angeles 54-28	P. Riley
1984–85	L.A. Lakers	4-2	Boston 63-19	K.C. Jones	L.A. Lakers 62-20	P. Riley
1985–86	Boston	4-2	Boston 67-15	K.C. Jones	Houston 51-31	B. Fitch
1986–87	L.A. Lakers	4-2	Boston 59-23	K.C. Jones	L.A. Lakers 65-17	P. Riley
1987–88	L.A. Lakers	4-3	Detroit 54-28	C. Daly	L.A. Lakers 62-20	P. Riley
1988–89	Detroit	4-0	Detroit 63-19	C. Daly	L.A. Lakers 57-25	P. Riley
1989–90	Detroit	4-1	Detroit 59-23	C. Daly	Portland 59-23	R. Adelman
1990–91	Chicago	4-1	Chicago 61-21	P. Jackson	L.A. Lakers 58-24	M. Dunleavy
1991–92	Chicago	4-2	Chicago 67-15	P. Jackson	Portland 57-25	R. Adelman
1992–93	Chicago	4-2	Chicago 57-25	P. Jackson	Phoenix 62-20	P. Westphal
1993–94	Houston	4-3	New York 57-25	P. Riley	Houston 58-24	Tomjanovich

NBA SCORING CHAMPIONS

Season	Pts/Avg.	Player	Team
1946–47	1389	Joe Fulks	Philadelphia Warriors
1947–48	1007	Max Zalofsky	Chicago Stags
1948–49	1698	George Mikan	Minneapolis Lakers
1949–50	1865	George Mikan	Minneapolis Lakers
1950–51	1932	George Mikan	Minneapolis Lakers
1951–52	1674	Paul Arizin	Philadelphia Warriors
1952–53	1564	Neil Johnston	Philadelphia Warriors
1953–54	1759	Neil Johnston	Philadelphia Warriors
1954–55	1631	Neil Johnston	Philadelphia Warriors
1955–56	1849	Bob Pettit	St. Louis Hawks
1956–57	1817	Paul Arizin	Philadelphia Warriors
1957–58	2001	George Yardley	Detroit Pistons
1958–59	2105	Bob Pettit	St. Louis Hawks
1959–60	2707	Wilt Chamberlain	Philadelphia Warriors
1960–61	3033	Wilt Chamberlain	Philadelphia Warriors
1961–62	4029	Wilt Chamberlain	Philadelphia Warriors
1962–63	3586	Wilt Chamberlain	San Francisco Warriors
1963–64	2948	Wilt Chamberlain	San Francisco Warriors
1964–65	2534	Wilt Chamberlain	San Fran.-Philadelphia
1965–66	2649	Wilt Chamberlain	Philadelphia 76ers
1966–67	2775	Rick Barry	San Francisco Warriors
1967–68	2142	Dave Bing	Detroit Pistons
1968–69	2327	Elvin Hayes	San Diego Rockets
1969–70	31.2	Jerry West	Los Angeles Lakers
1970–71	31.7	Lew Alcindor	Milwaukee Bucks
1971–72	34.8	K. Abdul-Jabbar	Milwaukee Bucks
1972–73	34.0	Nate Archibald	Kansas City-Omaha Kings
1973–74	30.6	Bob McAdoo	Buffalo Braves
1974–75	34.5	Bob McAdoo	Buffalo Braves
1975–76	31.1	Bob McAdoo	Buffalo Braves
1976–77	31.1	Pete Maravich	New Orleans Jazz
1977–78	27.2	George Gervin	San Antonio Spurs
1978–79	29.6	George Gervin	San Antonio Spurs
1979–80	33.1	George Gervin	San Antonio Spurs
1980–81	30.7	Adrian Dantley	Utah Jazz
1981–82	32.3	George Gervin	San Antonio Spurs
1982–83	28.4	Alex English	Denver Nuggets
1983–84	30.6	Adrian Dantley	Utah Jazz
1984–85	32.9	Bernard King	New York Knicks
1985–86	30.3	Dominique Wilkins	Atlanta Hawks
1986–87	37.1	Michael Jordan	Chicago Bulls
1987–88	35.0	Michael Jordan	Chicago Bulls
1988–89	32.5	Michael Jordan	Chicago Bulls
1989–90	33.6	Michael Jordan	Chicago Bulls
1990–91	31.2	Michael Jordan	Chicago Bulls
1991–92	30.1	Michael Jordan	Chicago Bulls
1992–93	32.6	Michael Jordan	Chicago Bulls
1993–94	29.8	David Robinson	San Antonio Spurs

NBA ALL–TIME RECORDS

ALL-TIME POINTS LEADERS
(THROUGH 1993–94 SEASON)

		Points
1.	K. Abdul-Jabbar	38,387
2.	Wilt Chamberlain	31,419
3.	X–Moses Malone	27,360
4.	Elvin Hayes	27,313
5.	Oscar Robertson	26,710
6.	John Havlicek	26,395
7.	Alex English	25,613
8.	Jerry West	25,192
9.	X–Dominique Wilkins	24,919
10.	Adrian Dantley	23,177
11.	Elgin Baylor	23,149
12.	X–Robert Parish	22,494
13.	Larry Bird	21,791
14.	Hal Greer	21,586
15.	Michael Jordan	21,541
16.	Walt Bellamy	20,941
17.	Bob Pettit	20,880
18.	George Gervin	20,708
19.	Bernard King	19,655
20.	Walter Davis	19,521
20.	X–Tom Chambers	19,521

X–Active

Leading Active Players Closing In

Karl Malone	19,030
Isiah Thomas	18,820
Hakeem Olajuwon	17,899
Eddie Johnson	17,658
Charles Barkley	17,528
Clyde Drexler	17,136
Terry Cummings	16,820

ALL-TIME REBOUND LEADERS
(THROUGH 1993–94 SEASON)

		Rebounds
1.	Wilt Chamberlain	23,924
2.	Bill Russell	21,620
3.	K. Abdul-Jabbar	17,440
4.	Elvin Hayes	16,279
5.	X–Moses Malone	16,166
6.	Nate Thurmond	14,464
7.	Walt Bellamy	14,241
8.	X–Robert Parish	13,973
9.	Wes Unseld	13,769
10.	Jerry Lucas	12,942

X–Active

Leading Active Players Closing In

Buck Williams	11,364
Hakeem Olajuwon	9,464
Charles Barkley	8,734

ALL-TIME ASSIST LEADERS
(THROUGH 1993–94 SEASON)

		Assists
1.	Magic Johnson	9,921
2.	Oscar Robertson	9,887
3.	X–John Stockton	9,383
4.	X–Isiah Thomas	9,061
5.	Maurice Cheeks	7,392
6.	Len Wilkens	7,211
7.	Bob Cousy	6,955
8.	Guy Rodgers	6,917
9.	Nate Archibald	6,476
10.	John Lucas	6,454

X–Active

NBA NATIONAL TV SCHEDULE

All Times Eastern

Day	Date	Game	Time (ET)	Network
Friday	Nov. 4	Charlotte at Chicago	8 p.m.	(TNT)
Friday	Nov. 4	Port. vs. LA Clippers at Yokohama, Japan	11 p.m.	(TNT)
Tuesday	Nov. 8	Houston at Cleveland	8 p.m.	(TNT)
Thursday	Nov. 10	Orlando at New York	8 p.m.	(TBS)
Friday	Nov. 11	Charlotte at Milwaukee	8 p.m.	(TNT)
Tuesday	Nov. 15	San Antonio at Denver	8 p.m.	(TNT)
Thursday	Nov. 17	Chicago at Houston	8 p.m.	(TBS)
Friday	Nov. 18	Seattle at Indiana	8 p.m.	(TNT)
Tuesday	Nov. 22	Golden State at Charlotte	8 p.m.	(TNT)
Thursday	Nov. 24	Golden State at Indiana	8 p.m.	(TBS)
Wednesday	Nov. 30	Phoenix at Chicago	8 p.m.	(TBS)
Friday	Dec. 2	New York at Orlando	8 p.m.	(TNT)
Tuesday	Dec. 6	Houston at Seattle	8 p.m.	(TNT)
Thursday	Dec. 8	Seattle at Sacramento	8 p.m.	(TBS)
Friday	Dec. 9	Chicago at Detroit	8 p.m.	(TNT)
Tuesday	Dec. 13	L.A. Lakers at Dallas	8 p.m.	(TNT)
Thursday	Dec. 15	Denver at Miami	8 p.m.	(TBS)
Friday	Dec. 16	New York at Phoenix	8 p.m.	(TNT)
Friday	Dec. 16	Orlando at Golden State	10:30 p.m.	(TNT)
Tuesday	Dec. 20	New Jersey at New York	8 p.m.	(TNT)
Thursday	Dec. 22	Phoenix at Houston	8 p.m.	(TBS)
Friday	Dec. 23	Indiana at Chicago	8 p.m.	(TNT)
Sunday	Dec. 25	Seattle at Denver	4 p.m.	(NBC)
Sunday	Dec. 25	New York at Chicago	6:30 p.m.	(NBC)
Thursday	Dec. 29	Orlando at Charlotte	8 p.m.	(TBS)
Tuesday	Jan. 3	Denver at Minnesota	8 p.m.	(TNT)
Thursday	Jan. 5	San Antonio at Utah	8 p.m.	(TBS)
Friday	Jan. 6	Seattle at Chicago	8 p.m.	(TNT)
Tuesday	Jan. 10	Indiana at New York	8 p.m.	(TNT)
Thursday	Jan. 12	Miami at San Antonio	8 p.m.	(TBS)
Friday	Jan. 13	Utah at Boston	8 p.m.	(TNT)
Tuesday	Jan. 17	Denver at Phoenix	9 p.m.	(TNT)
Thursday	Jan. 19	New York at Houston	8 p.m.	(TBS)
Friday	Jan. 20	Orlando at Denver	8 p.m.	(TNT)
Sunday	Jan. 22	Houston at Chicago	1 p.m.	(NBC)
Sunday	Jan. 22	Orlando at Phoenix	3:30 p.m.	(NBC)
Tuesday	Jan. 24	San Antonio at Chicago	8 p.m.	(TNT)
Thursday	Jan. 26	Chicago at Orlando	8 p.m.	(TBS)
Friday	Jan. 27	New York at Charlotte	8 p.m.	(TNT)
Sunday	Jan. 29	Phoenix at New York	Noon	(NBC)
Sunday	Jan. 29	Golden State at Chicago	2:30 p.m.	(NBC)
Tuesday	Jan. 31	Charlotte at Washington	8 p.m.	(TNT)
Thursday	Feb. 2	Seattle at Orlando	8 p.m.	(TBS)
Friday	Feb. 3	Seattle at Atlanta	8 p.m.	(TNT)
Friday	Feb. 3	Chicago at Phoenix	10:30 p.m.	(TNT)
Sunday	Feb. 5	New York at Orlando	1 p.m.	(NBC)
Sunday	Feb. 5	Houston at Phoenix	3:30 p.m.	(NBC)
Wednesday	Feb. 8	Chicago at Portland	8 p.m.	(TNT)
Thursday	Feb. 9	Golden State at Denver	8 p.m.	(TBS)
Friday	Feb. 10	All-Star Friday Night	10 p.m.	(TNT)
Saturday	Feb. 11	NBA All-Star Saturday	7 p.m.	(TNT)
Sunday	Feb. 12	All-Star Game at Phoenix	6:30 p.m.	(NBC)
Tuesday	Feb. 14	Utah at San Antonio	8 p.m.	(TNT)

Thursday	Feb. 16	Houston at Charlotte	8 p.m.	(TBS)
Friday	Feb. 17	Golden State at Phoenix	8 p.m.	(TNT)
Sunday	Feb. 19	Houston at New York	1 p.m.	(NBC)
Tuesday	Feb. 21	San Antonio at Houston	8 p.m.	(TNT)
Thursday	Feb. 23	Philadelphia at Denver	8 p.m.	(TBS)
Friday	Feb. 24	Chicago at Miami	8 p.m.	(TNT)
Sunday	Feb. 26	Chicago at Orlando	1 p.m.	(NBC)
Sunday	Feb. 26	Utah at Denver or Charlotte at Phoenix	3:30 p.m.	(NBC)
Tuesday	Feb. 28	New York at Orlando	8 p.m.	(TNT)
Thursday	March 2	Chicago at New York	7:30 p.m.	(TBS)
Thursday	March 2	Orlando at Houston	9:45 p.m.	(TBS)
Friday	March 3	Seattle at Phoenix	8 p.m.	(TNT)
Sunday	March 5	Houston at San Antonio or Milwaukee at New Jersey	1 p.m.	(NBC)
Sunday	March 5	Phoenix at Golden State	3:30 p.m.	(NBC)
Tuesday	March 7	Phoenix at Houston	8 p.m.	(TNT)
Thursday	March 9	San Antonio at Cleveland	8 p.m.	(TBS)
Sunday	March 12	San Antonio at Orlando	Noon	(NBC)
Monday	March 13	Houston at Atlanta	8 p.m.	(TNT)
Tuesday	March 14	Denver at New York	8 p.m.	(TNT)
Thursday	March 16	Phoenix at Charlotte	8 p.m.	(TBS)
Sunday	March 19	Chicago at Indiana or Utah at Charlotte	Noon	(NBC)
Tuesday	March 21	Phoenix at Orlando	8 p.m.	(TNT)
Thursday	March 23	Charlotte at Orlando	8 p.m.	(TBS)
Sunday	March 26	Golden State at Orlando	Noon	(NBC)
Tuesday	March 28	Chicago at New York	8 p.m.	(TNT)
Thursday	March 30	Atlanta at Golden State	8 p.m.	(TBS)
Sunday	April 2	New York at New Jersey or Phoenix at San Antonio	1:30 p.m.	(NBC)
Tuesday	April 4	Phoenix at Golden State	9 p.m.	(TNT)
Thursday	April 6	Seattle at Denver	8 p.m.	(TBS)
Friday	April 7	Indiana at Atlanta	8 p.m.	(TNT)
Sunday	April 9	Chicago at Cleveland or Charlotte at Indiana or Atlanta at Milwaukee	1 p.m.	(NBC)
		Houston at Denver or Phoenix at Portland	3:30 p.m.	(NBC)
Tuesday	April 11	Phoenix at Seattle	9 p.m.	(TNT)
Thursday	April 13	Golden State at Utah	8 p.m.	(TBS)
Friday	April 14	New York at Indiana	8 p.m.	(TNT)
Saturday	April 15	Orlando at Miami or Seattle at Golden St.	3:30 p.m.	(NBC)
Sunday	April 16	Atlanta at Charlotte or San Antonio at Den.	3 p.m.	(NBC)
Sunday	April 16	New York at Chicago	5:30 p.m.	(NBC)
Tuesday	April 18	Denver at San Antonio	8 p.m.	(TNT)
Thursday	April 20	New York at Charlotte	8 p.m.	(TBS)
Friday	April 21	Indiana at Orlando	8 p.m.	(TNT)
Saturday	April 22	Charlotte at Chic. or Denver at Golden St.	3:30 p.m.	(NBC)
Sunday	April 23	Orlando at New York	1 p.m.	(NBC)
		Atlanta at Indiana or Cleveland at Charlotte or Utah at Houston or Seattle at Phoenix	3:30 p.m.	(NBC)

INDEX

The NBA's Official Annual

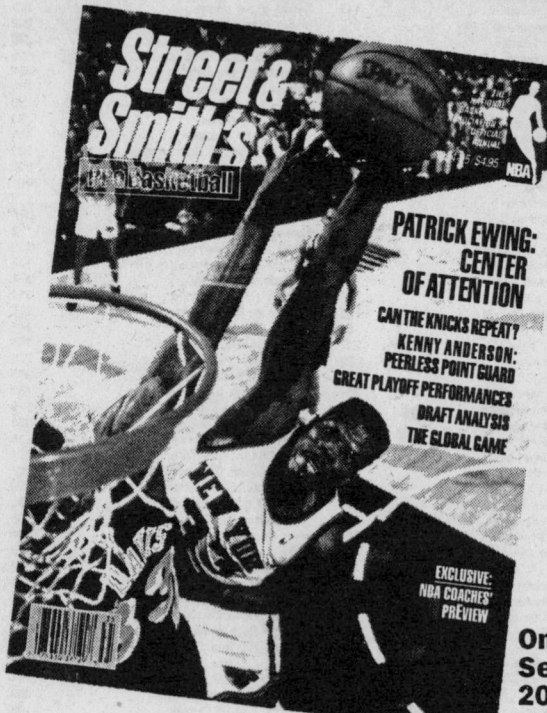

Street & Smith's Pro Basketball

THE NBA'S OFFICIAL ANNUAL $4.95

PATRICK EWING: CENTER OF ATTENTION

CAN THE KNICKS REPEAT?

KENNY ANDERSON: PEERLESS POINT GUARD

GREAT PLAYOFF PERFORMANCES

DRAFT ANALYSIS

THE GLOBAL GAME

EXCLUSIVE: NBA COACHES' PREVIEW

On Sale September 20